Edited by Elie Kedourie

436 illustrations, 135 in colour,

301 photographs, drawings and maps

THE JEWISH WORLD

Revelation, Prophecy and History

Texts by ELIE KEDOURIE · H. W. F. SAGGS · HYAM MACCOBY
ZVI YAVETZ · JACOB NEUSNER · AMNON SHILOAH
HAIM BEINART · A. GROSSMAN · SHELOMO DOV GOITEIN
AMNON COHEN · ARTHUR HYMAN · R. J. ZWI WERBLOWSKY
S. ETTINGER · EZRA SPICEHANDLER · T. CARMI · LIONEL KOCHAN
OSCAR HANDLIN · ARTHUR HERTZBERG · DAVID VITAL

THAMES AND HUDSON

ENDPAPERS: page from a Yemenite Bible of 1408 showing part of the Masoretic commentary arranged to form intersecting circles.
HALF-TITLE: page from a German Bible of the 13th century, showing the Masoretic commentary to the Book of Ezekiel in micro-writing arranged to form a lion of Judah.

Designed and produced by THAMES AND HUDSON, LONDON
MANAGING EDITOR: Ian Sutton BA
DESIGN: Pauline Baines MSIAD
EDITORIAL: Marcy Bourne BA
PICTURE RESEARCH: Georgina Bruckner MA
MAPS: Shalom Schotten MSIAD
TEXT set and printed in Great Britain by BAS Printers Limited,
Over Wallop, Hampshire
COLOUR PLATES originated in Switzerland by Clichés Lux, Neuchâtel
MONOCHROME originated by D S Colour International Ltd, London, and
printed in Great Britain by Balding & Mansell, Wisbech
BOUND in Great Britain by Webb & Sons, Glamorgan

T. Carmi's contribution is an abridgement of his Introduction to
The Penguin Book of Hebrew Verse (© 1979 T. Carmi) and is reprinted
by permission of Penguin Books, Ltd.

For copyright reasons this edition is not available for sale in
Belgium, France, Holland or Luxembourg.

Contents

Introduction

ELIE KEDOURIE

THE NINTH OF AB in the Jewish calendar (which usually but not invariably falls during the month of August in the Gregorian calendar) has been observed by Jews, for the last two thousand years or so, as a fast day. It is a day of mourning, commemorating two remarkably similar catastrophes, separated by some six centuries, which befell the Jews and Judaism. The first, in 586 BCE, was the handiwork of Nebuchadnezzar, king of Babylon, who destroyed Jerusalem and carried off its surviving inhabitants into captivity. The second, in 70 CE, was that of Titus (shortly afterwards to be proclaimed emperor in Rome), who likewise destroyed Jerusalem and its Temple, carried off the people into captivity and encompassed their dispersion. Titus's exploit was commemorated by a triumphal arch, which still stands in Rome as a landmark for tourists to gape at and Classical scholars to study. What Titus and his soldiers did is also still visible in Jerusalem in the Western Wall. This relic of Herod's Temple, which the Romans looted and burned, was thought until modern times to be all that had survived the destruction. But unlike Titus's Arch, which though unscathed is now no more than dead and inert stone, the fragment of a wall that escaped the Roman scourge is instinct with the devotion of Jews who believe themselves to be the descendants, in an unbroken line, of the people whom Nebuchadnezzar conquered, and Titus in his turn subdued and dispersed. At the service on the eve of the ninth of Ab there is recited at the Western Wall (as it is in synagogues the world over) the Book of Lamentations, which was inspired by the first destruction but which, since the second, is read to refer to both catastrophes. The Jews are the only people now living who recall and lament inflictions suffered at the hands of Powers whose pride bit the dust a thousand and two thousand years ago.

The lamentation on the ninth of Ab is not only on account of the fire, the rapine and the slaughter suffered on both occasions; nor is it because, on both, princes 'were hanged up by their hand' and foxes walked on the desolate mountain of Zion; nor because the terrible famine made the skin 'black like an oven', and

> They ravished the women in Zion
> And the maids in the cities of Judah.

Rather, and much more importantly, it is because both visitations are taken, in the perspective of Judaism, to have the self-same cause. It is true that Babylon's and Rome's were the hands that destroyed and killed. But Babylon and Rome were only agents sent on their mission by the Lord, who in his anger against Zion had 'swallowed up Israel', 'cast off his altar', 'abhorred his sanctuary', and 'given up into the hand of the enemy the walls of her palaces.' However, just as his anger had been called forth by the transgression and rebellion of his people, so his mercy and goodness will be extended to those that wait for him, to the soul that seeks him. Hence the Book of Lamentations is more than a sad, backward-looking commemoration. For the descendants of those who were carried off into captivity and Exile, it is meant to impart a lesson, the import of which is ever present and ever urgent, while Nebuchadnezzar and Titus, through whose instrumentality this lesson was driven home, have been long dead and gone.

By the time the Jews clashed with Rome they already had, and were aware that they had, a long history. In the course of this history they had come into contact, and been involved in contention, with many of the peoples and Great Powers of Antiquity, among others, Pharaonic and Ptolemaic Egypt, Assyria, Babylon, Persia, the Seleucids. Compared with such Great Powers, the Jews were politically puny and insignificant. But all these Great Powers – the loyalties they instilled, the ways of life associated with them – are now dead, while the Jews have lived to transmit from generation to generation a tradition in which Moses is seen as leading their ancestors out of slavery in Egypt, in which the Assyrian descends like a wolf on the kingdom of Israel, a tradition recalling those who by the rivers of Babylon sat down and wept, whom Cyrus the Great allowed to go back to the land of their fathers and on whom Antiochus vainly tried to impose a false idolatrous worship. The Jewish year is punctuated with solemn occasions and festivals, which keep alive the memory of these contacts and transactions: not only the ninth of Ab, but also Passover, which celebrates the signal deliverance from Egyptian bondage; the festival of Purim, when the Book of Esther is read, which, with its story of Haman and his unsuccessful plot to exterminate the Jews in the dominions of King Ahasuerus, is set in the context of Jewish life under Persian rule; and the festival of Chanukah, which commemorates the successful resistance of the Maccabees against the attempt by Antiochus Epiphanes to impose paganism.

The peoples and Powers of Antiquity with whom at one time or another the Jews became involved have now all disappeared. The history of each one of them has a beginning and an end, to be sure more or less clear, more or less defined. That they are wholly past makes them a more manageable object of study than their one-time contemporaries, the Jews, whose history goes back to remote times, but also extends to the present day. What is just as remarkable is that this small group, politically and militarily insignificant, has had an influence on the course of civilization which only Greece and Rome, among the peoples of Antiquity, have equalled. And while Christianity and Islam eventually absorbed large elements of Classical culture, this happened, so to speak, indirectly, since both these religions (which were to penetrate and largely dominate the world except for the Far East) decisively rejected the pagan gods: the God they acknowledged and worshipped as the one true God was the God of Abraham, Isaac and Jacob. Christianity (which claimed in due course to be the *verus Israel*) arose among Jews, and was to define and elaborate its dogmas by reference, and in opposition, to Judaism. The Prophet Muhammad's religious universe (as the Qur'ān attests) was wholly that of Judaism and Christianity, and the divine message, of which he announced himself to be the bearer, in his eyes only continued and completed the Revelation that mankind had received through the intermediary of Moses and Jesus. The Judaism out of which Christianity and Islam developed was essentially the same Judaism that has come down to the present day, with its biblical canon already established, with its Oral Torah supplementing the Written Torah and equal to it in authority, with the same rabbinical cast of mind, outlook and methods of argument already largely formed. It is this rabbinical Judaism that Christianity and Islam held to be both antagonist and point of reference. The Jews and Judaism, then, by reason of their position in world history, may be looked upon as the *trait d'union*, the buckle, which at once separates and unites ancient and modern in those societies to whose history such a periodization is applicable.

If Judaism 'gave birth' to Christianity and Islam, Jews had, following their clash with Rome and the catastrophe that ensued, to lead their lives in societies and states dominated by Christians and Muslims – societies where they were held at arm's length and where they were powerless. Their continued survival as a group in these dominant, attractive and yet very frequently hostile societies, where other groups sooner rather than later were lost without trace – as, for instance, the pagans of Greece, Italy and Western Europe, or the Christian populations of Anatolia and North Africa – must be adjudged remarkable. That such a group, utterly powerless as it was, did manage to survive for two millennia in a distinct and identifiable fashion is, on the face of it, a puzzle which calls for elucidation. The elucidation is to be found not so much in the conditions that the Jews faced in different times and places, with all their great variety, as in what Jews made of these peculiar conditions, what social arrangements they devised for the preservation of their group and the carrying on of their tradition. This is to say that the understanding of Jewish history requires that its divisions and articulations should follow its own autonomous movement, and be faithful to its own self-shaping spirit.

The disasters recalled by the Book of Lamentations were national disasters of the kind to which any polity, through mismanagement or bad luck, can fall victim. In this respect the Jews were no different from any other people. Nor were they different from the other peoples of Antiquity in closely linking religion and politics. For example, the polis and its tutelary deities formed a unity such that the prosperity of the citizens depended on the gods receiving due worship and propitiation. But the values enshrined in the religion of the polis were, so to speak, exclusively political. A defeat of the polis was, ipso facto, a defeat for its gods, and the destruction of a polis not only put the lives and possessions of its members wholly at the conqueror's mercy, but also left them spiritually naked and disoriented. Classical culture overwhelmingly put its trust in the life of politics and therefore had no defence against the inevitable vicissitudes of politics. But the Jews who wandered in the land of Assyria or wept by the rivers of Babylon or were taken by Titus into captivity, though their fate was as hard as that of any *polites* or *civis* whose polity suffered destruction, could draw on spiritual resources which enabled them to withstand, individually and as a community, the chances and changes of politics.

Their religion was marked by peculiar features which distinguish it sharply from other religions of Antiquity. For one thing, from the beginning, exile seems to figure in it as a leading motif. Abra(h)am, whom the Jews considered as their ancestor, breaks with his family and his ancestral religion and leaves his country in obedience to a divine injunction: 'Now the Lord had said unto Abram, Get thee out of thy country, and from thy father's house, unto a land that I will show thee' (Gen. XII:1). Later on it is foretold to him that his descendants will also experience exile and humiliation: 'Know of a surety that thy seed shall be a stranger in a land that is not theirs, and shall serve them, and they shall afflict them four hundred years' (Gen. XV:13). What Abra(h)am did was in response to a divine message of which he personally was chosen to be the recipient, and his election by God was ratified by a covenant in which his seed was promised a land of their own. But there is another, later, Covenant standing at the beginning of Jewish history which is of even greater significance. This later Covenant followed the departure of Abraham's descendants from Egypt, and in it God signified that he had chosen them for his people. This Covenant is between God and the children of Israel, each one of whom is responsible for keeping its terms. If the terms are not kept, we are told in Deuteronomy, various punishments will follow, and one in particular, that 'the Lord shall scatter thee among all people, from the one end of the earth even unto the other' (Deut. XXVIII:64).

Another theme in the traditional Jewish self-view serves to distinguish the Jews even more sharply from their neighbours and contemporaries. As the scriptural account has it, after Moses had led them out of Egypt the children of Israel were governed by elders and judges. In due course, Samuel received the divine calling and led the people. When he grew old, he appointed his two sons judges over Israel. But they proved unworthy, taking bribes and perverting judgments. The elders then applied to Samuel saying, 'give us a king to judge us.' The Bible hints that Samuel was taken aback and displeased by such a demand, but God told him to accede to it 'for they have not rejected thee, but they have rejected me, that I should not reign over them.' Such a passage is indicative of an outlook which considers not only that kings are not divine – divinity of the ruler was an idea common among the neighbours of the Jews – but also that divine rule is preferable to kingly rule. The biblical narrative also manages strongly to hint that this hankering after a king is somehow wrong and disreputable. When Samuel tries to persuade the elders that a king may prove to be a scourge rather than a blessing, they respond by insisting, like people obstinately bent on their own perdition: 'Nay, but we will have a king over us that we also may be like all the nations.' That a king was only a man capable of wrong doing and crime, and subject to Divine Judgment and punishment is a theme that recurs more than once in the Bible. The best known instance concerns David, whom the prophet Nathan rebuked harshly and to whom he promised retribution for committing adultery with Bathsheba and encompassing her husband's death (II Sam. XII:1–12). The arguments by which Samuel tries to deflect the elders from their purpose are remarkable. Samuel recites a whole catalogue of oppressive and despotic acts which may be expected from a king – and the Bible declares that in so doing Samuel was conveying the very words of God. The king will conscript the sons of the people to fight and to work his land, he will take their daughters for his service, he will levy taxes and appropriate land, 'and ye shall be his servants. And ye shall cry out in that day because of your king which ye shall have chosen you; and the Lord will not hear you in that day' (I Sam. VIII:10–18). These emphatic words about the disappointments, the mishaps and the disasters of politics are cast in the prophetic mode. The theme is repeated many times elsewhere in the Bible, where we find prophets using argument and exhortation at various critical junctures when internal disorder or external threat called into question the ability of the king or his judgment.

All through, then, we find expressed in the Bible mistrust of merely political authority, a questioning of its legitimacy and scepticism about the ability of rulers as such to act justly or safeguard the common weal. The prophets maintain a distance from current political arrangements, and deal with political power at arm's length: the attitude they articulate is that the body politic, a human contrivance and thus necessarily subject to decay and failure, is not that which gives meaning and coherence to human life. On the contrary, politics is perpetually under judgment, God's judgment revealed through prophets.

This peculiar duality, without parallel either in Classical Antiquity or among the Jews' immediate neighbours, paved the way for a situation quite as remarkable. The prophets spoke as the agents of Divine Revelation, the authority of which was supreme. This Revelation, the Torah, as it came to be designated, was held to have been given to Moses on Mount Sinai. This Written Torah was complemented by an Oral Torah, declared to have been revealed to Moses at the same time. This Oral Torah was of co-equal authority with the Written, and was transmitted like it to later generations: 'Moses received the Torah from Sinai and transmitted it to Joshua, and Joshua to the elders, and the elders to the prophets, and the prophets transmitted it to the men of the Great Synagogue' (Mishnah, Sayings of the Fathers).

Of this Oral Torah the guardians and expounders were the rabbis, whose decisions and conclusions were declared to be linked by an unbroken chain leading back to 'Moses our rabbi', so that what Akiba or Hillel or Shammai or their successors and their successors' successors expounded is all held to have formed part, *ab initio*, whether Moses knew it or not, of the original Mosaic Revelation. It is possible to go further. These rabbis, the heirs of the men of the Great Synagogue, who had received the Oral Torah from the prophets, who had received it from the elders, who had received it from Joshua, who had received it from Moses, were the ultimate authority as to the meaning of Revelation – a meaning to be clarified and ascertained in the course, and by means, of debate, disputation and commentary. A famous and remarkable passage in the Talmud records that in a disputation between rabbis, one of them, Rabbi Eliezer, sought to support his view by appealing to miracles. A carob tree was uprooted a hundred cubits from its place; his opponents said: 'No proof may be brought from a carob tree.' A stream of water flowed backwards; his opponents said: 'No proof may be brought from a stream of water.'

Then he said: 'If the *Halakhah* [i.e. the decision] agrees with me, let the walls of the school house prove it.' Thereupon the walls of the school house began to totter. But Rabbi Joshua rebuked them and said: 'When scholars are engaged in *halakhic* dispute, what concern is it of yours?' Thus the walls did not topple, in honour of Rabbi Joshua, but neither did they return to their upright position, in honour of Rabbi Eliezer; still today they stand inclined. Then he said: 'If the *Halakhah* agrees with me, let it be proved from Heaven.' Thereupon a heavenly voice was heard saying: 'Why do you dispute with Rabbi Eliezer? The *Halakhah* always agrees with him.' But Rabbi Joshua arose and said (Deut. XXX:12): 'It is not in heaven.' What did he mean by that? Rabbi Jeremiah replied: 'The Torah has already been given at Mount Sinai [and is thus no longer in Heaven]. We pay no heed to any heavenly voice, because already at Mount Sinai You wrote in the Torah (Ex. XXIII:2): "One must incline after the majority." ' Rabbi Nathan met the prophet Elijah and asked him: 'What did the Holy One, blessed be He, do in that hour?' He replied: 'God smiled and said: My children have defeated Me, My children have defeated Me.' (Translation in Gershom Scholem, *The Messianic Idea in Judaism*, 1971)

Intellectual poise and self-confidence are apparent in this passage, and the Talmud, the Midrash, the aggadic literature, the codes of law, the *responsa* and the commentaries upon commentaries which went on being written well into modern times indicate that this self-confidence and implicit belief in the high worth and relevance of their discipline continued to be the rule in rabbinical circles. Nor was the enterprise looked upon as simply academic. Following the disastrous clash with Rome, and the destruction of the Jewish polity in Palestine, the Jews became a collection of communities all over the Mediterranean basin and further afield. They were dispersed, small in number and politically powerless. With the official conversion of the Roman Empire to Christianity, and the subsequent rise of Islam, their position deteriorated further. In these new, far-flung political structures, membership of the body politic depended on professing the official faith, while those who did not do so were subject to various disabilities, the severity of which in practice varied from time to time and place to place, but which remained, until the 19th and 20th centuries, part of the public law of Christian and Islamic states. But these scattered communities managed to survive for centuries on end in these adverse and unpropitious circumstances. Not only to survive, but to maintain their cohesion, and, so far as they could, to govern themselves by means of communal organizations that were recognizably similar, however distant they were from one another in time and space. These communities, furthermore, were linked to one another by social, mercantile and scholarly networks which eventually became world wide. They constituted, and were aware that they constituted, a distinct group among the peoples of the world – a group which kept alive the traditional belief that it was the object of divine election.

It is the rabbis who, without benefit of state power or territorial base, provided and kept in repair the framework of belief, custom and law which allowed these small, dispersed communities, always vulnerable, often oppressed and occasionally terrorized, to maintain in unpromising conditions social cohesion and spiritual coherence. Nothing remotely comparable can be seen elsewhere in history. The Written and Oral Torah originated in and referred to a state of affairs in which the Jews formed a polity in a territory of their own. By submitting these materials to a centuries-long dialectic of interpretation and counter-interpretation, by engaging in detailed textual commentary and, eventually, by codifying the conclusions of debate and commentary, the rabbis built up a structure of law and custom, of injunction and prohibition, which regulated social, economic and religious life in conditions unimaginably remote and alien from those obtaining in, say, King David's time or that of the Hasmoneans – eras which form the original historical context of the Torah. This structure of communal regulation, which was in effect self-regulation, was maintained and transmitted over large areas and long periods. It has been the achievement of contemporary historians, such as Simon Dubnow, Salo Baron and most recently S. D. Goitein, to convey to their readers a detailed and vivid picture of the complex institutions and the sophisticated arrangements which enabled these communities to subsist for so long in such precariousness. And some of these communities continued to live in the traditional manner and according to the traditional arrangements set up and developed by the rabbis up to within living memory. One such community is that of Marrakech, the inner life of which, in the two or three decades preceding the Second World War, José Benech has so strikingly and with such penetration depicted in a little-known work, posthumously published shortly after the war, *Essai d'explication d'un mellah*.

As has been said, exile figures from the earliest times as a *leit motiv* in the Jewish self-view. Following the destruction of the Second Temple and the ending of Jewish autonomy, the fact, and the consciousness, of exile naturally became even more prominent. Through their own sins, successive generations of Jews were taught, they had brought this punishment upon themselves. But God is a merciful God, they were also taught, who will in his own time send the Messiah to redeem them and restore them to the Holy Land. The redemption here in question was an earthly one: it did mean that when redemption came the Messiah, the Anointed One, would once again sit in Jerusalem on David's throne, at the head of a divinely regulated polity when scarcity, famine, envy and war would disappear. In the words of the ancient blessing recited after the reading in the synagogue of the weekly portion from the Prophets:

> Rejoice us! O Lord our God, in the coming of thy servant Elijah the prophet, and in the kingship of the house of David, thine anointed. May he come speedily to gladden our hearts. Let no stranger sit on his Throne and let others no more claim his honour for their inheritance; for thou hast sworn unto him by thy holy name that his lamp shall never be quenched. Blessed art thou, O Lord, the Shield of David.

The blessing invokes God's ancient promise and supplicates for its fulfilment. It does not of course indicate when the Messiah will actually come. But, as may be suspected, the temptation to announce the tidings of his coming, especially in times of trial and suffering, was great. The rabbis, however, were firm in warning against such predictions. The Talmud and the Midrash forbid calculating the End, that is, forecasting the advent of the Messiah, or pressing for it, forcing its coming through human action. Jews are likewise enjoined not to revolt against the kingdoms of the world, and not to come up from exile 'like a wall', i.e. in a mass. In the twelfth of the Thirteen Principles of the Faith, which Maimonides codified and which are recited at the end of the prayers on the eve of the Sabbath, Jews profess their belief in the coming of the Messiah who will redeem those who await his final salvation. But Maimonides lays it down in a commentary that one must not determine a time for him, and he repeats the curse pronounced by the rabbis against those who calculate the End.

Belief that the Messiah must one day come to redeem Israel from exile and sit on David's throne in Jerusalem thus implied a concomitant political quietism which, inculcated by rabbinical teaching generation after generation, became, it is not too much to say, the ingrained attitude towards political action characteristic of Jewish communities everywhere. It is a surprising and unexpected sequel to a turbulent pre-Exilic history in which political issues had loomed so large – whether the issues had to do with reconciling political action with divine injunctions, or whether they had to do with negotiating the dangers posed by the ambitions of Great Powers. This is not to say that political passivity was always and invariably the rule. If that had been the case, there would have been no reason for reiterating the prohibition of calculating the End. From time to time belief in the imminent arrival of the Messiah would grip some community and plunge it into effervescence. One such Messianic movement which, in modern times, affected the whole of the Jewish world is that associated with Sabbatai Zevi (1626–76). Gershom Scholem has shown in his masterly study of Sabbatai and Sabbatianism, how the movement developed in an autonomous fashion out of kabbalistic doctrines. He has also shown how, within a year or so of Sabbatai's proclamation as Messiah in 1665, there was hardly a Jewish community in Asia, Europe or North Africa which was not more or less profoundly touched by the Messianic hope.

Sabbatai was proclaimed Messiah in May 1665; he was arrested in Constantinople by the Ottoman authorities in February 1666, and in the following September he turned Muslim. He thus disappointed the hope of redemption which had swept the Jewish world, and his followers were eventually confined to a group of outwardly Muslim secret believers chiefly in Salonica, and some others in central and Eastern Europe. But as Professor Scholem has argued, the Sabbatian movement is highly significant not only in what it indicates about the outlook and world view of Jewry, but in its intellectual sequels as well. Sabbatianism was antinomian in tendency, and its failure left a residue of disaffection towards rabbinical Judaism and a readiness to dismantle the fence round the Torah which the rabbis had so zealously erected, maintained and guarded for centuries. The fence was eventually, in large part, dismantled and destroyed. The role of Sabbatianism in this should alert us to the possibility that autonomous intellectual changes within Jewry had a role to play here as much as did the European Enlightenment and the policies that characterized Enlightened Absolutism and the Democratic Revolution – as the historian R. R. Palmer has called it – which followed.

During this latest period of Jewish history the main centres of Jewry were central and Eastern Europe, and subsequently the U.S.A. The political passivity which marked Jewish life under the aegis of the rabbis was increasingly abandoned. The democratic states and the democratic aspirations which became increasingly prominent in the 19th and 20th centuries offered a new promise and imposed new requirements. Democratic politics seemed to offer the prospect of Jews taking their place as citizens *à part entière* in a secular order where religion was a private matter, not an affair of state. This indeed has so far proved to be the case in the English-speaking world, and most notably in the United States. The Messianic vision of a *novus ordo saeclorum* seems to have received here a measure of realization, denied as yet to that which Jewish prayers have, these many generations, enshrined; and in this *novus ordo* Jews, like other citizens, sustain, indeed themselves are, the political order. Democratic politics elsewhere have proved more disastrous for Jews than Nebuchadnezzar or Titus had

ever proved to be. In the decades following the First World War the Jews of central and Eastern Europe found themselves far worse off in polities deriving their legitimacy from the popular will than they had been in the dynastic regimes the war had destroyed; indeed the regime that encompassed the holocaust issued from universal suffrage and continued to enjoy popular support to the very end. The Sabbath synagogue service includes a prayer for the ruler. As is well known, the Tsarist regime oppressed and persecuted Jews in various ferocious and ingenious ways. A certain rabbi in the Tsar's dominions, however, always insisted on saying this prayer with great fervour, explaining that one should always wish long life to the Tsar, since the next one was sure to be worse. This may apply, *mutatis mutandis*, to the promise and temptation of the life of politics as Jews have encountered it in so many places during this century.

Zionism is the other guise in which the life of politics has presented itself to the Jews of the modern world. Zionists hold that the Jewishness of the Jews demands the safeguard and the fostering care of a Jewish state. Considered historically, such an approach would reduce two millennia and more of life in the Diaspora to a mere hiatus between Solomon's kingdom and its restoration in the shape of the State of Israel; and this restoration, brought about as it has been by mundane means, may not perhaps be thought identical with that Messianic restoration the advent of which, the rabbis taught, may not be forced. However, the State of Israel exists, and in it lives a sizeable portion – though by no means a majority – of world Jewry. Israel came into existence in a world profoundly different from that known by the founders of Zionism; and it continues to exist amid circumstances which they did not envisage or even imagine. Their hope was that a Jewish state, by doing away with 'Jewish homelessness', would 'solve the Jewish problem' then becoming acute in a populist, and hence nationalist, Europe. But Israel has not, of course, abolished the Diaspora, which in fact is necessary to support and sustain it. In the thirty years of its existence so far, Israel has experienced with an ancestral fortitude the long forgotten splendours and miseries which attend the life of politics. As it continues to do so, it will be watched over with anxious solicitude by those kings of Judah and Israel, by those Hasmonean princes and those High Priests who, in their generation, had to deal and contend with Assyria and Babylon, with Seleucia and Rome.

EDITORIAL NOTE

In conformity with normal practice in the context of Jewish history, dates are designated BCE ('Before the Common Era') and CE ('Common Era'), corresponding to BC and AD of Christian history.

In the transcription and spelling of Hebrew words, we have been guided by usage and convenience rather than rigid consistency. Sub-script dots have not been used.

Biblical quotations have deliberately not been brought into conformity with any single version, but each author has been free to use the translation that he prefers; chapter and verse references make comparison easy if the reader wishes.

I
A PEOPLE AND A BOOK

Pre-Exilic Jewry

The Bible

A single event – the Exodus – is the key to the Pentateuch
and, indeed, to the whole of Judaism. For the Jews, this is the
crucial point at which the Divine irrupts into history, the point
to which the whole of creation was tending and from which all
subsequent history leads away. To what extent the stories of
the captivity and Exodus reflect real historical events is a
matter for debate. Yet it was the folk-memory of this
deliverance from Egypt that gave the Jews their unshakable
sense of destiny and mission and sustained them throughout
centuries of disappointment and tragedy. In this miniature
from the *Golden Haggadah* (Spanish, 14th century), the artist
portrays them leaving Egypt 'with a high hand' – a Hebrew
expression meaning 'triumphant', but here illustrated literally.
'And Pharaoh called for Moses and Aaron by night, and said,
Rise up and get you forth from among my people, both ye and
the children of Israel; and go and serve the Lord.' (1)

13

The God of the Israelites was probably an amalgam of several concepts of the Divine. Baal (*left*: a gilded bronze statuette of about 1200 BCE) seems to have been a fertility god, at first identified with Yahweh but later seen as an object of idolatrous worship whose name should not be applied to Yahweh. El, Baal's father (*above*: on a stele of the 13th century BCE) was the high god of the Canaanite pantheon and had developed some universal characteristics. As an object of worship among the Canaanites, he had receded into the background. His name was therefore retained in the Bible as a synonym for Yahweh. (2, 3)

The power of Egypt was felt all over the eastern Mediterranean, and is abundantly documented in both inscriptions and sculptured reliefs. Subject peoples are frequently shown in attitudes of submission before the pharaoh, but it is not normally possible to identify them with any certainty. Those shown here (*left* and *above*) from the tomb of Horem-heb at Saqqara, *c.* 1350 BCE, are very possibly Semitic. The man on the left is shackled and led by a rope round his neck; those in the larger relief are clearly imploring or entreating for something – one is prostrate on his stomach, another is on his back with arms raised in the air – and are conversing with Horem-heb, who was then commander-in-chief of the Egyptian army, through a man who is acting as interpreter. (4, 5)

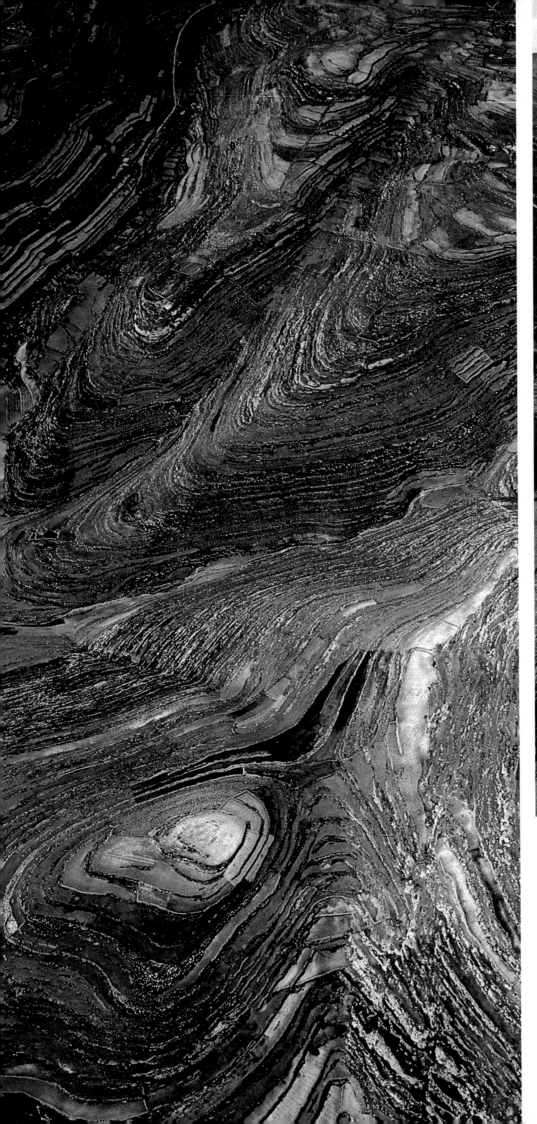

The desert and the sown

The move from the desert to the cultivated land of Canaan posed a series of profound questions for the Jews. Yahweh had been a god of the rocks and mountains of Sinai, manifesting himself on one of those gaunt and forbidding peaks (*above*) – its exact location has never been resolved – where he gave Moses the Tablets of the Law. The cult that grew up around him was adapted to these conditions; he had no fertility aspect. In Canaan, on the contrary, man depended on the cultivation of the soil. Agriculture, such as that of these Judaean terraces (*left*), which go back to ancient times, demanded knowledge of the seasons and careful attention to the processes of growth. Was this side of nature, too, under the rule of Yahweh, or were there other gods – like Baal, whom the Canaanites worshipped – to be placated and invoked? Was Baal independent of Yahweh

and equally powerful? Or were Baal and Yahweh different aspects of one divine power? The whole basis of Israelite monotheism lay open to question.

Traces of this critical period of Israelite religion remain in the Bible. It seems clear that at one stage Baal was equated with Yahweh, i.e. Baal was regarded as just another name for Yahweh. Both Saul and David gave one son a name based on the divine name Yahweh and another son a name based on the divine name Baal. In the end, however, this sycretism failed to work. The old associations, cult practices and mythology of Baal could not be forgotten. Baal was rejected as non-existent, and the name Baal lost all connection with Yahwism, though some of Baal's characteristics were retained in the figure of Yahweh. (6, 7)

Of Jewish life in the 8th and 7th centuries BCE, few traces remain. This strange incense-burner (*above right*, with detail *left*) was found at Tell Ta'annah, the Taanach mentioned in the 'Song of Deborah': 'Then Kings came and fought ... at Taanach by the waters of Megiddo' (Judges v:19). Its bizarre mixture of human and animal heads remains mysterious. (8, 9)

The transformation of a nomadic tribe to a settled community was now complete. This limestone inscription of about 950 BCE, found at Gezer, is an agricultural calendar, with appropriate activities grouped by months. (11)

A fertility goddess found near Rachel's tomb, Bethlehem, provides evidence of a similar kind. Hands holding breasts, she belongs to a type of Canaanite cult figure going back to a period before the Israelite conquest. (12)

After a brief golden age, when Israel, under David and his son Solomon (died, 922 BCE), was the major power in the Levant, the kingdom split into two – Judah and Israel. Within less than a century, Israel, menaced by the growing power of the Assyrians, declined to the status of vassaldom. Reliefs on a black basalt stele dated 841 BCE (*below*) show Israelites bringing tribute to King Shalmaneser III; they wear the western Semitic dress, with long over-garment, common to both Jews and Phoenicians. The tribute consists of silver, gold and vessels and bars of lead. (10)

In the Assyrian shadow

Assyria was the dominant power in the Middle East from the 9th to the 7th century BCE. Based at Nineveh, on the Tigris, the Assyrians, under a series of brilliant warrior kings, built up a vast empire which by 660 BCE included Egypt. The kingdom of Judah, however, maintained a precarious independence throughout this period. *Above left*: landscape between Judah and the Syrian desert, a scene that has changed little since those times. *Left*: King Jehu of Israel paying homage to Shalmaneser III of Assyria in 841 BCE. In the accompanying cuneiform inscription, Jehu is described as 'son of Omri', but we know from the Bible that he was only a successor. In 701 BCE, the Assyrian king Sennacherib attacked Judah and, according to his own record, destroyed forty-six cities. A relief from his royal palace at Nineveh (*above*) shows the fall of one of them – Lachish, south-west of Jerusalem. The king, enthroned, receives the surrender of the inhabitants. Jerusalem escaped the same fate only by the payment of a heavy tribute. These events are related in the Second Book of Kings, and form the background to the prophecies of First Isaiah. (13, 14, 15)

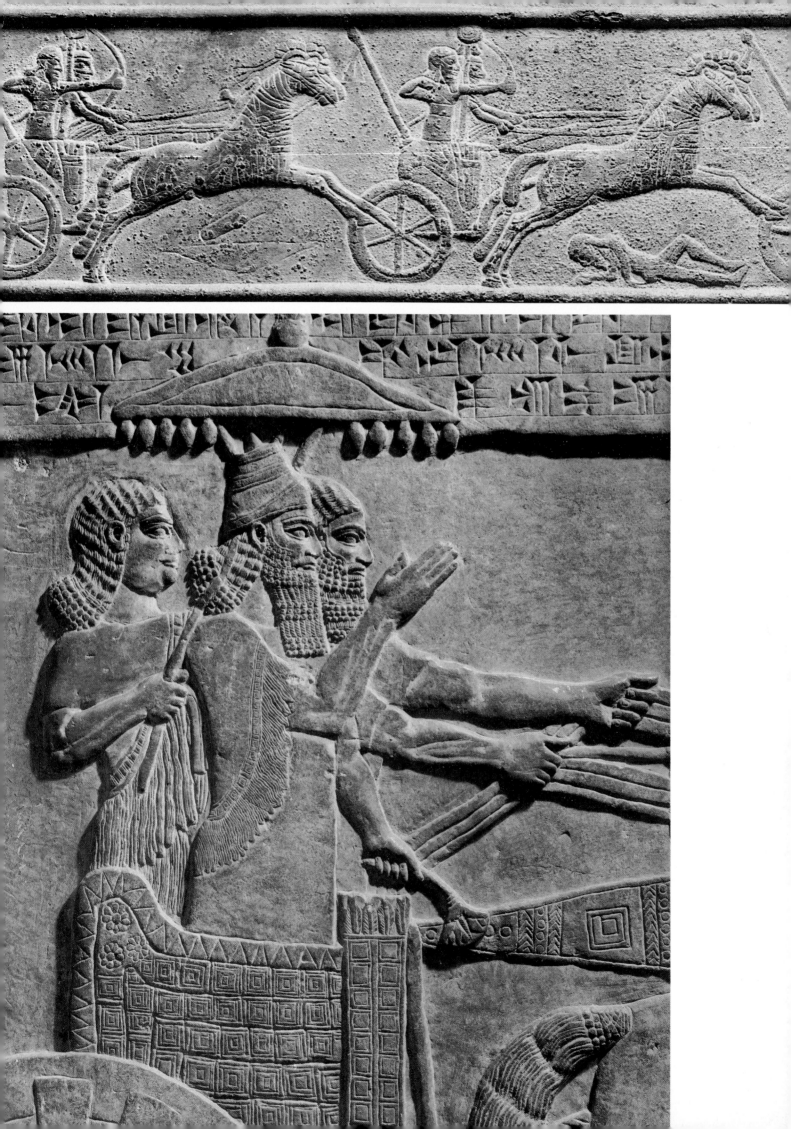

The road to Exile

The great kings of Assyria recorded their deeds in monumental reliefs which often bring the bare biblical narratives vividly to life. *Above:* Shalmaneser III in battle, a detail from the bronze gates of his palace at Balawat. (16)

Tiglath-Pileser III (*left*) reigned from 744 to 727 BCE. The Second Book of Kings (XVI:10) tells us: 'And king Ahaz went to Damascus to meet Tiglath-Pileser king of Assyria, and saw the altar that was at Damascus; and king Ahaz sent to Urijah the priest the fashion of the altar and the pattern of it. . . . And Urijah the priest built an altar, according to all that king Ahaz had sent from Damascus.' (17)

'Now the rest of the acts of Hezekiah, and all his might, and how he made the pool and the conduit and brought water into the city, are they not written in the chronicles of the Kings of Judah?' (II Kings XX:20). The 'conduit' is the Siloam tunnel, constructed by Hezekiah to ensure a water-supply to Jerusalem if it were besieged by Sennacherib in 701. In 1880 this very tunnel was excavated and an inscription (*right*) discovered, which describes how the workmen began at opposite ends and met in the middle. (18)

The end for Judah came in 586 BCE. In 611, Assyria was conquered by the new power of Babylon, and it was the Babylonian king, Nebuchadnezzar, who destroyed Jerusalem and sent the Jewish people into a second captivity. There are no reliefs of this event, but it must have been very like the scene at Lachish (*below*), when the Israelites were led away by Sennacherib. The prophecy of Jeremiah (XXXIV:2, 3) was fulfilled: 'Thus says the Lord: I am giving this city into the hand of the king of Babylon, and he shall burn it with fire. You shall not escape from his hand; . . . and you shall go to Babylon.' (19)

Mythology and nationhood

The meaning of Exodus and the significance of God's Covenant with Moses, and of his choice of the Jewish people as his instrument, permeated the literature of the Israelites from its earliest beginnings. It was probably during the Babylonian Exile that the work of collating the first Five Books of the Bible as we know it (the Torah) was completed. Since then, the crucial events of the national 'myth' have been represented again and again in literature and art, varying in style and emphasis but not in essence.

Shown here are two versions of Moses's crossing of the Red Sea, separated by about a thousand years. *Right:* a fresco from the synagogue of Dura Europus, on the Euphrates, *c.* 250 CE. Moses is shown twice, each time with the hand of God above him. On the left, the Egyptian army marches in pursuit of the Israelites; on the right, they are overwhelmed by the returning waters. (20)

The same scene (*below*) from a German Haggadah of the 15th century. The children of Israel are crossing the Red Sea on dry land, pursued by Pharaoh and his horsemen. A pillar of smoke separates the Israelites from the Egyptians (Ex. XIV:19). On the left is portrayed the 'strong east wind' (Ex. XIX:21) which caused the Red Sea to be divided. (21)

The bitter herb 'maror' from a Spanish Haggadah of the 13th century. The herbs are a symbol of the bitter slavery of the Jews in Egypt. The confection in which they are dipped symbolizes the clay and mortar with which the Jews had to make bricks, though this is a late rationalization, as a similar confection was used in the Hellenistic symposium. (22)

Matzah, unleavened bread, from an Italian 14th-century Haggadah. When the Israelites left Egypt they had no time to bake leavened bread, and had therefore to take only unleavened. Three matzahs feature in the Passover meal; two represent the bread of Sabbaths and festivals, the third (the one that is broken) 'the bread of affliction'. (23)

The beginning of the meal (*left*): the family sits with the bread, wine and herbs before them; below, the reader washes his hands. From a 14th-century Barcelona Haggadah. (24)

While a servant pours wine (*right*), the mistress of the house – in the right-hand margin – invites a group of poor people to take part in the meal. This page, from a Greek Haggadah of 1583, contains the passage in Aramaic where the poor are invited to the meal. (26)

The feast of the Passover, one of Judaism's three 'pilgrim festivals', commemorates the last day of the Israelites' captivity, when God slew the first-born of Egypt and allowed Moses to lead them forth to Sinai. The celebrations are spread over seven days (eight in the Diaspora), but the main event is a service called the Seder constructed round a meal eaten at home on the first night, during which the head of the family acts as reader. The distinctive features of the Seder are as follows (actions not specific to this festival are marked with an asterisk): (1)* sanctification (*Kiddush*), the blessing over the wine; (2) washing the hands (for eating the vegetables); (3) eating vegetables dipped in salt water; (4) dividing one of the matzahs and putting half aside as *afikomen*; (5) telling the story of the Exodus; (6)* washing the hands (for eating bread); (7) blessing over the unleavened bread and eating it; (8) blessing over the bitter herbs and eating them; (9) eating the matzah and bitter herbs together in accordance with the prescription of Hillel; (10)* eating the ordinary meal; (11) eating the *afikomen*, representing the paschal lamb; (12) saying grace; (13) Hallel (thanksgiving); (14) concluding prayer.

A Passover dish of pewter, 18th century, from Germany. In the centre are the blessing hands, below them the paschal lamb and round the edge the Hebrew words for Passover, bread and bitter herbs. (25)

The fourteen stages of the Seder are described on the opposite page. These miniatures (*right*), to be read from top right to bottom left, were painted in 1739 by the Moravian artist, Nathen ben Shimshon; the two final stages are combined. (27)

The Tablets of the Law

The Ten Commandments given by Yahweh to Moses on Mount Sinai are certainly among the oldest parts of the Bible, and may well go back to the time attributed to them there. Although not the oldest code of laws in the world, the Decalogue is peculiar in being a series not of legal decisions but of absolute commands and prohibitions.

Like the Exodus, the giving of the Law to Moses has been a constant theme of Jewish art from the earliest times. A Coptic wood-relief of the 6th or 7th century (*left*) shows a beardless and rather classical Moses holding the Tablets in one hand and surrounded by baskets of what seems to be manna. (28)

The Law is given to Moses (*left*), from the Regensburg Pentateuch, of about 1300. The illustration is allegorical rather than literal and relates to an idea in the Mishnah ('Sayings of the Fathers'): 'Moses received the Torah on Sinai, and handed it to Joshua, and Joshua to the Elders.' (29)

Moses descending the mountain bearing the Tablets (*opposite*), a page from the so-called Alba Bible, commissioned by Don Luis de Guzmán, in 1422, from Rabbi Moses Arragel of Guadalajara, who translated it, with commentary, from Hebrew into Spanish. The illustrations were probably painted by Christian artists, but certainly under rabbinic supervision, since many of them reflect specifically rabbinic interpretations, and may in fact go back to a lost Jewish iconography. On this page, the Commandments are written in Hebrew and seem to have been copied – by a Jewish scribe – from a double-page miniature, combining very awkwardly with the figure of Moses. (30)

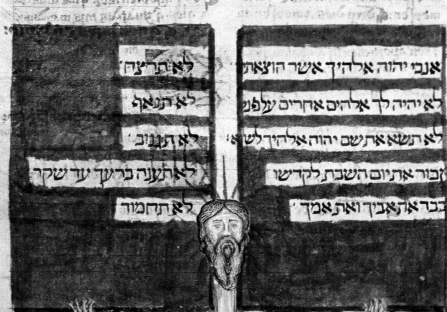

de malas condiciones e redrar los daños dela republica. de
del primero genero satisfazese ally do dixo yo so adonay tu dios
que te saque de tierra de egipto ca en este mandamiento se entiende
aver un solo dios infinito syn principio e syn fin del
qual dios que prima causa non ayan conosçimiento
ayudo las gentes catolica mente salvo en la ley
veyendo que quantos delos trezientos mandamien

tos o de todos seys sesenta e tres que en poner buenas opiniones çerca de
dios son dela espeçia deste primero genero. Ca el segundo genero es non
tener ome opinion errona çerca de la esençia de dios lo qual
se satisfaze en el segundo mandamiento que dixo non tenras
nin seran a ty dioses otros delante mi asy que se sigue que
quantos otros en los seys çientos e treze mandamientos
asy afirmativos como negativos este modo e apellido lle
varen son e se conduçen en este mandamiento. Ca el
terçero genero es commo
seamos ayuntados en
buenas condiçiones çer
ca dela gente lo qual
se satisfaze ally do dixo
onrra a tu padre e a tu
madre en el qual manda
miento se conduzen o a
ver onor alos omes
e a los mayores ygual
mente asy que
se sigue que quantos otros
mandamientos en los
seys çientos e treze
mandamientos este
modo e apellido llevaren
son de aqueste genero e non
cosa nueva. Ca el
quarto genero es quitar
alos omes de malas con
diçiones e redrar los
daños dela republica
lo qual se satisfaze en
los diez mandamientos
ally do dixo non mates
non fornigues non fur
tes e ca asy que se sigue
que quantos otros man
damientos en los seys
çientos e treze mandi
mientos que este modo
llevaren e apellido son
de aqueste genero e non otra
cosa nueva. Ca asy my
amigo que por estos x
mandamientos se man
te e mays de aquestos
mandamientos dio los
nuestro señor en las dos tab
las de piedra en los qu
ales sy ojos tienes la
ley fallaras en los x
mandamientos. Ca esta
es la segunda premissa
que te mande e en razon
de la declaraçion de los
mandamientos veo por
eso dixe eso mismo que
lo dexo de fazer por
los declarar en los otros
diez mandamientos que
fallaras escriptos en el
postrimero libro dela
ley: plaziendo a dios:

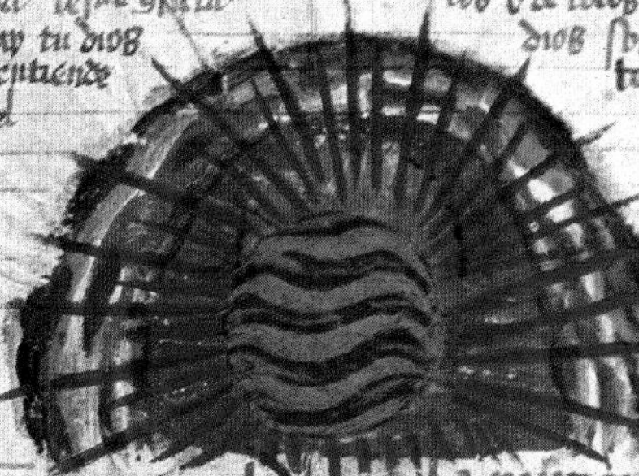

de tu conpañero. non cobdiçes la muger de tu conpañero nin
su siervo nin su sierva nin su buey nin su asno nin cosa delo de tu con
pañero:

Ca figura de moysen commo venia con las tablas dela ley en sus manos

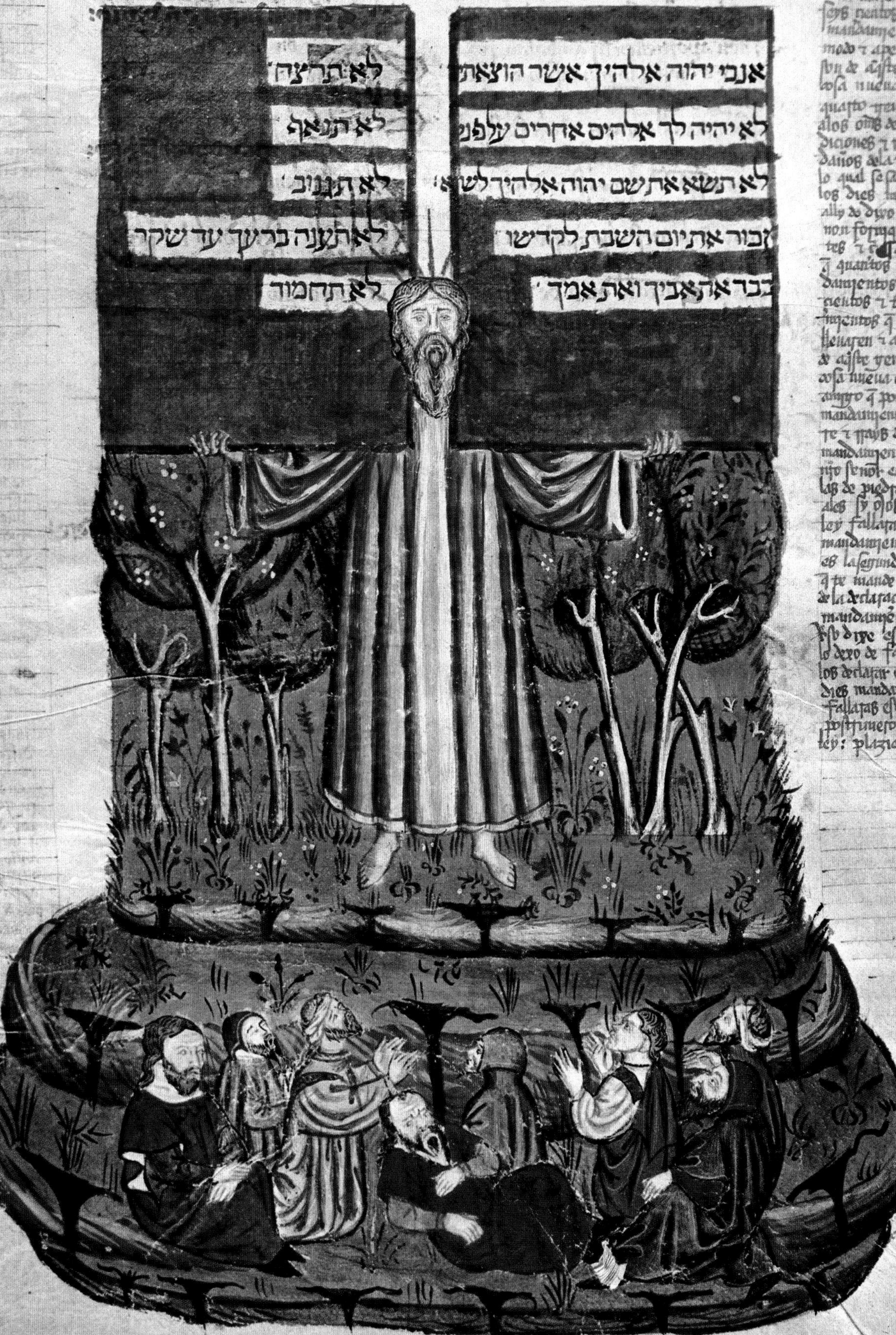

לא תרצח
לא תנאף
לא תגנב
לא תענה ברעך עד שקר
לא תחמוד
אנכי יהוה אלהיך אשר הוצאת
לא יהיה לך אלהים אחרים על פני
לא תשא את שם יהוה אלהיך לשוא
זכור את יום השבת לקדשו
כבד את אביך ואת אמך

The Torah scroll

The preservation of writing was a matter of concern to the Jews, for whom the written word was sacrosanct. The Tablets of Moses seem to look back to a time when writing was carved on stone or impressed into clay. But these media were cumbersome for the long texts that were becoming standardized after the Return from Exile. Papyrus had been employed in Egypt from very early times (25th century BCE). Parchment, more expensive but more durable, came into use in the 2nd century BCE. Both types of material were joined together to form continuous scrolls. When the bound book, or codex, was introduced (around the 1st century BCE), the scroll continued to be used for the Torah, as having a more venerable status, as it still does; for similar reasons, the Law had, and still has, to be hand-written, even after the invention of printing. At Dura Europus (*right*) even Moses is depicted holding a scroll instead of the Tablets. (32)

The oldest manuscripts of any part of the Bible are those found since 1947 at Qumran, on the Dead Sea. The Isaiah Scroll (*below*) is the longest and best preserved – seven metres long, containing fifty-four columns. Dating from about the 1st century BCE, it supersedes any text known hitherto, sometimes providing readings that clarify passages previously obscure. (31)

'Thy children make haste; thy destroyers and they that made thee waste shall go forth of thee.' So read Isaiah XLIX: 17 in the Revised Version, following the then accepted Hebrew text. But the Septuagint and the Vulgate both read 'builders' instead of 'children'. Did they have ancient authority for this reading? The answer has come from the Isaiah Scroll, where indeed it is the Hebrew word for 'builders' that occurs (detail *below*). The change has now been made in all translations, and the corresponding passage in the New English Bible, for instance, reads: 'Those who are to rebuild you make better speed than those who pulled you down, while those who laid you waste depart.' (33)

The scroll continued in universal use in the synagogue. Here, in a German Pentateuch of 1395, a reader (*ba'al qeriyah*), wrapped in the *tallith* or prayer-shawl, reads from an open scroll on a stand. (34)

To contain the scroll of the Law, elaborate cases were evolved during the Middle Ages, often among the richest works of Jewish art. This one, of copper inlaid with silver, was made in Damascus in 1565. (35)

Lifting up the scroll in an 18th-century synagogue (*below*). The scroll is displayed to the congregation after the reading, before being rolled together and put into its wrappings. (36)

A Turkish Torah-case of the early 18th century, in silver (*below*), closely follows contemporary Islamic forms and patterns. (37)

The Five Books of Moses – the Torah, or the Law – constitute the foundation of Judaism. Edited in their final form during the Exile, they relate the history of mankind from the creation to the entry into the Promised Land, together with the Ten Commandments and the Covenant established between God and his Chosen People. These splendid title-pages to the Five Books come from a 13th-century German Jewish Bible, and the letters are the opening words of each book. Their iconography is a curious, though characteristic, mixture of Jewish symbolism and Christian conventions.

Above left: Genesis. *Above right:* Exodus. *Below left:* Leviticus. *Below right:* Deuteronomy. Perhaps the most interesting imagery is that of Numbers (*opposite*). The four knights represent four of the Tribes, the leaders of the four camps of the Israelites (see Num. 11), Judah, Reuben, Ephraim, Dan, with their emblems on the flags – the lion for Judah, etc. In the corners are different kinds of seraphim (the word *seraphim* in Hebrew also means snakes); the one bottom right seems to be an ophan, a wheel-shaped angel (*ophan* = wheel) with many faces, as described in Ezekiel 1:15. (38–42)

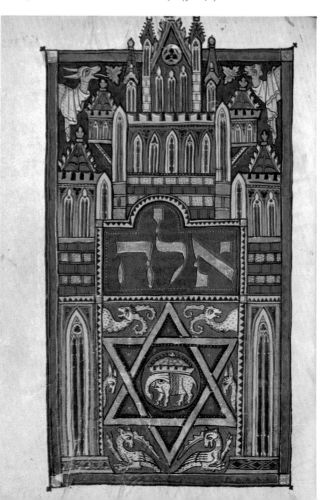

'Even so shall ye make it'

Together with the Law, God gave Moses detailed directions on the building of the Ark and the fashioning of its vessels and instruments: 'According to all that I show thee, the pattern of the tabernacle and the pattern of all the furniture thereof, even so shall ye make it' (Ex. xxv:9). When Jerusalem became the capital of a settled Israel, these were all given a permanent setting in the Temple. Almost unknown in Christian iconography, the Temple instruments and objects are frequently illustrated in Jewish Bibles.

The Ark is depicted (*left*) in a very early Bible, dated 929, written in Palestine or Egypt. The Ark itself is at the top, with the Tablets inside. Underneath is the menorah, and at the sides the jar of manna, an altar and Aaron's rod. (43)

The Messianic Temple: 'Happy is he who waits and comes to see it', runs (in part) the inscription round the edge of these two pages (*below*) from a French Bible of 1299. On the left, the altar in the outer courtyard of the Temple, used for animal sacrifices, with a sloping ramp at one side and the 'grate of brass' (Ex. xxxviii:4). Below it is the vessel containing water for washing, with its elaborate foot, and below that the 'firepan', 'flesh-hooks', spit and pots for sprinkling. In the next column is the golden altar inside the tabernacle, on which only incense was offered, with two trumpets and a *shofar*. On the right-hand page, two cherubim spread their wings over the Holy of Holies; below them, the Tablets of the Law inside the Ark; then two pans for frankincense; then the showbread with six loaves on each shelf. In the last column is the menorah, and at the bottom the staves of Moses and Aaron (flowering) with, between them, the vase containing manna. (44, 45)

'And thou shalt make a candlestick of pure gold. ...' For the menorah, too, exact instructions were laid down in Exodus: the seven branches, the position of the 'knops' or 'buds' (so labelled in Hebrew) and the tongs and snuff-dishes hanging from the lowest branch. This illustration (*opposite*) is from a Bible of 1385, written probably in Spain. (46) ▷

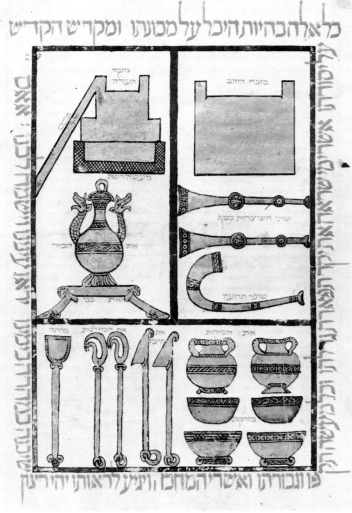

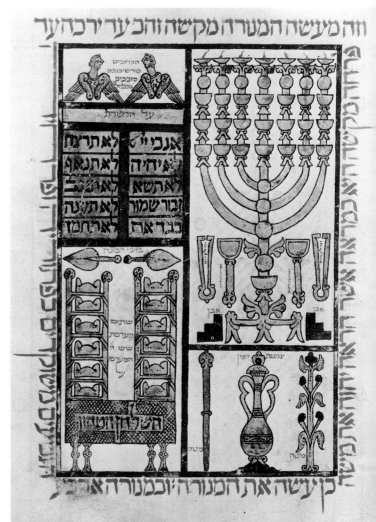

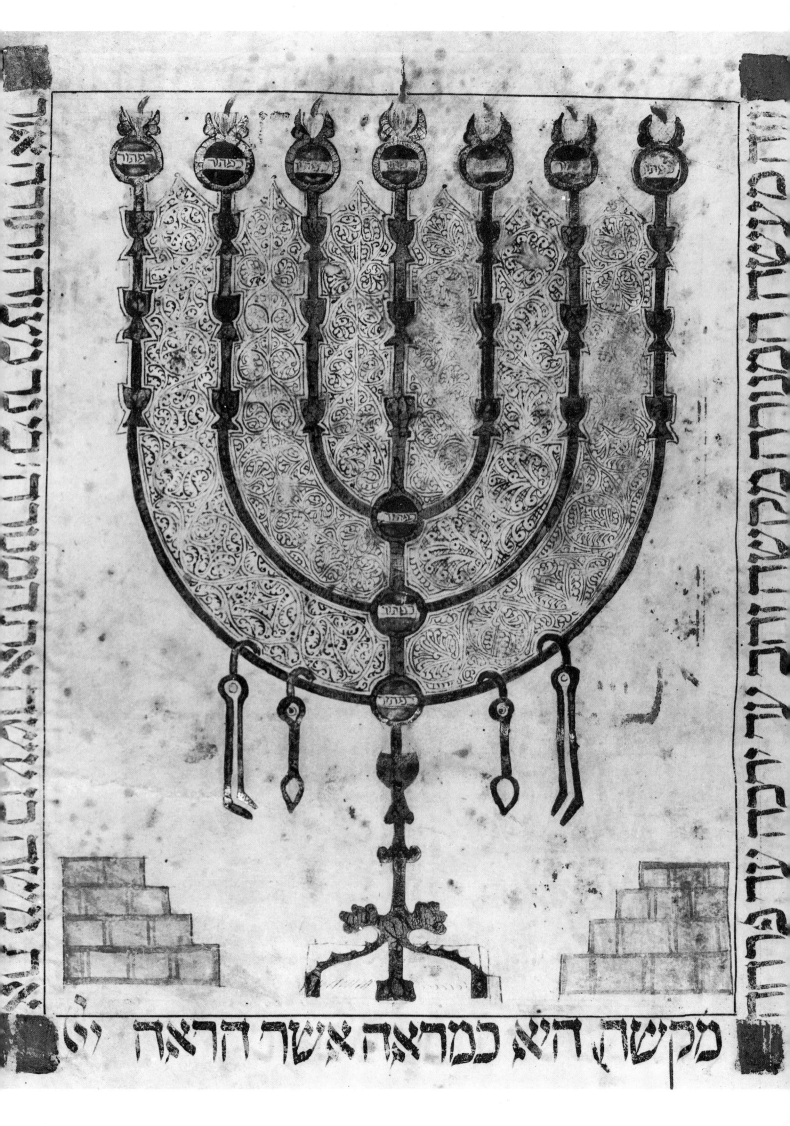

'One from among thy brethren shalt thou set king over thee.
. . . And it shall be when he sitteth upon the throne of his
kingdom, that he shall write him a copy of this law in a book
. . . and he shall read therein all the days of his life: that he may
learn to fear the Lord his God, to keep all the words of this law

and these statutes, and to do them; that his heart be not lifted up
above his brethren.' To the Jews, the king was a fallible human
being, often needing correction. This northern French
miniature of 1278 shows King Solomon reading his copy of
the Torah, as laid down by Deuteronomy. (47)

36

Chapter One

Pre-Exilic Jewry

H.W.F. SAGGS

ONE OF THE ENIGMAS of Near Eastern history, and indeed of world history, is that a politically insignificant entity, the ancient nation Israel, later known as the Jews, should have given birth to two of the world's major religions – Judaism and Christianity – and strongly influenced the concepts and institutions of a third – Islam. A standing reminder of this influence is the importance which the ancient Israelite capital, Jerusalem, continues to have in all three religious traditions.

The indisputable fact that the ancient Israelites came to have more religious significance for the world than any of their contemporaries sets them aside from other peoples and suggests the presence of some unique element in their culture. But, without accepting direct Divine Intervention, it is easier to recognize than to define that uniqueness, while, even if the divine element is accepted, there remains the problem of the events and institutions through which the postulated Divine Guidance operated.

The nomenclature for the people and culture under discussion can be confusing. Terms commonly used are 'Israel' and 'Israelite', 'Jew' and 'Jewish', and 'Hebrew'. Although in some contexts these terms may be used interchangeably, they are not synonyms and the three groups have separate histories and distinct connotations.

Within the biblical context the term 'Israel' is ambiguous. In its more restricted usage it is the name of the kingdom in northern Palestine, which existed alongside the sister state of Judah to its south during the two centuries before 722 BCE. But the term is also applied more widely, both in the Bible and by modern theologians, as a religio-ethnic term to subsume as a cultural group not only all the people of the two kingdoms mentioned, but also the ancestral groups from which the populations of those two kingdoms claimed descent. A related form, also occurring widely in the Bible, mainly in the sense of the wider religio-ethnic entity, is *bene Yisrael*, 'sons of Israel'; this is the basis of the common use of the term 'Israelite' as a designation of the people and culture to which in later phases the terms 'Jew' and 'Jewish' have come to be applied.

The term 'Jew' is derived from the Latin and Greek forms of 'Judaean', from the Hebrew *Yehudi*, found in Akkadian as *Ya(h)udai*. The Hebrew and Akkadian forms are known from the 8th century BCE, when the term specifically denoted a member of the population of the small state of Judah in southern Palestine, centred on Jerusalem, soon to be the only part of the old Israelite cultural area surviving as an independent political unit. Although the state of Judah represented only a part of the original Israelite body, there was an undoubted cultural and ethnic continuum between it and earlier Israel in the wider sense, on the basis of which the term 'Jewish' may properly be used as the later analogue of 'Israelite'.

The third term – 'Hebrew' – though sometimes used, not only in modern parlance but also apparently in the Bible, as a near synonym of 'Israelite', seems to have had a particular nuance, since in a majority of biblical occurrences the term is represented as having been spoken to, by, or in relation to foreigners. It could have originally denoted a wider ethnic community of which the Israelites considered themselves a sub-group. This possibility is suggested by the philological link between the term 'Hebrew' (*'ibri*) and the name of the person Eber (*'eber*, Gen. x: 24–5 and xi: 15–16), to whom was attributed a wide group of descendants including Abra(ha)m. But there is another possibility for the origin of the term. The earliest person to be specifically called a Hebrew (*'ibri*) in the Bible was Abra(ha)m (Gen. xiv: 13), in a context in which there is no positive indication that *'ibri* was an ethnic description, and where it could have been a term denoting social class. This admits the possibility that Eber as an imagined eponym and supposed ancestor of Abraham arose secondarily after *'ibri* had became misunderstood in an ethnic sense. Positive reasons for regarding *'ibri* as being originally a social description rest on extra-biblical evidence. In texts from the second millennium, there is widespread occurrence of a term *habiru*, which it is possible to link etymologically and perhaps historically with *'ibri*. The term *habiru* was certainly related to a particular social stratum rather than to an ethnic group, and its range of usage included the idea of 'landless wanderer', 'stateless person'. Such a description would have been appropriate for Abraham, to whom the descent of the Israelites, as well as some other groups, was traditionally traced.

The main, and for the earlier periods the only, sources for the history of the Israelites are to be found in the Bible. The wider aspects of the Bible and its meaning for Judaism are covered in Hyam Maccoby's chapter, but in assessing it as a historical source, its very complex literary history must be taken into account here also. It is not one book but a whole group of books, of different genres and periods of origin, edited on theological considerations. While recognition of this situation need

Megiddo was one of the largest of the Canaanite cities at a time when the Jews, according to the Books of Judges and Kings, were consolidating their power in the area. Although the Bible represents the two nations as unwavering enemies, there was clearly cultural exchange between them. In this ivory from the royal palace at Megiddo, c. 1200 BCE, a king is shown sitting on a richly sculptured throne. In front of him stand an official, a musician with a lyre and a warrior leading bound and naked prisoners.

in no way call into question the religious value of the Bible to Jew or Christian, it does necessitate acceptance of the possibility that what appear to be plain statements of historical fact need not be so taken.

Underlying the Bible in its final form are both written and oral sources, originating over a period of about a millennium. Some of the oral sources, particularly fragments of manifestly ancient poems, such as some embedded in the Pentateuch or the 'Song of Deborah' (Judges v), go back to before the end of the second millennium, while the latest parts of the Books of Chronicles and Daniel date from the 2nd century BCE. However, the fact that a book is demonstrably of late origin in its existing form does not preclude the possibility that it may incorporate traditions of considerable antiquity.

The major blocks of historical material in the Bible have been given a superficial unity by the latest editors, presenting an apparently straightforward account of God's dealings with the Israelites from the earliest times. In this account, Israelite traditions isolate or point up a number of formative phases. The most prominent of these in the early period are the Covenant with Abraham, the Exodus from Egypt, the giving of the Law on Sinai, and the settlement in Canaan (Palestine). These are presented as points on a continuous line of development, at which new stages in God's plan can be seen. God called Abraham to leave his home and migrate to Palestine, and there God made a covenant with him that his descendants should become a great nation occupying that land. This covenant was reaffirmed with Abraham's son and grandson, Isaac and Jacob. Circumstances took the descendants of the last-named into Egypt, where they became slaves. God led them out by Moses, to whom he had given a new Revelation, and renewed his Covenant with them on Sinai, amplifying it by a body of Law. He then guided them to conquer and settle in Palestine, where they dispossessed and subjugated the earlier inhabitants, the Canaanites.

This is all very pragmatic. Inside this overall and superficially unitary account, however, variant traditions and emphases are recognizable at many points, and a main task of modern scholarship is to probe beneath apparently incompatible data. Every one of the traditions down to the settlement has been contested as to its historicity, and even though the main currents of modern scholarship tend to accept some historical bases

for the main traditions, the detailed evaluation of those traditions varies widely.

The biblical sources are particularly difficult to evaluate as history. Besides the obvious problems of interpretation, which beset any group of ancient documents, there is a further difficulty. Because the Bible is a major element in the religio-cultural background of the Western world, biblical traditions about Israelite origins have become heavily overlaid by theological interpretations, Jewish, Christian or atheist. While this has not prevented modern literary and historical research from arriving at a consensus over wide areas, there remain areas in which major differences of interpretation persist, sometimes coloured by theological considerations, stated or unstated.

Abraham, Isaac and Jacob

It is with Abraham that Israelite origins are inseparably linked in biblical tradition. The historicity of the traditions of the Patriarchs, Abraham, Isaac and Jacob, therefore demands examination in relation to their value as evidence for early Israelite history. The problem here is two-sided: what historicity (and what chronology) is to be attributed to the patriarchal traditions, and in what sense are the Patriarchs to be accepted as ancestral to the later Israelites? If the traditional relevance of the Patriarchs to Israelite origins is accepted, there is a further problem as to the nature of patriarchal religion.

The biblical narratives offer chronological statements that would place the Patriarchs, Abraham, Isaac and Jacob, in the earlier part of the second millennium. The historicity of this tradition has been attacked by some modern scholars and strenuously defended by others. Those who reject the historicity of those narratives argue that they are substantially from a much later period, created for theological purposes. Those who defend them claim the indirect support of archaeological evidence, mainly from cuneiform texts.

There are two major collections of cuneiform texts seen as having particular importance in this connection. One is a group from around 1800 BCE, from the city Mari on the middle Euphrates, while the other comprises clay tablets from about 1500 BCE, from several sites near Kirkuk in Iraq, of which Nuzi is the most important. The former shed light on the end of a period in which nomads called Amurru (Amorites) had been settling in Mesopotamia, and the latter reflect the law and customs of a people called the Hurrians, widespread across northern Mesopotamia and northern Syria. The basic claim in the use of such data is that the patriarchal narratives reflect circumstances of life that the cuneiform texts (those mentioned and others) show to fit the first half of the second millennium rather than any other period. Adequate representation of the arguments would require a detailed study of technical points of philology and of social history, but, in brief, two of the main arguments turn upon forms of personal names and upon social customs. Thus, the cuneiform equivalent of the name Jacob is well attested in texts of the first half of the second millennium, and the form of the name Isaac equally fits there, although the name itself has not been found. Similar claims have been made for the name Abram (alternatively, Abraham), but here the situation is much less clear. In connection with customs, it is argued that some events recorded in the patriarchal narratives – such as Rachel's theft of her father's household gods in Genesis XXXI: 19 – are only meaningful in the light of customary Hurrian law reflected in the Nuzi texts, the particular argument in the case of Rachel being that there was some link between inheritance rights and the household gods. Some of the evidence has undoubtedly been pressed too far, and the Rachel incident is a case in point, since there is no definite proof that, as some scholars have claimed, physical possession of the household gods actually carried inheritance rights with it. None the less, a case does seem to have been made out for accepting that there are elements in the patriarchal narratives that do derive ultimately from traditions of the first half of the second millennium.

The conclusions reached upon this question determine the point at which one dates the beginning of Israelite culture. It is possible to recognize in the patriarchal traditions some genuine memory of a formative phase of Israelite culture, even if these are not accepted as direct historical records, and in that case Israelite beginnings can be placed before the mid-second millennium BCE. On the other hand, if any element of historical basis for the patriarchal traditions is totally rejected, and they are regarded as no more than a retrojection of the theological ideas of a later period, there remain no known strands of Israelite origins before (at the earliest) the Exodus from Egypt in the 13th century. The view taken here is that the patriarchal traditions are both so significant in our main source for early Israelite history – the Bible – and also so markedly in conformity with external evidence, that the beginnings of Israelite culture cannot be divorced from them.

The geographical and ethnic origins of the Patriarchs are obscure, though two important negative traditions are to be noted. One of these stresses that their ultimate place of origin was not Palestine; while it is possible that the emphasis given to this may reflect later religio-cultural tensions between Israelites and Canaanites, the underlying claim is so basic to the early traditions of origins that it cannot be disregarded. The second tradition, occurring in Joshua XXIV: 2, 14–15, specifically states that the ancestors of the Israelites before Abraham did not differ in religion from their neighbours; this is an indication that the Israelites thought of their more remote ancestors not as a separate group but as part of a wider cultural community.

The place of origin of Abraham is given in Joshua XXIV: 2 as 'beyond the Euphrates', and in the Hebrew text of Genesis XI: 31 and XV: 7 (but not the Greek version) more specifically as Ur of the Chaldeans; the latter is generally taken as the originally Sumerian city of Ur in southern Iraq. There are problems in this, particularly the fact that, since the Chaldean tribes did not enter the Ur area before 1000 BCE, 'of the Chaldeans' would be an anachronism at the posited time of Abraham. For this and other reasons, particularly the arbitrary hypothesis that Abraham must have been a merchant who would have come from a commercial centre linked with Haran (Gen. XI: 31), some scholars argue that Ur of the Chaldeans must denote a place in Anatolia to the north of Haran.

If the southern identification of Ur is accepted, it admits the possibility that Abraham was directly influenced by Sumero-Babylonian culture generally and by its religion in particular. Hypotheses have been propounded on this basis, which would have a bearing on the origins of Israelite culture. The most widely current hypothesis of this kind links Abraham's proto-monotheism with moon-worship. The basic argument here is that in both centres with which Abraham was associated – Ur and Haran – the chief temple was sacred to the moon-god, while it is claimed that some personal names in Abraham's cycle (Terah, Sarah, Laban, Milcah) had a lunar significance. But this lacks substantial basis. The supposed lunar connections of the names are based only on etymologies (some of them dubious) and are wholly hypothetical; and there are no indications until the middle of the first millennium BCE of the currency in either Ur or Haran of any ideas linking moon-worship with anything other than the usual broad ancient Mesopotamian polytheism.

It is equally speculative to attempt to attribute to Abraham's postulated link with southern Mesopotamia the incorporation into the Israelite literary tradition of elements of Mesopotamian myth, such as the Flood story, since there are many other possible and more probable periods and routes of transmission. While it may be accepted that the Abraham tradition of a link with the southern Ur has a historical basis, this need not imply more than that the pastoral clan to which Abraham belonged originally had a territorial range extending as far south along the Euphrates as Ur.

A more widespread tradition links the Patriarchs with the region of Haran, where northern Syria and Anatolia meet. There is extra-biblical evidence, which, though not proof, at least suggests that this tradition has some basis. This evidence comprises placenames, attested for the Haran area in cuneiform texts, which correspond with some personal names in the patriarchal stories; thus the personal name Nahor has an equivalent in the placename Nahuru, and there are several other examples. These seem to confirm a genuine memory of some link between Abraham's clan and the Haran area. The biblical tradition carries the patriarchal link with Haran beyond Abraham; according to this, when Abraham left Haran for Palestine, the remainder of his kinship group stayed there, and it was from among them that Abraham arranged for his son Isaac to obtain a wife, and his grandson Jacob married wives from the same area.

The Jacob tradition regards the Patriarchs' kinsmen

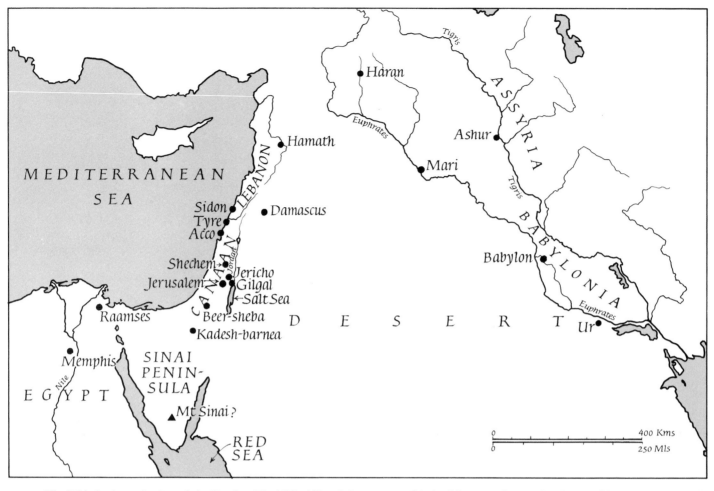

The Bible lands at the time of the Exodus. The biblical Ur of the Chaldeans remains somewhat of a mystery, but the site of Haran can be linked with the Patriarchs, and it is from there that the earliest Israelite tribes travelled across the Palestinian uplands to Canaan. It is possible that Hurrian tribes invading Syria and Mesopotamia from the north caused Jacob and his people to migrate to Egypt, where four centuries passed, of which almost nothing is known, before their miraculous Exodus, probably around the middle of the 13th century.

around Haran as being Aramaeans; this can be variously interpreted. Although Aramaean elements certainly existed in that area by the 11th and possibly by the 13th century, the evidence for a significantly earlier Aramaean presence there is dubious. Thus, unless Jacob is dated substantially later than 1500 BCE (which is about the latest date conforming to the main biblical chronology), there is the possibility that an old memory of a link between the Patriarchs and the Haran area has been coloured by the ethno-linguistic situation of a later time. Against this, note must be taken of a specific tradition, preserved in Deuteronomy XXVI: 5, that there was an Aramaean element in Israel's ancestry; in the text, the pious Israelite is required to say: 'A wandering Aramaean was my father.' The passage as we have it has received a secondary Deuteronomic elaboration implying that the 'wandering Aramaean' specifically meant Jacob; however, while this secondary element may be discarded, the original cultic formula is certainly ancient and its statement that there was a major Aramaean element in the initial stages of Israel's complex ethnic make-up must be taken into account. This again emphasizes that the Israelites did not think of themselves as ethnically distinct in origin from their neighbours. This absence of ethnic exclusiveness persisted among the Jews until after the Exile and there are many biblical references to intermarriage, or social relationships

implying the possibility of intermarriage, with peoples from most of the neighbouring nations. Not only did the Israelites think of themselves as descended from an Aramaean ancestor, but the two major Israelite tribes of Ephraim and Manasseh were traditionally part-Egyptian in origin, since their eponyms were sons born to Joseph in Egypt by an Egyptian wife (Gen. XLI: 50–2).

The nature of God

Because later tradition sees the Patriarchs as the vehicle of a Divine Revelation affecting all subsequent Israelite history, the nature of the religion of these figures is significant for the origins of Israelite culture. An earlier stage of scholarship saw patriarchal religion as a primitive animism, marked by the worship of sacred trees, stones and wells, of which (it was claimed) there are vestiges in the texts (trees, Gen. XII:6; XIII:18; XVIII:1; XXI:33; stones, Gen. XXVIII:18,22; wells, Num. XXI:17). But this fails to do justice to the powerful tradition associating the Patriarchs with some major religious development, and seeing Abraham as a major charismatic leader.

The patriarchal narratives apply a number of different names and epithets to the deity, and although these narratives seem to imply that the various terms were from the beginning alternative names of the one God, there are indications that the original situation was otherwise. A new approach to this question was introduced in an essay, 'The God of the Fathers', published by A. Alt in 1929. His analysis of the data was as follows. Before the entry of the Patriarchs into Palestine, the proto-Canaanites settled there had worshipped local deities (*'elim*; singular, *'el*) at particular cult-centres. Some of the clearest instances of early cults at particular places are El Bethel at Bethel (Gen. XXXV: 7), El Olam (translated as 'the Everlasting God' in the Revised Standard Version) at Beer-sheba (Gen. XXI:33), and El Roi (R.S.V. 'a God of seeing') at Beer-lahai-roi towards Kadesh (Gen. XIV:13–14). Although in the biblical texts these terms are applied to God as worshipped by particular Patriarchs, this was a secondary development, according to Alt. Alt saw the patriarchal concept of deity as quite different, of a special kind related to the nomadism (more recent scholars talk of semi-nomadism) of the Patriarchs. For Alt, it was a characteristic of this cultural stage that the deity had no personal name but was referred to by a title embracing the name of the first worshipper, of the type 'the God of Abraham' or 'the Mighty One of Jacob'. As a corollary of the nomadism of the original worshippers, the patriarchal type of deity was characteristically not localized.

Alt saw Abraham, Isaac and Jacob as, originally, three unconnected leaders of clans at this cultural stage. He argued that, after the settlement in Palestine of proto-Israelite tribal groups who preserved a memory of these clan leaders, the proto-Canaanite deities whom they found worshipped at local shrines in their area became identified with the form of deity associated with the name of their particular patriarchal ancestor. Thus, among the members of one group, El Bethel at Bethel became identified with the God of Jacob; another group saw El Olam of the sanctuary of Beer-sheba as the patriarchal god already known to them as 'the Fear of Isaac'; while in the Hebron area a proto-Israelite group including the tribe of Judah saw the local god of the sanctuary of Mamre as identifiable with the God of Abraham. With interrelations (Alt speaks of pilgrimages) between the proto-Israelite groups, the gods of Abraham, Isaac and Jacob, in time, became regarded as the same single deity; and, parallel to this, narratives developed to bring the Patriarchs Abraham, Isaac and Jacob into a father-son-grandson relationship.

There was, in Alt's view, a later development when the tribal confederation known as Israel came into being, with a god Yahweh; Yahweh could then be thought of as standing in the same relationship to all Israel as the divine power in the form 'the god of the Fathers' had stood to the particular groups of the earlier revelations. By this means it was possible to identify the patriarchal deity directly with Yahweh, for which reason this situation is presented in the biblical narratives in their final forms. On this view, the subsequent Israelite concept of deity contained three distinct original elements.

There has been an important subsequent modification to Alt's hypothesis. It is now recognized, from extrabiblical data, that such terms as El Bethel and El Olam in the context of proto-Canaanite religion would have denoted not different minor local gods but, rather, different manifestations of one god named El. This El was the supreme High God of the pantheon of the old settled peoples of Palestine and Syria. This has a significant bearing on the understanding of patriarchal religion. For direct syncretism to have been possible when proto-Israelites began to settle among proto-Canaanites, 'the god of the Fathers' must have possessed qualities compatible with those which were characteristic of El in the proto-Canaanite pantheon. But the main features setting El apart as we encounter him in the proto-Canaanite pantheon are that he was supreme in the pantheon, creator, and father of mankind. This implies that in the original patriarchal concept of 'the god of the Fathers' there existed (if only latently) the idea that the deity was lord of the universe and father of mankind as a whole. At the same time, while there is no indication that the patriarchal concept of the Divine explicitly predicated monotheism, there was no overt pantheon. Thus, though it would be going too far to say that patriarchal religion was universalistic and monotheistic, there are good grounds for holding that it already comprehended the seeds of universalism and monotheism.

One of the factors that contributed to producing this situation may have been the social form of the patriarchal clans. Social structure and religion were closely interrelated in the ancient world. Such a society as that of Mesopotamia was highly complex, and this was reflected in its religion. Originally, Mesopotamian civilization comprised numerous separate settlements in the form of city states, and long before the end of the third millennium it had developed a very complex social organization and much craft specialization; in this situation, not only did each original settlement have its own god or goddess, but each craft and each aspect of life also came to be associated with a deity of its own. Thus arose a multiplicity of deities, most of whom were restricted in their sphere of activity. The final Mesopotamian pantheon was a synthesis of a number of smaller local pantheons. In the total pantheon the High Gods from these local pantheons came together as a group of deities with universal aspects, though even here the need to interrelate them produced a tendency to regard the responsibility of each of these High Gods as restricted to a particular sector of the universe. A comparable situation, though with a much smaller pantheon reflecting the less complex background, prevailed in the mainly agricultural society of the proto-Canaanites, where El was the principal High God. In contrast, so far as the scanty evidence permits us to judge, the social form of the patriarchal clans was relatively simple. The clans were small in themselves, did not form part of a recognized larger social structure, and within them there was virtually no craft specialization or social stratification, apart from the distinction between the clan leader and the clan members. Thus, because there were no clearly demarcated aspects of life, stimulus was lacking for the concept of departmentalized aspects of the Divine controlling different aspects of life; the concept of the divine power could then remain undivided, reflecting the single undifferentiated clan under its leader.

In one respect the situation implied in patriarchal religion did not differ from that in the religion of the Patriarchs' contemporaries; El, for example, was creator and was much greater than a mere local god, as were

Anu, Enlil and Enki in the Sumero-Babylonian pantheon. Although these other High Gods were indeed universal, however, the fact that they were gods in an extensive pantheon had the consequence that their immediacy for mankind was much reduced by the presence of other departmental deities specifically concerned with particular aspects of human life. But in the patriarchal religion, with no overt pantheon, all that befell a man had to be the direct and immediate responsibility of the god who was the one effective divine being. Thus the traditions stemming from the Patriarchs came to see the patriarchal 'god of the Fathers' as intimately concerned with individual humans, in a way that the High Gods of pantheons, even such a one as the god El bearing the title 'father of mankind', were usually not. The Abraham tradition thus carried the germ of a new concept of the Divine as individual, single, and not merely creator of humankind in mythic time but intensely concerned for a particular human here and now. This in turn implied a new concept of the dignity and importance of the individual. This unity, universalism and ethical aspect of the Divine, latent in the patriarchal tradition, appeared in its fullness after the latter had coalesced with the dynamic cult of the god Yahweh, associated with the name of Moses.

Egyptian inheritance?

The Mosaic tradition is another area where widely differing interpretations of the data have been proposed. This tradition, though artificially linked to the Patriarchs by means of the Joseph story, is of separate origin; the biblical narrative itself shows this by the distinct break it sets (Ex. 1:6) between the Patriarchs and Moses.

Circumcision is first mentioned in the Bible (Gen. XVII) as a token of God's covenant with Abraham. Significantly, however, the rite is reintroduced by Joshua (IV:5) after the Exodus, and there is reason to believe that it was actually of Egyptian origin. This relief from Saqqara shows it being practised there as early as the third millennium BCE.

A tradition central to the Bible attributes to early Israel a period of residence in Egypt before final settlement in Palestine, and the evidence points to some important constituents of later Israel having undergone some such experience, although there are strong indications that, whatever the events were, they cannot have embraced all groups of the confederation that eventually became Israel.

There is no specific Egyptological evidence bearing upon the biblical tradition of the period in Egypt. The mention of the city Raamses in Exodus 1:11 as a store-city partly built by Israelite slaves does, however, offer a clue to the chronology, since it is known that Pharaoh Ramesses II (1304–1237 BCE) built a city Per-Raamses, which the biblical name must reflect. This would date the bondage and Exodus in the 13th century. In that same century, however, comes the first extra-biblical mention of Israel. This is found in an inscription of Ramesses's successor Mer-ne-ptah (1236–1223 BCE), who reports, of an Egyptian incursion into Palestine, 'Israel is laid waste, his seed is not.' It is not impossible chronologically that Israelites could have left Egypt during the reign of Ramesses II and been encountered in Palestine by his successor; on the other hand, this is not the only possible solution. The term 'Israel', in the Mer-ne-ptah inscription, could refer not to the tribal confederation so designated later but to an element, already in Palestine, whose name was afterwards applied to a larger group including clans that had subsequently arrived from Egypt.

It has been suggested that this early Israelite contact with Egypt had a direct effect upon the development of Israelite culture, and, in particular, that the rise of monotheism in Israel can be traced back to a movement inside Egyptian religion in the 14th century.

One would hardly expect monotheism to originate from Egypt, since from earliest times the religion of ancient Egypt was markedly polytheistic, particular prominence being given to deities representing some aspect of the sun. But at the time of King Amenophis IV (1379–1362 BCE), otherwise known as Akhenaten, there was a deliberate theological attempt to elevate one form of sun-worship to a position in which it would be the only cult. This reformed cult was centred on the sun-disk.

Some scholars have argued that Akhenaten's theology was a true monotheism and that it was this that influenced the subsequent teaching of Moses. This is, however, untenable on several grounds. Firstly, the whole basis of the Egyptian cult was that it was directed to a form of the sun, whereas in Mosaic religion it cannot credibly be argued that Yahweh was thought of as a solar deity. Secondly, the so-called monotheism of Akhenaten must be viewed in the light of the fact that he accepted divinity himself, an attitude completely contrary to that of Moses. Thirdly, the reform of Akhenaten had minimal effect, even upon Egyptian religion, away from Akhenaten's southern capital, or after his reign; it is thus inconceivable that it should have crucially affected proto-Israelites in the Delta of Egypt, far from Akhenaten's capital, a century after his reign.

The biblical texts, while firmly setting both Moses and Israelite origins against a partly Egyptian background, know nothing of any positive Egyptian influence on

Mosaic religion. The geographical area in which they place the main religious developments associated with Moses is, indeed, not Egypt at all but Sinai, although the texts as they stand suppose a direct connection between the events of Egypt and Sinai. However, it has been argued that this integration of the Exodus and Sinai traditions is secondary. This argument takes several forms. The most extreme would deny any direct link between historical events and either the Exodus or the Sinai traditions. On this view, the traditions as we have them do not derive directly from historical events at all but rather from the cult legends of festivals held at various places in Palestine. That is to say, at some cult-centre in Israelite Palestine (both Gilgal and Shechem have been proposed), a periodic festival took place celebrating the renewal of a covenant with Yahweh. Among its features was the reading of the divine law. At some stage the festival ritual was given a historical interpretation, and it was from this that the Sinai tradition as we have it arose. The Exodus-Passover traditions would be correspondingly explained. Against such an approach, however, is the consideration that, while traditions may well be preserved within a cult, there is no evidence that they can be created by the cult out of nothing. Thus, while accepting that the cult was important as a means of preserving ancient traditions, one may properly go behind the cult that preserves the tradition to look at the tradition itself and at its possible historical basis. Even with this approach, it is still possible to dissociate the Exodus and Sinai traditions; some would argue that, though the traditions as we have them do ultimately reflect actual events, they derive separately from the antecedents of two originally distinct groups of proto-Israelites.

The view dissociating the Exodus and Sinai traditions is based chiefly on the fact that, though both were clearly ancient, there are a number of instances in the Bible where one is referred to in apparent ignorance of the other. Such an analysis, however, which assumes two separate though parallel series of historical events, would necessarily divorce Moses from either the one or the other, and this would ignore significant parts of the evidence. The Revelation of Yahweh on Sinai, and the theophany in which the Law was given require a charismatic human figure as their vehicle, therefore Moses (or someone playing precisely the part attributed to Moses) must have belonged to the Sinai traditions from the beginning. When one turns to the Exodus events, one finds that the corresponding argument for an essential link with Moses is less strong; the traditions of the Plagues of Egypt and of the institution of the Passover are not organically tied to the figure of Moses. But, on the other hand, the name 'Moses' is of Egyptian origin, and this cannot be an invention of the traditions, since the Bible is so manifestly unaware of the fact that it offers a false etymology for the name, deriving it from Hebrew (Ex. II:10). Therefore, one cannot avoid concluding that Moses had genuine links with Egypt as well as with Sinai; to dissociate the Egypt and Sinai traditions creates more problems in the understanding of the traditions than it solves.

The Exodus narrative culminates in the institution of the Passover, a great festival characteristic of Israelite religion and Judaism throughout their history and one with major significance for the Christian theology of Good Friday and Easter. The Passover comprises two elements: the sacrifice of a lamb and the eating of unleavened bread and bitter herbs. There is an obvious cultural connection between the lamb and pastoralists and between unleavened bread and agriculturalists, and it seems a credible hypothesis that underlying the Passover ritual are two ancient festivals, originally distinct, one from a pastoral community and the other from an agricultural one, adopted after the settlement in Palestine. Exodus VIII:27 suggests that the proto-Israelites in Egypt already practised a pastoral sacrificial festival with a desert milieu before the time of the traditional institution of the Passover; this makes it probable that the memory of a traumatic departure from Egypt became tied in Israelite tradition to an even more ancient nomadic pastoral festival. Thus, before their final settlement, the proto-Israelites were already interpreting their history in terms of the purposes of their God. To see a plan in history became one of the distinctive marks of ancient Israelite thought, and it is therefore significant to see this indication of its operation well before the end of the second millennium.

According to the main tradition, Moses led the oppressed Israelites from Egypt to the Sinai desert. There, two main centres are mentioned: Kadesh-barnea and Mount Sinai (otherwise called Horeb). Kadesh-barnea is identifiable as a fertile oasis some fifty miles south of Beersheba; the site of Mount Sinai, on the other hand, is quite uncertain, though it was probably in one of the ranges of the Sinai peninsula.

As related in the biblical tradition, Sinai has two major associations of the highest significance for the ultimate development of Israelite religion and culture; first, the revelation of the name of Yahweh at the time of Moses's call; second, the Covenant with Israel and the giving of the Law after the Exodus. In terms of cultural history, these two are aspects of a single development.

Exodus VI:3 and III:13–15 clearly regard the revelation of the name of Yahweh as a momentous development in Israelite history. While there is the conflicting statement in Genesis IV:26 that Yahweh had been worshipped under that name from the most ancient times, the Exodus passages must reflect a formative religio-cultural stage in some group which had no prior tradition of Yahweh and which subsequently played a predominant part in the interpretation of Israel's traditions.

The human framework of the origin of the worship of Yahweh has been much discussed. Attempts made to see a form of the name Yahweh in cuneiform texts earlier than Moses have all been based on faulty philological analysis. A more tenable view is that the name ultimately derived from the Kenite clan among the Midianites in Sinai, south of Palestine, with whom Moses was closely associated in tradition. The eponym of the Kenites was the fratricide Cain, and Genesis IV:15 speaks of a mark placed upon him by Yahweh. This seems to indicate that there was a tradition that the Kenites had been worshippers of the god Yahweh from prehistoric times and that they were recognizable as such by some tribal tattoo or brand mark. Groups of proto-Israelites, long based in southern Palestine, acquainted from ancient times with Kenite neighbours to the south, would know of a tradition of the worship of Yahweh going back to primeval times; on the other hand, a clan leader such as Moses, coming into Sinai fresh from Egypt, could have met the divine name Yahweh for the first time at his encounter with the Kenites. However, to pursue this is unproductive, since it is indisputable that, even if a cult of Yahweh were known elsewhere and earlier than among the group associated with Moses, nowhere did it develop the significance that it did in Israel from the time of Moses.

What was of the highest significance was the manner in which Mosaic Yahwism, with its dynamic concept of a Covenant, backed by Divine Law, binding upon all members of the community, was able to come into relationship with the whole group, with its various antecedents, that ultimately became Israel. Among other strands that came to constitute Israel were those that carried the patriarchal traditions of 'the god of the Fathers', which in turn had come in association with the proto-Canaanite concept of the High God El. One theoretically possible way in which these three main strands could have come together would have been for their different concepts of the Divine to become interrelated within a pantheon. It has been argued with some credibility that there are slight traces of this, at least as between Yahweh and El. The clearest example claimed is Deuteronomy XXXII:8–9, where there is mention of the Most High (Hebrew, Elyon, a title of El) apportioning the nations among the sons of God (the pantheon), with Yahweh receiving Jacob (the nation Israel) as his heritage. However, even if all the few supposed instances of this kind are properly so to be understood, it is clear that this was a direction of development of no effective significance within Israelite religion. What actually happened, almost exclusively, was that the other ancient proto-Israelite concepts of the Divine were absorbed into, or merged with, that of Yahweh of the Mosaic Revelation.

It has been noted earlier that there is no evidence of any positive Egyptian influence upon the development of Israelite religion. It is possible, however, that some negative influence is to be seen. An Egyptian background could have been a factor in the failure of a pantheon to develop when the three different concepts of the Divine – Yahweh, 'the god of the Fathers' and El – came together. There has been much discussion as to whether or not the religion of Moses may properly be called monotheism; the main argument against is that there is no evidence, in the biblical traditions associated with Moses, of the absolute denial of the existence of any other god than Yahweh. There is, however, the strong tradition that for Moses Yahweh was a 'jealous god', who would not countenance the worship of any other deity alongside himself. Therefore, even if the term 'monotheism' is not strictly justified in this connection, it is quite proper to see Mosaic religion as anti-polytheistic. This could be linked to the mixed Hebrew-Egyptian background attributed to Moses, in which Moses (and the cultural group associated with him), acquainted with but not fully integrated into Egyptian culture, violently rejected the forms of Egyptian religion, with its marked polytheism and theriomorphism. An example of violent reaction to the latter may be seen in the story of Moses's destruction of the golden calf (Ex. XXXII:1–20).

The Decalogue

In the main tradition, when Israel under Moses reached Mount Sinai, a Covenant was effected, accompanied by the giving of the Law. On literary grounds, the origin of much of the existing corpus of Pentateuchal law is certainly to be attributed to the period after the settlement. The central element, the Decalogue of Exodus XX:2–17, repeated in Deuteronomy V:7–21, is in a different category, and there are no insuperable literary difficulties in accepting its origin (in its earliest form) as being in the Mosaic period, where tradition places it. Even so, it is nearly a millennium later than the earliest laws from the ancient Near East, which are now known from several collections earlier than the celebrated laws of Hammurabi (1792–1750 BCE). Thus the major significance of the Decalogue is not its date but its form and content. In form, it stands alone among corpora of ancient Near Eastern law. Other groups of laws, including some in the Pentateuch, are in casuistic form; that is, they are stated as decisions prescribed for particular offences or disputes. Such clauses were probably based ultimately on decisions made in actual cases by some judge (the ruler or his judicial representative), and we actually have an account of Moses himself giving such decisions (Ex. XVIII:16). Only in the Decalogue and some other sections of the Pentateuch are there laws in apodictic form, that is, in the form of absolute commands or prohibitions. However, while this form is not found elsewhere in laws, there are traces of it in international treaties between overlords and vassals. This has led some scholars to conclude that this concept affected the literary form of the Decalogue, seen as the terms of a treaty between the overlord, Yahweh, and his vassals, Israel. But even if this explains the form of the laws, it is highly significant that this concept of law as a treaty or covenant arose only in Israel. This suggests a difference in basic attitudes. Some other ancient Near Eastern collections of laws were, indeed, regarded as ultimately deriving their validity from a god, but their form – for example, 'If a man has harboured a lost slave ... in his house ... that house-owner shall be put to death' (Hammurabi's Laws) – contained the implication that, even though there may have been divine sanctions in the background, the obligations a man owed were to society or to individuals. In the Decalogue, on the contrary, while the subject of command or prohibition might relate to society or to individuals, the situation presented was that any failure to conform to the prescribed conduct was an offence directly against Yahweh himself.

It could be argued that this merely indicates that in Israel God was the personification of society or the community, which would correspond with the view of the sociologist Durkheim that religion is a way in which individuals represent the nature of their society and its relationship to themselves. But even if Durkheim's view be accepted as substantially valid as a sociological analysis, the situation still reveals a significant difference between the way Israel and its contemporaries looked at society. The difference implies that in Israel the whole of life was felt to be directly under the control and care of the Divine, whereas in Mesopotamia human institutions, represented by the apparatus of statecraft, were interposed between man and the Divine.

If we accept that the Decalogue in its origin goes back to before the final settlement in Palestine, it follows that there must already have existed some community to whose life these laws were central. The Bible in its final form presents this community as already being Israel. However, it seems clear as a historical fact that, before the settlement, there were several separate groups carrying traditions that became those of the later cultural entity, Israel; it avoids confusion to refer to these early separate groups as proto-Israelites, rather than anachronistically to lump them together as a single body, Israel, or, alternatively, to select one particular group for that designation.

To sum up the situation before the settlement: we may see certain attitudes already existing among the proto-Israelites, either actively operating or latent, which developed later as a part of what marked off Israelite thought from that of its contemporaries. Thus, in the group of the Egypt experience there were already traces of a belief in divine guidance in history. In the group of the Sinai theophany (probably the same group, though some scholars dispute this) there was a belief that Yahweh had made a Covenant with them by which men accepted Yahweh's sole governance and gave him their allegiance, while Yahweh made them his special people. Among the groups associated with the patriarchal traditions there were the seeds of universalism and monotheism.

These ideological strands came together after the settlement; by this term we mean the phase in Israelite development when the Tribes of Israel finally appear in Palestine, occupying or claiming certain territories and beginning to act as groups accepting mutual responsibilities. The beginning of this phase may be placed at the end of the 13th century BCE. The settlement presents certain historical problems, and some scholars, regarding the process not as a gradual movement but as a military invasion, would reject this term and speak of a conquest. The main basis for such a view is that Joshua I–XII does in fact present the situation as a conquest, and excavation shows that a number of towns mentioned in those chapters as attacked by the Israelites were destroyed at a date that might be within the supposed period of the Israelite military movement. However, the latter argument is very dubious; not only were most of the sites excavated before modern archaeological techniques were developed, and for this reason the dating of destruction levels is very uncertain, but the identification of some sites with towns named in Joshua I–XII is not beyond doubt. Moreover, there is no proof that the destruction of those towns was at the hands of Israelites rather than Philistines, who entered Palestine at about the same period. Against the supposition of a sudden Israelite conquest of Palestine are a number of other biblical passages, such as some pointing to immigration from the south, rather than via Transjordan as in Joshua I–XII, and another group of traditions supposing patriarchal clans dwelling in Palestine long before the Mosaic period. These traditions taken together contradict the idea of a sudden military conquest and indicate that the nation subsequently known as Israel coalesced from diverse groups, which entered Palestine by different routes and in different periods and circumstances.

A significantly different view of Israelite origins has been propounded by G. E. Mendenhall, who denies any major relevant immigration into Palestine, and sees the so-called 'settlement' or 'conquest' as a process of social change within the land. Mendenhall first challenges the usual view that the tribal form of Israel presupposes an earlier nomadic background, and then reinterprets the 'conquest' in the light of the Amarna letters. These are 14th-century documents written by the rulers of city states in Palestine and Syria to the Egyptian pharaoh, until then the overlord of that region; they contain warnings of attacks on the city states by people called Habiru, generally taken to be invaders. Mendenhall, however, shows that this is an unproved assumption and argues that, substantially, they were disaffected peasantry who had renounced their allegiance and withdrawn politically from the existing city state regimes. He sees the development of what came to be called 'Israel' as a corresponding process a little later. On this view, most of subsequent Israel derived not from immigrating nomadic tribes but from communities long settled in Palestine. Politically, this was not a conquest but a peasants' revolt. The ideology was provided by a small dynamic immigrant group who had escaped from slavery in Egypt, and, having no superior human community to protect them, had made a covenant with a god Yahweh. The various peasant groups who joined them, taking over the central concept of the covenant with Yahweh, became 'tribes' of Israel. This hypothesis, while providing a framework in which the terms 'Habiru' and 'Hebrew' could neatly interlock, rests heavily upon unproved assumptions about the nature of the Habiru of the Amarna letters, and takes inadequate account of a number of biblical traditions.

On all interpretations of the settlement traditions, it is accepted that it was the latest arrivals, those associated with the Exodus and Sinai events, who introduced Covenant Yahwism into Israel. Leaving aside the exact details of the mechanism of its introduction, it is clear that it was a popular ideological movement, of a kind not attested before (and only rarely after) in the ancient Near East. As far as can be traced, this was the first time that the idea was articulated of a relationship with the Divine which involved all members of the community, making claims upon individuals. This is not to deny either that there had been earlier ideological movements or that other earlier peoples were subject to divinely established codes of conduct. But the codes of conduct were thought of as part of the scheme of things and were not terms directly decreed by a god in historic time in a setting that made every individual personally responsible for observing them. As to earlier ideological movements, such as the religious reform associated with Akhenaten in Egypt, or the questioning of values in Egyptian and Sumero-Babylonian Wisdom literature, these never affected more than a small élite, not the whole community.

Yahweh and Baal

The Israelite settlement in Palestine, whatever its nature, introduced tensions: the dominant ideology of a group with a tradition of life in the desert encountered an agricultural and, subsequently, urban basis of life. These tensions had interrelated social and religious dimensions.

In the immediately religious area, a major problem concerned the relationship of the Divine to agricultural fertility. Among the old settled Canaanite population there were cults emphasizing the relationship of Baal and other deities with fertility. But the original connections of Yahweh, the god of the new ideology, were with the desert and the mountains of distant Sinai, with no tradition of a fertility aspect. Thus, until the existence of Baal became denied absolutely, there was the standing question: was Baal another god alongside Yahweh, with powers relevant to an agricultural community which Yahweh did not possess, or were Baal and Yahweh different aspects of one divine power? This latter solution – direct syncretism, Yahweh being equated with Baal – certainly occurred. Such good Yahwists as Saul and David might give one son a name based on the element Baal and another son a name based on Yahweh; for example, Saul's sons Eshbaal and Jonathan (= 'Yahweh gave', I Chron. VIII: 33), and David's sons Beeliada (= 'Baal knows', I Chron. XIV: 7) and Jedidiah (= 'Beloved of Yahweh', II Sam. XII: 25). There were even Hebrew personal names that actually stated the equation 'Yahweh is Baal' (Bealiah, I Chron. XII: 5). Although this syncretism was acceptable at the beginning of the monarchy, it came to be emphatically rejected by the prophets, as spokesmen for the mainstream of Mosaic Yahwism. While historical factors contributed to this, the main factor was that the equation produced theological problems. Among the proto-Israelites, identification of 'the god of the Fathers' with El had been possible without significant tension, largely because El was becoming otiose in the Canaanite and related pantheons. In texts from Ugarit of about 1400 BCE, reflecting early Canaanite religion, El, although High God, is much less prominent in the current mythology than Baal, and his mythological associations were clearly already fading into the background. Consequently, by the time of the Israelite settlement, current mythology within Palestine did not stress characteristics of El that were incompatible with the idea of the Divine deriving from the patriarchal tradition. But Baal was dynamic, with a fully operational mythology and an associated cultus containing elements incompatible with and abhorrent to the Yahwism of the Sinai Covenant group.

Perhaps the most conspicuous element of Baalism incompatible with the worship of Yahweh was cultic prostitution. The concept of the Divine associated with patriarchal religion and early Mosaic Yahwism shows no indication of any sexuality, and it had escaped this probably because it was not the end-product of a continuous religious evolution from prehistoric times. Outside early Israel, the feminine element in the concept of divinity was widespread in the ancient Near East and went back into the Neolithic period and even earlier, being well evidenced by figurines of mother-goddesses from many prehistoric sites. Within the historical period, although the role of goddesses in general gradually diminished, reflecting the male-dominated society that had developed, goddesses directly related to sexuality remained prominent. This was reflected in sexual activity as part of the cultus, which was particularly marked in the Canaanite area. This aspect of Canaanite religion, though always proscribed by official Yahwism, was so intimately related to the agricultural background of life

in ancient Palestine that it was impossible to eradicate it wholly, and during the monarchy it became an accompaniment of Yahwistic cultus at the local shrines known as High Places, and even gained a foothold within the Temple in Jerusalem; as late as the last quarter of the 7th century BCE, King Josiah found it necessary to destroy 'the houses of the cult prostitutes which were in the house of Yahweh' (II Kings XXIII: 7).

Alongside this tension of a directly religious nature, there were other tensions, which, although expressed in religious terms, were basically social. Palestine has an exceptionally large number of ecosystems for a small area, with climates ranging from subalpine to tropical, and physical features varying from complete desert to (in ancient times) both temperate and tropical forest. The Israelite community came to occupy a greater proportion of the whole than any single previous group. Thus, although the main aspect of life was agricultural and in part urban, there was no single standard pattern; other ways of life could exist, which emphasized and perhaps idealized the earlier semi-nomadism in the desert with which the traditions of pre-settlement Yahwism were associated. This ensured that the social institutions of agriculturalism and urbanism – the latter with its tendency to subordinate the individual and the family to the state – remained subject to criticism. We see this most directly among a group called the Rechabites, who deliberately followed nomadic ideals, living in tents and refusing to drink wine, build houses or cultivate the soil (Jer. XXXV: 8–10). This movement played some part in a violent anti-Baalist dynastic revolution in the northern kingdom in the middle of the 9th century (II Kings X: 15–17). The Rechabites were an extremist minority, but some of the same aspects of social criticism are seen in a more balanced and influential manner among the prophets. Amos (V: 21–VI: 6) protested against things done in Yahwism that related to an agricultural form of society, which had no part in the religion of desert days; Hosea (II: 14–15) contrasted Israel's condition in his time with the circumstances of 'the days of her youth' in the wilderness; Isaiah (V: 8) protested against abuses arising from the greed to own land.

The tension between old Yahwistic pre-settlement attitudes and those of a long tradition of agriculturalism and urbanism represented by the Canaanites is dramatically illustrated in the story of Naboth's vineyard (I Kings XXI: 1–16). This turned upon a question of land tenure. King Ahab of Israel wanted a vineyard next to his palace belonging to Naboth, and quite fairly (from the commercial point of view) offered him a better one or money payment in exchange. But Naboth refused on the ground that it was ancestral land; in the old Israelite concept, land was the property of Yahweh alone, held by particular families to whom Yahweh had entrusted it at the settlement, and so inalienable. Ahab, although displeased, accepted this. But to Ahab's wife Jezebel, a princess from Sidon, holding the concepts of the urban society of the Canaano-Phoenician commercial cities of Tyre and Sidon, land was property which could be sold like any other. The illegal measures she took to obtain the vineyard for Ahab were abhorrent to Israelite traditions, and triggered a major clash between old Israelite and Canaanite social concepts, or, in religious terms, between the ideologies of Yahweh and Baal.

Tensions of this kind served to limit the extent to which Israelite religion became shackled to a particular form of society or ecosystem. Thus, to a significant extent, it remained the fundamental principles of Yahwism that were emphasized; because of this, Israelite religion, more than any contemporary religion, developed in a form based on fundamentals that, in practice, could be strongly linked with particular institutions and places, but in essence were not tied to considerations of period or institution or place. This was a factor in the survival of Israelite religion, in the form of Judaism, after the traumatic events of 586 BCE, when the Holy City of Jerusalem and its Temple were destroyed, the apparently central institution of kingship ceased to operate and the most influential parts of the population were removed far from their land.

Israelite kingship

Israelite religion, though not tied to a particular political system, needs to be looked at in the context of the political situation in which it operated. We, therefore, need briefly to look at Israelite history from the rise of the monarchy to the end of the kingdoms. Despite problems of detail, this is basically straightforward. Pressures from surrounding peoples led to the rise of charismatic war leaders, one of whom, Saul of the Tribe of Benjamin, was anointed king just before 1000 BCE. After Saul's defeat and death in battle against the Philistines, he was succeeded by David. Under David and his son Solomon, Israel became briefly the major power in the Levant. At Solomon's death (922 BCE), the northern Tribes broke away to form a separate kingdom, Israel, while the southern Tribes remained in David's dynasty as the kingdom of Judah. These kingdoms maintained commercial, military and diplomatic contacts with their neighbours, particularly the Phoenicians of the coast of Lebanon and the Aramaeans of Damascus and Hamath. In the mid-9th century, Israel, in alliance with Hamath and Damascus, had its first military encounter with Assyria, an expanding state, which in the second half of the 8th century spread out to make all the states of Syria and Palestine its vassals. Assyria brought the kingdom of Israel to an end in 722 BCE, but the Davidic dynasty continued in Judah until 586 BCE, when that kingdom was extinguished by the Babylonians under Nebuchadnezzar.

Two of the major points for consideration from the period of the kingdoms are the consequences for Israelite development of the institution of kingship, and the effects of cultural contacts with neighbouring nations. While these were new factors, the Israelite reaction to them was conditioned by earlier history.

The institution of kingship was forced upon Israel by external pressures. This is beyond doubt historically and accepted by the biblical texts. Similar factors may well have operated in other nations, but different antecedents produced different consequences. In Israel, the combination of the idea of a Covenant relationship with Yahweh and the institution of kingship produced two conflicting reactions. One treated the old Covenant as re-enacted between Yahweh and the Davidic dynasty; this reinterpretation was doubtless promoted by the royalist party. But another reaction was one of hostility; the human king was seen as now usurping the authority that,

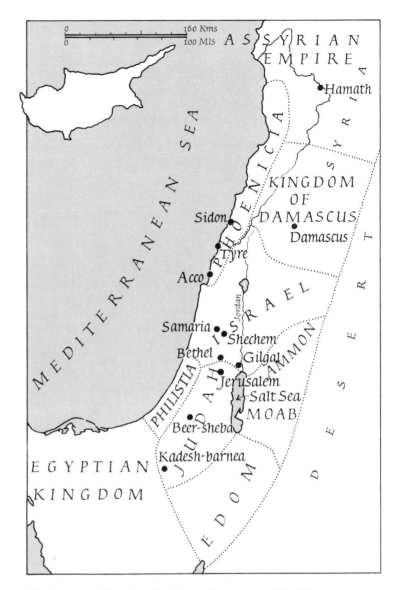

The kingdoms of Israel and Judah c. 785–745 BCE. The differences between the two kingdoms of Judah and Israel may, to some extent, account for the survival of Judah after the fall of the northern kingdom. Although Judah was far smaller, and her land less fertile, the population was homogeneous, loyal to the Davidic dynasty and united by the worship of Yahweh. The northern kingdom was also weakened by struggles with its neighbours to the north, the Aramaeans of Damascus. In the end, Damascus was crushed in 732 BCE by Tiglath-Pileser, the ambitious king of the Assyrian Empire, Israel in turn falling to his successor ten years later.

since the enactment of the Covenant, had belonged to Yahweh alone, as divine overlord. These two conflicting ideas are clearly represented in the biblical texts. The resultant tension had important social consequences: it contributed to making it impossible for an Oriental despotism to arise; when the threat of such a development became apparent, as at the end of the reign of Solomon, or subsequently in the northern kingdom under Ahab, influenced by Jezebel, the old ideology reasserted itself and overthrew the threatened tyranny. Because kingship was introduced at a very late period and the earlier tradition of direct governorship by Yahweh remained alive, it was always remembered that the king in Israel or Judah was a man among men and subject to the laws of Yahweh; he was never, like the king of Tyre (Ezek. XXVIII:2), himself a god and

47

absolute. Thus, King David himself was rebuked by a prophet in the name of Yahweh, and accepted the rebuke (II Sam. XII: 13). The fact that the king was, equally with the poorest in the land, subject to the laws of Yahweh, emphasized the equality of all men, and contributed to the development of the idea that the individual was important in himself and not merely as part of a social group (Ezek. XVIII: 19–20).

A second consequence of the ambivalent attitude to kingship was that Israel as a cultural entity did not grow to depend upon this institution for its existence. As already noticed, this became important for the perpetuation of the concept Israel after the final elimination of the monarchy at the fall of Jerusalem in 586 BCE. Although the king had been at the centre of the cultus in Jerusalem for four centuries, in the last resort the essential heart of Israelite religion and civilization could live on without the king.

The administrative machinery accompanying kingship proved to be one of the main channels for cultural contacts with other nations and for the penetration of foreign institutions into Israelite life. Solomon introduced a civil service based on Egyptian models, bringing Egyptian cultural influence in its wake. When the Bible enlarges on Solomon's 'wisdom' (I Kings IV: 29–34), it specifically compares it (favourably) with 'the wisdom of Egypt', and, as further amplification, explains that Solomon 'spoke of trees, from the cedar that is in Lebanon to the hyssop that grows out of the wall; he spoke also of beasts, and of birds, and of reptiles, and of fish.' These details indicate that the literary genres forming the background of this are traceable to both Mesopotamia and Egypt, the immediate influence in Solomon's case being Egypt. Indeed, within the Book of Proverbs, traditionally linked with Solomon, one section (XXII: 17–XXIII: 12) is generally accepted as showing dependence upon a known Egyptian composition.

Kingship also brought foreign influences in its wake by means of diplomatic marriages; it was alleged that the chapels Solomon built for foreign wives introduced religious practices opposed to the Israelite tradition (I Kings XI: 1–8). In fact, Solomon's building of Yahweh's Temple probably brought in at least as much foreign influence; the logistics for providing the timber from Lebanon entailed considerable contact of Israelites with Phoenicians (I Kings V: 8–12), while the fact that the bronze-work was entrusted to a craftsman of Phoenician descent (I Kings VII: 13–14) gave obvious scope for the introduction of Phoenician religious symbols, such as the bronze pillars Jachin and Boaz (I Kings VII: 15–22).

Commercial or military relations established by Israelite rulers must also have exposed Israelites to foreign cultural influences, as well as potentially making other peoples acquainted with Israelite concepts. A tradition that Solomon built store-cities in Hamath (II Chron. VIII: 3–4) may reflect a memory of Israelite merchant-colonies in Syria, while I Kings XX: 34 specifically mentions such colonies established by Syrians in Samaria and by Israelites in Damascus. A military alliance between Israel, Damascus and Hamath, to oppose an Assyrian invasion in 853 BCE, is recorded in the Assyrian sources, and a similar alliance between Israel and Damascus over a century later is mentioned in

II Kings XVI: 5. When the Assyrian power became dominant in Palestine, the status of vassaldom of the Israelite kingdoms brought further contacts, potent for foreign influences; we know from an Assyrian monument that King Jehu of Israel, or his representative, personally paid homage to the Assyrian king in 841 BCE, while just over a century later, Ahaz of Judah made a visit to his suzerain, Tiglath-Pileser III, in Damascus, which is specifically said to have resulted in cultic changes in Jerusalem (II Kings XVI: 10–15).

The need for change

Not only was Israel open to foreign ideas, but it was almost inevitable that Israel should also borrow and adapt institutions from its neighbours, since the form of society associated with Mosaic Yahwism in its formative phase did not of itself offer the full range of institutions needed for settled life in Palestine. This last point was consciously recognized in some quarters, one possible conclusion from it being that, because original Mosaic Yahwism did not provide a full social framework for settled life on an agricultural basis, then settled life on an agricultural basis was wrong. This was, of course, the very view taken by the Rechabites. The more generally held view was less extreme, and accepted the need for new institutions. As we have noted, some of the groups that merged into the entity known as Israel had taken no part in the Egypt-Sinai wanderings and were already agriculturalists, with their own traditions and practices. These constituted one potential basis for the way of life of the whole later Israelite community, provided they could be fitted into the framework of Mosaic Yahwism. This called for their scrutiny in that light. The result was that some old agricultural practices, such as the festival of Unleavened Bread, were reinterpreted and accepted, this particular institution becoming part of the Passover festival. Other practices, which had dangerously offensive associations with Canaanite religion, were proscribed. An example of the latter is the prohibition, repeated three times, against cooking a kid in its mother's milk (Ex. XXIII: 19; XXXIV: 26; Deut. XIV: 21), probably singled out because it was a magical fertility practice in Canaanite religion.

This need to adopt institutions, but at the same time to scrutinize them in the light of Mosaic Yahwism, was another aspect of the tension already mentioned. It had important consequences, which eventually contributed to differentiating the people of Israel from their contemporaries. In no other ancient society was the spirit of criticism and rejection as strongly articulated as in Israel.

No ancient society was completely static; it was necessary for all to adapt to changing circumstances in order to survive, but most ancient societies were markedly conservative. A good example of this is ancient Mesopotamia, where the situation was linked to the predominant view that the pattern of existence had been preordained by the divine powers: deliberate change acknowledged as such would thus tend to be associated with the disturbance of the proper order of things. The changes which – despite this world view – inevitably occurred were, therefore, usually not consciously innovative but, rather, were gradual, often almost imperceptible, and usually non-explicit. It must be granted that even in Mesopotamia there were occasional deliberate attempts to reform old institutions, but these were rare and seldom significant; the changes that did actually come about were generally not explicitly presented as being in conflict with earlier practices or practices elsewhere, and did not entail an acknowledged rejection of older, or other, ways. A good example is the Mesopotamian response in the late first millennium to an eclipse of the moon. By the period mentioned, the mathematics of the motions of the moon were sufficiently understood for lunar eclipses to be predicted well in advance, yet a religious ceremony was still performed to drive off the demons attacking the moon. Because of Mesopotamian conservatism, the logically incompatible old and new understandings of the eclipse continued side by side.

One of the major factors in the development of this kind of conservatism in both Mesopotamia and Egypt was the very long period of organized civilized life and institutions that lay behind, giving a sense of continuity and permanence. Israel, by contrast, was an upstart as a civilized state (or, later, states), and its people were consciously aware that their traditions lacked some institutions relevant to statehood, which they needed to adopt from their neighbours. There was no feeling that the way of life in which they now lived had been that of their ancestors since primeval times, and so the very different historical antecedents of Israel resulted in less reverence for old ways of life. Thus, instead of feeling a compulsion to preserve all the old ways and to reconcile them with the new, the Israelites at the time of the settlement and after could, more readily than peoples of the ancient settled civilizations or more recently settled peoples who had come under their cultural influence very strongly, make a deliberate explicit rejection of old concepts or practices that conflicted with concepts currently and directly significant to their way of life.

Had Israel, under the impetus of Mosaic Yahwism, not taken this attitude, enabling it consciously to reject, it is clear from the historical record that syncretism and cultural contacts would have converted Israelite religion into just another aspect of what we commonly refer to as Baalism, with the states of Israel and Judah leaving no more significant legacy for world history than did their contemporary states in Palestine and Syria. Indeed, looking at events from the political side, it could be said that the state of Israel, in which major elements had resisted Canaanite religio-cultural influences less successfully than more remote Judah, did eventually meet this fate; although it has to be taken into account that some aspects of the northern kingdom – for instance, some of its traditions, notably those of the Elohist strand of the Pentateuch, and some of its population (Jer. XLI: 5) – continued to play a part in Judaean Yahwism and the subsequent development of Judaism. For Yahwism to preserve its identity in the face of the forces of political developments and of syncretism, it was necessary for it to reject and to criticize.

The spirit of rejection and criticism is reflected in various ways in the Bible; one sees it in the prohibition of images of the deity, reflecting a view on practices which were certainly well known to the Israelites, while it also underlies the hostile reaction in some quarters to the institution of kingship, already mentioned. But, above all, this attitude was consciously articulated through the prophets.

The role of the prophet

Prophecy as a religious phenomenon was not peculiar to Israel; the giving of a message from a god through an inspired person, usually in a state of ecstasy, is attested from several other parts of the ancient Near East over a long period. In all ancient Near Eastern civilizations people sought communication with the supernatural, which in this connection might be thought of as either an impersonal fate or a specific deity or group of deities. The objective might be to give the worshipper knowledge of the future so that he might arrange his activities to the best advantage or, alternatively, to induce the divine powers to intervene for the benefit of the worshipper. Originally, prophecy was only one technique among several that Israelites might employ for this kind of purpose, the alternatives most commonly favoured being dreams and 'urim and tummim' (Deut, XXXIII: 8; I Sam. XXVIII: 6), the last mentioned operating probably by random choice of one of two stones, on the principle of drawing lots or tossing a coin. But, eventually, prophecy in Israel underwent a development that made it unique.

While it is not possible to offer a complete explanation of the unique development of prophecy in Israel, factors can be identified which contributed to this. As already indicated, it was not necessary for divination to operate on the basis of a divine personality, and in various parts of the ancient Near East there were forms of divination that, even though deities might formally be mentioned in connection with them, presupposed an impersonal fate behind the course of events; such forms of divination could have existed among proto-Israelites, and 'urim and tummim' may in origin have been one such, later given a Yahwistic interpretation. However, with the general Israelite adoption of the ideology of Mosaic Yahwism, the intense Israelite belief that the god Yahweh was at all times zealously overseeing the nation's destiny required that the only acceptable form of divination was a message given directly by Yahweh. Although 'urim and tummim' could be reinterpreted in this sense, the mechanism which most clearly fulfilled this need was prophecy, that is, a message through an individual in a psychological state indicating that he had been seized by the god, who was speaking through him. While this same phenomenon was attested at Mari early in the second millennium, there it was of only secondary importance, inasmuch as messages purporting to come from the god by prophetic means had to be checked by liver-divination. This was because liver-divination had a long history behind it, and a corpus of associated texts, with all the resultant prestige to be expected in a society dominated by a long scribal tradition. In Israel, with no corresponding long period of literate civilization, there was no factor tending to subordinate prophecy to other divination mechanisms, so that, with the particular Israelite need of a direct personal message from God, prophecy could develop unchallenged.

With the importance that these factors gave prophecy in Israel there was a tendency for the prophet to develop an association with the cult. How far this became general and formalized is a matter of controversy; an extreme view holds that the cultic status of prophets was so general that even the canonical prophets of the Bible were cult prophets with an official status. Certainly there were prophets who played an official part in state affairs, as I Kings XXII:5–12 shows; this speaks of the king of Israel formally consulting four hundred prophets for guidance before a proposed military campaign.

Originally, and typically, the kind of message a prophet gave, whether in Israel or elsewhere, was brief and in relation to a particular problem, like that just quoted. But, from an early stage, certain Israelite prophets went on to interpret their own message in the light of the tenets of Mosaic Yahwism. The prestige of the Israelite prophet, and his closeness in many cases to the central state administration, put him in a particularly powerful position to use this means to comment upon, or criticize, the behaviour of the king and government circles, or Israelite society more widely. In such a situation, the prophet, as the vehicle of a message from God, enjoyed some measure of immunity even if his message gave offence, since only the most ruthless ruler would dare to act against such a man. It has already been noticed that as early as the reign of David the prophet Nathan, claiming to speak in the name of Yahweh, was able to rebuke the king for adultery and murder (II Sam. XII:9). In the following century, the prophet Elijah was the mouthpiece for the condemnation of the land-snatching perpetrated by Ahab and Jezebel (I Kings XXI:19), while, according to one biblical tradition (II Kings IX:1–13), Elisha was instrumental in bringing about a dynastic revolution in Israel in reaction to such abuses.

This spirit of rejection and criticism reached its highest expression in the canonical prophets of the 8th century. By the middle of that century, the prophet Amos was criticizing a wide range of aspects of life in Palestine, extending beyond the two Israelite kingdoms: he condemned such matters as brutality in war (Am. I:3,6,11,13; II:1) and economic oppression of the poor (II:6–7; IV:1; VIII:6) as well as abuses more directly linked to the cult. With Hosea, shortly after Amos, although much of the message is specifically related to cultic matters, in that it is directed against syncretism with Baalism, this is linked with condemnation both of the social evils caused by departure from the tenets of Mosaic Yahwism, and of the involvement in international politics, which was one dimension of the rejection of the old theocratic ideal. Within the oracles of Isaiah, equally trenchant against social evils, the political aspect was more strongly marked, reflecting the historical situation in which, by the period of Isaiah's main activity in the final third of the 8th century, Assyria had spread out to take the two Israelite kingdoms fully into its orbit. Isaiah now applied the principles of Yahwism even to international political relations and to other nations.

Despite this social dimension of the teachings of the prophets, it would be misleading to think of them as being primarily social (or even political) reformers in intention. Their motivation was clearly not any specific programme of reform as such but to reassert the values of Yahwism and to judge and challenge all institutions and developments on those standards. This kind of prophetic criticism of behaviour at variance with Mosaic Yahwism, however, was potentially a powerful social force. Other nations of the ancient Near East were not without social mechanisms by which accepted values could be asserted, or even means by which public opinion could be brought to bear upon rulers, but so far as our evidence goes, Israel (in the wide religio-cultural sense) was the only nation in the ancient Near East in which society as a whole, and its leaders, were regularly exposed to public judgment in this way. It was a significant characteristic of the Israelite way of life, and one contributing to its survival in the form of Judaism, when all its contemporaries ceased to exist as recognizable nations, that its values and principles were explicit. This gave it a framework within which a society could be rebuilt after the disaster of the fall of Jerusalem to Nebuchadnezzar, and the destruction of the old social order headed by the king, in 586 BCE.

This spirit, of the judgment of institutions, events and men in the light of the demands of Yahwism, though particularly vividly represented in prophecy, is also present in some Israelite writing outside this category. One such genre is the biographical history found in parts of the Books of Samuel, particularly II Samuel IX–XX, recounting events relating to King David, and probably from not long after his reign. There are no close contemporary parallels to this literary form. It is true that the beginnings of historical records are found by this time or earlier in other ancient Near Eastern cultures, but these do not bear comparison with the vividness and objectiveness of the Davidic court history; the Israelite material has the spirit of epic with the directness of biography. Where historical records concerning kings begin to emerge elsewhere in the ancient Near East, they are predominantly put into the mouth of the king himself and are usually limited to describing the king's achievements (real or claimed) in the military, economic and cultic fields. Unlike the situation in the stories concerning David, there is no attempt at representing a personality, revealing the weaknesses of the king to set his strong points in relief and show the whole man. This aspect of Israelite historiography reflects the different Israelite attitude to the importance of the individual: the king himself is to be judged as a man on the basis of his strengths and weaknesses. He is measured against a standard – the ideology of Yahwism. This is not a mere matter of difference between Israel and other nations in regard to checks upon the power of the king. Such checks did exist elsewhere; among the Hittites it was specifically prescribed that the king should be subject to law, while from Mesopotamia there is a literary composition dealing with the ill consequences which would follow royal oppression. But these involved considerations relating to royal conduct as a general issue, whereas such a piece of historical writing as II Samuel IX–XX was particular; it included the biographical record of one particular individual who, though king, was judged as a man.

A Divine Plan for the Jews

It has frequently been argued that a distinctive Israelite attitude is to be seen not only in the category of writing just discussed, but in ancient Israelite literature as a whole. This claimed distinctiveness has been formulated in various ways; some – such as the glib antithesis that Yahweh acted in history while other gods acted in nature

– were so oversimplified as to ignore much of the evidence. A more acceptable formulation is to say that the Israelites saw history as the unfolding of a Divine Plan, whereas other ancient Near Eastern nations saw human life as being played out within a static framework divinely decreed once and for all in primeval times. But even this statement requires some qualification. It has to be accepted that this distinction was not absolute; undoubtedly, there are traces of the alternative attitude on each side. Thus, the Bible knows of a number of primeval divine decrees which set a permanent framework for human life; the procession of the seasons was so decreed (Gen. VIII: 22); so was the institution of the blood-feud (Gen. IX: 6); so was marriage (Gen. II: 24); so were birth-pangs (Gen. III: 16); so was the decay of the body to dust after death (Gen. III: 19). On the other side, other nations were not wholly ignorant of the concept of a Divine Plan in history. This element is often quite clearly expressed in Assyrian royal inscriptions, typically in relation to the intention of the national god Ashur to maintain the royal dynasty and to extend the Assyrian Empire, which does not differ at all in principle from Yahweh's intention to maintain the dynasty of David and to preserve the Israelite people. Thus the difference in attitude between the Israelites and their contemporaries was a matter of emphasis rather than something absolute. Such difference as there was may be linked with the fact, already observed, that the basis of Mesopotamian society (and of most other ancient Near Eastern societies) was markedly more conservative than Israelite society and did not see change and development

as inevitable components of human life. This distinction in attitude, although not to be taken as absolute, was sufficient to put a distinctive mark upon Israelite thought. Thus, virtually the whole of the Pentateuch is coloured by the view of history as the working out of a Divine Plan. So are the books known in Jewish terminology as the Former Prophets, that is, Joshua, Judges, Samuel and Kings. In Judges in particular, the view that God controls human history is set out with great clarity; adversity leads the Israelites to call to Yahweh, Yahweh raises up a deliverer, the deliverer achieves security for the people, security results in slackness and departure from the ways of Yahweh, and this brings adversity, with a repetition of the cycle – though it is not a mechanical cycle, as there is a direct intervention by Yahweh at every stage.

The very title, the Former Prophets, for Joshua, Judges, Samuel and Kings is diagnostic; these books are not mainly about prophets nor do they claim to be written by prophets, and by modern analysis they would be thought of as basically historical works. They are, however, from the ancient Israelite point of view, of a piece with prophecy, in that they see historical events as the working out of a plan that Yahweh is controlling. This oneness of history with prophecy, with the common element of the revealing of God's Plan, is also reflected in the fact that Abraham, the recipient of the Divine Promise, which became effective in later Israel, was called a prophet (Gen. XX: 7), while Moses, through whom was given the Divine Law, was thought of as the greatest of the prophets (Deut. XXXIV: 10).

Chapter Two

The Bible

HYAM MACCOBY

THE JEWS REGARD THE HEBREW BIBLE as the central and definitive revelation of God, needing to be supplemented not by any further substantive revelation, but only by the explanations, decisions, reforms and clarifications which the Jewish community, through its bodies of decision, has formulated through three millennia of practical experience of living in the light of the Bible. This view, of course, differs widely from the way in which Christians regard what they call the 'Old Testament'. To Christians, the 'Old Testament' represents an incomplete and provisional stage of revelation. Its concepts of 'salvation', 'redemption' and 'justification', on this theory, find their full meaning only in the revelation embodied in the New Testament. At the same time, the 'Old Testament' is the record of the repeated failure of the Israelites (later called the Jews) to understand or put into practice the mission and revelation entrusted to them; a failure culminating in the rejection of Jesus described in the New Testament, by which the Jews ceased to be the special instrument of God. Jews, on the other hand, regard the failings and backslidings of Israel, as described in the Hebrew Bible, as forming a record that induces humility and precludes complacency, but does not imply in any way that the Jews have ceased to function as the people chosen by God.

We are concerned here only to describe what the Hebrew Bible means to the Jews and how it has affected and even formed their culture and history. We are immediately confronted with the question: 'Which Bible?' Do we mean the Bible as it was finally edited and canonized in the period from Ezra to the composition of the Mishnah (400 BCE to 200 CE), or do we mean the Bible in the various stages of its formation? What did the Bible mean in the time of Moses? What did it mean in the time of King David? Or at the time of the reforms of King Josiah, in the 7th century BCE? Or in the time preceding and during the Babylonian Exile, when the prophets Isaiah, Jeremiah and Ezekiel were at work? For the Hebrew Bible (unlike, for example, the Qur'ān) is not the composition of a single period or a single person, but a compilation covering a period of about a thousand years, a period equivalent to the entire history of English literature from Beowulf to T. S. Eliot. Does it even make sense to talk of the influence of such a long and heterogeneous literary succession on a people or culture? Is there a unitary theme in the Bible, any more than in English literature taken as a whole?

Here, we have to take into account an influential modern theory of the Bible associated chiefly with the name of Julius Wellhausen (1844–1918). Wellhausen took the view that the Hebrew Bible has no unitary theme, but shows throughout a conflict between tribalism and universalism. The prophetic movement sought to inculcate a universal monotheism; the people, on the other hand, and the non-prophetic writers were unable to rise above a tribal religion, in which Yahweh was merely the god of the Israelite nation. At the time of the Babylonian Exile, however, a change of heart took place. The people as a whole (now called Jews, not Israelites) forsook idolatry and became monotheists. However, Wellhausen argues, after the Exile, under the influence of Ezra and the priestly caste, a new form of particularism arose, which was to be typical of Judaism (a name now for the first time appropriate). This was a nationalistic form of monotheism, in which God, despite his universal character as Creator of heaven and earth, took interest only in his Chosen People, the Jews, the rest of the world being abandoned to damnation or oblivion. Judaism, as developed by Ezra and the priests, on this view, was legalistic and ritualistic, since legalism and ritualism served both to differentiate the Jews from other people by setting up barriers of observance and purity, and to confirm the Jews in their sense of chosenness by allowing them to pile up credits with God by the meticulous observance of innumerable regulations. It was the post-Exilic priests who produced the P (Priestly) document of the Pentateuch and who combined it with the previous materials to form the Torah. The prophetic books of the Bible, however, still remained, for they had acquired too much authority to be jettisoned, and there were even some lone voices against particularism (e.g. Jonah) in the post-Exilic period. But post-Exilic Judaism developed, on the whole, in the spirit of Ezra, eventually producing the Talmud, allegedly the acme of legalism and particularism. The true heir to the universalistic strain in the Hebrew Bible was held to be Jesus and the Christian Church which he founded.

A unified view

Research in the 20th century, especially in archaeology, has shown that this theory is almost entirely wrong. It is now acknowledged that the chief influence shaping Wellhausen's theory of the development of biblical religion was Protestant Christian theology, which made it seem axiomatic that any preoccupation with law or ritual was a sign of religious degeneration. Consequently, portions of the Bible that showed such preoccupation were assigned a late date by Wellhausen, and, in general, the priestly P document is regarded as having no roots in early Israelite religion. Archaeology has proved, however, that, for example, the Tabernacle of the wilderness, which the Wellhausen school regarded as a figment of the imagination of priestly writers, is based on authentic tradition, since similar tabernacles have been found in ancient Semitic religion. Moreover, archaeology has disproved Wellhausen's theory that the sacrificial system of P is late. Sociology and anthropology, too, have contributed to an increased respect for the role of law and ritual in religion, and, indeed, in culture generally.

Nevertheless, Wellhausian theory still has a great influence outside scholarly circles, and even lingers on within them in certain contexts. Very many humanists who do not believe in Christianity nevertheless believe it to be superior to Judaism in the way Wellhausen proposed. We find frequent references to 'the tribal God of the Old Testament', a popularization of Wellhausen with half of his dialectical opposition omitted. The notion that Judaism after the time of Ezra neglected the message of the prophets and became legalistic and particularist is still very widespread, despite the refutations of George Foot Moore, Travers Herford, James Parkes and, recently, E. P. Sanders.

Yet the climate of opinion has changed significantly, and it is now possible to give an account of the Bible and of its effect on Jews and Judaism without recourse to a theory of split personality. The Hebrew Bible is not hopelessly divided but presents a unified view of life, in which both universalism and particularism exist in harmony with each other, and even implying each other. This unified view of life was handed on to the time of Ezra and to post-biblical times and provided the inspiration of all later Judaism. The dichotomy between Israelites and Jews is a false one; the religious culture of Israel is indivisible.

This does not mean that there is no progress of thought within the Bible itself, or in later Judaism. But it is progress within a single well-defined *Weltanschauung*. It is the continuous working out of an idea based on an overwhelming communal experience. Nor does recent reconsideration of Wellhausen mean that we must return to traditional pre-critical views about the Bible, such as that the Torah was written down word for word by Moses at the dictation of God. The part of Wellhausen's work that consists of the sifting of documents is still largely valid. The existence of four main sources for the Pentateuch (J, the Jahwistic; E, the Elohistic; D, the Deuteronomic; and P, the Priestly) is still accepted by most scholars. The human origin of the Bible, its gradual accretion by editing and redaction, the fact that many of the documents involved were written far later than the events they describe and were not written by the authors to whom tradition has assigned them – all this is established, and only means that the scientific study of the Bible must adopt the same criteria that are employed in the study of other ancient literary compositions. Yet such study does not preclude the possibility that the corpus of literature so studied may turn out to have certain qualities not paralleled in any other corpus.

The sources

How then did the Hebrew Bible take shape, and when did its influence on the people of Israel begin? The answer seems to be that there existed among the Israelites, from very ancient times, holy writings of one kind or another, but that they did not take shape as a book to which central importance was assigned until about 700 BCE, shortly after the great disaster in which the northern kingdom was swept away. It was not until this time that the remaining people of Israel, in the territory of Judah (from which they took the name of Judahites, or Jews), began to become the People of the Book.

It is clear that there was a lively literature among the Israelites at least from the time of the early monarchy (about 1000 BCE). Some of the war poems, such as the 'Song of Deborah', come from an even earlier period, the time of the judges. Many writings, now lost because they were not included in the canon, were composed in this period. All we have of them is their titles, which are mentioned tantalizingly in the Bible from time to time: 'The Book of the Wars of the Lord' (Num. XXI:14), 'The Book of Jashar' (Josh. X:13 and II Sam. 1:18), 'The Chronicles of the Kings of Israel' (I Kings XIV:19), as well as many prophetic writings. Moreover, the Israelite writings presuppose a knowledge of the literature of other more ancient nations of the Near East. The account of the Flood in Genesis is based on a Babylonian classic, though it is much altered to conform with Hebrew monotheism. Very recently, fascinating confirmation has been found of the antiquity and authenticity of the literary sources behind the Bible. The excavations at the site of the city of Ebla have shown that the account of the Five Cities of the Plain (including Sodom and Gomorrah) found in Genesis XIV is based on fact. It is extraordinary that the sources on which the Bible writers drew have now been shown to go back as far as 2250 BCE – and these must have been written sources.

A very interesting example of the use by the Bible of earlier material is the account in Genesis of the generations before the Flood. This makes use of the tribal records of the Kenites, with the difference that Cain, the revered primal ancestor of the Kenites, is treated in the Bible as a murderer because of his sacrifice of his brother Abel (cf. Romulus and Remus).

Since the Bible makes use of written records going back long before the time of Moses, there is no reason to rule out the possibility that it also incorporates or at least transmutes written material dating from the time of Moses, or even composed by Moses himself.

A whole genre of biblical literature that derives from non-Israelite culture is the Wisdom literature (e.g. the Book of Proverbs). This has been shown to derive largely from the Wisdom literature of Babylonia and Egypt. Indeed, there is no attempt in the Bible to disguise the non-Israelite origin of this genre, since much of it is ascribed to non-Israelite characters (Job, Agur, Lemuel, Ethan, Heman, Calcol, Darda).

There was thus an Israelite literature before there was a Bible. Some of these pre-biblical writings, however, had cultic significance. Especially holy were the stone Tablets of the Law which were kept in the Ark in the Holy of Holies. There seem to have been some other writings, too, which were regarded with great reverence and were preserved as 'memorials' or 'testimonies'; one of them is referred to in Exodus XVII : 14: 'And the Lord said unto Moses, "Write this for a memorial in a book, and repeat it in the ears of Joshua. . . ." ' Some of the writings of the prophets, who recorded their visions, were carefully preserved as oracles. Moreover, there were codes of religious law, which embodied what were thought to be the commands of God on Sinai; but these differed from region to region, and were not collated into a single authoritative book.

The change came with what has been called the 'Deuteronomic movement'. In the reign of King Josiah of Judah (640–609 BCE), as the Second Book of Kings (XXII) records, a 'book was found', and was brought to the king. On reading it he was struck with dismay, and began a great reform in accordance with the instructions of the book. The fact that the book was 'found' shows that at this time the existence of a holy book or Bible was by no means common knowledge. The fact that the king was struck mainly by the threats of punishment for idolatry, contained in the book, indicates that the book was not the whole Pentateuch but only the Book of Deuteronomy, which contains a series of such threats. Many scholars have thought that the book was not 'found' at this time, but actually composed. Various considerations make it likely, however, that the book was composed somewhat earlier, in the reign of Josiah's grandfather Manasseh, who was a renegade against the God of Israel, and even converted the Temple in Jerusalem into a place of idolatrous worship. Manasseh's father had been the pious King Hezekiah, whose reign had assumed Messianic stature when the kingdom of Judah was miraculously saved from the onslaught of the Assyrians. In the shock and guilt of Manasseh's apostasy, the Book of Deuteronomy was composed as a rallying-point for the faithful, and became the nucleus of the Bible.

Older writings containing stories of the Patriarchs, of the Exodus from Egypt, of the Revelation on Sinai, and also corpora of laws, all of which had long been in circulation in various regions without ever attaining full, central, canonical status, were gathered by members of the Deuteronomic movement and edited into one five-volume book which became the Torah (literally: teaching). The Deuteronomic movement also undertook the editing and composition of books of history, on the basis of existing written records, telling the story of the people of Israel from the time of their entry into the Promised Land down to their own day. At this time, the writings of the literary prophets were not yet part of the canon, but were circulated and treated with reverence as oracles (see, for example, the attitude shown towards the prophecies of Micah, who prophesied during the reign of Hezekiah, as evidenced by Jeremiah XXVI : 18).

The answer, then, to the question of the early influence of the Bible, appears to be this: the religion of Israel was not from the start a religion centred on a book; Judaism was built on an event, namely the Exodus from Egypt, and, while this event early gave rise to writings of various kinds, it took a very long time, about 700 years in fact, before a book took shape, enshrining the event and its consequences, and assuming the position of centrality in thought and worship that the Bible-book has had ever since. The appearance of this book was a response to

danger, rather than an expression of the primary energy which gave birth to the religion. The book came from the religion, not the religion from the book.

The above statement should not be taken to mean that there is a radical distinction to be made between Judaism before the crystallization of the Bible and Judaism after it. On the contrary, it means that the Bible is only one of the institutions in which the thrust of Judaism has expressed itself. It is certainly a very important form of expression, for in the Bible the energies of Judaism find their most conscious formulation; and once it was created as a canon, the Bible became a centre of energy in itself, implying as it did a whole programme of education, a mode of study, scholarship and intellectuality, and a fortress of culture, which could act as a substitute, in times of exile and distress, for the more tangible institutions and strongpoints, the Land, the Temple and the Priesthood. It is a great mistake, however, to think, as many have done, that the Deuteronomic movement, or that other great movement that ran parallel to it, the Prophetic movement, was the founder of Jewish monotheism. The Bible is rather the end-point of one long phase of Israelite monotheism – a phase that in some respects had greater vitality than subsequent periods. In order to understand this point fully, it is necessary to enquire (before going further into the qualities and divisions of the Bible itself) into the nature of the primal experience which lies behind the Bible, and, in the last resort, gives it its chief themes, its unity and its principle of development.

The implications of deliverance

Everything in the Bible goes back to one thing: that the people of Israel were once slaves in Egypt, and they experienced a great deliverance. This is the great event which Israel experienced as the irruption of the Divine into history. This event gave all human history a meaning: all previous history led up to it and all subsequent history led away from it; it was not just an event in the history of one nation, but an event in the history of the world. The one God of the universe, Creator of heaven and earth, 'heard the cry' of the children of Israel, suffering under oppression, and intervened to help them, the lowliest, smallest and least-esteemed nation on earth (Deut. VII : 7):

> Ask now of the days past, which were before thee, since the day that God created man upon the earth, and from the one end of heaven unto the other, whether there hath been any such thing as this great thing is, or hath been heard like it? Did ever a people hear the voice of God speaking out of the midst of the fire, as thou hast heard, and live? Or hath God assayed to go and take Him a nation from the midst of another nation, by trials, by signs, and by wonders, and by war, and by a mighty hand, and by an outstretched arm, and by great terrors, according to all that the Lord your God did for you in Egypt before thine eyes? (Deut. IV : 32–4)

Such an unheard-of event was not purposeless: it could not have been a mere matter of political freedom, but the election of Israel (through no merit of their own, Deut. IX : 5) for a great destiny. They were to be the people of God, who would implement a new Law of love and justice in a Holy Land. They were to lead mankind to a new ideal of communal living. The deliverance from Egypt brought with it a sense of tremendous mission, and an iconoclasm that respected nothing the ancient world thought worthy of admiration.

The Hebrew Bible cannot be understood without realizing the basic fact that it is the saga of the Exodus. It is in the Pentateuch that the story of the Exodus is given, and that is why the Pentateuch (or Torah) is for Jews by far the most important part of the Bible (just as for Christians the Gospels, which describe the event or saga of Christianity, are the most important part of the New Testament). It is true that the Bible does not begin with the Exodus, but with the story of mankind since the beginning. But this does not reduce the centrality of the Exodus from Egypt. On the contrary, it enhances it, for it shows the Exodus in a universalist setting, as the event towards which the creation of the universe and of man was tending. And this universalist presentation is all the more striking in that the people of Israel do not, like other nations, trace back their origin as a nation to the beginning of the world. They are frankly portrayed as a parvenu nation, Johnny-come-latelies compared with the great civilizations of Egypt and Babylonia. There is no attempt to equate the history of Israel with the history of the world. On the contrary, emphasis is laid on their insignificance and unworthiness. It is the event that is important, not the human participants in it. It is the implications of the event, theological, moral and political, that turn the story of the Exodus into a teaching, or Torah, a programme and agenda for humanity.

We see, in the rest of the Bible, that whenever the morale of the people of Israel flags, either through misfortune or through their own failings, it is to the story of the Exodus that they turn for renewal and spiritual refreshment. 'When Israel came forth out of Egypt, the house of Jacob from a people of strange language, Judah became His sanctuary, Israel His dominion' (Ps. CXIV). At times of dedication, it is this story that the prophets and leaders recall. 'For they are Thy people, and Thine inheritance, which Thou broughtest forth out of Egypt, from the midst of the furnace of iron' (I Kings VIII: 51). Exactly what historical facts lie behind this Israelite conviction of having been the subject of the most awe-inspiring event in the history of mankind, has been much argued over by scholars. Some have denied that the Exodus ever really happened; they see it as a 'historicization' of a spring festival of Canaanite origins, or as a myth of rebirth. We need not discuss this question here, except to say that the persistence and strength of such a conviction do seem to point to an actual historical event, which may have been a huge natural cataclysm enabling the Israelites enslaved in Egypt to escape. At any rate, from the very earliest period to which we can penetrate in the history of Israel, the conviction of the delivery from Egypt existed, and it was this conviction that made Judaism and made the Bible.

The fact that the religion of Israel began as a slave revolt is of the utmost importance in assessing both the religion and the Bible. The Hebrew Bible constantly adjures the Israelites never to forget that they were once slaves in Egypt. Even the Sabbath is grounded in this memory ('. . . remember thou wast a slave in the land of

The earliest extant Hebrew manuscript of the Bible (apart from the Dead Sea Scrolls) is the Codex Cairo, from the Karaite synagogue at Abbasiya. The manuscript was written in 895 CE by the well-known Masoretic scholar Moses Ben-Asher of Tiberias, and comprises only the Former and Latter Prophets. This page contains Joshua V: 12–VI: 12, about the fall of Jericho.

Egypt . . . therefore the Lord thy God commanded thee to keep the sabbath day,' Deut. V: 15). Wherever kindness is enjoined towards the poor and the stranger, the reminder is given to remember Egypt (e.g. Deut. X: 19). The experience of slavery was never to be forgotten, for otherwise the Egyptian style of tyranny would appear in Israel itself. Every year, at the festival of Passover, the experience of Egypt had to be relived.

An important way in which the consciousness of past slavery was translated into action and social behaviour was in the new attitude towards leadership, which developed in Israel. In Egypt, the king was a god. This was utterly excluded by the monotheism of Israel. Because there was only one God, all human beings were put on a single level, as God's creatures. The Hebrew Bible is the embodiment of this new attitude. In the Book of Samuel, the institution of the monarchy is regarded as a sign of failure, as the acceptance of the second-best (I Sam. VIII). The Hebrew Bible criticizes the Jewish kings mercilessly. Even the best of them, even those who were regarded as Messiahs and saviours, such as David and Solomon, are treated as fallible human beings, whose sins are recorded in full.

The king was no longer a magical being, providing a link between the world of the gods and the world of men. He was merely a human being who happened to have power, and who had to be watched jealously in case he misused his power. The king, according to Deuteronomy (XVII: 18–20), had to have a special book of the Law for his constant perusal, 'in order that his heart

Page from the earliest Palestinian Targum (a loose translation of the Bible into Aramaic, with occasional commentary). This work, a translation of the Pentateuch only, is considered by many scholars to be contemporary evidence of the religion and spoken language of the Jews at the time of the birth of Christianity. It was thought lost, but one complete copy of it was discovered in the last century, and is known as Codex Vatican (Neofiti 1). The page contains Genesis IV:14–V:1. Each verse begins with the two opening words in Hebrew followed by the translation of the whole verse into Aramaic. The Targum literature developed out of the custom of translating and explaining in Aramaic the weekly portion of the Torah and Prophets read out in the synagogue.

be not lifted up above his brothers'. Always watching the king, and ready to rebuke him if need be, was the prophet, such as Elijah, an outsider and non-establishment figure who was nevertheless recognized and revered. The king was not allowed to act as priest. The delicate threefold division of power by which authority was divided among king, priest and prophet (or teacher) was the result of a preoccupation with freedom, the legacy of the period of slavery in Egypt.

By saving the Israelites, God had made them his own slaves. They could, therefore, never be slaves to any human being henceforward. 'For they are My servants, whom I brought forth out of the land of Egypt; they shall not be sold as bondmen' (Lev. xxv:42). Slavery was thus abolished within the nation of Israel, though it was recognized as a continuing institution among the other nations of the world, who had not been set free by God; one day, however, in the almost unimaginable future, all nations would be free. The biblical principle that servitude to God means freedom from servitude to man was used in later Judaism to justify all principles of social freedom. For example, the Babylonian rabbi, Rav, of the 3rd century CE, used it to prove that a labourer was entitled to withdraw his labour at any time, even in the middle of a day's work.

Psychologically, the story of the Exodus expresses a striving towards adulthood and responsibility. Deliverance, or salvation, is regarded as a beginning, not as a release from struggle into a painless heaven. In the wilderness, the Israelites yearn at times for 'the fleshpots of Egypt', that is, for the infantile dependency of slavery. Freedom brings with it hard trials and a long process of education, in which Moses, the teacher, struggles to inculcate difficult values. Even the entry to the Promised Land is not a happy ending, but the beginning of a long struggle to translate the lessons of the desert into social and political reality. Reinforcing the Exodus story are the myths and legends with which the Bible surrounds it. Adam, ejected from the garden of infancy, finds he has to live by the sweat of his brow, having learned to distinguish between good and evil. There is guilt in the acquisition of this knowledge, but there is also the possibility of achievement. Man, says God to the angels, 'has become like one of us' (Gen. III:22). One must beware of reading this story in the light of the later Christian theology. The sin of Adam removed him from his protected status, but it also made him into a responsible being, capable of receiving the Torah. Without the Fall (as Christians call it, though this term is absent from the Jewish sources), there would have been no Sinai.

The theme of responsibility, its glory and its difficulty, is implicit in the early stories in which the youngest son yearns to be the eldest (Jacob, Joseph), and, by this yearning, supplants his elders and becomes the focus of decision and responsibility. Israel itself, the baby of the nations, supplants the great empires, hoary with antiquity, Egypt and Babylonia, and becomes God's 'first-born son' (Ex. IV:22). Though Jacob is a 'supplanter' (the very meaning of the name), this is not out of greedy ambition, but because he has a vision of adulthood far beyond that of the elder brothers. The ancient nations are sunk in idolatry, which means dependence. Their elaborate systems are essentially static, since they are meant to fit man within the scheme of nature regarded as cyclic, harmonious and unchanging. The hierarchy of society, with the god-king at its head, reflects the hierarchy of the heavens. Israel sweeps away both the earthly hierarchy and the heavenly hierarchy. The stars in their courses, the sun and the moon, worshipped by all the nations of the ancient world, become to Israel mere fellow-creatures, inferior in status to man himself, the crown of creation. The umbilical cord tying man to nature is snapped. Man is let loose in an unpredictable world, facing ultimate reality, or God, who, in the pagan systems, had remained in the background as the impersonal Fate, pitiless and inexorable, which eventually brought doom to both gods and men, but could be left out of everyday reckonings. Israel, however, comes into personal relationship with this ultimate Power, by-passing all schemes of security, and in the Exodus this Power intervenes in human history, with stupendous force, setting it on a course no longer cyclic but progressive. Along this straight line, Israel is now to stumble, with many backslidings and failures, towards a dénouement that will make sense of the human venture away from the animal kingdom into rationality and freedom.

The 'salvation' embodied in the Exodus is an earthly salvation. Judaism is not an other-worldly religion. The extraordinary absence in the Bible of reference to life after death or other-worldly bliss cannot be explained as a 'primitive' lack of spirituality. It was a deliberate reaction against the other-worldly emphasis of other ancient religions, especially that of Egypt. The Exodus was a deliverance from the actuality of physical slavery, and no definition of freedom that locates it in the purely spiritual realm (thus rendering programmes of material, political liberation unnecessary) has been acceptable to Judaism. The 'saviours' who appeared from time to time among the Israelites (for example, Gideon, Samson) were all saviours from material thraldom, like the first of the 'saviours', Moses. The tone of Judaism is thus anti-mystical. The problem of life is not conceived to be how to escape from the material into a world of the spirit, but how to convert the material into a world of freedom and justice. This is implicit even in the Hebrew story of the creation. Since man was created 'in the image of God' (Gen. 1:27), his life was valuable in purely human terms. The Torah, considered as Law, is intended for creatures with bodies, emotions and desires; but these are all consecrated by God's approval, and are therefore of cosmic significance. There is thus what has been called a 'normal mysticism', i.e. a mysticism of ordinary things, each of which has a part to play in the shaping of the truly human life. There need be no straining, therefore, for extra-human experience or for union with the Divine in the type of self-surrender or self-annihilation common in non-Jewish forms of mysticism. Man can achieve a valid independence from God, by which, like Abraham, he can become God's 'friend', or even God's critic (see Gen. XVIII:25: 'Shall not the Judge of all the earth do justly?'). This sense that man has been given his own task, the arena of which is earth, is expressed in the Psalms: 'The heavens are the heavens of the Lord; but the earth he hath given to the children of men' (Ps. CXV).

The overwhelming experience of the Exodus was thus set in a framework of cosmogony and legend, all reinforcing the determination of a band of runaway slaves under an inspired leader to set up a society based on the dignity of man, not based on the ethic of the ant-heap or on a static hierarchical perfection drawn from the motion of the stars. The basic symbols of the Exodus, the giving of the Law, the wilderness, the Promised Land, form the music of the Bible and shaped the Jewish religious consciousness to such an extent that their working can be discerned even in the thought of Jews (such as Karl Marx) who reject their own Jewishness. In place of a mythology of gods and goddesses, the Jewish mythology becomes human history itself, moving through its various eras towards the reconstitution of the Garden of Eden, when 'the desert shall blossom as the rose' (Is. XXV:1). The idea of a Messianic era, in which human effort will reach its fruition, when all mankind will grow to adulthood and live without war or exploitation, is implicit in the Exodus itself, but finds its full expression in the visions of the prophets.

Deuteronomy: the pivot

We may now turn to consider how the Hebrew Bible developed towards its completion. We have seen that the pivot of this development was the Book of Deu-

From the Aleppo Codex of the Bible, a very important early manuscript written about 920 CE by the famous Masoretic scholar, Aaron Ben-Asher. The page contains Deuteronomy XXXI:28–XXXII:14, comprising the beginning of the farewell 'Song of Moses', together with the prose introduction to it. The decoration on the top left marks the beginning of a new weekly portion. The distinctive way of setting out both the introduction and the Song is important for establishing the authenticity of the manuscript as the work of Aaron Ben-Asher. The Aleppo Codex contains about two-thirds of Scripture.

teronomy, which was probably composed about 700–650 BCE, during the traumatic reign of Manasseh. Before this time no central, canonical book existed. Many literary materials did exist, however, possessing greater or lesser sanctity, and there were also many orally-transmitted materials. These, both written and un-written, took many forms, depending on the use to which they were put: collections of commandments, prayers, psalms, blessings, accounts of the Exodus, chronicles of judges and kings, oracles delivered by prophets, sagas of pre-Exodus times, laments, hymns, declarations recited on dedicating gifts to the Temple and many more (the unearthing of these proto-materials from the text of the Bible into which they have been woven is known as 'form-criticism'). These materials might differ in detail from region to region, and according to the circles who used them (e.g. priestly, prophetic, popular, courtly), but they all had a common outlook and common presuppositions: the election of Israel, the deliverance from Egypt, the giving of the Law on Sinai, the Oneness of God. The Bible did not exist as such, but a kind of diffused Bible did exist, in the literature, communications and cultic utterances of the whole people. These materials eventually entered into the composition of the Bible, so that, to a large extent,

This page (Deut. XXXIII:25 to the end) is from an important 10th-century manuscript of the Bible, written by an unknown scribe in Iraq or Syria. The Masora Magna (textual notes) concludes by giving the number of verses in the entire Torah: 5,845.

the people of Israel created the Bible out of their experience of salvation and their daily experience of the workings of a salvation-society.

The Book of Deuteronomy was the first attempt to gather this material into a single book, which would henceforth function as a permanent, central institution of Judaism. It is in Deuteronomy that we find the only explicit references to the 'Book of the Torah'. Instructions are given (Deut. XXXI:26) that 'this Book of the Torah' should be kept in the Holy of Holies 'beside the ark of the Covenant' – the Ark, or chest, which contained the Tablets of the Ten Commandments. These two Tablets of stone may be regarded as the original Bible, the first written canon. Now they were to be supplemented by a book (a scroll written on parchment) which would have the same sanctity and authority.

The Book of Deuteronomy is a literary masterpiece. It is given unity, drama and pathos by the form in which it is cast, that of a speech made by Moses, shortly before his death, to the assembled children of Israel. Moses tells the story of the Exodus and the wanderings in the wilderness, not consecutively, but as they naturally arise in the course of a moving exhortation. Such a composition could be made only if its intended readership were entirely familiar with the whole saga, which is taken for granted (just as a Homeric bard could take up the 'matter' of Troy at any point, knowing that his audience would know the background story). The simplicity and intensity of the eloquence of this book are quite remarkable and have the stamp of an individual style, so that when we find the same style in key transition passages of the historical books we know that they have been edited by a Deuteronomic hand.

The appearance and acceptance of Deuteronomy gave the impetus to the compilation of a complete Torah-book, which would tell the Exodus-story in full, set it in an outline of universal history, and give a compendium of the Revelation given on Mount Sinai. Thus the other four books of the Pentateuch came into existence, largely on the basis, as it would seem, of two quasi-canonical texts, one circulating among the people (JE a combination of J and E), and the other among the priests (P). The work of collating these texts began before the Babylonian Exile, and was probably completed during it; so that when the Jewish state was reconstituted under Ezra in the 5th century BCE, it began with the Torah, or Pentateuch, as its main pillar and spiritual support. Under Ezra and his successors, further canonical books were added, bringing the history of the people of God up to date. Yet the 'book of Moses' (as it is called in Ezra, Nehemiah and Chronicles) retained its pre-eminence as the primary Revelation and as the account of the miracles of redemption by which the presence of God was validated in the formation of Israel as a people.

Contents of the Bible

The contents of the Hebrew Bible, as it thus developed, may best be described in accordance with the genres which it came to comprise.

Historical writings. These are the books of Joshua, Judges, Samuel and Kings, which form a continuous chronicle from the death of Moses to the destruction of the Temple and the Babylonian Exile. These books are known as the Former Prophets (because they were thought to have been composed by prophets) though their content is not 'prophetic' in the sense of being vatic or oracular. (The truly prophetic books of the Bible are known as the Latter Prophets.) There are also some historical passages embedded, as islands of prose, amidst the poetry of the prophetic writings. The two Books of Chronicles are in a separate category, as they were written much later, in the 4th century BCE, in the period of the Second Temple.

The historical writings, though written in a simple and sometimes prosaic style, are in some ways the most remarkable part of the whole Bible. The rise and fall of nations is conceived as the working out of a task divinely entrusted to man. These are no mere court annals (such as those of the Babylonian Chronicle) but a scheme of universal history, pointing to some final fulfilment. Yet despite the schematization (by which national misfortunes are ascribed to national sins, which are accordingly often much exaggerated), these historical writings convey a vivid sense of authentic human activities. These are real human beings – suffering, rejoicing, loving, hating, helping, betraying, intriguing, fighting, fleeing. The stories of these writings have become imprinted on the imagination of the Western world: the death of Samson, the childhood of Samuel, David's defeat of Goliath, the death of Absalom, the prayer of Solomon, the visit of the Queen of Sheba, the confrontation of Elijah and Ahab, and many more. The sense of actuality, combined with the overarching purpose, conveys the fusion of universalism with particularism, which is characteristic of Judaism: the idea that it is in the struggle of material life, with all its setbacks and misdirections, that God's purpose must ultimately work its way to a solution.

Poetry. National epics or sagas are usually written in verse. The fact that the main narrative of the Hebrew Bible is in a plain, sober prose is symptomatic of its 'normal mysticism', its harnessing of everyday life for purposes elsewhere regarded as appropriate only for gods or demi-god heroes. Yet poetry does form an important part of the Bible. It appears at moments of special emotion or inspiration: the celebration of a triumph, or the lamentation of a defeat, the illumination of a prophetic oracle, the serious ceremony of a cultic rite. Poetry is an older form of expression than prose; consequently, some of the oldest passages in the Bible are poetical. Examples are the Song of the Sea (Ex. xv), the Blessing of Balaam (Num. xxiv), the Blessings of Jacob and of Moses (Gen. xlix and Deut. xxxiii), and the lament of David over Saul and Jonathan (II Sam. i). Hebrew poetry is sharply differentiated from prose. It uses a different rhythm and even a different vocabulary. Yet it is not metrical, like Greek verse, with strict regulation of syllables and accents. It is much more like free verse, though certain underlying rules have been tentatively discerned by scholars. Its chief device is rhythmic repetition, or parallelism; e.g. 'How goodly are thy tents, O Jacob, thy tabernacles, O Israel!' It often uses a riddling, oracular style, but can also transpose into a directness of high emotion, whether of indignation or of pathos. It is essentially a lyrical form, and even long poetical works, such as the Song of Songs, or the books of prophecy, are really collections of relatively short poems. The exception is the Book of Job, which is partly in prose, but contains the most sustained poetic composition in the Hebrew Bible and has the unifying form of a drama.

While the prophetic writings (see next section) contain a public poetry of religio-politics, the Book of Psalms is the great collection of personal verse. Though many of these poems were intended for musical performance in the services of the Temple, their style is mostly that of individual devotion. It is noteworthy that there is no magical intent in these Psalms. There are no incantations or magical formulae, intended to produce quasi-automatic results, by the operation of laws inherent in the nature of supra-human reality. Instead, there is an interpersonal encounter between the human individual and God. The poet lays his agony before God, or expresses his joy and gratitude, or his personal reaction to the story of the Divine Intervention in history. The whole Hebrew Bible is anti-magical, but it is in the Psalms that we see most plainly the effects on the spiritual life of this rejection of magic.

A book of poetry that seems in a category of its own is the Song of Songs, a collection of love lyrics with no religious reference. These beautiful and sensuous poems probably arose from the folk-celebration of weddings, with their praise of the bride and dialogues of love. The

Page from the earliest complete Bible manuscript, Codex Leningrad B 19a, written in 1008. This is considered to represent the vocalization of the Ben-Asher school of Masoretic scholars, regarded by Jewish authorities as superior to the Ben-Naftali school (both were of Tiberias). It was made the basis of the third edition of the Biblia Hebraica *(Stuttgart, 1937), in preference to the rabbinical Bible of Jacob ben Hayim ben Adoniya (published by Bomberg). The page contains Genesis XV: 14–XVII: 4. Chapter beginnings are marked by a large letter* (samekh) *in the right-hand margin. The Masora Parva is in the margins, and the Masora Magna is above and below.*

final editing is late, but much of the material is early. Here we are in contact with the folk-art of the Israelite people, contributing their lived experience to the Bible. Later commentators used the method of allegory to connect even these poems of the Song of Songs with themes of election and salvation. Yet even in their secular meaning as songs of human love, they are not inappropriate in a Bible which so exalts the delights of this-worldly life (see especially Psalm civ).

The prophetic writings (the Latter Prophets). A category of poetry that has no parallel in any other literature is that of the writings of the prophets. Some general similarities in style can be observed to oracular, ecstatic utterances in other ancient languages, but there is no parallel to the ethical preoccupation and the universalist vision.

The figures of prophets (e.g. Elijah) appear prominently in the historical writings of the Bible, but more in the role of wonder-workers than in the role of teachers. Of the great literary (or book-writing) prophets, only Isaiah (and possibly Jonah) is even mentioned in the historical writings of the Book of Kings. It seems, therefore, that the literary prophets formed a movement distinct from the Deuteronomic movement that produced the historical writings. The first literary prophet was Amos, who lived in the 8th century BCE. In his work appear some of the characteristic themes of the

Codex Hilleli, a Spanish manuscript of the Bible, was written in 1241 by Israel ben Isaac ben Israel from a very ancient manuscript in Toledo known as 'the Hilleli', written some time before 1000 by Hillel ben Moses ben Hillel. The page contains Exodus VI:29–VII:10. The decorated letter on the left marks the end of a section. The word on the top left of the page is va-'er'a, the title of the Torah portion for the week, of which the page forms part.

out Israel for a purpose. Only gradually did it become apparent what the purpose intended by such a God might be. The election of Israel seemed at first a signal grace, a high destiny which could not be expected to extend to the rest of mankind. The idolatrous nations could not even be blamed for their idolatry, for only the special experience of Israel had enabled her to rise to the monotheistic conception. But the growing realization of the ethical nature of God brought with it the expectation that all mankind, out of their common feeling for morality, might be led to monotheism, and to a world-wide regime in which 'the knowledge of God' would take the form of universal peace and brotherhood. Such an idea had certainly not been absent from earlier Judaism (for example, in the prayer of Solomon, I Kings VIII:41), but it becomes central only in classical prophecy, especially Isaiah:

> For out of Zion shall go forth the law,
> And the word of the Lord from Jerusalem. . . .
> Nation shall not lift up sword against nation,
> Neither shall they learn war any more.

This eschatological vision, the logical outcome of monotheism with its unification of mankind and of the warring impulses of the human psyche, was never lost from Judaism.

Wisdom literature. Another kind of universalism is seen in the Wisdom literature of the Hebrew Bible. As mentioned earlier, this stands outside the framework of the salvation-history of Israel, and rests on a wisdom common to all humanity. It is monotheistic (for it regards both polytheism and atheism as foolishness), but it returns to the monotheism of an ancient (fictitious) primeval world, before polytheism arose. Solomon, the archetype of the wise man, to whom the authorship of both Proverbs and Ecclesiastes was credited, was an Israelite, but this is not emphasized in these works. The Book of Job belongs partly to this genre, Job being a non-Israelite sage; but this book transcends the genre by denying the association of virtue with prosperity. In the Book of Job, Wisdom literature questions its own assumptions. Job's agony of questioning produces in the end an epiphany of God; wisdom has broken through to the *Sturm und Drang* of revelation – to a world where nothing can be understood except that God has broken silence.

Apocalyptic literature. The Book of Daniel is the only example within the canon of a type of literature that proliferated during the period of the Second Temple. This is the apocalyptic literature, which purports to show, by means of visions, how all things will come to the dénouement of a final catastrophe and Judgment. These visions are distinguished from classical prophecy by their concentration on 'secret' information rather than on Utopian aspirations; they abound with ciphers and coded messages. Apocalyptic writings arose from a sense of impotence. Why was the triumph of Israel over idolatry delayed so long? The answer lay in elaborate schematizations of history into epochs. When the full scheme had worked its way out, deliverance would come. Classical prophecy was not concerned with this, but rather with the rededication of Israel by reproof and

movement: the primacy of morality over cultic pre-scriptions, the declaration of doom against a society which is not based on brotherhood, the polemic against the upper classes. Later literary prophets added another theme: the eventual conversion of the whole world to the religion of Israel.

The literary prophets represent a development or mutation in Israelite religion, though not in the way that some scholars have argued. They were not the founders of monotheism, for this had been the creed of Israel ever since the Exodus. They were not the first to connect monotheism with ethics, for this, too, was an early development, seen in the story of Sodom and Gomorrah, in the denunciation of David by the prophet Nathan, and of Ahab by Elijah, as well as in the moral prescriptions of the law-codes. But they were the first to see ethics as the supreme expression of monotheism, and to make a clear distinction between the worship of God by cultic means (which they regarded as merely symbolic, though they did not oppose it in its due place) and the worship of God by acts of 'lovingkindness' (Hebrew, *hesed*) to one's fellow-men, which they regarded as the essence. The development of monotheism, by its own inner logic, was towards ethical monotheism, but this was not entirely apparent at first. The emphasis, in early generations, was on 'the mighty deeds' of God, by which he had singled

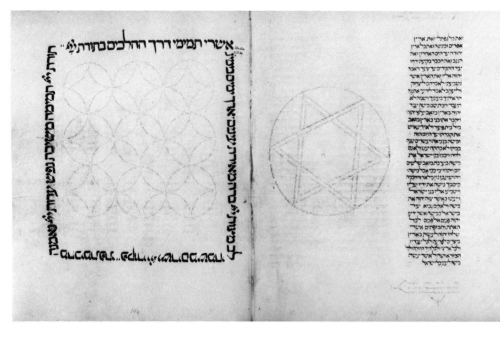

Two pages from the Merwas Bible, written in 1307 by Joseph ben Yehuda Merwas for a distinguished courtier of King Alfonso of Castile, Moshe ben Joseph Yehuda ha-Nassi (the Prince). The right-hand page contains the end of Deuteronomy, with micrographic designs made out of the words of the Masoretic material. The square of bold lettering on the left is made up of the following biblical verses: Psalms CXIX:1, Psalms XIX:8–9, and Proverbs III:16 (last letter omitted for lack of room). All these verses are in praise of the Torah.

doom-laden warnings related to the religio-political situation of the time. Some apocalyptic elements are found in Ezekiel, but his standpoint is still that of prophecy; he may be wafted on a wind and see visions, but his aim is to deliver a topical message to Israel. The great mass of apocalyptic writings were excluded from the canon as without true inspiration, and even Daniel (which is only partly apocalyptic) was not allowed prophetic status, but relegated to the 'Writings'. The chief sects influenced by the apocalyptic writings were the Dead Sea Scrolls sect, and the Christian Church, which preserved such works after Judaism had abandoned them.

Legal writings. The extra-Pentateuchal writings which we have been describing and classifying contain little of one type of composition – legal materials. This is not because law was considered unimportant in post-Mosaic times; on the contrary, law was considered so important that it was confined to the most sacred part of the Bible, the Pentateuch, or Torah, where it was given the full authority of the primal Revelation of Sinai. No prophet, other than Moses, was considered sufficiently great to be the vehicle of Divine Law. What is even more remarkable, bearing in mind the practice of other Middle Eastern states, is that not a single law promulgated by a king is preserved in the Bible. Law was not a matter of civil order but of the spiritual life. Law lies at the centre of the religion of Israel.

This high valuation of law did not begin after the Exile, as some scholars have argued, but was part of the structure of the religion from the beginning. Many religions are based on the conviction that freedom and love are incompatible with law; Israelite religion had just the opposite conviction: freedom and love can find expression only through law. The radical remodelling of society, made urgent by the release from slavery and the rebirth of the Exodus, required a new constitution based on new principles of brotherhood. Great renewals (such as the French Revolution and the American Revolution) are always a stimulus to law, especially when the basic inspiration is not world-negating but the outcome of respect for the human body and the human community.

The Law transcendent

The Law of the Torah was in many respects radically different from contemporary systems of law. It made law transcendent by deriving it directly from God. It thus abolished the distinction between law and morality, and also between secular and religious law. The fusion of the secular and the religious was accomplished by making central the idea of a Covenant, which involved not only individuals but the whole people in an undertaking to observe the Law. All law thus became constitutional law, and every individual was pledged to uphold the constitution. This meant that every man was required to study and know the Law. All these features are found in the very earliest stratum of the Torah Law, i.e. the Covenant Code of Exodus.

The new value given to the individual (an outcome of the Utopian spirit of the law) is reflected in the Law itself. The highest value is now not property but life. Offences against property are treated with surprising leniency, but the offence of murder cannot be compounded as in neighbouring codes by monetary compensation or by substituting other persons as objects of vicarious punishment. To commit murder is regarded not as an offence against man, but as an offence against God.

Judaism, under the inspiration of the Hebrew Bible, has always felt that law is the mainspring of the religious life. High-sounding sentiments, even those found in the Hebrew Bible itself, such as, 'Thou shalt love thy neighbour as thyself' (Lev. XIX:18), are regarded as useless without definition in a code of behaviour. The object of law is to consider all human situations with a view to discovering what constitutes loving behaviour in all possible circumstances. Law is thus a science of behaviour, the leading principles of which may be found in the Bible, but which requires constant development in new times and circumstances. A stock of knowledge about practical ways of expressing love of neighbour is built up and handed on, so that each generation does not have to start from scratch with the help of mere good intentions and well meaning maxims.

In addition to laws of morality and obligation and redress for injuries or deprivation (see especially Ex.

A Samaritan Pentateuch, written in Nablus by Ab Nasanah ben Sadakah in 1468–9, contains this page from Leviticus XIII:20–49, dealing with the laws of leprosy. The scribe carelessly omitted part of verses 25–6 (right-hand column) and added the missing material in the margin (there is a similar mistake in the left-hand column). At the bottom right of the right-hand column, the scribe has arranged the material so that the repetitions of one word (ha-neteq, 'the scab') appear vertically in line. Despite errors, the script is written in a bold, attractive style.

XXI–XXIII), the Torah also contains, especially in the Priestly Code, ceremonial regulations. These comprise the observance of a calendar of festivals and Sabbaths, and the cult of a central shrine, with priests, vestments, and an order of animal sacrifices, together with regulations for the observance of purity within the precincts of the Temple. These laws are contained mainly in the Book of Leviticus. Many of the details of these observances were taken from the cults observed in other nations of the Near East. The worship of the One God, it was felt, should not lack any of the beauty and dignity which was lavished on the worship of idols; nor should the people of God have a yearly cycle less stately or joyful than those of pagan nations. Yet the borrowings were not made in a way that compromised monotheism. The pagan ceremonies were given a new meaning. The sacrifices, for example, had no magical significance in Judaism. They did not atone in themselves, but merely marked the fact that atonement had been achieved by restitution and repentance. The laws of purity had no significance of exorcising demons or warding off evil forces. They were regulations of self-respect and of regard for the seemly conduct of the Temple services. Moreover, the whole realm of ceremonial observance was subordinated to the realm of morality. The prophets, the guardians of authentic Judaism, continually inveighed against tendencies to regard ritual as having substantive, rather than symbolic, value. This was not a new attitude invented by the literary prophets, for we find the same attitude in older sources (see I Sam. XXI:4–6, where David reminds the High Priest that the preservation of human life takes precedence over the holiness of the showbread; see also I Sam. XV:22). The innovation of the literary prophets was, rather, their idea that moral failings would bring about the destruction of the state, not merely individual retribution.

The criticism of the Hebrew Bible, that it advocates a narrow ritualism, thus has no basis in fact. Even the Priestly Code does not do this. Other common criticisms of the Hebrew Bible require some mention. Some are simply mistakes arising from confusion or ignorance. For example, because old-fashioned Calvinists who were

devotees of the 'Old Testament' were also hell-fire preachers, many people are under the impression that the 'Old Testament' is full of threats about Hell and Satan. Yet there is not a single mention of Hell in the Hebrew Bible (how could there be, when, in the words of a contradictory charge, it 'has not yet risen to the conception of an after-life'?). The word 'hell' does occur several times in the Authorized Version, but this is a mistranslation of the Hebrew *sheol*, which means usually 'the grave', or perhaps sometimes 'the underworld', a place not of torment but of shadowy existence for the dead. The real source of Calvinist hell-fire sermons (common enough in other denominations too) is the New Testament (e.g. Matt. V:22). Nor is there any mention of the Devil in the 'Old Testament'. He is not among the *dramatis personae* of the Fall, and he, or Satan, features only once as a tempter, in the post-Exilic Book of Chronicles (I Chr. XXI:1). It was from the New Testament that the Christian figure of Satan was derived. The Hebrew Bible and its successor, the Talmud, do not succumb to the dualistic idea of a realm of evil directed by the Devil, though this idea can be found in Jewish works that were excluded, probably for this very reason, from the canon.

Equally beside the mark are criticisms of the 'fierce, tribal, jealous God of the Old Testament'. The God of the Hebrew Bible is not in the least tribal, but is throughout, from the first verse of Genesis, the God of the entire universe. He has chosen Israel as his special instrument and 'treasure', but this doctrine of undeserved election (as Bruce Vawter has remarked) 'is as far removed as may be from the notion of a superior people or race.' The word 'jealous' has shifted in meaning since it was used in the Authorized Version, when it was closer to the cognate word 'zealous', a better translation for the Hebrew *qan'a*. It means something like 'uncompromising'. God in the Hebrew Bible is not exactly a cosy figure; he can be like a high-voltage cable, which it is unwise to approach carelessly. Nor does he fit easily into human categories of morality. Yet his quality of mercy is continually stressed, as is his fatherly love for humanity, to whom he has provided a means of justification, the

מקץ

רש"י

אבן עזרא

מסרה

Daniel Bomberg, a Christian from Amsterdam who settled in Venice, printed a rabbinic Bible in 1525, his second attempt, which became the prototype of all later rabbinic Bibles. Edited by the learned Jacob ben Hayim ben Adoniya, it was the first printed text to include the Targums (Aramaic translations), the leading Jewish commentaries and the Masora. This page (Gen. XLIII:29–XLIV:11, about Joseph and his brothers) has the commentary of Rashi on the right, and that of Ibn Ezra on the left. The text of the Bible is the right-hand column of heavy type, while the adjacent column is the Targum Onkelos. The Masora is in two parts: Masora Parva (very brief comments on the inside margin) and the Masora Magna, above the text and left, bottom. The clear printing of the tiny marks of vowels, accents and musical notation was a very great technical achievement at the time.

observance of the moral law and repentance, without the necessity for terrifying self-mutilations, offerings of human sacrifices, or semi-divine redeemers. He is not an abstract principle, like the unmoved mover of the Greek philosophers, but a person who feels love, anger, joy and grief, and who can be affected by prayer. He is not remote, but 'nigh unto all them that call upon Him' (Ps. CXLV). He does not require from men self-abasement or excessive guilt, for the means of attaining his grace are not hard: '. . . it is not hidden from thee, neither is it far off . . . but the word is very nigh unto thee, in thy mouth, and thy heart, that thou mayest do it' (Deut. XXX:11–14). By entering into a Covenant with God,

Israel has become very close to him, so that the people of Israel spend all their lives in his presence. They thus experience both his love and his wrath with a special intensity, like a favourite child who risks incurring a special kind of disappointment on the part of his father.

But they are not the exclusive object of his love. Prophets (e.g. Elijah, Jonah) are sent to give divine messages to non-Israelite nations. Proselytes from the nations are accepted (e.g. Ruth, the ancestress of David). Non-Israelite sages and saints are protrayed (e.g. Noah, Job, Jethro). God, as Father of the Universe, loves all humans and all animals: 'His tender mercies are over all his works' (Ps. CXLV:9).

The colophon of a Hebrew Bible was the place where the scribe or illustrator would occasionally sign his name or indulge in some gratuitous pattern-making. This one, from a Bible of 1299–1300, reads 'I, Joseph the Frenchman, illustrated and completed this book', in grotesque letters made up of animals, birds and fishes.

Against the legal code of the Hebrew Bible the charge is often made that it is cruel and revengeful, being based on the principle of retaliation. This arises from the misconception that the injunction, 'Eye for eye, tooth for tooth, hand for hand, foot for foot, burning for burning, wound for wound, stripe for stripe' (Ex. XXI:24–5), was interpreted literally. Other parts of the code show that this was not so; such as verse nineteen of the same chapter, which provides for monetary compensation for a near-mortal injury. In the very ancient pre-Israelite code from which the expression 'eye for eye' was derived, a literal meaning may have been intended, but in the Israelite code (and indeed in parallel codes such as that of Hammurabi) such expressions were meant only to convey the basic moral principle that he who commits an injury must internalize the injury, and, out of the revulsion and repentance of such vivid conceptualization of the pain his neighbour has suffered, pay appropriate and adequate damages. This is the psychic reality underlying later Jewish formulations such as that of Hillel (60 BCE – 20 CE), 'What is hateful to you, do not unto your neighbour.'

A common charge against the Hebrew Bible that has some basis in fact is that it contains aggressive passages directed against the enemies of Israel. Such are the curse against Amalek (Ex. XVII:14), the prayer for vengeance against Babylon in Psalm CXXXVII and the prophecy of Nahum against the Assyrians. These passages certainly fail to rise to the heights of internationalism found in First Isaiah. In the depths of defeat and despair they are nevertheless understandable. A parallel in the New Testament is, for example, Jesus's curse against Capernaum (Matt. XI:23).

More serious is the alleged approval given to genocide in the injunctions to annihilate the Canaanites. In Exodus, the Israelites are enjoined not to exterminate the Canaanites but to 'drive them out' (Ex. XXIII:28–32). Instead of battening on the defeated as a new ruling class (the usual role of conquerors), the Israelites were to make a radically new start. The permission to 'dispossess' the Canaanites was never extended into a general permission to dispossess all unbelieving nations. Only the Holy Land was to be cleared of idolatry. Many of the Canaanites, in historical fact, joined the Israelite community. The use made of the Israelite conquest to justify Christian conquests in South America and elsewhere has no ground in the biblical text. It has long been recognized by scholars that the expressions in the writings of the Deuteronomic school which seem to enjoin the extermination of the Canaanites were 'created at the writing-desk' (Weinfeld) as part of a polemic against idolatry following Manasseh's apostasy in the 7th century BCE, when the Canaanites had long ago been assimilated.

In the Hebrew Bible there is certainly a great deal of violence. People do not turn the other cheek, but fight hard when attacked, or in defence of what they think good. In the fervour of a revolutionary atmosphere, cruel things are done; but there is also a strong sense of the limits of violence and of the sacredness of human life. Arbitrary revenge is banned as an expression of hate and self-indulgence; instead there is the universal rule of law, by which private feuds are banished, and even punishment becomes a form of love, since it is directed against the crime, not against the man, who achieves atonement by paying the due penalty.

A criticism often made nowadays against biblical law is that it is anti-feminist. Many charges under this head are misunderstandings; for example, Deuteronomy XXII:20 does *not* mean that an unmarried woman was executed for losing her virginity – how then would the law requiring a man to marry a woman he has seduced (Ex. XXII:15) ever come into operation? Biblical law cannot be understood apart from its accompanying case-law (any more than the Roman law can be criticized on the basis of the Twelve Tables, or English law on the basis of the Common Law). In general, the laws relating to women were enlightened for their age and were continually improved in practice, as the evidence of Apocrypha (books not included in the canon) and Talmud shows. The Bible gives high honour to women: the Four Matriarchs, Miriam, Deborah, Hulda (all prophetesses), Hannah, Abigail, Ruth, Esther. See also Proverbs XXXI for a eulogy of an ideal woman.

Completion of the canon

The actual Law-codes of the Torah are extremely simple and summary. They could never have been the whole of the law by which society was administered.

There must have been many supplementary codes or collections of case-law, embodying the development of the law in changing circumstances. What happened to all this supplementary case-law? The answer is that it became what is called the Oral Law. It was only after the creation of the biblical canon that emphasis was laid on the oral transmission of case-law. The existence of a written canon gave rise to a reluctance to circulate in any official way any writings that might seem to rival the canon. Such writings were therefore committed to memory and written down only in a mnemonic form.

Meanwhile, it was only gradually that the canon of Scripture reached its final dimensions. The Torah was the first part to become accepted as Holy Writ. This was fully accomplished by the time of the Return and the construction of the Second Temple, as we see from the books of Ezra and Nehemiah. The second section of the canon, known as 'the Prophets' (*Nevi'im*), comprising the Former Prophets (or historical books) and the Latter Prophets, was well on the way to completion by this time, but was not actually completed until the 4th century BCE, with the addition of the post-Restoration Prophets, Haggai, Zechariah and Malachi. The rest of the canon after this consisted of what were called the 'Writings' (*Ketuvim*), and these were in a state of flux until a much later date. This section was not fixed until about 100 CE, and there is some evidence that its boundaries were uncertain even later (the Talmud refers on one occasion to Ecclesiasticus as being one of the 'Writings'). The sages of mishnaic times disagreed occasionally about which books should be included among the 'Writings' (disagreements are recorded about Ecclesiastes, and the Song of Songs), but there was never any disagreement about the canon of the Torah, and among the Prophets the only disagreement was about Ezekiel, because of its heterodox law-code.

Evidence of the development of the canon in the 3rd century BCE comes from the Greek Septuagint, the earliest translation of the Hebrew Bible, started when the canon had not yet reached its final form, but continued by later translators until after the beginning of the Christian era. The Septuagint, however, follows an arrangement (after the Torah) that differs from that of the Hebrew canon, being arranged in three sections by topic: historical, poetic, prophetic. Also, the Septuagint includes several books that the Hebrew canon excludes (e.g. Tobit, Judith, Maccabees), though the number of these additional books differs in the various editions. The earlier translations included in the Septuagint give valuable evidence of the state of the text (or rather one recension of it) at an early period, and the Hebrew text can often be corrected by reference to the Greek, though no general preference can be given to the Greek over the Hebrew. The Septuagint translation was made for the needs of the Hellenistic Jews of Alexandria, but eventually it was abandoned by Jews and taken over by the Christian Church. The Hebrew Bible then became the sole source of other translations (made into Greek and Aramaic) used by Jews.

When it was finalized, the Hebrew Bible consisted, traditionally, of twenty-four books, this number being arrived at by counting the twelve Minor (i.e. shorter) Prophets as one book, and by counting Ezra and Nehemiah as one. The division of Samuel, Kings and Chronicles into two books each was late, as far as the Hebrew Bible was concerned (Bomberg edition, 1521), though in the Septuagint these divisions are found. Many variations are found in the order of the prophetic books and of the 'Writings'. It was not until the invention of printing that the present order crystallized. (The English Bible follows roughly the order of the Septuagint.) The Bible, for centuries, was not a single book but a collection of scrolls (so the question of the correct order of the books was probably a matter of library storage). The first codices, or continuous books, of the Hebrew Bible did not appear until the early Middle Ages. To this day, the Torah is written by hand on a parchment scroll for synagogal use in the reading of the Law, as are certain other biblical books known as the Five Scrolls (*Megilloth*): Song of Songs, Ruth, Lamentations, Ecclesiastes and Esther.

The story of the transmission of the Hebrew text of the Bible is highly complicated. Much light has been thrown on it by recent discoveries at Qumran and Masada. These confirm that the text was in a state of considerable fluidity during the period of Persian and Greek domination, but that the type of text that was later fixed as canonical for Jews by the labours of scribes and the Masoretic school of textual experts is at least as ancient as any other, and is less in need of emendation than was previously thought.

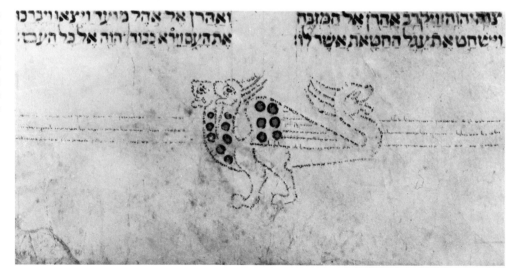

Micro-writing, script so minute as to be practically invisible to the naked eye, became a curiously widespread fashion in medieval Jewish manuscripts (see p. 130, pl. 5). The colophon of a Bible written by Joshua ben Abraham ibn Gaon of Soria, in Spain, 1301, is given the form of a multiheaded bird, composed of lines of tiny writing.

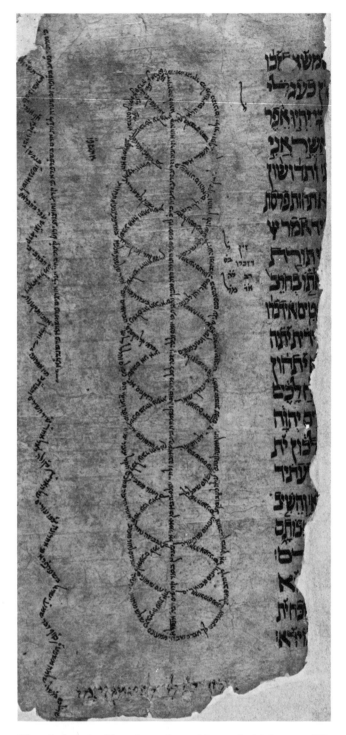

The colophon of a Yemenite scribe, writing at San'a' in 1474. His name is incorporated into interlocking circles of micro-writing. The manuscript is of the Latter Prophets.

first of the scribes, was a priest, the scribes rapidly lost their priestly character and became a classless intellectual élite, recruited by merit alone, and making their appeal to the brighter intellects of the whole nation. There was nothing esoteric about the learning centred on the Bible. There were no mysteries to be acquired by initiation or by special signs of qualification. There was no unbridge-able gap of specialization between the scholar and the ordinary people. On the contrary, the scholar was expected to make himself intelligible, not only by public discourses, but by putting his knowledge into public practice as a judge and arbitrator of disputes. Scholarship for its own sake was not prized.

Secondary literature

This ceaseless and massive study of the Bible led eventually to a huge secondary literature which also became the subject-matter of study. The Oral Law (as explained above) sprang into being by the very fact of the appearance of the Written Law; it was the material, explanatory and supplementary, that was left out of Scripture but remained essential to its operation in practical, legal life. This material was 'handed down' (to use an expression found in Josephus and in rabbinical literature) partly by word of mouth, partly by sheer imitative custom, and partly in the form of written collections, made unofficially for the use of individuals. This traditional material was itself supplemented by a huge body of new decisions and new exegetical remarks, until, in the end, the inhibition against the official embodiment of all this material in written form was broken down, and in the 2nd and 3rd centuries CE, the Mishnah (legal) and the Midrash (exegetic) began to take form. Among the Hellenistic Jews of Alexandria, on the other hand, another kind of supplementary literature appeared, based on Greek forms of philosophy and literary criticism. This literature, composed in Greek, was written down without inhibition, since it clearly could not be taken as rivalling the canonical status of Scripture.

The chief figure in this Hellenistic Jewish exegesis of the Bible, by which it was explained allegorically and related to the categories of Greek philosophy, was Philo, whose later influence was not on Jews but on the exegetes and theologians of the Christian Church.

The history of Jewish exegesis of the Bible is a vast subject. The eventual repository of the Oral Law and of post-Ezra Palestinian exegesis was the corpus of the Talmudim and the Midrashim, which incorporated not only the collections of the 2nd and 3rd centuries CE, but also the further work of legalists and exegetes up to the 6th century CE. To be a scholar now meant not only to know the Bible, but to know all this supplementary literature. Bible study itself now came to be thought of as elementary education, the first step in the educational ladder. Talmudic methods of exegesis were refined into a science and a methodology.

There was resistance, however, against this swamping of the Bible. Not only were there protestant movements rejecting the extra-biblical learning (especially the Karaites, whose movement arose in the 8th century CE) but even among Talmudists there was a constant tendency to resist the subtleties of exegesis and return to the plain meaning of the text. This led to a theory of

The appearance of the Hebrew Bible in its final form (and even before it reached its final form) had a profound effect on the mentality and character of the Jewish people. Henceforward, they became a literary people. Study of the Bible became a hallowed activity, and the figure of the scholar acquired great prestige. Yet, because study was never regarded as the prerogative of a particular class, this emphasis on study led not to social stratification but to an ideal of universal education. The Bible became the focus of a nation-wide effort towards literacy. In practice the new class of sages, or scribes, or rabbis, came from every social group. Though Ezra, the multiple meaning, by which the text could be interpreted on several different levels, one of which was always that of plain literalism ('A Biblical text never loses its literal meaning,' says the Talmud). This theory of multiple meaning became so firmly and confidently assimilated that it was even possible to put forward playful (punning) meanings, which were regarded as the outcome of a loving relationship with the text, rather than as truly inherent in it. Thus, by the Middle Ages, a wide repertory of exegesis was available: the allegorical, the mystical, the legal-hermeneutical and the playful. Yet there was a strong tendency from the 11th century onwards to revert to the literal, and to read the Bible (with the aid of a developing scientific grammar of Hebrew) in isolation from its talmudic and midrashic commentaries and on its own terms. The leading figures in this movement of return to the text were Rashi and David Kimhi, whose biblical commentaries were much used by the Christian Hebraists of the Reformation.

On the other hand, side by side with this literalist tendency and not in conflict with it, was a tendency to find mystical, esoteric meanings in every word of the Bible – a tendency culminating in the Zohar, the main kabbalistic text, which takes the form of a mystical commentary on the Torah.

In all generations, movements of renewal in Judaism have returned to the fountain of the Bible and have drawn from it new vigour. The very multitude of these past responses, available in the vast literature of exegesis, may sometimes stand in the way of a personal encounter with the Bible. Yet there is always one way in which the Jew can experience such an encounter: in the liturgical services of both the synagogue and the home, in which the Hebrew Bible plays so great a part. In the Seder service of Passover, the experience of the Exodus is

The Torah must still be hand-written on a parchment scroll. This etching by E. M. Lilien shows an old scribe in Poland or eastern Galicia during the First World War.

relived. In the great yearly cycle of readings from the Torah, the Covenant is renewed. Through the Psalms, very many of which are included in the prayer-book, the Jew expresses devotion, gratitude, praise and contrition. And in the daily *Shema*, the basic message of Judaism is repeated in the words of Deuteronomy, the focal book in the formation of the Bible: 'Hear, O Israel, the Lord our God, the Lord is One. And thou shalt love the Lord thy God with all thine heart and with all thy soul and with all thy might.'

II
THE MAKING OF JEWRY

The Jews and the Great Powers of the Ancient World

The Talmud

The Ritual and Music of the Synagogue

Jewry and Rome: a Classical capital supporting a slab bearing the carved menorah (candlestick), *shofar* (ram's horn), *lulab* (palm branch), and *ethrog* (citron) symbolizes the way in which Judaism learned to co-exist with the Great Powers of the Mediterranean world. It was under Cyrus, the Persian, that the Jews returned from their Babylonian Exile in 538 BCE. The Persian Empire was destroyed by Alexander the Great in 330. His brief reign was followed by two centuries of uneasy rivalry between his Hellenistic successors, the Seleucids in Syria and the Ptolemies in Egypt. In the 1st century BCE they in their turn were forced to submit to the universal power of Rome. Throughout this whole period of over five hundred years, the Jews maintained their integrity as a nation, sometimes by compromise, sometimes by playing off one power against another. When fortune was kind, as during the period of the Maccabees, they contrived to assert their political independence. More usually, they were subject to one or other of the Great Powers, preserving only a limited autonomy. Finally, in 70 CE, the great turning point in Jewish history, all attempts at compromise and diplomacy failed: the Temple was destroyed, the Jews were deprived of their homeland and the focus shifts away from Palestine to those Jewish communities established in other lands ... the Diaspora.

Each of the three great empires – Persian, Hellenistic and Roman – left its mark upon Jewish culture, though not upon doctrine or belief. Judaism could adopt Classical trappings while conceding nothing to Classicism. This column (*opposite*), with its acanthus leaves, volutes and bead-and-reel mouldings, stood at one side of the apse of the synagogue at Ostia, near Rome. Its foundation seems to go back to a period before the destruction of the Temple, but the present remains date from the 3rd or 4th centuries CE, when Ostia was a thriving cosmopolitan port. Between the columns probably hung the curtain that concealed the Ark. (1)

Under three empires

Of the Persian period few material traces survive and we must rely on the evidence of written history and coins. *Below:* a silver coin, 4th century BCE, struck in Jerusalem and bearing an eagle with the inscription 'Yehud', the official Aramaic name for Judaea after the Return. (2)

'Yehiskia', says the inscription on this silver coin of the Persian period, possibly referring to a High Priest mentioned by Josephus. *Below:* coin of the same date, with unidentified head. (3, 4)

In the Hellenistic world the Jews lived for the most part peacefully and prosperously. Jewish communities flourished in the great urban centres such as Alexandria. Jewish thinkers, such as Philo Judaeus, wrote in Greek, and a Greek translation of the Bible (the Septuagint) made the Law and the Prophets accessible to a non-Jewish public. The Jews in their turn adopted many elements of Hellenism. The rebuilt Temple, under Herod, was largely Greek in style, and so were the tombs and mausolea which began to be erected in the cemetery of Kidron, outside Jerusalem, from the 2nd century BCE. The so-called 'Tomb of Absalom' (*above*) is partly rock-cut, with Ionic columns and a Doric frieze, and partly built. The 'Tomb of Zechariah' (*below*) is also cut from the living rock. Behind these monuments lie smaller graves and catacombs. (5, 6)

'Year two' and 'Year three' say these two coins minted in Jerusalem between 67 and 69 CE. The first (*above*) is of silver and shows a chalice; the other is of bronze and bears an amphora. The years of Jewish freedom were to number only four. (8, 9)

Compromise ended in 66 CE, when rebellion against Roman rule flared up in Jerusalem. Defeat – as many Jews foresaw – was inevitable. It came in the year 70, and it ended Jewish political freedom for nearly nineteen centuries. The Romans tore down the Temple and as a symbol of their victory carried off its treasures, including the menorah (*above*), to Rome. (7)

The last rebellion was that of the Messianic leader Simeon Bar Kokhba in 132. The coins (*below*) issued during his government bear witness to Jewish hopes of a new age. They show the Temple, two trumpets and a lyre. But within three years he, too, had been crushed by the Romans. The Jews of Palestine virtually ceased to exist. (10, 11, 12)

The arts of peace

Herod's palace-fortress of Masada, a huge rock in the desert country close to the Dead Sea, has become legendary because of the heroic events of 73 CE. Here, after the fall of Jerusalem, the Jewish freedom fighters held out for three years against a vast Roman army. When defeat was closing in they committed mass-suicide. But before this, Masada had been a luxury retreat for Herod, built and decorated in the prevailing Hellenistic taste, including frescoes (*above*). The palace took ingenious advantage of the rock formation with apartments (*opposite*) descending by a series of natural steps. (13, 15)

The Judgment of Solomon: the presence of this traditionally Jewish story among the decorations of a Pompeiian house (*below*) seems to imply a well established Jewish colony there before 79 CE. On the other hand, there is a strong element of caricature in the painting, which makes it unlikely to be directly Jewish inspired. Solomon sits on a dais between two counsellors. The real mother kneels and pleads at his feet, while a soldier behind her prepares to chop the child in half. (14)

'The place of assembly'

Synagogue is the Greek word for the Aramaic *kenishta*, meaning a place where people come together. Before the destruction of the Temple, synagogues were merely rooms for teaching and prayer; after the destruction, when prayer replaced sacrifice as the key point of the Jewish liturgy, they became the only centres of communal religious observance. *Above:* carved panel from Kefr Yasif, with a series of abstract patterns and – top left – a stylized menorah and snuff-dishes. *Above right:* main entrance to the synagogue of Bir-Am, 3rd century CE. *Right:* reconstructed remains of the synagogue at Capernaum, then a thriving town on the shores of the Sea of Galilee. (16, 17, 19)

'No Gentile to enter the precinct of the Temple. Anyone caught doing so is responsible for his own ensuing death.' This inscription, in Greek (*below*), seems to have been placed on all the gates leading from the Court of the Gentiles into the Court of the Jews, and the rule was maintained under the Roman governors. (18)

'There is one God': a Greek inscription from a synagogue in Palestine asserts Jewish monotheism amidst the prevailing polytheistic religions of Greece and Rome. (20)

Flanking the Ark of the Covenant stand some of the familiar symbols that now formed the standard repertoire of Jewish iconography: the menorah, the *shofar* and the incense shovel. This mosaic formed part of the pavement of a synagogue at Beth-shaan, and dates from the 6th century CE. (21)

A puzzling mixture of Jewish and pagan elements occurs in the decoration of these early synagogues, comparable to the mixture of Jewish and Christian elements that we have seen in medieval illuminations. A mosaic at Ma'an (*below*) consisted originally of fifty-five medallions, of which only a few survive. The menorah, the lions of Judah, the *shofar* and two *ethrogim* (citrons) are fairly clear. But why the doves, the bird in the cage and the elephants? It has been argued (by E. R. Goodenough) that many of these symbols, including even the lions and the grapes, belonged to a popular form of mysticism adapted to Judaism from Hellenistic cults. (23)

'The seat of Moses' was by tradition set up in synagogues and reserved for the teachers of the Law. One of the Christian Gospels refers to the fact that 'the Scribes and Pharisees sit in Moses' seat.' The inscription on this one from the synagogue of Chorazin commemorates the name of Judah ben Ishmael, who provided 'this stoa and its staircase.' (22)

The medieval synagogue

As the centres of religious observance, the synagogues became the focal points of Jewish community life in the European Middle Ages. In a 14th-century Spanish Haggadah (*left*) a rabbi on the left holds the Torah scroll in his draped hands. Below him are the Tablets of the Law. The congregation shows men, women and children together, though in reality they would have been segregated, unless they are just entering en famille. (24)

The oldest synagogue still standing in Europe is the so-called Old-New Synagogue in Prague (*opposite*). It dates from the 13th century, and is close in style to the prevailing Gothic of Christian buildings. The nave (reserved for men – the women sit in a gallery at the end) has a rib-vault and is divided into two by columns. The centre is screened off by an iron grille. At the end of the room is the Ark containing the Torah scrolls. (27) ▷

Reading the sermon in a Spanish synagogue of the 14th century. Much of the décor, e.g. the hanging lamps, reveals an Islamic source. (26)

An Italian Haggadah (*left*), illuminated in 1435, shows a scene with men and youths wearing the *tallith*. In front of the tabernacle, a rabbi holds the Torah scroll wrapped in a red cloth. The animals in the corners probably represent the four 'camps' into which the twelve Tribes were divided. (25)

'**And it came to pass** when the evil spirit from God was upon Saul, that David took the harp and played with his hand: so Saul was refreshed and was well, and the evil spirit departed from him.' The power of music is well attested in the Bible. Numerous musical occasions are described and a whole array of instruments mentioned. But how did it sound? The question will probably never be answered. Outside Europe hardly any written music exists before the 19th century. The attempt to reconstruct ancient music by studying folk-traditions is bound to be hazardous.

A terracotta plaque (*left*), now in the museum of Aleppo, has been convincingly identified as the young David, although the word translated as harp (*kinnor*) is now thought to have been an instrument of the lyre family. (28)

Woodwind and strings were certainly known in ancient Israel. Crude figurines of the 9th–7th centuries BCE (*below*) prove this much, though they tell us little about their exact form or how they were played. The first, a figure playing a small lyre held against the chest, is from Ashdod; the second, two women playing a tambourine and a double pipe, comes from excavations at Akhzir; the third is a detail from an incense-burner showing probably a double pipe and lyre player. (29, 30, 31)

'**And David danced** before the Lord with all his might.' The Second Book of Samuel (Chapter VI) tells how David brought the Ark into Jerusalem, thereby making the city the centre of the nation's religious life: 'So David and all the house of Israel brought up the ark of the Lord with shouting, and with the sound of the trumpet. And it was so, as the ark of the Lord came into the city of David, that Michal the daughter of Saul looked out at the window, and saw king David leaping and dancing before the Lord; and she despised him in her heart. And they brought in the ark of the Lord, and set it in its place, in the midst of the tent that David had pitched for it: and David offered burnt offerings and peace offerings before the Lord. And when David had made an end of offering the burnt offerings and the peace offerings, he blessed the people in the name of the Lord of hosts. And he dealt among all the people, even among the whole multitude of Israel, both to men and women, to every one a cake of bread, and a portion of flesh, and cake of raisins. So all the people departed every one to his house. Then David returned to bless his household. And Michal the daughter of Saul came out to meet David, and said, How glorious was the king of Israel today, who uncovered himself today in the eyes of the handmaids of his servants, as one of the vain fellows shamelessly uncovereth himself!' This strange marble relief, made in Egypt around the 2nd or 3rd century CE, seems to have had a function in the Feast of the Tabernacles. In the centre is King David, naked and holding what look like castanets. Round the rim are a woman's head (Michal looking out of the window), a dead calf (he had earlier sacrificed 'an ox and a fatling'), olive branches (the peace offering) and eleven of the 'cakes of bread'. (32)

Music sacred and profane

'**The prophetess Miriam,** Aaron's sister, took a tambourine in her hand, while all the women went out after her with tambourines, dancing; and she answered them with the refrain: Sing to the Lord, for he is gloriously triumphant; horse and chariot has he cast into the sea.' So Exodus describes the triumphal dance of Miriam after the crossing of the Red Sea. It is one of our earliest accounts of a musical occasion, frequently represented in Haggadahs. This miniature (*opposite*) is from the 14th-century Spanish *Golden Haggadah*. (33)

The shofar is one of the most ancient instruments in the world. It is mentioned in the Bible and in spite of its limitations – it can make only the most rudimentary sounds – it has continued in use for the New Year and Day of Atonement festivals. In kabbalistic literature it is credited with the power of softening the Divine Judgment and dispelling the forces of evil – something that it appears to be doing in this 13th–14th-century miniature in a German Yom Kippur rite. Placing one foot on a stool was believed to dispel the power of the devil in his attempt to confuse the blower. (34)

Tiny grotesque figures, many of them playing musical instruments, inhabit the letters of this *siddur*, or prayer-book, written in Germany in 1471. One has a pipe like a recorder, another a lute and another, near the middle, an instrument like a violin played with a bow. The medieval convention of 'inhabited letters' has been clearly adapted to the Hebrew script, using animals for the diacritical marks. (35)

Five musicians (*below*) decorate a page from a 15th-century Haggadah produced in Barcelona. The first plays the tabor and pipe, the second a violin, the third a lute closely resembling the Islamic *'ud*, the fourth bagpipes and the fifth kettledrums. The page on which it appears begins the section of the Passover service devoted to the matzah, or unleavened bread. (36)

The kid that father bought for two zuzim.

Then came the cat that ate the kid.

Then came the dog that ate the cat.

Then came the stick that struck the dog.

Then came the fire that burnt the stick.

Then came the water that quenched the fire.

Then came the ox that drank the water.

Then came the butcher who slew the ox.

Then came Death who slew the butcher.

Then came the Holy One, blessed be He, who slays the Angel of Death. (This frame is left virtually blank, since God can neither be represented nor named.)

'The kid that father bought for two zuzim' is an old Jewish song chanted at the end of the Haggadah, each verse repeating the previous ones. Like many folk-songs, its apparently nonsensical words conceal an allegorical meaning. Some critics believe that it goes back to the period of the Great Powers, and reflects the rise and fall of empires – Babylon, Persia, Greece, Rome – that had wronged Israel and perished. These illustrations come from a Haggadah made in Rotterdam in 1739. (37)

שמחת בית השואבה

אנשים משח   צורת הקידה   חסידים

The dance, following David's example, has continued to be an accepted expression of religious celebration. Part of the Sukkot (Feast of the Tabernacles) is called 'The Drawing of Water', and the Talmud relates that Rabbi Simeon ben Gamaliel, the president of the Sanhedrin in the 1st century CE, would juggle with eight burning torches, 'throwing them in the air and catching them.' This 18th-century embroidered hanging shows other acrobatic feats recommended by the rabbi for this occasion. (38)

Jewish bands became a familiar sight in 17th- and 18th-century Europe. Often organized into guilds, they took part in family rejoicings and festive occasions such as weddings. This watercolour (*right*) was made in Poland in 1830 and shows a group of cellist, cymbalist, zither player and violinist. (39)

For the Hasidim, life is a gift from God, to be celebrated with dance, song and rejoicing. The great age of Hasidism was the 18th century, but it is still alive. These members of the sect were sketched by Chaim Gross in 1941. (40)

The vine

The symbolism of vine, vineyard and grapes has been part of Jewish iconography since the days of Moses. Isaiah uses the metaphor of the Gardener and the Vineyard for God's disappointment with the people of Israel: 'My wellbeloved hath a vineyard in a very fruitful hill. ... And he planted it with the choicest vine ... and he looked that it should bring forth grapes, and it brought forth wild grapes. ... I will tell you what I will do to my vineyard. I will take away the hedge thereof, and it shall be eaten up. ... And I will lay it waste: it shall not be pruned nor digged. ... For the vineyard of the Lord of Hosts is the house of Israel, and the men of Judah his pleasant plant' (Is. v). Vine leaves or grape clusters figure on Jewish coins, with a similar meaning. *Above left:* a coin of the first Jewish revolt, 68 CE. *Above right:* Vine leaves and grapes on the tympanum of the Old-New Synagogue in Prague. Twelve bunches of grapes stand for the twelve Tribes. (41, 42)

A stucco frieze in the Synagogue of the Transito in Toledo, 1366, with parallel inscriptions in Hebrew and Arabic is a poignant witness to the harmony of the two cultures at that time. The artists were probably Muslim. (43)

'**Plant vineyards** that may yield fruits of increase,' says Psalm CVII. Vineyards were a sign of settled peace and prosperity, the vintage a symbol of God's blessing. Shown here are four examples of the grapes motif used in different contexts. *Right:* the embroidered border of a Torah-cover, dated 1741, from Prague, with the vine scroll encircling a salamonic column. (47)

'**And they came** unto the valley of Eshcol, and cut down from thence a branch with one cluster of grapes, and they bore it upon a staff between two.' The story of the spies who brought back grapes as proof of the fertility of the promised land (Num. XIII:23) is frequently illustrated. A rabbinical peculiarity of the Alba Bible (*above*) is that it interprets 'between two' to mean two staves, not two men, and so shows eight men, four to each staff. (44)

Grapes as a symbol of the Tribe of Levi (*right*) on a Persian silk rug of about 1850 (see p. 157, pl. 84) and (*below*) on a tombstone in the Jewish cemetery of Prague. (45, 46)

As an evocation of the Covenant between man and God, the hands raised in blessing is a symbol that runs through the whole of Jewish history, and can be traced back to pre-Jewish origins. A Canaanite stele of the 13th century BCE (*left*) shows a pair of hands reaching upwards to a disc and a crescent, symbols of the Canaanite moon-god, Jehovah's defeated rival in the story of Elijah. The stele was found at Hazor, near the Sea of Galilee. (48)

The last blessing: hands are among the commonest symbols to be carved on Jewish tombstones. This one (*left*) dates from the 17th century and is in the old Jewish cemetery of Prague. The priestly blessing, 'May the Lord bless you and keep you,' was one of the few functions remaining to the priests after the destruction of the Temple. (49)

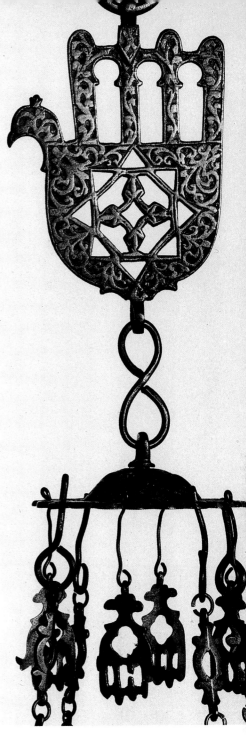

In the ritual of the synagogue the blessing priestly hands occur on a variety of liturgical objects. *Above:* a silver and gold Torah crown dated 1793. The custom of decorating Torah scrolls with crowns is especially characteristic of Eastern countries, though this example comes from no further east than Germany. It is engraved with the name of the donor and enriched with jewels. *Right:* a hanging lamp from a southern Moroccan synagogue incorporates an Islamic hand, a symbol equally widespread and equally beneficent. *Below:* part of a stained glass window installed in the Great Portland Street synagogue, London, in the 1960s. *Below right:* cover of a manuscript Haggadah, written in Germany in 1740, with a design that includes the crown and blessing hands. (50–53)

The Talmud consists of Mishnah and its commentary, the *Gemara*. Taken as a whole, it is second to the Bible in authority. This page is from a 14th-century German manuscript of Asher ben Jehiel's commentary on the Mishnah. It is the opening of the tractate called *Yevamot* ('Sisters-in-law'), which deals with the legal complications that can arise when a man is bidden to marry his deceased brother's widow (what if she is his own daughter?). The word illuminated with such exotic fancy is 'Five' (in fact the first half of 'Fifteen'), and the little figure at the bottom may be intended either for the commentator or the original author. (54)

Rabbis Gamaliel and Eleazar, marginal portraits from a Greek Haggadah, probably written in Crete in 1583. (55, 56)

Chapter Three

The Jews and the Great Powers of the Ancient World

ZVI YAVETZ

IT IS A TRUISM THAT the ignorance of modern historians often derives from the abundance of material, just as the ignorance of ancient historians derives from its paucity. The problem is rampant in topics connected with foreign policy, and it is not necessarily characteristic of Jewish history. There were no ministries of foreign affairs in Antiquity, and no archive dealing with the formulation of foreign policy has survived. Moreover, rarely do we know anything about the way of thinking of those who influenced the directions of foreign affairs. What we do know is all too often fragmentary and its preservation is purely accidental. Scholars interested in what political scientists depict as the 'decision-making process' are at a loss when it comes to Antiquity.

What joy classicists would find in the discovery of an inscription or a papyrus containing some record of informal talks among Senators at a dinner party! It would be no less valuable to acquire information regarding conversations among Senators on their way to the Senate and gossip in the lobbies, than the analysis of every comma in a Senatus Consultum, which revealed the end-product of a process but nothing of the raw material that went into it. While a lack of source material is one problem, another is that ancient historians, who recorded in depth the growth of political institutions and the behaviour of social groups, did not excel when handling topics that are today regarded as foreign affairs. Thucydides is certainly the exception who proves the rule. To this day, historians find it difficult to explain the revolutionary leap from the naïve interpretations by Herodotus, concerning the outbreak of the Persian Wars, to the classic description of Thucydides of the Peloponnesian Wars. Rarely have modern scholars pin-pointed the underlying motives for the outbreaks of war as convincingly as did Thucydides: fear, aspiration for glory and ambition for wealth. It is sad to concede that, after Thucydides, few historians followed his example. Most of them saw, in the territorial aspirations of one or another leader, sufficient reason to explain the outbreak of the war. In Josephus we read simply that an Egyptian king went to war because he wished to conquer Asia. A Roman historian saw Hannibal as not only the *casus belli* but also the *causa belli* of the second Punic War. A description of the political, strategic and economic interests that might have played a decisive role in an outbreak of a war is usually conspicuous by its absence.

What is most disturbing is that the social background is totally deficient. No one can be satisfied by a cliché – 'the Jews wanted . . .' or 'the Romans aspired. . . .' It is essential to know which Jews and which Romans, since there never was a monolithic approach to foreign policy. At the time of every war there are fierce advocates of the war, there are those who are less enthusiastic and there are those who oppose it altogether. An analysis of the social group that clamoured for war might teach us more about the hidden objectives of the foreign policy than a dry juridicial document preserved in an archive. One illustration: it is an accepted fact that the Punic Wars (264–241 BCE and 218–202 BCE) were a turning point in Roman history. For the first time, tremendous resources were expended overseas. The wars were extended and Roman peasants became their first victims. They could not afford to stay away too long from their plots. We do not know what arguments took place in the Senate before it was decided to cross the Straits of Messina and no one knows what weighed on the mind of each individual Senator. All we know is that there was a heated discussion and that the Claudian family were the 'Jingoes'. Even the writings of a historian as important as Polybius do not satisfy our curiosity, and the fragmentary writings of Livy, 230 years after the events, do not come to our rescue. With the help of detailed prosopographic studies, attempts were made to reconstruct the composition of the various factions. This kind of research gave ancient history an important boost, but did not solve the problem. For in many cases, names of Senators rather than their opinions are known.

Hence, there are more conjectures on the essential questions – such as whether Rome embarked on a series of overseas campaigns as a consequence of long-term strategy or was accidentally dragged into an adventure – which seem to one generation to be more valid than to another, than there are substantive answers based on hard-core evidence. No wonder that more cautious historians, less prone to generalize, blamed their more audacious colleagues for having put the cart before the horse, for having proposed intentions on the basis of consequences and for having rested their case on the notorious *post hoc ergo propter hoc* principle. Cautious historians preferred to profess their own ignorance rather than to hazard guesses. They dedicated their efforts to fact-finding, thus providing future generations with raw material to mould and interpret. They also recommended the study of the topics for which authoritative evidence could be found, and looked with suspicion on those who introduced contemporary

'Shema, servant of Jereboam': the inscription on this seal documents it as belonging to the reign of Jereboam II (783–743 BCE). The kingdom of Israel was then in a characteristic position, poised between three powerful empires – Assyria, Babylonia and Egypt – and preserving its autonomy by a mixture of compromise and diplomacy.

terminology into ancient history. Their criticism was to some extent well founded, because some scholars did not hesitate to use terms like 'Roman imperialism' (Tenney Frank), 'ancient anti-Semitism' (Heinemann), 'Roman bourgeoisie' (Rostovtzeff), 'socialism and communism in the ancient world' (Poehlman). This criticism was not always justified. Rostovtzeff knew very well that the Hellenistic bourgeoisie was not the bourgeoisie of the French Revolution and Tenney Frank knew very well that Roman imperialism of the 2nd century BCE was different from British imperialism of the 19th century. All that they wanted was to illustrate ancient phenomena for the non-professional reader, and each of them would point to the old master (Mommsen), who never hesitated to use the term 'Roman Junker'. Therefore, attempts to approach ancient history in modern terms were never completely abandoned. As historians two centuries ago rebelled against antiquarians, so do scholars in our own day protest against those who abide by the principle, *quod non est in actis, non erat in vita*. The truth is that not everything recorded in ancient sources is accurate, and the testimony of an ancient historian that so-and-so intended to achieve such-and-such an objective is not yet acceptable evidence. In most cases, it is wiser to depend on facts rather than alleged intentions, and if Polybius asserted that the Romans went to war with the Dalmatians because they did not wish their army to become effeminate, his statement should be taken with a grain of salt. However, attempts to deduce intentions may occasionally be rewarding if the point is not pressed too far. It is also important to emphasize that the absence of a concept in ancient texts is no proof that the problem did not exist in Antiquity. It is often circumscribed, and by asking the right question we might get some satisfactory answers. This actually happened in a recent, refreshing and rather convincing book by E. Luttwak on the 'Grand Strategy' of the Roman Empire.

Obviously there is no term 'Grand Strategy' in the writings of Livy and Tacitus, but after reading Luttwak's book, no classicist will find it easy to deny Luttwak's basic assumption that the Romans had no need of a

Clauswitz to subject their military energies to the discipline of political goals. One will also have to admit that without the knowledge of 'systems analysis' the Romans were capable of designing a large and complex security system, whether by intellect or traditional intuition. Careful scrutiny of the ancient sources leads us to the fact that the Romans understood all the subtleties of deterrence and also its limitations. In this case one may go one step further. A Chinese scholar who would like to analyze Roman strategy could easily prove that the Romans behaved according to the principles laid down by a Chinese sage: 'To subdue the enemy without fighting is the acme of skill. This which is of extreme importance in war is to attack the enemy's strategy. Next best is to disrupt his alliances. His army should be attacked only as a last resort.' Tiberius Caesar never read Sun Tzu, but one could easily provide some Latin quotations from Tacitus to prove that (at least on the German frontier) he acted along those lines.

These introductory remarks have been made to clarify the difficulties with which Greek and Roman historians are faced when dealing with foreign policy and strategic problems, but these difficulties are negligible when compared to a consideration of the foreign policy of the First and Second Jewish Commonwealths. At first, it would appear that the difficulties in studying Jewish history are not as complicated. Jews know more about their ancestors than Frenchmen, Yugoslavs, Romanians and Turks know about Gauls, Illyrians, Dacians or Cappadocians. Hebrew and Aramaic sources have survived; the Talmud and the Midrash constitute a mine of information for Jewish spiritual, intellectual, legal and even social history. But for political history, and especially for the problem of orientation towards the Great Powers, these sources are utterly inadequate. Greek and Latin authors on the other hand are inadequate in a different way; they are usually biased (who is not?); what is more serious is not their bias, but their lack of interest in or understanding of internal political problems, without which it is impossible to analyze foreign policy. It seems that the topic was not rated by them as sufficiently important. Here, we shall try to take up some problems that certainly preoccupied the leadership of the Second Jewish Commonwealth, even if the problems were not formulated in our own jargon.

The problem: Egypt, Assyria and Babylonia

There were times in which Howard Fast was highly esteemed in Soviet literary circles; his books were not only praised but used as an example for Soviet writers and poets. His novel of the Hasmonean Revolt, however, has never been translated into Russian. Once, when asked for an explanation, a Soviet critic replied that this is precisely the kind of book that is far removed from socialistic realism. No little nation can defeat a great one (unless it acts as a stooge and is used by a Great Power) and the Hasmonean slogan of the few having defeated the many should once and forever be exposed as invalid.

We are not going to discuss the validity of this statement here, but it is necessary to emphasize right away that the Soviet critic put his finger on a major political problem that haunted the Second Jewish Commonwealth – from the Return of the exiles from Babylonia (538 BCE) to the destruction of the Second

Temple (70 CE). How can a small nation survive in freedom and autonomy, surrounded by other – not always friendly – small nations, and situated in an area that has always attracted hegemonical interests of one or more greater powers, which transformed the Middle East not only into a thoroughfare, but all too often into a battlefield? The possibilities are many but not unlimited. The obvious ones may be mentioned: (1) a small nation can survive by depending on one Great Power, and by conscientiously surrendering maneouvrability in foreign policy; (2) it is possible to make an alliance with the smaller neighbouring countries, to thwart interference from any Great Power; (3) it is possible to conduct a more aggressive foreign policy, conquer the smaller nations and become a mini-empire of the area, and afterwards signal to one of the greater powers how advantageous it would be for them to lean on the mini-empire; if more than one Great Power is interested in the area, the mini-empire might try to play both ends against the middle; (4) it is possible to try to stay out of the wider political arena, to surrender all initiative in foreign policy, to convince the Great Powers that this kind of neutrality is not directed against any of them; it is directed towards the realization of the best interests of a small people, and as a consequence is in the best interests of all parties.

These 'models' are not figments of the imagination. One need look no further than the Balkans to find a parallel situation and to prove that such possibilities existed in fact. It was never easy for the Romanians, Bulgarians and Serbs to navigate their ship of state through the troubled waters of foreign intervention – from the perilous Ottoman encroachment into the area to the period of growing interest on the part of Tsarist Russia and later to that when the Austro-Hungarian Empire began to concern itself with what was happening to them. Were Jews after their Return from the Babylonian Exile aware of these problems? They must have been, because the history of the kingdoms of Israel and Judah provided instructive examples. Whatever Jews may have lacked, it was never a quarry of historical memories.

The last years before the destruction of the First Temple can briefly be depicted and, for reference, short passages from the Scriptures may be used. One can hardly prove that an organized pro-Babylonian or pro-Egyptian party existed; we shall also never know the content of the discussions that undoubtedly took place between the various groups. Quotations from the Bible can only prove that kings and prophets were aware of problems of orientation.

David's kingdom did not last. It emerged in a period in which Egypt was weakened by internal struggles, the Hittites were heavily engaged in turning back invaders from the sea, Babylonia was not yet a Great Power and Assyria was on the threshold of becoming an empire. David took advantage of the vacuum, but this sort of political pattern did not reappear after King Solomon's death. From the 8th to the 6th century, Assyria and Babylonia played decisive roles in the north, Egypt in the south. The kingdom of Israel was torn apart by the dilemma of whether to join the nearby king of Aram or to become a vassal of the further away, but more powerful, Assyria. During the years 735–733 BCE,

King Uzziah had ruled the kingdom of Judah from 807 to 754 BCE, and the story of his reign is told in the Second Book of Kings. During the period of the Second Temple his bones were reburied in Jerusalem and this inscription placed over them: 'Hence were brought the bones of Uzziah, King of Judah. Not to be opened.' It is our only tangible link with the pre-Exilic Judaean monarchy.

Pekah, the son of Remaliah, aligned himself with Rezin, king of Aram, rebelled against the Assyrian, Tiglath-Pileser, and tried to force the king of Judah to join the anti-Assyrian alliance. This is a classic attempt to form a small entente against the Assyrian giant, but the prophet Isaiah warned the king of Judah not to embark on that adventure:

> Take heed, and be quiet; fear not, neither be faint-hearted, for the two tails of these smoking firebrands, for the fierce anger of Rezin with Syria, Ephraim and the son of Remaliah have taken evil counsel against thee, saying: let us go up against Judah, and vex it, and let us make a breach therein for us, and set a king in the midst of it, even the son of Ta'be-al: thus saith the Lord God. It shall not stand, neither shall it come to pass. For the head of Syria is Damascus and the head of Damascus is Rezin and within three score and five years shall Ephraim be broken, that it be not a people. (Is. VII:4–7)

In this phase, Judah was saved and even in the kingdom of Israel the pro-Assyrian party won the day. Pekah, the son of Remaliah, was murdered, and in the Annals of Tiglath-Pileser we find the laconic statement, 'they killed their king Pekah and replaced him by Hoshea.' But Hoshea, the son of Elah, did not last long. In the days of Shalmaneser (726–722 BCE), he was enticed by the king of Tyre to rebel against Assyria. Punishment was not long in coming. In 724, Shalmaneser showed his claws by besieging Samaria. The capital of Israel withstood for three years, but finally fell in the days of Sargon. The kingdom of Israel was turned into an Assyrian province; the élite of the people, high functionaries, priests and

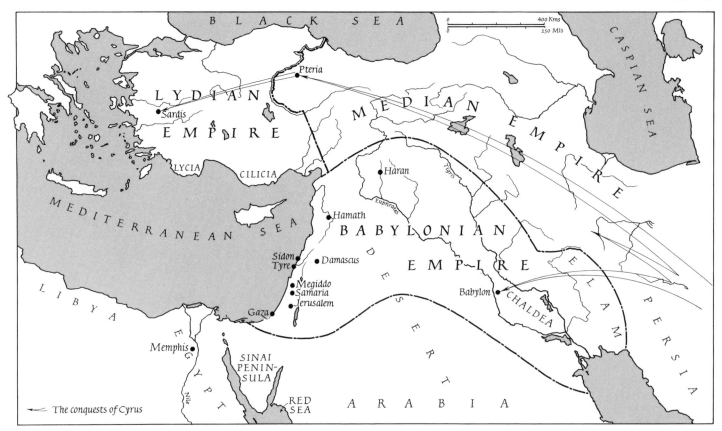

The Babylonian Empire to the beginning of the Persian conquest, c. 612–539 BCE. With the fall of Nineveh, in 611 BCE, the Chaldean, Nabopolassar, gained possession of an empire vaster than any hitherto known. Nebuchadnezzar, his son, subjugated Syria, Palestine and Phoenicia and, in 586 BCE, razed Jerusalem, sending into exile in a pagan land many thousands of Jews, so called after this date because, of all the Tribes, only part of Judah remained. But the glory of the Babylonians was brief, for Cyrus moved swiftly to conquer first the empire of the Medes in the north, then Lydia and, finally, the Babylonian Empire in 538.

iron-smiths were banished to Mesopotamia and were replaced by other tribes. A military colony was established in Samaria. The events have been almost identically depicted in II Kings and in the Annals of Sargon – the latter adding only that the number of exiles was 27,960, for what the exactitude is worth. The kingdom of Israel was never resurrected and the fate of the ten Tribes became a central theme in myth and romance.

Nor did the Assyrian Empire survive. In 611 BCE, Nineveh, 'the dwelling of the lions', fell (Nah. II:11). Babylonia took its place. In Judah, the young and energetic Josiah reigned, and he was faced by a dilemma similar to that of Pekah, the son of Remaliah, one hundred years earlier; instead of wavering between the nearby Syria and the far-off Assyria, however, he had to choose between the nearby Egypt and the far-off Babylonia. He must have remembered not to trust Egypt, 'the bruised reed on which if a man leans, it will go into his hand and pierce it' (II Kings XVIII:21). It is plausible to ascribe to him the logical assumption that, by leaning on a remote Babylonian king, he might gain more freedom of action than under the vigilant eye of the nearby Egyptian. These intentions can be conjectured fairly. Some biblical quotations, however, speak for themselves and the problem does not seem to be overwhelmingly complicated. As long as Assyria was the only strong northern power, Egypt supported any potential opponent to Nineveh; therefore, the relations between Judah and Egypt were not hostile. After the downfall of Assyria, the situation changed. Josiah did not want to allow Pharaoh Necho to use Palestine as if it were a thoroughfare that belonged to him. He tried to stop him at Megiddo, was wounded accidentally at the outset of the battle and succumbed to his wounds in 609 BCE. Not many years later, the Egyptian king was crushed by the Babylonians (604 BCE) but it is very doubtful whether history would have taken a different course had Josiah not fallen in battle. The closer the Babylonians came to the borders of Judah, and the heavier their oppressive arm, the more likely was a rebel to arise. Indeed, from the battle of Megiddo to the destruction of the First Temple (586 BCE), and perhaps to the murder of Gedaliah, the problem of orientation towards a Great Power did not cease to haunt the kings of Judah.

Political scientists may say that more than one 'model' has been exemplified. Details are lacking but the basic facts are well known. A fairly powerful pro-Egyptian faction came into being, and the warnings of the prophets were not heeded; in vain did Isaiah cry out, 'for the Egyptians shall help in vain and to no purpose, therefore have I cried concerning this, their strength is to sit still' (Is. XXX:7). None heeded Jeremiah: 'Pharaoh King of Egypt is but a noise; he hath passed the time appointed ... Egypt is like a fair heifer, but the destruction cometh, it cometh out of the north' (Jer. XLVI:17–20); and his resolute exhortation, 'serve the King of Babylon, and live, wherefore should this city be laid waste?' (Jer. XXVII:17), turned him into a traitor in the eyes of the ruling establishment.

However, there is no doubt that a pro-Babylonian faction existed alongside the pro-Egyptian faction. It must have been decidedly weaker, but in the short periods of catastrophe it held the upper hand. Such was the case after the first Exile, in 597 BCE, when the inhabitants of Judah learned that Jeremiah's dire prophecy came true: 'the King of Babylon shall certainly come and destroy this land' (Jer. XXXVI:29). The new king enthroned by the Babylonians, Zedekiah, one of Josiah's sons, scarcely showed enduring loyalty to his patrons. This time, Zedekiah did not turn to the Egyptians. He possibly had not forgotten what the Egyptians had done to his father in Megiddo. He tried to establish a little entente, to free itself from the fetters of the Great Powers. In 593 BCE, representatives of Ammon, Moab, Tyre and Sidon met in Judah. Details of the discussions are unknown, but what is clear is that the endeavour fell through. In 588, Zedekiah lifted the banner of revolt alone against Babylonia, and the outcome is only too well known and does not need further elaboration. In 586, Jerusalem was conquered, the Temple burned, the city walls destroyed and the leading personalities of the country exiled to Babylon. Zedekiah's attempt to escape failed. He was caught, his sons tortured in front of his eyes, and he went into exile in chains. A governor, Gedaliah, the son of Ahikam, was appointed over Judah, who tried with what remained of his strength to rehabilitate Judah, while remaining loyal to Babylonia. Most of those who remained in the country were the poor, as testified by Jeremiah: 'Nebuzaradan, the captain of the guard left of the poor of the people which had nothing, in the land of Judah, and gave them vineyards and fields at the same time' (Jer. XXXIX:10).

Not everything seemed to be lost, but Gedaliah was murdered by a group of people that would not reconcile itself to the surrender to the Babylonians. There is no proof that the murderers of Gedaliah acted in the service of Egypt, nor is there evidence that the Ammonites had a hand in the plot. The truth is that we know nothing of their motives, but it is impossible to leave the affair without conjecturing. The murderers of Gedaliah were certainly fanatical about Judaean independence. They refused to accept the transfer of the central administration from Jerusalem to Mizpah, a symbol of treason; they also refused to recognize Gedaliah as the legitimate ruler of Judah, opposed fiercely the confiscation of lands that belonged to the exiles and were against the handing over of those lands to the paupers of Jerusalem and Judah. It is possible that they hoped to achieve a political goal by that assassination, but their hopes were in vain. The Babylonians tightened the yoke over rebellious Judah. Jeremiah made unavailing efforts to calm the population. Many were in a state of panic, fearful of retaliatory acts by the Babylonians, and fled to Egypt, dragging the old prophet Jeremiah along with them. He was never heard again. Thus ended the history of the First Commonwealth.

Was it all inevitable? And do we have to agree that all that happened, had to happen? Certainly not, but two thousand years of hindsight hardly gives us licence to advise.

It is possible that in 586 BCE nobody envisaged the approaching collapse of Babylonia. The fact is that it happened, but when it happened, there was no longer a

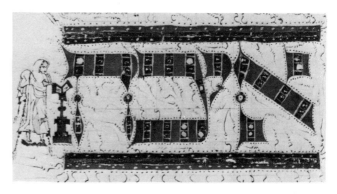

The Book of Lamentations was written in response to the destruction of the First Temple, but in Jewish ritual is normally read as applying to the Second as well. This detail from a German manuscript of 1344 is its opening, and includes a Jew wearing the tallith *to recite it.*

Judah to reap any benefits from it. Under the Persian hegemony, everything had to begin anew. Nobody knows what would have been the course of Jewish history without the destruction of the First Temple, but one is haunted by one question – did the prophets anticipate the entire process? It seems that the attempts to depict Jeremiah and Ezekiel as practising 'Realpolitik' failed. To reduce their prophecies into the narrow framework of political expediency is a gross over-simplification. Socrates brought upon himself the wrath of the Athenian authorities in 399, not only because he was a friend of Critias and Alcibiades, nor only because his public image was that of an enemy of the 'new democracy'. Neither did the prophets of Israel pour out their wrath for political motives only. From their point of view, the king of Judah had abrogated Jewish moral principles to the highest degree, principles that were sacred in the religious sense. The king of Judah had obligated himself to the king of Babylonia to remain faithful to him. He did not fulfil this obligation and thus breached his covenant. Ezekiel explicitly warned against this:

> [The king] despised the oath by breaking the covenant . . . he had given his hand, and hath done all these things, he shall not escape. Therefore thus saith the Lord God: As I live, surely mine oath that he hath despised and my covenant that he hath broken, even it will recompense upon his own hand. And I will spread my net upon him, and he shall be taken in my snare, and I will bring him to Babylon, and will plead with him there for his trespass that he hath trespassed against me. (Ez. XVII:18–20)

It is possible that these words of rebuke did not fall on deaf ears. After having learned their lesson the hard way, a tradition entrenched itself not to breach covenants for reasons of opportunism. From then on, Jews made an effort to appear in the eyes of the Gentiles as a people who remains loyal to its benefactors and does not breach its solemn covenants. This tendency clearly survives in the legendary tradition of Alexander's conquest of Palestine in the 4th century BCE. Josephus tells us that, after the conquest of Damascus, Sidon and Tyre, Alexander dispatched a letter to the High Priest of the Jews, requesting him to supply his army with provisions and give him the gifts which were formerly sent to Darius as tribute. 'The High Priest refused, because he had given an oath to Darius not to take up arms against him.' From the aspect of 'Realpolitik', it was doubtless expedient to ignore the commitment to Persia, then in its decline, and no doubt at that time the political dependence of Judah on Persia was no less than Gedaliah's need to depend on Babylonia. Moreover, a cuneiform tablet informs us that, in the day of Artaxerxes III (during his campaign against Egypt in 345 BCE), many Jews had been deported to the Caspian Sea, and thus a grudge against Persian rule may have been justifiable. Nevertheless, the leaders of Judah were in no hurry to break the covenant with Persia in order to win Alexander's favours, and it is possible that this dignified behaviour impressed Alexander more than the opportunistic stratagems of the Samaritans. But this is anticipating. We should return to the story of Judah (henceforth more commonly known as Judaea) from the days of Cyrus to the Hellenistic period. A new type of relationship towards a Great Power emerged.

Persia, Alexander and the Hellenistic monarchies

It is possible that the decline and fall of Babylonia implanted into the hearts of the Jews a sense of confidence that whosoever will insult and persecute them will not escape retribution.

In the first place, Jews suffer because they are punished for their own sins, but in good time the Almighty will pour out his wrath on those who have tortured his people. The Ten Plagues and the Exodus were not the last examples. Assyria savagely destroyed the kingdom of Israel, but she in turn was crushed by Babylonia within a short time. Babylonia destroyed Judaea only to be crushed by Persia, etc.

One could go on with a catalogue of oppression and retribution from the Roman Empire to our own day. Indeed, on Passover night, Jews chant a song of 'the cat that came and ate the kid that father bought for two zuzim . . . then came a dog and bit the cat . . .', and in the opinion of many, this is an allegory of the rise and decline of empires that had wronged Israel.

Jews did not suffer physically in Exile in Babylonia. According to Berosus, King Nebuchadnezzar assigned to the captives dwelling places in the most convenient locations. Jews built houses, planted vineyards and prayed for the peace of the country in which they lived. Spiritually, however, they cried by the waters of Babylon and swore never to forget Jerusalem, and in the deepest national sense had no reason to bewail the collapse of Babylonia. The Persians were received with open arms by the Jewish exiles.

King Cyrus epitomized pagan liberalism and polytheistic tolerance. In 538 BCE, he issued the famous declaration permitting Jews to return to their land. This declaration is immortalized in Jewish history, and, in passing, it is worth mentioning that it is less ambiguous than many modern ones.

Cyrus permitted Jews to rebuild the Temple. He permitted them to perform sacrifices and to bring back the holy vessels which were pillaged by Nebuchadnezzar. He ordered the expenses to be paid from the king's treasury, but explicitly forbade the rebuilding of the city walls. Nowhere in the declaration is there even a hint of renewal of political freedom and autonomy. To quote a few extracts from the text:

The Lord of heaven hath given me all the Kingdoms of the earth and he hath charged me to build him a house in Jerusalem, which is Judah. Who is there among you of all his people, his God be with him and let him go up to Jerusalem . . . and build the house of the Lord. . . .

It is not necessary to assume with some modern theologians that, during the Persian rule, the Jews ceased to be a nation and became a religious community. Nor was Judaea an ecclesiastical state. The Temple did not possess any real estate, and the priests lived on the voluntary offerings of the believers. Priests and Levites were influential and the Persian government preferred them to a military aristocracy. What happened is that, henceforth, only the spiritual authority remained in the hands of the High Priest. The political supremacy remained in the hands of the satrap, appointed by the Persian king. It should never be forgotten that even Ezra was a royal commissioner, appointed to investigate conditions in Judaea, and also endowed with the authority to promulgate the Law of Moses among the Jews (Ez. VII:14, 25). The Temple was restored not only according to the commandment of the God of Israel but also according to the decree of the Persian kings: Cyrus, Darius and Artaxerxes (Ez. VI:14).

Nehemiah, of course, acted as an appointee of the king and not as a representative of the Jewish population. When his term was over, he was replaced by a non-Jewish satrap by the name of Bagoas. It would be difficult to claim that the rule of the satraps was ideal and that the Jews of Israel were happy under their rule. First of all, their country was very small. The district of Judaea (and it was no more than a district) comprised about one thousand square miles, extending from Bethel to Beth-zur and from the Dead Sea (Salt Sea) to the lowlands in the area of Lydda. In the sources, there are many hints that at least the first satraps ruled with an iron hand and extorted heavy taxes. But they had released the Jewish leadership from the dilemma of finding an orientation towards another empire, a dilemma which had haunted them in the final century of the existence of the First Temple. In 525 BCE, Cambyses conquered Egypt. The Middle East entered a period of a Persian peace from India to Ethiopia (Est.1) – a peace which rendered futile any hope of liberation from the Persian yoke, or of regaining freedom and autonomy with the aid of another Great Power. There was no other Great Power. This fits our first 'model', with the reservation that the Jews did not choose this position of their own volition, but had it imposed on them.

Priority was given to spiritual and religious crystallization and social and economic consolidation. The activities of Ezra and Nehemiah confirm this. Even the squabbles with the Samaritans had a strong religious nuance, despite the fact that, in the background, economic and political overtones were not lacking. The competition with the Samaritans expressed itself especially in the attempt to win the favour of the great king, but no one had entertained the thought of a rebellious step towards independence.

This situation did not change after the conquest of Judaea by Alexander the Great. This time, the competition between the Jews and the Samaritans expressed

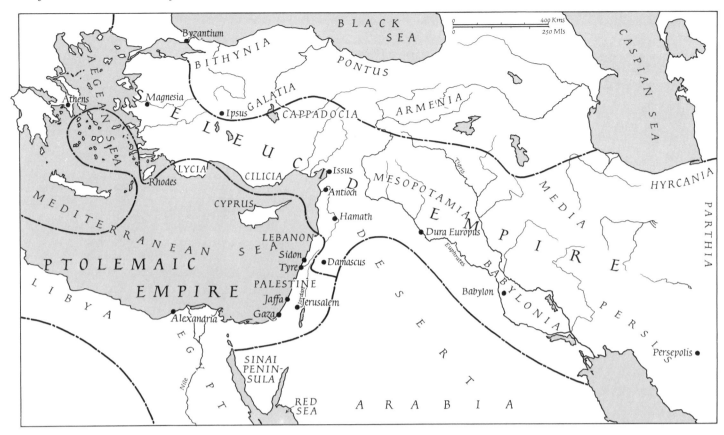

Rivalry between the kingdoms of the Ptolemies and the Seleucids c. 187 BCE. During the time of Alexander 'the earth was quiet before him', but chaos followed his death, and the Jews were at the centre. Coele-Syria became the first line of defence for the Ptolemies, but they were defeated by the Seleucids, led by Antiochus III. The Jews helped him to drive the Egyptians from the citadel of Jerusalem.

itself in the legendary meeting between Alexander the Great and the High Priest of Jerusalem. The story is full of anachronisms and fantasies, and this is not the place to analyze them. It is not difficult to prove that Alexander never visited Jerusalem and thus never bowed before the High Priest, but the implications are important. For one thing, the story was intended to spread the news that Alexander the Great allowed Jews to live according to the customs of their forefathers. He exempted them in the fallow years from taxes. He also acceded to their requests to grant permission to the Jews of Babylonia and Persia to live according to their own traditions. In due course, he refused to recognize the Samaritans as Jews, although told by the former that they were the sons of Manasseh and Ephraim. And Josephus adds with contempt, 'such was the habit of the Samaritans. When the Jews were in distress, they held aloof from them, but when their lot was good, they remembered their descent from Joseph, Manasseh and Ephraim.'

Jews received Alexander cordially, as befitted a distinguished guest, but let it be known that this reception was not a breach of their covenant with the Persians. As already mentioned, this dignified approach impressed Alexander considerably. No reliable sources from this period have survived, but from everything we know, we can surmise that Jews were not yearning for the days in which the area was torn between two antagonistic powers tyrannizing the smaller nations. If the Persian rule had to give way to Macedonian rule, it did so without causing any unnecessary crisis.

The 'happy days' of life under one Great Power were short-lived. The kingdom of Alexander disintegrated immediately after his death, and Palestine became a disputed territory between the Ptolemies in Egypt and the Seleucids in Syria. In 320 BCE, Ptolemy invaded Palestine, consciously or intuitively pursuing the policy of the pharaohs, who frequently aspired to bring Syria under their control. One would like to know more about the intentions of Ptolemy, who might have anticipated Napoleon's dictum that domination over Palestine was indispensable if one wished to protect the Valley of the Nile. Diodorus (in keeping with our introductory comments) is very laconic: 'Ptolemy perceived that the geographical situation of the countries Phoenicia and Coele-Syria (it included the whole of Palestine from the mountains of Lebanon to the Egyptian border) was excellent in relation to Egypt and therefore threw all his energies into an endeavour to gain control of those places.'

Details cannot be given here, but it is worth noting that during the wars of the Diadochs Palestine changed hands several times, that the local population suffered a great deal and that stabilization came only after the battle of Ipsus (301 BCE).

After many years of senseless bloodshed, it was evident that no one could rule a united Alexandrian Empire and that peace could be established only on the basis of partition and compromise. Cautious Ptolemy did not participate in the last battle and was not entitled to claim from the spoils which fell into the hands of the victors. However, he did not sit idle. Before Seleucus had time to lick his wounds, Ptolemy had conquered Coele-Syria. This is not the place to adjudge who was right or wrong in this quarrel nor whether it is true that the formal right of authority over Palestine remained in the hands of Seleucus and that only de facto was she in the hands of Ptolemy.

A crucial passage in Diodorus is significant for an understanding of what was to happen: 'Seleucus did not intend to raise the matter for the moment, because of his friendship for Ptolemy, but in time he would return and attend to it and would then decide what course he should adopt towards friends who came with exasperated demands.' It seems that Seleucus gave up Palestine reluctantly and never forgave Ptolemy his avarice.

Indeed, the 3rd century represents a period of continuous tension between Syria and Egypt. Five wars are testimony to this tension, and Palestine was not a minor issue in the conflict. It came up especially during the diplomatic negotiations in 218 BCE, between Antiochus III of Syria and Ptolemy IV Philopator of Egypt. Between 221 and 219 BCE, Antiochus III pushed southward, conquered Tyre and Acre and besieged Dor. The Ptolemies tried to resolve the conflict through negotiations but diplomatic efforts bore no fruit. After a lull, Antiochus resumed his offensive, conquered upper Galilee without difficulty, crossed the Jordan, eventually taking Beth-shaan and Mount Tabor, then reached Samaria. The Ptolemies reorganized their forces, counter-attacked and smashed Antiochus at Rafiah in 217 BCE.

Once again, Palestine returned to Egyptian rule, but this time for a short period only. After the death of Ptolemy IV, Ptolemy V Epiphanes, a five-year-old child, ascended the throne (204 BCE). Antiochus III immediately exploited Egypt's weakness at a time when the regents could not restore law and order. He invaded Coele-Syria in 201, and avenged the humiliation of Rafiah by defeating the Egyptian general, Scopas, near Panion and by causing the final expulsion of the Ptolemies from Palestine. In 199, Seleucid hegemony began.

Jerusalem fell into Antiochus's hands without resistance. Moreover, the Council of Elders received him with acclamation. This turn-about calls for an explanation. Firstly, it was not sudden. Secondly, it should not be assumed that the acclamation was exactly unanimous, and that, after a hundred years of Egyptian rule, there was not a residual pro-Egyptian element. And thirdly, it is worthwhile to investigate the pro-Seleucid faction and find out what motivated them to turn their backs on the Ptolemies.

We have shown that in the period of the First Temple a pro-Egyptian faction struggled against a pro-Babylonian one, but paucity of sources precluded an analysis, supported by first-hand citations, of the social composition of each faction. The inability to associate social and economic developments with reversals in foreign policy inevitably led to a narrative more informative than illuminating.

In this chapter, we are on more solid ground but even here there are pitfalls of conjecture. A passage in the Book of Daniel (XI:14) obscures more than it clarifies but leaves little doubt that the struggle to find an orientation towards a Great Power – a struggle which disappeared under the Persian rule – re-emerged in a sharp form: 'And in those times many shall stand up against the King of the South, also the CHILDREN OF THE VIOLENT among

thy people shall exalt themselves to establish the vision; but they shall stumble!' Whether 'BNEI PARITZEI' should be translated as 'children of the violent' or merely 'robbers' is still disputed in modern scholarship. St Jerome, however, in his commentary on the Book of Daniel, was less troubled by uncertainties and stated: 'When Antiochus the Great and Ptolemy's generals were at grips, the land of Judah was drawn in two opposite directions: some supporting Antiochus and some the Ptolemies.' At the head of the pro-Antiochus faction was the High Priest, Simon the Just, and his loyalty was well rewarded. The king was impressed by the eagerness of Jews to serve him, by the splendid reception they gave him when he entered Jerusalem and by the favourable attitude of the Council of Elders – which helped him to expel the Egyptian garrison in the Citadel and furnished an abundance of provisions for his soldiers and elephants. And the Jews were promptly compensated: on account of their piety they were granted an allowance of sacrificial animals, wine, oil, fine flour, wheat and salt. The king ordered work on the Temple to be completed (including the porticos and any other part that was found necessary to build). Imported timber was to be exempt from toll charges. The members of the Council of Elders, the priests, the scribes and the temple singers were to be relieved from poll-tax, crown-tax and salt-tax. A decree aimed at repopulating Jerusalem promptly exempted those living there, and those committed to return within a certain period of time, from taxes for three years. These and many other privileges were granted en bloc in a series of decrees – and they can all be summed up in one sentence: Jews were allowed to live according to their ancestral laws.

Was this indeed so very different from the conditions that prevailed under the Egyptian regime; had the Ptolemies forced the Jews to disavow their ancestral tradition? The answer is emphatically negative. The period of the Ptolemies was generally a period of tranquillity and there were no rebellions. Under Persian rule, there was no chance for Jewish political leadership to develop and thus the mediator between Judaea and the Hellenistic monarchy was inevitably to be the High Priest. Granted that the High Priest was deeply respected, the Ptolemies nevertheless did not think that he alone should be the sole liason between the Egyptian authorities and the population of Judaea. Other centres of power emerged, and this will be discussed below. Suffice it to say at this point that Antiochus introduced one essential change. He recognized the Jewish High Priest and his Council of Elders as the supreme representatives of Judaea and Jerusalem. Not only was the personal position of the High Priest strengthened by the king's orders, but the other priests also enjoyed more privileges than previously: they were exempted from taxes, for example. What is of even greater importance is that the Commandments of the Torah were given the validity of official law:

> It is unlawful for any foreigner to enter the enclosure of the Temple which is forbidden to the Jews, except to those of them who are accustomed to enter after purifying themselves in accordance with the law of the country. Nor shall anyone bring into the city the flesh of horses or of mules or of wild or tame asses, or of

leopards, foxes or hares, or in general of any animal forbidden to the Jews. Nor is it lawful to bring in their skins or even to breed any of these animals in the city. But only the sacrificial animals known to their ancestors and necessary for the propitiation of God shall they be permitted to use. And the person who violates any of these statutes shall pay to the priests a fine of three thousand drachmas of silver.

This may well explain the tendency among priests, scribes and interpreters of the Law to prefer Antiochus to Ptolemy, but this is not enough to explain the influence of a pro-Seleucid faction, whose existence can hardly be doubted.

We have to seek our answer in other directions and not in the religious sector. One of the most significant processes, without which we cannot understand the period at all, is the process of Hellenization of a certain social class in Judaea. This process did not start with the fall of Jerusalem into the hands of Antiochus, but many years earlier.

It was accepted years ago that the agents of the spread of Hellenic culture in the East were the Greek and Macedonian settlers, who emigrated to the Orient after the death of Alexander the Great and concentrated mainly in cities. It was assumed that this development did not bypass Palestine. Indeed, at least thirty Greek cities were founded during the Hellenistic period and it is worth mentioning some of them: Acco, Straton's Tower (later Caesarea), Apollonia (near Herzliah), Jaffa, Ashdod, Ashkalon, Gaza and Rafiah along the Mediterranean coast; the Decapolis in the north and east of the country (Transjordan), e.g. Scythopolis (Beth-shaan), Hippos (Sussita), Pella (Fahil), Philadelphia (the ancient Rabbat Amman).

Many a myth has been shattered in the careful scrutiny of Hellenic culture in the East in the last fifty years, and it has been found that Greek culture did not seep through to the lower classes of Asia and Africa, who remained loyal to their religion, their language and the customs of their forefathers. The rural population everywhere is usually more conservative, and is loth to detach itself from ancestral tradition. The Orient was no exception. This is perhaps one of the reasons why a hundred years of existence of Greek cities in Palestine left no imprint on Judaea, but other factors, too, have to be taken into account.

The number of native Greeks and Macedonians who actually settled in Palestine was small. Some of them were discharged soldiers, who chose to remain in the East after many years of campaigning. Others were impoverished farmers from the Greek mainland, or merchants whose luck had failed them, and who aspired to improve their standard of living by immigration. They were not missionaries of Greek culture and civilization and did not go East in order to propagate Homer's poetry and Plato's philosophy among the barbarians. It is unlikely that they were themselves versed in it. Their principal legacy to the Greek cities founded after the death of Alexander was the language itself – Greek became the official language – and such institutions as the boule (city council), gymnasium, ephebeion, etc. were founded. The majority of the urban population was primarily of Oriental extraction and

A tombstone from the Jewish cemetery at Rome. The representation of the menorah was common, that of the Ark with the scrolls of the Law less so. The inscription is in Greek, the lingua franca *of the Roman world.*

accepted these external features of Hellenistic civilization, but nothing more. This holds true for the area as a whole. As a matter of fact, the majority of the inhabitants of the Greek cities in Palestine were Syrians, former Phoenicians, who were descended from the Samaritans, Edomites and Philistines. One should not be unduly impressed that the name of a city was Apollonia. Her chief deity was neither Apollo of Delphi, nor the Delian Apollo, but the ancient Phoenician Reshef. Only the outside shell was Greek, the kernel remained Oriental, and a religious syncretism developed, to fascinate scholars to our own day. Apollonia is just one example. The chief deity of Ashdod remained Dagon; of Ashkalon, Ashtoret; and since these deities were not exactly novelties for the population of Judaea, very few Jews were seduced to abandon the God of Israel for a Dagon or a Reshef. Hellenism penetrated Judaea, but in a different way: not as a result of a decisive influence of the Greek cities, but as a result of personal relations which developed between some Jews and the Ptolemaic authorities. As in all Oriental countries, the first to be influenced were the rich and the powerful.

These were the rich and powerful people mentioned in the writings of Ben Sira, who exposed the tension that existed between them and the lower strata of the population, a tension that was not a phenomenon originating in the Hellenistic period. It appears in the writings of Nehemiah, and it was against these rich and powerful Jews that his social reforming was directed: 'Then I consulted with myself, and I rebuked the nobles and the rulers [*horim* and *sganim*] and said unto them: Ye exact usury, everyone of his brother. And I set a great assembly against them' (Neh. v:7). Abolition of debts always hurt the wealthy money-lenders but only for a short period of time, since a reform of this kind was never intended to change the basic structure of society and its property laws. After a temporary alleviation, everything remained the same – the rich remained rich, and the poor remained poor. This is how wealthy 'sheikhs' emerged in Palestine and Jordan to exert their unquestionable influence on the rural population.

The Ptolemies could not afford to govern Palestine through the High Priest only. They went to great lengths to seek additional allies and found them among those wealthy landowners. Some of them are known to us by name from various papyri – Jeddous was a very powerful man and Tobiah, the father of Joseph son of Tobiah, was to play a central role in the dissemination of Hellenism in Judaea. The process can easily be explained. The Tobiads were Jews who lived in Transjordan, and their estates were in the area of Rabbat Amman, but they never severed their relations with Jerusalem. When one of the Tobiads married a daughter of the Oniads, the family of the High Priests of Jerusalem, these relations became even closer. In contrast with the Jerusalemite aristocracy, the Tobiads were more cosmopolitan, with closer relationships with the Gentiles who lived in their vicinity. In the middle of the 3rd century BCE, when a sharp dispute broke out between the High Priest and the Egyptian king over taxes, Joseph the son of Tobias promptly offered his services, went down to Egypt and arrived at a compromise acceptable to both parties. He himself did not lose out in the affair – he was appointed tax-gatherer by the king, who chose that way to show his esteem. The system of appointing a local dynast as a tax-gatherer was certainly expedient for the Egyptian government. From now on they had a competent agent for tax-collecting and were absolved from the need to set up a bureaucratic apparatus, even if they were obliged to put at the disposal of the local tax-gatherer a small armed force to serve as a whip over the recalcitrant population.

People such as the Tobiads had to go down to Egypt frequently, and thus it is to be assumed that they learned the local Greek dialect, and, when invited to dine at the tables of their Alexandrian hosts, it is hardly likely that they insisted on strict adherence to the Mosaic dietary laws. They remained Jews, but very different Jews from those in Jerusalem who insisted on the most rigorous adherence to every Mosaic precept. So the situation continued for some fifty years without any serious upsets between Judaea and Egypt.

Ptolemaic Egypt, however, was a centralistic and bureaucratic kingdom. Most lands in Egypt were royal lands, the king was himself the chief banker, leaving little room for private initiative, freedom or autonomy. The Greek city was far from uppermost in Egyptians' minds, for, with very few cities in Egypt, its concept had made little impact on their politics.

The Seleucid monarchy, on the other hand, was not as homogeneous and therefore not as centralistic. Government was based on three different instruments of power: cities, peoples and princes. The central government was much more fragile, and it seems that this pluralistic system appealed to the population of Judaea more than the monolithic centralism of Egypt. They awaited the opportune moment when the weakening Egypt would coincide with a simultaneous Seleucid option. Moreover, restive under the increasingly heavy hand of Alexandria, even the pro-Egyptian element of the aristocracy felt that they might have more freedom of action under the Seleucids.

Of course, not all the Tobiads were disappointed with the Ptolemies. One of the brothers, Hyrcanus, remained loyal to them to his last day; however, once his older brothers and the Oniad family of the High Priest had switched their loyalties, Judaea was virtually ripe for the taking by Antiochus III, the Seleucid. He was well received in Jerusalem and hence his generous decrees. However, the ideal relationship between Jerusalem and Antiochia did not last. Antiochus IV (Epiphanes) was not like his predecessors; nor was the role of the High Priest cast in the same mould. Judaea entered into one of the stormiest periods in its history. The road led to independence, and the problem of relationships with the Great Powers took a different shape. In 190 BCE, Antiochus III was defeated at Magnesia. Rome appeared on the horizon, having conquered the western basin of the Mediterranean. With the justification of defending the freedom and autonomy of the Greek cities against Hellenistic monarchs, she conquered Greece and then challenged Antiochus.

Alexander of Macedon came upon the Middle East with a great noise, but Rome entered the area with a cat-like tread, to the extent that her entry went unnoticed. It is against this background, and the growing influence of the Hellenizers in Jerusalem, that the Hasmonean Revolt should be studied.

Independence

External and internal factors alike were at work in the exchange of Ptolemaic hegemony for Syrian hegemony in Judaea. On the one hand, Egypt was so weakened that she turned again into 'the bruised reed'. New hope was arising in the north, not evil, as once prophesied by Jeremiah (Jer. VI:1). A faction favouring the Seleucids rather than the Ptolemies emerged in the rifts between the members of the upper classes. Some Oniads and some Tobiads helped Antiochus to conquer Jerusalem. The High Priest, Simon the Just, played the principal role in this turning point, with consequences that were swift in coming. The High Priest was from now to be not only the highest religious official, but also the central political figure of Judaea. It is doubtful whether this had been his preconceived intention; having been set in motion, however, this trend moved on its own dynamic. Once the Priesthood became a magistracy of political importance, it became the target of political intrigue. The Tobiads did not share the religious ideals of the Judaean priestly clan, of the Levites and the scribes, their aims being decidedly more material and political. They intended to influence the choice of the High Priest, and left no stone unturned to get their way.

This is the place to insert a methodological remark: important scholars were most impressed by the cosmopolitanism of the Tobiads, their openness and their tolerance, in contrast with the bigotry, narrow-mindedness and xenophobia of the Hasidim. One phrase from the Book of Maccabees (I, 1:11) led them to think this way: 'Let us make a covenant with the Gentiles about us, for since we have been different from them, we have found many evils.' These scholars assumed that the Hellenizers resembled the *aufgeklärtes Reformjudentum* of Germany in the 19th century, as opposed to Orthodox Jews, who do not deviate from the Halacha. Their mistake is compounded. The Hellenism of the Tobiads was not of a higher standard than the Hellenism of other countries. There, as in Palestine, only the external features of Western civilization were adopted. Euripides and Aristotle were never the concern of the Jewish Hellenizers, who preferred a gymnasium to an academy and a hippodrome to a theatre. The truth is, firstly, that Jewish Hellenism was one of the first manifestations of Levantinism. And, secondly, that the Jewish Hellenizers did not consider themselves to be any more the carriers of Greek culture and civilization than the Greek immigrants to the East. The Tobiads who had turned to the Seleucid monarchy did not betray the Ptolemies because they hoped to spread Greek culture in Judaea with the help of the Seleucids. All that they wanted was to manipulate with greater ease the High Priesthood, with the help of the Seleucid king. They regarded the High Priesthood as a political rather than a religious function, as the fulcrum of political rather than spiritual power.

This is hardly surprising. Great wealth was concentrated in those days in the Temple, and Jews from Asia and Europe had been sending their contributions to the Temple from time immemorial. There were no other public resources, apart from the sacred funds, and the attempts (in scholarship) to distinguish between political and religious affairs in the days of the Second Commonwealth are not very convincing. Politics and religion were closely interwoven, and, at the moment when the High Priesthood became also a political function, corruption was not far off. There always had been a time of confusion between private deposits and public contributions, because both had been transferred to the central treasury in the Temple. There was no other treasury.

As long as there was harmonious co-operation between Oniads and Tobiads, the economic and political importance of the High Priesthood went unnoticed. But from the moment that Onias III, the son and successor of Simon the Just, sided with Hyrcanus, the renegade of the Tobiads who had remained faithful to the Ptolemies, the pro-Seleucid Tobiads schemed against him. They added to their following by attracting an influential family headed by three outstanding brothers – Menelaus, Simon and Lysimachos. First and foremost they had to topple Onias III. They succeeded in persuading Jason, the brother of Onias III (whose Hebrew name was formerly Josua), to go to Antiochus Epiphanes and to buy from him the High Priesthood. Loyalty to Syria was obviously *conditio sine qua non* of the whole operation, but there was a no less significant corollary. For the first time, a foreign interloper was to be a factor in the appointment of the High Priest in Jerusalem. The source for this is an obscure, and for many years a controversial, passage:

> When Seleucus died, and Antiochus called Epiphanes succeeded to the Kingdom, Jason, brother of Onias, supplanted his brother in the High Priesthood. He promised the king in his petition 360 talents of silver and 80 talents from other sources of revenue. In addition to this he promised to pay another 150 if he might be given to set up a gymnasium and ephebium and to register the Antiocheans in Jerusalem [alternative interpretation: to register the Jerusalemites as Antiocheans]. The king assented to this and he took

office. Immediately he started out to convert his countrymen to the Greek way of life.

It seems plausible that Jason got the Priesthood by bribing the king, and at the same time received permission to convert Jerusalem into a Greek 'polis' called Antiochia.

All this happened in 175 BCE, the year that is usually identified with the Hellenistic reform in Jerusalem. What was the real meaning of this reform? It was not meant to abolish the so-called 'Orthodox Judaism' and to replace it by a more progressive one. The reform that was connected with transforming Jerusalem into a Greek city was not cultural in its essence. It implied the closer integration of Judaea into the Seleucid Empire and it led to political and economic oligarchies headed by Jason and Menelaus. Till 175 BCE, the status of Jews in the Seleucid Empire was a status of an 'ethnos' (people); however, in the Seleucid pluralism, 'ethnos' was a marginal type of institution. An 'ethnos' could enjoy the right to live according to an ancient tradition, but that was all. Cities were the base of the Seleucid Empire and they were the pillars of the political structure. Cities had more autonomy, had their own city council and had the right to strike their own coins. The upper classes stood to benefit most from the elevation of Jerusalem to a 'polis', since not all inhabitants of Jerusalem would have automatically become citizens. The lower classes would have become 'metics' or 'katoikoi', second class citizens. The lower classes cleaved to the ancestral tradition, were less assimilated and had no interest whatsoever in Hellenistic reform. This led to new tension between the more traditional urban and rustic plebs of Judaea and the aristocratic Hellenizers in Jerusalem. The common people clearly opposed reform.

Jason objected to being merely a tool in the hands of Antiochus, and, at a certain moment, refused to place the Temple treasury at the king's disposal. His attempt to show some independence was discovered and he had no way out of the trap set for him. Menelaus instituted a series of intrigues and succeeded in casting Jason aside just as Jason had cast Onias III aside. Jason fled to Jordan and Menelaus became High Priest, a submissive servant of the king. This situation alone could explain the revolt of the lower classes against the Hellenizing oligarchy. The Hasmonean Revolt will be understood even more easily in the light of two additional factors: the weakening of Antiochus's international prestige and the evil decrees against the Jewish religion. This is the moment to focus on Antiochus's campaign against Egypt and Rome's appearance on the scene.

After the battle of Zama, in 202 BCE, Rome's supremacy in the western basin of the Mediterranean was absolute. Carthage was not allowed to expand beyond her borders in Africa. The Numidian Massinissa became a client king of Rome; Sicily, Corsica, Sardinia and Spain were transformed into Roman provinces. Rome could confidently turn eastward.

The phrases 'divide et impera' and 'balance of power' do not appear in ancient texts. Considering the international relations of those days, however, it is not surprising that these expressions were (erroneously) attributed to Rome. The simple truth is, that from the 3rd century BCE Rome did not allow any of her neighbours to become a Great Power. She would go to war against a neighbour who merely gave the smallest semblance of imperial aspirations. At the beginning of the 2nd century, Rome silenced the king of Macedonia; and her victory over Antiochus III in Magnesia (190 BCE) put an end to the Seleucids' dream of becoming a world power.

The Peace of Apameia (188 BCE) exacted from Antiochus III a tribute of 10,000 talents of gold and 90,000 bushels of grain, forced him to evacuate Asia Minor as far as the Tauros mountain range, to give up his navy and his elephants and, most important of all, to undertake never to attack an ally of Rome. From Magnesia to the days of Antiochus IV, the Seleucids tried to reconcile themselves to Roman supremacy and to take precautions not to provoke Rome or to disturb the sleeping lion. The great change came in 169, when Antiochus IV Epiphanes invaded Egypt after Ptolemy IV had made an attempt to recover Palestine. In 169, Rome did not intervene; she was preoccupied with Perseus of Macedonia. After the victory of Pydna (168 BCE), however, she decided to put an end to Antiochus's ambitions. A Roman envoy, C. Popillius Laenas, presented a point-blank command to Antiochus to call off his attack and, when Antiochus proceeded to argue the matter, Popillius devised a new method of diplomacy: he drew a ring round the king with his stick and bade him give his answer before he stepped out of the circle. In his youth Antiochus had been a hostage in Rome, where he had received his education. He understood Rome's attitude towards the East, and knew that Popillius was not joking; he evacuated Egypt without further demur. A humiliated king retreated to Syria, but on his way home he decided to restore law and order to troubled Jerusalem.

The Jewish national uprising had social overtones. The Maccabees and their supporters revolted first and foremost against the Jewish Hellenizers in Jerusalem, the oligarchy that tried to transform Jerusalem into a Greek city and the poor section of the population into second class citizens. The Hellenizing oligarchy was considered a stooge in the hands of Antiochus, and the rebels were determined to expel them from the High Priesthood and to re-establish the traditional way of life in Judaea. It is futile to separate political, social and economic factors from religious ones. They were all interwoven and this is how the passage in the Book of Maccabees should be understood. 'Mattathias the Hasmonean gathered unto him a congregation of Hasidim, a great force in Israel, every man that obeyed the law.' In that way, the banner of revolt was raised.

It has been suggested lately that the chronology of the Hasmonean Revolt should be reconsidered and that the traditional view, holding that the revolt started as a reaction against the evil decrees of Antiochus, is completely erroneous. A. Tscherikover thought that it was precisely the other way around: when Antiochus came to Jerusalem and found that the Hasidim had started guerilla warfare against his protégé, Menelaus, he decided to weaken the rebels by a series of decrees, such as the prohibition of the Sabbath observance and rite of circumcision. He further ordered the erection of high places and altars on which swine and other animals were to be sacrificed, and the 'abomination that maketh desolate' (Shikutz Meshomam; Dan. XI:31). From then

on the rebellion spread and turned into a war of independence.

The first stage of the Hasmonean Revolt lasted three years, and after a series of impressive victories Judas Maccabaeus controlled the whole country of Judaea, captured Jerusalem, with the exception of the fortress Akra (not taken until 142 BCE), purified the Temple and restored the cult of the God of Israel. An independent state was established after hundreds of years of servitude. But the survival of the infant state was far from certain. An international breakthrough came with the recognition granted to the recently established state by the Roman Empire. The contract between the mini-state of Judas Maccabaeus and the Roman Empire, signed in 161 BCE, may be quoted in full:

May it be well with the Romans and the Jewish nation on sea and land forever. May both sword and enemy be far from them. If, however, war shall be declared against Rome first, or against any of her allies, in any of the domains, the Jewish nation will be expected to fight at their side as allies, as the occasion shall dictate to them, whole-heartedly. To those who start the war, they shall neither give nor supply grain, arms, money or ships, as Rome shall decide. They shall keep their stipulations without receiving anything in return. On these same conditions, if war falls to the lot of the Jewish nation first, the Romans will assist as allies faithfully, as the occasion shall dictate. No grain, arms, money or ships shall be given to the enemies as Rome shall decide. They shall keep these stipulations without deceit. Thus, on these conditions, the Romans have established a compact with the Jewish people. If hereinafter either party shall decide to add or subtract therefrom, they shall do so of their own volition and whatsoever they add to or subtract therefrom shall be valid. Moreover, concerning the atrocities which King Demetrius is perpetrating against you, we have written to him saying: 'Why have you made your yoke heavy upon our friends and allies the Jews? If they again appeal to us against you, we will demand satisfaction for them and will make war upon you by sea and land.'

This seems a suitable point to interrupt the thread of the narrative, and to consider once more the statement of the Soviet critic referred to at the beginning of this chapter, that a small state can never defeat a big state. This truism gives us as little insight into the Hasmonean Revolt as the nationalistic and almost mystical approach, which sees the victory as one of a just minority, remaining faithful to the One God and his worship, over a corrupt and sinful majority.

But since the number of historians who speak in all seriousness about 'the miracle of the victory of the Hasmoneans' is decreasing, it is more important to take up the issue with the 'super rationalists'.

It would be a mistake to underestimate the Hasmonean Revolt and the establishment of an independent Hasmonean state. It was more than an intermezzo between the fall of the Seleucids and the emergence of the Roman rule, as Eduard Meyer thought. It would be vulgar to label a small nation fighting for its existence and independence as merely a tool of some Great Power.

In 1859, Napoleon III was interested in weakening Austrian influence in Italy. He supported Italian national aspirations and his soldiers fought in Magenta and Solferino. Would anyone conceive of 'Young Italy' as being the tool of French hegemonial interests? In 1917, the Germans were interested in the cessation of hostilities on the Eastern Front, in order to transfer all their forces to the West. They were instrumental in smuggling Lenin into Russia, but it would be grotesque to suggest that the Bolshevik Revolution was merely a German manipulation.

The emergence of the Hasmonean state was the historical consequence of intrinsic developments which took place not only in Palestine but over a wide area. Nowhere were the roots of Hellenism strongly implanted, and the more the central government of the Seleucids weakened, the wider was the disintegration. Zipoetes of Bithynia, Mithridates of Pontus and Ariarthes of Cappadocia were local leaders who seceded from the empire and established eventually independent states headed by royal families. The upper classes in all the countries took on the external trappings of Hellenism; most of them spoke Greek, established Hellenistic institutions and were influenced by Greek religion, but they never surrendered their national interests and fought for an independent Bithynia, Pontus or Cappadocia. The Hasmonean state was no exception. Judas Maccabaeus fought tooth and nail against Apollonius, who established in Jerusalem a cleruchy of foreigners, 'a nation of a foreign God', and converted Jerusalem into an 'abode of aliens'. The settlers were not Greeks from the Greek mainland, but Syrian soldiers who served in the Seleucid army. Their god was not Zeus, but the Syrian Baal Shamin; this was the meaning of the term 'abomination of desolation' in the Book of Daniel. Mattathias and his sons rose up against their oppressive acts and not against Greek culture and civilization. As a matter of fact, the later Hasmoneans showed no antagonism towards Hellenistic civilization. They did not scorn Greek names (Hyrkanos, Aristobulos, etc.) and Greek political customs and institutions. Their aim was, as an eminent scholar once said, to build a Hellenistic state on a Jewish national foundation.

From the outset, the Hasmoneans showed a shrewd understanding of the system of international relations prevailing in the area. The treaty between Rome and Judas Maccabaeus, of 161 BCE, is proof of this. The circumstances which led to Judas Maccabaeus being regarded as an equal in the treaty may briefly be described.

In 162 BCE, Demetrius I of Syria, the older brother of Antiochus Epiphanes, ascended the throne. The Roman state was unhappy about this development and supported Timarchus, the satrap of Babylonia. Demetrius fought back and tried to consolidate his authority first and foremost by the destruction of the independence of the Hasmonean state. He assigned the task of destroying Judaea to two of his best officers, Bacchides and Nicanor (the governor of Judaea). The king occupied himself with the eastern front. On the thirteenth day of Adar, 161 BCE, Judas Maccabaeus won a resounding victory. Nicanor fell in battle and the day of the victory was celebrated for many generations as a national holiday. But Judas Maccabaeus knew only too well that Judaea

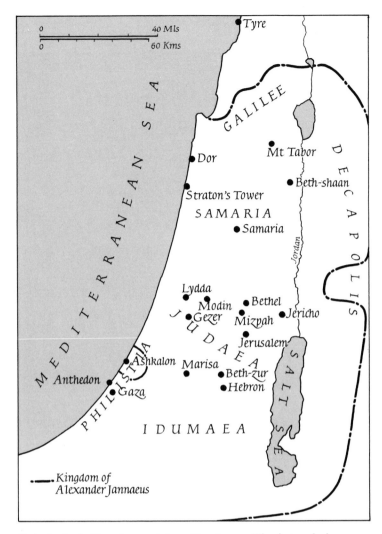

Palestine in the Maccabean period c. *168–163* BCE. *The glorious deeds of the Maccabees are commemorated annually by the festival of Chanukah, instituted by Judas Maccabaeus on the occasion of the purification of the Temple. The political skill shown by Judas Maccabaeus in making an alliance with Rome led for the first time to true, though short-lived, independence. In the end, internal quarrels brought Judaea under Rome's heavy yoke.*

could not hold out alone indefinitely against the Seleucid Empire and the hostile Greco-Syrian population of Palestine. This is why he was set on the attempt to make a treaty with Rome. The initiative came from him. He chose to send Eupolemus, son of John, and Jason, son of Eleazar to Rome. Their mission was to convince the Romans that 'the kingdom of the Greeks was reducing Israel to slavery' and that a treaty with Judaea would not be incompatible with Rome's interests. The Book of Maccabees records what befell the mission as follows:

> They journeyed to Rome, though the way was very long, and entering the Senate House, they began and said: Judas Maccabaeus, his brothers and the Jewish people have sent us to you, to effect an alliance and peace with you, so that we may be enrolled as your allies and friends.

Allowing for rhetorical gloss, the document is undoubtedly authentic. The text was flawed because of frequent translations back and forth. The text reached us in a Greek form and was translated into Hebrew (for I Maccabees) from the original Greek. The original document was in the archives of the Temple, and the author of I Maccabees had no difficulty in tracing it. Since similar documents – similar treaties between Rome and smaller countries – are known to us from various inscriptions, there is no reason to question the authenticity of the document. Moreover, it is clear that the treaty was also in Rome's best interests – Rome, refusing to recognize Demetrius, the enemy of Judaea. This is fully confirmed by a Roman historian: 'When the Jews rebelled against Demetrius and asked for Rome's friendship, they were the first to achieve independence in the east, because in those days the Romans were generous at the expense of others.'

Nowhere is there substantive evidence to support an allegation that Judaea acted as a tool of the Roman Empire. The contrary is true. Judas Maccabaeus understood, either by properly assessing the situation or by instinct, that the Syrians and the Egyptians were so weakened that they hardly rated as empires any more. Such circumstances had occurred in the days of the First Temple as well, and the kingdoms of Judaea and Israel flourished when they were able to overcome their smaller neighbours. Against empires like Babylonia or Syria, they had no chance. In the days of the Maccabees, the situation was no different. The characters changed but not the plot.

Rome was a mighty power, who willingly made treaties with enemies of her neighbours. When Rome fought Pyrrhus, she allied herself with Carthage only to turn on Carthage after Pyrrhus had been defeated, and it is not surprising that she entered into a treaty with Judaea, when her enemy was the Seleucid king.

It is regrettable that so little is extant concerning what Romans knew about Jews, and what Jews knew about Romans in the 2nd century BCE. In both cases, it was presumably not very much. Not only did Jews find the social fabric of Roman life incomprehensible, they did not even know that two consuls, not one, headed the Roman state. They certainly did not grasp the significance of *clientela*. A client may be described as an inferior entrusted to the protection of one more powerful than he, and rendering certain services and observances in return for his protection. The Romans called this state *in fide alicuius esse. Fides* implies trust and was basically a moral obligation with no legal implications. The origins of *clientela* are shrouded in mist, but its validity in Roman social and political life cannot be exaggerated. It is easily discernible not only in the relationship between a manumitted slave and his patron who has set him free, but also between a whole community that surrendered in war and the more powerful victorious city (or state).

Since the appearance in 1958 of E. Badian's *Foreign Clientela*, which has become a classic, nobody can investigate Roman foreign policy without taking into account this special relationship. We frequently read of treaties between mighty Rome and some small country, in which both parties appear as equals. Such treaties are known as *foedus aequum*, but one should not be led astray by terminology. When the Romans cited a small partner as *socius et amicus* (ally and friend of the Roman people), they did not consider it to be an equal. In this case, the term friend meant client, and the Romans expected that it should conduct itself as such. Not all 'friends' immediately appreciated this and it was a hard lesson to learn.

That is how the treaty between Rome and Judaea should be understood, and related to the treaties between Rome and three other small independent communities: the city of Kibyra in Asia Minor, the city of Methymna (Lesbos) and the island of Astypalaea in the Aegean Sea. The third of these was signed in 105 BCE, and in many clauses there is a close similarity to the treaty between Rome and Judaea in 161 BCE. Fortunately, the inscription has been preserved and a quoted passage might be instructive:

> If anyone makes war upon the people of Astypalaea, the Roman people shall assist the people of Astypalaea. And if anyone first makes war upon the Roman people, the people of Astypalaea shall render assistance in accordance with the treaty and oaths existing between the Roman people and the people of Astypalaea. If the people and Senate [of either party] wish by common consent to add or take away from this treaty, whatever they desire shall be permitted. . . .

It is indeed a wry joke to read that an island of about forty square miles will render assistance to mighty Rome, but it can be assumed that a treaty of this kind certainly raised the morale of the Astypalaeans.

The situation with Judaea in 161 BCE was no different. Practical advantages from the treaty were not immediately forthcoming and Judaea had to travel a long and hard road before gaining genuine independence. But formal recognition by the greatest power on earth must have given a tremendous boost to Judaean morale.

After the fall in battle of Judas Maccabaeus, his brother Jonathan was still considered a Syrian official and was at pains to manoeuvre among the various Syrian rulers. Only with Simon was complete political independence obtained. In 142, the Akra was captured, and in 140, 'the Great Assembly [Knesset] of the Priests and the people [of the rulers and the people and elders of the land] elected Simon as High Priest, military leader [Strategos] and leader of the people [Ethnarches].'

In the days of Simon and his son, John Hyrcanus, the territorial expansion of Judaea commenced, but only after the death of Antiochus VII (Sidetes) did the Seleucid influence cease in Palestine. In 104 BCE, Judah Aristobulus assumed the title 'King', and under Alexander Yannai, the Hasmonean kingdom controlled the whole of Palestine from Galilee in the north to the Egyptian frontier in the south. Jaffa was conquered by Simon, who transformed it into a Jewish port and secured for the Jewish state an outlet to the sea. John overran Idumaea, compelling the Idumaeans to convert. Aristobulus conquered the Ituraean people, who dwelt near Lebanon, and forced them to become Jews. Yannai took Gadara, Pella, Serasa and Gamela, in Transjordan, Rafiah and Anthedon, on the Mediterranean coast, and destroyed Gaza. For the sake of the historical record, it is worth stating that the Hasmoneans did not consider themselves conquerors. When Antiochus Sidetes demanded that the towns of Jaffa and Gezer should be returned, the answer preserved in the First Book of Maccabees is typical: 'We have not taken foreign soil, but the inheritance of our fathers, which fell into the hands of our foes unjustly, and now the land has returned to its first owners.'

Throughout these conquests, the Hasmoneans never abandoned their relations with the Roman Republic. In the time of Simon the Hasmonean, the Roman consul published a proclamation in favour of the Jews, sending it to various lands and to the Greek cities where Jews resided. It is known from official documents that, in 134, John Hyrcanus renewed the traditional alliance with Rome. The Roman Senate, on the other hand, was no less interested in curtailing the expansionist aspirations of Antiochus VII. This comes to light in a formal decision of the Senate:

> Whereas . . . the envoys of the Jews – worthy men and allies – have discussed the matter of renewing the relation of good will and friendship which they have formerly maintained with the Romans, and have brought as a token of the alliance a golden shield . . . it has been decreed to form a relation of good will and friendship with them [Jews] and to provide them with all the things which they requested and to accept the shield which they have brought.

But the Hasmoneans did not rely on remote Rome only. When sallying forth against the Seleucids, they sought good relations with the Parthians and the Ptolemaic court and, in parallel with this wise foreign policy, pursued the strengthening of their armed forces. It is not surprising that, at the end of the 1st century, Judaea became a military power to be reckoned with.

There are those who believe that if only the Jews had preserved internal unity, had not deviated from the principles laid down in the Torah and had followed in the footsteps of the first Hasmoneans, they would have held out for many more years. However, with the increasing social polarization (which is depicted in the Book of Enoch), the growing conflicts between Pharisees and Sadducees and the popular resistance to the concentration of political and religious power in the hands of the Hasmonean king, the country was so weakened that it fell to Pompey like a ripe fruit.

According to this view, the civil war between Hyrcanus II and his brother Aristobulus, which broke out in 67 BCE, the treacherous role played by Antipater the Idumaean and the approach of Pompey to mediate put an end to Judaean independence. This view could be questioned in the following way: has history any example of a continuing period of conquest not having affected the social fabric of the conqueror? Was Athens before the Attic-Delian alliance the same Athens of the Athenian Empire? Were the conquests of the Roman Republic not the direct cause of the social agitations which brought about the appearance of Gracchi in 133 BCE? And is it conceivable that the conquests of John Hyrcanus and Alexander Yannai failed to influence social relationships in Judaea?

Even if harmony had prevailed – and there is no doubt that the disharmony depicted in Josephus is so grossly exaggerated because it originated from a hostile (anti-Hasmonean) source – is it possible to conceive that a united Judaea would have thwarted Rome's policy of limiting the expansion of small states? It is difficult to answer these hypothetical questions. They are not posed to elicit simplistic answers, but to warn against over-simplifications which are bound to arise if these questions are not asked.

To return to the facts: the civil war made Pompey's intervention that much easier, but even had there been no civil war, Rome would still have curtailed the freedom of action of her overweening Hasmonean client. Pompey, having conquered Jerusalem and having entered the Holy of Holies without touching the Temple treasury, truncated the territory of Judaea. The Greek cities along the seashore and east of the Jordan were placed under the direct jurisdiction of the governor of the newly established province of Syria. Hyrcanus II was deprived of his monarchical title; he remained in charge of his diminished territory only as High Priest. Judaea was not yet converted into a Roman province, but Hyrcanus was subject to the control of the Roman governor of Syria. The days of *foedus aequum* between Rome and Judaea were over. The last Hasmonean king became a client prince, a system of controlling remote territories that the Romans preferred to annexation. It was to end in annexation, but this was to happen many years later and only after the Romans were convinced that all other ways to subdue the territory had failed.

Rome and Parthia

The question that persists throughout this chapter is whether the road from the loss of independence in 63 BCE to the destruction of the Temple in 70 CE was unavoidable. But before essaying an answer, it is important to point out that from one point of view the situation in 63 BCE might appear similar to 538 BCE: Pax Romana instead of Pax Persica with the hazards of choice in foreign policy pre-empted for Judaea.

The whole Middle East fell into the lap of one powerful empire. Had Judaea acquiesced, as they acquiesced in the days of Ezra and Nehemiah, it would have been possible to survive and to avert the tragedy of Exile. Like most analogies, this one is erroneous, too. The 6th century BCE was not the 1st, Rome was not Persia and on the horizon there was Parthia to kindle some small hopes for those who refused to acquiesce. But what is most important is that Judaea, once having tasted independence, would hardly accept again the humiliation which had prevailed before the Maccabees. There is no doubt that there was popular opposition to the last Hasmoneans and that the majority of the subjects never forgave the king for refusing to surrender the High Priesthood, but the horror stories associated with Alexander Yannai should be read with some circumspection. Josephus, in those chapters, relied heavily on Nicolaus of Damascus, who, in order to praise Herod, excessively vilified the Hasmoneans. But the truth can not be suppressed.

After the conquest of Jerusalem by Pompey and after the growing influence of Antipater and his sons over Judaean policy, sympathy for the Hasmoneans revived until it occasionally reached irrational heights. The sins of the later Hasmoneans were soon forgotten and the name Maccabee became synonymous with freedom and autonomy.

The main features of the period 63–40 BCE are: Hyrcanus reigned de jure only, the de facto power was in the hands of Antipater the Idumaean; the political line was clear-cut – total loyalty to Rome. However, Aristobulus, Hyrcanus's brother, never gave up the struggle with Rome. He escaped from his imprisonment, and did not find it difficult to recruit supporters in Judaea. There were many people left who considered Hyrcanus a traitor who sold out independence to Rome. Eventually, Aristobulus's attempts failed and he was transferred to Rome as a prisoner.

In Roman history, this is a period of the struggle of political dynasts, or, as it is called in textbooks, the time of the triumvirates. It was not easy for Antipater to read the political map in Rome and he had to handle his alliances with the various dynasts with great caution. Loyalty to one led to ruptures in the relationships with the others and it was very difficult to prophesy who might win the upper hand. In the beginning, Antipater remained faithful to Pompey, but when he found out about the latter's defeat at Pharsalos, in 48 BCE, he went over to Julius Caesar without batting an eye. Hyrcanus influenced Egyptian Jews to support Caesar and thus won the favours of the dictator. At the outset of the struggle between Caesar and Pompey, Aristobulus joined Caesar, and who knows what the outcome of this alliance would have been, had Aristobulus not been poisoned by Pompey's friends. Caesar, on the other hand, after he saw that Hyrcanus and Antipater served him loyally, abandoned Antigonus, the son of Aristobulus, and pushed him into the hands of the Parthians.

Meanwhile, Antipater consolidated his power in Judaea. He appointed his sons, Herod and Phasael, as Strategoi in Jerusalem and Galilee respectively. This opportunism paid off. Caesar left Hyrcanus in his position as High Priest but appointed Antipater as Procurator (Epitropos). Permission was granted to the Jews to rebuild the walls of Jerusalem, and, at a later stage, territories which had been taken from them by Pompey were restored. Most important was the restoration of Jaffa, 'which the Jews had possessed from ancient times since they made a treaty of friendship with the Romans.'

It is accepted that Jews enjoyed a sympathetic rapport with Caesar, and Latin sources testify that Jews mourned when Julius Caesar fell to the daggers of assassins in 44 BCE on the Ides of March. Indeed, compared with their lot in the days of Pompey, the period of Julius Caesar was an amelioration. Hyrcanus was recognized as Ethnarches and High Priest, and these two positions were promised to his scions, and the Jews were allowed to live according to their customs and the ways of their forefathers. Hyrcanus was given the title *socius et amicus populi Romani*, Judaea was given the right to exact taxes, and customs duties at the port of Jaffa, and Hyrcanus was exempt from the obligation to provide garrison for the Roman armies in Judaea. But the general mood in Judaea was not altogether as genial as it might appear. Otherwise, the emergence of the first Zealots – described as 'robbers' by Josephus – cannot be explained. The fact remains that their leader, Ezechias, was put to death by Herod, with many of his companions and without a trial, an outrage that had far-reaching historical consequences. Ezechias the Galilean became the forerunner of a great anti-Roman movement and was venerated by all those who refused to surrender to Roman rule.

The obligation to pay land-tax was regarded by the Zealots as a token of servitude and, therefore, of humiliation, and this symbolized Roman rule to them rather than the honourary titles that had been awarded to Hyrcanus. Jews never forgave Herod's contempt for Jewish legal procedures while trying Ezechias, nor his haughty conduct before the Jerusalem Sanhedrin. However Herod might try to be the accepted leader of the Jews, his efforts were doomed to fail. He was to become king of the Jews, but was never recognized as a Jewish king.

After the murder of Julius Caesar, Antipater (poisoned in 43 BCE) and his sons were confronted with a new dilemma. The Roman government, far from being stable, was behaving erratically and it was not easy to decide whom to support.

In this period of civil war in Rome, the petty princes and client kings in the East vacillated from one dynast to another. In the beginning, it seemed that Brutus and Cassius would win the day, but they were defeated at Philippi in 42 BCE. The East fell to Anthony, but in Rome, Octavian (the adopted son of Julius Caesar) continued to consolidate his position. Hyrcanus, Herod and Phasael would not indulge in speculative exercises. Anthony was near and won their support without delay. Indeed he nominated Phasael and Herod as tetrarchs of the Jewish territory. Peace still escaped the area, however. In 40 BCE the Parthians overran the whole of the Near East, and Antigonus, the son of Aristobulus, with no chance of regaining power under Roman domination, persuaded the invaders from the East to reinstate him as the legitimate ruler of Judaea.

This intermezzo (40–37 BCE) can be described briefly. When Antigonus appeared on the Judaean scene, enthusiastic supporters rallied to him, just as they did to his father. Phasael and Hyrcanus tried to negotiate with Antigonus but were arrested and put in chains. The more sceptical Herod escaped to Petra. The Parthians put Antigonus on the throne, cut off the ears of Hyrcanus to prevent him from again becoming High Priest and exiled him from Judaea. Herod did not despair. He succeeded in reaching Alexandria, sailed from there to Rome, won the favour of Octavian and, in 40 BCE, was officially recognized in a plenary session of the Senate as king of Judaea. At the same time, a provisional understanding was reached between Anthony and Octavian, and Herod found it easy to make his peace with both of them.

In Asia Minor, in the city of Samosata, he met Anthony, who ordered Sossius to offer Herod all the military aid for the reconquest of Judaea. There is no doubt that Antigonus was far more popular than Herod in Judaea, but whether the people were happy with the Parthian occupation is another question. Robbery and pillage committed by the occupying Parthian forces gave rise to resentment and hatred no less than that felt towards the Romans. In 37 BCE, Jerusalem fell to Sossius and Herod, who had meanwhile married Mariamne, the granddaughter of Hyrcanus the Hasmonean. Antigonus was taken prisoner and put to death in Antiochia.

The same cruel fate befell the last of the Hasmoneans as that met by Zedekiah, the last of the Judaean kings in the 6th century BCE. Had there been a prophet in the days of Antigonus he would have depicted the Parthians as the 'bruised reed'. The Parthian invasion was not anchored in firm Parthian interests to conquer the Near East. It was an episode that originated in the efforts of the Roman renegade, Labienus, to unite the Parthians

There were synagogues in Jerusalem before the destruction of the Second Temple in 70 CE, but only one remnant of them survives. This Greek inscription records the building of a synagogue, guest-house and ritual bath by a leading Jewish citizen whose name, too, is rendered in Greek: Theodotus

against Rome; but Labienus's success was short-lived. Parthia was not a centralistic empire and the Parthian king had difficulty in harnessing the numerous Parthian princes, who preferred separatism to national interests. From that time, no serious statesman had any illusions that, with the aid of the Parthians, they would expel the Romans. The small, suriving, pro-Parthian element must have been persuaded by the turn of events to abjure all hope. Herod, however, had no such hesitations. For him, there was one orientation only, the orientation to Rome; and the question as to whom to support, Anthony or Octavian, disappeared after Actium, 31 BCE. Herod resolved the problem with that inimitable cunning that characterized his entire reign. He certainly would have described his approach to foreign policy as pragmatic. He remembered that he had to remain loyal to Rome without committing himself to one or another dynast.

Between the years 37 and 31, Anthony ruled the East. Herod was loyal to him but derived little joy from his loyalty. In order to appease Cleopatra, Anthony had to be generous at Herod's expense. Cleopatra received Chalcis, the Phoenician cities along the shore and the valley of Jericho. These territorial excisions hurt Herod's prestige. Not surprisingly, he did not follow Anthony enthusiastically once the hostilities broke out between Anthony and Octavian. He could attribute his neutrality to his preoccupation with wars against the Nabatean tribes. When he learned of the result of the Battle of Actium, he joined the victorious camp without demur, remained faithful to Octavian and was generously rewarded for it.

Octavian returned to Herod the valley of Jericho, Gaza, Antidon, Jaffa, Straton's Tower, Samaria and the cities of the Decapolis in Transjordan, which had been severed from the kingdom of Judaea in the days of Pompey. Now it was obvious that any alternative in foreign policy would be inadmissable, and no one was ready to repeat the adventures of Antigonus. The Romans were always grateful to Herod and this was emphasized at a meeting of the Senate, recorded by Josephus:

> Messala and Atratinus convened the Senate and, presenting Herod, dwelt on the good deeds of his father, and recalled the loyalty which Herod himself

had shown towards the Romans. At the same time they brought accusations against Antigonus, whom they declared an enemy . . . because he had received his kingly title from the Parthians, thus showing no regard for the Romans. And when the Senate had been aroused by these charges, Anthony came forward and informed them that it was also an advantage in their war with the Parthians, that Herod should be King. And as this proposal was acceptable, *to all*, they voted accordingly.

This information is reconfirmed by many other sources, but one should not be led astray by the title 'King'. Herod was a king – but a typical client king as the Romans understood it. A client king had limited authority, especially in foreign affairs. He was permitted to legislate his own laws, to strike coins and even to go to war on his own if the aims of the war did not conflict with the greater interests of Roman policy. He was not subject to the authority of the governor of the nearest Roman province. He himself was responsible for the internal security and the protection of the natural resources of his own country, but he was obliged to pay a regular annual tax. Herod was generally cautious and wise enough not to overshoot his mark; however, in 9 BCE, he dared to go to war against the Arabs without having sought Roman permission. Augustus became angry, wrote a very harsh letter to Herod and stated bluntly 'that whereas formerly he had treated him as a friend, he would now treat him as a subject.' This was the real meaning of being a *rex socius et amicus populi Romani*.

From a strictly legal point of view, Herod did not enjoy more autonomy under Augustus than Hyrcanus had under Julius Caesar. In certain respects, it was even less. While the High Priesthood and the ethnarchy were promised to Hyrcanus and his descendants, in the case of Herod, the agreement with Rome was personal to him, and would not be valid after his death.

Nevertheless, there is no comparison between the authority exerted by Hyrcanus and that by Herod. The dominating personality of the latter, his exceptional sense of public relations and the recognition by the Romans that he was serving their interests in the best way possible transformed him into one of the most powerful rulers of the Near East.

At the same time as he succeeded in representing himself on inscriptions as a lover of Romans (Philoromaios) and a lover of the emperor (Philokaisar) he failed to endear himself to the Jewish people. His image in Jewish tradition and history remained essentially negative and that was not only for his Edomite extraction. The people never forgave him for his systematic extermination of the Hasmonean family, and no power on earth could obliterate the scars left behind by his cruelties. Josephus summed up his reign in one brief remark. 'He was a man who was cruel to all alike and one who easily gave in to anger and was contemptuous of justice.' Even Augustus was appalled by his cruelty and once said that he would sooner be Herod's pig than Herod's son. (The jest, especially if uttered in Greek, had its sting: *Hys-Hyios* means pig, *Hyios* means son, and Herod, as Jew, would never touch pig's flesh.) In Jewish tradition he was depicted as being as cunning as a fox and no one was sorry that he died like a dog. They could not even muster admiration for his efforts to boost the Judaean economy and to renovate the Temple in a splendour never known before. He was hated by the Jews not only because of his cruelty and tyranny; the rift between the leading Pharisees and Herod went much deeper. Herod was a typical, absolute and autocratic, Hellenistic ruler, who deliberately limited the influence of the Sanhedrin and the High Priesthood, and who forcibly wedged Judaea into the structure of the Pax Romana. He believed in Rome's mission to impose peace among the nations of the world, saw no conflict between Roman and Jewish interests and conscientiously became one of the pioneers in the East of the cult of the emperor.

In this view, any minor affronts to Jewish tradition were negligible in comparison with the advantages that would accrue to the Jewish people were they fully to integrate into a flourishing Roman Empire. There lay the roots of the conflict. Such redemption was foreign to the spirit of the Jewish nation. They continued to believe that real redemption is not in human hands but in the hands of God, who will bring redemption on earth through his Messiah, at a time when Jews will be worthy of him. That will be the genuine and final redemption, and no compromise with any different reality could be accepted. No wonder that several Messiahs arose among such a people, and it is against this background that the history of Messianism should be studied.

This conflict winds like a continuing thread through Jewish history of the 1st century CE, from the days of Herod to the fall of Masada in 73.

It is impossible to relate in this framework the detailed events after Herod's death: the transformation of Judaea into a Roman province; the hopeful episode of the reign of Agrippa I; the sufferings and privations of the Jewish people at the hands of the Roman procurators; and the emergence and growth of the movement of the Zealots. This is the central theme of Josephus's literary work and a careful analysis of *The Jewish War* might induce us to formulate the pivotal question this way: on the one hand Josephus maintained that the purpose of his *The Jewish War* was to console those who were conquered by the Romans (i.e. the Jews), and to deter others who might be tempted to revolt. But the real motif throughout his whole work is that the Jews and the Romans are two great nations, that war between these two nations is not inevitable, and peaceful co-existence was a real possibility, if wild extremists on both sides – criminal Zealots on the one hand and greedy procurators on the other – had not dragged the nations into an unnecessary clash. In other words, there were good and bad people on both sides, but tragedy arose from the fact that the villains on both sides gained the upper hand.

Josephus typifies Titus as the good Roman who never intended to burn down the Temple; in conflict with Jewish tradition, he was depicted by the Romans as the darling of mankind. On the Jewish side there was Ananus, the senior of the chief priests. He is depicted as a man of great sagaciousness, who might possibly have saved the city of Jerusalem had he escaped from the hands of the murderous extremists.

It is not possible to enter into the question of the authenticity of Josephus's historical writings, but this has to be said: Josephus lied only when he had to apologize for his own behaviour during the war. He knew that no one would forgive his treachery and his desertion to the Roman camp. He would have liked to have appeared in Jewish history as another Ananus, whose misfortune it was to recognize at an early age the hopeless circumstances. He tried to explain that no one would have listened to his advice anyway, and had he remained in the Jewish camp and fought for his ideas his fate could have been similar to that of Ananus. Josephus failed in his attempt to pose as another Jeremiah. Jews were never prepared to compare a renegade, who acted as an advisor of moderation in Titus's headquarters, to a Jeremiah, who preached for an understanding with the Babylonians from within the besieged walls of Jerusalem. But his treacherous character does not condemn him automatically as a poor historian, nor does his ethics detract from his capacity to analyze the political situation.

In this respect, it is difficult to fault him. He understood that, throughout the history of Jewish independence, the Jewish state could never defeat an empire such as Babylonia, Assyria or Egypt. It was possible to defeat Ammonites, Moabites and Philistines, but at the same time it was imperative to ensure a friendly attitude on the part of some Great Power, preferably remote and far away. This is precisely the policy adopted by Judas Maccabaeus, who, while fighting the Seleucids in their decline, sought an alliance with Rome. To use Tacitus's observation: 'When the Macedonians were by degrees enfeebled, when the Parthians' state was in its infancy, and the Romans were yet at a distance, the Jews seized the opportunity to erect a monarchy of their own.'

The war that led to the destruction of the Second Temple was hopeless from the outset, just as there was no chance of success in the war against Babylonia in 586 BCE. This was the message that Josephus wished to convey, putting into the mouth of Agrippa II a speech 'in order to bring misguided persons to reason and a better frame of mind, and to prevent virtuous citizens from reaping the consequences of the errors of a few.' Agrippa II states in that speech that the justified accusations against individual Roman procurators do not justify a war with Rome. Firstly, because many great states have already submitted to Rome (Athens, Sparta, Macedon, etc.), and from this point of view the Zealot passion for independence is a belated one. And, secondly, because there is a difference between a war against a small neighbouring nation and a war against an empire: 'Do you really suppose that you are going to war with Egyptians or Arabs? Will you shut your eyes to the might of the Roman Empire and refuse to take measure of your own weakness?' And, eventually, it is impossible to wage war against Rome alone and without allies. Nobody will join Jews in a war against the Roman Empire. Not even the Jewish Diaspora will lift a finger. Thus the war is lost before it is fought.

Modern historians have in futile fashion tried to explain the fall of the Second Commonwealth by alluding to civil war, internal conflicts and personal rivalries among the Jews. While one hesitates to introduce an 'if' into historical investigations, it is reasonable to say that even had a harmonious coalition of all Jewish factions existed, the Roman Empire would not have been defeated. The Jewish freedom fighters were certainly virtuous, but they did not grasp the magnitude of Roman power. A Herod would never have rebelled. There were indeed many Jews (and it is not necessary to analyze here their social composition) who praised the deeds of the Romans in Judaea. They spoke with appreciation of the market-places they built, of the bridges and their bath installations. Indeed, the Talmud does not shrink from giving some credit to the benefits of Roman rule. Many other Jews, however (and they seemed to have been the majority), were not so impressed. The Talmud preserves another tradition as well: 'All they have instituted [the Romans] they have instituted only for their own needs. They have instituted market-places to place harlots in them, baths for their own pleasure, bridges to collect toll.'

Zealots are never convinced by rational arguments, and the price they pay is always heavy. It is possible to ascribe the catastrophe to Jewish intransigence, intolerance and a fanatic adherence to their religion. Not for nothing did Tacitus emphasize that 'the obstinacy of that stubborn people filled Vespasian with resentment.' But it should never be forgotten that the fiercest conflicts between Jews and Gentiles in Antiquity erupted against kings who were considered enlightened, liberal and tolerant. Antiochus Epiphanes, Titus and Hadrian are typical examples. All three persecuted Jews with the declared objective of compelling them not to be different from other peoples. Thus, even these 'well-meaning' rulers had fallen victims to the disease of dislike of the unlike, the epitome of intolerance.

It is futile to ask what would have happened had the Jews compromised. The answer oscillates between nothing and anything. It was a tragic story and tragedy is but the difference between what was and what might have been. The fact remains that without having read Seneca, *Praeferenda est spurcissima mors, servituti mundissimae* (*Epistulae ad Lucilium* LXX:21), many Jews would have subscribed to his dictum: the foulest death is preferable to the fairest slavery.

Chapter Four

The Talmud

JACOB NEUSNER

AFTER THE TANAKH ('Scripture', or 'Old Testament'), the Talmud is the single most influential document in the history of Judaism. This is for both religious and cultural reasons. The Talmud, viewed as part of the Revelation of the Torah (the Pentateuch) to Moses on Mount Sinai, has from the time of its redaction been treated as the authoritative interpretation of Scripture and as a corpus of revealed Law in its own right. The cultural traits inculcated by the Talmud, moreover, defined the shape of the civilizations of the Jewish people in many different lands. These traits – respect for reason, belief in the orderly and logical character of the good life, reverence for rational discourse and a high sense of the potentiality of the human intellect – derive in particular from the study of the Talmud. They include, as well, moral and ethical teachings about love of neighbour, respect for law and order and the conviction that the good life consists in studying Torah, keeping the Commandments, both those now seen as ritual and those perceived as moral, and doing deeds of lovingkindness, acts of grace beyond the measure of the Law. The Talmud thus defined for the Jews the way in which the good life would be conducted. The Talmud constitutes the principal, formative element in the life of the Jewish people.

But, in point of fact, we err when we treat the Talmud as a single document. It is true that, when most people refer to 'the Talmud', they think of the Babylonian Talmud, a compilation, produced in Babylonia in the 6th and 7th centuries CE, consisting of the Mishnah, a Palestinian law-code of the late 2nd century CE, and the *Gemara*, or commentary on the Mishnah, accumulated in the following three or four centuries. But there is another Talmud, the one produced in the Land of Israel (in Palestine: the Jerusalem, or Palestinian, Talmud) towards the end of the 5th century CE, also consisting of that same Mishnah, but with its own *Gemara*, the Mishnah-commentary produced in the Land of Israel from the 3rd to the end of the 5th century. The Mishnah is a sizeable autonomous document which originally existed on its own. Around it gathered not only the *Gemaras* but also another body of law and theology known as the *Tosefta*, or supplement (to the Mishnah), independent of the *Gemaras* and in fact cited in them. At the same time as this literature (Mishnah, *Tosefta*, Palestinian Talmud, Babylonian Talmud) was being written, the same authorities, in the same religio-legal institutions, were also producing sizeable corpora of exegesis and interpretation of the Tanakh. These are put together into collections of interpretations of various books of the Pentateuch, e.g. *Genesis Rabbah* and *Leviticus Rabbah*. Attributed to the authorities of the Mishnah, moreover, are interpretations of the legal passages of Exodus, Leviticus, Numbers, and Deuteronomy, known as *Mekhilta* for Exodus, *Sifra* for Leviticus, and *Sifre* for Numbers and Deuteronomy. And when we turn to the sorts of materials put together in the *Gemaras* of the Babylonian and Palestinian Talmuds, furthermore, we discover not a single, unitary and harmonious discussion, but a fairly wide variety of types of materials, each serving its own purpose. It follows that before us is a considerable corpus of literature. Calling the whole 'Talmud' or even 'talmudic literature' is misleading. And even if we do, the Talmud is only one document produced by the Judaic authorities of late Antiquity, and we cannot be sure that, from their perspective, it was their central and most important creation.

These authorities are called rabbis. The form of Judaism that bears their imprint and definition is known as rabbinic (or talmudic) Judaism. Previously there were other kinds of Judaism, but rabbinic Judaism has grown until, today, it predominates among nearly all those Jews who draw upon the Revelation of Moses and view the world from within the religious system based on that Revelation. As an example of an earlier form of Judaism, if the priests of the Temple of Jerusalem before 70 CE were asked to describe their central religious act, it surely would have been the sacrifice of animals to the Lord in the Temple. If the Messianic teachers of the Essene community, whose library was discovered at Qumran, by the Dead Sea, could tell us what activity was most important in their kind of Judaism, it probably would have been the communal meal, eaten in a state of cultic purity in accordance with the purity-taboos of Leviticus, and the study of the meaning of Scripture in, and to, the life of their commune. Obviously, to those Jews who believed that Jesus was the Messiah promised of old but who also saw themselves as Jews, the Church of Peter in Jerusalem, at the heart of Judaism, will have been yet another quite distinctive symbol. To the rabbis – of ancient times as of today – the central symbol of Judaism is Torah, the most important activity is the study of Torah, the principal authority is the learned man, the rabbi, and the ancient Scriptures are read as the record of the masters of Torah, from Moses, whom they called 'our rabbi', onwards. Clearly, calling Moses 'our rabbi' indicates a considerable rewriting of the history of biblical Israel and tells us that the Talmud stands in the very centre of a massive reformation of Judaism, past present, and future.

The Mishnah

To gain a clearer picture of the complex literature produced by the rabbis of late Antiquity, let us isolate the single component of that literature viewed by the ancient rabbis as most important. It is undoubtedly the Mishnah, which the rabbinic account of the history of rabbinic or talmudic literature assigns to Judah the Patriarch, ruler of the Jewish community of Palestine in the late 2nd and early 3rd century. Mishnah stands out because it is called part of the Torah revealed by God to Moses at Sinai. That is an extraordinary claim. For one thing, how can Mishnah be attributed to Judah the Patriarch and also be received as 'Torah revealed to Moses on Sinai'? We must wonder about the conception of revelation contained within this contradictory statement, and, in due course, we shall plumb its meaning.

Mishnah, a corpus of sayings divided into six principal sections, which themselves are subdivided into sixty-three tractates in all, contains its own theological verification. The opening chapter of the tractate called the 'Sayings of the Fathers' (*Pirqe aboth*) explicitly links the authorities of Mishnah itself upwards to Sinai:

> Moses received Torah [not: *the* Torah, the *written* Torah] on Sinai and handed it on to Joshua, and Joshua to elders, and elders to prophets, and prophets handed it on to the men of the great assembly.

Rabbi Yose of Galilee, one of the great sages whose opinions are recorded in the Talmud. This imaginary portrait occupies the margin of a Spanish Haggadah of the 14th century.

The men of the great assembly, supposed to have lived in the 4th century BCE, then are succeeded by such non-biblical paragons as Simeon the Righteous, Antigonus, Yose ben Yo'ezer and Yose ben Yohanan, Joshua ben Perahiah and Nittai the Arbelite, Judah ben Tabbai and Simeon ben Shatah, Shema'iah and Abtalion, and, finally, Hillel and Shammai. With Hillel and Shammai, we find ourselves at the threshold of the 1st century CE. The disciples, or 'Houses', of Shammai and Hillel stand at the beginning of the numerous and important names to which Mishnah attributes the bulk of its materials, so that by beginning with Moses and coming down to Shammai and Hillel, the apologists of Mishnah lay claim to origination of their document not only in ancient times, but on Sinai. Mishnah is part of the Revelation to Moses on Sinai, but clearly a part that was not written down – since the Scriptures do not contain anything like Mishnah – and hence is deemed to have been formulated and transmitted orally.

According to this account, therefore, Mishnah is part of the Torah revealed to Moses on Sinai, and hence must be understood as a major document in the history of Judaism. Together with its commentaries and appended materials (*Gemara*), it constitutes the true beginning of Judaism, since Judaism has been defined – from ancient times to the present – as Scripture interpreted by the talmudic rabbis.

How then does Mishnah and its related documents define and explain the meaning of Torah? By Torah is meant both a *book* and an *activity*. The book is the written Scripture, the Tanakh. The activity is the unwritten Revelation of God to Moses 'our rabbi' on Mount Sinai,

which produces, in time, the Mishnah. Thus 'Torah' refers to 'the whole Torah of Moses our rabbi', a Torah in two parts, distinguished by the forms of the formulation and transmission. The one part is written down. The other part is memorized. The two together constitute Torah, and it is by combining both that one learns Torah, principally through memorization and critical inquiry into what is memorized (that is, the paramount mode of the *second* half of Torah). Accordingly, for talmudic Judaism, literary texts constitute the data of religion, and interpreting them defines the quest for, and experience of, the sacred. It follows that, to the ancient rabbis and their continuators, one seeks God through the worship effected in a particular kind of learning of a distinctive sort of literature.

The reader will be helped at this point if we clarify the meaning of Torah, which already has been used in more than one sense, and which, in the history of Judaism, bears a variety of meanings. In the beginning, Torah meant teaching or instruction, but very soon after the creation of the Torah-literature, about 450 BCE, Torah becomes 'the Torah', the Pentateuch or the Five Books of Moses, Genesis, Exodus, Leviticus, Numbers and Deuteronomy. In Judaism today, the Torah as a physical object, a scroll, contains these five books. They constitute the sancta, sacred objects, of the synagogue worship, being kept in the place of honour and carried in procession, then handled and proclaimed, at the very centre of the divine service. But when the concept of the whole Scripture came into being, towards the end of the 1st century CE, then 'Torah' came to refer to the whole of the written Scripture known, as we pointed out, as the

'Old Testament'. Now, in using the word Torah to mean Divine Revelation, rabbinic Judaism reverted to the most ancient usage and claimed on behalf even of its holy documents and teachings the status of *torah*, Divine Revelation. To speak explicitly of Mishnah: when Mishnah is referred to as part of Torah, it is claimed that, when Moses received Torah from God on Mount Sinai, he received Torah in two parts, one in writing, the other to be memorized. This much is clear, of course. It will follow that Mishnah as a distinct document, and Mishnah as part of Torah must be kept separate. Mishnah as a distinct document existed before Mishnah was assigned a place in the Torah of Moses. The Talmud, attached as it is to Mishnah, likewise joined in that Torah of Moses because it is deemed to be part of the Oral Torah, and much that came into being later on likewise was deemed to be holy, therefore to be Torah. So, while Mishnah came to closure *c.* 200 CE, and the Talmud of Palestine *c.* 450 CE, and that of Babylonia *c.* 500 CE (all these dates are merely guesses and stand upon very little firm evidence), the whole found its way into the Torah of Moses on Sinai. It is this curious fact that we must now try to appreciate.

To the talmudic rabbis Torah – Revelation – remained open, an uncompleted canon, as late as the early 3rd century CE, if not later. Mishnah was regarded as part of it by people who personally knew the authorities of Mishnah. Samuel and Rab, who could have known Rabbi Judah the Patriarch himself, know Mishnah as Torah. No wonder, then, that they could deem Torah-learning to be the chief locus of the open way toward the sacred, for it is through the processes of *qabbalah* and *massoret* – handing down, 'traditioning' – that they claim on behalf of Mishnah its status as part of Mosaic Revelation: *Torah-learning is a mode of attaining Revelation of Moses on Sinai*, and transcendence by rabbis is defined as receiving Divine Revelation. Mishnah itself is called Mosaic and assigned to Sinai by people who stand within decades of the work that brought Mishnah into being, an amazing fact. Accordingly, so far as the talmudic rabbis are concerned, Torah is, as I said, an unfilled basket, a canon still open and uncompleted. Because Judah, Meir, Simeon, Yose and Simeon ben Gamaliel of the mid-2nd century are the main authorities of Mishnah, it means that the 3rd- and 4th-century rabbis cannot have supposed the processes of revelation had closed a thousand or more years earlier. Not for them the route of pseudepigraphy, assigning their great ideas to Adam or Enoch or the sons of Jacob. Nor do they even take the trouble to put the language of Mishnah into the forms and syntax of the biblical tongue, as do the masters of the Essene community at Qumran. They do not imitate the forms of the sacred literature of old nor hide themselves in the cloak of pseudepigraphic anonymity. For to them the sacred and Revelation are as available as to Moses. Nothing said to Moses may not also be said to them.

Mishnah is a work formulated in the processes of redaction. That is, the particular linguistic formulation of Mishnah took place among the men who combined and collected its materials into a well composed and orderly document. These materials dated from the previous two or three centuries, but the forms that were imposed on them in earlier times were not totally obliterated by men wholly in command of themselves and confident of their own superior judgment of how things should be put together and worded. Mishnah is set out in highly stereotyped sentences. The range of such sentences is very limited. We can list their paramount forms on the fingers of one hand. The patterned sentences, e.g. 'If x is so, then y is the rule, and if x is not so, then y is not the rule,' will run on in groups of threes or fives. When the pattern shifts, so does the topic under discussion. The patterns are so worked out and put together that it is exceedingly easy to memorize Mishnah. Just as the authorities of Mishnah, speaking in their own names, do not take the trouble to put their ideas into the mouths of Adam, Enoch, or their own heroes, e.g. Moses and David, and just as they do not bother to copy the formulary patterns of Scripture, so they take decisive action to wipe out the traces of the literary and aesthetic forms in which intellectual materials, then nearly three centuries old, had come down into their own hands.

What the redactors and formulators of Mishnah do, they do only in Mishnah. The companion compilation, *Tosefta*, does not reveal equivalent traits of formulation aimed at facilitating memorization. Nor, in the later rabbinic documents, do we find equivalent linguistic structures encompassing whole chapters and even larger units of redaction, though, to be sure, brief formulae seem to have been memorized throughout. Mishnah is unique. It alone was made into literature for memorization, and on its behalf alone was the claim laid down, 'Moses received Torah on Sinai, and handed it on to Joshua, and Joshua to the sages, and sages to the prophets', and so on down to the named authorities who stand within the pages of Mishnah itself, including, as we have seen, such recent figures as Shammai and Hillel.

Exactly how do the framers of Mishnah facilitate memorization? Let me state first what they do not do. They do not give us rhyme-schemes. Although probably meant to be sung, the text does not follow disciplined rhythms. Its principal forms consist of arrangements of words in certain syntactical patterns, not of the repetition of the same words with some stunning variation at the start or end of a thought. It is the presence of these recurrent syntactical patterns that makes it easy to memorize. They are deeply embedded within the structure of language, rather than expressed superficially. The mishnaic mnemonic is defined by the inner logic of word patterns: grammar and syntax. Even though Mishnah is to be handed on orally and not in writing, it expresses a mode of thought attuned to highly abstract syntactical relationships, not concrete and material ones. Rabbis who memorize Mishnah are capable of amazingly abstract perceptions, for their ears and minds perceive regularities of grammatical arrangements running through a whole range of diverse words. What is memorized is a recurrent notion expressed in diverse examples but framed in a single, repeated rhetorical pattern. The diverse cases are united by a principle that is contained within all of them. But that principle is seldom made explicit. Rather, it is embedded in the deep structure of thought and language and has to be discovered there by the mind of the person who memorizes and studies the several cases.

Mishnaic rhetoric creates a world of discourse distinct from the concrete realities of a given time, place and

society. The exceedingly limited repertoire of grammatical patterns imposed upon all ideas on all matters gives symbolic expression to the notion that beneath the accidents of life are comprehensive, unchanging and enduring relationships. It is through *how* things are said, therefore, as much as through *what* is said, that Mishnah proposes to express its message. Mishnah is made out of meaningful statements, the *form* of which is meant to convey deep meaning. The framers of Mishnah expect to be understood by keen ears and active minds. They therefore convey what is fundamental at the level of grammar, independently of specific meanings of words and cases. They manifest confidence that the listener will put many things together and draw the important conclusions for himself. Mishnah assumes an active intellect capable of perceiving implications and of vivid participation. Apart from the message memorized, Mishnah demands the perception of the unarticulated message contained within the medium of syntax and grammar. And the hearer is assumed to be capable of putting the two together to create still deeper insights. The cogent syntactical pattern underlying statements about different things expresses a substantive cogency among those diverse and divergent cases.

There are, then, these two striking traits of mind reflected within Mishnah: first, the perception of order and balance, and, second, the view of the mind's centrality in the construction of order and balance. The mind imposes wholeness upon discrete cases. Mind perceives meaning and pattern, because, to begin with, it is mind – the will, understanding and intention of man – that *imparts* meaning to the world. To give one concrete example: to the rabbis of the 2nd century CE, it is human intention, not material reality or the automatic working of mindless laws, that defines what is unclean or clean. In one area of the law of purities after another, the conclusion is reached that what man *thinks* is determinative of what can be made unclean and definitive of the processes of contamination. For instance, Scripture states (Lev. XI:34, 37) that if a dead creeping thing falls on dry food, the food is unaffected, but if it is wet, it is made unclean. The late 1st- and 2nd-century rabbis add, however, that food that is wet accidentally is not affected by the source of uncleanness. It is still clean and insusceptible. Only when a man deliberately draws water and intentionally applies it to grain, for example, does the grain become susceptible to uncleanness. It follows that, if you have two stacks of grain, one on which rain has fallen, another which a man has watered, and if a dead creeping thing falls on both, only the latter is unclean. The two sorts of grain are identical, except for man's intention. That is one among literally hundreds of examples of the same viewpoint.

The claim for Mishnah, laid down, as we have seen, in Aboth, Mishnah's first and most compelling apologetic, is that the authority of Mishnah rests upon its status as received tradition of God. This tradition, handed on through memory, is essential to the whole Torah. In a world in which writing was routine, memorization was special. What happens when we know something by heart, which does not happen when we read it or look for it in a scroll or a book, is this: when we walk in the street and when we sit at home, when we sleep and when we wake, we carry with us, in our everyday perceptions, that

Woodcut showing the Temple, from the edition of Maimonides's Mishneh Torah, *the great codification of talmudic Law, printed in Venice in 1524.*

memorized saying. The process of formulation through formalization and the coequal process of memorizing patterned cases to sustain the perception of the underlying principle, uniting the cases just as the pattern unites their language, extends the limits of language to the outer boundaries of experience, the accidents of everyday life itself. Wise sayings are routine in all cultures; but the reduction of all truth, particularly to wise sayings, is not.

To impose upon these sayings an underlying and single structure of grammar corresponding to the inner structure of reality is to transform the structure of language into a statement of ontology. Once our minds are trained to perceive principle among cases and pattern within grammatical relationships, we further discern, in the concrete events of daily life, both principle and underlying autonomous pattern. The form of Mishnah is meant to correspond to the formalization perceived within, not merely that imposed upon, the conduct of concrete affairs. The matter obviously is not solely ethical, though the ethical component is self-evident. It also has to do with the natural world and the things that break its routine. In Mishnah, all things are a matter of relationship, circumstance, fixed and recurrent interplay. 'If x, then y, if not x, then not y' – that is the datum by which minds are shaped.

The way to shape and educate minds is to impart into the ear, thence into the mind, perpetual awareness that what happens recurs, and what recurs is pattern and order, and, through them, wholeness. How better to fill the mind than with formalized sentences, generative of meaning for themselves and of significance beyond themselves? In such sentences meaning rests upon the perception of *relationship*. Pattern is to be discovered in the multiplicity of events and happenings, none of which themselves state or articulate pattern. Mind, trained to memorize through what is implicit and beneath the surface, is to be accustomed and taught in

Page from the Talmud printed in Basel between 1578 and 1580, upon which all later editions are based. In the middle is the text of the Mishnah and Gemara, *surrounding it ('the hedge round the Torah') are the commentaries, that of Rashi on the right.*

such a way as to discern pattern. Order *is*, because order is discovered, first in language, then in life. As the cult, in all its precise and obsessive attention to fixed detail, demonstrated that from the orderly centre flowed lines of meaning to the periphery, so the very language of Mishnah, in its precise and obsessive concentration on innate and fixed relationship, demonstrated order deep within the disorderly world of language, nature, and man.

While rabbinic Judaism is commonly described as a highly 'traditional' kind of religion, and while Mishnah, with its stress on memorization and obedience to the Law, is treated as a document of tradition, Mishnah is hardly traditional; as we shall see, the *Gemara* preserves for its part an equally independent frame of mind vis-à-vis Mishnah itself. The Talmud as a whole is anything but traditional, in the commonplace sense of tradition as something handed on that bears authority over us simply because it has come down to us from old. The foundation of Mishnah's world view is the claim that revelation continues to occur and is embodied in the work of men of the recent past. It, therefore, is the *contemporaneity* of Mishnah – a contemporaneity effected through the detachment of its cases from specific time and place and even particular linguistic context – that is its principal trait. The later history of Mishnah, its capacity to generate two large Talmuds as commentaries, its unfathomed implications stirring later generations to

produce their commentaries on Mishnah and on *its* commentaries, their responses to specific questions of Torah-law, and their efforts to codify the law – these testify to the permanent contemporaneity of Mishnah.

Accordingly, we must ask, 'why is it that Mishnah, while being accepted as Torah, escapes being fossilized as tradition?' In my view, the chief reason is to be found in the intentions of Mishnah's own framers, who do not present their ideas as ancient tradition but in their own names as living Torah, and who, therefore, keep open the path of continuing receptivity to revelation through continuing use of the mind. I think it is done deliberately, just as the authorities of Mishnah intentionally reject the names of old authorities and the linguistic patterns of ancient, holy documents.

By stating Mishnah in terms essentially neutral to their own society (though, to be sure, drawing upon the data of their context), Rabbi Judah the Patriarch sees to it that his part of the Torah will pass easily to other places and other ages. Through patterned language, Mishnah transcends the limitations of its own society and time. There is, however, a second side to matters. What makes Mishnah useful is not only its comprehensibility, but also its *incomprehensibility*. It is a deeply ambiguous document, full of problems of interpretation. Easy to memorize, it is exceptionally difficult to understand. Mishnah not merely permits exegesis. It demands it. That accounts for its Talmuds. We can memorize a pericope of Mishnah in ten minutes. But it takes a lifetime to draw forth and understand the meaning. Mishnah contains within itself, even in its language, a powerful statement of the structure of reality. But that statement is so subtle that, for eighteen centuries, disciples of Mishnah, the Talmuds and the consequent literature of exegesis have worked on spelling out the meaning (not solely the concrete application) of that statement.

It is no accident at all that the most influential works of Jewish intellectual creativity, such as the Zohar, the 13th-century corpus of mystical lore laid down in the names of 2nd-century authorities, and Maimonides's legal code, and the *Shulchan Aruch* of Joseph Caro, link themselves specifically to Mishnah. Zohar claims for itself the same authorities as those of Mishnah, as if to say: 'This is the other part of Mishnah's Torah.' And Maimonides's work, the *Mishneh Torah*, is in the model of, but an improvement upon, the language and structure of Mishnah itself. Nor should we forget that still a third religious genius of Judaism, Joseph Caro, heard the Mishnah personified speak to him and wrote down what the Mishnah had to tell him. These are diverse testimonies to the ineluctable demand, imposed by Mishnah itself, for further exegesis. The first, pseudepigraphic, the second, an imitation of the language and form, and the third, a curious personification of the document; all look backwards, not forwards. For each is a way taken earlier in response to the written Torah. The Zohar takes the model – as to its authority – of the pseudepigrapha of the 'Old Testament'. Maimonides, like the sages of the Essene community at Qumran, takes the model of the inherited linguistic choices of the holy book. Joseph Caro, of course, in his hearing the personification of Mishnah talking, will have been at home among those who talk of Torah or wisdom personified.

Babylonian Talmud: Mishnah and Tosefta

Having seen how and why Mishnah not merely requires, but actually generates, commentaries, we now turn to the most important one, which is the Babylonian *Gemara*. What we shall see, first of all, is that Mishnah as Mishnah – an autonomous part of Torah – is submerged into the processes of amplification and discussion of individual units of thought – pericopae – of Mishnah. The document thus loses its independent character. The commentary, with its atomistic and line-by-line exegesis of the text, obliterates the character of the text as a document with its own literary, legal and theological traits. The second interesting trait of the *Gemara* (not evident in the particular selection we shall examine) is its critical stance towards Mishnah. Just as Mishnah takes up its independent position vis-à-vis the written Torah, not imitating the language of the written Torah and not adducing, as proof of the correctness of Mishnah's propositions, texts of the written Torah, so the *Gemara*, while commenting on Mishnah, establishes its own viewpoint. What strikes the *Gemara* as interesting in Mishnah is the absence of proof-texts, leading from Scripture to the propositions of Mishnah. It therefore chooses, wherever possible, to provide proof-texts, which Mishnah, for its part, deems unnecessary. Mishnah claims to be an independent unit of Torah, half of the whole Torah of Moses our rabbi, and, by its exegetical interest, *Gemara* subverts that claim by setting Mishnah forth as essentially secondary to, and dependent upon, the proofs – the truths – of the written Torah.

The best way to come to an assessment of the character of *Gemara* is to examine a sample of its immense literature, to see how it is put together and conducts its inquiry. Because Judaism takes the conduct of every detail of life with utmost seriousness, we shall consider how the Talmud considers a matter of ritual law, rather than a more practical, ethical or moral issue. This passage allows us to see the solemn character accorded to small matters of religious life, how one says a blessing over wine, for example. It shows, in a concrete way, how talmudic discourse treats various injunctions that constitute the practice of Judaism. To be sure, it is easy enough to consider what follows as an instance of hair-splitting or nit-picking, and, viewed from some perspectives, a discussion such as this is nothing more than that. But if we consider that, to the rabbis of the Talmud, the good life is orderly, logical and rational, and that to them no detail of everyday life is exempt from the criticism of applied reason, we cannot be surprised that nits too must be picked and hairs split. We, therefore, take up a brief unit of Mishnah-tractate *Berakhot*, which deals with diverse blessings, and shall consider, in sequence, first, a pericope of Mishnah, second, the corresponding supplement of *Tosefta*, and, third, the Babylonian Talmud's treatment of that same Mishnah. This will allow us to see how one small part of the Babylonian Talmud works, the modes of argument and of practical logic that generate the bulk of that immense work. Before us is the opening pericope of the eighth chapter of *Berakhot*:

> A These are the things which are between the House of Shammai and the House of Hillel in [regard to] the meal:

> B The House of Shammai say, 'One blesses [says the blessing for] the day, and afterwards one says the blessing over the wine.'

> And the House of Hillel say, 'One says the blessing over the wine, and afterwards one blesses the day.'

The chapter begins with a superscription, A, which announces the subject and identifies the authorities whose opinions are to be given. No one can suppose that the only laws 'in regard to the meal' derived from the Houses, or that no one thereafter raised issues or formulated opinions on the same subject. Nor are these the only points about meals on which the Houses differed. The *Gemara* lists others. What we have are elements of a much larger tradition, which have been chosen for redaction and preservation. What we do not have, by and large, are the items omitted or passed over by those editors responsible for the document in our hands. To some measure, these omitted materials are preserved in other compilations of rabbinical traditions, or occur as single items, not in collections, in the *Gemara*; they will be signified as deriving from the authorities of the 1st and 2nd centuries, called Tannaim ('repeaters' – the Aramaic root, TNY, is equivalent to the Hebrew SHNY, thus Mishnah teachers), masters whose opinions were formulated and included in the Mishnah, or in the stratum of materials from which the Mishnah was finally selected.

The first difference, B, concerns the order of blessing the wine and saying the Sanctification of the Sabbath day. The House of Shammai say the Sanctification comes first, then the blessing for the wine. The House of Hillel rule contrariwise. The Mishnah explains nothing about these requirements and their meaning. We are supposed to know that 'say' means reciting the Sanctification, 'wine' means saying a blessing over the wine.

Since we have already noticed that Mishnah is formulated so as to facilitate memorization, we can hardly be surprised to observe an obvious mnemonic at B. The opinions of the Houses are verbally identical except for the order of the operative words, day/wine as against wine/day. The remainder of the chapter exhibits similar mnemonic devices. If we give the Hebrew letters in their English equivalents, we have for B the following:

MBRK ʿL HYWM WʾHR KK MBRK ʿL HYNN
MBRK ʿL HYYN WʾHR KK MBRK ʿL HYWN

These words preserve a fixed order and balance from one House-saying to the next, as is obvious above.

As we have seen, although the Mishnah is the primary component of the Talmud, there is a second, almost equally important collection of traditions, also attributed to 1st- and 2nd-century masters: the *Tosefta*, the supplement to the Mishnah. Indeed, the *Gemara* centres more on the analysis of the *Tosefta* than on the Mishnah. The Mishnah supplies the form and structure for the Talmud as a whole. But our chapter cites the *Tosefta* and that document provides the focus of interest.

The passage of *Tosefta* which serves our unit of Mishnah is as follows (*Tosefta Berakhot* V:25):

> A [The] things which are between the House of Shammai and the House of Hillel in [regard to] the meal:

> B The House of Shammai say, 'One blesses over the day, and afterwards he blesses over the wine,

The largest and most lavish edition of the Talmud ever printed is the Vilna edition of 1880, of which this is the title-page. It drew upon dozens of early manuscripts and included a wealth of notes and commentaries by later rabbis.

then the day. The House of Hillel are given a second reason for their ruling. The man must always bless wine before he drinks it, on any day of the week. Therefore, the requirement of blessing the wine is continual or perpetual. He first carries out a continuing obligation, then the one that is not continuing, for the former takes precedence under all circumstances. The final decision is then given by D. The Law, as is mostly the case, will be observed according to the opinion of the House of Hillel.

The *Gemara* will combine the two sets of traditions and discuss their contents. But it takes for granted that the whole is a seamless fabric of Law. It is not going to perceive that the relationships between the traditions and the ways in which they are formulated pose problems for literary analysis. We now review the Mishnah and compare the *Tosefta's* materials pertinent to it. The *Tosefta's* additions to the Mishnah's language are given in italics.

Mishnah (VIII:1)	*Tosefta* (V:25)
A These are the things which are between the House of Shammai and the House of Hillel in [regard to] the meal:	[The] things which are between the House of Shammai and the House of Hillel [as regards] the meal:
B The House of Shammai say, 'One blesses the day, and afterwards one blesses over the wine.'	The House of Shammai say, 'One blesses the day, and afterwards one blesses over the wine, *for the day causes the wine to come, and the day is already sanctified, but the wine has not yet come.*'
And the House of Hillel say, 'One blesses the wine, and afterwards one blesses over the day.'	And the House of Hillel say, 'One blesses over the wine, and afterwards one blesses the day, *for the wine causes the Sanctification of the day to be said.* *'Another matter: The blessing of the wine is continual, and the blessing of the day is not continual.'* *And the Law is according to the words of the House of Hillel.*'

The relationships between the mishnaic and the toseftan versions of the Houses' disputes are fairly clear. The *Tosefta* tends to expand the Mishnah's terse laws. Mishnah VIII:1 / *Tosefta* V:25 – the expansion takes the form of an addition to the Mishnah.

Babylonian Talmud: Gemara

This brings us to the Babylonian Talmud's treatment of our Mishnah pericope. For reasons of space, we consider only the first part of the Talmud (Babylonian Talmud *Berakhot* 51B) to our Mishnah. The Talmud is written in two languages, Hebrew and Aramaic. The use of the one rather than the other is by no means accidental. Normally, though not always, the sayings attributed to the Tannaim and statements of normative law will be in Hebrew. The comments and analyses of the Amoraim and stories will be in Aramaic. The editors' own remarks will be in Aramaic. To signify the differences, Hebrew will be in regular type, Aramaic, in italics.

To begin with, we must know that the presupposition of the Talmud is that nothing will be stated that is obvious; redundancy, it goes without saying, will not occur. But the Talmud also objects to the inclusion of well known facts. This is regarded as bad style. The reference to the 'echo which has gone forth' alludes to a story about the House of Shammai's and the House of

'for the day causes the wine to come, and the day is already sanctified, but the wine has not yet come.'

C   And the House of Hillel say, 'One blesses over the wine, and afterwards he blesses over the day,

'for the wine causes the Sanctification of the day to be said.

'Another explanation: The blessing over the wine is continual [always required when wine is used], and the blessing over the day is not continual [but is said only on certain days].'

D   And the Law is according to the words of the House of Hillel.

The *Tosefta* supplies reasons for the rulings of the Mishnah. The opinion of the House of Shammai is explained by B. You have to have the wine in order to say the Sanctification of the Sabbath. On an ordinary day, not the Sabbath, the man is not required to have wine before the meal. Therefore, the 'day', that is, the Sanctification, supplies the occasion for the wine to be brought. The day is already sanctified, for at sunset one no longer works. The Sabbath day has already begun. The Evening Prayer for the Sabbath has been said before the meal. So the Sanctification is said first. Then comes the recitation of the blessing over the wine. The House of Hillel, C, argue that what is essential is the blessing of the wine. Without wine you do not say the Sanctification of the day at all. Therefore, you bless over the wine first,

Hillel's debating for three years, until heaven intervened with the Divine Announcement, delivered by an echo, that both Houses possess the words of the living God, but the Law follows the House of Hillel. Supernatural intervention into legal matters is commonplace. The Talmud was created in a world that took for granted that heaven cared about, therefore influenced or interfered in, the affairs of men, particularly the affairs of the people of Israel, and especially those of the rabbis, who were believed to study Torah on earth exactly as it was studied by Moses 'our rabbi' in the Heavenly Academy.

Gemara (5 1 B)

A   *Our rabbis have taught:*

B   The things which are between the House of Shammai and the House of Hillel in [regard to] a meal:

The House of Shammai say, 'One blesses over the day and afterwards blesses over the wine, for the day causes the wine to come, and the day has already been sanctified, while the wine has not yet come.'

And the House of Hillel say, 'One blesses over the wine and afterwards blesses over the day, for the wine causes the Sanctification to be said.

'Another matter: The blessing over the wine is perpetual, and the blessing over the day is not perpetual. Between that which is perpetual and that which is not perpetual, that which is perpetual takes precedence.'

And the Law is in accordance with the words of the House of Hillel.

The *Gemara* opens with a simple citation of the *Tosefta* we have already studied. It then proceeds to analyze the passage.

C   *What is the purpose of* 'Another matter'?

The first peculiarity is simply the second 'reason' assigned to the Hillelites. Why should we require *two* reasons for their position, while we have only one for the Shammaites?

If you should say that there [in regard to the opinion of the House of Shammai] *two* [reasons are given], *and here* [in regard to the opinion of the House of Hillel] *one, here too* [in respect to the House of Hillel], *there are two* [reasons, the second being]: 'The blessing of the wine is perpetual and the blessing of the day is not perpetual. That which is perpetual takes precedence over that which is not perpetual.'

The *Gemara* reads into the Shammaite saying two separate reasons, and so explains that in order to balance those two reasons, the Hillelites likewise are given two.

D   'And the Law is in accord with the opinion of the House of Hillel.'

The statement of the final decision is cited from *Tosefta*, but this poses a new problem. For the Law normally will follow the Hillelites. Why say so?

This is obvious [that the Law is in accord with the House of Hillel], *for the echo has gone forth* [and pronounced from Heaven the decision that the Law follows the opinion of the House of Hillel].

Now the question is spelled out. In rabbinic lore, it was believed that, a few years after the destruction of the

Temple in 70 C E, a heavenly echo had announced that the Law follows the House of Hillel.

E   *If you like, I can argue* that [this was stated] before the echo.

F   *And if you like, I can argue* that it was after the echo, and [the passage is formulated in accord with the] opinion of [52A] R. Joshua, who stated, 'They do not pay attention to an echo [from heaven].'

Two answers are given. The first is that the final decision was formulated before the echo had been heard; the second, that it came afterwards but accords with the view of those who none the less deny supernatural intervention into the formulation of the Law, for instance, Joshua ben Hananiah, who lived at that time and was alleged to have rejected the testimony of supernatural signs.

Let us review the whole pericope.

The Talmud opens with a citation, A, of the *Tosefta*'s parallel to the Mishnah. Our chapter consistently supplements the Mishnah with the *Tosefta*, primarily in order to analyze the latter. The *Tosefta* is cited with the introduction of A, a fixed formula that indicates that a tannaitic source is quoted. Other such formulae include *We have learned*, the formula for introducing a citation to the Mishnah; *It has been taught*, introducing a teaching attributed to the authority of Tannaim, though not necessarily to a specific mishnaic teacher. These Aramaic formulae function like footnotes, providing information on the source of, or type of authority behind, materials cited in the text.

In B, the *Tosefta* we have already examined is simply stated. Then, C undertakes the analysis of the passage. The explanation and elucidation are ignored; it is assumed that these are clear. What C wants to know is why the House of Hillel give two reasons for their opinion. The 'two reasons' of the Shammaites are (1) the wine is brought on account of the Sabbath, and (2) it is already the Sabbath, yet the wine is still lacking. The Hillelites' reason then is cited without comment.

The analysis of the toseftan passage is continued by D. The statement that the Law follows the House of Hillel is regarded as obvious, since normally that is so.

A simple, 'historical' answer is provided by E: D was included before the echo had delivered its message; F then gives a somewhat more substantial response: some rabbis opposed accepting supernatural signs of the determination of the Law by heaven. Chief among these is Joshua ben Hananiah (*c.* 90 C E), who, when presented by Eliezer ben Hyrcanus with supernatural evidence on behalf of the latter's position, proclaimed, 'It – the Torah – is not in heaven' (Deut. XXX:12). Thus D is credited to Joshua, who would not accept the heavenly decision and, therefore, had to provide earthly counsel based on reason.

The Palestinian Talmud

We now consider the equivalent treatment of the Palestinian Talmud for the same unit of Mishnah.

Mishnah (VIII: 1)

The House of Shammai say, 'One blesses the day and afterwards one blesses over the wine.'

בָּרוּךְ אַתָּה יָיָ אֱלֹהֵינוּ מֶלֶךְ
הָעוֹלָם בּוֹרֵא פְּרִי הַגָּפֶן

The famous Bird-head Haggadah, *produced in the Upper Rhine about 1300, illustrates the ritual observances to be carried out during the Passover service, but in order not to infringe the law forbidding images, human beings are shown with the heads of birds. This miniature relates to the blessing over the wine by the household head.*

And the House of Hillel say, 'One blesses over the wine and afterwards one blesses the day.'

A *What is the reason of the House of Shammai?*

The Sanctification of the day causes the wine to be brought, and the man is already liable for the Sanctification of the day before the wine comes.

What is the reason of the House of Hillel?

The wine causes the Sanctification of the day to be said.

Another matter: Wine is perpetual, and the Sanctification is not perpetual. [What is always required takes precedence over what is required only occasionally.]

The *Gemara* first cites the available toseftan explanations for the positions of the two Houses. All that is added is the introduction, 'What is the reason. . . .'

B R. Yose [*c.* 150 CE] said, '[It follows] from the opinions of them both that with respect to wine and *Havdalah*, [the prayer marking the end of the Sabbath day and the beginning of the week of labour], wine comes first.'

Now, Yose begins the analysis of the two opinions. He wants to prove that both Houses agree the wine takes precedence over *Havdalah*. That is, you bless the wine, then you say *Havdalah*.

'*Is it not the reason of the House of Shammai* that the Sanctification of the day causes the wine to be brought, and here, since *Havdalah* does not cause wine to be brought, the wine takes precedence?'

Since the Shammaites hold that the reason wine comes after the Sanctification is that the Sanctification is the cause, then, when the prayer is *not* the reason for saying a blessing over wine, as in the case of *Havdalah*, the wine will normally take precedence over the prayer.

'*Is it not the reason of the House of Hillel* that the wine is perpetual and the Sanctification is not perpetual, and since the wine is perpetual, and the *Havdalah* is not perpetual, the wine comes first?' Similarly, since the Hillelites say what is perpetual takes precedence over what is episodic, they will agree the wine takes precedence over *Havdalah*. So both Houses will agree on this point.'

C. R. Mana [3rd century] said, 'From the opinions of both of them [it follows] that with respect to wine and *Havdalah*, *Havdalah* comes first.'

Now Mana wants to turn things upside down. The opinions of both Houses are such that they will agree *Havdalah* takes precedence over wine – the opposite of Yose's claim!

'*Is it not the reason of the House of Shammai* that one is already obligated [to say] the Sanctification of the day before the wine comes, and here, since he is already obligated for *Havdalah* before the wine comes, *Havdalah* comes first?'

The Shammaites' principle is that a person carries out the obligation that already applies – the Sanctification – before the obligation that does not *yet* apply. The reason the Sanctification comes before the wine is that, as soon as the sun sets, you are obligated to say the Sanctification. But the wine only comes later.

'*Is it not the reason of the House of Hillel* that the wine causes the Sanctification of the day to be said, and here, since the wine does not cause the *Havdalah* to be said, *Havdalah* comes first?'

The Hillelites are going to agree with Mana's proposition, for they say wine comes first when it is the pretext for some other prayer. But the wine is not the pretext for saying *Havdalah*.

D. R. Zeira [3rd century] said, 'From the opinions of both of them [it follows] that they say *Havdalah* without wine, but they say the Sanctification only with wine.'

Zeira draws from the foregoing the necessary consequence: you may say *Havdalah* without wine. But you may say the Sanctification only in connection with wine. The House of Hillel make this point clear: wine is not the pretext for saying *Havdalah*. Therefore, *Havdalah* may be said without wine. The House of Shammai say that the Sanctification of the day supplies the pretext for reciting the blessing over the wine. The *Havdalah* does not. So they will agree also. Zeira's point seems well founded.

    E   *This is the opinion of R. Zeira, for R. Zeira said, 'They may say Havdalah over beer, but they go from place to place [in search of wine] for the Sanctification.'*

Now Zeira's rule is applied. You must go in search of wine for Sanctification. But *Havdalah* may be said over beer.

Let us now review the argument as a whole.

Once again, we observe that the Talmud's interest is to find the reasons for the Laws. These will be elucidated, then criticized according to logic and finally tested against the evidence supplied by related rules. Like the Babylonian *Gemara*, the Palestinian one draws heavily upon the *Tosefta*. Its inquiry into the *Tosefta*, however, tends to be more thorough and systematic than the one we have seen in the Babylonian version. The opinions of both sides are examined; questions addressed to the one will be brought to the other. Thus a perfect balance is maintained throughout. Then new issues will be raised and worked out.

The stage is set by A for what is to follow, rapidly reviewing the reasons given in the *Tosefta* for the opinions of the respective Houses. Then B, C and D draw conflicting inferences from the foregoing in respect to *Havdalah*.

Yose's view, B, is that both Houses agree that the wine comes before *Havdalah*. The Houses' principles are reviewed. As to the Shammaites: which one supplies the pretext for the other? *Havdalah* does not require wine, therefore the wine will take precedence. As to the Hillelites: what is 'perpetual'? The wine. The wine, therefore, is going to precede *Havdalah*. So both Houses will agree that the order is wine, *Havdalah*.

Mana, in C, takes the opposite view. If the reason of the House of Shammai is that the obligation to say the Sanctification is already present, then *Havdalah*, the obligation of which *likewise* is already present, will come first. If the reason of the House of Hillel is that wine comes first on the evening of the Sabbath because the Sanctification may not be said without it, then at the end of the Sabbath, *Havdalah* will come first, for it *may* be said without wine. The dispute is made possible, therefore, because both Houses give two reasons for their opinions. Yose concentrates on one of the reasons for each of the Houses, Mana on the other.

Zeira, D, then concludes that, in the opinion of both Houses, *Havdalah* may be said without wine, but Sanctification may not. Then E provides an abstract formulation of Zeira's view.

Theology and literature

The literary character of Talmud has emerged from an examination of the development of a single unit of thought. It remains briefly to state the fundamental theological conviction of the Talmud.

The supposition of the Talmud is that order is better than chaos, reflection than whim, decision than accident, rationality than force. The Talmud's purpose is so to construct the disciplines of everyday life and to pattern the relationships among men that all things are made intelligible, well regulated and trustworthy. Its view is that order and rationality are not man's alone. Man is made in God's image. And that part of man that is like God is the thing separating man from beast: consciousness. It is when we use our minds that we act like God.

All reality comes under the discipline of the critical intellect; all is therefore capable of sanctification. Torah, represented by Mishnah, reveals the way things are, whether or not that is how they actually may be at some particular time or place. Reality surpasses particularities and derives from the plan and will of the Creator of the world, foundation of all reality. God looked into the Torah and created the world, just as an architect follows his plan in making a building. The single whole Torah, in two forms, underlies the one seamless reality of the world. The search for the unity hidden by the pluralities of the trivial world – the supposition that some one thing is revealed by many things – these represent in intellectual form the theological and metaphysical conception of a single unique God, creator of heaven and earth, revealer of one whole Torah, guarantor of the unity and ultimate meaning of all human actions and events.

God supplies the model for our mind. Man, therefore, through reasoning in Torah penetrates God's intent and plan. He attains revelation by learning Torah. The rabbis of the Talmud believe they study Torah as God does in heaven; their schools on earth replicate the Heavenly Academy. Just as God puts on *tefillin* (phylacteries), so do they. Just as God visits the sick, comforts the suffering and buries the dead, so do they. In studying Torah they seek the heavenly paradigm revealed by God in his image and handed down from Moses and the prophets to their own teaching. If, therefore, the rabbis of Mishnah and Talmud learn and realize the divine teaching of Moses whom they call 'our rabbi', it is because of the order they perceive in heaven: the rational construction of reality. Torah reveals the mind of God, the principles by which he shapes reality. Torah is revealed in the principles of reality. These were discovered even by the most modern-thinking men, the rabbis of the 2nd century who make Mishnah and know they are making Mishnah, yet who call it part of the Torah God revealed to Moses on Sinai.

The modes of learning are holy because they lead from earth to heaven, which synagogue prayer, or fasting, or other, merely tolerated, holy rites cannot. Reason is the way, God's way; the holy person is the one who is able to think clearly and penetrate profoundly into the mysteries of Torah, and, especially, its so very trivial laws. In context, those trivialities contain revelation and serve to impart to the one who grasps them the fully realized experience of the sacred. The task, as I said at the outset, is to surpass ourselves: to undertake the reconstruction of reality through the interpretation of what *is*, in terms of what can and should be. The experience of sanctification both through the intellect and of the intellect is the mode of the transcendent laid open, once for all time, by the rabbis of the Talmud.

Another detail from the Bird-head Haggadah, *showing the household head washing his hands before eating the vegetables dipped in salt water. The whole ceremony of the Seder meal is described and illustrated on p. 26.*

Theology and history

It remains to ask: what is the shape of this world of meaning so carefully and precisely constructed by Mishnah and its accompanying Talmud? What the Talmud has to say about the world is summarized in one word: 'holiness'. And the question raised by the Talmud is how man achieves holiness, how he becomes like God, in the ordinary and everyday world. We already have noticed that central to the talmudic view of life is the conception that man plays the crucial role in imparting meaning and significance to ordinary and unimportant things. The reason is that the intention and will of man transform what is ordinary into what is holy. To take one unimportant example: if one has a pile of a hundred apples and sets aside two of them for whatever purpose, those two apples are not thereby made holy, sanctified or consecrated. But if, when setting aside those two apples, one has the intention of setting them aside *for the priest as the heave-offering* from that pile of one hundred apples, then those two apples become holy and cannot be eaten by ordinary folk or used for secular purposes. Again and again, in diverse areas of Law, the importance of the human will comes to the fore.

To Mishnah and the commentaries that flow from it, what one wants constitutes a fundamental norm of reality, because when Mishnah took shape all that was left for ancient Israel was the unfettered will of the people, the hope of Israel to endure. The most important fact about the Mishnah and the Talmud is that they come into being after the destruction of the Second Temple in 70 CE, and after the devastation by the Romans of the southern part of the Land of Israel, the territory of Judaea, a consequence of Bar Kokhba's disaster of 132 CE. The former brought out, in all their stark and urgent character, the issues of sin and punishment, atonement

and reconciliation, originally encountered by the ancient Israelites in the aftermath of the destruction of the First Temple in 586 BCE. But now, it is clear, the biblical message required repetition and amplification. For, in olden times (586), the people had sinned and atoned, and God had forgiven them, they believed, by restoring them to the Land and by allowing them to rebuild the Temple. After 70 CE the question of why the disaster had come about, and what sin punished thereby, necessarily arose, but the question was now more difficult to answer. The reason is that, having sinned, suffered, achieved atonement and found reconciliation with God one time, the Israelites could not so readily re-enter the trying process without some sense that the old meanings yet endured, that the whole system had not, in fact, collapsed in the ruins of the Temple. The disorder of a formerly orderly world is best symbolized by the Temple, where not a stone was left upon stone in the aftermath of its ruin.

The stress on exactness, precision and order revealed in mishnaic language and literature, on the one side, and in talmudic analysis and argument, on the other, has to be seen against the background of the chaos of the 2nd century CE and beyond. In a time when old meanings and ancient certainties seemed no longer to explain and construct meaning, Mishnah's stress on the reconstruction of a world of precision and order constituted a firm response, an assertion that, amid chaos, the order of language is yet available. It will then follow that what effects the orderliness of the world is the will of man, which, through careful speech and careful deed, imposes regularity and trustworthiness upon ordinary life. The everyday deeds of men living their mundane lives constitute the last realm over which the Israelite ruled, lacking now a government, a Temple, an administration of his own. It then would be in that one remaining area of inner autonomy, the commonplace life at home and in the village, that the Israelite would construct the world of meaning and would transcend the vagaries of history, with its disasters and its disappointments. Here at home, through patterned language and a life of infinite structure, he would find his way to a world above history and beyond time. A much later folk-song states the rabbinic view very clearly: the nations of the world think that their kings are kings, but the Holy One, blessed be He, is the King of kings of kings. The Israelites would be ruled by that supreme monarch, and the effects of his dominion would be seen in their every deed and gesture, whether in the realm of morality or ritual, whether at home or with Gentiles.

When we turn to the concrete details of mishnaic and talmudic Law, we see the main lines of the delineation of the divine realm of dominion, the definition of the reality subjected to God's rule. Mishnah itself, as we noticed above, is divided into six parts. These six divisions describe for us the aspect of life and of metaphysical reality to be sanctified and consecrated to the Divinity through the will and right intention of man. The six are *Zera'im*, seeds; *Mo'ed*, seasons; *Nashim*, women (thus: family life, personal status); *Neziqin*, torts; *Qodoshim*, holy things; and *Tohorot*, purities. The issues of the Law, to state matters somewhat more broadly, are in three parts: (1) agriculture and the passage of time; (2) family, home, property relationships, civil and criminal affairs; and (3) the cult and purity laws, principally affecting the cult but additionally concerning the table at home, to be conducted in a state of cleanness as if it were the Lord's altar in the now-devastated Temple. The first of the three divisions makes clear that Mishnah proposes to subject to Divine Law, and so to sanctify, the economy of the people, which was chiefly agricultural, and the passage of time and the seasons. It begins with these for the obvious reason that the life of the Israelite society rested upon the foundation of agriculture and took shape in the differentiation of days, weeks and months through the agricultural calendar. The second division concerns practical matters of society, which also have to be subjected to close regulation and sanctification: the status of the individual, the rights to property and the transfer of property, the creation of the family, the protection of man's property and life from criminal trespass, and the proper organization of social institutions of government. The third division treats the service of the Lord in the Temple, through the conduct of the cult, and the protection of the cult from unseen forces of danger and contamination already described in Leviticus.

This last division of course makes the question urgent: who kept this Law? For we realize that there was no Temple at the time that Mishnah came into being, and vast areas of the Law in fact lay in desuetude. Mishnah then describes a world out of relationship with ordinary, everyday reality. Those parts of its Law that can be kept are kept. But the study of Mishnah and its accompanying Talmud encompasses the whole. And what that means is that Mishnah and Talmud constitute principally a document describing a reality that is within, on the one hand, or in time to come, on the other. People enter that reality by learning about it, before they actually experience it. The whole of being is subject to inner processes of learning and reflection, even though, in practical fact, a negligible part of the whole may be brought into concrete being. The whole realm of literature and Law, learning and deep human anguish and yearning, is meant to reconstruct that ancient, now ruined realm of cult and priesthood, to serve God through the continuing study of his Revelation and through the making of that study into the motive and definition of the purpose and meaning of Israelite life.

Chapter Five

The Ritual and Music of the Synagogue

AMNON SHILOAH

THE SURVIVING HERITAGE OF JEWISH MUSIC represents an intricate web of groups and congregations and a baffling variety of styles. This variety is a direct consequence of the long period of dispersion, frequent forced migrations and the repeated uprooting of large communities. The resulting confrontations with different musical cultures inevitably left their imprint on the musical traditions of the Diaspora.

The question that faces us at the outset is whether it is possible to detect any common denominators within this multiplicity, and to uncover, beneath the dust of the Diaspora, a path that leads back to the music of ancient Israel. This thorny question has been the subject of prolonged research, but the answers remain in the realm of speculation. They all suffer from one very serious drawback: the lack of musical evidence. Before the 19th century, very few examples of musical notation have survived outside the European tradition. The recent discovery of a notated Oriental chant transcribed by Obadiah, the 12th-century Norman proselyte, is of very great interest, but is only a drop in the ocean of Jewish musical history. We are still groping in our search for concrete examples of even the recent, let alone the remote, past.

Some scholars believe that one last resource remains – the study of Jewish music preserved in oral tradition, mainly in the Near Eastern countries, on the assumption that it contains traces of more ancient forms. The success of this exercise will depend on being able, firstly, to compare each individual tradition with the indigenous music of its host country in order to determine its peculiarities, and, secondly, to compare all the resulting Jewish traditions together in order to arrive at a common denominator, if any. Such an intensive investigation has not yet been carried out. An attempt on a smaller scale was made some sixty years ago by the pioneer Jewish ethno-musicologist A. Z. Idelsohn. He recorded, analyzed and compared the many musical traditions still existing in Jerusalem. His work was valuable in many respects, but his belief that the different extant biblical cantillations can all be traced back to a common pre-Exilic archetype remains doubtful.

The families of Jewish music

Today, in that same Jerusalem, on the spot that witnessed the highest achievements of the music of ancient Israel, the same traditions continue to live side by side, though affected by the process of change resulting from new contacts. In front of that venerated remnant of the Temple – the Western Wall – one can still see individuals of various physiognomies and provenances intoning day and night the same Psalms of David, scanning them with the same accents and devotion, although in different intonations. Common texts, common language, common functions and principles of rendition, both in these Psalms and in other biblical cantillations and prayers, combine to give an image of unity to diversity. The more we move towards the sophisticated liturgical forms of the hymnody, the more acute are the differences of style, which become decisive in the non-synagogal music. In this latter category, the multitude of languages and musical idioms reflects the diversity of neighbouring styles much more than any specifically Jewish tradition. In view of the difficulty, therefore, of treating Jewish music as anything like a homogenous entity, I shall attempt to divide it into families according to style. These stylistic families will be found to correspond roughly to the families of Jewish dialects. Although we often find several stylistic layers within the same family, because of the intermingling of groups arriving from different places at different times, these differences tend to diminish and disappear in time, becoming assimilated into the predominant style. In certain cases, however, they do continue as ramifications of the original style.

We can distinguish seven broad musical traditions or styles.

The Yemenite tradition: this musical tradition is one of the oldest. The first Jews in the Yemen emigrated from Palestine between 100 BCE and 70 CE. They lived in relative isolation, although their music was influenced by Negro and neighbouring tribes before and after the advent of Islam, as well by features of Ethiopian and Indian music, due, respectively, to the long occupation of the Yemen by the Ethiopians and to trade relations with India. Nevertheless, their biblical cantillation, which displays only major divisive accents, provides evidence for the earliest stages of the system of Masoretic accents – the *te'amim*. Their hymns and songs are rich in poetical forms and genres. In performing them, men and women distinguish themselves in antiphonal and responsorial singing, rudimentary polyphony and special tone quality. This community is known for its great talent for the dance, in which it takes profound delight. Yemenite steps have become the model for new folk-dancing in Israel. Ramifications of the Yemenite style are to be found in the tradition of the small community of Cuchin (India) and the Ethiopian Falasha.

The Babylonian tradition: the Jewish colony in Babylonia dates back to the destruction of the First Temple in the 6th century BCE. This oldest Diaspora settlement played a dominant role for many centuries, but its very ancient traditions could hardly withstand the overwhelming influence of the music established after the advent of Islam in the 7th century CE. Only a few archaic elements have survived, notably in certain forms of lamentations and chanting. It is possible that some other features of the distant past still exist in the repertoire of some Kurdistani Jews of the area. Yet, despite certain particularities and local stylistic differences, the style elaborated in contact with the music of the world of Islam can be considered common to the communities living between Turkey and Tunisia. The secular music of Kurdistani Jews does not fall into this category. As a result of recent migrations of Iraqi Jews to Southeast Asia, ramifications of this tradition are to be found there.

The Persian tradition: this tradition, whose roots go back to the biblical period, is a meeting-point of different musical styles. It displays more or less the same features that have characterized Persian civilization down to the present day, that is, special musical expressiveness mingled with a feeling of sorrow and mystical exaltation and an ideal of voice colouring characterized by rich vocal production. This style has migrated to Jewish settlements in Afghanistan, Bukhara, Georgia and the Caucasus, where it co-exists with other styles.

The western Mediterranean tradition: on the western shores of the Mediterranean, old communities in Italy, Greece and Turkey preserve remnants of traditions formed after the destruction of the Second Temple. These remnants continue to co-exist with later and more powerful traditions.

The Maghribi tradition: the Jewish settlements in southern Morocco and the Atlas mountains are said to go back to the period of the Second Temple, but the style now prevalent in this region is to some extent impregnated with Berber elements. The plain biblical cantillation differs considerably from the pan-Sephardi chant practised in other parts of the Maghrib. The music of this area and the folk-music of other North African countries were not affected by the Andalusian style, which predominated in the urban centres.

The Sephardi and Portuguese style: the period between 900 and 1492 CE witnessed the efflorescence of Jewish sacred and profane music in the Iberian peninsula. With the Expulsion of the Jews from Spain and Portugal, a rich legacy of typically Castilian hymns and folk-songs migrated with the exiles and was faithfully preserved in their new homes. One wave spread over the Ottoman Empire, where in the course of time it was absorbed into the Turkish tradition. A second wave reached Morocco; a third made its way through Portugal to Italy, Amsterdam, Hamburg and London, where it was Westernized to a very large extent. However, in all three

ramifications, several hymns, particularly those of the high holidays, are still sung with the same basic melodies. The Judaeo-Spanish *romancero* was confined to a more restricted area, and the art music of Andalusia, notably that of the *nuba* (a form of suite), was perpetuated in the corpus of *bakkashot* (supplications) in many Jewish Maghribi centres.

The Ashkenazi tradition: the most recent of the traditions to develop is that of the Ashkenazi Jews. It begins at the end of the Carolingian epoch, after 900. The first settlement was in the German and French Rhineland. In the 14th century, mass emigrations to Poland and Russia took place as a result of persecution. In this new environment, the influences from Slavonic music led to the establishment of the Eastern branch. Although a distinction between the Eastern and Western branch must be recognized, there was a constant interaction between them and they always shared many common features. Their biblical cantillation distinguishes itself by giving each accent a distinct melodic motif. The consolidation of the Ashkenazi tradition of sacred song culminated in the school of Jacob ben Moses Moellin (*c.* 1356–1427), commonly called the Maharil, to whom are ascribed the traditional melodies named *mi-Sinai* tunes; he is also considered as the patron of Askenazi *hazzanut* (the musical style of the precentor).

'The ancestor of all who play'

Our major source for knowledge of the music of ancient Israel is the Bible. The first musical reference, ascribing the invention of music to Yuval, 'the ancestor of all who play the *kinnor* and *'ugav*' (Gen. IV:21), occurs in the creation stories. This legend is the source for medieval speculations on the origin of music. Later Jewish and Muslim commentators viewed the invention of music with some hostility, associating it with the depravity and satanic delusion that led to the Flood. Interestingly, in Muslim sources the credit of the invention was transferred to Yuval's father, Lamech, and his lament (Gen. IV:23–4) is quoted as the first song performed by man.

After the Flood, music clearly appears in connection with a variety of different functions. In battle we find the trumpets and the *shofar* (ram's horn) used as noise-maker and strategem to frighten enemies. In victory rejoicings, women sang and danced to the accompaniment of frame drums. The singing of dirges by male or female mourners is strongly attested. Stringed instruments (lyres) were used in early periods to stimulate prophetic inspiration and for therapeutical purposes. In the cult, the priests' trumpets participated in ritual functions, in sacrificial ceremonies and also in royal coronations. In the same context we find the use of tintabulating little metal plates attached to the tunic of the High Priest. At a later stage, towards the end of the First Temple, occur certain forms of organized cult music performed by families of Temple singers and instrumentalists.

A significant change in this cult music occurs after the Return from the Babylonian Exile and the establishment of the Second Temple. It takes the form of an artistic sacred act. Post-biblical sources, such as the Mishnah, the writings of Philo, Josephus, and the sectarians of Qumran, as well as actual archaeological remains of musical instruments, complement our knowledge and furnish us with a profusion of accurate details on the large musical ensemble that participated in the cult, and on the status of the musicians. They were organized in twenty-four watches. Each watch counted at least twelve principal singers, occasionally reinforced by additional singers, especially including boys' voices. The vocal ensemble was accompanied by twelve instrumentalists, who played on nine *kinnorot,* two *nevalim* (types of lyre) and one pair of cymbals. According to our sources, the Levites, who were in charge of this musical cult, guarded their art jealously and abstained from teaching it to others. The Book of Psalms provided the bulk of the texts used in the cult music of the Temple. Many of the Psalms contain musical indications and names of instruments, but some of these indications, which appear mainly at the heads of Psalms, were already enigmatical by the time of the Septuagint. Some modern musicologists agree with the assumption of Jewish medieval commentators that they refer to modes or pre-existing known songs. As to the instruments named in the Psalms, they belong to the nineteen identifiable instruments mentioned in the Bible, including two types of lyre, the trumpet, clarinet, drum, cymbal and the *shofar.* With the destruction of the Second Temple in 70 CE, the music that enhanced its services disappeared forever, together with the Levites who cultivated it. Out of the whole instrumental ensemble, only the *shofar* survived in Jewish usage. Limited to the performance of rudimentary signals and formulae, the *shofar* is mainly used on the occasion of the New Year holiday and the Day of Atonement. Its ancient magical virtue has been considerably reinforced by symbols and mystical concepts elaborated in the kabbalistic literature, namely its function of softening the Divine Judgment and fighting against the forces of evil.

Detail of an ivory plaque from Megiddo (the whole object is reproduced on p. 38) showing an early type of hand-held lyre, 12th century BCE.

The development of synagogal music

The establishment of the synagogue as a place of divine service preceded the destruction of the Second Temple, but only after the Exile did it become the focal point of worship where music became involved in many ways. In this place of meditation, intimate prayer replaced the pomp of the Temple's music and the refined instrumental art of the Levites; the musical element was reduced to a discreet support of the spoken word and simple chanting of the prayer. At this early stage any member of the congregation could lead the prayer as a 'delegate of the community' (*sheliyah zibbur*). In addition to the plain prayer tunes there were certain basic forms of chanting related to the rendition of the Psalms, the Pentateuch and other biblical books.

The performance of Psalms, or the psalmody, was conditioned by their poetic form and structure. The psalmody, which became an important element of Jewish and Christian worship, gave rise to certain musical patterns characterized by a bipartite structure, a recitation note framed by an initial motif and final cadence. The pronounced bipartism contributed to the development of various responsorial ways of performance, with the text distributed among groups of singers. The ancient surviving pattern of psalmody disregards the detailed accents later added to the Psalm text by the Masoretes. It may be noted that in later periods the singing of Psalms became variegated and took different forms according to the function it fulfilled. Thus, for instance, Psalm XXIX is sung like a solemn march on Sabbaths and holidays during the procession that accompanies the scroll of the Torah back to the Holy Ark. In Aleppo, on the occasion of the celebration of *bakkashot* (see below), Psalm XCII, amplified by additional texts, served as a point of departure for sophisticated vocal improvisation and frequent passage from one mode to another.

The reading of the Pentateuch, the Prophets and certain other books of the Bible in worship and in study is always enhanced by musical intonation governed by fixed rules and practices. The practice of Bible chanting is attested as early as the 2nd century CE. This cantillation was based upon conventions handed down by oral tradition. The musical element in this chanting had to be entirely subordinated to the text. Written reading accents developed from the 6th century onwards; out of different graphic representations, called *te'amim*, the Tiberian system, codified by Aaron and Moses Ben-Asher (10th century), became the single accepted system and was imposed upon the whole of Jewry. In none of the systems was an attempt made to establish a specific melodic motif for each accent; the vague musical motifs admitted were principally meant to sustain the disjunctive and conjunctive accents and to emphasize the grammatical and syntactical function of the text. In practice, a certain margin of flexibility was left to the individual reader. Furthermore, separate conventions exist for the Pentateuch, the prophetic books and for several of the Hagiographa. In fact, except for the Pentateuch, the rendition of the accents is partial and selective. The style of rendition is also affected both by regional styles (such as the Yemenite, the south Moroccan, the northern Mediterranean, the Sephardi and the Ashkenazi) and by the context of performance, which determines certain variants. For instance, the intonation used in the collective cantillation learned by children in *heder* (religious school) differs from the solemn and ornate style used on some specific and festive occasions.

The emergence of the piyyut

The *piyyut* (a religious hymn specially composed by the cantor as an elaboration of the biblical readings) made its first appearance in Palestine in the 6th century, and quickly became an integral part of synagogue liturgy and a determinant factor in the development of synagogal and paraliturgical music. In contrast to the simplicity of the prayer and biblical cantillation tunes, whose principal aim was to emphasize the meaning of the text, the musical setting of the *piyyut* opened the way to a new approach and new developments. The recourse to organized poetical constructions and symmetrical structures necessarily led to an increase in the importance of the musical component. According to a practice still vigorous in oral traditions, text and melody were usually created by the same individual, who also publicly performed the fruits of his talent. Hence, the *piyyut* demanded the virtuosity of a gifted creator and soloist and the response of the congregation, encouraging him to compose and to gratify their expectations. Consequently, the new function of the professional solo singer, the *hazzan* (precentor), came into existence. In the earliest stage, the singing of the *piyyut* was essentially solo. Gradually, however, the discreet participation of the congregation increased and in certain genres of the *piyyut* led to the introduction of sections of a refrain character; this seems to indicate the presence of an institutionalized small choir complementing the solo performance of the *hazzan*. As to the music used on these occasions, we know nothing about its nature and provenance. The long period separating this epoch from the banishment of music from synagogal worship, after the destruction of the Temple in 70 CE, permits us to assume that the precentors may have had recourse, at least in part, to the contemporary music of their environments.

In the 10th century, a new period of efflorescence began for the *piyyut* on the soil of the Iberian peninsula. It was through contact with Arabic literature that the poet and grammarian Dunash ben Labrat (after 950) introduced the prosody and forms of Arabic poetry into Hebrew. The period between 900 and 1400 witnessed the blossoming of a Hebrew religious poetry of hymnodic character, which has survived in the liturgy of almost all Jewish communities. The emergence of the new strophic forms of *muwashshah* (*shirei ezor* in Hebrew) with their fresh popular flavour, also left an imprint on religious hymnody and on semi-religious and popular songs. Many of these strophic songs have survived or were imitated in the Maghribi corpus of *bakkashot*, the Jewish Yemenite hymnody and the like. The occurrence today

In this unusual miniature from a Hebrew Psalter written in medieval Italy, the choirmaster, in the margin, conducts his five singers across a column of text. The book in front of them shows Hebrew letters and neumatic notation.

among Sephardi communities, spread over an extensive area, of common tunes in the singing of some lamentations and penitential hymns seems to indicate an affiliation to a common source, which is the tradition established in Spain. In the domain of folk-song, it is obvious that the typical Castilian element is still discernible in the corpus of the Judaeo-Spanish *romancero*, despite the modifying influences of the new host countries.

The 16th century marks an important new step in the development of the *piyyut* in a mystical environment—the small Galilean town of Safed, where the Kabbalists and mystics fixed their centre. Some of the fundamental kabbalistic concepts provided an impetus for the enhancement of the musical significance of certain prayers and celebrations and influenced the development of liturgical and extra-synagogal music. The holiness and symbolic meaning of the Sabbath – 'the Queen' – gave rise to such religious hymns and *zemirot* (songs sung at home) as 'Lekhah dodi', 'Assader bishvahim', 'Yedid nefesh' and 'Yah ribbon 'alam'; these, as well as the celebration of the three repasts of the Queen, have spread throughout the Diaspora. The favourite theme of the song at midnight, when the Holy One enters the Garden of Eden to delight with his righteous ones, was influential in the development of the midnight vigil as well as the night-time singing of pious brotherhoods, such as the 'watchers of Dawn' in Italy, the 'Singers of *barukh she-amar*' in Bohemia and the singing of *bakkashot* in Syria, Turkey and Morocco. In these centres, the singing of *bakkashot* has become the highlight of musical life, where the best musical talents display a sophisticated art music not very different from that of the host countries, but often perpetuating features that have disappeared from the borrowed repertoire. One of the foremost poet-musicians of the Safed kabbalistic circle was Rabbi Israel Najjara (1550–1620), who fostered music in its broadest meaning. Many of his hymns were written to the tunes of secular Spanish and Turkish songs.

The science of music

The first scientific treatment of music in Jewish literature appeared at the same time as the emergence of the first known Arabic musical treatises. The few theoretical chapters and passages written by Jewish authors living in countries under Muslim domination show obvious indebtedness to Arabic writings. Indeed, the earliest example of this kind, the chapter on the eight rhythmical modes and their influence on the human soul contained in the *Book of Beliefs and Opinions* by Saadya al-Fayyūmī Gaon (died, 942), is little more than a compilation from a work by al-Kindī (died after 870). However, Saadya's interest in the science of music extended to biblical exegesis, and he provides intriguing explanations of some obscure musical passages. Still following in the footsteps of the great Arab theorists, some later Jewish writers, such as Moses ibn Ezra, put forward the claim that all musical theories and knowledge, as well as musical instruments, originated in the Bible. In later periods, this view led to the belief among Provençal and

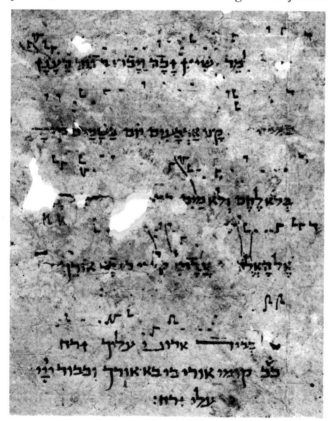

A unique document shedding light on medieval Jewish music has recently been discovered. This is an excerpt from the piyyut, 'Mi 'al har Horev', intended for Shavu'ot or Simhat Torah. Its melody in neumes was notated by the 12th-century Norman proselyte named Obadiah. The text is by a certain 'Amr and the composition, of unknown authorship, is in the style of the western monodic chant of the Middle Ages. It is one of the earliest notated documents in the history of Jewish music.

Italian Jewry that their fervent cultivation of the art and science of music meant the recovery of their own ancient possession.

Between the 12th and the 14th centuries, the main scene of musical activity moved to the areas of northern Spain, southern France and the north of Italy. Here, an additional influence, that of Latin culture, left its mark – for instance in the treatise *De numeris harmonicis* written by Levi ben Gerson (1288–1344) at the request of Philippe de Vitry, and the Hebrew translation by Judah ben Isaac of a comprehensive Latin treatise on musical theory. Of greater importance are the notated examples by Obadiah the proselyte (12th century) and the transcription of *te'amim* in square notation by Solomon Minz (1483) and the non-Jewish humanists J. Boeschenstein (1500), J. Reuchlin (1518) and S. Münster (1524).

The hazzan and hazzanut

Al-Samaw'al al-Maghribi, a 12th-century author who converted to Islam, made a distinction between the prayer chanted by the delegate of the congregation without melody and the *hizāna*, which consists of rendering the *piyyutim* with melody and with response from the congregation. This statement shows the direct and close relationship between the *piyyut* and the emergence of the function of the *hazzan* (precentor), who was supposed to command a good deal of musical and poetical creativity. But in the communities outside Europe we can observe a clear separation between the function of the *hazzan*, who leads the prayer and whose competence is judged by his piety and personal respectability, and the *paytan*, the singer of *piyyutim* and perhaps creator of new hymns. The latter, who might be a professional musician, also participates in family rejoicings. His role in the synagogue is limited and counterbalanced by the spirit of prayer and devotion. He may sometimes be one of the two assistants (*somekhim* or *mezammerim*) who support the *hazzan* on festive occasions.

The term *hazzanut*, used to designate specific melodies and the musical style of the solo singer, is attached rather to the Ashkenazi tradition, whose norms are ascribed to the Maharil, the legendary patron of Ashkenazi *hazzanut*. To him are attributed the traditional melodies called *mi-Sinai*, which became the common heritage of the Ashkenazi synagogue in both Western and Eastern Europe. This tradition is also characterized by the use of typical synagogal modes, called *shtayger* (a Yiddish term equivalent to mode and manner). The custom of providing the cantor with two assistants underwent special development in Ashkenazi synagogues. From the 17th century onwards, one of the two assistants was a boy descant, called 'singer', the other an adult, called 'bass'. They accompanied the cantor with short improvised figures, which opened the way to the introduction of polyphony into synagogal music. The Eastern branch of Ashkenazi *hazzanut* developed a style characterized by emotional and dramatic power mingled with a certain virtuosity, provoking a rabbinical reaction that accused the *hazzanim* of 'theatrical' or 'operatic' modes of performance. Nevertheless, until the contemporary change towards a spirit of formal artistry, the traditional solo style known as 'Polish' *hazzanut* preserved most of its typical features, notably the composition of melodic cells that proceed like a chain of small movements, the predominance of the principle of variations and a certain rhythmical freedom.

As a result of the process of Westernization, Ashkenazi *hazzanut* has undergone significative changes. Towards the middle of the 18th century, cantors started to write new *hazzanut* compositions of their own, designed to suit the demand for virtuosity and coloratura display. Although the basic structure remains in the line of the tradition, the melodies were principally borrowed from post-Baroque music.

The Hasidic niggun

Hasidism arose in Eastern Europe in the middle of the 18th century, a distressing time for the Jews, and rapidly gained favour among the masses. Its doctrines are discussed at greater length in another chapter. They had strong affiliations to the Kabbalists of Safed, and the expression of exuberant joy was regarded as a chief religious duty. Musically, Hasidism is notable for the ecstatic dance and for the *niggun*, a form of song, often sung to meaningless syllables, based on the synagogue modes and Ukrainian and Slavic folk-songs and dances. It was conceived as bridging the gap between the sacred and the profane, leading the soul to mystical exaltation. The emotional meaning of the music was considered superior to and stronger than the spoken language, so that the *niggun* was believed capable of expressing the inexplicable to the ignorant, who in turn could convey through it his naïve thoughts, wishes and prayers. Most of the Hasidic leaders were fond of music and talented enough to create new *niggunim* of their own. The foremost inventors of *niggunim* were Yehiel Michael of Zloczov (died, 1761), and Shneur Zalman of Ladi (died, 1813). Nevertheless, the substantial part of the material for their songs was drawn from the folk-music of the non-Jewish environment. By so doing, the Hasid believed that he was saving the tune from its impure state and sanctifying it through certain transformations. Hasidic music has exerted a considerable influence on Jewish art music compositions and Israeli popular music.

Music, synagogue and society

The invasion of synagogal worship by art music at different times and places had to face rabbinical opposition, which varied in degree according to the circumstances. Even in the early stages the rabbis regarded the principal exponents of *piyyut* singing with a certain suspicion. From the time of Hai Gaon (*c.* 1000), most Talmud commentaries and legal decisions uttered repeated warnings against the sensual and destructive power of music, a power incompatible with the true feeling of devotion. But, apart from a few cases of intransigence, there were tacit or discreet concessions respecting private rejoicings, such as weddings and circumcisions, as well as some festive occasions, such as the carnival-like feast of Purim, the festival of Simhat Torah (rejoicing of the Torah) and the semi-religious holidays. This tolerance gave rise to certain abuses, as the numerous rabbinical condemnations testify.

The active participation of Jewish professional musicians in the musical life of their respective countries seems to have been a determinant factor in the

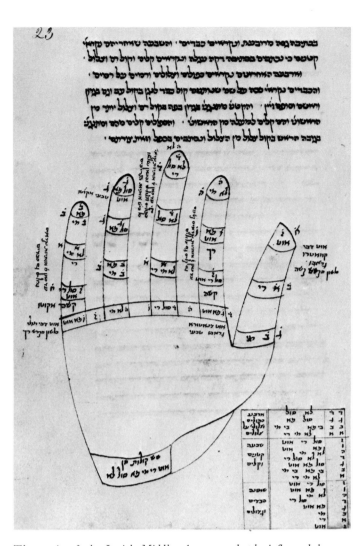

The music of the Jewish Middle Ages was deeply influenced by contemporary writings. This diagram from a 13th-century treatise by Judah ben Isaac is a Hebrew version of the so-called 'Guidonian hand' (after Guido of Arezzo, the 11th-century Benedictine theorist), used for teaching the hexachord: the teacher pointed with a finger of one hand to the joints of the other, twenty in all, to remind his pupils of the order of the notes.

introduction of art forms to Jewish music. Indeed, whenever and wherever Jews were given free access to musical life, gifted musicians appeared and left the direct or indirect imprint of the heritage of their own community. Even in certain Muslim countries, where the religious attitude was strong enough to restrict the activity of professional Muslim musicians, particularly the playing of instruments, Jewish musicians found ways of displaying their talents. Thus, we find flourishing Jewish bands in Morocco, Persia, Bukhara, Turkey and, at a later date, Iraq. Though discredited and even held in reproach by their fellow Jews, these musicians were always called upon to enhance rejoicings, and even participated in the synagogal worship and other religious celebrations, like the singing of *bakkashot*. In Andalusia, professional Jewish musicians were active in both Muslim and Christian society.

From the 16th century onwards, Western musical techniques were increasingly integrated into synagogal music. This movement is first attested in northern Italy. In the prospering communities of Mantua, Ferrara and Venice, the new current was endorsed by the ideological assessments and legal decisions of two rabbis: Judah Moscato (died, 1590) and Abraham Portaleone (died, 1612). The former, in a sermon entitled 'Higgayon bekhinnor' ('Meditations on the Lyre'), demonstrated the legitimacy of musical art in Judaism; the latter, in his book *Shiltei hagibborim* (*Shields of the Heroes*), extolled the Levitic song and the musical instruments of the Temple. Outstanding among the numerous Jewish musicians and composers who participated in musical life was the famous composer Salomone de Rossi (*c*. 1565–*c*. 1628). He wrote thirty-three hymns for three to eight voices for the synagogue in the characteristic style of the epoch under the title 'hash-shirim asher li-Shelomo'. These choral synagogal compositions were not designed to replace the traditional synagogal chant.

An analogous phenomenon occurred in another Jewish centre, Amsterdam, where the flourishing Portuguese community included gifted musicians and commissioned festive cantatas from both Jewish and Gentile composers. One of the best-known Jewish composers is Abraham Caceres, who in the early 18th century wrote compositions for the synagogue in contemporary style.

In the area of popular and semi-professional music, the band of *klezmerim* (a term deriving from the Hebrew *kli zemer* = musical instrument) played an important role in the process of Westernization in central and Eastern Europe. Such bands, sometimes organized in guilds, were active from the second half of the 17th century onwards in both Jewish and non-Jewish society. They enhanced family rejoicings and certain festive occasions, they played at fairs and in taverns, in processions and solemn celebrations. Known for their particular skill and virtuosity, these music-makers exercised various musical styles from elegiac tunes to frivolous dances, on their violins, cellos, clarinets and cymbalum.

The reform in the synagogal chant and worship

As we shall see in later chapters, at the beginning of the 19th century, a movement for social emancipation began among the Jewish communities of Western Europe. The spirit of the French Revolution and the German philosophical school as well as the Napoleonic synagogal constitution stimulated the already existing tendencies to revise the synagogue service. Animated by a desire to integrate into surrounding society, the Reform movement in Germany sought to beautify Judaism and to remove from synagogal worship all 'ugliness of medievalism', regarded as a symbol of the condition of exile incompatible with social emancipation. The first notable reformer of the synagogue ritual was Israel Jacobson (1768–1828). In 1801, he established in Seesen, Westphalia, a boys' school giving formal instruction in music. The pupils formed a choir that sang German chorales to organ accompaniment. Jacobson abolished the traditional cantillation of the Pentateuch and Prophets as well as the prayer modes and replaced them by a plain declamation; he also excluded the function of the *hazzan*. Jacobson's reform was soon taken up in Hamburg where the new trend was consolidated. Here and elsewhere, the corale-like hymns for the Temple were mostly composed by Christian composers, and were performed on special occasions by a mixed choir. Numerous choral collections of this sort appeared during the first half of the 19th

century. In 1845, the young Reform rabbis recommended the employment of instruments in the synagogue even on Sabbaths and holidays, arguing from a spiritual and religious standpoint.

The radical reform introduced by Jacobson stirred up stormy opposition and, in fact, did not go beyond a certain sector of the larger communities. Later, in its new centre in the United States, the Reform movement became a promoting agent for the creation of important new compositions by such composers as Ernest Bloch, Arnold Schoenberg and Darius Milhaud and has been a powerful force in encouraging scientific research in Jewish music.

The moderate and less far-reaching reform of the chief cantor of Vienna, Salomon Sulzer (1804–90), became a model for many European synagogues and left a deep impression on the subsequent generations of cantors in Europe and in America. Sulzer, a gifted musician and a friend of Schubert, did not aim to abolish the traditional chant but to remodel it in a dignified and musically satisfactory shape. He explains his programme in the introduction to his collection of synagogal chants: *Shir Zion* (Volume I published in 1840, Volume II in 1866). The collection contains choral compositions and recitatives with organ accompaniment. He achieved his purpose by renouncing the coloratura brilliance of the cantorial solo and eliminating the improvised accompaniment of the two assistant singers (*meshorerim*). He replaced all these by compositions based on conventional 19th-century harmony, which needed well rehearsed part-singing. In this process, Jewish music lost some of its traditional features, such as its modal character, and became melodic in the Western European sense. Among the most distinguished representatives of this trend are Louis Lewandowski (1823–94), who was the first to introduce authentic organ music to the synagogue, and Samuel Naumburg (1815–1880). Sulzer's favourite disciple, E. Birnbaum, transported the music of the 'improved service' to the United States.

Music in the synagogue

The musical items that have a place in the synagogue services may be roughly divided into two types – biblical texts, and prayers and hymns.

Of the first, the most important is the cantillation of the lessons from the Pentateuch on the Sabbath and on festivals, followed by the Haftarah, a passage from the Prophets, which has its own mode of cantillation. Certain passages from the Pentateuch, like the 'Song of Moses', are sometimes chanted in the course of services apart from this.

On specific occasions, books from the third category of biblical writing, the Hagiographa (i.e. everything not included in the Pentateuch and the Prophets), are intoned to their respective tunes; Esther at Purim (since that festival celebrates the deliverance of the Jews through Esther); the Song of Solomon at the evening service of the Sabbath from Passover to Pentecost; and Lamentations on the ninth day of Ab, when the destruction of the Temple is commemorated.

Special musical performances of Psalms take place on various occasions. Psalm XXIX, for instance, is sung at the Sabbath evening service and – to a different tune – to accompany the procession of the Torah in several

Eastern communities. Specific Psalms open the solemn service of the three pilgrimage festivals. Psalms CXIII–CXVII together make up the Hallel, or thanksgiving service, sung on certain festivals.

The second type of music – prayers and hymns – consists of eight categories:

1   The 'Eighteen Benedictions', a collection of prayers which seems to have grown up during the period after the destruction of the Second Temple. These are repeated by the precentor. They include the so-called *trisagion* – 'Holy, holy, holy' – and the Benediction of the Priests. On high holy days several hymns are added and there is usually an introductory hymn.
2   The *Kaddish*, a prayer in Aramaic, which formed the basis of the Christian 'Lord's prayer', and is occasionally chanted by the precentor.
3   *Kabbalat Shabbat* (the welcoming of the Sabbath); this includes the mystical hymn 'Lekhah dodi', chanted to various melodies.
4   Hymns that close the service, such as 'Yigdal Elohim', 'Adon 'olam' and 'Ein Kelohenu'.
5   Hymns for the invocation of rain (Feast of the Tabernacles) and dew (Passover).
6   Lamentations, the commemoration of the destruction of the Temple, noted above.
7   Special and penitential hymns (*selihot*) sung at the New Year and Day of Atonement services.
8   The *Hakkafot* (circuits) sung at the festival of the Rejoicing of the Torah, the day when the annual cycle of the readings from the Pentateuch has come to an end with the last verse of Deuteronomy and begins again with the first verse of Genesis.

In search of a Jewish musical style

The early 20th century marks the beginning of attempts to create a 'national' Jewish music. Under the influence of the national Russian school, Joel Engel in Moscow and the group of young Jewish composers and musicians who made up the Petrograd Society for Jewish Folk-Music (1908–18) started collecting and arranging Jewish folk-tunes for concert performance. This led to the integration of this material into their own compositions, with the object of establishing a typical national style. Members of this group were also involved in writing incidental music for the Yiddish and Hebrew theatre.

Jewish musical tradition has descended to modern times through many different channels, all greatly modified by regional and national styles. That of Russia was one. Marc Chagall sketched this Jewish violinist at a wedding in 1911.

The group dispersed after 1920. In 1938, J. Engel and J. Stutschewsky went to Palestine, where they played a prominent role in musical life, but their style was soon overshadowed by other national tendencies, namely the Mediterranean school. In America, L. Saminsky, J. Ahron and J. Yasser were much encouraged by American synagogues, who sponsored the composition of a new synagogue music.

The transcription and publication of oral material had started in the middle of the 19th century, and was mainly the work of historically minded cantors who were concerned by the rapid propagation of the new style of *hazzanut*. The first serious exploration of traditional Jewish music was carried out by E. Birnbaum in America. In 1905, his disciple A. Z. Idelsohn went to Jerusalem, where, as we saw earlier, he recorded and transcribed the musical repertoires of many Oriental communities. His *Thesaurus of Hebrew Oriental Melodies* in ten volumes became a corner-stone for Jewish ethno-musicological research. A second wave of systematic documented recordings emerged after the creation of the State of Israel in 1948. Continuing research on Jewish musical traditions has already produced rich fruit in historical and ethno-musicological studies.

III
DIASPORA:
JEWS UNDER CHRISTIANITY & ISLAM

The Jews in Spain

The Jews in Byzantium and Medieval Europe

The Jews under Islam
6th – 16th centuries
c. 1500 – today

The dilemma of co-existence faced the Jews throughout the whole of the Middle Ages, whether they lived under Christian or Muslim rule. In both communities the Jews were an alien minority, never free from the threat of hostility and active persecution. In this situation there were two conflicting pressures. One was to assimilate, to conform, to adapt to the life-style of the host country, with the accompanying danger that they would lose their identity and compromise the purity of their beliefs. The other was to withdraw, to separate, to insist on the absolute exclusiveness of Judaism, thus provoking more fear, misunderstanding and aggression in their Christian or Muslim neighbours. The history of the Jews in Spain, for all its achievements, shows the tragic impossibility of reconciling these two attitudes in a world where religious passions were all-pervasive. After attaining positions of trust and power under the Muslims, after weathering the transition to Christian government during the Reconquista, the Jews were expelled in 1492, to initiate a new Diaspora.

One of the most interesting examples of co-operation between the two communities in Spain is the Alba Bible, some illustrations of which have already been reproduced in earlier sections. It was commissioned in 1422 by Don Luis de Guzmán, Grand Master of the Order of Calatrava. Dissatisfied with existing translations of the Old Testament into Castilian,

he approached Rabbi Moses Arragel of Guadalajara to prepare a new translation from the Hebrew, with commentary and illustrations. To help with the Christian interpretation of difficult passages he arranged for two theologians of Toledo to be available. Rabbi Moses agreed, and the work was eventually finished on 2 June 1430, when the manuscript was handed over. The magnificent full-page illumination reproduced here commemorates that event. Don Luis sits enthroned in the centre. At the sides, in front of the two towers, stand a Franciscan and a Dominican, the two theologians. Between them, on a smaller scale, are members of the Order of Calatrava performing the Acts of Mercy – feeding the hungry, clothing the naked, visiting the sick, consoling the bereaved, burying the dead. At the bottom of the whole page, we see the ceremony of delivering the manuscript. Surrounded by members of the Order, Don Luis receives it from a kneeling Rabbi Moses. Curiously, the page at which it is open – Chapter I of Genesis – is shown neither in Hebrew nor in Castilian, but in the Latin of the Vulgate.

The fact of this happy collaboration between Christians and Jews is as surprising as it is impressive. Savage persecutions had been a feature of Spanish life for at least thirty years, and only sixty more were to elapse before every Jew in Spain would have to face the awful choice of apostasy or exile. (1)

comer. beuer. caltcar. uestre. visitar. confolar. enterrar.

Spain: the promise

A hybrid culture seems to lie at the very roots of Spanish civilization. *Above:* a trilingual inscription on a sarcophagus from Tortosa dating from about the 5th century CE. In Hebrew, Latin and Greek, it commemorates a girl called Meliosa, daughter of Rabbi Jehudah. (2)

Islamic art gave much to Judaism, including a delight in abstract pattern. Typically, however, in this 15th-century biblical page (*right*), the Jewish scribe has transformed the endless interlace into words – it is micro-writing containing verses from the Psalms. (5)

Christian rulers claimed the allegiance of Jews. The coat-of-arms on a seal of Todros ha-Levi (*below*), one of a Toledan family equally renowned as statesmen and Kabbalists, incorporates the three towers of Castile. (4)

Jew and Muslim pay homage to the life of a Christian king. These inscriptions (*above left*) in Arabic and Hebrew, separated by a band bearing the lion and the castle, emblems of León and Castile, adorn the walls of Ferdinand III's royal chapel in Seville Cathedral. A similar point is made by the decoration of

The words 'this matzah' proclaim this to be a page from the Haggadah (*below*), but the grid of ingeniously interlocking lines is, like the example on the left, purely Islamic. In the centre is the most curious detail of all – a door with hinge and keyhole, very like that of an alms chest. (7)

the Transito Synagogue in Toledo, where a commemoration plaque (*above right*) records the Jewish benefactors of the synagogue beneath the same royal coat-of-arms; the stuccoists were almost certainly Muslims, and some of the words are Arabic written in Hebrew letters. (3, 6)

The Holy Land remained a potent symbol to the Jews of Spain and many tried to return there. This detail from the Catalan World Atlas of 1375–7 shows the coast of Judaea, Jerusalem, the Jordan and the Dead Sea. The cartographers, Abraham and Yehuda Cresques, were Jewish. (8)

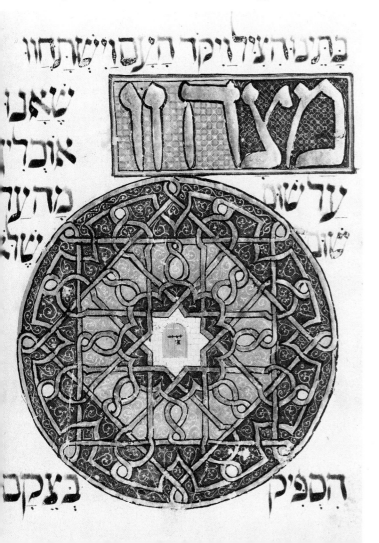

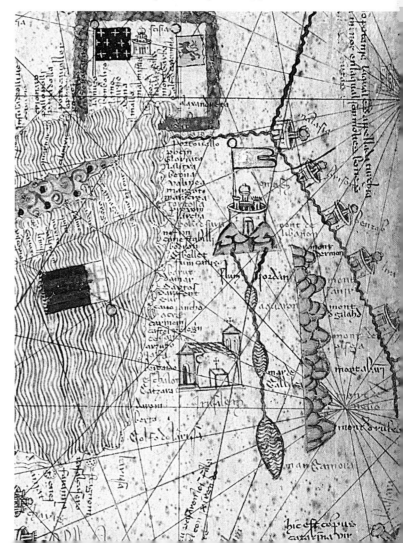

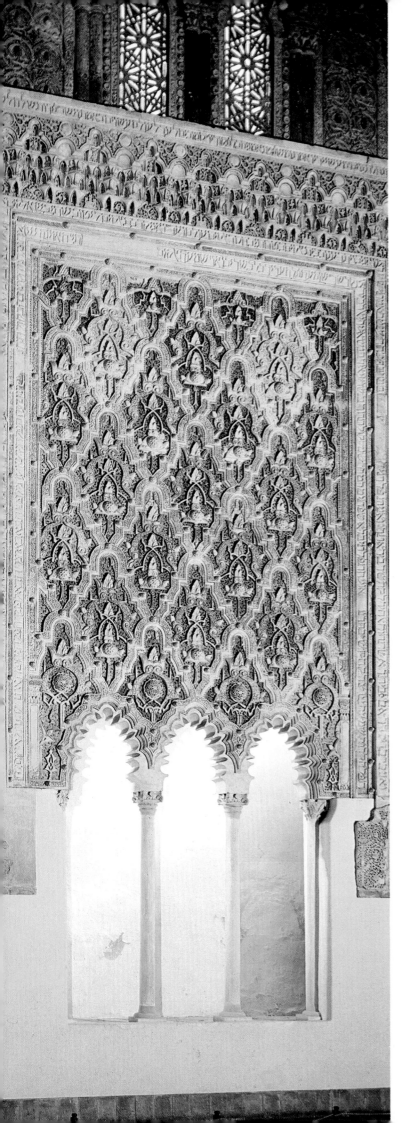

Medieval Spain presents such a web of cultural influences that many works defy attribution to a single religious group. The Transito Synagogue (*left*) is probably the creation of Muslim craftsmen working to a Jewish commission. Of the inscription framing the central panel, parts are in Hebrew, parts in Arabic using Hebrew letters. A Portuguese Bible (*above*) may well have been produced by a similar arrangement with Christian illuminators; the familiar arms of Castile and León appear at the foot of the page, which contains the end of Kings II. *Below:* the decoration of this Seder plate includes four Hebrew words, of which three are misspelled. Was the Muslim artist badly briefed or simply careless? (9, 10, 11)

The splendid synagogue carpet
from Spain, now in Berlin (*right*), is
one of the mysteries of Jewish art.
Dating from the 14th century, it is
among the earliest of all Spanish
carpets. Its connection with the synagogue seems proved by the resem-
blance of the repeated pattern to the
form of the Ark, and the stem holding
them together is clearly a stylized Tree
of Life. A modern Jew would hesitate
to place such a representation on the
floor where it might be walked on.
Yet it is certain that the Ark was
included in mosaic floors in the
Roman and post-Roman periods (for
instance, at Beth Alpha). Some of the
Ark shapes incorporate the six-
pointed star, and to complicate matters still further there is a band of
ornamental *kufic* lettering round the
border. (12)

Rabbi Moses receives instruction from one of Don Luis de Guzmán's experts, the Franciscan Brother Arias. (It is interesting to note that, although clearly a highly respected man, he still has to wear the discriminating badge on his shoulder, seen also in the frontispiece, pl. 1.) Christian interpretations of the Old Testament naturally had to be included in the rabbi's commentary, along with the Jewish views. But it was a true cultural exchange. Rabbi Moses constantly introduces traditional Jewish interpretations. The death of Moses, for instance, is thus described in Deuteronomy XXXIV: 'So Moses the servant of the Lord died there in the land of Moab, according to the word of the Lord. And he buried him in the valley of the land of Moab over against Beth-peor: but no man knoweth of his sepulchre unto this day.' The words translated 'he buried him' can also mean 'he was buried', but Rabbi Moses considers it most likely that God himself buried Moses, as he is seen doing in this miniature. (13, 14)

When the Christians reconquered the Spanish peninsula (a long and bitter process lasting many centuries) the position of the Jews became more precarious. But the possibility of peaceful co-existence was never closed. Many Christians appreciated the value of the Jewish contribution to culture and society, and even the most bigoted had to recognize their economic usefulness. Jews acted as tax-farmers. Court Jews were often important and trusted members of the government. In 1465, Nuno Goncalves included the judicial head of Portuguese Jewry (*below*) in his St Vincent Altarpiece showing the court of Henry the Navigator. (15)

But Christian hostility to the Jews, actively encouraged in Spain by the Church, hardened from the 14th century onwards. Grotesque stories of their hatred of Christ and the Virgin circulated and were believed. *Above:* three episodes from a manuscript produced at the court of Alfonso x. A Jew steals a picture of the Madonna and Child from a shrine outside a church; he is about to put it down a well when he is seized by devils who forthwith cart him off to Hell. Stories of the desecration of the eucharistic host were common. In a Valencian painting (*below*), the Jews try in all possible ways to destroy it – hammering it, slicing it with a sword, boiling it over a fire – but in vain. *Right:* detail of a Catalan work of the 14th century, specifying the wilful errors of the Jews. The text in the panel is part of the Hebrew Bible (dealing with Korah's rebellion and Aaron's rod), which the Jews persist in 'misinterpreting' (i.e. not seeing it as a prefiguration of the True Church) because they have been blindfolded by devils. Motivated by beliefs such as these, Christian crowds rioted in Seville in 1391 and thousands of Jews were murdered. For a hundred years the process was to be repeated, periods of bloodshed alternating with periods of illusory peace. (16, 17, 18)

The Expulsion order (*below right*) was signed by Ferdinand and Isabella on 31 March 1492, shortly after the conquest of Granada. The Jews were given three months to leave a land where they had lived for more than a thousand years. (19)

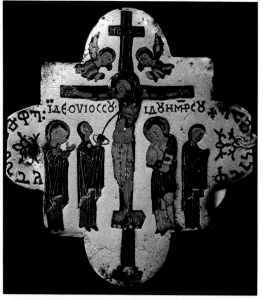

Christian attitudes were inevitably conditioned by the Church's understanding of the Jews' role in God's plan. On the one hand, the Hebrew Bible (which Christians called the Old Testament) contained the preparation and prophecy of Christ's coming. On the other, the Jews had rejected Christ (a view vigorously propounded in the Gospels) and thereafter persisted in wilful blindness. The representation of Ecclesia, the Christian Church, as a woman looking clear-eyed to God, and the Synagogue as a similar woman, blindfolded and holding a broken staff, became a commonplace of Christian iconography. One of the earliest examples is this Byzantine enamel (*left*), where Ecclesia catches Christ's blood in a chalice while Synagogue, not yet blindfolded, turns away from him. (21)

In theory the legal position of Jews in medieval Europe was better than it usually turned out to be in practice. Outside Spain, the earliest Christian legislation concerning Jews is that of Byzantium, where a Jewish community had been established for centuries. *Above left:* an 8th-century gold medallion from Byzantium, bearing a menorah, a *shofar*, a *lulab* and the enigmatic inscription in Greek: 'For the vow of Jacob the leader, the pearl-seller.' (20)

The 'Sachsenspiegel', or 'Mirror of the Saxons', is a unique code of laws compiled between 1220 and 1235, though the earliest extant manuscript dates from the 14th century. Two miniatures from it (*right*) illustrate laws relating to Jews. In the first, the Jew is confirmed as legally equal to the non-Jew; wearing his pointed hat, he stands with a group facing the Count of Saxony. In the second, anyone who kills a Jew incurs execution. (22, 23)

136

Marriage certificates survive from an early date. This one, written in 1342, comes from Krems, in Austria. Such documents go back to talmudic times, and were part of the legal requirements of a Jewish marriage. They served primarily to protect the wife's interests, setting out the financial obligations of the husband and specifying the amount due to her in case of a divorce. (24)

The tax position of Jews was unenviable. Taxes, often harsh, were imposed upon Jewish communities as a whole, and it was the responsibility of their own councils to see that the taxes were paid. Some (called *korobka*, or 'shopping basket') were levied on consumer goods, particularly slaughtered animals, others directly on income. These collection boxes (*right*), built for safety in the gallery of the Old-New Synagogue in Prague, are from the 17th century. (25)

Inside the community

The ghetto phenomenon, contrary to popular belief, is not something that goes back to the Middle Ages. It began in 16th-century Venice ('Ghetto', meaning 'Foundry', is the district where the Jews were obliged to live in 1516) and spread rapidly in Italy, Germany and Eastern Europe. Often the ghettos were walled and furnished with gates that had to be locked at night. While this was a burdensome restriction on Jewish liberty, it could also work for their protection. Most of the old ghettos have now been demolished, but in many cases the cemeteries remain. That of Prague (*below*) contains the tombstones of several cemeteries crowded together – a poignant symbol of ghetto-life itself. (26)

'Rabbi Jacob ben David', reads this tombstone from Basel, 'killed on the Sabbath day. His reward is in the Garden of Eden with the other saints of the world.' The implication is that he was killed in a persecution. (27)

Trades are represented on these two tombstones at Prague, of an apothecary (*above*) and a tailor. (28, 29)

'Weighing in the scales' was a metaphor of judgment. This page from a German prayer-book of 1379 contains the end of one *piyyut*, dealing with repentance and atonement, and the beginning of another, relating to Sabbath Shekalim, the collection of money for charity. (30)

The wealth of many 16th- and 17th-century European Jews was a result of their special status, financial expertise being one of the few skills they were allowed to cultivate. *Above:* a gold coin struck in the royal mint of Wroclaw, by the Prague Jew, Isaac Meit, between 1546 and 1549; and a Jewish marriage ring of the same date, with inset jewels and Hebrew inscription. (32, 33)

For alms: a strongbox built into the wall of the Stara Synagogue in Cracow, Poland, in the 17th century. Outside pressures upon the Jews had the effect of encouraging a high standard of community care. (31)

Spice-boxes, used in the *Havdalah* ceremony, at the close of the Sabbath, were often of intricately worked silver. This Bohemian example (*below*) is modelled on a tower with four corner spires. (34)

A bizarre imagination often transformed the Hebrew letters into creatures of a fantasy world. *Above:* two facing pages of a 13th-century Spanish Haggadah with, on the right, a line of script made up of writhing patchwork monsters with human and animal heads. On the left, two human-headed birds balance on poles which emerge from the mouths of gryphons. To the right, another human-headed creature confronts a dog, while below, a multicoloured lion supports another pole ending in a human face. On a third page from the same manuscript (*left*), the letter *aleph*, first in the Hebrew alphabet, is cleverly turned into a rider on a horse. (35, 36, 37)

עֲמֹק אוֹיְמֵיהּ שַׁבָּת שַׁבַּתּוֹ לְקַיְּמֵיהּ

Assorted devils, a bird pecking a flower and a blue-faced Jew wearing a pointed hat are some of the weird images embodied in the letters of a German 14th-century *machsor*, a prayer-book for festivals. (38)

When the Jews of Constance waited upon the newly elected Martin v in 1417 (*below*), offering the Torah, with a request that their privileges be restored, he said ungraciously, 'You have the Law, but understand it not. The old has passed away and the new been found.' (39)

For the Jews of Germany, the later Middle Ages was a time of renewed persecution. At the time of the Black Death, a terrified population accused them of poisoning wells in order to destroy Christendom, an accusation revived in the 16th century (*below*). (40)

The 'miracle' of the Geniza

In 1896, two English ladies on holiday in Cairo came across some fragmentary Hebrew manuscripts for sale, and bought them as curiosities. Returning to Cambridge, they showed them to the Reader in Rabbinics at the University, Solomon Schechter. He realized the antiquity of the find, journeyed to Cairo and located the place from which the manuscripts had come – the *geniza*, or storeroom, of an old synagogue. It had always been Jewish practice not to destroy any sacred text, but simply to relegate it to a store. The Cairo Geniza not only contained far more than liturgical texts: it had lain practically untouched for nine hundred years, a huge treasury of records going back to the 10th century, dealing with every aspect of Jewish life – religious, professional, social and literary.

Schechter crated 100,000 fragments and shipped them back to England. This photograph shows him sitting in the midst of the collection soon after it arrived in Cambridge. The condition of the manuscripts makes study difficult, but historians have extracted a vast amount of fresh information from them, and there is enough to occupy several more generations. Suddenly a Jewish community in medieval Cairo has become as intimately known as one of today. (41)

Some spectacular pages of the Geniza manuscripts had been taken before Schechter's arrival by private collectors and are now to be found in libraries all over the world. These three (*left* and *right*) are in Leningrad. They are from a copy of the Pentateuch written on parchment in 1008 CE. In the first, verses from Isaiah have been arranged to form a diagonal pattern, with the Masoretic commentary going round the circumference. The other two pages contain tributes by the scribe, Samuel ben Jacob, to his patron, Mevorah ben Joseph ha-Cohen, one in a six-pointed star, the other in a stylized version of the Ark. (42, 43, 44)

From medieval Egypt, too, come these leaves from Bibles written in the 10th or 11th century. One (*above*), from Deuteronomy XIX, derives from the Karaite sect, which regards the Torah as uniquely authoritative and rejects the Talmud. It is in three columns, with the Masoretic commentary in smaller script at the bottom. The other (*below*), from Psalm LXIX, was once decorated along the right-hand margin and bottom. (45, 46)

The thriving life of the Jewish communities in Egypt is vividly illustrated not only by the Geniza documents but also by such material remains as these doors from a synagogue at Fustat. They date from the 12th century, their deeply undercut panels showing an artistry indistinguishable from Islamic work of the same period. The lintel above was made in the following century and has an inscription referring to a rabbi called Solomon: 'Our master and teacher, Solomon, who died in his youth. May God let him rest in peace and may God's spirit give him peace.' Fustat's period of prosperity was by this time coming to an end; from the 8th to the 12th century it was the chief commercial centre of the whole Fatimid Empire, but finally had to yield to the younger city of Cairo only a few miles away. (47)

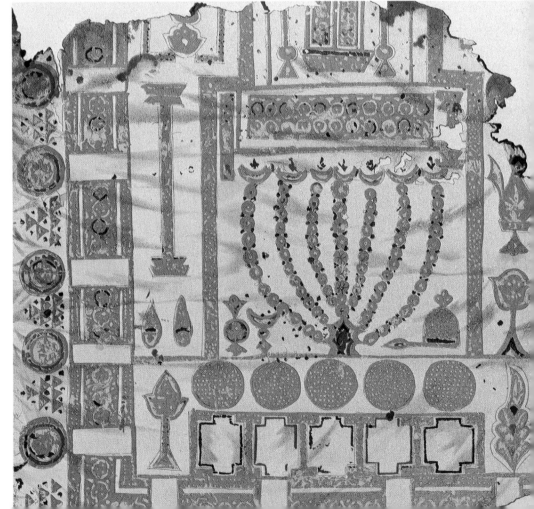

'To Abraham and Masliah the sons of Maimon': the dedication of what must have been a particularly rich copy of the Pentateuch (*above right*). The scribe was Solomon ha-Levi, the date 930. *Below:* another fragment from the same manuscript, showing the Temple instruments, including the menorah (see p. 210, pl. 30). Like the pages shown earlier, these were among the Geniza fragments taken to Leningrad before Schechter could acquire them. (48, 49)

Wedding and home

A marriage contract dated 1128 (*left*) was one of the documents recovered from the Cairo Geniza. It begins with seven lines of highly ornamental script, reproduced on a larger scale (*opposite*), with the letters arranged in groups divided by a sign like a fleur-de-lis; this section, in rhyming verse, conveys good wishes to the bridal pair. After that come the more prosaic details, written in less elaborate but still beautiful script. It lists the objects that a young couple belonging to the Jewish middle class could expect to possess, and on the rest of this double page are shown examples of the things mentioned, dating from approximately the same period. (50, 51)

The necklace and metal dish (*below*) could have been owned by Jew or Muslim indifferently. The necklace is of silver with three pendants containing pearls and semi-precious stones. The dish incorporates the six-pointed star, but this is an Islamic as well as a Jewish symbol. (52, 53)

בשעה מעולה ‏ ועונה מהוגה ‏ ושמחה וצהלה
וידרשם שתהלה ‏ ומילולי שאלה ‏ לאדונינו
ראש ישיבת ‏ גירון עולה ‏ גאון יעקב
יברכהו שוכן מעלה ‏ בן אדונינו ‏ שלמה ה
ראש ישיבת גאון יעקב ‏ נשמתו בעדן
ולדתו הלכמה ‏ ולבית הקהלה ‏ ישישו
יציעו ויפרחו ‏ יזהירו ויזרחו ‏ יבורו יצלחו

Objects for display and for use: a silk cloth, a ceramic pot with the inscription 'perfect blessing' (which could equally well have been Jewish or Muslim) and an ornamented brass vessel, again with the six-pointed star. The Geniza documents reveal a closely integrated society, with lawyers, physicians and merchants co-operating readily for mutual benefit. Jews in Muslim countries, as in Christian, were by this time almost exclusively town-dwellers. (54, 55, 56)

To teach the alphabet to the young Hebrew scholar, this book was produced in 10th-century Egypt. The menorah forms the frontispiece. On the facing page are the first three letters (compare the *aleph* with the highly fanciful one in pl. 37), with different vowels indicated by subscript marks. The scribe sketched the contours, while the child filled them with colours. In this playful way he learned to read and write. (57)

The 'carpet' page of a Karaite Bible of the 10th century (*left*) could be mistaken for the first page of a Qur'ān. And, indeed, the Hebrew text of this manuscript is written in Arabic characters. (58)

The Dayyenu is a traditional poem going back to the early Middle Ages, which found its way into the Seder ceremony. Its theme is the goodness of God, and it consists of a repeated formula beginning with 'If': 'If he had not saved us from Egypt ... taken us across the Red Sea ... given us the Torah ... etc.' – still 'it would have been enough' (the meaning of the word *dayyenu*). On this page from a 12th-century Haggadah, the opening word 'If' (reading from right to left) is singled out for ornamental treatment. (59)

Babylon continued to shelter a Jewish community after the Muslim conquest. *Below:* page from an 11th- or 12th-century Bible in a Babylonian or Persian hand. The text, from Deuteronomy XXXII, is surrounded by a prettily coloured border, and there are other patterns, including the six-pointed star, between the columns. The Masoretic commentary is made into a series of semicircles at the bottom. (60)

The Yemen became a distinctive centre of Jewish cultural life, notable especially for its schools of mysticism. In this 'carpet' page (*below right*) from a Pentateuch produced at San'a' in 1469, the top and bottom panels carry an Arabic inscription giving the date and the name of the scribe. (61)

Under Ottoman rule

The Jews of the Ottoman Empire attained positions of wealth and influence in many fields – finance, trade and the professions. In 1547, a French traveller wrote that most of those who practised medicine were Jews. This coloured etching (*below*), dating from a few years later, 1568, bears witness to the solid prosperity of Jewish doctors. The caption tells us that the hat is 'a high topped cappe died of redde scarlet.' (64)

Kalfas of the harem were frequently Jewish. This one, holding her staff of office, is dressed in the height of fashion for around 1720–30. (63)

◁ **Before the Ark** of an Ottoman 18th-century synagogue, hung a curtain (*left*), which at first sight could be an Islamic prayer-mat. At the top, words from Psalm CXVIII; but the niche underneath could be a *mihrab*, and is the design in the centre a menorah or a group of mosque lamps? (62)

A Jewish tombstone in a cemetery near Istanbul follows conventional Ottoman design but has a Hebrew inscription. (65)

Jewish goldsmiths and jewellers were common throughout the Ottoman Empire in the 16th and 17th centuries, in contrast to Christian Europe, where they were debarred from entering the guilds. During the 19th century, however,

The entertainers of the sultan's court were often Jewish. In another page from the 'Book of Festivals' we see a procession going round the Hippodrome of Istanbul (identified by the column and the three-headed serpent); it includes three Jews wearing the red hats already mentioned. Two of them are acting as gaily caparisoned hobby-horses. (66)

The Muslim attitude was not one of complete sympathy and toleration for the Jews. The Qur'ān contains several derogatory remarks about them, and in lives of the Prophet they are represented in humiliating defeat after a battle at Medina. In this 16th-century miniature of the incident, they wear contemporary costume with the red fez. (68)

they tended to be squeezed out of the more lucrative professions by restrictive laws. This detail showing Jewish jewellers in a booth is from Murad III's 'Book of Festivals', a record of entertainments in 16th-century Istanbul. (67)

The synagogues of the Ottoman Empire reflect contemporary mosque design, as those of European countries reflect that of churches. In this example at Istanbul, the *bimah*, the platform from which the Torah is read, is on the left and the Ark is on the right, with the carved Tablets of the Law above it. (69)

The stereotyped image of the Jew, which gained currency in the 19th century, may perhaps be attributed to popular reaction at non-Muslims being made equal to Muslims. *Left:* two puppet-figures showing a Jewish musician, with tambourine, and a rich Jew, holding the key to his money-box. (70)

153

Syria: a 17th-century Purim jug for wine, in etched amber glass. The inscription on the neck is in Arabic, on the body in Hebrew. (71)

The Yemen: early 19th-century marriage certificate (*right*), elaborately decorated with pictures of Jerusalem and the other holy places. The actual text is enclosed in an arch entirely composed of lettering. (72)

Salonica: an 18th-century Chanukah lamp, with Neo-Classical scroll and acroterion forms. The eight depressions at the bottom are for the oil lamps, the holder on the left for the single lamp from which the others are lit. (73)

Baghdad: another marriage certificate, dated 1815. In contrast to the Yemenite example, this one is wholly abstract in design, relying entirely on fine calligraphy. (74)

The Jews of Salonica were among the longest established and most influential of the Ottoman Empire. Although in 1912 the city passed from Turkish to Greek rule, old photographs show the traditional ways of life continuing in the 20th century.

A prosperous family in Salonica in the 1890s. The father wears the Turkish fez; mother and the older girls have dresses reflecting the fashions of Western Europe, while the old woman and children show the influence of local Greek costume. (75)

Community welfare has a long history among the Jews under Ottoman rule, and such organizations were maintained under the Greeks. *Above:* two orphanages in Salonica, photographed in 1926. The motto on the wall reads 'May you merit to live many years.' (76, 77)

Sarajevo, 1910: a wealthy Jewish family in the Serbian capital poses at a wedding. There is outwardly little to distinguish them from the local population. (78)

Education and medicine (*right*) were organized by charitable bodies financed from both within the Ottoman Empire and outside. In the upper picture a school play is being performed, possibly on the theme of Judas Maccabaeus. (79, 80)

The Jews in Persia drew close to their Muslim neighbours in many details of their daily lives, adopting their dress, artistic conventions and language. In these two portraits of a bride and bridegroom (*left*), the inscriptions are in Judaeo-Persian, i.e. Persian written in Hebrew characters. The bride, making up her eyes, is called Rachel, the bridegroom, playing the guitar, ben Solomon. The date is about 1840, and the style – Qajar – very typical of Persian art of the period. *Below:* a marriage contract of roughly the same time, 1860; the language here, as was customary, is Aramaic, but the design incorporates the national emblem of Persia, the lion and the sun. (81, 82, 83)

Persian and Jewish cultural traditions unite in this splendid ▷ silk rug made in central Persia around 1850. The main subject is the meeting of Solomon and the Queen of Sheba. On the steps below are pairs of animals made of gold, mentioned in a midrashic text as occupying these positions. Across the top and down the two sides are the symbols of the twelve Tribes (some repeat in reversed form left and right – in one case, the lion of Judah, reversing the lettering too). These symbols finish with the clump of trees (Reuben), and other subjects, also duplicated, continue the sequence – the Burial Place of the Patriarchs, the Grave of Rachel, Rama and the Grave of Samuel and, at the bottom (here the two sides differ), two synagogues called 'The House of Jacob' and 'The Pride of Israel'. Along the bottom border are the Sacrifice of Isaac and the Finding of Moses by Pharaoh's Daughter, with between them the Western (or Wailing) Wall of the Temple. (84)

The coasts of North Africa were a refuge to some 50,000 Jews expelled from Spain in 1492, but Jewish settlement there goes back to far earlier times. The village of Hara Kbira is inhabited exclusively by Jews, who have adopted many features of Islamic life. In the cemetery are tombs of Jewish 'saints' hardly distinguishable from those of Muslim 'holy men'. (85)

Dressmaking workshops in Algeria (*below*) were among the activities promoted by Alliance Israélite to maintain Jews in profitable work during a period of economic hardship. The Alliance was founded in 1860, partly through Adolphe Crémieux's efforts, to defend Jews from persecution and 'to encourage the pursuit of useful handicrafts.' (86)

The Maghrib

The daughters of two affluent Jewish families in Tangier and Algeria (*right*) display their festival dress: basically Moorish with a touch of the exotic. The first wears a *hezam*, a wide stiff belt of embroidered velvet, the second a plastron, the heavily decorated front part of the bodice. *Below right*: a family of about the same date, photographed at Constantine, Algeria. (87, 88, 91)

Objects for the liturgy descend from a long tradition, only slightly modified according to period and local styles. All these are from the Maghrib and date from the late 19th century. *Above*: Chanukah lamp of silver; the eight candles or tiny oil lamps are progressively lit during eight days until all eight are alight. *Above right*: silver pointer used for marking the place in the daily reading of the Pentateuch. *Right*: wedding ring; the hollow cube is for holding aromatic spices. *Far right*: Torah crown, encircling the case in which the Torah scroll is kept. (89, 90, 92, 93)

אֵין זֶה כִּי אִם בֵּית אֱלֹקִים

'This is no other** than the house of God'; the inscription on these 18th-century glazed tiles from Isfahan comes from the Genesis account of Jacob's dream. The style is typically Persian for that date. An interesting detail is that the name of God, *Elohim*, has been deliberately misspelled *Elokim*, a conventional practice when the name of God is used outside religious services and benedictions in order to avoid 'taking the name of God in vain.' (94)

An Algerian synagogue in the 1830s suggests a life-style so deeply imbued with Islamic culture that it might easily be mistaken for a mosque. But there would be no benches in a mosque, and the curtained enclosure at the back seems to be the space reserved for the Ark. The women's gallery is at the back. This synagogue, in the rue Chartres, Algiers, was demolished in 1837. (95)

Chapter Six

The Jews in Spain

HAIM BEINART

THE MOST IMPORTANT FACT ABOUT SEPHARDI, or more exactly Hispano-Portuguese, Jewry is the sheer length of its settlement in a single territory, the Iberian peninsula. Beginning, to the best of our knowledge, in the 1st century – possibly before the destruction of the Temple – it grew naturally and organically. First came small-scale settlements in coastal towns such as Tarragona and Tortosa; then more widespread colonization inland, in hundreds of villages, towns and cities all over the Peninsula. After the Muslim invasion, Jews became prosperous and powerful in both the Christian and Muslim areas of Spain, contributing generously to the cultural and social life of both. All this came to an abrupt end in Spain in 1492 with the Expulsion, and in Portugal five years later with the forced mass conversions. What we shall try to define in this chapter are some of the corner-stones on which this Jewry based its life and creative activity; how the Jews influenced and were in turn influenced by their neighbours, Christian and Muslim, and how they lived with them, sometimes in strife, sometimes in harmony.

The first Jewish settlers in Iberia had come from the Holy Land, either directly or via Rome. They brought with them a Palestinian tradition inherited from the late Roman period, a tradition later reinforced by influences from the Jewish national centre in Babylonia as long as it flourished. From this very early period in Spain we have a fair number of material remains, including inscribed ossuaries and tombstones. One trilingual inscription on a sarcophagus from Tarragona reads, 'Peace be on Israel and on us and on our children, Amen', a unique survival outside the homeland of Israel. Another, also trilingual, found at Tortosa, tells us of a girl named Meliosa, the daughter of Rabbi Jehudah. And at Elche, a mosaic inscription in Greek in a synagogue uses the word *Archisynagogus*. These three inscriptions are only a fraction of the total. Together they help to build up a picture of these Jewish communities at the end of the then known world.

More can be deduced from the deliberations of the 4th-century Synod of Elvira (Illiberis), some clauses of which tried to regulate the relations between Jews and Christians. Jews, for instance, were forbidden to bless the fields of Christians; a Christian who permitted such a thing was liable to permanent excommunication. What did this mean? It seems as if a blessing – a Jewish blessing – by a Jewish farmer on a field cultivated by a Christian was something to be sought after, perhaps because of the advice given by the farmer as much as the power of the blessing. Further clauses forbade Christians and their priests to share in the same meals as Jews, and attempted to set up other barriers against social communication between Jews and Christians. These restrictions were pointers towards things to come.

The period of Visigothic rule in Spain lasted from the early 5th to the early 8th century. Active persecution did not begin until King Reccared renounced his Arian creed and converted to Catholicism in 586. Three years later his first anti-Jewish laws were issued. Church and State were now united in forging an anti-Jewish policy, which became more severe from one Synod to the next. In 613 King Sisebut decreed that the Jews in his kingdom should either accept Christianity or leave. Many Jews crossed the Straits to North Africa. Those who stayed behind formed the first converso community in Spain. Another Synod, the Fourth of Toledo, held in 633 in the reign of Sisenand, proclaimed a new series of restrictions: 'those who are from the Jews' (i.e. the conversos and their descendants) were forbidden to hold any public office that gave them authority over Christians. We do not know to what extent Jews had hitherto held public office, but this was clearly an expression of mistrust. Its main importance, however, lies in its delayed effect centuries later when, in the 15th century, it was publicly debated whether conversos could legally hold public office in a Christian society. The remainder of Visigothic rule in Spain represents one long period of persecution, a period in which no Jewish creativity was possible, in which Church and State united in imposing the idea of a purely Christian society in which there was absolutely no place for Jews. Yet, strangely enough, the form of a Jewish oath, used by Jews and conversos up to 1492, was accepted as part of the declaration made by conversos that they undertook to lead a purely Christian way of life.

The Visigothic state ended with the Arab conquest of 711, when almost the whole Peninsula fell into the hands of the invader like a ripe fruit. Spanish historians of the 15th century accused the Jews of collaborating, though there is no evidence that it was they who invited Moussa and Tarik to cross the Straits. Did the totalitarian Visigothic regime expect a persecuted population to resist a liberator who offered an end to that persecution? As we shall see, it was a lesson that a later Christian society signally failed to learn when it tried once more to forge a state of one faith and one nationality.

Al-Andalus and the Reconquista

The Muslim invasion created new conditions for Jewish life to re-establish itself in the Iberian peninsula, but for this early period we know little about the Jews who emigrated to Al-Andalus (Muslim Spain). We know more about those who remained in the Christian pockets in the north or in Marca Hispanica, a zone established by Charlemagne on the slopes of the Pyrenees as a barrier to Muslim expansion. Documents show that Jews owned arable land and vineyards, which they could buy, sell, acquire by lease or rent out, and that they worked on their land. Plots of land were exchanged with Church bodies, convents, bishops or vicars of parishes, and sometimes deeds were drawn up in Hebrew and signed in Hebrew by the Jewish party to the contract. (In fact a Jewish oath given in Hebrew or a deed signed in Hebrew was in many cases acceptable to Christian authorities right up to the Expulsion.) It seems to have been a peaceful and neighbourly life. As the Christians began to win back the land that had been taken in the Reconquista, Jews were among the pioneer settlers, and were granted land in full ownership by virtue of this. Working the land was indeed their primary source of livelihood.

In the parts of Spain controlled by the Muslims, on the other hand, Jews were rapidly excluded from holding land through prohibitive taxation, and they became more and more city dwellers. It was not long before this process had its effects. As early as the 10th century, Al-Andalus was witnessing a great upsurge in Jewish cultural activity. Under Abd-ar-Rahman III (912–61) and his son Hakam II (961–76), Cordoba, a city of about half

'*Then sang Moses and the children of Israel this song*' (*Ex.* xv): *the* '*Song of Moses' surrounded by painted borders, from a Toledan Bible of 1246. Toledo was at this time a flourishing cultural centre and contained the most important Jewish settlement in Spain.*

a million inhabitants, became a centre of learning, and specifically of Jewish learning, under the leadership of Rabbi Hisdai ibn Shaprut (c. 915–c. 970). Hisdai was a famous physician, scholar and diplomat. He cured Sancho, king of León, of his obesity, receiving as a reward ten fortresses on behalf of his own sovereign. He negotiated with two important foreign missions, one from Byzantium, and one sent by the Emperor Otto I in 953; gravely concerned with the fate of his brethren in the Byzantine Empire, he intervened with Helene, daughter of Romanus I Lecapenus, for the Jews of southern Italy. It was Hisdai who wrote a famous letter to Joseph, king of the Khazars, a Central Asiatic nation who had converted en masse to Judaism, expressing his desire to visit the Khazar kingdom. His palace became a centre for those first Jewish poets who renewed Hebrew poetry in Spain. He was the first court Jew of Muslim Spain.

In the next century, the most striking personality was Samuel ha-Nagid, poet, scholar and statesman, who from humble origins rose to be vizier to the emir of Granada. He considered himself a tool in the hands of Providence, sent by God to fight for his people. When the Jews in neighbouring emirates, such as Almeria and Seville, were subjected to persecution, he made it a casus belli for Granada and personally led the army into battle to rescue his brethren. These were the great days of Jewish pride, of flourishing talmudic colleges and centres of learning like Alisana (today's Lucena). Not for nothing was Granada called 'Granata-al-Yahud'.

Another great centre was Saragossa, the home of Yekutiel Abu Isaac ibn Hassan, counsellor to Mundir II, the last of the Tujjib Dynasty, who was also a Jew. It was in places like Saragossa that the foundations of Hebrew studies were laid; as the bard, Solomon ibn Gabirol wrote: 'Hebrew has all that other tongues possess, and more.' Yet this prosperity was precarious. In 1039 Rabbi Yekutiel, a scholar of great learning, versed both in Jewish studies and in general culture, was beheaded. Nor was the fate of Jews under the Christian rulers more secure.

The situation in the north was transformed by the discovery of the reputed remains of St James, and their burial at Compostela led to the opening of a highly lucrative pilgrimage route. Jews were among those who settled the lands recovered from the Moors in this area, and were granted privileges to encourage them to do so. For example, the fine to be paid for killing or injuring a Jew was at times as high as that for killing a knight (*infanzon*) or a priest, though the inhabitants of some towns tried to get it lowered to that for an ordinary farmer. Each district had its own customs, but the Jews generally managed to acquire the means to protect themselves. In Navarre, in cases of dispute between Jews and Christians, the ruler himself undertook to provide a champion (*bastonarius*) to fight on behalf of the Jews.

The second half of the 11th century, especially the reign of Alfonso VI, was a period of great expansion in Jewish settlement in the regions of northern Spain, and this pattern continued in the 12th century as the Reconquista extended to Aragon and Catalonia.

Toledo was conquered by Alfonso VI in 1085. The Jews of Toledo remained in their quarter in the south-west corner of the city, where they had a fortress. Before long, Toledo had become the foremost Jewish settlement in Spain, partly owing to the presence of a great

Jewish personality then in the service of King Alfonso, Yosef ha-Nassi ben Ferrizuel, better known by the name Cidellus. Born at Cabra, near Granada, he became Alfonso's personal physician, and was appointed *nassi*, or head, of all the Jewish communities in his realm. He was able to aid the Jews of Guadalajara when it was taken by Alfonso, and encouraged those of Muslim Spain to emigrate and settle in the Christian north. In one of the first poems to be written in Romance (the forerunner of Spanish), the great Jewish poet Yehuda ha-Levi compared Cidellus to 'a fresh breeze, a ray of sunshine, in Guadalajara'.

As *nassi*, Cidellus wielded a great deal of power. In the interests of Jewish unity, he excluded the Karaites (a dissident sect who rejected the Talmud and advocated a return to the Bible) from centres of Jewish settlement. His position – administrative leader, official representative of the Jews at the royal court in matters of taxation and chief appeal judge in cases involving Jews – continued to exist in Castile under the title of Rab de la Corte, until the Expulsion. It had its counterpart in Portugal under the name 'Arrabi môr'. Needless to say, not every *nassi* or Rab de la Corte was worthy of his office, or sufficiently learned to deserve the title of Rabbi.

The status and rights of Jews in Spain and Portugal were determined not solely by legal enactments but also by the corpus of local laws and customs, known as the Fueros, which were recognized by the Crown. These are, indeed, of particular importance since they represent an organic growth, spanning many centuries and containing many clues about the problems of Jewish settlement in different parts of the Peninsula. What is striking is the absolute equality of Jew and Christian in the definitions of the Fueros. The onus of proof by witnesses fell equally on both litigating parties; Jewish oaths were accepted; and market activities were regulated with complete impartiality. Spain's uniqueness should be recognized here.

During the 12th and 13th centuries, Toledo became one of the centres of European culture. The process had begun in the days of Alfonso VI, but reached its peak under Alfonso VIII (1126–57), when Archbishop Don Raimundo, with a group of learned Jews and Christian clerics, founded a college of translators, which immediately gained renown. Many key works of Arabic and Hebrew literature were here translated into Latin, and Jewish participation in the work of translation was strong. The well-known mathematician, Juan de Sevilla, was the Jewish convert to Christianity Juan Avendeuth, or Ibn David. He translated texts on medicine, philosophy and astronomy, bringing to the knowledge of the West many of the works of Plato and Aristotle. He also translated *The Fountain of Life* by 'the Jewish Plato', Solomon ibn Gabirol, a work which drew together strands of thought from several traditions (it was originally written in Arabic, which Ibn Gabirol handled as easily as Hebrew). Another group of translators, which included the Jew, Maestro Pedro of Toledo, translated the entire Qur'ān in the course of a single year, 1143. Hebrew often served as a sort of intermediary language until well into the 14th century. Maimonides's great work, *A Guide to the Perplexed*, completed about 1190, was written in Arabic, but became known through its Hebrew translation and only then was rendered into

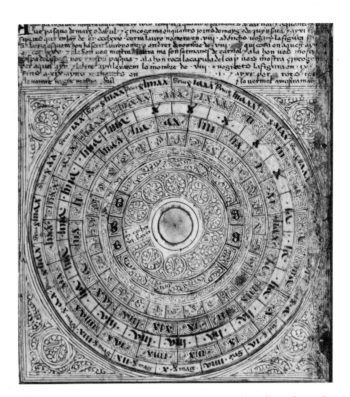

Abraham Cresques, the 14th-century cartographer, drew charts for Henry the Navigator, and created the Catalan World Atlas in 1381. A detail from the first of eight long leaves in the atlas includes astrological tables.

Latin. Its impact on Christian scholasticism was enormous, influencing Albertus Magnus and Thomas Aquinas, in particular.

Another contributor to Spanish culture was Shemtov ben Isaac ibn Ardutiel, better known as Santob de Carrion, who lived in the days of Alfonso XI (1312–50), and was equally fluent in Hebrew and Spanish. His Hebrew *Vidduy* became part of the Mussaf service of Yom Kippur, according to the Sephardi rite, while his Spanish *Proverbios Morales*, applying Hebrew ethics to daily life, is one of the seminal works of the Spanish language, and a key document for Jewish influence on the culture of the Middle Ages. Through this book, Jewish ideas penetrated into the literature and philosophy of Spain. Many other names could be mentioned – in mathematics, for instance, that of Abraham bar-Hiyya of Barcelona; and in cartography that of Abraham Cresques (died, 1387) of Majorca, his son Yehuda Cresques and Abraham Zacut of Salamanca, whose *Almanach perpetuum* at the end of the 15th century helped Columbus in the calculations for his great voyage. There was reason in his day for the poet Fernán Pérez de Guzmán to call Jewish Spain – in this case Cordoba – 'another Athens'.

Inside the community

Is there a particular character that can be associated with Spanish Jewry? Most of its features were, after all, shared by the Jewish communities of other countries. Jews lived in villages, small towns and cities. They could be rich, moderately well-off or poor (the latter supported by the public); they could be scholars, students or learned religious dignitaries; physicians, merchants or artisans practising the widest variety of crafts; freeholders, leaseholders or peasants. Social tensions existed for them as they did for any other community. Yet the suggestion of stability would be deceptive. Conditions for Jews varied considerably from period to period and from region to region. Changing political conditions often led to their founding new centres and new congregations. In the cities and villages recovered in the Reconquista, there would be old communities who now had to adapt to living in a Christian rather than a Muslim state. Such, at least, was the case for many centuries. In the last phase, the war against Granada, this was already a thing of the past. The Catholic monarchs did not have the slightest intention of calling on the Jewish element in settling conquered Granada. They had already decided upon total expulsion. It was the logical outcome of a process that had begun in 1391, a process involving pogroms and forced conversions, or the voluntary abandonment of creed and nation. The 15th-century crisis in Spain heralded a profound change in Jewish life all over Europe, whose effect was to be felt for hundreds of years.

Let us now look at the structure of Jewish community life, beginning at the top. The phenomenon of the 'court Jew' has already been mentioned. Every Christian king in Spain had his court Jew, an arrangement that could work in favour of the Jews, since it meant that they had access to the Crown, but which was set up primarily, of course, for the benefit of the king. Jews played a central role in the fiscal system as providers of funds, either directly or indirectly through the supervision of the taxes. For hundreds of years Jews were the 'farmers' of the taxes that they were supposed to deliver. It was not simply a question of a regular annual tax to be assessed and gathered by Jews: whatever the Crown needed – from the salaries of the royal entourage to pocket money for a spendthrift queen or prince – was collected through the same channels. The result was that the Jews became identified with financial impositions and unjust demands, and with all the cruel practices that these often entailed – a major cause of anti-Jewish feeling. In December 1491, when the Expulsion was being decided upon, new regulations had to be drawn up to remove Jews from their positions as tax farmers so that the necessary funds for Castile and Aragon would continue to flow in afterwards. Tomás de Torquemada was the architect of this prescient move.

In many ways these great financiers were spokesmen for their Jewish brethren. Some of them were great personalities in their own right, true and devoted protectors of Judaism. A generation that had leaders like Mosheh ben Nachman (known as Nachmanides), the bailiff of King Jaime I in Gerona, or Solomon ben Abraham Adret in Barcelona, was indeed fortunate. Only a character as strong as Nachmanides's could have withstood the pressure of the Barcelona disputation in 1263. This was a debate arranged by King Jaime and a Jewish convert to Christianity, Pablo Christiani. It lasted four days, and there can be no doubt that Nachmanides was intellectually the superior. He, nevertheless, had to flee because of a charge of blaspheming the Christian religion. He went to the Holy Land, became committed to the doctrine that it was the duty of every Jew to return to the Holy Land and founded a synagogue in Jerusalem. There were many other such men, who contributed to the religious life of Jewry and helped to maintain Orthodox doctrine.

Of course, not every court Jew was a model figure in his community. Some were bullies who oppressed their own people and aped the Christians – and their children were not slow to follow such examples. The borderline between assimilation and conversion was easily crossed. It was to counter such tendencies that Menahem ben Zorah wrote his *Food for the Journey* (1376), a short and simple summary of basic Judaism. Yet the patron to whom it was dedicated, Don Samuel Abravanel of Seville, was shortly afterwards baptized and became Don Juan Sánchez de Sevilla. He was not alone. These were the people to whom Jews looked for guidance and in many ways it is at their door that we should lay responsibility for the crisis of Spanish Jewry at the end of the 14th century. From involvement in the affairs of state in a Christian society it was only a short step to conversion.

During all this period, the Jews played an important role in resettling the conquered areas. There are even examples of Jews forming part of the armies that drove out the Muslims. In such areas as Murcia, Valencia, La Mancha, Andalusia, Extremadura and the Balearic Islands, they were given plots of land and shops on condition that they settled there with their families.

The privileges granted by Spanish kings made possible the development of communal organizations unique to Spanish Jewry. Barcelona, for instance, had a 'Council of Thirty' composed of upper, middle and lower classes. There were similar councils in Saragossa, Gerona, Perpignan and elsewhere, and executive committees of representatives, called *neemanim*, carried out the policy that they decided. These *neemanim* were chosen for their moral rectitude, since in theory all public affairs depended upon them. In practice, however, it was normal for a group of aristocrats, the 'great men', to exert a controlling influence on local affairs: one might call it an oligarchy with democratic tendencies. Special officers called 'Berurei Averoth' in the documents – literally: 'sin magistrates' – were appointed to summon those who had transgressed the Jewish Law. This was a specifically Catalan institution, which was transferred after the Expulsion to the Jewish communities of the Ottoman Empire. There were also *dayanim*, magistrates chosen either for life or for a certain term, who judged according to Jewish Law and precedent, but who could also act in cases of mixed Jewish-Christian litigation. Castile had its 'Closed Council' (Consejo cerrado), composed exclusively of members of distinguished families, governing through boards of elders. It had complete control of communal affairs and was supported by the Castilian monarchs, who considered it a means of maintaining order in the Jewish community, as well as a moderating force in Christian society.

The social order of the Jewish communities in Spain found detailed expression in a series of Statutes drawn up for the management of their affairs and the determination of their way of life. This was a people who knew what faced them and knew how to adapt their Jewish ways to prevailing conditions. The Statutes tell us how they did it: they defined internal jurisdiction; they fixed the limits of personal relations; they demarcated the duties of the individual to society. Each community had its own Statutes; they were accepted voluntarily, and this gave Spanish Jewry one of its unique characteristics. It was from such voluntary traditions and from associations of craftsmen, joining together for communal work, that union for mutual help and charity developed. Thus we find in Saragossa a fellowship of the 'Doers of Mercy', another of the 'Pursuers of Righteousness', a third of the 'Nights of Vigil' (to pray for the coming of Messiah). At Huesca the ordinances of the 'Grave Diggers' were promulgated by the king. There were cases where associations would have been useful and were lacking – there was none for the 'Redemption of Captives' for example, nor for 'Bridal Funds'; these needs were dealt with in other ways. They did not form a land organization, as was proposed in the kingdom of Aragon after the Black Death pogroms, or in Castile in the 1430s. Nevertheless, taken as a whole, the Statutes show us a close web of public and private relations, which suffered at times from inner crisis and yet was capable of coping with most problems of Jewish existence in the Diaspora. They were in force for many generations, and the Jews who left at the Expulsion took them to new communities in North Africa, the Ottoman Empire and elsewhere.

A word must be said about Jewish creative and cultural activity in Spain. Spanish Jewry received its cultural inspiration from the great centre of Jewish studies in Babylon, which it actively supported. Hebrew literature in Spain is characterized by a deep love and yearning for Zion, a memory of its past glories and Messianic expectation in the future. Some of its great names – Solomon ibn Gabirol, Samuel ha-Nagid, Yehuda ha-Levi and Ibn Ezra – are described in Chapter 12.

Spanish Jews were equally illustrious in legal studies. Isaac Alfasi (1103–65), one of the first codifiers of Jewish Law, was born in Morocco and settled in Muslim Spain. The work of Maimonides (1135–1204), a tremendous philosophical, literary and spiritual achievement, was actually produced at Fustat (Cairo), but his intellectual background was essentially Sephardi. Another great legalist was Yaacov ben Asher (died, 1340), who left Germany in the 1290s with his father and family and settled in Toledo, where he created his *Four Turim*, a compendium of religious practice, ritual and civil laws which skilfully combines Ashkenazi and Sephardi learning. Ashkenazi traditions found their way into Spain by several other paths. In the 14th century, ascetic views on life, characteristic of the Ashkenazi, and such doctrines as the Kiddush ha-Shem (literally: Sanctification of the Name, the glorification of God through martyrdom) were adopted in Spain. Their effects were apparent later in the days of trial – the 1348–9 massacres, the 1391 pogroms and the Expulsion in 1492. Finally, to conclude this brief survey of Jewish Law in Spain, we should mention Joseph Caro (1488–1575); born at Zamora, but forced to leave Spain in his infancy, he eventually settled at Safed in Palestine. His magnum opus, the *Shulchan Aruch* (literally: Laying the Table), was a virtually definitive codification of talmudic Law, selecting from among the mass of conflicting rabbinical judgments and establishing rules that were widely accepted for the next two centuries. (It was said that Moshe Isserles of Cracow, another great legal mind, 'only added the table-cloth'.)

Perhaps the greatest contribution of Spanish Jewry was in the field of the Kabbalah, of such immense significance to Judaism and to the human spirit in general. Spain was the cradle of Jewish mysticism, and from there it spread to every corner of the earth where Jews lived. But this subject is explored more fully in Chapter 10.

The rift with Christianity

From the 14th century onwards, relations between Jews and Christians steadily worsened, culminating in the Expulsion of 1492. Who was chiefly responsible for that deterioration? There can be no doubt that it was the Church whose voice was loudest in calling for a reduction in tolerance and a stiffening of anti-Jewish regulations and restrictive laws. Pope Innocent III gave free reign to such measures, and they continued under Gregory IX. Implementation was easy in the rest of Europe, but took longer in Spain. Local political considerations and the necessities of the Reconquista had the effect of moderating the Church's demands, though at times the government of Castile or Aragon would heed those demands to the extent of initiating anti-Jewish policies. Attitudes towards Jews were often taken as criteria of obedience to the Church and the Pope, and this constant pressure succeeded in reducing Jewish communities in many localities to stagnation.

During the 14th and 15th centuries, several circumstances combined to affect the situation of the Jews adversely. There was a relaxation of the struggle against the Muslims, whose territory eventually dwindled to Granada and its region only. The Black Death and the pogroms that followed it left deep scars on Spanish Jewry. Castile, with its tougher religious policy, began to outweigh Aragon. And in the civil war between Pedro the Cruel and his bastard brother Enrique II, anti-Jewish propaganda became for the first time a major issue. Enrique used anti-Jewish slogans against Pedro, accusing him of being a puppet in Jewish hands. An atmosphere hostile to the Jews was engendered, and although Enrique, after gaining power and killing his brother, subsequently changed his policy, the seed had fallen on fertile ground. Seville saw many local disturbances and anti-Jewish riots in the late 1370s, forerunners of the great pogrom of 1391.

With Judaism, this was a period of spiritual disintegration, both communally and socially, which in some ways prepared the ground for the mass conversions that were to follow the pogroms. According to one anonymous writer, for many wealthy and powerful Jews, Jewish life had lost its inner meaning. Another book already mentioned, Menahem ben Zorah's *Food for the Journey*, suggests a similar atmosphere. There is little doubt that the roots of the crisis that now overtook Spanish Jewry went back deep into the past. Physical attacks on Jews came at a time when, within the community, something like a rejection of Jewish values was taking place.

Riots started in Seville on 4 June 1391. Urged on by a fanatical priest, Ferrant Martínez, the mob looted and burned Jewish property and murdered four thousand Jews. From Seville, the violence spread all over Spain like a wild forest-fire. Many communities were totally destroyed. Thousands of Jews remained strong in their faith and suffered martyrdom. Thousands more converted to Christianity to save their lives. The presence of these 200,000 unwilling Christians was to constitute one

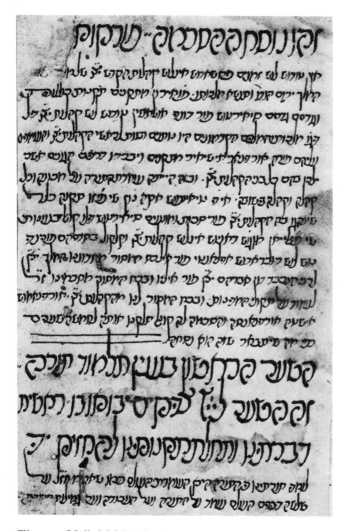

The 1432 Valladolid Synod ordinances, of which this is the beginning (written in Hebrew and Spanish in Hebrew characters), were drawn up in order to strengthen Jewish leadership and restore the community structure that had been destroyed in 1391. The communities of Castile were invited 'to send trustworthy people from amongst them to safeguard the ways of justice and to take counsel together.'

of the gravest social and religious problems in Spain and the Spanish possessions overseas.

Many formerly flourishing centres, including Barcelona, never recovered. The philosopher and talmudic scholar Hisdai Crescas succeeded in re-establishing communities in Valencia and Burriana. Majorca accepted a settlement of 150 families from Portugal in 1394, but this was again destroyed and dispersed in 1435. Many fled to North Africa and a wave of emigration started towards Eretz Israel. This was the foundation of Sephardi Jewry outside Spain.

Immediately after the mass conversions, both Church and Crown made efforts to erect barriers between those recently baptized and their former Jewish brethren. Jews and converts were ordered to live in separate quarters – an order that was to be repeated as late as 1490, and in fact it was only the Expulsion that finally succeeded in separating them. Pressure mounted to force the remaining Jews to convert. In 1412, the so-called Laws of Valladolid were issued, stipulating that they should live in closed quarters, forbidding them to practise medicine or any handicraft or to trade with Christians, and abolishing Jewish courts of law. The convert Pablo de

Santa Maria was the instigator of these laws. In 1413, anti-Pope Benedict XIII convened the notorious Tortosa disputation. In this twenty-two-month-long debate, the most learned Jews of Aragon were obliged to argue with the scholastic theologian Jeronimo de Santa Fé (another convert, formerly Yehosua ha-Lorki). Since the arbiters of the argument were Christians, there was never much doubt about the result. The Jews were arraigned for blasphemy and threatened with death. At the same time, the Dominicans renewed their campaign of terror. It wrought havoc among the Jews all over Spain. Singly and in groups they went to Tortosa to be baptized, and it seemed as though the end of Spanish Jewry had come. A ship stood waiting in Valencia to go to Majorca to bring Vicente Ferrer to the Spanish mainland, so that he could have the honour of baptizing the last Jews of Spain, and thus solve the problem once and for all. But the problem was not to be solved so easily.

These terrible events prompted a reappraisal of Jewish life in Spain. Josef Albo, a pupil of Hisdai Crescas who had taken part in the Tortosa disputation, wrote his *Book of Principles*, where he tried to evaluate the tenets of Judaism anew. Shlomo Alami's *Ethical Letter* attempted to define the causes of the disasters that had overtaken Spanish Jewry – 'let us look into our ways' – and found them in inner disintegration. Another author, Shemtov ibn Shemtov, called his book *The Book of Beliefs*, and placed responsibility for the crisis upon the growth of philosophical enlightenment. The *Book of Principles* was an analysis of the foundations of faith, providing answers to those who cast doubt upon it, but the other two were specific investigations into the roots of the evils that had befallen the Jews. Such exercises in introspection were to continue for generations to come.

Yet Spanish Jewry had great inner powers of recovery. In 1422, Rabbi Moses Arragel began his Spanish translation of the Bible, with commentary, at the suggestion of Don Luis de Guzmán, head of the Order of Calatrava. He was aided in this exegetical work by two friars, a Franciscan and a Dominican. This unique work shows how, despite the prevailing attitude to the Jews and the looming problem of the conversos, personal initiative could still carry great weight in Judaeo-Christian relations. It was carried out in a small town in Castile, Maqueda, and illuminated by a Christian painter after Rabbi Moses had completed his translation and commentary. It furnishes us with a living picture of Castilian Jewry in those days.

Another notable achievement was the convention called by Abraham Bienveniste of Soria, the Rab de la Corte, which took place in Valladolid in 1432. Here, an attempt was made to create a new constitution for the Jewish communities – to organize Jewish education, to renew the Jewish legal system and public taxation, to form a basis for action against those who harmed the Jewish community from within and to fix standards of modesty in dress and behaviour. This constitution, written in Hebrew letters in a mixture of Hebrew and Castilian, is not only a cultural heritage of exceptional value in the evolution of the spoken language of Spanish Jewry, but also an attempt to found a national organization. The Jewish communal leaders sought to lay foundations upon which Jewish communal life could be re-established. But it was too late. Jewish life did not revive according to the lines laid down. No government aid was forthcoming. Both Castile and Aragon were passing through grave crises, which affected Christians as well as Jews.

The Expulsion

The failure of Christian society to deal with the problem of the conversos was blamed upon those Jews who remained faithful to their laws and their past. It was in the 1460s that Alonso de Espina, an Observantine friar, put forward the idea of the total expulsion of all Jews from Spain. Jews had been expelled from England in 1290 and from France in 1306. If these kingdoms had managed without Jews for so many years, so could Spain. The prospect was brought closer to reality when the Catholic monarchs, Ferdinand and Isabella, succeeded to the thrones of Aragon and Castile and by their marriage united the two kingdoms into a Christian state – 'one flock and one shepherd'. This goal could only be achieved on three conditions: firstly, the integration of the conversos, secondly, the conquest of Granada, thirdly, a solution to the Jewish problem. In pursuing these aims, the state had two powerful allies. One was the Dominican friar Tomás de Torquemada, prior of Santa Cruz in Segovia and father-confessor to Queen Isabella; the other was the Santa Hermandad, an organized police force, which existed in many towns and whose pupose was to keep the peace by forcibly restraining rebellious gangs and marauding nobles.

The Spanish Inquisition started to function in Seville in 1481. Two years later, in an attempt to segregate the conversos from their Jewish brethren, the Jews were expelled from Andalusia. We do not know where they went. In the struggle against Granada, the Jews were called upon to contribute heavily. In fact, the whole burden of the war fell upon the shoulders of the dwindling communities until Granada fell in 1492. Simultaneously came a wave of persecution and anti-Jewish propaganda, which reached its peak in the so-called blood libel of 1490–1 of the 'Santo Niño de la Guardia'. Jews and conversos were accused of having killed a Christian child, whose body was never found. The story was a complete fabrication; the Inquisition hoped to prove that they were conspiring to destroy Christendom. There was even an attempt to implicate Abraham Senior of Segovia, the last Rab de la Corte, and one of the most trusted counsellors of Queen Isabella, in the plot. Although the Crown put a stop to these insinuations, a group of Jews and conversos was in fact burnt at the stake.

On 2 January 1492, Ferdinand and Isabella entered Granada in triumph. On 31 March they signed the order of Expulsion. A month more passed in desperate negotiations, in which Isaac Abravanel and Abraham Senior took part, to annul the order. But they were opposed by Torquemada and his followers. The die was cast.

The order states that the Jews themselves are responsible for their own expulsion. As long as Jews remain in Spain there can be no hope of the conversos freeing themselves from the Jewish past. The Jews are thus blocking the assimilation of the conversos into Christian society. It is important to emphasize that the Expulsion order had no economic cause. On the contrary, it emptied whole areas of their inhabitants at a time when the authorities could find no replacements. It had been thought that the conversos would supply the deficiency, but this was a vain hope.

The Expulsion order dealt in detail with departure arrangements; the authorities saw as well to what routes were to be used, how guards should be hired, what the Jews were permitted to take with them. Those who drafted the order assumed that some would convert rather than leave, and so they did. The rest saw their going as a second Exodus; they expected God to work miracles as he had done for the Jews leaving Egypt.

Here the greatness of a people is to be seen. A royal decree, instigated by the Church, suddenly put an end to more than a thousand years of life and creation. Disillusioned, they went their way, leaving this rich heritage behind. Immediately upon publication of the order, whole families began preparing for the road. After negotiations, 120,000 Jews crossed into Portugal; about 50,000 went to North Africa; others went to Navarre and the rest to Papal Avignon, Italy or the Ottoman Empire. In all, about 200,000 Jews left Spain by sea or land. Their last day on Spanish soil was 31 July 1492, – the seventh day of Ab, which, being so near, is added to the ninth, when Jews commemorate the two ancient destructions of the Temple. To Sephardi Jewry, this was a third destruction.

How did ordinary Jews react to the Expulsion, and to what extent were they prepared for it? A study has recently been made of one Jewish community on the eve of the Expulsion, that of Trujillo, in Extremadura, a town with about fifty Jewish households, some 150 miles from the Portuguese border. Here the Jews seem to have been taken completely by surprise. Their leaders had no idea of the plans maturing in the minds of the Catholic monarchs. The community, up to the very last moment, was busy with internal quarrels and open disagreements in which the civil powers were often called in to adjudicate. These civil powers were in fact doing their utmost to pacify the country and lull the Jews into a sense of security, in order to strike the more effectively when the time was ripe. They were led to believe that after the fall of Granada a new Renaissance would dawn. The blow, when it fell, was against all expectation, seemingly against all logic. Yet Spanish Jewry did not surrender to despair. Undaunted in spirit, they began preparations to leave the land which had been their own for over a millennium. Three months were enough for them to take leave of their past. Even a priest like Andrés Bernaldéz, no friend of the Jews, could not help marvelling at their deep faith, as he saw them marching off with joy, accompanied by timbrels, to face an unknown future.

The refuge which many thought to find in Portugal proved delusive. Not many years were to pass before the Sephardi settlers there, and Portuguese Jewry itself, met a similar fate. In a sense, this was for the expelled a new beginning – a Diaspora within a Diaspora. It grew to encompass the whole Mediterranean, and in the 16th and 17th centuries spread out to new lands, opening up fresh horizons for Jewry in general. But the story of Spanish Jewry up to the Expulsion has a classic, saga-like dimension of its own. It is a unique page of Jewish history, telling of indestructible spiritual values, of down-to-earth realism and of the deep sense of Jewish responsibility and mission.

Chapter Seven

The Jews in Byzantium and Medieval Europe

A. GROSSMAN

JEWS WERE FOUND IN EUROPE as early as the Roman era, mainly along the Mediterranean coast – in Italy, the Balkan peninsula and Spain – and in smaller numbers further north in Europe, in France and even in Germany. Some Jews, particularly those who had settled in Germany, left when the Roman cities were destroyed in 476; but in northern and southern France, Jews remained, though in small numbers.

Jewish settlement in Europe was renewed north of the Pyrenees in the 9th and 10th centuries, following migration from three main centres of settlement, where Jews had dwelt for hundreds of years: Asia Minor, southern Italy and the Balkans. Others came from Spain, via Provence, and were indirectly influenced by the large waves of migration in the Muslim caliphates westward from Babylonia to North Africa and Spain, which explains why names of Oriental Jewish origin were found among the Jews in 11th-century France and Germany. While no complete or exact information is available on the extent or course of these migrations, it is obvious that their underlying motives were mainly economic and that the Jews were accepted willingly by the Carolingian rulers. Charlemagne and his son, Louis the Pious, were dedicated to the development of trade and the reconstruction of the cities. The Jews, with their expertise in languages and their connections in the East – with Jews in the Muslim caliphates – were qualified to play the role of successful international traders.

Some of these Jews received a 'charter of rights' (*privilegium*) from the king, in which they were promised protection of life and property, the possibility of observing the commandments of their religion, commercial privileges, exemption from taxes and other concessions. Others received land as a *feudum*, as well, and became landowners within the framework of the feudal system.

The important role played by the Jews in commerce and in the development of cities – which began to grow and flourish at the end of the 10th and beginning of the 11th century – was still recognized at the end of the 11th century. Rudiger, Bishop of Speyer, granted to the Jews of his city in 1084 a charter of rights in which he explained why he was interested in their migration to his town. 'I thought that I would increase the honour of our locality a thousand-fold by bringing Jews also to live here' (*Putavi milies amplificare honorem loci nostri, si et Iudeos colligerem*; Aronius, *Regesten*, No. 168).

The Jewish communities in these cities were generally small, most of them consisting of only a few hundred Jews. Relatively large population concentrations occurred in the towns of Provence in the south of France, in the region of Champagne in the north of France, in the towns of the Rhine in Germany and in northern Italy. In the first half of the 11th century, Jewish communities already existed in parts of Poland (Cracow) and Russia (Kiev).

The estimated number of Jews at the end of the 11th century was approximately 20,000 in Germany and a few more in communities throughout France, including Provence. In the whole of Europe (including Italy and England, where Jews arrived after 1066) the number of Jews did not reach 100,000. In other words, there were far fewer Jews there than in the countries of the Muslim caliphates, especially Babylonia.

Nevertheless, Western European Jewry in the 11th and 12th centuries developed important institutions for the internal organization of its communities and distinguished itself in intellectual creativity, in certain spheres even surpassing the magnificent achievements of the Babylonian centre.

The pogroms and massacres during the Crusade of 1096 had a considerable impact on the Jews' political status and security but the map of their settlement hardly changed.

During the 13th century, there were hundreds of communities in Bavaria and Bohemia, and the area of Jewish settlement was expanding eastward to the Slavic countries and Poland. In England, the number of Jews living there in 1290, at the time of the general expulsion order, is estimated at between 5,000 and 10,000. In southern Italy, tax returns for 1294 enable us to calculate a population of at least 10,000 Jews. In Byzantium, persecution came to an end in 1261 and Jews were given a good location in Constantinople.

The general picture that emerges is thus one of an increase in the number of Jews in Europe in the 12th and 13th centuries. In fact, the 13th century was a period of growth in terms of the number of Jewish settlements and the size of the Jewish population in Western Europe. At the end of the century (1290), the Jews were expelled from England and at the beginning of the 14th century (1306), from France, but were permitted to return in 1315. A substantial change for the worse, from a settlement point of view, occurred following the harsh decrees of 1348, when the Black Death raged through Europe. Hundreds of communities were stricken with the Plague and thousands were killed during the pogroms. German Jewry sank to an ebb at that time, coming close to annihilation. Decrees of expulsion were issued to many Jewish communities, though many towns later expressed their readiness to accept Jews again – but with conditions that were more harsh. In many towns the 'Jews' Street', their residential area, was restricted in size.

Because the expulsions occurred repeatedly, the places where Jews dwelt acquired a temporary character. Many communities attempted to attract new residents in order to spread the burden of taxation and extortion, whose weight was now heavier than in the past. Moshe Mintz wrote in 1456: 'In this town, house-owners are few and the burden [of taxes and maintenance of the community] is heavy upon us. We are courting house-owners who will share the burden with us.' Expulsions also took place among the French communities.

At that time, migration to Poland increased, encouraged by two particular factors: the waves of persecution in European towns, especially during the 14th century, and the urgent need to resettle the towns of Poland after the destruction caused by the Tartars' invasions. At the end of the 15th century, there were approximately sixty Jewish communities in united Poland-Lithuania, and the number of Jews greatly increased over the course of the 16th century and the first half of the 17th. This was the first time that Ashkenazi Jewry achieved a large population in any European state. Jewish settlement increased in the Ukraine, too, and around 1648 there were 115 Jewish settlements consisting of over 50,000 people.

The Jewish centre in Poland-Lithuania and the centre in the Ottoman Empire (which absorbed many Jews who had been expelled from Europe) were the focal points of Jewish intellectual and material creativity near the end of the Middle Ages and the beginning of modern times.

The political, social and economic status of the Jews

The most important centres of Jewish life in Europe from the beginning of the Middle Ages up to the 9th century were Byzantium and southern Italy, in Apulia and Calabria (a region largely under Byzantine rule).

Various literary sources show that these Jewish populations were relatively large, containing many religious scholars. They filled an important commercial role and their economic and political circumstances were generally good. The Jews of these areas maintained regular contact with Benevento, the capital of Lombardy and with other Italian towns in the western and northern parts of the peninsula, as well as with countries in the eastern Mediterranean, including Eretz Israel. At that time, southern Italy served as a sort of bridge between the Christian and Muslim worlds (and part of it was even conquered by the Muslims).

In Italy, Jews generally enjoyed the freedom to organize their community life as they wished, including freedom of worship. A number of serious outbursts against them took place, however, especially under the kings Heraclius, in 632, Basil, in 873, and Romanus Lecapenus, in 932–6, which dealt serious blows to Byzantine Jewry. The persecutions of Romanus Lecapenus led to the exodus of Jews from the towns of southern Italy within the Byzantine Empire to Italian towns further north.

The migration to inner Europe, which began in the 9th century, brought about a discernible change. The centre of gravity gradually moved westward and the cultural supremacy passed in the 11th century to the towns of the Rhine. The Jews were in demand mainly as international traders, a fact that found its expression in charters of rights, which have been preserved since then. The trade included bringing merchandise from the East, particularly expensive clothing, spices (which were very important in those days as a food preservative), luxury goods and slaves.

The merchants were the dominant element in Jewish society in Western Europe, as is clearly witnessed by the literature of the period. Thus, for example, a customs order of the second half of the 9th century states: 'The merchants, i.e. Jews and other merchants, shall pay a market tax', identifying merchants as such with Jews.

In France, many Jews engaged in vine-growing and some of them were the owners of feudal estates. Louis the Pious, in a decree of 839, ordered the granting to a Jewish family, of royal documents, 'by which we shall proclaim and command that the aforementioned Hebrews and their descendants shall be the masters and owners of the aforesaid estates and everything belonging to them' (Aronius, *Regesten*, No. 602).

Although the Jews of the Carolingian kingdom were regarded as free people, there was a legal distinction between them and Christians because they could not take the explicitly Christian oath of allegiance to the emperor. For the same reason they had to swear a special form of oath (*more judaico*) when giving evidence against Christians.

It was the Christian clergy – especially the higher clergy – who were mainly responsible for the general decline in the political and social status of Jews. In 938–9 they made an unsuccessful attempt to initiate anti-Jewish legislation, but the imperial authority acted as a counterweight. In the disastrous pogroms of 1096, Henry IV's officials tried to protect the Jews. However, the influence of the Church gradually increased, both with the masses and with the royal house itself. Another factor counting against Jewish interests was the increase in the power of the urban class, especially in the second half of the 11th century. The struggle between the State and the Church – which reached its height when Henry IV went to Canossa in 1077 – strengthened the power of the town-dwellers and Henry resorted to using them when suppressing the revolt of the Saxon aristocracy. These townfolk regarded the successful Jewish merchants as competitors.

Notwithstanding these 'official' attitudes, we possess much evidence of social relationships and friendship between Jews and their neighbours in everyday life: the exchange of gifts and greetings, assistance in times of need and other manifestations of mutual sympathy. A Church Council held at Metz in 888, approved regulations for the prevention of joint meals with Jews and Christians, which clearly testifies to the frequency of the phenomenon and the fear of its effect. In the 9th and 10th centuries, many Jews, especially women, were given

Public disputations between Jewish sages and Christian clergy, sometimes virtually constituting a trial and sometimes a debate, vacillated between abuse and apparent friendship. In this 16th-century woodcut, Jews are debating with humanists.

Christian names or nicknames. The fact that Jews did not live in their own special districts – especially up to the mid-11th century – also helped to promote social communication. It is not to be wondered, therefore, that there were Jews who converted to Christianity of their own free will and Christians (including priests) who converted to Judaism. Cultural contacts also existed between Jews and the higher Christian clergy, as demonstrated in the works of Agobard of Lyons, written between 820 and 828, referring to ideas found in Jewish works. At the same time lived Rhabanus Maurus of Fulda, who made great use, in his own biblical exegesis, of the commentary of one of his Jewish contemporaries (*Hebraeus moderni temporis*). The public disputations that were held between Christian clergymen and Jewish sages doubtless acquainted each side with the other's literary works. These disputations continued in France, Germany and England as late as the 11th century. In 1012 and 1015, Jews participated in the burial rites of two archbishops in Magdeburg, Germany, and again in 1075 in Cologne. And even during the 1096 persecutions, quite a number of Christians hid Jews in their homes.

The pogroms of 1096 and their consequences

The cruel massacres in the First Crusade of 1096 constituted a turning point in the history of the Jews in Europe. These were the first pogroms that knew no bounds. They encompassed almost all the countries of Jewish settlement in the realm of Christianity in Western and central Europe, and they revealed the full force of the hostility of the masses towards the Jews. For the masses, not the nobility nor the clergy, were the motive power in these pogroms. There were, indeed, some junior monks

who preached against the Jews, but this was not representative of the official Church attitude, which generally followed the principle laid down by Gregory the Great (pope between 590 and 604) that one should humilitate the Jews and put mild pressure on them and tempt them economically in order to persuade them to accept the Christian faith, but not kill them or burden them excessively with anti-Jewish economic edicts. But to the common people, Jews were now the Christ-killers and enemies of God.

The impression left on Jewish life by these persecutions was deep. From this time on, the estrangement between the two camps grew. The Jews' fear of their Christian environment increased and they became further removed from it. The Jews began to segregate themselves from their surroundings more than in the past, and social contact between people of the two religions virtually disappeared. The partition that had been erected lasted for many generations.

A symbol that re-emerged and whose value received greater emphasis was martyrdom – Kiddush ha-Shem – the willingness to die rather than give up one's faith. Actually, there were some who, to save their lives, outwardly converted to Christianity; most of them returned to Judaism after a short time, with the permission of Henry IV. But many Jews killed themselves and their families, including young children. They regarded themselves as a distinguished and elect generation charged with undergoing the trial that Abraham underwent at the time of the binding of Isaac.

In these persecutions, the empire turned out to be almost the only power in the Christian world ready to defend the Jews. There were some bishops, too – in fact the rulers of the towns – who protected them or tried to, but they were few. The protection afforded by the empire had a considerable influence on the Jews' political and legal status from the 12th century onwards. It constituted one of the factors in turning the Jews into 'Serfs of the chamber' (*servi camerae*). In other words, they were regarded as the king's property. He possessed the right of ownership over the Jews and their property in exchange for a promise on his part to provide them with protection and defend their lives and property. It was an arrangement that stemmed from the interests of royalty itself, since the Jews' taxes provided it with a valuable source of income.

Emperor Frederick I used this concept as an illustration of the kingdom's duty to ensure the well-being of all its citizens, in the introduction to the *privilegium* to the Jews of Regensburg in 1182:

> It is the duty of our empire, as well as a requirement of justice and intelligence, to observe the rights of each of our loyal subjects, not only those who believe in the Christian faith but also those who do not agree with our religion but live according to the customs of their forefathers' tradition. We must try to enable them to observe their customs and ensure their well-being – both physical and monetary. Accordingly, we hereby proclaim to all loyal subjects of the empire, today and in generations to come, that we are most concerned about the well-being of all the Jews who live in our empire who are recognized as belonging to the empire's exchequer on the basis of the special right of our gracious rule. (Aronius, *Regesten*, No. 314a)

The words of Frederick II are even more emphatic:

> Since one honours a master through his servants, whoever acts with grace and kindness towards the Jews, our servants, will certainly find favour in our eyes. (Aronius, *Regesten*, No. 403)

However, examples are not lacking of Jews being made to pay heavy taxes on the very pretext that they were the emperor's property. And their protected status left them powerless to hold back the increasing hostility of the Christian masses towards them, a hostility exacerbated by the fact that they now began lending money at interest. This process had begun in the 11th century. In England and France, money-lending was the principal profession of the Jews by the 12th century, and in other countries of Europe by the 13th and 14th centuries.

How did this phenomenon come about? To be a farmer under the feudal system required a (Christian) oath of allegiance to the lord of the manor, which Jews automatically could not take. Their opportunities in agriculture were therefore limited. They were also gradually squeezed out of local and international trade, both in Italy and in Western Europe, by the growth of the cities and the preferential conditions granted to local merchants. The latter were generally exempt from paying taxes, whereas Jews were compelled to pay them, sometimes very heavy ones. The guilds of merchants or artisans were established as Christian co-operative associations and they refused to accept Jews into their ranks.

Another factor was the deterioration in security on the highways, especially after the pogroms of the First Crusade in 1096. Many Jews feared to continue travelling for purposes of trade. The question of the religious-legal status of a woman whose husband went on a journey, and disappeared without leaving a trace, was repeatedly raised in the *responsa* literature of the time. (*Responsa Prudentia*, a major branch of rabbinical criticism, consisted of answers – *responsa* – given to questions sent by Jewish communities to learned rabbis.)

Usury, the lending of money at interest, was strictly forbidden by the medieval Church, especially from the 12th century onwards. There were, indeed, some Christians (the Lombards, the inhabitants of Cahors in southern France and other places) who evaded this prohibition, but they were few and were unable to meet the great demand that existed for money. This demand was due to the increase in the size of the cities and in the number of their inhabitants who engaged in commerce. The many obstacles in the path of the Jewish trader who wished to continue in his vocation, together with the great thirst for money in Christian society and the difficulties in obtaining it, gradually led to Jews being cast in the role of money-lender. Granting loans involved taking pawns and selling them when the loan was not repaid; interest at the time was extremely high. All this intensified the hatred for the Jews and led to their being conceived of as blood-sucking leeches, an image that remained for centuries. The kingdom itself benefited from this situation because it collected a large portion of the Jews' income. Its opposition to their money-lending activities was often mere lip service.

In England, which was at that time the most orderly of all European countries from an administrative point of view, special arrangements were made for keeping promissory notes under royal supervision. This even enabled the king to increase his income from the Jews. But in 1275, Edward I issued a law which prohibited Jews from lending money at interest. Fifteen years later, after their wealth had dwindled away because of the heavy taxes that he himself had collected from them, he expelled them from England.

In all European countries there were Jews who continued to engage in commerce during the 13th, 14th and 15th centuries. Some of them based their trade on the Slavic east while others acted as intermediaries in the sale of village produce to the city merchants. But they were now a minority in Jewish society.

Blood libels: the growing terror

The hostility to the Jews which has just been described had at least some basis in economic reality. It was now to be overlaid by a hatred that was entirely superstitious. Under the instruction of the Church, the people were encouraged to see the Jews literally as devils, creatures in the image of Satan. This is the background of the most famous libel against the Jews in the Middle Ages – the blood libel. They were depicted as drinkers of little Christian children's blood or as the users of such blood for ritual purposes and acts of witchcraft. The accusation first appeared in Norwich, England, in 1144, and afterwards reappeared in various places in Europe. It was of no avail to the Jews that they were found to be completely innocent after a thorough investigation carried out by Frederick II in the wake of a blood libel in Fulda in 1235, or that Pope Innocent IV opposed the blood libels and declared them to be untrue. The libels appeared again and again in various places. Belief in them was so deeply rooted in the consciousness of the masses that they found expression in various branches of Christian art in the Middle Ages. The Jews who tortured Christ, and the sages who gave the silver to Judas Iscariot for his betrayal were often drawn and carved in such a way that they resembled the Jews who then dwelt among the Christians. Devils and destructive angels were given the images of contemporary Jews. Later, plays were produced describing Jesus's torment, and the treacherous Jews in them were also presented in the images of contemporary Jews.

Church leadership became increasingly aggressive towards the Jews. Particularly strong anti-Jewish legislation was passed at the Fourth Lateran Council in 1215, under the leadership of Pope Innocent III. Among other things, he ruled that Jews must wear on their garments in a visible place a badge that would distinguish them from Christians: 'The order is given them', he wrote, 'to let the Jews wear clothes by which they might be distinguished from Christians, but not to force them to wear such as would lay them open to the danger of loss of life.' Such was, however, the effect of the order, since the badge marked them as inferior and undesirable. This anti-Jewish activity led to the burning of the Talmud in the early 1240s. Only after some years did the Jews succeed in obtaining permission from Pope Innocent IV to possess the Talmud and prevent its burning.

All these developments in the 12th and particularly in the 13th century provided the background for the

A Jew-baiting Franciscan, preaching in Trent in 1475, produced such a strained atmosphere that a rumour about a missing infant named Simon rapidly turned into a blood libel; the trial, torture and expulsion encompassed the entire community of Jews. This contemporary woodcut illustrates the supposed Jewish atrocities.

violent outbursts against the Jews between 1298 and 1348, especially in Germany. The libels and persecutions came in waves and culminated during the Black Death of 1348–9. This Plague (which lasted for five years) wrought havoc among the populations of Europe. The number of people who died in Western Europe was estimated at twenty-five million, i.e. approximately a quarter of the entire population. No rational explanation of the phenomenon – which originated in Central Asia and was brought to Europe mainly by merchant ships – was available at the time. The Jews, who had been depicted all the time as Satan's offspring, were soon accused of having poisoned the wells in order to bring about Christianity's destruction. Suitable 'confessions' were obtained under torture. News of the so-called Jewish guilt spread rapidly throughout Europe and led to bitter attacks on the Jews throughout the continent, from Spain to Poland. The most severe blow was dealt in the German Empire, where thousands of Jews were burnt to death. Hundreds of communities throughout Europe were practically liquidated.

Enlightened Christians protested against the false accusations of the Jews. Pope Clement VI opposed them strongly and spoke of 'certain Christians who were incited by the devil to discover the cause of the Plague, with which God has afflicted the Christian people for its sins, in acts of poisoning on the part of the Jews.' He explicitly testified that 'avarice motivated some Christians to profit on the account of these Jews, to some of whom they owed large sums of money.' Thus these terrible pogroms partly had an economic background too. The pope proved the innocence of the Jews by the fact that the Plague had struck in other parts of the world where no Jews were to be found and that Jews were themselves among its victims. He also threatened to excommunicate anyone who dared to harm the Jews again. However, even such valuable protection did not prevent the accusations and anti-Jewish attacks from continuing.

Many towns that had expelled Jews agreed to receive them back, at least for limited periods of time. However, many Western European communities, especially those in Germany, never recovered. The pogroms and expulsions encouraged Jewish migration to new locations in Eastern Europe and the Mediterranean region. Migration to Poland, which had been taking place all the time, now grew considerably, for Jews had come to regard Poland as the safest place for them – a place 'whose gates no foe or oppressor would enter.'

The status of the Jews in Poland–Lithuania

Some of the events that characterized the history of the Jews in 9th–12th-century Western Europe repeated themselves in the history of Polish Jewry: participation in a commercial activity that was essential for the country, and at first improved the Jews' status, was followed by a gradual deterioration of position until envy and hostility towards them became widespread. The Jews played an important role in commercial contacts between Poland and Hungary and Bohemia on the one hand and between Poland and the Italian colonies along the Black Sea coast on the other. The conquest of Constantinople by the Turks in 1453 increased the importance of the land route from Constantinople through Poland to central and Western Europe. In the Polish towns themselves, Jews increasingly penetrated the various branches of commerce, and their status as important merchants was recognized in the various charters of rights. Their success, however, caused great tension between them and the town inhabitants, and in May 1494 attacks broke out on the Jews of Cracow. A year later they were expelled from Cracow as well as from other Lithuanian towns for a certain time. But generally speaking their status remained firm.

Another reason for the improvement in their status was the great number of Protestants in Poland–Lithuania and the substantial power that they possessed up to the 17th century. The religious tolerance shown towards Protestants indirectly helped the Jews to achieve similar treatment. The economic connections between them and the Polish aristocracy, who had great power, helped them too at the time. Later, their association with the hated upper classes was to bring fresh calamities.

From the mid-16th century, the Polish aristocrats began to make safe the highways and to cultivate steppe land of the present-day Ukraine. This needed considerable sums of money, for which they often relied on loans from Jews. In many cases they pledged their estates as a security for the loan, and the Jew from whom they had borrowed it was sometimes asked to manage the estate because he was regarded as a good administrator. Because they represented the exploiting nobleman, though, the Jews were the object of detestation to the harshly exploited rural population. This tension was later to be reflected in the terrible pogroms of 1648, which followed the Cossack revolt; large sections of the Jewish population of the Ukraine were destroyed and a certain migration began to the West.

At the end of the Middle Ages, three important new developments occurred in the status of the Jews, symbolizing the transition from the Middle Ages to modern times.

1. The ghetto was established in Italy: at first in Venice in 1516 and later in other Italian towns and other places in Europe. The Jews were settled in a special quarter, which was closed off and officially separated from the other parts of the town by a wall and gates. Jews were prohibited from living outside the ghetto and at certain times even from leaving it. It was a development charged with significance for the future. True, in the past, Jews had lived together in one street or one district for religious, security and social reasons, but the actual *obligation* to segregate themselves within walls symbolized, on the one hand, their inferiority and degradation, their being different from the others (it was not by chance that the Church initiated the establishment of the ghetto), and, on the other, their insecurity and the need to lock them away for their own protection.

The ghettos were overcrowded and insanitary. (In Venice alone, the ghetto held approximately five thousand people in the middle of the 17th century.) Sometimes, the rulers did not permit the expansion of the ghetto, even when its population grew, so that it became necessary to add additional storeys to existing houses, which occasionally collapsed.

2. The Christian Reformation caused the break-up of the unified Catholic framework, from 1517 onwards. Catholicism had emphasized the view that the Jews were a foreign and unusual element in society. Now Christians, too, had become different from each other; different groups of Christians had to live side by side in something like religious tolerance. Neither of the two camps – each of which sought to win a victory over the other – ever thought of including Jews in this framework but, in practice, the very existence of different camps and sects facilitated the creation of conditions that enabled the Jews to integrate into modern society.

The personal attitude of Martin Luther towards the Jews changed from one extreme to the other. At first, he offered them his own type of Christianity and preached better treatment of them (especially in his book, *Das Jhesus Christus eyn geborner Jude sey*). But when they did not respond, his tone changed to one of virulent hostility; not being restrained by the long papal tradition of moderation, he was soon surpassing the Catholics.

3. Communities of Marrano Jews, or conversos, who had migrated from Spain, sprang up in the Protestant Netherlands. At the end of the 16th century, they began to return openly to the Jewish faith. At first they congregated at Antwerp, but this was soon replaced by Amsterdam, which became one of the most important centres of Jewish life in Europe. Many of these Marranos belonged to rich and distinguished families in Spain and Portugal and they were very successful in various economic spheres, especially in all branches of international trade.

At the beginning of the 17th century, groups of Marranos left for north-west Germany and established a few communities there, the most famous one in Hamburg. The Marranos maintained contacts with Spain and Portugal as well as with their Marrano brethren in Western and central Europe, in Italy and North Africa and the Turkish Empire. These contacts were the principal foundation of their great success in trade, and they also had an important cultural impact.

The Jewish community in medieval Europe

The Jewish community in Western Europe appeared from the start as a living body, uniting all its members within it. The concept of a communal organization originated in Eretz Israel in the period of the Second Temple. Its authority and control encompassed all spheres of individual and public activity; in fact, the individual's destiny was bound up with the community from cradle to grave. Some of its elements, which were already fashioned in the 10th–11th centuries, influenced Jewish communities throughout Europe for centuries.

The community had three important aims: observance of the commandments of Judaism and concern for religious needs; concern for the safety of life and property; and mutal aid in times of need. Much effort was spent in achieving these aims: many institutions were established (such as charity funds, educational institutions, synagogues, ritual bath-houses and cemeteries), regulations were enacted in various spheres, taxes were imposed and judicial institutions and a penal code were established. The community was thus a state within a state.

The development of the community in medieval Europe may be divided into three main periods: the 10th–11th centuries; from the 12th to the beginning of the 14th century; and from 1348 onwards.

In the first period – before the organization of urban society began in Christian Europe – various procedures and institutions were already established in the community. Clear evidence of this is found in the *responsa* of Meshullam, son of Kalonymus, who lived and worked in Lucca, northern Italy, in the second half of the 10th century. By this time, the communities were imposing their authority on individuals by means of excommunication and by fines, despite the fact that the Babylonian sages opposed this custom outside the borders of Eretz Israel. Noteworthy among the first arrangements made by the community was the 'Stopping of the Services', i.e. the right of every community member to hold up the prayers in synagogue until his complaint about some injustice done to him had been discussed to his satisfaction. This was only one of the democratic features that were adopted by the community from its beginnings. Other sources relate how all the members convened in the synagogue to discuss their affairs together. By the beginning of the 11th century, it had already been decided that the majority had the right to enforce its will on the minority. 'An individual is overruled and the majority is entitled to impose an oath, to ban, to confiscate money and to enact other regulations' (a *responsum* from the first half of the 11th century, Kol Bo, Chapter 142). Moreover, it was decided that one community had no right to intervene in the affairs of another one, even if it was numerically larger or had more scholars. Every community was sovereign and could enact regulations in accordance with its needs. It was explicitly stated that the leaders of the community were those who were elected even if they did not excel in their religious knowledge. Rabbenu Gershom, 'Light of the Exile' – one of the greatest sages of German Jewry in the Middle Ages – stressed this point: 'Even the simplest of men, if appointed leader of the community, is the most important of men.' At this time a nation-wide joint leadership existed, which met when the great fairs were held in the large towns, in order to discuss the common problems of all the communities. Almost all the leaders known to us from this period were the descendants of a number of distinguished families. There were even sages who explicitly emphasized that the majority's right of decision depended on 'notables' among them, distinguished by study and social status. The communities of the time, therefore, cannot be described as complete democracies.

In the second period, from the 12th to the beginning of the 14th century, the Jewish community changed in ways that reflected changes taking place in Christian society, where towns were gaining greater autonomy. The absolute power of the majority was restricted, though it usually continued to operate in practice. Instead of a single leader, communities in the 13th century began to be represented by a community head and a council, called the Elders of the Congregation, corresponding roughly to the mayor and council (*Rat*) of a German town.

The third period, following the Black Death, was marked by new penal laws, harsh persecutions and repeated expulsions. Communities were no longer allowed to elect their leaders as a matter of course, but had to buy the privilege for a large sum of money. Judicial rights, e.g. the right to collect taxes independently and the right to deliberate on criminal cases, were curtailed. The state exacted a levy on fines imposed by Jewish courts. In 1407, King Ruprecht appointed an official Chief Rabbi, a move bitterly resented by the Jews. At the same time, however, internal tensions brought about a decline in the status of the rabbinate.

All these factors led to attempts, from the end of the 14th century, to establish a central authority. Where this succeeded, it meant that the influence of the rich families (in Italy, for instance, the great banking families) on communities grew stronger.

Polish communities generally observed the Ashkenazi tradition concerning organization and form of leadership, but relationships among communities were different and more complicated. At first, the communities in Poland concentrated around large 'mother communities', which were responsible for the smaller ones. In the eastern parts of Poland, even greater councils were established in the 16th century – originally four councils of various regions, or 'lands' (Greater Poland, Little Poland, Russia and Lublin), later increased to ten. In the middle of the 16th century, the regional councils united for common action and were called the Council of the Four Lands. This council possessed secular as well as religious authority, including a high court for the Jewish communities of Poland. The Council of Lithuania was established in 1623.

The communal leadership consisted of three authorities: (1) the heads, a small number of leaders – responsible for the community before the authorities – who rotated the headship by the month; (2) the 'good ones', next in importance; and (3) the communal officials, including the religious judges and directors of the communal institutions, such as book-keepers and custodians of orphans.

Regulations enacted in Cracow in 1595 reveal that the community's authority encompassed all spheres of Jewish life: the manner of trading, the rate of interest on loans, education, charity and even the cleanliness of the streets. Rules for electing leaders differed from place to place, and, in fact, at least a quarter of Polish Jewry had no vote.

The councils of Poland and Lithuania were virtually 'governments', dealing with extensive and important matters affecting the whole Jewish community, and they convened fairly frequently (twice a year in Poland, once every two years in Lithuania). Their powers, including powers of punishment, were great, their status higher than any other communal organization of medieval Jewry.

The community's importance in the consciousness of ordinary Jews is demonstrated by the fact that hundreds of *responsa* of various sages from every area of Jewish settlement deal with it. By the middle of the 11th century, the sages of Germany and France decided that obedience to the enactments of the community was to be regarded as a religious commitment. Even if a person had previously sworn an oath that he would not obey a regulation, his oath was cancelled and he had to obey it, notwithstanding the extraordinary severity with which breaking an oath was regarded. The community member was thus commanded 'from Mount Sinai' to accept the authority of the community. There was no doubt an ulterior motive for this. For the Jews who were persecuted in the Middle Ages, the freedom to organize their internal life was a symbol, a sort of reminder of the past when they were a free people in their own country.

Jewish society and the Jewish family

The structure of Jewish society in medieval Europe differed from place to place and time to time. It was certainly not rigidly hierarchical, like 11th-century Babylon. But to say that it was essentially democratic would be an exaggeration. There was neither social equality nor equality of opportunity. Family status counted for much. In the 11th century, members of only seven families of Mainz and Worms consistently occupied all the senior positions all over Germany and France, as leaders of the community, heads of *yeshivas* and teachers of Torah. It is possible to trace their descent for five generations down to the persecutions of 1096.

In a question sent from the community of Troyes in the region of Champagne, it is written that 'the little ones among us listen to the great ones and have never gone against them in any matter.' From the context, it is clear that the 'great ones' are those of distinguished status and origin. Even the great sages – including Rashi, the greatest sage produced by medieval French Jewry – wrote in a very humble and deferential way when corresponding with the members of these families.

The value and importance of the family cell and family lineage for early German Jewry are reflected in its social structure and exercised an obvious influence on its intellectual life. Children strictly observed the customs of their forefathers even when they did not understand them. Their deeds and manners were regarded as a binding precedent from which no divergence was possible. Italian Jewry, too, contained a dynasty of sages, about which unfortunately little is known.

A change took place in the 12th century. Among the Tosaphists (Talmudic commentators whose work was offered as *tosaphot*, or 'supplements', to that of their master, Rashi of Troyes) in France and elsewhere were those who did not come from a distinguished lineage. On the other hand, in 12th- and 13th-century Germany, an extremely hierarchic ladder, based strictly on status and family lineage, existed among the Hasidei Ashkenaz. Although they sympathized with the common folk and advocated bringing them closer to the Torah, they preached the separate residence of the 'good ones' and intermarriage within their own group only:

In one place, only good people came together and they had good leaders. An old man said to them: 'If we marry others and others marry us, our children will follow their evil ways. Let us therefore impose a boycott so that nobody shall give his daughter in marriage to anyone who is not from this town lest it corrupts its inhabitants; nor shall we take a woman in marriage from another place.' (*Sefer Hasidim*, ed. Wistinetzki, Chapter 1301)

From the 13th century onwards, the influence of the wealthy members of the Jewish communities grew. The fact that this produced so little tension between the classes is apparently due to two factors. Firstly, the privileged status of the leading families did not confer on them any rights of control over their lesser brethren, nor any material benefits, nor did they mingle with non-Jewish society and imitate its ways, as was the case in Spain. A few Jews served at the royal court of Germany, but their numbers were not significant. Secondly, student life broke down class-barriers. In the *yeshivas*, young men from all backgrounds met together in a friendly atmosphere; an obscure student could challenge a teacher no matter how distinguished, could live in his house and accompany him on his journeys. All this was true of the Christian schools as well.

Outwardly closest to the court Jews of Spain was the Jewish intelligentsia of Provence, highly educated, economically secure and at ease with its Christian neighbours. But the inner life of the community was very different from Spain, and social conflict on the Spanish model never occurred in Provence.

In Poland, the great economic expansion of the 15th and 16th centuries led to a way of life typical of wealthy people. Some moralists protested against the licentiousness which, in their opinion, had infiltrated the lives of Jewish leaders. They claimed that too much expensive clothing was being worn, too many grandiose feasts and banquets were being held and that the Jews were living in houses which were more suitable for the Polish nobility than for Jews. It was even claimed that this way of life 'diverted attention from the redemption.' The conflicts that arose in Poland, however, were not as bitter as they had been in Spain, despite the marked class polarization and the existence of certain groups that had acquired a preferential status owing to their wealth.

The rabbinate, meanwhile, was undergoing a period of stress. In Poland–Lithuania, where community organization was strong and certain prominent rabbis were highly revered by the public, it enjoyed great prestige. But in Germany, where the rabbinate in the 15th and 16th centuries was becoming professional, i.e. the rabbi was actually an employee of the community, that prestige suffered noticeably in the struggle for authority.

Women enjoyed a high social status from the beginning of Jewish settlement, in the 9th and 10th centuries, until the 13th century, after which their status declined somewhat. At the beginning of the 11th century, two regulations were enacted, apparently by Rabbenu Gershom, which had a considerable effect on the structure of the Jewish family: marriage with more than one woman and the divorce of a woman against her will were both prohibited. Other regulations of the time show that the situation of the woman in Jewish society was better than in any other religious group in the Muslim caliphates. This is also reflected in the amount of money that a husband agreed to pay his wife, in the marriage contract, in case of divorce or his death, in the expensive jewellery that women possessed and in the vital role that they played in the household economy and in relationships with the Christian environment. In certain cases, the wife's status in the family, as far as household arrangements and upkeep were concerned, was clearly superior to that of the husband. An important regulation introduced into Germany and France in the 11th century prohibited the annulment of a betrothal. Since engagement at an early age was usual, there was a reasonable fear that one of the sides would wish to break it off after a number of years. On the other hand, the communities feared that cancellation might be interpreted as evidence of a flaw in the lineage of the family concerned. In small communities, such as those in Germany at the time, such an event would gain rapid publicity and make it difficult for the members of the family to marry. The fact that the Church, too, opposed the annulment of betrothals probably had some influence on Jewish society's behaviour. The communal leaders, in these and other regulations, explicitly stated that their purpose was 'not to shame the daughters of Israel.' In fact, many Jews in France and Germany, as they specifically stated, aspired to resemble the Christian knights and their womenfolk in their way of life.

As mentioned, this development suffered a certain setback in the 13th century, except in Hasidei Ashkenaz circles. Here, the husbands' tender feelings for their wives, the high level of women's education and the important role that they continued to play in various fields recall the conditions of two hundred years earlier in the communities of Italy, Germany and France. The Hasidim considered themselves an élite in Jewish society, differing from the accepted norm in several other ways, which are discussed below.

Intellectual creativity

The Middle Ages was a period of great artistic and intellectual achievement for the Jews. Many works produced then are still regarded as classics, exerting their influence on present-day Jewish life and outlook.

At the root of all this creativity lies the devotion given by European Jewry to study of the Torah. To read the Bible, the Midrash and the Talmud was regarded not only as a most valuable activity from a religious point of view but also as one of the outstanding ideals of medieval Jewry everywhere. Hence the great concern of parents for their children's education. Large sums of money were invested in it by the community and the individual. Even in the 11th century, every pupil had his own book, despite their exorbitant price at that time. This concern for education is particularly notable considering that illiteracy was the lot of the non-Jewish masses.

German and northern French Jewry developed in a way very different from that of Spain and Provence, yet the two areas were by no means isolated from each other. Close commercial links existed from the 10th century onwards. Many German and French Jews travelled on business to Spain as well as to the Muslim caliphates of the East. These merchants served as an important bridge between the different cultures and transmitted oral traditions and written works, which shows that the different developments in the sphere of intellectual creativity and the apparent disregard of one centre for the other were conscious and intentional. All parts of the Diaspora shared a common denominator, namely, an intense devotion to the various types of Jewish legal literature: talmudic exegesis, legal works and *responsa*. There were differences in these spheres, too, but no essential contradictions; these emerged mainly on the question of the attitude towards philosophical study and rationalism in general.

First one centre and then another took the leadership, according to the political, social and economic status of the Jews in each centre. The supremacy of a centre was established by the questions on religious law referred to its sages from other centres and by the recognition of these sages as a higher authority. But European Jewry, especially from the 12th century onwards, considered itself a single body with one Torah and one way of life.

From the 9th to the 10th century, an important centre of study existed in southern Italy within the Byzantine Empire. Part of it later moved to central and northern Italy. Like Byzantine Jewry as a whole, the Jews of this centre were influenced by the Babylonian Geonim (judicial authorities), but because of the easy sea communications they also had very close cultural contact with the tradition of Eretz Israel. The written language of Italian Jews was Hebrew and a revival of the Hebrew language took place in the 8th century, as can be seen from Hebrew, rather than Greek, inscriptions on contemporary gravestones.

A few literary remnants from this period show that Italian Jewry engaged in almost all branches of halachic literature: commentaries on the Bible and Talmud, the writing of halachic works, liturgical hymns and homiletic literature. Byzantine Jewry engaged in the last more than any other Jewish centre at that time, or even later. Historical literature is represented by the *Josippon Chronicle* in Italy, in 953, and the genealogical table of the Ahimaaz family. And the first evidence of the study of Jewish mysticism in Europe is found in southern Italy. In the 13th century, a prolonged preoccupation with philosophy may be added.

The role of Italian Jewry in the intellectual life of medieval European Jewry was important for two reasons. Firstly, its diversification into all fields of creativity was almost unparalleled elsewhere. Secondly, it constituted the principal channel for the transmission of the spiritual legacy of Babylon and Eretz Israel to the whole of Western Europe. Italian Jewry made an especially important contribution to the development of the magnificent centre of religious learning that was established in Germany in the second half of the 10th century.

This German centre flourished and grew extremely rapidly. Until the end of the 10th century, most of the sages of Europe (including Provence, France and Germany itself) were associated with the important Jewish centre at Lucca in northern Italy; but at the beginning of the 11th, the leadership passed to the magnificent *yeshiva* at Mainz, with Jews from northern France, Provence and even Italy coming to study under its sages. The various traditions were integrated and fertilized each other. Here, too, under the influence of the Italian immigrants, all shades of contemporary Jewish literature were studied. At this time, the Bible was still a most important source of halachic decision in everyday life. It was not until the mid-11th century that Germany followed the rest of the Diaspora in placing supreme reliance on the Babylonian Talmud. Nor do we find any trace of the kind of exact theological study known in Christian circles as scholasticism – presumably because the rise of scholasticism coincided with the time when the Jews began to seclude themselves from general society.

In Provence, too, an important spiritual centre emerged in the 11th and 12th centuries, but its connections with Babylon were closer than those of Italy and Germany. The surviving literature shows that this centre engaged in Midrash, too, and it had apparently come under the influence of Italy. In all these areas the Jews were in the vanguard of cultural progress. While only the first buds of such blossoming were to be seen in Christian society, all Jewish communities in Europe, including Muslim Spain, were imbued with religious learning and general education – the two great ideals of Jewish life. The destruction of the Torah centres in Germany during the persecutions of 1096 dealt the fatal blow to the current and future intellectual development of Ashkenazi Jewry.

The 12th century saw a cultural flowering all over Europe, and this applied to both Christian and Jewish society. But the directions of development were only partly comparable. In the first half of the century, chronicles were written in Germany describing the heroic stand of the Jewish martyrs in the First Crusade and they contained a bitter attack on the Christian faith. Such polemical literature was the first of its kind among Western European Jewry and, though not to be regarded as an important branch of Jewish cultural activity, it continued to develop in different forms. In Byzantium, another type of polemic, originating in Babylonia, had developed as early as the 10th century – against Karaism.

The most important work written in 12th–14th-century Europe was that of the Tosaphists, which began in France and spread to Germany and England. It essentially constituted a deeper study of the meaning of the talmudic questions. The Tosaphists regarded themselves as adding to and complementing the great commentary of Rashi on the Talmud, which was written in the second half of the 11th century, but in fact they introduced a new type of fundamental and sharp-witted study of talmudic exegesis, owing much to the legal and scholastic methods that flourished in Christian society at the time.

Another cultural branch which blossomed at the time was biblical exegesis. Beginning in the Ashkenazi *yeshivas* of the 11th century, it reached its height in northern and southern France in the 12th and 13th centuries. This exegesis, too, was influenced decisively by Rashi's commentaries on the Bible, which even affected some Christian biblical commentators. However, it developed in the direction of emphasis on the literal meaning of the Bible, whereas Rashi relied heavily on the Midrash. In Provence, an attempt was made at combining the various schools of biblical exegesis. On the other hand, in religious poetry in Germany and France, a certain decline took place after the zenith it had reached in the 11th century, when it constituted a vital force in forming the ideals of Jewish society.

Another aspect of intellectual life which was started in Provence and Spain and blossomed in the 13th century was the study of mysticism, discussed in Chapter 10.

In 12th- and 13th-century Germany, a most important movement emerged which was to affect certain circles throughout the Jewish world for hundreds of years. This was the movement of Hasidei Ashkenaz. Although it was uniform neither socially nor philosophically, and was marked by various shades of thought originating in different ages and from different people, yet certain clear dominating trends can be recognized. Many popular stories and fables are based on the aspiration to go beyond the letter of the law, beyond the requirements of the Torah applicable to all Jews, and to belong to a moral élite. At the same time, the Hasidim emphasized the need to understand one's fellow men and to show consideration to all, even Gentiles. Thus, for example, they opposed taking high interest from Christians, then the usual practice, and their doctrine contained a bitter social criticism of those leaders who, in their opinion, were not behaving properly and were concerned only with their own status and honour. Nevertheless, they preached the preference of those chosen for their family lineage and way of life. As we have seen, they even advocated the intermarriage of the 'good ones', i.e. those who followed Hasidic teachings and methods.

The compilation of halachic books, arranged by subject or in the order of the tractates of the Babylonian Talmud, which had begun in Spain in the 11th century and reached a peak in the work of Maimonides in the 12th, was carried out in Provence and Germany during the 13th and 14th. Why? Such compilations, as Maimonides himself suggests, always tend to accompany a period of decline in talmudic exegesis. In the tragic times following the Crusades, there was a need for summaries of the laws which could be used by people who were not themselves brilliant scholars.

The 13th century, in general, saw a great controversy over the question of philosophical education. It arose from the impact made by Maimonides's *A Guide to the Perplexed* on Orthodox belief and practice. By stimulating national enquiry, Maimonidean philosophy was thought to lead (and in certain cases did lead) to the neglect of some of the commandments and to the reinterpretation of parts of the Bible as allegory. The dispute came to a head in 1232. In that year the rabbis of northern France imposed a total ban on the study of philosophy, including *A Guide to the Perplexed*. Enlightened reaction was immediate. Jews all over the world realized that the fate of Jewish scholarship and culture was at stake. Each side was sure that even from a religious viewpoint it was absolutely right. The debate continued even in the most difficult hours of persecution and expulsion (such as the expulsion from France in 1306). Finally, a ban was maintained in some places but the general retreat from rationalism in the 13th century in Christian Europe, too, and the harsh persecutions of the Jews in the 14th and 15th centuries led to the whole question dying a natural death.

An important encounter between the Ashkenazi and Sephardi cultures took place from the 13th century onwards, and especially in the 15th century, mainly as a result of the expulsions. Various immigrants from Spain and even Western Europe turned to the Ottoman Empire and to Italy. Mutual acquaintance led to mutual influence but, on the other hand, revealed contrasts and discord. Despite the fact that each group tried to preserve its cultural uniqueness, each was influenced by the other.

In the 16th century, Poland rapidly became the most important centre of Torah study in Europe. Despite the fact that Polish Jewry regarded itself as the continuation of Ashkenazi Jewry, its *yeshivas* developed along rather different lines and included a variety of points of view.

The curriculum was limited almost entirely to the Talmud. No lessons were given on the Bible and even of the Talmud only a few tractates, mainly those that had some bearing on everyday life, were studied. The method of study was dispute and casuistry, which had first appeared in the German *yeshivas* in the 15th century. Underlying it was the assumption that the various sources in the talmudic tractates had to be entirely consistent, in accordance with the strict rules of logic, and in complete unity and harmony, and that by comparing and examining the various sources all the discrepancies that appeared among them could be adjusted. The students resorted to far-fetched intellectual exercises, whose main achievement was more often intellectual pungency than clarification of the problem under discussion.

Apart from talmudic exegesis, the only other flourishing area of study was ethical literature. The main purpose of this was to show man the desirable way of life, but it also took into account contemporary social and intellectual conditions. Some of it was written in Yiddish – an innovation compared with the early period in Germany, when all works were written in Hebrew. (In the Muslim caliphates, Arabic had always been the principal language alongside Hebrew.)

Another literary genre saw a notable development in the 15th and 16th centuries – Jewish historiography. Following the lead given by Italian Renaissance historians, Jewish writers learned to look critically at their material and to use secular and non-Jewish sources in examining traditional views. The upheaval experienced by Spanish Jewry after the Expulsion, in 1492, also played its part.

Some of the works produced in medieval Europe in the field of rabbinical literature, liturgy and philosophy are regarded to this day as the zenith of Jewish creativity in these fields. It is this achievement, brought to fruition despite all the enormous difficulties that stood in its path, that makes the Middle Ages so decisive a period for Jewish cultural history – more decisive than it is in the cultural history of Western Europe as a whole.

Chapter Eight

The Jews under Islam
Part one   6th – 16th centuries

SHELOMO DOV GOITEIN

JEWS AND JUDAISM stood at the cradle of Islam. This fateful conjunction had a lasting impact on the character of the new religion and greatly affected the destinies of the Jews who were to live under its shadow.

The Prophet Muhammad created a religion – Islam; a unique book – the Qur'ān; and a state with a powerful army. His greatest creation, however, and the precondition of all the others, was his belief in himself as the Messenger of God, called upon 'to bring' a book that would save the Arabs from Hell. To be sure, this is the way *we* put things. For the true believer it was God who wrought all this, not the man, who said of himself: 'I am only flesh like you' (Sūra XVIII: 110).

The greatness of the new faith may be gauged from its achievements. Politically, it changed the map of the world. Spiritually, through fourteen centuries, it provided countless millions with the tranquillity of religious certitude, stirred the elected few to mystical elation and served all as a safe guide to moral conduct.

The Companions of the Prophet felt that with him a new world had come into being. Soon after Muhammad's death they established a new era of chronology. As its beginning they chose the year 622, in which Muhammad and his followers left their native city of Mecca for the oasis of Medina, whose inhabitants had become receptive to monotheism by the presence in their midst of several flourishing Jewish settlements.

No one doubts today the originality of the Arab Prophet. This does not imply, however, a creation out of nothing. Quite the reverse. Muhammad never tired of emphasizing – in his earlier period – that he brought to the Arabs what others had received before, and – after his stunning successes – that he accomplished what others had begun.

The Arab character of the new religion expressed itself in the language of its holy scripture, in the adoption of Mecca, and the holy sites around, as its central sanctuary and in numerous Arab social notions and laws incorporated in its system. It is, therefore, all the more remarkable how thoroughly Islam absorbed elements of the Judaic heritage. From beginning to end, the Qur'ān is replete with biblical ideas, stories and phraseology. Telling references to post-biblical, specifically Jewish teachings, are included. The belief in the redeeming power of the book and in Moses as his predecessor in transmitting a heavenly scripture dominated the Arab

Prophet in his initial, formative period. He remained 'Judaic' throughout his career.

Islam shares with Judaism its stern monotheism, which abhors the 'association' with God of any other supernatural being. Muslims, like Jews, misunderstood the nature of the Trinity, regarding it as polytheistic, and abhorred its figurative representation as idolatry. The word *Islam* means exclusive and complete dedication. As the second *sūra* of the Qur'ān shows, the term originated in the story of Abraham, who is described in the Jewish tradition as a completely devoted servant of God. (The same Semitic root *slm* is used to express the idea of total dedication.) As in Judaism, the service of God consists of the fulfilment of his commandments, moral and, especially, ritual, which have to be carried out in an exactly prescribed manner. The study of these commandments, as laid down in the holy law, is worship. Islam, like Judaism, is a religion of deeds and study.

The Jews living under Islam were not unaware of this affinity. One can point to Abraham, the son and worthy successor of Moses Maimonides, who speaks of the Muslims as 'those who have adopted our type of religion' (literally: who walk in our ways), and notes with regret that some of the pious of Islam were worthier successors of the prophets of Israel than many Jewish contemporaries. Such attitudes found their expression in deeds. An 11th-century Hebrew family chronicle tells of a learned and well-to-do member who used to make donations for the illumination of the Dome of the Rock in Jerusalem. Such gifts were nothing exceptional: Muslim law books discussed the question whether it was permissible to accept such donations and answered it in the affirmative.

The fateful encounter
Such close affinity presupposes considerable personal contacts between the fledgling Prophet and representatives of the earlier religions. Although the Meccan opponents of Muhammad made repeated allusions to his mentors, we have no detailed information about such relations. 'The disbelievers say: "This is nothing but a fraud which he has devised: other people have helped him with it." They have also said: "These are stories of the ancients, which he has written down for himself; they are recited to him every morning and evening"' (Sūra XXV:4–5). 'It is only a human being who teaches him.' To this Muhammad retorts with the naïve, but most

significant, refutation: 'The language of him they hint at is foreign, but this is clear Arabic speech' (Sūra XVI:103). The language-minded Arabs would lend their ear only to pure Arabic, not, for instance, to the *ratāna*, or specific dialect spoken by the Jews. 'Verily this is a revelation by the Lord of the Worlds . . . in clear Arabic speech. Is it not a sign [a proof] to them that the learned of the children of Israel know it? If We [God is speaking] had sent it down through one of the foreigners and he had recited it to them, they would not have believed it' (Sūra XXVI:192–9).

In any case, during the centuries preceding the advent of Islam, there were many Jews in Arabia, and their influence was felt. Mention has already been made of Medina (where, according to his Muslim biographers, the Prophet passed his childhood). This Hebrew-Aramaic word is derived from *dīn*, law, and designates the place where lawsuits were settled, that is, the capital. From there the Wādī al-Qurā, the Valley of the Villages, stretched northward, and was also inhabited by Jews. Another great oasis was Khaybar, where, as in Medina, the Jews were date-palm growers and lived in fortress-like tower-houses. There were other Jewish settlements in and near northern Arabia, like the fishing villages of Maqna and Elat, which, of course, is the gate to Palestine.

Not only did Medina harbour the two 'priestly' tribes of Qurayza and Nadīr (called al-Kahīnān, Kohens, by the Arabs), who were farmers, but also a landless community of goldsmiths and silversmiths, the Qaynuqā'. In the days of Muhammad we hardly hear anything about Jewish merchants. In a rabbinic source of the 3rd century, the Jews of Arabia are described as possessing camels and incense, but no land. This means that they were engaged in great international trade at the time, which was later taken out of their hands by such local people as the enterprising citizens of Mecca.

In pre-Islamic South Arabia, which was generally referred to then as the land of the Sabeans (the biblical Sheba) or the Himyars, the Jews were particularly influential. Muslim and Christian sources speak about Himyarite kings who had converted to Judaism, and there are Sabean inscriptions that seemingly confirm this assumption. While in pagan inscriptions a multitude of gods is addressed, there are others dedicated to Rahmān, 'the All-merciful', alone, and some describe him as the 'God of the Jews'. Rahmān was a local deity, but in the Talmud it is the regular word for God, and it is to be understood as such in these monotheistic inscriptions.

A thorough examination of these inscriptions reveals, however, that the Himyar kings and nobility did not embrace Judaism. They cultivated a Judaizing monotheism, deeply concerned with life after death and centred around a local sanctuary, similar to the new religion subsequently propagated in Mecca. Had the famous last 'Jewish' king of Himyar, Dhu Nuwās, 'the man with the side locks' (in the inscriptions his name is As'ar), remained victorious, the Jews probably would have fared neither better nor worse under his Judaizing monotheism than they did, later, under Islam.

Fortunately, a bilingual Himyarite-Hebrew inscription by a professing Jew came to light in South Arabia recently (1969), enabling us to form an idea about the religious world of the pre-Islamic Arabian Jews. It describes the dedication of a house, which also served as a synagogue, to which other Jews ('Israel') had made a contribution.

'Judah YKF [family name] built, founded and completed his house YKRB [name of the house, possibly meaning "May it be blessed"] . . . through the power and grace of his Lord, who has created his soul, the Lord of the living and the dead, the Lord of heaven and earth, who has created everything, and with the aid of his [Judah's] people Israel, and with the authorization of his lord . . . the King of Sheba . . ., and the authorization of . . . and his tribes. . . .'

The Hebrew addition is short: 'Written by Judah, may he be remembered with blessings, Shalom [Peace], Amen.'

This concern with the soul and life after death and the awe before God, who effects everything, characterizes the spiritual atmosphere in which Muhammad perceived his call.

Recent scholarly work on the religious and political biography of Muhammad should be reassessed. It seems to be commonly assumed that it was the refusal of the Jews of Medina to recognize him as Prophet that forced Muhammad to give up his universalistic approach to monotheism and to form a militant religion of specific Arab character. Montgomery Watt, a modern biographer of Muhammad, goes so far as to argue that, had the Jews of Medina not been so proud, but a little bit more obliging, Islam would have become a Jewish sect and world history would have taken a different course.

A closer study of the Qur'ān and the trustworthy historical tradition of the Muslims provides another picture of Muhammad's development as Prophet and national leader. His original approach was indeed universalistic; that is, he believed that the one God had only one book to give; the different religions were versions of the same book, and he, as a language-minded Arab, saw himself called upon to bring a version in pure, easily understandable Arabic. Moreover, as a God-fearing man he had a natural attachment to the Ka'ba, the ancient sanctuary of his native city of Mecca. However, when he attacked the polytheism of his compatriots, the religion of their fathers, and began to argue with them, he was forced to make a closer study of monotheism, which he himself professed. To his dismay, he discovered that not only Jews and Christians, but the various Christian denominations, too, did not regard the other faiths as valid versions of their own; each claimed to be the exclusive possessor of God's message, and, consequently, also refused to accept Muhammad's claim to be a prophet sent to the Arabs. This discovery caused him great anguish; he wrestled with the problem for years: how could God's revelation cause discord and hatred among his believers instead of unity and co-operation? Muhammad's qualms were resolved thus: it was God's inscrutable will that his revelations would entail disunity. But if so, Muhammad's own message, as the last one, was final. The other monotheistic religions were legitimate, but they had to recognize the superiority of Islam. This religious reorientation of Muhammad happened in his native city of Mecca, long before he and his followers were forced to emigrate to Medina.

Muhammad's religious reappraisal had political consequences. Islam must rule; all other faiths must be subdued. The first to be affected by this new concept were the Jews of northern Arabia, for there were no compact Christian settlements nearby. When the emissaries of the few newly converted Arabs of Medina came to Muhammad to discuss with him the prospective emigration of his followers to their oasis, they were shocked to learn that he intended to liquidate their Jewish neighbours. 'You will come to Medina,' said one of them, 'annihilate the Jews and, after having succeeded with your plans, return to Mecca and leave us unprotected by our confederates.' Muhammad assured them that, once settled among them, he would never give up Medina and return to his native city. He kept his word, but the fate of the Jews of Medina was sealed long before Muhammad put his foot on the soil of that oasis.

If this was the true course of events, why then are the Medinese sections of the Qur'ān, by far the major part of the book, replete with orations addressed to the children of Israel, meaning the Jews, often also Jews and Christians together? The answer is that these orations were destined for the ears of the Arabs of Medina. For them it was no easy matter to betray their confederates of old and to see a number of them robbed and expelled and others liquidated. Many passages in the Qur'ān and in the writings of Muslim historians show how difficult it was for Muhammad to obtain the acquiescence of the local Arabs. Naturally, materialistic aspects were also involved. The houses, fields, date-palm groves and other possessions of the Jews were coveted spoils, especially for the landless émigrés from Mecca.

However, this revised approach to the biography of the Prophet does not change the fact that the Qur'ān, the holy book of Islam, which is read and memorized day in day out by millions of Muslims, contains, in addition to many approving passages about the 'children of Israel', derogatory and hostile remarks about the Jews. Naturally, in subsequent centuries, such remarks were used to justify attitudes towards the Jews.

When Muhammad's realm expanded beyond Medina to far away places, another approach to the treatment of non-Muslims was required. They were left where they were, granted security for their lives and possessions, but had to hand over their weapons, armour and horses, and pay heavy annual tributes. For instance, the Jews of Khaybar had to deliver half of the crop from their palm groves, and those of Maqna a quarter of their dates, their fishing and the fine cloth woven by their women. These arrangements created a precedent, but, as will be immediately seen, by no means a strict model, for the treatment of non-Muslims under Islam.

The price of protection

Although the Qur'ān contains numerous passages unfavourable to Jews, the Muslim law books do not discriminate between Jews and Christians. The reason for this might be found in the situation during the early formative period of Islam, when Jews actively supported the Muslim armies while the Christians were regarded as hostile or, at least, suspect.

As the examples of Khaybar and Maqna show, legally binding agreements, or, rather, concessions granted by the victors, were made immediately after the conquest. Indeed, regulations with regard to the position of non-Muslims belong to the most ancient parts of Islamic law. Because the situation differed from one place to another

and constantly changed during the 150 years or so of Muslim expansion, it is almost impossible to trace the development of these regulations until they first appear in the law books around 800. This was not the end, but rather the beginning of discriminatory legislation. The Muslim rulers promulgated ordinances from time to time that further aggravated the lot of the non-Muslims, but, favoured by propitious socio-economic circumstances, they often succeeded in evading the harshness of the law. By the late Middle Ages, however, the Muslim state prevailed. By making the life of its non-Muslim subjects intolerable, it succeeded in reducing their once flourishing communities to powerless minorities, whose miserable existence served to remind the Muslims that their religion was superior, or, rather, was the only true religion.

This was indeed the intention of the original law concerning 'those who have been given the Book' (Jews and Christians), as laid down by Muhammad at the end of his life, when, at the height of his success, he spoke of God and himself in one breath: 'Fight those who do not believe in God and not in the Last Day, and do not prohibit what God and his Messenger have prohibited, and do not embrace the true religion, namely those who have been given the Book, until they pay the [poll] tax . . . while they are in a state of humiliation' (Sūra IX:29). The endless vexations described here and in the section on the late Middle Ages are only variations of the theme broached in this verse. On the other hand, the humiliated state of the Christians and Jews was considered the price for their protection and for the toleration of their religion.

In practice, laws against non-Muslims were created from time to time as the physical and spiritual needs of the Muslim community dictated. In the early phase of the wars of conquest, the local population was requested not to wear arms and to deliver all war materials; it was made defenceless. In return, the conqueror promised protection. This protection was called *dhimma*, meaning responsibility; consequently, Jews and Christians and their like were described as *ahl al-dhimma* or *dhimmīs*, people enjoying this privilege. Good Muslim rulers and upright jurists took this 'responsibility' seriously and protected the minorities against the outbursts of the mob or the fanaticism of less enlightened scholars.

War materials included horses. The *dhimmīs* were prohibited from riding horses at all or at least with the saddles used by Arabs. In later times, and for reasons other than providing safety for the invading Muslims, a plethora of vexatious regulations concerning riding grew out of this prohibition.

Another safety measure was the injunction that no *dhimmī* should array himself or dress his hair like an Arab. He should be easily recognizable by wearing a belt, so that no treacherous attack on stray Muslims might occur. This was the beginning of a periodic reiteration of laws specifically designed to discriminate against the infidels.

In order to control the masses of Christians and Jews, a poll-tax was imposed on each of them. This, like numerous other impositions, was inherited from the preceding empires. In South Arabia, Muhammad himself taxed each adult, male or female, one dinar (a gold coin) or its equivalent. This was probably the practice of the Persians, who had ruled the Yemen before him. When the Arabs conquered Syria, they found that the Jews, male only, paid the Byzantine government a staggering poll-tax of one, two, or four dinars in accordance with their means. The victors preferred this system, which became standard in the law books, though not always in reality.

One or two gold pieces a year appears to be a modest imposition. It was not. A large section of the population, townspeople included, lived at starvation level. A schoolmaster often would not earn more than five dirhems (a silver coin) a week, the equivalent of about six dinars a year. If he had only two sons of the age of, say, eleven and thirteen, all regarded as adults by the tax collector, his poll-tax amounted to three dinars. The ancient law books prescribe that the poor should be exempted from the obligation to pay the tax. As the letters and documents of the Cairo Geniza (see below) prove, this humane ruling was not observed even during the 'liberal' Fatimid period (969–1171). The poor went begging for their poll-tax more frequently than for food. If they did not pay, they were thrown into prison, where they suffered maltreatment and even death.

When the Muslims came out of Arabia into the great cities of the Fertile Crescent they were overawed by the splendour of the cathedrals and the solemnity of religious functions, and even funeral processions, that they witnessed. Moreover, the thoughtful among them began 'to ask the People of the Book'. In view of the form the biblical stories took in the Qur'ān, it is easy to imagine that the answers received aroused new questions. Finally, out of necessity, the administration of the newly conquered provinces remained for a long time in the hands of the officials who had previously run it; a Muslim could find himself bowing to the authority of a non-Muslim. It was not the physical safety, now, but the inner security of the true believer that was threatened. The situation was quickly remedied by a long series of provisions in Muslim law, designed to limit contact with non-Muslims.

Following Byzantine legislation concerning synagogues, the erection of new houses of worship was prohibited; about the repairs of old ones, opinions were divided. Public display of religion, such as processions or blowing the *shofar* in a Muslim environment, were forbidden. In the new cities founded by the Muslims, churches and synagogues were built, of course, since the Christians and Jews living there could not do without them. But they were inconspicuous and concealed by huddles of surrounding buildings. Apostasy from Islam was punished by death, and non-Muslims trying to propagate their faith among Muslims were liable to incur the same fate. As soon as it appeared feasible, the employment of *dhimmīs* as government officials was prohibited, an ordinance that had to be renewed again and again over the centuries.

The more the power of the caliphs declined, the more did they try to make themselves conspicuous by harassing all the non-Muslims. The wretched al-Mutawakkil decreed that Christians and Jews should wear yellow badges on their garments (*c.* 850). Clearly this decree was not generally observed, for the wearing of badges had to be reintroduced by another caliph half a century later. Under the Fatimids of Egypt, the discriminatory laws on clothing seem to have fallen into desuetude. However, during the great persecution of non-Muslims by the eccentric caliph, al-Hākim (996–1121), these laws were renewed and aggravated. For instance, because women were known to be concerned with their appearance, they were singled out for particularly offensive humiliation, such as being forced to wear shoes of different colours. Al-Hākim himself soon called off the persecution, but the ingenious invention concerning women's shoes was taken up again by a caliph of Baghdad about a hundred years later. The Ayyubid rule of Egypt and Syria (*c.* 1171–1250) was a period of transition. In the late Middle Ages, the occupation with the mistreatment of non-Muslims became an obsession of rulers, jurisconsults and the population at large.

Socio-economic conditions

Oppressive as it was, the position of the Jews under medieval Islam cannot be compared to their position in Western Europe. Massacres and mass expulsions, so common there, were practically unknown in Islamic countries. The reason for this difference can be found in the totally different socio-economic conditions of the Jews in the two areas. In Europe, the Jews formed tiny colonies of foreigners, separated from the bulk of the population not only by religion and culture (they used Hebrew, not Latin, as their language of literary expression), but by their confinement to a few hateful occupations, which put them outside of and in opposition to the population at large. Under Islam, the Jews were not the only minority; the presence of far more numerous Christian communities preserved them from excessive isolation. Moreover, in the countries of Islam the Jews were indigenous old-timers, and active almost in all walks of life. The Cairo Geniza, a treasure-trove of letters and documents mainly from the 10th to the 13th century, mentions about 450 occupations in which Jews were engaged – of which about 250 were manual – that is, jobs for craftsmen and artisans of all types. The division of labour in those days was phenomenal. This explains why we find Jews in so many different occupations.

The notion that Jews were confined under Islam to 'despised' manual professions, such as tanners, dyers, butchers, or cobblers, or to work connected with precious metals, such as goldsmiths and money-changers, is unfounded, as far as the high Middle Ages are concerned. Muslims, even from scholarly families, were engaged in all these occupations as well. Dyeing was a different matter. Colour (and not the cut) was the pride of the medieval costume, and, with the primitive (mostly natural) dyeing materials then available, dyeing was an art, of which Jews were reputed to possess certain secrets. The Geniza shows, indeed, that they specialized in various dyeing processes such as purple-making, and that there were dyers of high socio-economic standing. The most common 'learned manual professions' of Jews were those of the pharmacists and the makers of medical potions.

The pronounced professional and economic diversity of the Jewish community had the effect that the Jews did not represent a distinct social class but were fairly well distributed among the various layers of the population. A statistical examination of the family papers preserved in the Geniza reveals that about 15 per cent of the people represented in them were destitute, 45 per cent lived in modest circumstances, 20 per cent belonged to the lower middle class, and about 16 per cent to the upper middle class, while the real rich comprised about 4 per cent of the total.

This stratification of Jewish society created close contact with the Muslim population. A Jewish baker would get a loan from a Muslim miller; Jewish and Muslim merchants co-operated and even concluded partnerships (although this was disapproved by most of the religious codes); physicians of the two creeds worked together as colleagues in the same hospital; and even the official representatives of the two religions, the judges and their like, respected one another (unless they had reason not to do so). Geniza letters of Jewish divines, referring to cadis, and the famous poem in honour of Moses Maimonides written by the chief cadi of Cairo, Ibn Sanā' al-Mulk, are cases in point.

It was fortunate for Jewish history that Babylonia (Iraq) and the neighbouring countries, which harboured the main stock of the Jewish people, as well as its central institutions, became the political, economic and cultural core of the Islamic world. Unfortunately, however, our information about this period, the 8th and 9th centuries, is extremely scanty. The terrible upheavals and persecutions during the last century of the Persian Empire, the horrors of the conquest by Bedouin hordes and the subsequent oppressive administration must have had dire consequences for the *dhimmīs*. It was during this period, the 6th and 7th centuries, that the last remnants of the Jewish farming population were dispossessed, and, like others, fled to the cities, where they formed a proletariat. In any case, not long after the advent of Islam the Jews had become a purely urban society.

On the other hand the Jewish merchant class, which had come into prominence around 200, made good use of the opportunities offered by the conquests and, later, the economic efflorescence of the Muslim Empire. When the Arabs raided the island of Rhodes in 672/3 and carried away from there its famous Colossus (one of the seven wonders of the ancient world), they sold its metal to a Jewish merchant. It weighed 880 camel loads (about 44,000 pounds). Only a very wealthy man could have been able to make such a deal. The most stupendous example of Jewish enterprise was the company of the Radhanites, whose undertakings, by sea and by land, encompassed almost the entire world known at the time – from France, Spain and North Africa in the West, to Iraq, Iran, India and China in the East. They also visited Constantinople, the capital of Byzantium, and the land of the Khazars, a Turkish people occupying south-eastern Russia at the time. The acceptance of Judaism by the rulers and nobles of the Khazars was certainly due to the influence of those great Jewish merchants. A recent study on them has shown it likely that their base was Iraq.

Under the Umayyads of Damascus a Jew was already in charge of the caliphal mint (*c.* 695). Throughout Islamic history, Jews remained connected with the mints (mostly as entrepreneurs, not as officials). As the weakest of the communities under Islam they could be trusted. They knew well that no one would protect them in the case of any misdeed. The loans provided to the caliphal treasury by the famous Ibn Phineas family of Baghdad

(early 10th century) should not induce us to believe that the Jews were the Rothschilds of the Islamic world. In general, we hear more about loans taken by Jews from Muslims than vice versa.

In the course of the 10th century, Iraq and Iran became devastated as a result of internecine wars and bad administration. The well-to-do Muslims and Jews moved westward. Soon we find 'Easterners' being the leading Jewish families in North Africa, Egypt and, later, in Aden, South Arabia. Owing to their capital and business experience a flourishing Jewish trade developed in the Muslim countries of the Mediterranean. By the end of the 11th century, however, the Italian maritime cities had driven the Muslim navies, and with them their merchant-men, off the sea. The enterprising Jews turned to the route to India, importing spices, medical herbs, dyeing materials, iron and other Oriental goods. The 12th century was the great time of the Jewish India trade. By the 13th century this trade became more or less monopolized by the Muslim India 'Hanse' of the Kārim. In general, the range of Jewish occupations and enterprises became very much narrowed in the late Middle Ages, a fact which had an adverse effect on their social position.

Communal organization

The high Middle Ages also witnessed far reaching changes in the communal organization of the Jews under Islam. At the beginning, the central institutions of the Jews in Babylonia that developed during late Antiquity, the exilarchate and the *yeshivas* (for higher learning), were still in operation. The exilarch, the *resh galutha*, should not be described, as he frequently is, as the secular head of the Jews, because the Jews were a religious, not a political, community. He was a kind of monarch, claiming to be a descendant of King David, a claim recognized by the Muslim authorities. He appointed, or, rather, confirmed the appointment of the *gaons*, the heads of the two *yeshivas*. These were not educational institutions (no 'student' was ever admitted), but rather corporations of learned members, who studied texts assigned to them and discussed and decided questions submitted to the *gaons*. Both the *resh galutha* and the *gaons*, after having received the approval of the Jewish community, were installed by the caliphs, which was done by the delivery of an appropriate document and the investiture with a robe specific to each office. By the 10th century, the exilarch and the two *gaons* had their seats in Baghdad. The Jewish population of Iraq and adjacent countries was divided into regions, each of which made contributions to one of the three dignitaries.

A third *yeshiva* was in Jerusalem. After the conquest of Egypt and Palestine by the Fatimids (969), its *gaon* was recognized by the Fatimid caliphs as the head of the Jews in their empire with the right to appoint the judges and lower officials and to supervise the religious and communal affairs of the Jews within their realm. Both he and the judges needed a new letter of installation whenever a new caliph ascended the throne.

In the countries once belonging to the Byzantine Empire, such as Syria, Palestine and Egypt, the local communities were under the authority of the Jerusalem *yeshiva*. In addition, because of the influx of Jews from

Part of a court record written by Abraham Maimonides, son of the great philosopher Moses Maimonides, which was found among the Geniza documents at Cairo. Abraham practised medicine, as did his father, and succeeded him as chief physician to the Jewish community in Egypt.

Iraq and Iran, 'Iraqian' synagogues were founded everywhere. In communal affairs, such as the care of the poor and the education of their children, the two local communities mostly co-operated. In many places there existed a third congregation, namely that of the Karaites (see below).

The local congregation, the *kehilla*, like the *yeshiva*, was a pre-Islamic institution. It was a corporation headed by a Council of Elders, who took care of the financial affairs and social services. They assisted the spiritual leader, called *dayan*, judge, or, when he was learned, *haver*, that is, member of the *yeshiva*, in his juridical and other duties. Those rabbinical courts, mostly composed of experienced merchants, often with overseas relations, were effectual and contributed much to Jewish autonomy and interterritorial cohesion.

In the course of the 11th century, that is, long before the advent of the Crusaders, Palestine became completely devastated through the incessant wars between the Fatimids and various insurgents, and, finally, between them and the Seljuks and Turkomans. The *yeshiva* was forced to leave Jerusalem (*c.* 1072) for Tyre, Lebanon, and, later, Damascus, a blow from which it never recovered. At the same time, approximately, Mevorakh ben Saadya ha-Rofe, an honorary member of both the *yeshivas* of Baghdad and also that of Jerusalem, himself a physician in attendance at the Fatimid court, became the official and spiritual head of the Jews of Egypt and the adjacent countries. He and his successors appointed the local judges and other officials, made all the decisions on

religious and public affairs and intervened for Jews wherever needed. From the time of Abraham, the son of Moses Maimonides (early 13th century), this dignity, called *nagid*, or prince, became hereditary in the family of Maimonides, an unhealthy practice based on Islamic models.

A similar development can be observed at the local level. The *dayan* became like a cadi, replacing, with his functionaries, the laymen leaders by taking care of the financial affairs and the social services of the community. The ancient Jewish 'religious democracy' gave way to Islamic authoritarianism.

The Babylonian *yeshivas*, too, participated in the general decline of the country in which they had their seat. As their incessant letters requesting help indicate, they were often reduced to utmost poverty. However, from the reports of the Muslim historians it is evident that, during the first half of the 13th century, *gaons* were still regularly installed in their office by the 'Abbasid caliphs, the last one known to us in 1250. With the conquest of Baghdad by the Mongols, in 1258, and the murder of the last 'Abbasid caliph this relationship, naturally, came to an end.

Cultural transformation

As in the case of communal organization, the cultural development of the Jews under Islam was a combination of indigenous Jewish elements, continuing and even flourishing, and Islamic models, which were followed and assimilated. This Judaeo-Islamic symbiosis had a decisive impact on the formation of classical Jewish thought and practice.

In Jewish historiography, this period, because of the overwhelming authority enjoyed by the Babylonian *yeshivas* and their leaders, is called the 'Gaonic' period. Everywhere in the Diaspora, Jews wished to live in accordance with the Law of God; but all the time problems arose, either created by new situations or by incomplete or controversial interpretation of the sacred texts. Questions of individual scholars or communities, sifted by the highest religious authority in each country, and accompanied by donations, were sent to Baghdad, and, after having been discussed in the *yeshivas*, were returned by the *gaons* together with their 'opinions'. Thousands of pieces of correspondence with such Muslim countries as Spain, Morocco, Tunisia and the Yemen have been preserved. Together with collections of legal opinions (*responsa*), written by several *gaons* in Aramaic and Hebrew, they form the corpus of traditional Jewish learning created in that period.

Meanwhile, however, Islam had developed its own law. The Jewish judiciary formed a part of the juridical system of the Islamic state, and some co-ordination was necessary. Saadya al-Fayyūmī (882–942) and other *gaons* wrote systematic treatises on Jewish law (civil as well as ritual) in Arabic, using, of course, Islamic legal terms and principles of arrangement. Moses Maimonides's great and 'definite' Code of Jewish Law and Belief, written in Hebrew, is a synthesis of traditional Jewish learning and Islamic systematization.

The text of the Hebrew Bible, its vocalization and cantillation, was finally established during the 8th and 9th centuries, through the efforts of the Masoretes, the bearers of Jewish tradition. It was, however, the example of the language-minded Arabs that induced the Jews to study the grammatical structure and vocabulary of biblical and, soon, also post-biblical Hebrew. This activity started in the East, again with Saadya Gaon, but reached its perfection in the Muslim West, especially in Spain, that 'border province' of Islam with its passionate dedication to pure, classical Arabic. The occupation with Hebrew became a major concern for the Jewish intellectuals of that country. The work of the Jewish linguists there, mainly during the 10th century, remained unsurpassed until modern times.

Hebrew traditional poetry, the *piyyut*, reached its zenith in Palestine in late Byzantine times and continued to flourish during the early centuries of Islam. It was the zeal for the holy language that motivated pious Jews to introduce secular, sometimes even frivolous, topics into Hebrew poetry while using Arabic forms of versification and modes of expression. This new poetry was created almost entirely in Spain. The real acme of Judaeo-Arabic symbiosis, however, was attained in Spanish Hebrew *religious* poetry, in which Jewish tradition, belief and emotion were fused with Arabic form and rhetoric in a superb way.

Judaism never constituted a solid block of beliefs. It was, however, the example of Islam with its multitude of sects and heresies that brought those divisions within Judaism into full light. The most important Jewish heresy was that of the Karaites, who rejected the authority of the talmudic sages, the rabbis, and claimed to accept that of the Bible alone. The Karaites, many of whom were well educated (and also rich and powerful), were the first to make prolific use of argumentation as found in Islamic theological literature. They contributed much to the intellectual assimilation of the Jewish intelligentsia.

In late Antiquity and early Islamic times, Jewish thought was expressed in the form of the Midrash, comments on a great variety of topics based on verses of the Bible, and connected with one another in a purely associative way (a characteristic word, etc.). Systematic, logical thinking, such as that of Philo Judaeus of Alexandria, who wrote in Greek, did not reach the Aramaic speaking Jewish populace. Christian theology, however, absorbed Greek philosophy, and Islam followed suit. Arabic became the depository for logical thinking. Muslim, Christian and Jewish intellectuals in Baghdad of the 10th century convened to discuss purely philosphical topics. If the Jewish populace was not to lose its intelligentsia, Judaism had to be presented in a form acceptable to it. This was done, in the course of three hundred years, from Saadya Gaon to Abraham Maimonides, in a series of works on Jewish thought, differing widely in character, scope and quality. They had, however, one thing in common: they were all written in Arabic. The abundant quotations found in them presupposed complete familiarity with biblical and post-biblical Hebrew literature; Moses Maimonides had shown in the sections on belief in his great Code that it was perfectly possible to express abstract thought in the Hebrew language. But, by the fifth century of Islam, Arabic had become the means of literary expression for most Jews living under its shadow. This deep-rooted assimilation of the Jewish intelligentsia to its Arabic environment was not without consequences.

The disastrous late Middle Ages

In the late Middle Ages the pagan Mongols overran large parts of the Muslim and Christian worlds; the ancient Muslim system of the rule of soldier castes, consisting of imported slaves, reached its zenith in the domination of Egypt, Palestine and Syria by the Mamluks (1250–1517); epidemics, beginning with the catastrophic Great Plague of Egypt in 1201–2, culminated in the Black Death of 1348–50; finally, a new world power, Ottoman Turkey, comprising most of the Arab world and much of Europe, came into being. Powerful rulers displayed great splendour, but large sections of the population experienced incredible misery; the Jews, the most vulnerable section, were particularly hard hit.

Basically, the wrath of the Muslims was turned against the Christians. It was the end of the Crusader period in the Levant; in the critical half century prior to the conversion of the western Mongols to Islam (c. 1295), they co-operated with the Christians; the Muslims were driven out of Spain; and European rulers attacked North Africa. However, Muslim law and popular attitudes made no distinction between the Jewish and Christian *dhimmīs*. Whenever heavy fines or new harassing restrictions were imposed on Christians, when their houses of worship were temporarily closed or destroyed, or when they were attacked by the mob, Jews suffered together with them. Moreover, Christian kings who had diplomatic relations with Islamic rulers intervened with them for their co-religionists. Jews did not enjoy such protection.

The rise of religious fanaticism during the late Middle Ages, to be observed in Islam and in Christian Europe, induced the rulers to take the lead in the persecution of the infidels. The Muslim historians provide us with an unending list of edicts, promulgated by governments, destined to humiliate the *dhimmīs* and to make their lives unbearable. In 1301, the yellow colour was reserved for Jews, while dark-blue was made obligatory for Christians. Already around 1250 a Geniza letter reports from Cairo that, on a Sabbath, a government town-crier proclaimed in the morning and evening that any Jew or Christian walking in the street without his distinctive badge or a belt had forfeited his possessions and his life. *Dhimmīs* were forbidden to ride, not only on horses or mules, but even on donkeys worth more than ten dirhems. Soon they were prohibited from riding altogether (except when travelling overland), an extreme humiliation, especially for a man of standing. For the year 1247, a Muslim historian reports that a *gaon* in Baghdad, after having received his investiture from the vizier and chief cadi, went home with his retinue on foot, but when the mob attacked them with stone throwing the culprits were imprisoned and punished. Stone throwing on such occasions was accepted practice, but, clearly, the historian reports this detail because the protective measures of the government were exceptional and therefore noteworthy.

A visitor to Egypt around the middle of the 13th century reports that most of the Jews there were either government clerks or physicians. A hundred years later: 'Every customs official is a Jew.' These statements are exaggerated, but they demonstrate the vulnerability of those professions; on the one hand they carried with them a certain measure of authority, on the other, they brought those who were engaged in them into daily contact with the population at large. Muslim religious writers fulminated against the employment of *dhimmīs* as government clerks or physicians, and the rulers promulgated ordinances from time to time, leaving their officials the choice only between dismissal or conversion. Edicts prohibiting Jewish physicians from treating Muslims were less frequent, but the propaganda against them was poisonous and widespread, and without attending Muslim patients a Jewish doctor could not make a livelihood.

The outcome of all this was that a very large section of the Jewish (and the Christian) intelligentsia, and not only physicians, converted to Islam. The late Middle Ages produced voluminous Muslim biographical dictionaries containing thousands of life stories, and not a few of them tell the story of a Jewish convert. This was a multifaceted phenomenon, which deserves a special study. Firstly, the Jewish intellectual had a somewhat sceptical view of the absolute truth of revealed religion. The Jew Sa'd ibn Kammūna, in his brilliant *Examination of the Three Faiths*, published in Baghdad in 1280, collected all the 'proofs' for and against the truth of Judaism, Christianity and Islam – and demonstrated that both the pros and cons were futile. Secondly, some intellectuals were disgusted with certain aspects of Jewish life, such as the bickerings about the *shehīta* (the ritual killing of animals), and developed a self-hatred not unknown in other quarters. Thirdly, conversion to Islam was, from the theological point of view, less heartbreaking than to Christianity with its Trinity. Finally, as demonstrated by both the Cairo Geniza and Muslim sources, Islamic pietism and mysticism attracted religiously minded people. Abraham Maimonides had tried to reform Judaism in that direction, but failed. In the main, however, the sarcastic Sa'd ibn Kammūna might have been right in asserting: 'We never see anyone converting to Islam except when in fear, or out of quest for power, or to avoid heavy taxation, or to escape humiliation, or because of infatuation with a Muslim woman.'

In 1335 and 1344 (a period of the rise of a new dynasty), the Jews of Baghdad were exposed to brutal persecutions:

The Egyptian Jews formed one of the oldest and most deeply rooted communities, but declined under Mamluk rule in the 15th century. In this woodcut after a drawing of about 1500, from the travels of Arnold von Harff, various nationalities are shown, the Jew on the right.

their property and personal safety were in jeopardy, the synagogues were demolished, precious libraries destroyed and anyone who counted was forced to convert to the ruling religion. A comment on Hebrew elegies written in those days states: 'No Jew in Baghdad could keep his religion, except those who were not conspicuous by money, knowledge or rank.'

The defection of a large part of its intelligentsia (which was certainly duplicated by the lower classes) emasculated the Jewish community under Islam. By no means did scientific and literary activities cease, but they were largely of an epigonic character. The situation was remedied when, from the 14th century onwards, refugees and emigrants from Spain and other Christian regions settled in the countries of Islam. North Africa was the first area to benefit from this inner Jewish migration. Around 1500 this had become a mass movement. The 16th century witnessed a general revival of the Jewish community under Islam.

The Jews under Islam
Part two   c. 1500 – today

AMNON COHEN

Jewish life under Islam during the second half of the second millennium concentrated almost exclusively in the Ottoman Empire. Beyond its eastern and western borders, in Persia and Morocco, there were two important and old Jewish communities, which, in spite of the vicissitudes of the political and military strife between these competing Islamic states, could still maintain some of the traditional economic and other links with their co-religionists across the borders. Numerically and otherwise, however, they were inferior to and influenced by the overwhelming majority of Oriental Jews living under the Ottoman sultans. The Ottomans ruled over parts of European Jewry also (Hungarian, Bulgarian, Romanian, Balkan, Greek), thus making them even more important from a wider Jewish perspective. And on top of all that, the Ottomans were also the masters of the Holy Land, the importance of which in Jewish eyes could hardly be exaggerated, quite apart from the actual number of its Jewish inhabitants.

Jewish life under the Ottomans dates back to the very early stages of the growing state. During the 14th century, not only did the Ottomans become rulers over Jewish communities, but they also encouraged the influx of Jews from the coastal areas into their newly established centres of administration (Brusa, Edirne). This policy was implemented even more systematically after Istanbul (Constantinople) had become their permanent capital (1453): as part of a general scheme aimed at the increase of the population of Istanbul, Jews were also invited to come over from other parts of the empire and settle there, which they actually did in increasingly impressive numbers stretching for well over a century. A certain influx may also have occurred as a consequence of the invitation extended by some prominent Jews in Istanbul to their European kin to come and share with them their secure and prosperous life. All of these, however, turned out to be only minor elements – quantitatively and otherwise – in the demographic picture of Ottoman Jews. The factor that became overwhelmingly important in this respect was the arrival of those who had been expelled from Spain. The majority of the 200,000 expelled by Ferdinand were welcomed by the Ottoman sultan, who regarded them as a major contribution to the development of his economy, thus combining religious tolerance with economic expediency. The newcomers proved this approach to be more than valid. Some were instrumental in the establishment and promotion of industries such as fire-arms, gunpowder and artillery, and most conspicuously

in the various stages of the manufacture of textiles (most prominent and productive in this respect was Salonica, with its overwhelming Jewish presence, especially during the 16th century); other Jews used the capital and their widespread commercial contacts to foster the flow of merchandise to and from the main ports of the empire. In the middle of the 16th century they were described as follows: 'They have in their hands the most and greatest traffic of merchandise and ready money that is in the Levant.' A most outstanding example at that time was the Mendes family, who through their banking system controlled a large proportion of the European spice and wool trade. Doña Gracia, the head of the family, though using both Jewish and Muslim funds in her financial consortium, could base her activity on the capital that she managed to bring over from Europe. In the same century, another lady, Esther Kyra, amassed most of her huge capital in Istanbul by farming the collection of customs and various taxes as well as by actively participating in international trade. In later centuries, when other communities became equally involved in international trade (and in some cases even surpassed such financiers), there were still Jewish bankers in the capital (and elsewhere, e.g. Yehezkel Gabbay from Baghdad) who had impressive resources at their disposal, which they successfully employed both in trade and industry.

Ottoman attitudes

What was the extent and what were the limitations of Ottoman toleration of the Jews? At the outset one should point out that the Jews under the Ottomans did not suffer collectively from outbursts of aggression even reminiscent of the persecution and pogroms their kin were exposed to in many parts of Christian Europe. Being regarded as *ahl al-kitab*, they were protected by the state, but the protection was two-edged and resulted in wide discrimination by both the authorities and the public. The bright careers of those Jews highly placed and very influential in their time crashed immediately after the replacement of their benefactors; their fortunes were confiscated and not infrequently they met untimely death. Being underprivileged meant that they were liable to special taxes, such as the poll-tax, *jizya*, which was replaced in 1855 by a compulsory exemption tax from military service, the *bedel*. Social and other restrictions were imposed on the Jews in the spirit of the 'Covenant of 'Umar'. Jews were not allowed to possess slaves of any denomination or to build houses unless specifically

186

authorized to do so, and only then if they were a quarter lower than those of Muslims. The erection of new synagogues was forbidden altogether. A Jew should never ride a horse or use a boat that had more than three pairs of oars. Special attention was given to the way they dressed: official decrees specified the shape and colour that their headgear and shoes should take, and even when they frequented the public bathhouse they had to put on certain signs (clogs, bells, etc.) to distinguish them from all the others. Yellow was very often the colour they were supposed to use, either for their headgear or other clothing, and as a general regulation (on some occasions even under the threat of the death penalty) they were several times forbidden to wear expensive garments. Finally, there were blood libels (accusation of ritual murder), which can be traced back to the 16th century (in the towns of Amasya or Tokat in Anatolia), and which became most prevalent in the 19th century (Damascus, 1840; Beirut, 1862; Istanbul, 1864–5; Edirne, 1872; Aleppo, 1875). The immediate source of the story was often a Christian one, and needless to say it always proved to be false, but in the meantime Jews were insulted and maltreated, and in some cases (notoriously in Damascus, 1841) influential international Jewish figures had to intervene in order to attain their formal (though never final) exoneration by the Ottoman authorities.

The more we learn of the realities of Jewish life under Islam the clearer it becomes to us that many of the restrictive regulations mentioned above were circumvented. Though usually forbidden, the riding of horses was a privilege enjoyed by a few exceptional Jews (e.g. Yehezkel Gabbay in the 19th century); upon the conquest of Cyprus Jews were permitted by the sultan to purchase slaves (and Jews from Cairo and Damascus are reported to have widely exercised this privilege); some synagogues were closed down by the authorities towards the end of the 16th century (in Jerusalem, Damascus and Cairo), but new ones were either especially built or introduced into private houses, later officially sanctioned by the government (in Istanbul, Salonica, Jerusalem); contrary to the general belief, Jewish testimony was accepted in the local courts of justice in civil as well as in criminal cases; the very recurrence of orders specifying the colour and shape of their dress (with changing details through the ages), along with other information, indicates the relatively low degree of implementation of these regulations. Local or highly placed contacts, external pressure and ample sums of money were resorted to alternatively or concurrently, in order to abolish acts of oppression perpetrated by local governors in the various provinces throughout the centuries. Still, arbitrary harsh measures were often applied to the Jews either by the authorities (thus the execution, by sultan's order, of the rabbi who had brought an unsatisfactory amount of taxes from Salonica in 1636), or, more frequently, by various local elements, mostly Muslims, and sometimes Christians.

The upper echelons

Intensive Jewish involvement in banking, money-lending and trade, both interprovincial and international, should not be misinterpreted as an expression of economic segregation of any form. Until the

Doña Gracia Mendes-Nassi, c. 1520. Head of a financial consortium based in Istanbul, controlling Jewish and Muslim funds, Doña Gracia was welcomed by the Sultan and played an important role in aiding other endangered Jews. A bronze medallion by Pastorino, Ferrara.

18th century, Muslims were widely active in the various types of trade with Europe, while Jews were welcomed, and actually widespread, in almost all other professions. Some of the financial experts referred to above, it should be noted, were regarded by their sultan, grand viziers or other dignitaries of the empire not only as advisers in this field, but also as being highly reliable from other points of view, including the political. Don Joseph Nassi was granted Naxos, and some of its neighbouring Aegean islands, as well as Tiberias in Palestine, wherefrom, according to old tradition, Jewish redemption would start.

Not less influential in later years, in the 16th century, were Salomon Ashkenazi, Salomon ben Ya'ish and Esther Kyra. Jews never again reached this height of achievement, but two hundred years later some of them were still influential in Istanbul, either with the sultans (e.g. the Carmona family) or with the Janissary corps (the Adjimans). In some instances this influence was initially gained as a result of their being the private physicians of the sultan (most famous were the Hamons in the 16th century, when it was reported that the number of Jewish doctors in Istanbul was higher than Muslim). Jewish doctors, however, were equally popular in the provincial centres, such as Cairo and Jerusalem. They all contributed, undoubtedly, to create an impression like that reported in 1547 by a French doctor, Belon: 'Those who practise medicine in Turkey . . . and in other towns in Turkish territory are, for the most part, Jews.'

As well as finance and medicine, another official Jewish role within the Ottoman administration was the management of several sectors of the state economy: various monopolies, like the wine or bees-wax trade; the mint (*dar al-darb*) in Egypt, almost as a matter of tradition, and that of Damascus, occasionally; the customs of many ports and other commercial centres (Istanbul, Bursa, Buda). Official decrees refer to the last phenomenon as a matter of fact when they mention, in 1577, that all the intendants in the port of Suez are

Jewish; this is perhaps even better summarized in a firman to the cadis of Istanbul, dated 12 October 1583: 'Most of the intendants [*emin*] of the ports and the customs, as well as the purveyors and contractors, are Jews, while their co-religionists occupy the posts of supervisors, wards and other services.'

Artisans and tradesmen

Turning from the impressive, though numerically limited, members of the upper echelons of the economic and administrative pyramid, to the much more prevalent professions on the lower scale, one may safely generalize that Jews were to be found in almost all fields of economic activity. Until 1910 they were excluded from military service (though during the Napoleonic wars and the Greek War of Independence Jewish seamen were drafted). They usually lived in urban centres, which meant that the extent of Jewish agricultural activity was limited. Their vital importance in all types of commerce did not recede for many generations. Widespread among Jews, from Morocco to Istanbul, were silversmiths and goldsmiths. Of equal importance were blacksmiths and butchers, tailors and cobblers, pharmacists, weavers and masons, carpenters, millers and bakers (the latter even had a separate guild to avoid any infringement on the Jewish Kasherut regulations). The numbers of those in productive professions decreased during the 18th and 19th centuries, but even then, partly as a result of efforts on their behalf by Jewish charitable organizations (Alliance Israélite), they never ceased to constitute a constructive element in the economy.

Two additional categories deserve mention: Jewish musicians and entertainers (dancers, singers), and Jewish printers. The latter introduced the profession into the empire early in the 16th century, published hundreds of books in Hebrew in most of the main cities (though relatively speaking those in the eastern provinces turned out to be much more prolific than their North African kin) and when, early in the 18th century, the Ottomans overcame their religious inhibitions and started printing books in Arabic characters, they could and did draw on the experience and knowhow of the Jewish printers in Istanbul.

The Sephardim

Both the economic and the administrative achievements of the Jews in the Ottoman Empire, by 1500, were due to the massive influx of Jews and Marranos from Spain and Portugal (Sephardim, literally: those [who came over] from Spain) around that date. Though Sephardi Jews

A Moroccan amulet in the shape of a hand shows the silversmith's skill. In the centre: a Hebrew word for God.

had been immigrating to the Islamic lands earlier, this had always been done on a very small scale. Even at this initial stage Ottoman Jewry was not monolithic; it consisted of several, separate elements, and became more conspicuously heterogeneous from then onwards. There were the Karaites, regarded as outsiders by halachic tradition, and there were the communities left over from the Byzantine times, the Greek-speaking Romaniot Jews. In the Arabic-speaking countries, their equivalent was the Musta'riba Jews, those who spoke and probably dressed like the Arabs. And there was a fourth element, Jews who had arrived from various parts of Christian Europe and were of non-Sephardi origin. Some of these – Ashkenazi (of German origin), Italian and French – had already been there before 1500, and were later reinforced by waves of newcomers resulting from further expulsions: those who fled after Ottoman conquests of additional territories, or those who sought refuge from the Chmielnicki massacres of the 17th century.

As may be inferred from the last examples, these, as well as all the others, continued to be regarded as separate communities, distinguished according to their countries or even provinces of origin. By the same token, the Sephardi Jews, for many years to come, referred to themselves as the congregations of Catalonia, Castile, Cordoba, etc., living together in compounds bearing their respective names and praying in their own synagogues. For some time they even insisted on the printing of separate prayer-books, which differed in liturgical details, not necessarily substantial ones. During the 16th century some of these differences seem to have died away, and one could speak more safely of Sephardi Jews as a whole. In Morocco (Fez) and Algeria the fusion between the various elements was more rapid, though the arrival of newcomers in Tunisia from Livorno, as late as the 18th century, was the cause for the creation of an entirely new congregation, distinct from the original Twanisa. The distinction prevalent in North Africa, between the original Jews wearing a turban (or Ba'ale Hamitznefet) and the newcomers wearing a round hat (Ba'ale Hakapos), seems also to have been valid in the other parts of the Ottoman Empire, as a Capuchin friar described towards the end of the 17th century: 'There are . . . two kinds of Jews in Turkey, that is to say, those who are native or aboriginal, and strangers, so called because their ancestors came from Spain and Portugal. The former wear a turban like the Christians, made up of many colours. . . . The latter wear a ridiculous head-dress resembling a Spanish hat without a brim.'

The local Romaniot Jews did not hide their criticism and contempt for the liberal approach to life and religion, which they blamed on the Sephardi Jews; both communities looked down on the European Ashkenazi Jews, whom they referred to as *Tudesco* (a shortened form of the Italian for Ashkenazi: *Tudesco mallo*, meaning bad and, also, an unclean person, thereby implying contempt for their behaviour and appearance). Before long, however, the Sephardi Jews, who gained prominence in terms of numbers, resources and intellect, became uncontested as the leaders in the eyes of both the Jews and the government.

The insistence of the various congregations on the preservation of their individuality and independence, to the extent of forbidding their members from leaving

The Jewish cemetery at Istanbul, 'Sepulture de giudei', lies across the Golden Horn from the city: detail from a woodcut of about 1520.

their own group or marrying into the other, could not stand in the way of the general process by which the largest of them all first influenced, then absorbed, most of the others. The Portuguese, Italians, Hungarians, sections of the French and the Germans were gradually drawn towards the solid Sephardi mass until they reached total fusion. The Romaniotes were the last to give up their separate entity: the process was more rapid in the smaller towns, while in Istanbul, their traditional stronghold, they did not succumb until late in the 17th century. It was then, as a result of a series of recurring fires in Instanbul (1630, 1660) in which the Jewish quarters were very badly hit, that they were forced to leave their old quarters and look for new houses. Their separate synagogues (like all the other buildings) having been burnt down, members of the two congregations had no alternative but to intermingle, share the same synagogues and rites, which were, of course, those of the Sephardim.

Community life

During the last two hundred years of the Ottoman Empire there were three distinct Jewish groups: the overwhelming Sephardi majority, the small Ashkenazi minority (regarded by the Sephardim as inferior to them), and an insignificant, marginal Karaite group. Each was established along lines that were basically similar to the larger variety of communal organizations existing among the Ottoman Jews in earlier times. It would be pertinent, therefore, to draw at this point the general outlines of these separate communal voluntary organizations, which were all similar in principle.

The most conspicuous trait of the Jewish community in the Ottoman Empire was its elaborate, effectively arranged, intensive internal life, reminiscent in many respects of self-government. Each community (*kahal*) administered its own affairs and those of its members, covering many aspects and a vast variety of fields. The synagogue (not infrequently located in a private lodging) was not only a place of worship, but a centre where most of public and much of private life was conducted:

circumcision, betrothal, marriage, elections, enactment of regulations. The head of the community, the rabbi (*hakham, dayan*), was in charge of the synagogue, as well as of affiliated institutions of learning, though in the latter he was often helped by another teacher (*melamed*). The rabbi was not only the highest religious authority, but he also participated in the promulgation of laws and ordinances, administered justice, supervised the execution of wills and inheritances and represented the community as a whole. He was aided by several executive administrators (*parnassim*), who were entrusted with the practical aspects of the civil, financial and religious affairs of their *kahal*. Other officials designated and remunerated by the community were the ritual slaughterer (*shohet*), and the cantor (who sometimes performed other tasks, like teaching). Among the congregational societies, who looked after the needs of the poor and the helpless, was the burial society (*Hebra kadisha*), which took care of the burial rites and the funerals, including the cemetery (though, in the case of very small Ashkenazi communities, they were allowed to bury their dead in the Sephardi cemetery upon a certain payment).

The two most important forms of regular activity within the community were education and litigation. Jewish learning and free education for the orphans and the poor were disseminated in the Talmud Torah (literally: learning of the holy book). Affiliated to the synagogue as it was, it consisted of one class only in small towns, whereas in larger centres, such as Salonica, there was a whole building in which courses were given from elementary school up to the highest level (*yeshiva*). These were usually financed by donations from affluent families, bequests and incomes from properties, either from within the same town or abroad. The students came usually from the community itself, but the highest institutions were frequented by students attracted to them from distant places. Salonica's *yeshivas* were regarded as a centre for the whole of the Balkans, whereas Jerusalem attracted students from overseas.

Jewish courts tried civil cases between Jewish litigants, and, although they had no executive power, their authority was sufficiently high, and they could always resort to the most expedient, though seldom used, means: excommunication. In mixed civil cases, in criminal cases and even in disputes among themselves, there was at least a tendency to refer the case to the Muslim court. This was resented by the Jewish courts, and in certain cases (Salonica, 1558) was even formally forbidden by the leaders of the communities. But many references in the Muslim court archives in all parts of the empire indicate a surprisingly high degree of cases brought up for the perusal of and decision by the Muslim judge. Ordinary daily life, however, was regulated within the community itself, and external intervention was resorted to as little as possible. Various taxes were paid, not only governmental (either in kind or in coin, like the poll-tax, *jizya*, exacted from every grown-up male), but also special taxes for community purposes (*gabella*, a levy on food, mainly on meat and cheese, which was charged to the Jewish consumer by the butcher or the producer). On a broader scale, one could speak of a high degree of self-government, the main instrument of which was the communal ordinance, *takkana, haskama*, enacted by the congregation, and aimed at the regulation of all aspects of life, both materially and spiritually. Many regulations were stipulated in order to avoid any unnecessary friction within the community itself. Most famous of them all were those intended to minimize competition among the members on the limited number of houses for rent (or other real estate for lease or purchase) by the application of the principle of *hazaka*, that is, self-denial by all community members of the right to acquire a place after it had been rented by a Jew for a certain given period (usually three consecutive years). Through these various means the Jewish communities could reach and maintain a high degree of cohesion, which, in turn, enabled them to sustain the difficulties inherent in their very existence as a tolerated minority within the Muslim state.

The years of Ottoman decline

During the 18th and 19th centuries there was a general deterioration in the conditions of the Jews of the Ottoman Empire, which in many ways goes side by side with the deterioration of the empire itself. They lost certain rights, most of them were underprivileged and an increasing number among them became economically deprived of many opportunities they had enjoyed in bygone days. As the British Consul in Jerusalem described them in 1839: 'The spirit of toleration towards the Jews is not yet known here to the same extent it is in Europe . . . still a Jew in Jerusalem is not estimated much above a dog.'

Yet, on balance, the Jews of the Ottoman Empire were satisfied with their lot. Why? Firstly, they could not forget the very warm welcome their ancestors had encountered when they emigrated from Spain and Portugal. This should be put in an even wider perspective: the Ottoman conquest of the Arabic-speaking countries also brought about a very substantial improvement in the conditions of those Jews living there, from Cairo to Baghdad. Secondly, they could easily compare their situation with that of their co-religionists in Christian Europe, where the 'toleration'

mentioned above was very late to emerge even in its formal version; a comparison with the Christian subjects of the sultan, their immediate neighbours, would have led them to identical conclusions about being much better off. Thirdly, many of their reported sufferings were either intentionally exaggerated by themselves, in order to gain the sympathy and the financial help of their brethren in Europe, or misinterpreted by the foreign observers, who could not know to what extent these were patterns of administration applied equally to other subjects of the sultan, or else relatively easy to avoid and tolerate. Fourthly, they elaborated a whole system by which poor communities, such as those living in the Holy Land, were financially upheld and guided, either from Europe or by their more prosperous relatives in other towns (Istanbul, Salonica, Smyrna). This help, extended to them from outside, did not impinge upon the high degree of autonomy that they enjoyed within the *millet* system. Both the general concept, and most of its elements, existed as early as the beginning of the 16th century. But they were, as noted above, applied by each community separately. There is little evidence to suggest an overall Jewish authority until the second quarter of the 19th century, for there was no Jewish equivalent to the Armenian or Greek-Orthodox central religious or communal leadership. It was only for approximately a hundred years, that the *Hakham Bashi* in Istanbul was officially approved by the Sublime Porte as the head of the Jews of the empire. Many of the privileges granted to him had, for many years, been practised by each local rabbi in his respective community; but, here, they were codified and became part of a general system, directed and headed by this Chief Rabbi. Jewish autonomy in all matters of worship and belief, personal status, justice and local administration was formally recognized in the office of the *Hakham Bashi*.

This attempt to define and mould more clearly the Jewish *millet* should be seen in a wider context, that of the Tanzimat reforms of the 19th century. Generally speaking, the 17th and 18th centuries witnessed a steady decline in the position of Jews in the empire, as both a result of an increase of the relative importance of the Greeks and Armenians, and an outcome of the deterioration of the general living conditions. External pressures and internal needs triggered off a series of reforms, of which one important aspect was the attempt to improve the lot of the religious minorities. Though lagging far behind the high hopes and spectacular declarations of the sultans in 1839, 1856 and 1876, substantial results were attained: additional security to body and property, greater freedom of worship and higher degree of autonomy, creation of various representative bodies within the communities and limited Jewish presence in the provincial councils and even in the parliament. However, the ultimate goals were not reached: Jews never achieved political equality or religious freedom. Because the whole concept and conduct of the empire, until its very end, remained based on religion – on the superiority of Islam – all the above-mentioned achievements could be only partial and precarious. However, the fact that the 300,000 Jews living there at the end of the 19th century (out of a world population of seven to eight million Jews) could turn nowhere else was of great consequence. It resulted in a high degree of identification (verbal, at least) with the empire in which they lived, and adjustment to their status as a small religious community. It also meant that, since they proved to be more loyal than the Christians (who demanded political rights as well as equality), there was a greater readiness, on the part of both the Ottoman government and the Muslim public, to respect them, rely on them and even reward them.

An end to tolerance

Jewish presence under the Ottoman rule was regulated in accordance with certain administrative, social and economic concepts, but these concepts were themselves subordinate to the all-embracing religious perceptions of Islam. The constitutional reforms of the 19th century had only a limited success, as far as the minorities were concerned; Jews were continuously looked upon as a group that, by definition, was bound to remain inferior, despised, downtrodden, if not persecuted. This being the case, one might have expected a general trend of progress and improvement for the Jews to enjoy as a result of the developments of the 19th and 20th centuries. It was during the former that the Ottoman Empire lost some of its provinces to European Christian rule, both in Europe (Greece, Bulgaria) and in Africa (Algeria, Tunisia, Egypt). What remained of the Muslim Empire after the First World War was replaced by a Turkish state and several political entities that were to be administered by the British and the French. Unfortunately, the introduction of nation states into the Middle East and North Africa turned out to lead, paradoxically enough, to the termination (with insignificant exceptions) of the long history of Jewish life under Islam. This, one should underline, came about as an abrupt change in the course of events, which took the Jews by bitter and painful surprise. In spite of attempts to ignore or minimize the meaning of the new developments and regard themselves as an exception to the rule, they had to admit fairly soon that reality was running counter to both their experience and their wishes. Following the elementary rules of self-preservation, they drew the only possible conclusion: they should emigrate, mainly, though by no means exclusively, to Israel.

Though their expectations may have been short-sighted and somehow naïve, it was not unnatural to hope for a better future in the former provinces of the Ottoman Empire that had been taken over by Western Powers. Egyptian economy, after the British occupation in 1882, must have amply compensated those foreigners who were drawn there by the prospect of building their own future; thus the Jewish community (mostly foreign subjects) increased from 25,000, at the end of the 19th century, to 60,000 in 1917. In Iraq, they welcomed the British occupation, drew direct economic benefit from it and did not hesitate to sign a petition asking the British to remain. This step should be regarded, inter alia, as an illustration of the political immaturity which characterized the Jewish communities in the East. It was apparently also regarded in this light by Arab eyes. During the first decade of Mandate in Iraq, Jews were granted equal rights by the constitution, were represented in the parliament and filled many positions in the civil service; there was even a Jewish minister of finance for several years. It is no wonder that in certain Jewish circles one could discern a conscious attempt, during the 1920s and 1930s, to assimilate culturally and politically with Iraqi society. In Turkey, Jews had to give up publicly their status of minority, and between the two world wars they became increasingly involved in various aspects of both the material and the intellectual life of the country. (One should note that most Jews seldom resorted to speaking Turkish during the time of the Ottoman Empire; Ladino was their mother tongue. Though not giving it up altogether, in republican Turkey they adopted Turkish as their first language.) One should not be misled by these, and other, expressions of greater affinity between the Jews and the countries where they were born and of which they were subjects.

Basically, however, their main interest was economic rather than political, and their general preference (partly as a result of their education) was for European culture and languages rather than for the symbols of the local national movement. This applied also to the Jewish national movement, Zionism, which, unlike the situation in Europe, attracted only negligible interest in the few countries (Egypt, Iraq) where it showed any activity at all. Nevertheless, Jews were regarded as lackeys of the imperialist powers and affiliated to the international Zionist – thus anti-Arab – movement. Discriminatory steps were, therefore, undertaken against them from the mid-30s, such as in independent Iraq. In hind-sight these could be regarded as preliminaries to the abrupt outbreak of pogroms against the Jews of Baghdad in June 1941. In the wake of the Rashid 'Ali al-Kailani episode of a brief pro-Nazi rule in Iraq, the disappointed crowds were allowed (if not encouraged) by the highest local authorities to attack the Jews, who had nowhere to turn for help. Within two days of the 'Farhud' of Baghdad hundreds of Jews were killed and property worth over half a million pounds was looted. The local community later resumed its normal activity, being led to consider this an exceptional case. Unfortunately, it was, in fact, a forerunner of the anti-Jewish outbreaks that were to follow: Cairo riots on 2 November 1945; pogroms in Aden in December 1947. The local communities involved suffered much death and destruction.

The foundation of the State of Israel only exacerbated the situation, providing the Arab governments (with the exception of Lebanon) as well as the mobs with what they regarded as sufficient grounds to persecute the Jewish population of their own countries. The inevitable outcome of this was massive emigration – either illegal or with the consent of the government.

In Iraq, for instance, within a year following the promulgation of the law of March 1950, more than 100,000 Jews renounced their citizenship, lost all their properties and left the country. Around the middle of the 20th century, within a decade or two, there came an end to most of the ancient Jewish communities in the Muslim countries. Out of about half a million Jews in North Africa in 1945, only 30,000 stayed; a mere handful were left behind from over 350,000 Jews who had been living in the Arab countries. About 100,000 Jews who remained in the Middle East, basically unmolested and unharmed, stayed in Turkey and Iran (a similar number having gone to Israel in recent years). These are the only living vestige of what had been for many centuries a long and rich history of Jewish life under Islam.

IV
THE INNER WORLD

Jewish Philosophy

Jewish Mysticism

The Jews and the Enlightenment

A double strand, of revelation and reason, runs through the whole complex web of the Jewish intellectual tradition. Bible and Talmud, prophetic utterance and rabbinical question, the Zohar and *A Guide to the Perplexed* – every stage of Jewish history can show both a living, direct response to the Divine Will and a cold, logical analysis of it. In a sense, therefore, it is misleading to speak of philosophy, mysticism and the Enlightenment in a Jewish context as if they were separate concepts. The values that the Bible conveyed in myth, parable and symbol were those that the philosophers of the Enlightenment sought to present in terms of rational inquiry. Controversy, however bitter, never stepped outside that area of basic agreement. 'Love of the Law', as Moses Maimonides stresses, is the foundation of all wisdom. When his great work, the *Mishneh Torah*, was illuminated, probably in the studio of Mateo da Cambio of Perugia, about 1400, the artist placed at the head of Book II, called the 'Book of Love' (*opposite*), a small figure dressed in the *tallith* and embracing the Torah scroll, with the inscription from the Psalms, 'Oh how I love thy Law.'

Maimonides, more than any other thinker before or since, succeeded in combining every aspect of the Jewish tradition into a single, consistent body of doctrine. Born in Cordoba in 1135, he migrated to Fustat, in Egypt, where he remained for the rest of his life. By profession he was a doctor, and an outstandingly successful one, but he found time to master the whole of Hebrew literature and a great deal of Arabic, which at that time included all that was known of Greek (Aristotle made his impact on the Muslim world a century before Christendom). In the *Mishneh Torah* (literally: Second Law) he provided a systematic summary of the Talmud, bringing together its scattered decisions and showing how every part of it derived from the Bible (this was a blow against the Karaites, who rejected the Talmud as having no authority). In *A Guide to the Perplexed* he achieved something even more far-reaching, an interpretation of Judaism that incorporated all the latest Aristotelian ideas and made it a 'modern' religion capable of complete rational justification. But while many Jews welcomed Maimonides as an intellectual saviour, others condemned him for dragging the Unknowable down to the level of human intelligence. It was a debate that was to flare up again in the 18th century, and whose repercussions are still with us. Yet Maimonides denied neither the supernatural nature of God's Law nor the role of the prophetic imagination in bringing it to mankind. (1)

מה אהבתי תורתך כל היום

היא שיחתי

ספר שני   והוא ספר

אהבת

הלכותיו ששׁו זהו סדורן
הלכות   הלכות קריתשמע
תפלהו וחתהיות   הלכות תפלה תגלחׁ וחזר

Pomegranates and flowers decorate a carved menorah from the 4th-century synagogue of Hammath, near Tiberias, again uniting the images of candlestick and tree. Exodus does in fact mention the 'flowers' of the menorah (xxv : 31). (2)

The candlestick is one of the oldest symbols of Judaism. Placed immediately in front of the sanctuary of the Temple, it represented the light of God and of judgment. But it goes back to a yet more ancient symbol of the seven-branched Tree of Life, a fact of which at least some Jewish mystics seem to have been fully aware. A manuscript of the Pentateuch, written in Germany in 1298, contains three full-page illustrations made up of micro-writing, all closely associated with the menorah. In the first of them (*right*), men who wear the pointed hats of the Jews pluck olives from the Tree and extract oil from them in a press. (7)

The symbolic menorah appears in Jewish funerary art from an early date. *Above:* graffito from a Roman catacomb, *c.* 300 CE, with menorah, *ethrog, shofar,* amphora and *lulab.* A lead coffin from Jerusalem (*below*) additionally includes the incense shovel. (3, 5)

Glass pendants, possibly amulets, from the 4th century CE bear the same array of conventional emblems. But the menorahs found carved in synagogues (*below*, from Caesarea, 4th century CE; another example from Ostia is shown on p.69) seem to represent the destroyed Temple, symbol of the unity of Jewish religious life, for the rebuilding of which Jews still pray. (4, 6)

Oil from the Tree of Life is carried to light the menorah (*right*). On this page, from the same manuscript as that shown above, the High Priest, holding the same vessel into which oil had been pressed, stands in a kind of arbour flanked by heraldic animals, one grasping a sacrificial knife. (8)

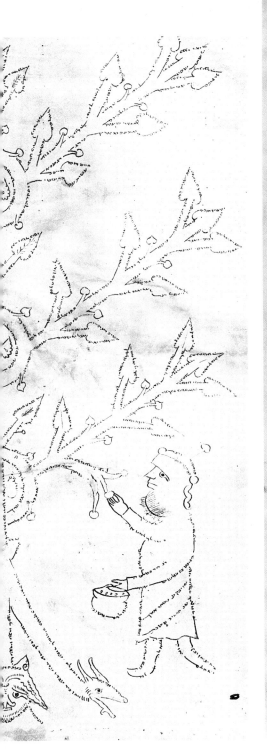

A superb menorah forms the third of the illustrations mentioned opposite. The scribe's name is known, Solomon ha-Cohen, and his style is marked by a rich and freely expressed imagination, with exotic foliage and strange animal heads. (9)

'God be merciful unto us, and bless us, and cause his face to shine upon us.' The words of the whole of Psalm LXVII are given the form of the menorah (*right*) in this Italian prayer-book of 1397. The Hebrew alphabet itself had great significance for the mystics, who saw the shape of the letters as well as their various combinations as having meanings. The base is formed by verses from Genesis. (10)

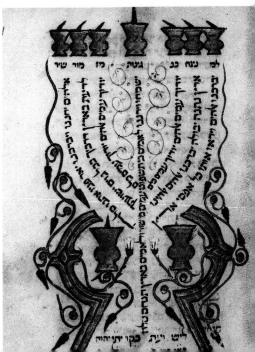

Divine Intervention was represented in Jewish art by a hand descending from Heaven. In this fresco from Dura Europus, the first figure is a literal illustration of Ezekiel xxxvii: 'And the hand of God was upon me, and he carried me out in the spirit of the Lord and set me down in the midst of the valley; and it was full of bones. . . . And he said unto me, Son of man, can these bones live? And I answered, O Lord God, thou knowest.' This conversation seems to be represented by the second figure of Ezekiel with one hand raised, the other lowered. 'Again he said unto me, Prophesy unto these bones, Behold, I will cause breath to enter into you and ye shall live. . . . So I prophesied as I was commanded: and as I prophesied, there was a noise, and behold an earthquake and the bones came together . . . but there was no life in them' – as shown in the right-hand section of the fresco. (11)

'And the Angel of the Lord called unto him out of Heaven, and said, Abraham, Abraham.' Again, in this version of the story of Abraham and Isaac from the 6th-century Beth Alpha synagogue (*left*), the effective presence of God is indicated by the hand. The mosaicists, Marianos and his son Hamina, are the earliest Jewish artists known by name. (12)

God's hand delivers the Tablets of the Law to Moses (*right*): a miniature from the so-called Parma *machsor* (prayer-book) of 1450. The fence in the foreground is of particular interest. When God entrusted the Tablets to Moses, he told him (Ex. xix: 12): 'And thou shalt set bounds unto the people round about, saying, Take heed to yourselves, that ye go not up into the mount, or touch the border of it.' The notion of erecting bounds ('a hedge round the Law') played a considerable role in later rabbinic legislation and practice. (15)

'**Lo, I come unto thee** in a thick cloud.' So God spoke to Moses. And so every mystic knew. The illustrators of both the German *Bird-head Haggadah* (*left*) of *c.* 1300 and the 14th-century Spanish Haggadah (*right*) included this cloud, with the hand symbolizing the Divine Presence. In the *Bird-head Haggadah*, other pages of which have already been seen in previous chapters, Moses too is represented symbolically, or at least aniconically. In the Spanish example he listens to God in the burning bush, his flocks around him; he has half carried out God's command: 'Put off thy shoes from off thy feet', and is hiding his face 'for he was afraid to look upon God.' (13, 14)

Mysticism and magic shaded into one another in the popular mind – and in the minds of many Kabbalists themselves. Rabbi Löw of Prague, an eminent scholar and thinker whom later legend transformed into an all-round Renaissance magus rather like Shakespeare's Prospero, was credited with having made a *golem*, a man-like automaton, to carry out his commands. Löw's grave in Prague (*above*) is still an object of veneration. (16)

Zodiac signs written in an occult script (*below*) were part of 'practical Kabbalah', through which the powers governing the physical universe could be controlled. (17)

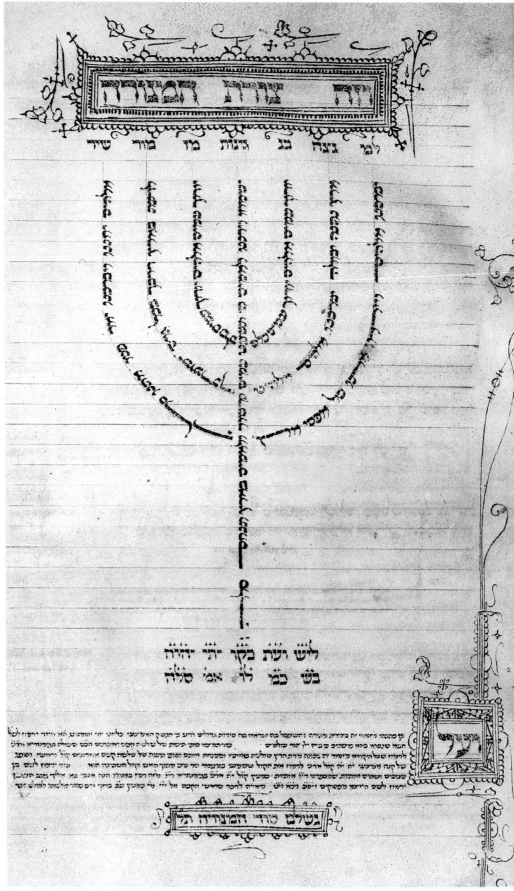

The Mysticism of words: in a 15th-century liturgical manuscript from Florence, the words of Psalm LXVII are arranged to form a menorah. In addition to being made into a picture, the letters are given numerical values (since each Hebrew letter also functions as a number): thus, the seven branches of the candlestick can be 'added' and the resultant number translated back into words. The elaborate results of this esoteric game are explained in the inscription at the bottom. The final number equals the name of God. (18)

The Kabbalah is the most important product of Jewish mystical thought. It is a strange and complicated system, combining many elements, and its basic text is the Zohar, once believed to date from the 2nd century, but now generally held to have been written in Spain in the late 13th century. The Zohar's doctrines were developed to their furthest extreme by Isaac Luria (1534-72), of Palestine, and the diagrams on this page are all by his disciples.

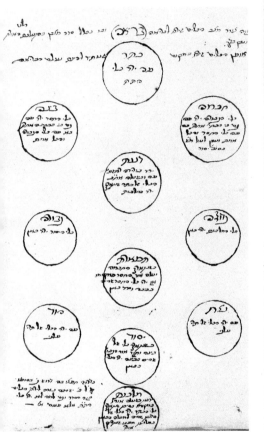

The Godhead is conceived in terms of ten aspects or manifestations, the *sefiroth*, represented (*above*) by ten circles, together with one non-*sefirah*, centre line second from top, which is Knowledge. It is the interaction between the *sefiroth* that gives the Godhead its dramatic inner life, in particular that between *Tif'ereth*, in the middle of the centre line, the hub of the whole system – Sun, King, Bridegroom – and *Malkhuth*, at the bottom, where the divine sphere meets the non-divine – Moon, Queen, Bride. The union of these two is seen as a sacred marriage, *hieros gamos*. (19)

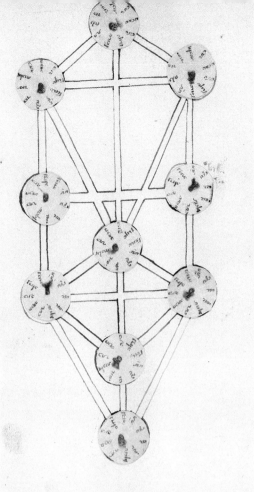

The first step in Luria's ideas was to link the *sefiroth* by paths setting out the relationships between them. In this diagram each *sefirah* contains the names of all, indicating that, in spite of the criticisms of some Orthodox critics, the essential unity of the Godhead is not compromised. This emphasis on unity was the more important as the *sefiroth* tended to be personified. (20)

The separation of *Tif'ereth* and *Malkhuth* is the greatest disaster that can be imagined, but precisely this is the consequence of Adam's sin. *Below:* Luria's system at a relatively early stage of elaboration. (22)

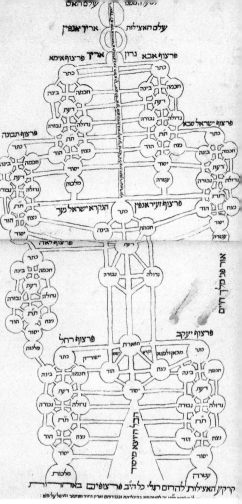

The ultimate complexity of the Lurianic system may be judged from this drawing by his pupil Hayyim Vital, showing eight *sefiroth*-clusters. He is demonstrating how the cosmos may be reconstructed after the 'shattering of the pipes', the primal, pre-Adam, catastrophe. (21)

Man too is involved in the cosmic process. This diagram equates the *sefiroth*-system with the trunk and limbs of *Adam Kadmon*, the celestial archetype of Adam. (23)

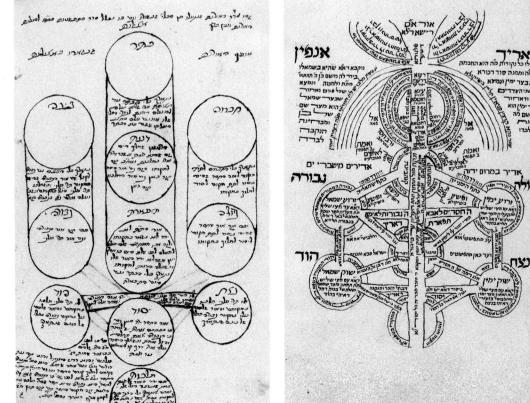

The sacred portal

The door into another world is a deeply symbolic image going back far into the religious history of the Near East. In Jewish art it holds many meanings: the doors of the Temple sanctuary, the Holy of Holies, the dwelling place of God; the doors of the Ark of the Covenant, which was kept there, and which contained the Tablets delivered to Moses; and, by an easy transition, the doors of the Torah shrine in the synagogue, which contains the scroll of the Law. *Left:* an engraved gold glass from Rome showing the Torah shrine between two lions, and beneath it the usual collection of Judaic symbols. (24)

The Ark itself is represented realistically in this carved stone from the Capernaum synagogue. Built originally by Moses (Ex. xxv: 10), it was carried from place to place before being permanently enshrined in the First Temple. (25)

At Dura Europus the portal (*left*) is positioned above the niche which housed the Torah shrine, with on each side of it the menorah and the sacrifice of Isaac. Some of the most important themes relating to the Judaic Covenant with God are thus figuratively brought together – the Temple, the Ark, sacrifice and the Law. (26)

Ark and portal merge and become impossible to separate in the mosaic floor of the Beth Alpha synagogue (*above left*). Placed as it is at the far end of the synagogue, close to the Torah niche, these doors must stand, at the deepest level, for the entry leading to the realm of the Most High, the 'gate of Heaven' mentioned in Genesis XXVIII: 17, and in Psalm XXIV. 'Lift up your heads, O ye gates, and be ye lift up, ye everlasting doors, and the King of Glory shall come in.' Other instances in

Jewish art suggest a similar interpretation. *Above right*: detail from the Spanish 14th-century synagogue carpet shown on p. 133. *Below left*: detail from the mosaic floor of the Hammath synagogue, 4th century CE, with curtains that seem to point to the veil of the Temple. *Below right*: page from an Egyptian manuscript of the 10th century, with lines of micro-writing, incorporating part of the Masoretic commentary, integrated into a door-like design. (27-30)

By the 18th century Jewish isolation was being eroded from both within and without. As the power of the Church waned, so did hostility towards the Jews, and in the new atmosphere of critical inquiry, some men of all religions recognized a common humanity. The effect of these ideas within Judaism was the Haskalah, an outgrowth of the European Enlightenment, aimed at purifying the faith, freeing it from prejudice, reducing the authority of the talmudic scholars and increasing that of reason. Thus, as secular governments moved towards toleration, Jewish communities in many Western countries were ready to move forward to meet them. *Above:* a medal commemorating the Edict of Toleration issued by the Emperor Joseph II in 1782, when Jews were recognized as fellow citizens, and some restrictions on where they lived were lifted. Protestant, Catholic and Jew stand equally protected by the wings of the Imperial eagle. *Below:* a Chanukah lamp of about the same date, in which the emperor's portrait and the Habsburg eagle are prominently displayed. The cut-out soldiers at the sides perhaps allude to the enlistment of Jews into the Imperial army for the first time. (32, 33)

Time-change: the addition of an 18th-century belfry and Western-type clock to the 16th-century Jewish Town Hall of Prague is indicative of the changing climate of ideas. The clock with Hebrew numbers goes in the direction we should call 'anti-clockwise'. (31)

Moses Mendelssohn (*above*, a drawing by Daniel Chodowiecki), the leading philosopher of the Haskalah (born 1729, died 1786), saw Judaism as a faith closer to 'natural religion' than any other. His theories aroused some suspicion in more traditional circles, but were profoundly influential in Western Europe in the years following his death, often in ways of which he would have disapproved. (34)

Farewell to the ghetto. *Above right:* Jews begging Helvetia (Switzerland) for protection in 1765. *Below:* trade-card of Abraham Delvalle, tobacco merchant of London, in a beautiful Chinese-Rococo frame. *Below right:* two rural synagogues at Endigen and Leungnau in Switzerland. (35-38)

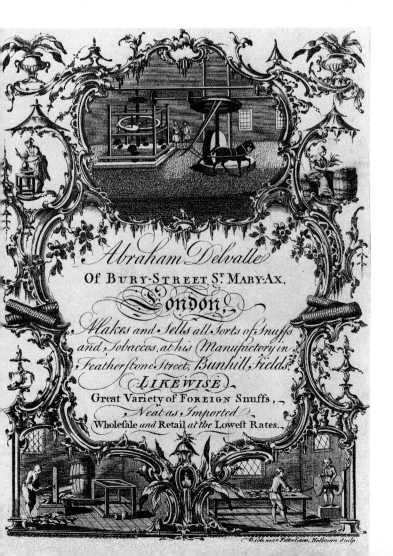

Abraham Delvalle
Of BURY-STREET Sᵗ. MARY-AX.
London,
Makes and Sells all Sorts of Snuffs and Tobaccos, at his Manufactory in Featherstone Street, Bunhill Fields
LIKEWISE
Great Variety of FOREIGN Snuffs, Neat as Imported Wholesale and Retail at the Lowest Rates.

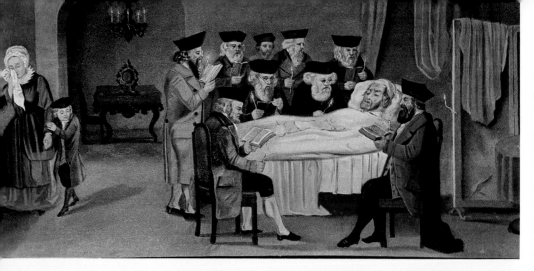

Bohemian Jewry was among the strongest and best organized communities of Europe.

This series of panels was commissioned by a Prague burial society in the late 18th–early 19th century. Burial societies, to which only the most distinguished members of the community were admitted, gained considerable influence in central Europe, often becoming semi-official councils. Burying the dead was considered one of the major religious commandments and acts of charity, following God's example, who himself buried Moses (see pl. 14 p. 134). Hence a burial society was called a 'Holy Company'; they held their annual meetings on the seventh of Adar, the traditional day of the death of Moses. Members contributed funds for their own funerals and for those who could not afford to pay for themselves. In the first picture a member has just died. On the left, his widow and young son steal sorrowfully out of the room. Next, the corpse is taken on an open bier to the cemetery, where the rabbi holds a funeral service. The panel at the bottom is a group-portrait of the members, whose activities were by no means always funereal. *Below*: a burial society jug, dated 1726, with a funeral scene running round the sides, and the words 'Hebra Kadisha' – 'Holy Company'. (39-43)

The body is lowered into the grave. It has now been put into a coffin. This was a requirement of Austro-Hungarian law, but it was not at the time the Jewish custom, though Maimonides and the Talmud allow them. Rapid burial was normally the rule, within twenty-four or thirty-six hours of death. Since the 16th century, under kabbalistic influence, coffins had gone out of use, though previously used in most Jewish communities. (44)

France was officially closed to Jews at the end of the 14th century, though the Sephardim of the south were officially recognized as Jews in the middle of the 18th century. Some splendid synagogues were built, sometimes on the foundations of those abandoned over three centuries earlier. That of Cavaillon (*below*) is a masterpiece of the *style Louis XV*, with fine Rococo wood-carving and wrought iron. The pulpit, with the Ark behind it, is reached by elaborate steps. (45)

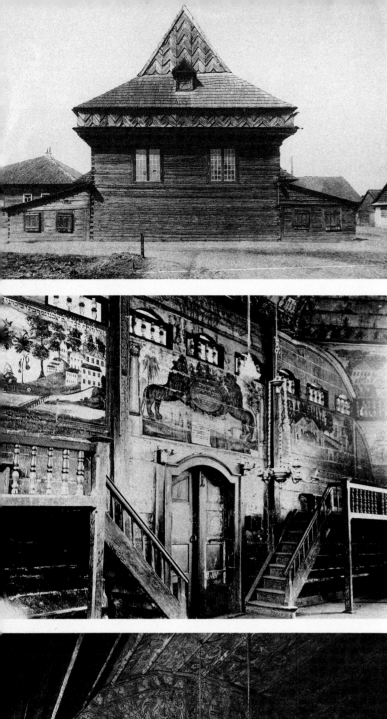

A Jewish pedlar decorates a target used for shooting-practice. His head is the bull's-eye. Made in Moravia, 1747. (49)

In Eastern Europe the Jewish Enlightenment, the Haskalah, confronted Orthodoxy and conservatism. *Left:* from top to bottom, the rustic synagogues of Zabludow and Grojec, both in Poland, and of Kirchheim in Germany, painted by an artist from Galicia. Here ancient ways were too deeply rooted for the new ideas to be easily accepted. (46, 47, 48)

A Hasidic doll – for a non-Hasidic household? The little wooden figure, wearing the characteristic fur hat, vibrates on his spring in parody of the Hasidic dance. Hasidim were generally enemies of the Enlightenment, but had their own enemies among the Orthodox, who composed songs mocking them and who may have made this doll. On the other hand, the Hebrew writing suggests there was no hostile intent. (50)

The Jews of Poland suffered terribly in the 17th century, when whole communities were wiped out in savage pogroms. It was not an atmosphere to encourage rational discussion and reform. Men took refuge in mysticism, Hasidism and the Messianic movement of Sabbatai Zevi. In the 1790s, parts of Poland became Russian. Jews were confined to the Pale of Settlement and every effort was made to induce conversions to Christianity. *Right:* faces of Polish Jews during the reign of Nicholas II, a painting by Piotr Michalowski. (51)

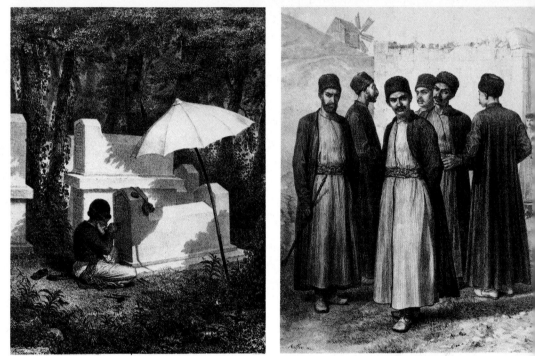

Hungary: a Hungarian circumcision book of 1819 still shows signs of the occupation of Hungary by the Turks. By now they were citizens of the enlightened Habsburg Empire. (52)

South Russia: the partitions of Poland in 1772, 1791 and 1793 brought Jews within the Russian Empire for the first time since the end of the 15th century. Alexander I encouraged them to settle in the sparsely populated lands of south Russia. Some of them were Karaites. *Above:* Karaite stone-cutter in a cemetery, and Karaite merchants. (53, 54)

Odessa probably had a higher concentration of Jews than any other city in Russia. Founded in 1794, it had a Jewish element from the beginning, and in the 19th century was a meeting-place for Jews of every type – Orthodox, Maskilic, Hasidic, Karaite. This scene (*right*) is dated 1837. Journals were published in Hebrew, and it was one of the birthplaces of Zionism. It was also the unhappy focus of Russian anti-Semitism; between 1871 and 1905 there were three appalling pogroms. (55)

יהוה

וינקה יי צבאות במשפט

שמרו · משפט
כי קרובה · ישועתי לבוא

ומשר צדקה

אשר שומרי משפט

וגל כמים · משפט

משפט שמור אם רל ואם עשיר · זמרת אלהים רהי כנכלי שיה · · ברכת יי היא אשר תעשיו ·

'Open thy hand to the poor': almsgiving had been a basic tenet of Jewish morality from ancient times and was reinforced both by rabbinical teachers and by the philosophers of the Enlightenment. This triptych was commissioned by Isaac Aboab of Amsterdam, a wealthy East India merchant, and is painted in oil on parchment. The imagery is traditional, but there is an unusual emphasis on water. In the first panel, the hands represent giving, the curtains secrecy, with a verse from Isaiah (v:16): 'And the holy God is sanctified by charity.' In the second, the palm tree alludes to Psalm xcII: The righteous shall flourish like the palm tree'; above it is the Tetragrammaton, and the texts are from Proverbs (III:18): 'It [wisdom] is a tree of life for those who grasp it and happy are those who retain it' and from Isaiah (Lv:1): 'all who thirst go to the water.' The third panel bears the scales of justice, with two more quotations: 'Let justice well up like water' (Am. v:24) and 'Keep justice, for my salvation is near to come' (Is. Lvi:1). Around the whole triptych is a contemporary rhyming poem conveying such precepts as: 'If thou wouldst rise on the wheel of Fortune, then keep judgment whether rich or poor.' *Below*: the collection of alms at a burial in Prague, from the same series as that shown earlier. The corpse is being brought out on the left; on the right are members of the burial society. (56, 57)

Chapter Nine

Jewish Philosophy

ARTHUR HYMAN

JEWISH PHILOSOPHY began in the Hellenistic Jewish community of the 2nd century BCE and continued there until the middle of the 1st century CE. It flourished for a second time during the Middle Ages: from the early 10th century to the beginning of the 13th in the Islamic world, and from the early 13th century to the beginning of the 16th in Christian countries. It entered its modern phase in the 18th century and continues today.

Jewish philosophy arose when Jewish thinkers became conversant with the general philosophic teachings of an outside culture. Convinced that philosophy ought to play a role in the life of an enlightened person and noting that there were similarities, as well as differences, between the teachings of the philosophers and their own beliefs, Jewish philosophers investigated how the opinions of the philosophers could be related to their own tradition. These concerns imposed upon them a twofold task: to interpret and formalize the teachings of Judaism by means of philosophic concepts and arguments, and to refute philosophic, as well as religious, teachings when these conflicted with Jewish beliefs and practices.

Jewish philosophy takes its place beside other Jewish exegetical traditions – the Aggadah of the rabbinic sages and the speculations of kabbalistic mystics. But it also had to present the case for Judaism in the face of other religions and other philosophies of life and to show that, properly understood, it contained a noble vision of human life and required practices designed to produce human happiness. Against Christian trinitarianism and Zoroastrian dualism it maintained the absolute unity of God, and against Christian and Muslim beliefs in the respective pre-eminence of Jesus and Muhammad it affirmed the supremacy of Moses. Finally, Jewish philosophers had to defend the study of philosophy itself against the attacks of some of their fellow Jews who held that the study of philosophy leads to unbelief.

Jewish philosophy is essentially, and has been during most of its history, a religious philosophy, concerned with harmonizing religious and philosophic ideas. But with the advent of secularism and attendant secularist conceptions of Jewish life, there were philosophers who based their speculations on a secularist, rather than a religious, understanding of what Judaism is.

The term 'Jewish philosophy' may suggest that Jewish philosophy is unitary and monolithic, but this by no means is the case. Even those philosophers who saw Jewish philosophy essentially as religious did not always agree on what Judaism is. Here the sharpest distinction occurs between those ancient, medieval and modern philosophers who had a supernaturalist conception of Judaism and some medieval and many modern philosophers who embraced a naturalistic approach. According to the former, God is an omnipotent, omniscient and benevolent being, who freely created the world, exercises providence, performs miracles, sends prophets, rewards and punishes, elected the children of Israel for a special mission and communicated his will through the Written and the Oral Torah. By contrast, the latter consider God as an impersonal principle, which does not interfere in the process of nature and history; for them, prophecy is the manifestation of human genius, and the Written and the Oral Torah the result of human experience, creativity and reaction to historical changes.

Diverse in their conception of Judaism, Jewish philosophers were even more diverse in their philosophic orientation. In Hellenistic times, Jewish philosophers were primarily influenced by Platonic and Stoic ideas; during the Middle Ages there were Mu'tazilite Mutakallimūn (Muslim theologians who used philosophy to solve certain scriptural problems, including divine unity and justice), Neoplatonists, Aristotelians and philosophic critics of Aristotelianism; and in modern times there have been Rationalists, Idealists, neo-Kantians, Pragmatists and Existentialists. The philosophic orientation of a philosopher was often determined by the philosophic literature available to him or by the philosophic climate of his day. At all times, however, Jewish philosophers argued their position with philosophic rigour.

What, then, united Jewish philosophers through the ages was not a set of common doctrines, but a certain programme and certain common issues. As philosophers, they were convinced that Judaism was capable of philosophic interpretation and, more than that, that it was their obligation to understand Judaism in a philosophically sophisticated fashion. Varied as their interests were, the subjects of their investigation can be classified under the following three headings: purely philosophic issues, such as categories and arguments of logic, the division of being, the structure of the universe; issues common to other religions and metaphysics, such as the existence of God, divine attributes, creation, prophecy, and the human soul; and, finally, purely Jewish issues, such as the prophecy of Moses, and Jewish conceptions of the Messiah and the after-life.

Philo Judaeus and Hellenistic Jewish philosophy

Our knowledge of Hellenistic Jewish philosophy is rather scant, since, in most cases, only fragments of philosophic works have been preserved. The notable exception is Philo Judaeus (*c.* 20 BCE–50 CE), thirty-eight of whose works are extant. Writing in Greek, Hellenistic Jewish philosophers undertook to show that the Jewish conception of God is spiritual, and Jewish ethics, including the ritual laws, rational, and they polemicized against polytheism and pagan practices. For their interpretation of the Bible they had recourse to the allegorical method.

Conversant with Greek philosophy, especially Platonic and Stoic ideas, Philo was the author of commentaries on the Pentateuch, works on biblical topics and independent philosophic treatises, but because of the unsystematic presentation of his thought, interpreters have differed concerning the complexion of his philosophy. Some have considered Philo as a philosophic preacher, others as a philosophic eclectic, still others as a mystic, but H. A. Wolfson, the eminent historian of religious philosophy, has presented him as a systematic philosopher, and, in fact, the founder of religious philosophy in Judaism, Christianity and Islam.

Central to Philo's method is the assumption that the Bible, as the revealed Word of God, has an apparent meaning addressed to the masses of believers and a hidden meaning which philosophers can discover by means of the allegorical method of interpretation. But Philo's use of this method is complex. It seems to have been his opinion that although most biblical passages have a literal as well as an allegorical meaning, some (e.g. certain parts of the creation story) can be interpreted only allegorically, and in the case of anthropomorphic descriptions of God, such as the hand of God, the eyes of God, he holds that these must always be taken only in a spiritual sense. While he allegorizes biblical names, persons and events, he also accepts most of the biblical stories in their literal sense. In Philo's attitude towards the observance of the precepts of Jewish Law there is a certain ambiguity. While there are passages in which he advocates the observance of the totality of the Mosaic Law, there are others in which he describes certain laws (for example, Ex. xxii:25–6) as trivial in their literal sense, maintaining that these have only allegorical meaning.

Philo's conception of God and the universe shows strong Platonic influences and he developed notions that became characteristic of Neoplatonism later on. Emphasizing God's transcendence, Philo describes him as one, self-sufficient, eternal, incorporeal and unlike any of his creatures. His essence is unknowable, indescribable and unnameable, and any human description of him can only refer to his actions. But God is also good and in his benevolence he freely created the world.

While the Bible ascribes creation to God directly, Philo maintains that the world was created through the intermediacy of a logos, also called wisdom. Invoking the Platonic notion that eternal, unchanging ideas, rather than the transient, changing substances of the perceptible world, are the foundations of reality, Philo holds that the ideas exist, first of all, as patterns in the mind of God. They are next independently existing beings between God and the world and they are, finally, forms inhering in the world. Since ideas must belong to a mind, Philo posits a logos in which the ideas inhere. But just as the ideas exist in threefold fashion, so does the logos. It exists firstly as an attribute of God, then as a being intermediate between God and the world and, finally, as immanent in the world. Creation for Philo is an atemporal process, and when it is said that God is prior to the world, that statement means that he is its cause. God created the perceptible world out of matter, but it is not clear whether Philo considers this matter as eternal or as created by God. The world functions in accordance with natural laws, but, if God so desires, he can change them in miraculous fashion.

As part of his creation, God created souls of varying kinds. The purest of these souls remained incorporeal and became angels, the messengers of God, while less pure souls were joined to human bodies. But through speculation and practice the human soul can free itself from the confines of the body, ascending upon death to the angelic world and even beyond.

Like Plato, Philo divides knowledge into sensation or opinion, rational knowledge and knowledge of ideas. Whereas for Plato knowledge of ideas comes through recollection, for Philo it comes through prophecy. But prophecy is also concerned with prediction of the future, expiation for the people's sins, promulgation of law and the vision of incorporeal beings. Of the varying forms of prophecy, some can be attained by Gentiles, but prophecy through the voice of God is reserved for Jews. Prophecy can be accompanied by ecstacy and frenzy and it is here that Philo's mystical sentiments come to the fore.

With the philosophers, Philo affirms that human happiness comes through the acquisition of the moral and intellectual virtues and requires obedience to the law. But, while human laws produce only inadequate human happiness, the Law of Moses, divine in origin, produces it perfectly. To the philosophic virtues, the Law of Moses adds virtues of its own, among them faith, piety and holiness, and it requires prayer, study and repentance. The Law of Moses is the constitution of a state consisting of citizens and non-citizens, ruled by a king, High Priest and a Council of Elders. However, God is the real ruler of this state, and earthly rulers only interpret and administer the Divine Law. While the Mosaic state was, at first, only the state of the Jewish people, in Messianic times it will provide the pattern of a state for all mankind.

Medieval Jewish philosophy: the impact of Islam

In less than a hundred years after the death of Muhammad in 632 CE, Muslims, through military conquests, established an empire that extended from India in the East, through North Africa, to Spain in the West. These conquests brought a number of religious and intellectual communities under Muslim rule and, as the political situation became stable, 'Abbasid caliphs encouraged and supported Arabic translations of Greek and Hellenistic works. Translators, active from *c.* 800–1000 CE, produced Arabic versions of Platonic dialogues, virtually all the works of Aristotle, commentaries on Aristotle, Neoplatonic writings and works by Galen. Since these works contained incidental discussions of Stoic, Epicurean and Sceptic ideas, Muslims became familiar with these philosophies as well.

The knowledge of Arabic, current among Jews, provided access to this literature in translation as well as to philosophic works composed by Muslims, and the advent of the new learning inevitably produced a certain intellectual turmoil in Jewish thinkers. Many of the most important works of medieval Jewish philosophy are written in Arabic.

Saadya Gaon (882–942), head of the rabbinical academy of Surah (near Baghdad), is generally considered the first Jewish philosopher of the Middle Ages. Author of an Arabic translation of the Bible and commentaries on it, liturgical works, rabbinic *responsa*, books on Hebrew grammar and polemical writings, Saadya presents his philosophic ideas primarily in his *Book of Beliefs and Opinions*, a work based on the views of the Muslim dialectical theologians, the Mu'tazilite Mutakallimūn.

Aware of the sceptical temperament of his day, Saadya begins his *Book of Beliefs and Opinions* by showing how doubts concerning sense perception and human reason can be removed and by offering a definition of belief, the opposite of doubt. 'Belief', writes Saadya,

> is an idea arising in the soul as to what an object of knowledge really is: when the idea is clarified by speculation, Reason comprehends it, accepts it, and makes it penetrate the soul and become absorbed into it; then man believes this idea which he has attained, and he preserves it in his soul for another time or other times. . . . (trans. A. Altmann)

But beliefs may be true or false, so that sense perception, self-evident first principles, inference, or reliable tradition are required to distinguish true from false beliefs.

Saadya proves the creation of the world in order to derive from it the existence of God. Four proofs appear in the *Book of Beliefs and Opinions*: from the finiteness of the world, from its composition, from accidents and from the nature of time. Typical of these proofs is that from finiteness, according to which the finite universe requires a finite force for its preservation, and everything possessing a finite force must have a beginning in time. A created world requires a creator, God, who is distinct from his creation and who created it out of nothing. God, the creator of the world, is demonstrated to be one, yet he is described by many attributes, such as life, power and knowledge. To resolve the apparent conflict between God's unity and the multiplicity of his attributes, Saadya holds that God and his attributes are, in reality, one, though the inadequacy of human language requires that he be described by a multiplicity of terms.

In his kindness, God provided man with a Law, the Torah, as a guide to temporal happiness and eternal bliss. The Torah consists of rational commandments, such as gratitude and the prohibition of murder and theft, and traditional commandments, such as Sabbath, festivals and dietary prescriptions. The former are applicable to all men and are the product of reason, while the latter are required only of Jews and are the result of the Divine Will. Since the divine commandments are not discoverable by human reason, prophets, whose mission is attested by miracles, are required for their promulgation. The Torah in its totality is eternal and unchanging.

For Saadya, human freedom is the central topic of his account of man. If Divine Omnipotence required that all human acts be caused by God, God would be unjust in punishing sinners for their evil deeds. (This is the problem of Divine Justice.) In support of human freedom, Saadya argues that man, in his actions, does not feel himself compelled and that without human freedom man cannot be held responsible for what he does. God's foreknowledge is compatible with human freedom, since to foreknow something is different from being its cause.

Turning to eschatology in the latter sections of his work, Saadya discusses the resurrection of the dead, redemption and the World to Come. Accepting the resurrection of the body in its literal sense, he holds that this miraculous event will occur after Israel has been redeemed. Redemption will be brought by the Messiah and in Messianic times Israel will return to its own land and the Temple will be rebuilt. The final stage will be the World to Come in which the righteous will be rewarded and the wicked punished. Unlike some Jewish philosophers, who held that only the incorporeal human intellect will exist in the World to Come, Saadya, in more traditional fashion, maintained that, in this state, body and soul will exist eternally together. Throughout his work, Saadya polemicizes against views that diverge from his own.

Like Saadya, the Karaites followed the opinions of the Mu'tazilite Mutakallimūn, but unlike many later Jewish philosophers, they never accepted Aristotelianism, since, in their view, it was incompatible with the teachings of the Bible. Joseph ben Abraham al-Basīr and his disciple Jeshua ben Judah (both of the 11th century) developed a philosophical system more rational than that of Saadya, and they differed from his Aristotelian physics by holding that the world is ultimately composed of atoms. The outstanding Karaite philosopher was Aaron ben Elijah of Nicodemia whose *Tree of Life* (written in 1346) was a kind of Karaite answer to Maimonides's *A Guide to the Perplexed*. Taking issue with Maimonides, he argues for the validity of proofs for the creation of the world, for the positive signification of divine attributes, for the extension of God's providence not only to men, but also to animals, and for the immortality of the soul, not only of the intellect.

Neoplatonism, a second major philosophic movement, began with Saadya's older contemporary, the Kairouan physician, Isaac ben Solomon Israeli (*c.* 835–*c.* 955). While accepting the Neoplatonic doctrine of emanation (which will be explained in our discussion of Ibn Gabirol), he imposed upon it certain features of his own. God, according to Israeli, created the world in time and out of nothing by means of his will and power, which are attributes of God, not separate substances (hypostases). Two simple substances, first matter and first form, proceed directly from God and these two combine to form the next hypostasis, intellect. Next come soul and nature (for Israeli, identical with the heavens) and then the perceptible world. The purpose of human life is the soul's ascent to the spiritual world from which it came and this is accomplished by turning away from the emotions, illumination by the intellect and union with supernal wisdom.

The most important Jewish Neoplatonist was the poet and philosopher Solomon ibn Gabirol (*c.* 1021/2–57, possibly *c.* 1070) with whom the setting of Jewish philosophy shifted to Spain. He was the author of *The Fountain of Life*, a metaphysical work on matter and form, which in its Latin translation influenced Christian scholastics, the *Improvement of Moral Qualities* and of the Hebrew philosophic poem, the *Kingly Crown*. Central to Ibn Gabirol's thought is the doctrine of emanation, according to which God's creation of the world is compared to the emission of rays of light by the sun.

At the summit of Ibn Gabirol's emanationist scheme stands God, who, transcending all, can only be described by negation. From God there issues forth the Divine Wisdom (logos) as an independent substance (hypostasis) and from it comes the Divine Will. While it appears that Ibn Gabirol introduced the notion of the Divine Will to safeguard God's free creation of the world, there are passages in which he appears to maintain that the world came to be through the necessity of the Divine Nature.

Ibn Gabirol holds that after will come universal matter and form, then three spiritual substances – intellect, soul and nature – and, finally, the perceptible world. It was distinctive of Ibn Gabirol's thought that everything other than God, Divine Wisdom and Divine Will is composed of matter (not to be confused with corporeality) and form. As did other Neoplatonists, Ibn Gabirol held that the soul's return to the spiritual world from which it came is the goal of human life and this is accomplished through correct conduct and philosophic speculation. Some of Ibn Gabirol's ideas influenced later kabbalistic thought.

Towards the end of the 11th century there appeared a devotional manual which, unlike the more technical philosophic works, had great popularity among the masses of the Jews: Bahya ibn Pakuda's *Duties of the Heart* (the mystical aspects of which are discussed in another chapter). Distinguishing between 'duties of the

The Spanish poet-philosopher, Yehuda ha-Levi, had a profound influence on 12th-century thinking. This manuscript fragment, in his own hand, shows that he wrote in Arabic, using Hebrew characters.

limbs', those commandments of the Torah which require overt actions and 'duties of the heart', those which demand certain beliefs and attitudes, Bahya notes that while there existed many books devoted to the former, the latter had not been discussed in any systematic work. To remedy this Bahya composed his work, devoting a chapter to each of the following commandments: belief in the unity of God, examination of the world to understand God's wisdom and goodness, service to God, trust in God, sincerity in serving God, humility, repentance, self-examination, abstinence and, finally, love of God.

The most important figure of the first half of the 12th century was the poet and philosopher Yehuda ha-Levi (1080–1141?) who presented his views in the *Book of Arguments and Proofs in Defence of the Despised Faith*, popularly known as *Kuzari*. Using the historically attested conversion of the king of the Khazars in the early part of the 8th century as his framework, ha-Levi casts his book in the form of a dialogue between the king and a Jewish scholar. At the beginning of the *Kuzari*, an angel appears to the king in a dream telling him that his beliefs are pleasing to God, but his deeds are not. At first the king interprets the dream to mean that he should be more zealous in his observance of the Khazar religion, but when the angel appears with the same message a second time, he understands that he must look for a new way of life. The king then invites an Aristotelian philosopher, a Christian and a Muslim – only when he finds their presentations unsatisfactory does he turn to a Jew.

Unlike the Aristotelian philosopher, who had described God as an impersonal principle who is uninterested in the world, the Jewish scholar begins his presentation by affirming his belief in a personal God who directs the processes of history.

Closely related to his conception of God is ha-Levi's account of prophecy and the nature of the Jewish people. Unlike the Aristotelians, who ascribe prophecy to man's natural powers, ha-Levi posits a separate prophetic faculty which distinguishes the people of Israel from all the other nations. While prophecy is the gift of God, it must take place in the Land of Israel (or at least be about the land), and its recipient must observe the commandments of the Torah.

While the philosophers had advocated philosophic speculation as the goal of human life, ha-Levi held that only the faithful adherence to the commandments of God can achieve this goal. Hence the pious individual rather than the philosopher is ha-Levi's ideal. Ha-Levi accepts the Mu'tazilite distinction between rational and traditional commandments, but he assigns to the former only a preparatory role. The servant of God, ha-Levi holds, is like a king: he apportions to each part of his soul and body its due. Advocating moderation in all of man's activities, ha-Levi nevertheless states that man's joy on the Sabbath and the festivals is no less pleasing to God than his affliction on days of fasting. In accordance with his belief that the full Jewish life can only be led in the Land of Israel, the Jewish scholar, at the end of the *Kuzari*, declares his intention to settle there.

In the second half of the 12th century the climate of Jewish philosphy began to change and under the influence of the Muslim philosophers, Alfarabi, Avicenna and Avempace it turned in an Aristotelian direction.

Abraham ibn Daud (*c.* 1110–80), the author of *Sublime Faith*, is generally considered the first Jewish Aristotelian. Critical of Ibn Gabirol and influenced by Avicenna, Ibn Daud begins his work with an exposition of metaphysical, physical and psychological notions, proceeds to a discussion of the existence of God, his unity, divine attributes and actions, prophecy, and the allegorical interpretation of terms comparing God to creatures, and concludes with a discussion of ethics.

Maimonides and his successors

Ibn Daud was soon overshadowed by Moses Maimonides (1135–1204), easily the greatest Jewish philosopher of medieval times. Maimonides presented his philosophic ideas, in popular fashion, in his legal works, but his more technical exposition is reserved for his *A Guide to the Perplexed*. Addressing a disciple who is perplexed by the literal meaning of biblical terms and parables, Maimonides shows that his perplexity can be resolved by proper interpretation of the biblical texts. In addition, Maimonides states that his work is devoted to the inner meaning of the Torah, which he identifies with physics and metaphysics. Since these secrets of the Torah should be taught only to a philosophic élite, Maimonides wrote his book in enigmatic fashion.

Maimonides begins his *Guide* with a lengthy exegetical section in which he shows that a comparison of biblical verses reveals that anthropomorphic terms applied to God have a spiritual meaning already in the Bible. Proceeding to a philosophic exposition of divine attributes, he holds that essential attributes, such as God's existence, unity and life, must be interpreted as negations, while accidental attributes, such as his mercy and anger, must be understood as referring to God's actions.

Before presenting his discussion of the existence, unity, and incorporeality of God and of creation, Maimonides summarizes earlier discussions of these topics, at the same time offering his critique. His own proofs of the existence of God are based on Aristotelian physical and metaphysical principles and he presents proofs from motion, the composition of elements, necessity and contingency, and potentiality and actuality. All these proofs start with some observable property of the world and argue to the existence of a first principle, which is identified with God. Maimonides accepts the biblical notion of creation out of nothing, but only after he has convincingly shown that the philosophers did not have a conclusive argument for the eternity of the world.

Turning to prophecy, Maimonides rejects both the traditionalist notion that prophecy is miraculously given by God and the view of the Aristotelians that it is natural, stating his own opinion that the attainment of prophecy is natural, but that God can prevent prophecy in someone who is prepared for it. While, according to Maimonides, the prophet must be a consummate philosopher, he is also required to have a well developed imagination, for it is through his imagination that the prophet formulates the parables necessary for the instruction of the masses. Moses was singular among the prophets in that he brought the Torah, while it was the function of the other prophets to admonish the people to observe its precepts.

The handwriting of Moses Maimonides: several of the responsa *found in the Cairo Geniza turned out to be answers by Maimonides himself (written at the bottom of the page in a mixture of Hebrew and Arabic in a Syro-Rabbinic hand) to questions prepared for his judgment.*

To account for evil, Maimonides invokes the Neoplatonic notion that it is the privation of good, and, since most evils in the world are political or moral, they are, at least in principle, under the control of man. Closely related to the problem of evil is that of divine providence. Here Maimonides affirms that God's providence extends to individual human beings, though the amount of providence is determined by the degree of intellectual perfection that the recipient has attained.

In his philosophy of law, Maimonides rejects the Mu'tazilite distinction between rational and traditional commandments, holding that all the commandments of the Torah are expressions of the wisdom of God, though the reasons for some commandments, particularly the ritual ones, can only be discovered with difficulty. The purpose of the Torah is the well-being of the soul (intellect), which is obtained through the acquisition of true beliefs, and the well-being of the body, which comes to be through the observance of the practical commandments. There are, however, particular commandments that lack any reason and, hence, are the arbitrary demands of the Divine Will. In an extensive discussion of the commandments, Maimonides holds that many ritual laws, such as the prohibition of wearing garments made of wool and linen, were ordained to counter ancient pagan practices.

While eschatological discussions are notably absent from the *Guide*, Maimonides develops his views concerning these matters in other writings. The Messiah is an earthly king, descended from the House of David, who will bring the Jews back to their own land and will initiate a period of peace and tranquillity for the world. The Messiah will die after a long life and will be succeeded by his descendants. Maimonides's attitude towards resurrection is somewhat enigmatic, but he seems to affirm the resurrection of the dead in traditional

While Maimonides did not accept all Aristotelian thinking, he did base his proofs for the existence of God on Aristotelian principles. Here, the teacher Aristotle is seated on a chair covered with six-pointed stars – an illumination in A Guide to the Perplexed, *from Barcelona, 1348.*

fashion. However, the real after-life is the World to Come in which the human intellect will exist without the body, engaged in the contemplation of God. Maimonides's philosophic ideas influenced Christian scholastics through the Latin translation of his *Guide*.

With the decline of the Jewish community in the Islamic world, the setting of Jewish culture, and with it the setting of Jewish philosophy, shifted to Christian lands – Spain, Provence and Italy. With these geographic shifts, the knowledge of Arabic was gradually forgotten by Jews and they turned to Hebrew as the language of their philosophic writings. As a first step, the numerous scientific and philosophic works that had been written by Jews and non-Jews were translated from Arabic into Hebrew. The major philosophic influences of the period became Maimonides's *A Guide to the Perplexed* and the numerous commentaries on Aristotelian works by the Muslim Averroes (1126–98). Under the influence of Averroes, Jewish philosophy took a more naturalistic direction and there arose Jewish philosophers who attempted to harmonize the opinions of Maimonides and Averroes when these two differed.

Maimonides's rationalistic interpretation of Judaism gave rise to controversies between his followers and their opponents, which lasted throughout the 13th century into the early 14th. There were bans and counterbans, the most famous of which was that of the rabbi of Barcelona, Solomon ben Abraham Adret who, in 1305, prohibited the study of physics and metaphysics prior to the age of twenty-five. During the early 13th century, some philosophers were still active in the Islamic world, among them Abraham, Maimonides's only son, who wrote in defence of his father's views and who, in his *Comprehensive Guide for the Servants of God*, advocated a Jewish pietism.

Of special interest is Hillel ben Samuel (*c.* 1220–95), one of the first Jewish philosophers active in Italy. As did other Italian Jewish philosophers, he knew Latin and this enabled him to draw on the Christian scholastic tradition. In his *Rewards of the Soul* he follows Aristotle in holding that the soul is the form of a natural organic body; however, along with Avicenna and the Platonists, he maintains that the soul emanated from God through the intermediacy of the supernal soul. Using arguments received from Aquinas, he criticizes the Averroean doctrine of the unity of the material intellect, according to which this intellect is one for all mankind, holding instead that each man has his own material intellect. Hillel also holds that only the incorporeal human intellect is immortal and that its ultimate happiness consists in union with the active intellect. Isaac Albalag (second half of the 13th century) followed Averroes in accepting such naturalistic doctrines as the eternity of the world, and he seems to have been a proponent of the theory of the 'double truth', according to which religion and philosophy provide two independent truths which can stand in contradiction. He held that speculative truths are solely the province of philosophy and that the Bible is only required for the moral and political guidance of the masses.

The first half of the 14th century produced a debate concerning the freedom of the human will. Abner of Burgos, who later converted to Christianity, maintained that human actions are causally determined, while Isaac Pollegar defended human freedom. Moses ben Joshua of Narbonne (died after 1362), the author of an important commentary on the *Guide*, also attacked Abner.

Next to Maimonides, Levi ben Gerson (1288–1344), known as Gersonides, was the most important Jewish Aristotelian. Mathematician, biblical commentator and commentator on Averroes, Gersonides presented his opinions in his *Wars of the Lord*. Influenced by Averroes, he discusses topics that Maimonides had not explained sufficiently or for which Maimonides's solution was wrong. Beginning with a discussion of immortality, Gersonides reviews and criticizes various theories concerning the intellect, and reaches the conclusion that only the so-called acquired intellect survives death. But unlike Averroes, he holds that the human intellect is individual in its immortal state. Turning to prophecy and the prediction of the future, Gersonides holds that since the celestial spheres determine terrestrial events, particularly those pertaining to man, it is possible that certain individuals are able to predict them. But human life is not completely determined, since man is free in a certain respect and since his knowledge of the celestial spheres can help him avoid the evil influences they may have. In his discussion of God's knowledge of individuals in the sublunar world, Gersonides is critical of Maimonides's view that God knows these particulars, holding that since God knows only the order of nature, he can only know particulars insofar as they are determined by natural laws. Closely related to God's knowledge of particulars is the question of his providence. Here Gersonides rejects the notion that providence extends only to the species or that it extends to all men, maintaining, with Maimonides, that it extends only to those individuals who have developed their intellect. He differs from Maimonides, who had held that essential attributes applied to God must be understood as negations, by stating that they have positive signification. Yet these attributes are applied to God primarily, to man derivatively. In his account of creation, Gersonides agrees with Maimonides that Aristotle's proofs of the eternity of the world are not conclusive, but Aristotle's arguments are the best that had been offered so far. However, he presents arguments for the creation of the world that he considers better than those that Aristotle had offered for its eternity. Gersonides differs from most Jewish philosophers in holding that the world was created out of some pre-existent matter, rather than out of nothing.

While there had been earlier reactions to the teachings of the Aristotelians, Hisdai Crescas (died 1412?) was the most eminent critic among the Jews. In his *Light of the Lord*, he attacks certain Aristotelian notions, but to replace these he proposes certain philosophic notions of his own. In his philosophy he emphasizes observance of the commandments of the Torah and he holds that the love of God is the supreme goal of human life.

The structure of the *Light of the Lord* is influenced by a controversy that goes back to Maimonides. Maimonides had formulated thirteen basic principles of Judaism which, he held, every Jew was obligated to accept. After Maimonides had made this novel demand, Jewish philosophers extensively discussed whether, in fact, Judaism had mandatory beliefs and, if it did, whether their number was thirteen. Taking issue with Maimonides, Crescas held that there are only three basic principles (and these are basic to all religions), namely, the existence, unity and incorporeality of God. In addition, however, there are six principles required for a belief in the validity of the Torah, namely, God's knowledge of existing things, providence, divine omnipotence, prophecy, human freedom and purpose in the Torah and in the world; and there are eight true beliefs that every adherent of the Torah must accept. Among these are: creation, immortality of the soul, the superiority of the prophecy of Moses and belief in the coming of the Messiah.

Of special interest in Crescas's critique of the Aristotelians, is his conception of space and infinity. The Aristotelians had denied the existence of empty space, had maintained that the existence of an actual infinite was impossible and had considered the universe as finite in extension. Against the Aristotelians, Crescas argued that empty space did exist, that an actual infinite is possible and that the universe is unbounded. Crescas's belief in the possibility of an actual infinite invalidated most of the Aristotelian proofs for the existence of God, but he retained the proof from necessity and contingency, since it was not invalidated by his strictures. He also formulated proofs for the unity and incorporeality of God to replace those which he had rejected. Against Maimonides, Crescas affirmed that positive attributes can be applied to God.

The discussion concerning principles of Judaism was continued by Crescas's student, Joseph Albo (15th century), who in his popular, eclectic *Book of Principles* holds that the existence of God, revelation and reward and punishment are the three basic principles required for the existence of a divine law. From these there follow eight derivative principles and from these, in turn, six

branches. Medieval Jewish philosophy drew to a close with Isaac Abravanel who, after the Expulsion of the Jews from Spain in 1492, settled in Italy. Author of a commentary on *A Guide to the Perplexed*, Abravanel admired Maimonides greatly, but opposed his rationalist interpretation of Judaism, holding that immortality comes through the observance of the commandments of the Torah, not through philosophic speculation.

The Enlightenment and modernity

While modern Jewish philosophers shared many problems with their ancient and medieval predecessors, they differed from them significantly in their solutions. The development of modern science challenged the traditionalist conception of religion, and much of modern philosophy was less hospitable to religious speculations than was ancient and medieval thought. The Enlightenment, with its emphasis on the religion of reason, required that Jewish philosophers rethink some of their theological beliefs, and the emancipation made them investigate anew the nature of Jewish peoplehood. We shall consider five of the more important modern Jewish philosophers.

Moses Mendelssohn (1729–86), translator of the Bible into German, is generally considered the first modern Jewish philosopher. His early training was in traditional Jewish learning, including medieval Jewish philosophy, but he later studied mathematics, languages and modern philosophy. With the pre-Kantian Enlightenment, he shared the belief that metaphysical knowledge is possible and he wrote on the existence of God and the immortality of the soul.

In his *Jerusalem*, Mendelssohn advocated the separation of Church and State, held that religion is a private matter and maintained that both Church and State must guarantee freedom of conscience.

Religion, for Mendelssohn, is the religion of reason which, consisting of rational and moral truths, is available to all men. In its beliefs, Judaism is identical with the religion of reason, but in its practices it is revealed legislation. Traditionalist in his attitude, Mendelssohn holds that the commandments of the Torah are still binding on all Jews, and change can only come about through a new Divine Revelation. Judaism consists of three parts: beliefs, which it shares with the religion of reason; historical truths, which disclose the purpose of Jewish existence; and laws, the observance of which will bring happiness to all Jews. It is the purpose of Jewish tradition to promulgate the religion of reason and to unite the Jewish community.

Under the influence of idealist philosophy, Nachman Krochmal (1785–1840) presented a philosophy of religion and history in his *Guide to the Perplexed of the Times*. For Krochmal, all religions are concerned with the self-realization of human consciousness and all religions are based on a belief in spiritual powers. Judaism differs from the other religions in that it accepts belief in an infinite absolute spirit, God, while the other religions only believe in finite spiritual powers. Religious and philosophic truths are identical, but religion presents these truths through representation, while philosophy presents them through concepts. Judaism, from its beginnings, believed in the infinite absolute spirit, but its understanding of this principle advanced from a representational to a conceptual state.

According to Krochmal's philosophy of history, each of the historical nations is governed by a spiritual principle that determines its history and culture. The history of each nation manifests three stages: growth, maturity and decline. However, while in the history of the world the decline of one nation is followed by the rise of another, the Jewish people is eternal. Jewish history consists of cycles, each one of which manifests the principles of growth, maturity and decline, but once a cycle has been completed, a new cycle begins. It is the mission of the Jews to teach belief in infinite absolute spirit to all mankind.

Hermann Cohen (1842–1918), founder of the Marburg school of neo-Kantianism, presented his views of Judaism in his *Religion of Reason out of the Sources of Judaism*. In his early thought, Cohen considered religion as religion of reason, but in the Kantian sense of the term. Lacking a domain of its own, religion belongs to ethics. In their beginnings, the historical religions embodied a primitive form of ethics; however, as they developed they moved towards a more philosophical ethics. While Cohen always maintained that Judaism should preserve its identity, he saw little difference between liberal Judaism and liberal Protestantism (both as religion of reason) in his early thought.

In Cohen's later years his conception of religion underwent a marked change. He now assigned to religion its own domain. General in its nature, ethics only knows mankind, but it does not address itself to the feelings of guilt and sin of particular men. By advocating remorse and repentance and by fostering a belief in the mercy of God, religion enables man to correct his ways, thereby enabling him to recapture his moral freedom. Cohen's conception of God also underwent a change. Whereas for the early Cohen God was an idea required for man's moral task, he now is being. God, as being, is distinct from the world which is becoming. Asserting that God and the world will always be distinct, Cohen yet affirms that 'correlation' can exist between them. In the light of this new conception, he discusses creation, revelation and redemption. Creation signifies the world's dependence on God (though not its temporal creation by him), revelation refers to the human mind's dependence on God and redemption means mankind's progress towards the ethical ideal. Cohen never gave up his early conception of the religion of reason, but modified it by making room for more personal elements of religion.

The first half of the 20th century saw the emergence of existentialism, whose major Jewish exponents were Franz Rosenzweig (1886–1929) and Martin Buber (1878–1965). In his *Star of Redemption*, Rosenzweig advocates a 'new thinking', to which individual man with his suffering, anxiety and longing is central, rather than abstract ideas. Up to Hegel, philosophers had tried to show that the three elements of human experience, God, man and the world, share one essence, but Rosenzweig argues that they are distinct. However, the three can stand in relation: creation is God's relation to the world, revelation his relation to man and redemption man's relation to the world. These three relations form the substance of the historical religions. Expressing a rather novel point, Rosenzweig holds that Judaism and Christianity are parallel religions. Each of the two religions possesses only partial truths, and God's full truth will only be revealed at the end of time. Christianity and Judaism differ in their missions in the world. Born a pagan, the Christian becomes a Christian through baptism and he must join with other Christians to convert a pagan world. The Jew, by contrast, is born a Jew and he must testify by leading the life of his people. Christianity is the 'eternal way', Judaism the 'eternal life'. Christianity is immersed in history, Judaism transcends it. Judaism, for Rosenzweig is a religion of law, and law governs the Jew's relation to God. Yet, true to his existentialist orientation, Rosenzweig does not advocate blind obedience to the Torah: each man must study the traditional body of law with seriousness and respect, and then appropriate whatever, in conscience, he can.

Martin Buber is perhaps best known for his philosophy of dialogue which he presents in his *I and Thou*, published in 1923. There are two basic relations that man has to other men and to the world: I-Thou and I-It. I-Thou is a relation between two persons, I-It a relation between a person and a thing. The former is marked by reciprocity and mutuality, the latter by domination and use. Ideally all human relations should be I-Thou relations, but they often deteriorate into I-It relations. Buber also maintains that there can be I-Thou relations between persons and things. There exists, however, one I-Thou relation which does not deteriorate and that is the relation between the I and the Eternal Thou, God. There are no philosophic proofs demonstrating the existence of the Eternal Thou, he can only be discovered by human sensitivity.

God, according to Buber, is not encountered in supernatural occurrences, but in the events of day-to-day life. The dialogue between God and man is best attained by living in a community, and Judaism is the community within which God dwells and which is the bearer of the kingdom of God. One of the most problematic aspects of Buber's thought is his attitude towards Jewish law and it is here that he differs from Rosenzweig. Man, according to Buber, may consider Jewish law when it speaks to a given situation, but it is man's existential response that must determine what he ought to do. Within Judaism, the prophets and Hasidism provide the best example of the life of dialogue, and Buber wrote many works on biblical and Hasidic topics. It is fair to say that the current climate of Jewish philosophy is existentialist.

Chapter Ten

Jewish Mysticism

R.J. ZWI WERBLOWSKY

ONE OF THE MOST IMPRESSIVE PASSAGES in the whole Hebrew Bible is that which describes the 'numinous' vision of the prophet Isaiah:

> In the year that King Uzziah died, I saw the Lord sitting upon a throne, high and lifted up, and his train filled the temple. Above it stood the seraphims: each one had six wings; with twain he covered his face, and with twain he covered his feet, and with twain he did fly. And one cried unto another, and said, Holy, holy, holy is the Lord of hosts: the whole earth is full of his glory. And the posts of the door moved at the voice of him that cried, and the house was filled with smoke. (Is. VI:1–4)

Is this what we should today understand by a mystical experience? In one way it is, since it involves a sense of close communion with the Divine, but unlike most later mystical experiences it is by no means free from involvement and links with 'this world'. It is essentially – and this is true of most of the other prophets – an experience of vocation, of 'appointment', accompanied by a sense of sinfulness, inadequacy and impurity, followed by an act of purification:

> Then said I, Woe is me! for I am undone; because I am a man of unclean lips, and I dwell in the midst of a people of unclean lips: for mine eyes have seen the King, the Lord of hosts. Then flew one of the seraphims unto me, having a live coal in his hand, which he had taken with the tongs from off the altar. And he laid it upon my mouth, and said, Lo this hath touched thy lips; and thine iniquity is taken away and thy sin purged. (Is. VI:5–7)

But immediately we learn that this vision was not granted for its own sake. It was merely a kind of preparation. For coming to the purpose, the account continues:

> Also I heard a voice from the Lord, saying, whom shall I send and who will go for us? Then said I, Here am I: send me. And he said, Go, and tell this people, Hear ye indeed but understand not; and see ye indeed but perceive not. (Is. VI:8–9)

A similar analysis could be made of the powerful, albeit somewhat bizarre and disconcerting vision of the celestial throne in Ezekiel I. These two examples have been chosen very deliberately because they did, in fact, play a considerable role in the subsequent development of Jewish mysticism. The 'vision of the chariot' (i.e. the celestial throne) and of the heavenly spheres as practised by later mystics was undoubtedly indebted to Ezekiel and, for all we know, may have grown at least in part out of meditations or commentaries on this text.

Many Psalms, too, breathe a desire for closeness to God and, given the right spiritual climate, are susceptible to a near-mystical interpretation. 'As the hart panteth after the water brooks so panteth my soul after thee, O God. My soul thirsteth for God, for the living God: when shall I come and appear before God?' (Ps. XLII:1–2). But as the conclusion of the last sentence indicates, the kind of piety expressed in this Psalm is Temple-oriented. The worshipper seems to identify the boon of the presence of God with the privilege of appearing, possibly on a pilgrimage, in his Temple – which incidentally reminds us that Isaiah's mighty vision also has the Temple as part of its stage-setting.

But while we can easily speak of biblical forms of piety, it would surely be an anachronism to speak of biblical mysticism in the sense that we normally attach to that term. The typical prophet is not interested in his own states of communion with God. Very often he would much prefer to be released from his prophetic vocation altogether. This vocation is that of a messenger, charged with delivering God's message (laws, injunctions, exhortations, warnings and threats of dire punishment, promises of salvation and comfort, etc.) to a community. In the Jewish case, this community is the people of Israel. The prophet is thus, by definition, community-oriented. The essence of his vocation is not ineffable and unutterable but, on the contrary, the delivery of a very specific and clear message. His relationship to God is (to use Martin Buber's phrase) of the I-Thou type, both personally and on behalf of the community, rather than of the 'mystical union' type.

The prophetic mission

Mysticism, as generally understood, means a particularly intense form of individual, spiritual and/or emotional intercourse with the reality of the Divine, a quest for the closest possible contact or even union with the higher, purer and 'absolute' realms of the Godhead. Hence terms like adhesion (*devekuth*, in Hebrew) or even union (cf. the *unio mystica* of many Christian mystics) figure so largely in the vocabulary of mysticism. This remains true even in the case of mystics who raise disciples, influence circles of followers or even produce voluminous writings and found 'schools'. For one of the curious paradoxes of mysticism is that, in spite of the quest or actual experience of a reality that is said to be 'ineffable', 'unutterable' and 'unspeakable', many mystics have left an immense body of writings.

Prophetic religion, on the other hand, is basically 'dualistic' (God, the transcendent Creator, the 'wholly other', over against his creation); the relationship is one of both love and fear (e.g. 'fear of the Lord' in the sense of a genuine religious relationship and not, of course, as mere daemonic terror); its expression is loving obedience, seeking and doing his will and walking in his ways, faith, hope and prayer. And since it is in the nature of human existence to fall short of these ideals, therefore sin and awareness of sinfulness as well as the need for repentance and forgiveness inevitably play a considerable role in this type of religiosity. There is a sense of vocation not only of the individual but of the community as a whole (e.g. the 'Chosen People') and a concomitant sense of responsibility. This structure has wider implications and corollaries: a more social and historical orientation (which may produce a concept of history and of historic destiny and fulfilment leading to a full-blown Messianic ideology), an emphasis on ethics and on social values (e.g. justice and righteousness) and an essentially activist atttitude that may aspire to establish not only a God-willed national and social order but also a perfected world (the Kingdom of God on earth). Mysticism, by contrast, is often described as more monistically inclined (the essential unity of the soul with God or – as in the case of pantheism – of all Being, as such, with God), as more 'quietistic' and less preoccupied with ethics and social action. Virtues are valued less for their own sake than as preparatory stages on the road to spiritual perfection. Mystics tend to be less interested in history and the time-process, since they usually strive to rise above and beyond time and the sphere of change, to the sphere of the eternal, the 'everlasting now' or whatever it be called. The mystic does not live the life of faith, hope and trust, but the life of deeper (or higher) knowledge and of an actual and immediate spiritual realization even if he considers this realization as merely an anticipation of a fuller and more complete realization to be attained at a later stage (e.g. after death).

The period of the Second Temple

During the second half of this period we can trace the beginning of a tradition that can certainly be called mystical in the sense just described. New forms of spiritual life seem to have developed, partly as a result of suffering and persecution, partly under the influence of diverse Oriental and Hellenistic religions. One of these forms is known as 'apocalyptic', that is, revelations about the cosmos, about the celestial realms, about things to come and about the final dénouement of history, such as the last judgment, the resurrection of the dead, the descent of the new or heavenly Jerusalem, that were vouchsafed to visionaries. Even here we cannot always be sure whether the literature that has preserved these revelations is based in every instance on actual experiences and visions, or merely uses a current literary device. The visions preserved in the Book of Daniel make a fairly authentic impression on the reader. (The same would seem to hold true of the last book of the New Testament – the Revelation of John – very possibly a Christian reworking of some originally Jewish apocalyptic material.) Still, we must admit that the beginnings of Jewish mysticism are shrouded in obscurity, and much depends on how we date the various texts and how much 'early' material we assume to be preserved in texts whose extant versions are of a demonstrably later date (see below on the Mishnah *Hagigah* II:I).

As I have said, many of the visionary and prophetic experiences described in the Hebrew Bible were to play an important part in the development of later Jewish mysticism, but they do not form the beginning of a continuous mystical tradition. The earliest fully articulated system that can properly be called mystical is that of the *Merkabah*, which is found in Palestine and then in Babylonia from the first centuries of the Common Era to the 10th century. This system no doubt had its roots in the early rabbinic period, and beyond that to certain currents and trends that were rife in the period of the Second Temple.

Many factors combined to create a climate in which mystical lore could develop: the syncretistic mystical religiosity of the Hellenism of late Antiquity (including its Oriental components), popular forms of Neoplatonic and stoic philosophies, the 'lower' as well as 'higher' forms of magic current throughout the Hellenistic world (and which included angelology and demonology), speculations regarding 'wisdom' (*sophia*) as a divine or cosmic principle (derived, in part, from Proverbs VIII:22*ff.*), the combination of *sophia* with *logos* speculations – the divine logos, which played such a central role in the semi-mystical system of the Jewish philosopher Philo Judaeus of Alexandria and which underwent such a decisive transformation in the Prologue to the Fourth Gospel and in subsequent Christian theology – and, last but not least, Gnosticism. Such movements were widespread both within Judaism and outside it. The biblical Apocrypha and pseudepigrapha, as has been remarked before, contain writings of a visionary and apocalyptic kind and suggest the existence of circles cultivating esoteric doctrines and mystical disciplines. The Gnostic movements, about which the Church Fathers had so much to say, may be indebted to Jewish mystical speculations to a much greater extent than has previously been assumed. Philo of Alexandria (*c.* 20 BCE–50 CE) not only interprets Judaism in terms of Hellenistic mystical philosophy but actually describes a sect leading a semi-monastic life dedicated to meditation. There were no doubt considerable differences between the mysticism of the Hellenistic Jews and those of Palestine, and even within Palestine we can distinguish different types of esotericism. There is reason to believe that the Essenes described by Josephus possessed a secret lore, which consisted to a large extent of angelology and magic as well as certain eschatological doctrines. Most scholars hold the Essenes to be identical with the 'Dead Sea' or 'Qumran' sect, whose writings were found near Jericho from 1947 onwards, but there is, as yet, no conclusive evidence of any continuity between Essene doctrines and the forms of mysticism cultivated in rabbinic and other circles.

Mysticism and the Talmud

Rabbinic religion, as it developed from the pharisaic teachings to its final, normative crystallization in the talmudic literature, is anything but 'mystical'. A careful examination of, for example, the prayers composed or transmitted by the early rabbis, both for public liturgy and private devotion, bespeaks a profound piety but no mystical aspirations let alone flights of mystical enthusiasm. Yet the legal parts of the Talmud attest, or perhaps we should say betray, almost incidentally, as it were, the existence of certain disciplines that should not be taught in public and that were considered as esoteric lore reserved for initiates only. Thus the Mishnah, in the tractate *Hagigah* ii:i, rules that certain subjects may not be taught in public:

> . . . may not be expounded before three persons; nor the account of Creation (Gen. i) before two; nor the account of the chariot (Ez. i) before one alone, unless he is a Sage that understands of his own knowledge. Whosoever gives his mind to four things, it were better for him if he had not come into the world: what is above? what is beneath? what was beforetime? and what will be hereafter? And whosoever takes no heed of the honour of his Creator (by enquiring too closely into these things) it were better if he had not come into the world.

The rules formulated by this text, which dates from the 2nd century CE, were apparently accepted and traditional by that time.

The existence of other esoteric doctrines may be inferred from well established technical terms, though detailed descriptions of them survive only in later hymns and may not reflect exactly the practices and teachings of the early rabbis. The most important is the *Merkabah*, an ecstatic contemplation which culminated in the vision of the throne of glory. The idea of the heavenly journey comes from Ezekiel i. The ascent of the soul through the celestial spheres and palaces, and the attendant 'perils of the soul' encountered on this journey, is the theme both of later *hekhaloth* texts and of other mystical writings, including non-Jewish Hellenistic ones. St Paul, for instance (II Cor. xii:i–4), describes an ecstatic ascent which took him not, indeed, to the throne of glory but to the 'third heaven'.

Heavenly journeys involve cosmology, angelology, demonology and magic. The ascent takes place in a spatially conceived cosmos, divided into higher and lower worlds or spheres, often with palaces and gates, etc., peopled by all kinds of powers and angelic guardians; the adept has to use magical formulae and mystic signs to force his passage and subdue these supernatural beings who bar his progress. Esoteric speculations and ecstatic experiences of this kind were tinged with Gnostic elements; they were consequently viewed with misgivings and suspected of leading weaker spirits into heresy. The talmudic commentary on the Mishnah *Hagigah* and related texts provides much incidental information and illustrations. The strange story of the four great rabbinic masters who made this ecstatic ascent – one died as a result, one went mad, one became a heretic and only one, Rabbi Akiba (subsequently also famed for his martyrdom at the hands of the Romans), 'entered in peace and came out in peace' – is evidently meant to discourage dabbling in ecstatic mysticism, since only very few possess the required physical, mental and moral qualifications. But the story

also suggests, as Professor G. Scholem has pointed out, that this kind of 'gnosticizing' mysticism was practised not merely by marginal enthusiasts, sectarian oddballs and the like, but by the leading rabbis and teachers of the generation. Clearly, talmudic Judaism had its mystical side which, however, the rabbis considered as esoteric and hence did not wish to see popularized.

Since *Merkabah* mysticism is indebted to Ezekiel's vision of the divine throne of glory, it is not surprising that the figure of a man upon the throne (Ez. 1:26) should also have played a part, and speculations regarding this *Shi'ur Qomah* (i.e. the 'measure of the Godhead') and *Metatron* (who, from an apotheosis of Enoch became the 'lesser Yahweh' and a kind of demiurge) often bordered on heresy. It is characteristic of *Merkabah* mysticism that the experience of loving communion, so common in later mysticism, is completely absent. The deity is transcendent, mysterious, awesome and truly numinous: *rex tremendae majestatis*. After rising through spheres, worlds, heavens and celestial mansions, guarded by all sorts of terrifying angels, the initiate, if he be worthy, stands trembling before the supreme vision of divine Splendour.

The esoteric teachings and practices of the *Merkabah* mysticism did not survive into the later Kabbalah but their mark on the Jewish liturgy has been permanent. The daily repeated recitation of the *trisagion* 'Holy, holy, holy is the Lord of Hosts') and some of the most numinous hymns in the religious literature of the world are their contribution to the prayer-book of the synagogue. Incidentally, the *praefatio* to the *Sanctus* in the Christian liturgy, with its evocation of the community on earth joining the celestial choirs in praising the Lord, is an exact replica of the model provided by the ancient Jewish liturgical formula.

The *Sefer Yetsirah* (*Book of Creation*) stands outside the tradition we have been examining. Its mystical doctrine is one of letters and numbers: all reality derives from the ten primary numbers and twenty-two letters of the Hebrew alphabet, the ultimate elements from which the cosmos is constituted. The book was written in Palestine or Babylonia some time between the 3rd and 6th centuries, and it exerted a great influence on later Jewish thought. Its letter-mysticism was very close to the kabbalistic doctrine of the cosmic process as an unfolding of the name of God (i.e. of the Hebrew letters constituting his name), while on the other hand it linked easily with the theory and practice of magic, which sought to manipulate the world by spells based on these same Hebrew letters.

The Middle Ages: Maimonides, ha-Levi and Bahya

From Palestine and Babylonia some of these esoteric and magical texts and traditions spread to the Jewries of Spain, Italy and France, and led to the formation of the German 'Hasidism' that flourished in the 12th and 13th centuries. The word *hasid* already occurs in the Hebrew Bible, where it signifies a pious man, steadfast in his devotion to and trust in God. Later, the term was used for religious groups of great piety and fervour, such as the supporters of the Maccabean revolt (2nd century BCE) against the religious persecution of Antiochus Epiphanes. Subsequently, the term was used to designate the mystical and pietist movements that arose in 12th-century Germany and in 18th-century Poland. The mysticism of the German Hasidim was an eclectic mixture of ideas from the *Sefer Yetsirah*, from *Merkabah* mysticism (without its ecstatic practices), from magic and from misunderstood Aristotelian philosophy. In practice, it emphasized piety, humility, penitence and self-discipline, and its prayer made use of a technique of meditating on Hebrew letters and their numerological equivalents.

The ascetic mysticism of this circle profoundly influenced the life and the spirituality of a significant section of Ashkenazi Jewry. In fact, their practice of humility, penitence and piety is so reminiscent of certain forms of contemporary Christian piety, that influences from the latter – by what routes or by what kind of 'osmotic process' we do not know – cannot be excluded. In due course, German Hasidism merged with the new Kabbalah that developed in the 12th and 13th centuries, at first in the Languedoc part of southern France and subsequently also in northern Spain.

Before proceeding to the Kabbalah, however, some other forms of Jewish spirituality must be mentioned, and at this stage a brief discussion of medieval philosophy is inevitable for at least two reasons. In the first place because of the truism that certain types of philosophy lead to mysticism: they not only tend to become 'mystical philosophies' but systematically and almost naturally lead to a spiritual border-area where mysticism takes over from philosophy. In the second place, most forms of mysticism resort to philosophical concepts, doctrines, traditions and even systems whenever they want, or need, to reach out beyond mere experience to intelligible utterance. In fact, even the 'unutterable' experiences are often structured by the philosophical presuppositions that form part of the mystic's tradition. In addition, mysticism contains a great many implicit assumptions concerning the nature of the cosmos, of the soul, of the Godhead, and of the relations obtaining among them. At a certain point philosophical 'explication' becomes inevitable. Thus Neoplatonism, for instance, not only generated its own brands of mystical spirituality but also profoundly influenced the articulations of the mystical traditions and theologies of Christianity, Islam and Judaism. Even the ascendant Aristotelianism of the later Middle Ages was still to a large extent Neoplatonic.

The major figure of Jewish philosophy, Moses Maimonides (1135–1204) – a radical Aristotelian by medieval standards – provides an excellent example of how a philosophical spirituality gradually merges into mysticism. It is man's rational faculty, i.e. his capacity to unite himself to the 'active intellect' emanating from God, that makes him the image of God and that leads him to true contemplation of, knowledge of and communion with God. Maimonides identifies this stage of being lovingly united to God – an *amor intellectualis dei* that is at the same time an emotional experience – with prophecy.

This 'rationalist' type of mysticism, as some have called it, leads to another notion familiar to mystics. Maimonides, for strictly philosophical reasons, was at particular pains to dissociate himself from any suggestion of anthropomorphism. Even such innocent statements as 'God is great, good, powerful, etc.' were unacceptable to him and, indeed, pregnant with heresy,

since for an entity to have attributes entailed that it was an existent thing to which adventitious characteristics were added, making it composite. But God is absolute *One*-ness and, therefore, can have no attributes. The almost unbridgeable gulf between this, the philosopher's God, and the all-too-human God of the devout simple believer needs no emphasis. Philosophical mysticism finally came to speak of God as the 'great Nothing', and some mystics talk of communion with God in terms of mystical an*nihil*ation.

The opposite pole of mystical thought is represented by Yehuda ha-Levi (1080–1141?), whose poetry burns with an intensely personal love of God and individual longing for divine communion. Many of his liturgical compositions still figure among the gems of the Jewish prayer-book; yet he does not recoil from paradox when paradox can convey his meaning more adequately than normal logic:

> *Lord where shall I find thee?*
> *High and hidden is thy place;*
> *And where shall I not find thee?*
> *The world is full of thy glory.*
>
> *O Lord, before thee is my whole desire,*
> *Yea, though I cannot bring it to my lips.*
> *Thy favour would I ask a moment and then die.*
>
> *When far from thee, I die while yet in life;*
> *But if I cling to thee I live, though I should die.*
>
> *To meet the fountain of the life of truth I run;*
> *To see the face of my king is my only aim;*
> *Would I might behold his face within my heart,*
> *Mine eyes would never ask to look beyond.*

There is much else that could be said on ha-Levi's theology and in particular on his attack on rationalist philosophy. In fact, he is a kind of Jewish counterpart to Al-Ghazzali, and long before Pascal he had defined the difference between God as conceived by the Aristotelians – an abstract 'First Cause' or 'Prime Mover' – and the living God of Abraham as experienced in personal revelation. Ha-Levi's theology also provides a profound interpretation of Jewish existence – election, suffering, humiliation, persecution and hope of redemption – but these subjects are outside the scope of our present concern with the history of Jewish mysticism.

At least one more author should be mentioned here in order to do justice to the full range of Jewish spirituality, especially as popular interest in the Kabbalah has monopolized views on Jewish mysticism to such an extent that non-kabbalistic forms of Jewish mysticism tend to be ignored. Bahya ibn Pakuda (Spain, 11th century) was a judge at a rabbinic court, and was for that reason particularly alive to the dangers of mere external observance to which a religion of works and ritual practices was exposed. His book on the *Duties of the Heart* was written to expound the principles of religious life. Despite its extreme ascetic spirituality, calculated, one would imagine, to appeal only to a minority, it became widely popular with all types of readers. Fundamental subjects, such as the existence and unity of God, are given the conventional Neoplatonic treatment. But upon this groundwork, Bahya builds a system of complete and utter faith in God, which springs from Sufi traditions though it avoids the extremes of Sufism. All worldly

A Jew and his 'Bride', the crowned Synagogue (here blindfolded in the manner of Christian iconography), symbolize the betrothal of Israel to God, a relationship conceived in holiness and contracted to outlast even the end of days.

desires are condemned; they are an admission of 'secret polytheism', since they set up objects of intention and volition besides God. Indeed, any kind of activity is essentially bad because it assumes that nature is permanent and causality valid – assumptions that, according to Sufi piety, breach our immediate communion with the First Cause. Even duties prescribed by religion, such as working for a living, caring for one's family, etc., are fundamentally useless and valueless. They are merely chores laid upon us by God, and the natural order that they seem to imply is an illusion. When a physician gives medicine and a patient takes it, their correct attitude should be that they are merely behaving 'as if' the medicine brought about the cure. But to believe that it really does so is to be guilty of 'secret polytheism'; it is God alone who cures. The logical conclusion to such a theory is complete indifference to the world, total abandonment to God, and solitude. It is interesting to see how Bahya's Jewish Orthodoxy stops him following the Sufis all the way to this conclusion. How, in fact, can such a theory be reconciled to a religion that strictly enjoins marriage, communal prayer and a host of other duties and social activities? Bahya carefully qualifies his formulations. Solitude is not to be taken to extremes; it is meant only to loosen man's bonds with the world and prepare the soul for union with God. Conscience should be constantly examined, repentance and humility should be practised, but not to such a degree as to interfere with normal living. Mystical union in its extreme, classic form is totally excluded from rabbinic Judaism. The purpose of spiritual discipline is an intense all-absorbing love of God, defined as 'the longing of the soul and its yearning for the Creator, so that it may cleave to His supreme light.' A perfect state of indifference to the joys and sorrows of this world leads not to inactivity but to a supernatural knowledge by which the lover of God 'sees but not with his eyes, hears but not with his ears, feels but not with his senses, understands without ratiocination, dislikes nothing and prefers nothing . . . makes his will dependent on the will of God, and his love on the love of God, loving only what God loves and rejecting what God rejects.' Bahya's demands may seem extreme and his spirituality élitist. All the more noteworthy is the fact that his book on the *Duties of the Heart* was one of the most frequently copied, printed and reprinted manuals of the spiritual life.

The mysterious world of the Kabbalah

The Kabbalah is a strangely bizarre theosophical system, in which Neoplatonic, Gnostic and mystical elements have come together in a combination that is still difficult to disentangle, but it is undoubtedly the most influential and far-reaching of all forms of Jewish mysticism.

What are the mystical experiences that lie at the root of the Kabbalist movement? The early Kabbalists rarely talked about them and biographical accounts are extremely rare. But something can be gleaned from passages such as the following:

> [After hours of intense meditation] they would imagine the light of the Divine Presence above their heads as though it was flowing all around them and they were in the midst of this light . . . and whilst in that [state of meditation] they were all trembling as a natural effect but [spiritually] rejoicing in trembling, as it is written [Ps. 11:11], 'Serve the Lord with fear, and rejoice with trembling.'

At the centre of the kabbalistic system lies a distinction between two apparently incompatible conceptions of God, conceptions which we have already noted in contrasting Maimonides with Yehuda ha-Levi. One is the abstract 'rational' God of philosophy, so essentially 'one' that not even attributes can be postulated of him and nothing can be said about him. This God lacks the divine vitality; he had become a 'state', not a 'process', and still less a 'person'. The other is the living dynamic God whose relevance to man resides precisely in his personality and multiplicity. The Kabbalists, however, accepted both aspects of the Divine, combining them into a single theology – the hidden and unknowable *deus absconditus* and the manifest, self-revealing, accessible God of religious experience. Of the former not even existence can be postulated; it is the great divine Nothing. The Kabbalists called it *En sof*, the 'Infinite'. The mystery of its nothingness is never mentioned in the Bible, nor can it be addressed in prayer or approached in meditation.

Yet the Bible, God's Word, can only be the revelation or self-manifestation of the hidden God. To be existent at all, God must be manifest, revealed, capable of being apprehended by man. This process of manifestation is the process by which God – as comprehensible by man – comes into 'being'. Superficially understood, the Bible describes God's creation of the world and first dealings with it. More profoundly understood, by the Kabbalist, it describes the process of divine becoming: in the depths of the divine 'hiddenness', something occurs which makes it begin to turn outward, to unfold, to exist (*ex-*

stare), a process of extraversion in the introverted *En Sof*. This initial movement is described in a highly mystical passage of the Zohar, the most important kabbalistic text. The concentration or crystallization of energy in one luminous point bursts the closed confines of *En Sof* and the process of emanation has begun.

'Emanation' (rather than 'Creation') is a key term of kabbalistic theology. Though borrowed from Neoplatonic philosophy, it is used to refer, not to any intermediary or intermediaries between the spiritual One and the material Many, but, rather, to the process by which the divine Nothingness becomes the divine Being. Its totality is described as consisting of ten *sefiroth* – 'potencies', 'foci', aspects, stages or manifestations of the deity in revealing itself. These *sefiroth* interrelate dynamically, making up the intensely dramatic inner life of the Godhead, which yet remains essentially one in spite of its complexity. Orthodox critics were quick to complain that the Kabbalists had set up a tenfold God, which was even worse than the threefold God of the Christians, and indeed both the dualism inherent in the doctrine of the hidden and manifest God and the multiplicity in that of the *sefiroth* do look dangerously like denials of strict Jewish monotheism. But the Kabbalists, many of whom were themselves great luminaries of Orthodox talmudic learning, replied that they were speaking of a profound mystery – the mystical understanding of the divine unity in all its manifestations. The *sefiroth* were not gods; they were not even attributes. Yet, by the sheer inherent power of the kabbalistic system, they became more and more personified, and the emphasis on unity correspondingly more insistent.

The relation between two particular *sefiroth* – the sixth (*Tif'ereth*) and the tenth (*Malkhuth*) – is particularly important in kabbalistic thought and practice. *Tif'ereth* is in a way the central *sefirah*, the hub and pivot of the whole system, receiving power or influx from higher potencies, harmonizing them, and passing them down to the lower ones. Embodying the creative dynamism of the *sefiroth*, it is expressed exclusively in dominant or male symbols: Sun, King, Bridegroom, etc. *Malkhuth* is at the lower end of the *sefiroth*-cluster, occupying the point where the divine sphere meets the non-divine. She is the receptive womb, the Moon, Queen and Bride. Although the lowest of the *sefiroth*, she acquires authority in relation to the nether world, where her creative, active and 'royal' aspects are emphasized, and the Bride is also Mother.

Now the most striking feature of these kabbalistic writings is the frankly erotic quality of the relation between *Tif'ereth* and *Malkhuth*. It is a holy union, *hieros gamos*, between two aspects of the Divine, the essence of the unity of God. For *Malkhuth* to be separated from *Tif'ereth* means the destruction of that unity, the greatest catastrophe that the Kabbalist can imagine. But it is precisely this that was the consequence of Adam's sin. The fate of God, not just the fate of man, was sealed by that sin, and the whole of religion, including man's efforts in good works and in mystical contemplation, should be directed to repairing it, and to promoting the wholeness, i.e. the union of male and female, within God. The gravity of sin lies in man's capacity to disrupt the divine union. Such a union involves a whole philosophical system which cannot be expounded here, but in essence it is based on the correspondence or

analogy between microcosm and macrocosm. Man is the image of God, a belief that the Kabbalists interpreted to mean that the human frame reveals the same structure as the divine 'frame' of the *sefiroth*. This again links up with pre-kabbalistic notions of a divine *anthropos* or *adam kadmon*, i.e. the originally Gnostic concept referring to a divine or semi-divine celestial archetype of Adam, the First Man.

The significant thing about all this is that both in the image of man (cf. Gen. 2:17; 11:18, 24) and in the image of God, totality and perfection are only achieved by the union of male and female. This is a good example of how the Kabbalists added a new, mystical layer to the traditional Jewish doctrine that perfection was possible only in the married state. In fact, it seems that Kabbalah is the first system to develop a mystical metaphysics of the sexual act. Erotic mysticism, however, is limited to the sphere of the inner-divine (*sefiroth*) life; it has no place in man's relation to God. The Kabbalist knows no lover who ravishes him; he does not tell of the kind of experience known to us from Christian or Sufi literature. Instead of *union* with God, which was unacceptable to the Jewish tradition of monotheism, the Jewish mystic seeks *communion*, or *devekuth*, a turning to God, an awareness of his otherness, a loving clinging or adhering to him which implies no loss of identity. He achieves this by a kind of *imitatio dei*, by which his own integration follows the pattern and analogy of the Divine. Contemplation of the Divine, i.e. of the *Malkhuth* in the first instance, thus leads to a communion whose ultimate purpose is the *unio mystica* within the Godhead. It is the Kabbalist's task to promote this end by contemplative efforts and a holy life.

The later Kabbalah

One of the strangest paradoxes of the Kabbalah had always been its mythological element, derived partly from old, Oriental Gnosticism. Stranger still, in a religion which is usually considered the mortal enemy of myth, was the almost explosive reappearance of even more mythological notions in the kabbalistic systems of the 16th century.

Isaac Luria (1534–72) invented an elaborate new kabbalistic 'mythology', according to which, long before the beginning of the human race, a cosmic catastrophe occurred at the very heart of God's creation. The channels or 'pipes' by which the creative light of God poured into Creation-in-the-making, said Luria, collapsed or broke, and the divine sparks fell into chaos. Since then, these sparks yearned to return to their source, and the history of the world, with its progress and setbacks, is really the struggle for such a restoration. The two major setbacks had been the fall of Adam and the destruction of the Temple, but in fact it was not only Israel or mankind that was in desperate need of salvation, but every stone, every plant, the whole cosmos, even God himself.

What is the practical significance of this weird system, in which elements from so many disparate sources jostle each other? Firstly, it produced a cosmos in which God and man were bound together by much closer ties than in Orthodox theology. Sharing a common fate and destiny, they need one another equally. This is very different from the normal picture of a God completely independent of the world, bringing to it a kind of condescending, paternal benevolence. His interest and involvement in mankind had often been expressed by the rabbis, but never with such force as this. Secondly, it added a new dimension of meaning to the traditional image of Israel as God's Bride: that relation could now be seen as the earthly counterpart of one that was mystical and divine. The historical Israel 'is' *Malkhuth*, the symbol of a principle within the Godhead, and everything in the universe and in man corresponds to something in the divine sphere. The result is that every human act acquires a new and profound significance, directly affecting the Divine itself. Man is not just a sinner passively waiting on divine grace; he is not even just a free agent working out his own salvation; he is a factor in the universe, a being whose actions are vitally related to the inner life of the Godhead.

According to Luria, man was created after the primeval catastrophe, as God's helper in the struggle for the restoration of the perfect order and the conquest of 'daemonic' forces. Man's task – the task of Israel – consists in living a life of sanctity, mystical concentration and fulfilment of the divine Law, and by so doing bringing about the salvation of the world. God himself is incomplete as long as the divine sparks are imprisoned in fallen matter and fallen souls; God and man are united in the great work of salvation which will redeem the world, the soul, and God himself. This mystical framework was able to absorb in toto the whole traditional Jewish system of life according to the Law. For the Kabbalist, this tradition – its commandments, its ritual observances – was itself nothing less than the way by which the cosmos would be restored and re-ordered. 'Doing the will of God', which had formerly meant carrying out his commandments as laid down in the Covenant, and thereby acquiring blessing and long life, was now transformed by contemplative concentration into a process of mystical redemption. It represented a 'sacramentalization' of the life of even the humblest Jew.

Having said that much, one of the most interesting and important features of Lurianic Kabbalism should have become clear. Lurianism is essentially a Messianic mysticism. This point deserves special emphasis, since normally mysticism and Messianism are related in inverse ratio. In the mystical quest or fulfilment of supra-temporal life in God, the historic and Messianic dimensions tend to shrink or even disappear. Lurianism combined mysticism with the Messianic thrust, impetus, yearning and hope of Jewish tradition. It is a chemical compound that can produce dynamite and, indeed, the great Messianic outburst in the 17th century that centred round the figure of Sabbatai Zevi becomes comprehensible only against the background of Lurianic Kabbalism. The history of this astounding movement has been described and analyzed by G. Scholem in his magisterial *Sabbatai Zevi: The Mystical Messiah* (1973). Lurianism had been the dominant form of Jewish piety from the 16th century until the Sabbatean outburst, with its antinomistic excesses combining forms of antinomianism that are well known to students of both mystical and Messianic movements. The debacle of the movement and the spiritual disarray that followed it left the Kabbalah severely shaken, especially in its social role.

Mysticism reasserted itself in the last great religious movement of Judaism. The movement, which is known

The career of Sabbatai Zevi is one of the most extraordinary episodes in Jewish history. Inspired by his kabbalistic studies, he proclaimed himself Messiah and quickly won a following in his home-town of Smyrna. His wanderings through the Near East spread his fame to all corners of the world, and when he returned to Smyrna in 1665 (above) he was joyfully received. His later forced conversion to Islam did not, surprisingly, put an end to the movement.

as Hasidism, was initiated by Rabbi Israel Baal Shem Tov in the 18th century and flourished in Eastern Europe. It still continues, albeit in a degenerate form, to the present day. Hasidism saw itself as standing in the line of the kabbalistic tradition. In actual fact, however, and in spite of the use of kabbalistic terminology by the early Hasidic masters, the new mystical revival had shifted away from the classical Kabbalah in general and from the high-pitched Messianic fever of Lurianism in particular. The popular success of the movement was due in no small measure to its character of protest against talmudic scholasticism of the rabbinic élite, the bankruptcy of Lurianism after the Messianic failure and the spiritual hunger of the pauperized masses. Cleaving to God, the continual practice of the presence of God, the rejoicing in the communion with God – particularly as mediated by the Hasidic masters around whom 'sects' of followers congregated – these were among the ideals cultivated by the Hasidim. But decline was inevitable. Enthusiastic excess, the foolish superstitions that become part of every mass movement, the development of hereditary 'dynasties' of Hasidic masters combined with a degenerate but presumptuous theory of 'mediation' – all these helped to discredit the movement. Above all, Hasidism developed in a period when Judaism was about to cross the threshold to modernity: the new rationalism, the struggle for emancipation and civil rights and the need to formulate a Judaism that would fit into the social and cultural context of the 19th century were not propitious for the positive and constructive evolution of a mystical movement born of a very specific crisis situation in the East European ghetto. Whether 'modern' Judaism will be capable of creating meaningful 'mystical' dimensions of its religious culture only the future historians will be able to say.

Chapter Eleven

The Jews and the Enlightenment

S. ETTINGER

THE HASKALAH (JEWISH ENLIGHTENMENT) was essentially an outgrowth of the European Enlightenment, although its influence on Jewish life began to be felt at a relatively late period – namely, the end of the 18th and beginning of the 19th century. Like the European Enlightenment, it was a revolt against authority and tradition and an attempt to establish human reason as a yardstick for the judgment and appraisal of phenomena, taking rational inquiry, the critical examination of conventions and the rejection of 'prejudices' as its basic premises. The profound influence of Jewish rational philosophy during the Middle Ages, and its continued sway during the transition stage into the modern era, served as a support for the *Maskilim* (proponents of the Enlightenment) by allowing them to point to this already existing trend within the Jewish philosophical tradition. Indeed, the trademark of the Haskalah was the pronounced moderation of its criticism of tradition and, even more, of the nature of religion. Most of the first-generation *Maskilim* observed the standard injunctions of Judaism and few in the second and third generations went so far as to challenge the authority of the Talmud, while only a tiny minority reached the threshold of deist consciousness, i.e. rejection of revealed religion in favour of the belief in 'natural religion' (the proposition that certain religious principles are common to all men of reason).

Despite the hesitation of the *Maskilim*, the basic concepts of the Enlightenment did take root in their circles. Even those who wished to see Judaism become the 'true religion of Moses' (*reiner Mosaismus*), cleansed of its accumulated additions and 'prejudices', did not dare subject the Bible to criticism. Following Moses Mendelssohn, many tried to prove that, for one reason or another, Judaism was closer to 'natural religion' than were the other positive religions or that, judging by its fundamental precepts, it was a more 'rational' religion than the others. Yet despite the moderation of the *Maskilim*, the public impact of rationalist criticism was definitely revolutionary and soon led to a sharp confrontation between the advocates of the Enlightenment and the vast majority of the Jewish public.

This clash came about because consciously or otherwise the masses of Jewry began to perceive the fundamental change in approach implied by the Haskalah's mode of thinking – namely, the replacement of the theocentric world view by an anthropocentric outlook. For countless generations, the Jew had accepted upon himself the judgment of Providence,

borne the burden of 'this long and bitter Exile', and tried to mitigate his doom by repentance and good deeds or by an extreme asceticism that would presumably enable elect individuals to hasten the salvation of the world. For Jews, Christians and Muslims alike, religious imperatives guided the prevailing outlook. Now, however, the spectrum of opinions on the nature of religion and the role of the Church in the life of the state had broadened considerably in Europe, and man's reason and discretion became the judge of such matters. And so that man would not err, staggering down these new paths like a drunkard, the 'scientific method' came to his aid and was considered the supreme authority even in the investigation of metaphysical questions.

All this obviously applied only to elect circles of intellectuals, like those gathered around Mendelssohn, who frequented his home, or the cliques of youth studying philosophy at the University of Koenigsberg or medicine at the universities of Padua, Leipzig and elsewhere. At the same time, the *Maskilim* also arrived at the overall realization that the Jews could not continue to exist if the majority of them aspired to become talmudic scholars; it was thus necessary to teach the younger generation new occupations in agriculture, crafts and commerce. Moreover, it was imperative to reform the flawed Jewish educational system; and, both for the sake of maintaining a livelihood and to draw closer to and be accepted by the supportive Christian environment, special attention must be paid to deportment, cleanliness, a change in the style of dress and the ability to speak and write the language of the land. The sciences, too, must be tackled and mastered so that benefit could be derived from them. All this, the *Maskilim* contended, did not stand in contradiction to the precepts of the Jewish faith and tradition. On the contrary, it was quite in keeping with them, since some of the greatest talmudic scholars had supported themselves as craftsmen; the most renowned Jews had stood before kings and addressed them in their own language; and some of the most important works in Jewish culture had been written in Aramaic, Greek, Arabic and Spanish.

On the surface of it, what the *Maskilim* proposed was a change in manners and the improvement of methods of instruction, while in practice their programme implied a revolution in the entire character of Jewish life. Starting out from the proposition that it was not the talmudic scholar nor the rabbi who knew what was best for a Jew but the *Maskil*, who derived his authority from outside

Jewish society, the implications extended to the relative importance of the sciences and languages in the life of the individual Jew, to a change in attitude towards the rulers and the peoples among whom the Jews lived and to the adoption of new modes of conduct befitting occasions of joy and sorrow, thus creating a revolution in almost all the conventional dictates of Jewish life. The declarations of the *Maskilim* generated a sense of ferment, owing not only to the controversy which developed over various customs (e.g. deferment of burial, shaving on the intermediate days of festivals) but also to their approach, which was phrased neither in the dry, plodding language of the rabbinical scholars nor in the colloquial 'vernacular' (Yiddish) used in addressing women and lowly men – and which the *Maskilim* claimed was not a language at all but a debased jargon – but in the 'pure language' of the Bible, or something close to it.

Most Jews rejected the appeal and claims of the *Maskilim*; but from that time on, none could ignore or remain indifferent towards them, and the ferment generated by the *Maskilim* gradually became an integral feature of Jewish life.

Origins of the Haskalah

The earliest factor, and perhaps the most important, in terms of fostering trends characteristic of the spirit of Enlightenment, was the group of Jews who had been expelled from Spain and Portugal and Jews who had migrated from the Iberian peninsula in the 16th and 17th centuries and built up prominent economic, social and cultural centres in northwest Europe (Bordeaux, Amsterdam, Hamburg and London).

Most of these Jews were Marranos who had fled from the Iberian peninsula after having absorbed elements from the culture of their surroundings. They essentially continued to live within the two cultures – the European Christian and the Jewish – in their new homes as well, and the conditions of life forced them to engage in comparisons, examinations and critiques of them both. The frequent need to conceal their Jewishness, the mode of their economic activities and their ties with political circles required these Jews to continue fostering a knowledge of local languages (some of them even knew Latin, the language of culture and science) and keep up with developments in the fields of philosophy and science, economics and finance, literature and theatre. Resembling them from this point of view were many circles within Italian Jewry. Alongside the critical radicals were some Sephardim who, while rooted in the European Enlightenment, were fascinated by the destiny of the Jewish people and its historical and spiritual uniqueness and sought to imbue it with a special mission and purpose. They interpreted the essence of this mission by drawing on concepts that lay outside Jewish tradition, thereby providing a modern interpretation for the basic religious concepts of Judaism.

Another impetus to draw closer to the Christian surroundings and its culture resulted from the change in the occupations of many Jews in Western and central Europe. Developments in the means of transportation, the rise of new cities, the development of industry, a change in the character of financial transactions and the advent of commodities exchanges, insurance companies and the like gave rise to a new type of Jewish merchant and financier, whose knowledge of the surrounding society, its needs and habits became an essential part of his business and brought him into close contact with a non-Jewish milieu. In a number of European countries – and especially in Germanic states – the consolidation of centralist administrative bureaucracies and standing armies engendered a class of merchants who supplied the court and the army, and financial administrators in the service of the king, who were referred to as court Jews. Their contact with the rulers was constant, sometimes truly intimate, and it is therefore not surprising that their involvement was intense in both the affairs of state and life-style of the court.

The wealth and stature of these court Jews prompted them to emulate the fashions, mores and general way of life that prevailed in their non-Jewish surroundings; matters reached the point of mutual social calls, participation in family celebrations and sorrows and

The festival of Passover, as celebrated in the comfortable home of an enlightened 18th-century Sephardi family. They are shown reading from the Haggadah, surrounded by the traditional symbols of the festival, while a servant washes the food in the manner prescribed – a veritable blend of cultures.

shared recreations. In late 18th-century Berlin and Vienna, Jewish women from these circles played hostess to some of the salons that drew in the crème de la crème of German society. Moreover, centring around each of these court Jews and employed in their service were bevies of other Jews – administrators, clerks, doctors, teachers – who in turn assimilated the culture of their surroundings and copied the life-styles of their patrons; sometimes they even surpassed their masters, in their deviation from the conventional Jewish way of life. It was in these quarters that Judaism's traditional stance regarding a sense of exile and the yearning for salvation were totally undermined. These Jews did not regard the countries in which they resided as the Exile and, indeed, felt a permanent attachment to them. For them, Jerusalem became a matter of liturgical phraseology that had no bearing on reality, and much the same was true of Messianic longings.

Enlightenment versus mysticism

In contrast with those limited circles that hungrily absorbed the ideas promoted by the Enlightenment, the mainstream of Jewish society in the 16th–18th centuries was subject to influences and developments that tended to impede contact with the surrounding Gentile society and thus thwarted the opportunity for absorbing these ideas. An internal spiritual development, related to one of the most profound crises in Jewish history – the Expulsion from Spain and Portugal – had a very great impact on this situation. The Expulsions and the trauma that followed in their wake, the establishment of large centres of Marranos and the fervent expression of Messianic expectations, all served as the background for the swift spread of mysticism through broad sectors of the Jewish public and the magnified influence of the centre of Kabbalah, in Safed, on Jewish life.

Beginning at the close of the 16th century, and particularly during the 17th century, Lurianic Kabbalism spread to the communities of the Diaspora and became a powerful force in the intellectual and religious life of the Jews. This development neutralized the long-standing sway of philosophical thought, counteracted rationalist doctrines and revived the intellectual basis for Messianic yearnings – which had recently found expression in the outburst that swept through the communities of the

Diaspora during the era of Sabbatai Zevi. And though the conversion of the 'Messiah' and the consequent frustration of the Messianic movement had created a deep sense of crisis, the advent of the Hasidic movement in Eastern Europe provided a new channel for the mystical mood and longings for redemption, and considerably expanded the circles susceptive to the influence of the Lurianic Kabbalah. Even Jewish communities beyond the reach of Hasidism found ways to overcome the Sabbatean crisis and restore the Kabbalah and mysticism to a central position in their lives.

The deteriorating situation of whole classes of Jews in various countries, the undermining of their security in Poland and the Islamic countries and the collapse of their traditional livelihoods due to the forces of modernization and the early development of capitalism merged to create the climate for rising tension between the Jews and their non-Jewish surroundings. It was only natural that this should lead to the rejection of influences that penetrated from the outside world and to increasing self-segregation.

The problem of education

The first problem to which the *Maskilim* addressed themselves in their campaign to 'improve' Jewish society was education, and their choice was not random. Jewish education had made many gains during the Middle Ages, when new instruments were created to foster a traditional Jewish education (reading from the prayer-book, the weekly portion, the Mishnah, laws and, for many, even the ability to read a page of the *Gemara* together with the additions of its commentators). Moreover, these achievements were especially prominent in contrast with the prevailing ignorance of the surrounding society, in which a knowledge of reading and writing was limited to the clergy. None the less, by the 17th and 18th centuries it was the defects in Jewish education that began to stand out. The system whereby the community assumed responsibility for the education of youngsters – including the sons of the poor – in *heder* and Talmud Torah was still in effect in many places, and some way was found to provide the rudiments of learning for girls as well. Many communities even arranged for boys to continue their education after the age of Bar Mitzvah. More and more, however, study of the Bible and even the Mishnah was being neglected, and a grounding in grammar – which had occupied a respected position in the medieval Jewish curriculum – was abandoned altogether. Instead, the stature of the *yeshivas* (for studying the Talmud) was on the rise, and the foremost subject there was *hiluk* or *pilpul* (systems of dialectical logic). Some of the greatest Jewish scholars of the 16th and 17th centuries (the Maharal of Prague, R. Ephraim Luntshits) had bitterly attacked this system of education, but it none the less became the standard form of Jewish study in Eastern and central Europe. Secular subjects disappeared altogether from the curriculum of the *yeshivas*, in contrast to the schools in Italy, where they comprised an integral part of the study programme.

The interest of the *Maskilim* in education, however, did not derive primarily from the criticisms that had been voiced within Jewish society or from the proposal to reform methods of instruction. Their principal motive was the European Enlightenment's belief in the ability of education to forge the nature of both man and society. After the notion of 'innate' ideas was replaced by the certitude that man at birth was a tabula rasa, it appeared that the way was opened to fashion the character of a youngster according to the rationalist principles of education. The aim of the wise educator was to develop the student's reason and thereby enable him to perceive the principles of nature and society. Society would become enlightened not only when a large number of human beings were raised on these principles and aspired to perfection, but when such people attained positions of influence.

No less an influence on the *Maskilim* was their personal closeness to some of the figures of the European Enlightenment, as well as the administrative officials who were infected by a similar mood. After the publication of C. W. Dohm's famous work, *Über die bürgerliche Verbesserung der Juden (On the Civil Improvement of the Jews)*, in 1781, the subject of education among the Jews took precedence in all the deliberations of government circles in Prussia, Austria, and Russia on the 'improvement of the Jews'. This was likewise true of the laws promulgated on the status of the Jews. Thus the *Maskilim* could assume that in advancing their proposals they were acting in line with the desires of the authorities and could expect their support.

The centrality of the question of education was a function of the criticism that was being voiced against the Jews by hostile public opinion. There were those who regarded the Jews not only as deviants or sinners, from the religious viewpoint, but as morally blemished beings whose religion or character led them to do harm to Gentiles. The *Maskilim* felt obligated to defend the Jewish religion and prove that Judaism's command-ments contained no elements that might cause harm to the state or its citizens. On the contrary, the flaws of the Jews, they claimed, were a result of the persecution they suffered: the limitations imposed upon their choice of occupation, restrictions on their freedom of movement and settlement, and so forth. Thus education, together with tolerance and the abolition of discrimination against the Jews, is the primary means to 'improve' them.

'Pure language', be it Hebrew or the language of the land, is an important principle in education and in the formation of a man's character. This contention was obviously directed against Yiddish, which the *Maskilim* – especially of the first generations – did not consider to be a language at all, merely a jargon, a mass mockery. In a sense, their view was a corollary of the long tradition in Eastern and central Europe that held a knowledge of Hebrew (and Aramaic) to be the hallmark of a 'learned man', while Yiddish was the language of lowly men and of women. Yet it was also a reflection of current trends in the European states, which were undergoing a process of political, economic and cultural consolidation and centralization and tended to relate to local dialects with scepticism and distrust, accepting only the 'higher language' – namely, the language of literature (or the administration) – as 'a cultured tongue'. Hence, in this way as well, the aspirations of the *Maskilim* coincided with the aims of the administration. We must also take into account the propensity of the centralized regime to keep tabs on the activities of its subjects, while the existence of a separate language or dialect undoubtedly obstructed this kind of supervision. Indeed, accusations were voiced – some of them justified – that expressions borrowed from Yiddish served as a secret code for Jewish criminals (albeit they could just as well have used words from the 'pure' Hebrew language, but it was not common within the social strata that bred thieves) and eventually spread into the general world of crime. And what is far more important, Jewish merchants and money-lenders kept their books and issued their receipts in Hebrew and Yiddish, which, the authorities claimed, led to misunderstandings and a lack of trust between Jews and Gentiles. Thus the motive behind the prohibition of Hebrew and Yiddish in commercial documents and account books was, in fact, to remove the barriers and cultivate trust between the Jews and their surroundings – a goal that was highly coveted by the *Maskilim*.

Yet beyond these pragmatic considerations, the *Maskilim* believed that 'pure language' was important to the Jews themselves. According to the doctrines of the age, language was the classic expression of a man's way of thinking, his concepts and even his moral behaviour. Hence the *Maskilim* believed that the refinement of language was a way of overcoming errors and 'prej-udices', a medium to raise the intellectual level of the individual and the most efficient means of all for integrating the Jew into the society and state in which he lived.

It therefore becomes apparent that the seemingly innocent calls for the use of 'pure language' and improvement in the methods of education were actually an opening for revolutionary changes in the thinking and way of life of the Jews, though few of the *Maskilim* or their sympathizers actually grasped the full implication of their own proposals. The great ideal of Jewish society since the days of the Mishnah and the Talmud – the supremacy of Torah study above all other values and the image of the *talmid hacham* (scholar) as a revered person (even the poorest of common men was prepared to make great sacrifices so that his sons could attain that stature) – was summarily rejected. And in its place came the values of good citizenship and propriety, rational thought and familiarity with world problems, integration into the state and particularly in its affairs.

A Tractate of Jewish Rights was published in Nuremberg in 1741, dealing especially with monetary transactions. The Jewish merchants of the period, though in many respects almost indistinguishable from their Gentile counterparts, are shown here wearing the conical Jewish hat, not the tricorn.

Change of occupation

Here lies the importance of the change in the livelihoods of the Jews. Peddling and small trade, money-lending and the sale of liquor not only made the Jews an object of hatred in the eyes of their countrymen, they also corrupted morals and the soul – or so the *Maskilim* contended. To one degree or another, they accepted the claim, widespread among the enemies and critics of the Jews, that their principal income came from fraud, exploitation and encouraging the farmers to drink themselves into a stupor.

Once again we see the concord between the *Maskilim* and the ruling circles, if not over means to achieve their goal (many *Maskilim* opposed the severe economic regulations promulgated against the Jews), at least over the goal itself. The *Maskilim* enthusiastically promoted a transfer to agriculture, the livelihood of the Jews of Antiquity. Both in Austria (during the reign of Joseph II) and in Russia (during the reigns of Catherine II and Alexander I), plans were made to settle the Jews on the land so that they could take up agriculture, and agricultural colonies were, in fact, established. Yet there were tremendous obstacles to this solution: shortage of land appropriate for settlement in populated areas; inexperience of the Jews in agricultural labour; corruption of the government officials charged with implementing the programme; and, not least, the inferior and humiliating status of the farmers in these kingdoms, which to a large degree continued to maintain their feudal character. Thus, despite the initial enthusiasm of the *Maskilim* for a return to the soil, they soon realized that this was not a viable solution for the masses and shifted their emphasis to crafts.

But this also was far from simple, since most of the crafts were in the hands of the guilds, which were highly unreceptive to new members – especially Jews. The guild was not only an economic or professional organization but also an influential social organization in which religious rituals and the principle of mutual aid played major roles. Even the learning of a craft posed many problems, since it was customary to place a young apprentice in the home of an artisan, where he would live as a member of the family. Many obstacles stood in the way of a Jewish youngster, therefore, from the observance of the Sabbath and dietary laws to the basic problem of the spoken language. In the end, despite the enthusiastic talk about the importance of crafts, actual opportunities existed in only a limited number of branches. These included the so-called kosher crafts, in which Jews had engaged since Antiquity because they were related to the observance of religious injunctions (butchers, bakers, wine-makers, tailors – to prevent the unwitting transgression of the law forbidding the mixture of linen and wool), and crafts that were traditional to the Jews, who were evidently the earliest experts in them (silk-makers and dyers, goldsmiths, diamond cutters). There were also other relatively simple crafts into which the Jews had managed to penetrate (cobblers, harness-makers, hat-makers, blacksmiths). Yet, as already suggested, the principal difficulty and opposition to the proposals of the *Maskilim* arose from the fact that a change in the sources of livelihood meant shattering the existing hierarchy of values and giving a different meaning to the life of a Jew within the framework of a non-Jewish society.

New communal organizations

The proposed changes in language, education and occupations necessarily brought with them the need for a change in the intrinsic organization of Jewish society. For hundreds of years the Jews had lived within the framework of their own communities, which were government-recognized religious-social-economic corporations, whose leaders (rabbis, scholars, public officials) served as spokesmen for the Jewish nation. This arrangement suited the monarchs, for in the absence of an organized administrative apparatus the autonomous Jewish communal organization facilitated the enforcement of law and order among the Jews and assumed responsibility for collecting their taxes. With the rise and consolidation of the centralist states, however, came a permanent officialdom that embarked upon a struggle against all corporations, which, by their nature, came between the ruler and his subjects. Jurists and officials came out with the claim that the autonomous Jewish communal organization was not only superfluous and disruptive to the administration's work in enforcing laws and collecting proper taxes, but that it existed to the benefit of the wealthy Jews and their rabbis and to the detriment of the rest of the Jews, who were exploited by their leaders. Furthermore, they concluded, the Jewish public was deliberately kept in ignorance, and prejudice and religious intolerance were fostered among the masses precisely to ensure their subjugation.

The *Maskilim* attacked the autonomous Jewish structure even more forcefully than did the government officials. Their claims were based on a composite of principles and concerns that derived from their own unique position in Jewish society. In principle, the *Maskilim* preached religious tolerance, for only in a climate of tolerance could the Jews assume a position of respect in their countries of residence – and who if not the Jews had tasted the flavour of religious intolerance and victimization? The accepted means of achieving religious tolerance in Europe was by the separation of Church and State, and this was the goal of *les Philosophes* as well as the decisive majority of the *Maskilim*. Yet the Jewish community was a mixture of the two realms, wherein religious leaders were allowed to force their will on all the members of the community by using the *herem* (excommunication), economic domination and the courts – and all this with the complicity of the civil authorities! For these reasons the *Maskilim* demanded the abrogation of internal Jewish jurisdiction and economic regulations (the laws pertaining to the right of possession, taxation, etc.) and the transformation of the *kehilla* (autonomous communal authority) into a body that dealt exclusively with religious affairs and observance of the commandments. All other jurisdictions bound up with coercion were to be turned over to the state or municipal administration. Even the use of the *herem* for transgressions of religious law was discredited by most of the *Maskilim*.

Religious reform

The *Maskilim* were at pains to point out that no precept of Judaism prevented 'members of the Mosaic faith' from being loyal and upstanding citizens. There were many educated Europeans – and not just members of the clergy and die-hard traditionalists – who alleged that a Jew is obligated to harm Christians; that he cannot be a loyal citizen of the state because his king is the Jewish Messiah; that the Jewish calendar has more than two hundred holidays a year on which work is prohibited. Even enlightened liberals asked: how can we socialize with the Jews when they cannot take part in our festivals nor raise a glass with us in friendship and when they celebrate a different Sabbath and holidays? Until the Jews reform or accommodate their religious customs so that they can be full partners in the majority's way of life, they will persist in segregating themselves from society at large.

Those who aspired to be considered Frenchmen, Germans, Poles or Russians 'of the Mosaic faith' wanted to make the Jewish religion acceptable and respectable in the eyes of the Gentiles. But they were none the less disturbed by the fact that, owing to the success of the Haskalah's educational programme, Jewish youth, who had adopted the language of the land and was deeply involved in the local culture, had begun to hold the Jewish religion in contempt and to abandon the synagogue. Religious ritual performed in a manner more reflective of the aesthetic and cultural tastes of the Christian environment might, they felt, bring these enlightened and alienated youngsters back to Judaism and enable them to appreciate its spiritual and ethical value.

Yet while even these modest reforms met with opposition, the reformers realized that they were insufficient. In order for prayer truly to inspire the soul and evoke lofty religious feelings, it must be understood.

And because, according to the proposals of the *Maskilim*, only rabbis and elect laymen could devote their time to a profound study of the Hebrew language and Jewish literature, the proportion of prayers recited in the language of the land inevitably grew. Yet beyond the language of the prayers lay the question of the liturgy's content: what purpose was there in a modern enlightened man detailing the types of sacrifices carried out in the Temple? And a far-reaching problem: what is the relevance of the prayers for the return of Zion and rebuilding the Temple? Is the highest goal of Judaism still the return to the Land of Israel and the resurrection of the Hebrew kingdom? Are the countries of Europe in which the Jews reside – and aspire to become citizens with equal rights and responsibilities – to be regarded as the Exile from which every Jew longs to be redeemed? Is the Messianic Age an era when the Jews will live as a sovereign political nation in their land or, perhaps, an age of peace, brotherhood and friendship for the entire human race, a generation of knowledge and the rule of reason? Herein lies the motive behind the attempt to strike out the prayers for Zion and Jerusalem from the liturgy, which marked even the earliest Reform prayer-books.

The seeds of change: Germany, Galicia, Poland

In his introduction to Manasseh Ben-Israel's *Vindication of the Jews* (1782), Moses Mendelssohn had emphasized the relationship between the state of society and the advancement of the Jews: 'It is a felicitous coincidence that an improvement in the status of the Jews goes hand in hand with human progress.' In *Jerusalem, or On*

By all accounts, Mendelssohn's great charm won him many friendships, and in this 19th-century lithograph he is shown (left) with his close friend Lessing, with whom he collaborated on a philosophical treatise, and Lavater, the Protestant poet and theologian. Discussions and debates with both these men helped Mendelssohn to crystallize his own beliefs; Lessing used him as the model for the impressive figure of 'Nathan the Wise'.

Religious Power and Judaism (1783), he not only underscored the principle of separation of Church and State but even went so far as to define the nature of Judaism as 'revealed law'. He thus stressed that, judging by its religious principles, Judaism is based exclusively upon reason, meaning it is closer than any other faith to the rationalist 'natural religion'. At the end of the 1770s, Mendelssohn, in collaboration with a few of his followers, began to prepare a German translation of the Torah, accompanied by *Bi'ur* (commentary) in Hebrew. Although the *Bi'ur* basically did not deviate from the traditional exegesis, it met with sharp opposition from the rabbinical establishment and became a symbol of the Enlightenment's approach. By Mendelssohn's own admission, the reason for translating the Torah into German was to bring 'culture' to young Jews – that is, draw them closer to the German language and German thought. Thus it was not accidental that his translation was printed in Hebrew characters.

Other means of broadening influence were the founding of a 'Free School' (i.e. tuition-free) for Jewish youngsters in Berlin in the 1780s, soon imitated in other cities, and the establishment of a journal to spread the ideas of the Haskalah. In 1783, Isaac Euchel, together with Mendel Breslau and others, founded the Society of Friends of the Hebrew Language, and in the autumn of that year the journal *Ha'meassef* began to appear in Koenigsberg. Among the various subjects of controversy, *Ha'meassef* devoted attention to the question of postponing burial of the dead (to comply with the recently issued government regulation permitting burial only on the third day after death); and, of course, it underscored the importance of studying secular subjects and supported the reform of the Jewish educational system.

Its later issues were characterized by an aggressive stance towards the rabbis and tradition; and those of Mendelssohn's followers who published in German had no compunctions about staging an outright attack on religious laws. Their wish for 'a purified Mosaic religion' (as it was described, for example, in Lazarus Ben-David's book, *On the Character of the Jews*) led them to negate all the later Jewish tradition. In 1799, David Friedlander went so far as to approach the head of the Lutheran Consistory in Berlin with the suggestion that Jews be accepted into the church on the basis of the deistic principles common to all men of reason. When this proposition was rejected, some Jewish leaders in Berlin and other German cities searched for ways to draw closer to their non-Jewish surroundings by accommodating Judaism to their spiritual and social needs, through the religious reforms discussed above. But Berlin effectively ceased to serve as the model for the Jewish Enlightenment: the deliberate attempt by many German Jews to disguise their Jewish identity and the appalling rise in the number of coversions to Christianity caused the 'Berlin Haskalah' to become an ominous symbol, and deterred other Jewish communities from following in the footsteps of the 'Berliners'.

The Haskalah in Eastern Europe had drawn heavily on the centre in Berlin. Naphtali Herz Homberg, a member of Mendelssohn's coterie who was particularly close to the revered philosopher, was appointed supervisor of the special school for Jewish children established by government order in Galicia. Because the Jews resisted sending their children to these schools, the regime adopted a series of coercive measures designed to force their compliance. Homberg, however, published an appeal in Hebrew ('To the Shepherds of the Scattered Flock of Israel') in an attempt to convince the Jewish leaders of the benefits of the Haskalah. He failed – not surprisingly. The Jews viewed the duty of military service, recently imposed upon them by the Habsburg monarchy, as a harsh persecution; and the restrictions on economic activity in the villages – especially the prohibition of the sale of liquor, which was an important source of income for the Jews – certainly did nothing to reassure them that the regime was concerned for their welfare.

At the same time (the end of the 1780s), the 'Great Sejm' (Diet), or Four-Year Sejm (1788–92), was convened in still-independent Poland, and its education committee discussed proposals to improve the conditions of the Jews. These included a number of suggestions raised by both Jews and non-Jews, and the objective of most was to seek out ways of integrating the Jews into the Polish state – through education, abolishing the Jews' special style of dress, and through military service. In 1792, Mendel Levin of Satanov, who had played a crucial role in the advancement of the Haskalah in Galicia, placed before the Great Sejm a pamphlet in French on the enlightenment of the Polish Jews and on the refinement of their manners. Levin believed that the radical attacks of the *Maskilim* on the rabbis and on Jewish tradition only antagonized the Jewish public and turned it against the Enlightenment. The proper approach, therefore, was one of moderation. Cultured rabbis should be courted and drawn closer to the Haskalah. But a war must be waged on Hasidism – a breeding-ground of fanaticism, nonsensical beliefs and prejudices – with the leaders of the movement exposed and their books banned. He also recommended the establishment of Polish-language schools in which both Bible and general subjects would be taught.

The difficulties faced by the *Maskilim* in Galicia derived from the cohesive character of the Jewish public there and the powerful influence of Hasidism, which had always regarded the *Maskilim* as destroyers of the Law. Because of its unifying effect Hasidism exercised firm control over social and economic affairs within the community. Thus only Jews of independent means or those who relied on the government as their source of support could afford to hold out against the hostility and the machinations of the defenders of the faith. Under these conditions, it is not surprising that no basis was laid for religious reform in Galicia, and that the Orthodox communities preserved their exclusivity there.

The *Maskilim* in Galicia hit back by portraying the Hasidic leaders as charlatans and scoundrels. Josef Perl, in *Megalleh Temirin (The Revealer of Secrets)*, and Isaac Erter, in *Tzofe l'Beit Yisrael (The Observer of the House of Israel)*, wrote the classics of anti-Hasidic satire. But the power of the pen notwithstanding, the *Maskilim* in Galicia did not place great faith in their ability to counteract the influence or stop the spread of Hasidism; consequently, some of them sent memoranda to the authorities demanding government intervention to suppress the Hasidim. Perl even proposed such drastic steps as closing down their synagogues and ritual baths, subjecting all their books to censorship and forbidding them to serve as rabbis; but his proposals were not accepted by the regime.

During the second half of the 19th century, and particularly after the Jews of Galicia attained legal equality in 1868, the German language acquired an increasingly important standing in the intellectual life of Galician Jewry. Hebrew culture, the legacy of the Haskalah, however, held its ground until the nationalist movement began, which provided it with new outlets.

The Russian Haskalah

The 'Father of the Haskalah' in Russia was Isaac Baer Levinsohn (Ribal) from Kremenitz, in Volhynia, who had spent much time among the *Maskilim* in Galicia. His book, *A Mission in Israel*, provoked strong opposition and was published only in 1828. In it he criticized the existing methods of education, called for the study of languages and the sciences and advocated crafts and agricultural labour. The appearance of the book, together with the support Levinsohn received from government officials (with whom he had connections), inspired *Maskilim* scattered throughout western Russia to initiate action. In fact, they made little progress until the 1840s, when a circle of *Maskilim* consolidated in Vilna and even maintained a special *bet midrash* of its own. Its leader was the writer Mordecai Aharon Guenzberg.

The military draft law in Russia, which permitted the conscription of young boys (sometimes even eight- and nine-year-old children were torn away from their mothers), generated a deep hatred both of the authorities and of the *Maskilim*, who were alleged to be their agents. On the other hand, the Jewish communal leadership was charged with supplying the conscripts; and the arbitrary exercise of the great power placed in its hands led the *Maskilim* to launch sharp attacks on the *kehilla*. Levinsohn, the Hebrew writer A. B. Gotlober and the Yiddish writer I. J. Linetzky bitterly assailed Hasidism and the corruption of the community leadership. The government's decision to withdraw its recognition of the *kahal* (community leadership) and to establish Russian-language schools for Jewish children roused the hopes of the *Maskilim* that with the aid of the authorities they would succeed in attaining positions of influence in the Jewish community. Yet these hopes were realized only in that many *Maskilim* were appointed to teaching posts in the schools and rabbinical seminaries. Dr Max Lilienthal, a German Jew who had been appointed by the Russian government to implement the educational reforms, fled Russia when he realized that the authorities were not interested in educating the Jews but in having them

transgress against their faith ('to detroys the talmudic prejudices in them').

The activity of the *Maskilim* gave impetus to the development of Hebrew and Yiddish literature in Russia, as evidenced by the appearance of such talented writers and poets as Abraham Mapu and Judah Lev Gordon (Yalag) and, in the 1860s, Mendele Mokher Sefarim (Shalom Abramowich) and Peretz Smolenskin. With Alexander II's ascent to the throne in 1855 and the adoption of a more liberal policy towards the Jews, however, Jewish youngsters began to flood into the Russian schools and universities, and the swift Russification of educated Jewish youth led to the crystallization of a Russian Jewish intelligentsia. Soon thereafter Russian Jewish literature (i.e. works written in Russian on Jewish subjects for Jewish readers) began to appear. In 1863, the Society for the Spread of Education was founded, primarily to aid Jewish youth in obtaining a Russian education. In fact the trend towards Russification was so intense that by the 1870s Yalag was moved to publish a poem called 'For Whom Do I Labour?', bewailing the fact that the younger generation was abandoning the Hebrew language. Nevertheless, creativity in Hebrew and Yiddish continued in Russia, and with the growth of the nationalist and socialist movements among the Jews it gained fresh impetus and reached the pinnacle of its florescence (Bialik, Tchernikhovsky, Shalom Aleichem, I. L. Peretz).

The criticism of religious Orthodoxy voiced in the works of Yalag and Smolenskin and the religious reforms proposed by Joachim Tarnopol and Moses Leib Lilienblum did not lead to the establishment of a Reform trend within Russian Jewry. And despite the attacks of the *Maskilim*, the stature of Hasidism and Torah study in the *yeshivas* of Lithuania grew in the eyes of the Jewish public. Eventually, the proletarianization of Russian Jewry and the rise of a broad class of craftsmen occurred, not in response to appeals of the *Maskilim* but as a result of the way in which capitalism developed in Russia, undermining the Jews' traditional sources of livelihood.

In conclusion, we should note that the Haskalah strongly influenced the course of Jewish affairs in the 19th and 20th centuries. To a large degree it paved the way for the modernization of Jewish life; and while it undoubtedly stimulated movement towards acculturation and assimilation, it also opened up channels for all the other major trends that coalesced among the Jews during those centuries: *hochmat Yisrael* and neo-Orthodoxy in Germany; social and intellectual radicalism and the growth of the socialist movement among the Jews of Eastern Europe; and the nationalist movement – which from many points of view was the direct sequel to the Enlightenment.

V
TRADITION AND CHANGE

Jewish Literature: Fiction and Poetry

European Jewry in the 19th and 20th centuries

American Jewry

'If I am not for myself, who is? and if I am only for myself, who am I? and if not now, when?' Ben Shahn's *Identity*, 1958, with its quotation from Hillel, poses the basic questions of morality, but in a style, and with overtones, that belong to the 20th century alone.

The two hundred years that separate us from the Enlightenment and the Haskalah have witnessed fateful developments in Jewish history. The French Revolution encouraged the hope that Jews and non-Jews could form a single community, with separate religious beliefs but the same civil loyalties. In many ways the 19th century saw that hope fulfilled. Without compromising their heritage, Jews were able to take part in the public life of their countries of residence on a scale rarely known before; and in the arts – especially music – there was an astonishing flowering of Jewish talent. But this very success had its dangers. Pressures to assimilate completely grew stronger. Many prominent Jews no longer professed their religion. More ominously: anti-Semitism (a new 'scientific' version of the older anti-Judaism) made great strides. In Eastern Europe popular prejudice, restrictive laws and spasmodic pogroms brought two results important for the future: firstly, mass-emigration to America, so that by 1914 more Jews lived in the U.S.A. than in any other single country and, secondly, the revival of the old dream of a return to Israel.

In the 20th century, the pace of events quickened, and hardly a decade went by without questions involving the Jews occupying the forefront of the world's stage. In America the story has been one of steady and peaceful advance; in Israel one of courage and achievement in the face of daunting odds; in Europe one of tragedy so black that it casts two thousand years of suffering into the shadow.

The art of Ben Shahn seeks to crystallize and to come to terms with these events. Born in Lithuania, he was taken as a child to America and from there, physically safe yet deeply involved, followed the whole agony of European Jewry. Like the modern school of Israeli poets, he has seen the past through the present and the present through the past, intent upon reading a meaning in the unfolding pattern of history. Hillel's words, written in talmudic times, can therefore only gain in resonance when they are quoted today, after centuries spent examining and re-examining the question of 'identity', after the Nazi holocaust, after the State of Israel and a world-wide Diaspora: 'If I am not for myself, who is? and if I am only for myself, who am I? and if not now, when?' (1)

The sacrifice

Like reflections in a hall of mirrors, some themes appear and reappear all through Jewish history, changing their forms and acquiring new meanings. The binding of Isaac is such a theme.

Isaac bound (*above left*): an intaglio of the 3rd or 4th century CE, of ribbon sardonyx. Abraham turns to look at the hand of God and below it, close to a bush, is a large ram. (2)

From the Bird-head Haggadah (*above*): the same scene, *c.* 1300, with Isaac, Abraham and even the angel given birds' heads. (3)

'This is the sacrifice of Isaac, and Abraham and the ram caught by its horns': a roundel (*left*) from one of the finest of all Hebrew manuscripts, produced in France between 1280 and 1290. (4)

A ceremonial dish of silver gilt ▷ (*right*) shows the scene surrounded by the signs of the zodiac. It was used in the ceremony of Redeeming the First-born, first prescribed in Exodus (XIII: 13). The first-born were originally intended to act as priests, but the Levites took their place at the time of the giving of the Law. (6)

In Hebrew literature the subject of Abraham and Isaac has always been recognized as of special significance to the story of the Jews. One could compile an extensive anthology of poems on this theme (*akedot*), from talmudic to modern times, in which it serves as a metaphor for martyrdom – the pogroms of the Crusades, the *autos-da-fé* of the Inquisition, the extermination of more than half of all the Jews in the Yemen in the 17th century and the Nazi holocaust. In Amir Gilboa's 'Isaac' (see p.263), the language shuttles back and forth between past and present, biblical scene and real scene dissolving into each other: 'It is I who am being slaughtered, my son, and already my blood is on the leaves.'

The pictures on these pages offer a partial equivalent of the literary 'hall of mirrors' in visual terms.

A morality picture (detail *right*) painted in Amsterdam, in 1679, contains overtones of Isaac as a type of the sacrificial lamb, perfect (*tamim*) as the lamb is perfect. (5)

תמים תהיה עם יהוה אלהיך

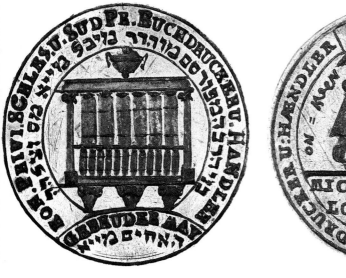

Jewish printers were among the pioneers of their profession. Many Hebrew books are numbered among the incunabula (books printed before 1500) and in several countries the first presses were operated by Jews. *Left:* two printers' seals from 18th-century Germany, both 'By Appointment' to the Prussian court. (7,8)

English trade-cards of the 18th and early 19th centuries indicate the wide variety of trades now adopted by Jews. Butchers, bakers, wine-makers and tailors had always practised the so-called 'kosher crafts'; silk-makers, dyers and goldsmiths were also traditionally Jews; other relatively simple occupations were now opening up to them. *Right:* a London fishmonger and a Bristol goldsmith. (12, 13)

A teacher of Hebrew (*left*) could support himself in the England of 1814. Other cards are those of a Liverpool engraver, a Boston watch-repairer, a Covent Garden embroiderer ('By Appointment'), a Newcastle optician and a London shipping agent. The little Staffordshire pottery figurine (*far right*) is a Jewish clothes pedlar. (9, 10, 11, 14-17)

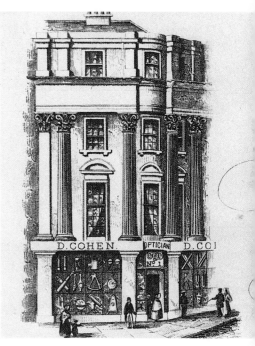

Jew and citizen

Napoleon's solution to the problem of integrating the Jews into society – like most of his solutions – did not lack boldness and confidence. In 1806 he summoned an Assembly of Jewish Notables, who declared that nothing prevented Jews from giving full allegiance to the French nation. Napoleonic propaganda (*above*) represented this as one more act of imperial magnanimity. Holding a copy of the new law for re-establishing Judaism, the Emperor raises the submissive Jewish people, her arm on the Ten Commandments, her back against the menorah, while grateful rabbis kneel at his feet. (18)

To indicate Jerusalem, the correct direction for prayer, Jewish households place a drawing or plaque on the wall. This one (*left*) is of interest because it contains an inscription to the Emperor Ferdinand, who reigned over the Habsburg Empire from 1835 to 1848. Although an epileptic and an incapable ruler, Ferdinand was surprisingly popular, especially among the Jews, and was nicknamed *der gütige*, 'the kindly'. (19)

Few outward signs were left to indicate Jewishness in the prosperous bourgeois world of the early 19th century. *Above*: the Nathanson family of Copenhagen, painted by C. W. Eckersberg in 1818. Social assimilation was virtually complete, but reservations on both sides made real rapprochement a delusion. (20)

The army and the arts were two careers that had formerly been unfriendly to Jews. Now the barriers dissolved. *Left*: portrait of Baruch Oppenheimer by his brother Moritz Daniel. Born in 1801, M.D. Oppenheimer rose to become Professor of Painting at Weimar, specializing in scenes with Jewish subjects. (21)

GRAND SANHEDRIN
XXX. MAI. MDCCCVI

Political involvement

The 'Grand Sanhedrin', convoked by Napoleon in 1806 on the model of the ancient high court of the Jews, is typical of the ambivalence of many such outwardly enlightened measures. It was a body of genuine authority (of its seventy-one members more than half were rabbis), making for real equality within the framework of the state. But its ulterior purpose was to encourage Jews to enlist in the army. The ambivalence is plainly, though inadvertently, expressed in this medal (*left*), in which Napoleon presents the Tablets of the Law to Moses – a blasphemy from which every Jew would recoil. Two years later, indeed, the wind changed and Jews were loaded with oppressive and restrictive regulations. (22)

The year of revolutions, 1848, found Jews prominently committed to political action. The first cabinet formed after the February uprising in Paris included two Jewish members – Adolphe Crémieux, Minister of Justice (*left*, far left in the centre row), and Michel Goudchaux (*above*). (23, 24)

Popular bigotry contradicted the move towards greater understanding. The troubled province of Alsace had been the home of Jews from Roman times, and they continued to live there when excluded from France in the 14th century. During the revolution of 1789 they were accused of being 'a state within the state', and when revolution came again in 1848 they were once again the victims. At Durmenach, 28 February (*right*), the crowd turned on them, tore the slates from their houses, broke down their doors and windows and threw their possessions into the street. (29)

Across the frontiers Jews continued to help their brethren irrespective of nationality. In 1840, Sir Moses Montefiore and Adolphe Crémieux led a deputation to Istanbul in order to defend the Jews of Damascus, who were accused of murdering a Christian friar and his Muslim servant. The exploit is commemorated on a magnificent silver centrepiece (details *above*), designed by Sir George Hayter in 1843; the scenes on it include Sir Moses interceding with the sultan and being thanked by Oriental Jews. (25, 26)

The Frankfurt Parliament of 1848, the short-lived voice of a democratic Germany, included Gabriel Riesser (*right*), a life-long champion of Jewish rights, and Moritz Hartmann, journalist, novelist and poet. (27, 28)

The paradox of Russia

Russian Jewry had suffered hardships throughout most of the 19th century, the degree of oppression varying with the character of the Tsar. One answer was emigration; another was radical political activity.

It is this last which may partly explain the amazing upsurge in the Jewish contribution to the visual arts which took place in the first decades of the 20th century. Isaac Levitan's *Spring Waters*, of 1897 (*left*), shows a painter completely Russian and completely professional, but a later painting by him (p.289) makes it clear that he had not forgotten his Jewishness. Altman and Lissitzky, illustrated below,. made deliberate efforts to recreate a Jewish style, undertaking expeditions to see wooden synagogues and country cemeteries at first hand. (30)

'The Sukkah Meal' (*right*) by Marc Chagall is characteristic of his early period, when he combined an adventurous avant-garde spirit with deep awareness of his Jewish roots. Born in 1887, he grew up in an Orthodox home in Vitebsk, studied in Paris before World War I, but returned to Russia between 1915 and 1922. Sukkot, or the Feast of the Tabernacles, is the Hebrew Harvest Festival, commemorating also the wanderings in the desert (Lev. XXII:43). (33)

The poetess **Anna Akhmatova** by Nathan Altman (*far left*), painted in 1915. Altman adapted Jewish folk-motifs to a modern idiom and played an active part in the growth of a Yiddish theatre in Moscow. (31)

The sculptor **Miestchaninov** by Chaim Soutine (*left*), 1923. Soutine's Jewishness is harder to define, since he avoided Jewish subject-matter, but Maurice Raynal found in his art 'an expression of a kind of Jewish mysticism through appalling violent detonations of colour.' (32)

El Lissitzky, born in 1890, came from Smolensk. His illustrations to the Yiddish story *The Kid*, based on the same song as that shown on p. 82, were published in 1917. It is interesting to note that in the last episode (*right*) Lissitzky, unlike the 18th-century artist, has not scrupled to represent the Lord killing the Angel of Death, who is represented as a skeleton. The inscription, in rhyming Yiddish, reads 'God, the Holy One, blessed be He, caused the Angel of Death to die.' (34)

Emigration for Jews in the late 19th and early 20th centuries was not the hopeful adventure that it had been in the Colonial period. It was primarily an escape – from poverty, intolerance and persecution. In 1922, Ilya Ehrenberg published a story called *The Boat Ticket*, describing the thoughts of an old man in Russia waiting for a ticket to America to be sent by his son. It was illustrated by El Lissitzky with a brilliant collage composition (*above*) that evokes the whole dilemma of an ancient tradition faced with radical change. The hand, as we have seen earlier, is a Jewish symbol that goes back into prehistory; the white Hebrew letters on it are those inscribed on tombstones for 'Here lies . . .'; and underneath it is a diagram itemizing the layout of the Temple. All this belongs to the past – the dead past. The future lies across the Atlantic – the liners, the flags, the ticket from Hamburg to New York. (35)

◁ **The experience** of emigration has sunk deep into the consciousness of modern American Jewry. As late as 1928, Lasar Segall published a series of etchings called 'Emigrants', of which this is one (*left*). (36)

Aaron Hart was born in London in 1724, joined the Canadian army and founded a bank at Three Rivers (*top right*). His son Ezekiel was the first Jew to sit in the Canadian Parliament. (39)

From their homes in central and Eastern Europe (*below*, Lemberg in Austria, now Lvov, Poland), the Jewish emigrants set out to one of the embarkation ports, of which Hamburg was the most important. *Bottom*: registering Jewish passengers in the emigration hall of the Hamburg-America line, *c.* 1909. (37, 38)

Their New Jerusalem.

There was resentment at the numbers of Jews coming to America. This cartoon from *Judge*, of 1892, while not unsympathetic to the plight of the victims of Russian persecution, shows them taking over New York and forcing the old-established Americans to head further west. (40)

'The most crowded spot in America', according to the cover of *Leslie's Weekly* for 23 April 1903, was New York's ghetto. Ludlow Street (*right*) consisted largely of the shops of Jewish tailors, hatters and sellers of cloth. (41)

The Colonial period

The first Jews in America came, like the settlers of other nations, to make their fortunes in a new land. Many succeeded. Most of the busy seaports of the East Coast – Newport, Philadelphia, Charleston, New York, Savannah – had prosperous Jewish families by the mid-18th century. At Newport, the community was rich enough to raise the Touro Synagogue in 1763 (*left*), named after the Touro family, who enabled it to be built. Other Jewish merchants at Newport included Aaron Lopez (*below*), who owned a fleet of more than thirty ships. The intellectual climate of the time was remarkable for tolerance, sympathy and enlightened interest. One of the most learned men of his time was Ezra Stiles (*right*), Congregational minister of Newport. The books behind him show the range of his mind – along with Newton, Plato and Livy is a volume of the Talmud, and on the wall an 'emblem of the Universe' incorporating the Hebrew word for God. Stiles's tutor in Hebrew was Rabbi Raphael Hyam Karigal, whose sermons at the Newport synagogue were widely acclaimed, and who influenced the rise of Hebrew studies at Yale. (42, 43, 44)

Rebecca Gratz (*right*), daughter of wealthy Jewish parents in Philadelphia, founded the first Jewish Sunday School in America and the Philadelphia Orphan Asylum. Sir Walter Scott is said to have modelled the character of Rebecca in *Ivanhoe* on her, after being told about her by Washington Irving. (45)

THE RUSSIAN JEWISH FARMER SETTLEMENT WECHSLER
BURLEIGH COUNTY DAKOTA TERRITORY.

Struggle and achievement

Opportunities for the poorer immigrants were few. Most of the newcomers went into industry and crammed the already overcrowded quarters of the big cities. But instead of understanding and respect, they met increasing dislike and prejudice which was not so much anti-Jewish as anti-foreign.

Agriculture: attempts were made to establish Jewish farm settlements (*left*) on the lines of other religious minorities, but they met with scant success. (46)

The garment industry absorbed a high proportion of immigrants. By 1900, almost all the country's clothing was produced by Jews. They worked either in squalid factories that became known as sweat-shops (*above left*) or at home. Others went in for cigar-making (*left*). These two historic photographs were taken by L. Hine and Jacob A. Riis. In the garment workers' strike in 1913 (*above*), Jews joined other national groups in the fight for better wages. (47, 48, 49)

The theatre was one road to success not already occupied by an establishment, and Jews were quick to take advantage of it. The Grand Theatre, New York, was a centre for Jewish entertainment in the years before World War I. (50)

Education continued to be of prime concern, and did much to hold the Jewish community together. *Right*: a school in Harlem. The poster reads: 'Beth Israel of Harlem Hebrew School. Open every weekday from 4.30 to 7, Sunday morning 10-12. Register your child NOW.' (51)

Big Business offered immense wealth to those with energy and imagination. In 1854, the three Straus brothers – Nathan, Isidor and Oscar – arrived from Bavaria. By the end of the century they had taken over Macy's (*right*), New York's biggest department store. *Below right*: the interior of L. J. Levy's dry goods store (i.e. drapers) of Philadelphia. (52, 54)

Organized religion tended to split into many factions in the free atmosphere of America. While the older generation remained Orthodox, the younger saw the need for modernization and reform. Rabbi Isaac M. Wise (seen *below* in the centre of a convention at Atlantic City in 1897) gave both publicity and rationale to this movement. (53)

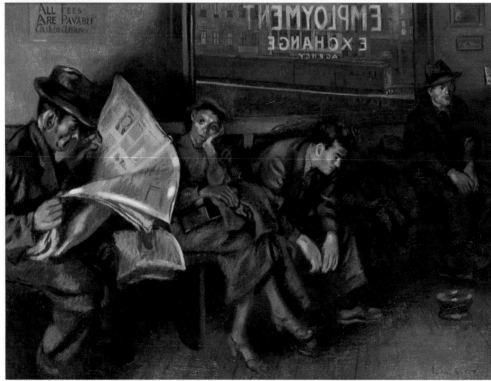

America: the Jewish experience in art

American Jews – now the leaders of the Diaspora and thus in some ways closer to tradition than the Jews of Israel – have become increasingly self-conscious and articulate in the 20th century. This page shows that self-consciousness reflected in the work of four leading American Jewish artists.

Max Weber: 'The Talmudists', 1934 (*upper left*). Weber emigrated from Russia to New York in 1891, at the age of ten. This painting is a memory of his childhood – old, serious men read, argue and meditate the fine points of the Law. (55)

Isaac Soyer: 'Employment Agency', 1937 (*left*). Soyer, too, came to America as a child. Many of his paintings spring from the days of poverty, hardship and struggle. (56)

מ ל ל א ש וליד א כ ה מ א כ א ו ה ל
מ ד ו נ ע נ כ ו ד ע י ש ב א ח י ל ל ח ל ב ו

Ben Shahn has already been briefly
described at the beginning of this
section. His *Sketch for a Mural*, 1958
(*above*), though designed for a synagogue, uses traditional Jewish
imagery – the creating hand, the
menorah, the *shofar* – to express a
message (from Mal. II:10) that is more
than merely Jewish: 'Have we not all
one father? Has not one God created
us? Why do we deal treacherously
every man against his brother, profan-
ing the Covenant of our fathers?' (57)

William Gropper: 'Tailor', 1940
(*left*): the world of work-people and
small traders. Gropper was a second-
generation immigrant, born in New
York in 1897. (58)

Mr Levi Strauss (*above*) arrived in California during the Gold Rush of the 1850s. Very prudently, however, he invested his time and energy not in prospecting but in providing tent canvas for the miners. This durable material soon became used for making trousers, and Levi Strauss jeans set out on the road to fortune. A photograph of about 1880 (*above right*) shows the firm's staff and premises at 14 and 16 Battery Street, San Francisco. The two sets of advertisements (*below*) date from about the same time. 'Spring bottom pants' were designed to fit over boots with a gentle flare in the cut of the leg. Note the little drawing, which became famous, to show the strength of the Levi Strauss 'patent riveted overalls' – two horses try in vain to pull them apart, with the motto: 'It's no use – they won't be ripped.' (59-62)

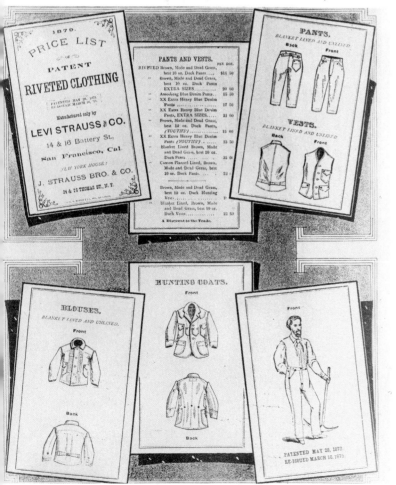

Chapter Twelve

Jewish Literature: Fiction

EZRA SPICEHANDLER

HEBREW NARRATIVE PROSE is a significant part of a prodigious Hebrew literature, which began to be written more than three thousand years ago and continues to our own day. The Hebrew Bible, the monumental product of its earliest phase, has become part of the cultural heritage of the West and still serves it as a model of literary excellence and a source of myth, symbol and metaphor. Subsequent Hebrew literature, on the other hand, was confined to the smaller and often isolated Jewish world, although Christian and even Muslim authors made sporadic use of its contents. Since the general reader may be assumed to be better acquainted with biblical literature than with these later works, I shall devote the greater part of the essay to them.

Biblical narrative, 1200–150 BCE

The Hebrew Bible is an anthology of a much larger literature and was more or less completed by the close of the 2nd century BCE. Even its earliest narrative portions may be considered to be a sophisticated literary reworking of oral folk-traditions.

Three major types of biblical narrative have been defined: legends that relate the origins of the world and progenitors of the human race (demythologized and infused with ethical import); historical stories about national heroes, becoming more realistic and less supernatural as the biblical text deals with more recent history; and stories explaining such things as physical phenomena (e.g. the desolation of the Dead Sea area by the destruction of Sodom), names (e.g. Moses – Moshe – from *msh*, to draw, because he was drawn from the river), tribal divisions or ritual.

Biblical narratives vary in length and complexity. The simplest tale may consist of no more than a ten-verse account of a simple incident involving two characters, as in the story of Jacob wrestling with the angel. The longer story may in contrast run the length of at least a biblical chapter, have more characters and involve more complex situations. The saga links a chain of tales and stories to a major biblical hero (Joseph or David, for example). The romance, a later genre, takes the form of a complete biblical book, e.g. Ruth or Esther. Jonah belongs to this category, although it includes a psalm-like poem, but Job, although its prose framework is a literary gem, does not, since its main body is poetic.

All types of stories are written in a sparse, elliptical style. Only the decisive points are emphasized. Yet the author will often repeat certain key words, scenes or actions within a single narration. Such repetition, once thought to be a sign of a primitive cultural level, is now recognized as a sophisticated literary device serving a variety of purposes; for instance, it can stress key ideas, reinforce dramatic intensity or present shifts in point of view.

Many episodes go through three stages – the action anticipated, the action itself and the action completed. Flashbacks are generally avoided, but there may be parenthetical insertions filling in past details. The development is circular, opening with a tranquil prelude, often linked to a preceding event, unfolding towards a climax and closing by a return to a situation of tranquillity.

Except for God himself, who moves outside the realm of human experience, the characters in biblical stories are rarely 'mythic' in the Greek or Germanic sense. The biblical hero is a mortal human being capable of virtue and sin. Unlike the Homeric hero, his physical characteristics are either entirely ignored or lightly sketched except when necessary for the development of the story. Dramatic rather than scenic techniques predominate. Although the speaker is frequently 'all-knowing', he prefers 'showing' to 'telling'.

The age of Aggadah, 100 BCE–700 CE

Following the canonization of the Bible, Jewish literature (which now comprised works in Aramaic and Greek as well as Hebrew) developed new literary forms, often based on extra-canonical traditions, either imaginative embellishments (Pseudo-Philo's *Biblical Antiquities* and the *Book of Jubilees*, for example) or original narratives (*Judith, Tobit, Susana,* for example). Jewish tradition distinguished between two major components of this literature: Halacha and Aggadah: Halacha, 'the going' (in the pathway), designated legal materials; Aggadah, 'the telling', the remaining non-legal elements. Halacha was considered to be the more significant.

The aggadic Midrashim, which were mostly of Palestinian origin, continued to follow the order of the biblical text and appear to be anthologies of sermons, or homilies upon its key passages. There are, however, aggadic materials which were not tied to a specific text. This was particularly but not exclusively true of stories about post-biblical events or personalities.

As Joseph Heinemann points out, 'for many generations, from the cessation of biblical poetry until the

The story of Esther is one of the most perfect examples of a biblical 'novella', a self-contained narrative with tense drama and a strong human interest. This unique miniature from a German Bible of 1344 shows the triumphant end of the story – the hanging of Haman and his ten sons, on the gibbet he had prepared for Mordecai.

beginning of the *piyyut*, it was the sole outlet of all poetic feelings and the only form of literary (though originally oral) creation among the Jewish people.' The narrative prose of the period included legends about biblical heroes, biographical anecdotes about great rabbis, pious men or even important enemies, parables, tales and moral *exempla*.

It also represented an endeavour to extract new meanings from the Torah for an age facing the disasters of the destruction of the Temple and the loss of national independence. The task of the scholar, whether Halachist or Aggadist, was to uncover the implied meanings hidden behind the biblical text. But whereas the Halachist was obliged to curtail his imagination to conform to a rigid technique, the Aggadist was generally not subject to these restrictions. 'One need not question an Aggadah' was a principle that unfettered the imagination of the Aggadist. From the Greeks he also learned the method of allegorical interpretation. Events and personalities of the biblical text became for him, as they did to an even greater extent for the authors of the New Testament, prefigurations of things to come.

Like the biblical tale, the great majority of Aggadot are short and episodic. Frequently the Aggadist strove

to fill in gaps left by the biblical narrator. His depictions of character and plot are far less objective. He idealizes his heroes and tries to explain away their moral shortcomings. Thus he insists that Bathsheba was a divorcee and that, consequently, David never committed adultery. In the same spirit, less sympathetic biblical personalities are made into arch villains (Balaam, for example).

The Middle Ages: story, legend and satire

In the massive literature of the Hebrew Middle Ages, which in the Jewish context may be defined as extending from the Islamic conquest in the 7th century to the age of Enlightenment at the beginning of the 19th, belles-lettres played a minor role. The Jewish literary imagination is best represented by the great medieval Hebrew poets. Works of narrative prose were largely addressed to a less sophisticated audience. The medieval Hebrew tale, however, cannot be described as folk-literature; rather, it is a reworking of the folk-tale into literary form. Composed in Hebrew, which like the medieval Latin of Christian Europe was the literary language of the Jews, it lacked the spontaneous and earthy quality of the various vernaculars spoken by the Jews.

Medieval authors rediscovered, perhaps through their Christian neighbours, sources that had generally been ignored by their predecessors. The Book of Maccabees now became the source for such works as *Megillat Antiochus* (*The Scroll of Antiochus*) and *Megillat Hannukah*. Stories and motifs are drawn from the *Book of Jubilees*, *Judith* and *Tobit*. To this group also belong such works as the *Romance of Alexander the Great* and *Josiphon*, a popular abridgement and rewriting of the histories of Josephus. Medieval Christian romances and tales of chivalry were not only translated and adapted into Hebrew but also left their imprint on original works. Messianic legends, based on apocryphal, talmudic and early mystical materials served as a source for *Zerubabel*, which wove them into a continuous narrative. Perhaps under Christian influence, its author introduced a new character into Messianic lore – the mother of the Messiah.

Although structurally related to the biblical tale, *Toledot Yeshu* (*The History of Jesus*) had a radically different motivation. Subject to conversionist harassments by the Church triumphant, the Jew struck out against the Jesus legend by composing a sarcastic, scatological version of the life of Jesus. Its anonymous author was obviously acquainted with the synoptic Gospels. Naïvely, he accepted as true all the miracles and events they recorded, but interpreted them away as being black magic performed by a villainous Jesus who made illicit use of God's ineffable name. Jesus became the traitor and Judas Iscariot the patriotic Jew who exposed the fraud.

The Story of Eldad, the Danite, introduced a new narrative genre: the fantastic travel tale, which had its counterpart in such works as the *Voyages of Prester John*. This legend about the remnants of the ten Tribes of Israel, living a life of freedom and sovereignty beyond the remote Black Hills, nurtured the wish-fulfilment fantasies of the medieval Jew and his Messianic yearnings to return to his ancient homeland. Folk-fantasy, also, was responsible for the very popular tale about a pope who was a clandestine Jew, who at a crucial moment rose to save his people from destruction.

During the 12th century, the *hasidic* movement in Germany (not to be confused with later Hasidism) developed the demonological tale, a genre that was clearly affected by the German medieval folk-tale with its witches, wizards, werewolves, etc. Holy men save the Jews by magical or kabbalistic powers from evil wizards and witches or from tyrannical Gentiles. The famous *golem* legend, about the creation of a monster by a pious rabbi to save the Jews, originated in this period.

Much of medieval Jewish narrative prose appeared in the form of a compendium of tales. The *Story of the Ten Martyrs* is a series of stories built about the alleged martyrdom of ten rabbis during the Bar Kokhba revolt; the *Midrash on the Ten Commandments* associates a pious tale with each of the commandments; the *Alphabet of Ben Sira* simply follows an alphabetical order. This latter work's anti-traditional posture is a unique phenomenon. Ben Sira, its hero, is the offspring of a sordid incestuous affair between the prophet Jeremiah and his daughter! Conventional Jewish heroes are also portrayed in a negative light. King David, for example, is described as a cunning hypocrite. Was the author satirizing traditional values because he belonged to some non-Orthodox sect? Scholars to this day have not explained his iconoclastic stance.

The *maqama*, an Arabic literary genre composed in rhymed prose, was introduced into Hebrew literature by Judah al-Harizi at the close of the 12th century. In its classical form, the individual *maqama* forms part of a compendium of *maqamat*, whose framework is based on the relationship of two key characters: *the hero*, a crafty, picaresque voyager, who is a talented poet and a charming rogue, and *his foil*, the narrator, who reports the antics of his companion. Many of the stories deal with secular themes: travel, romance, marital infidelity, and ribaldry.

At times the medieval Hebrew author employed the device of a nocturnal journey into the heavenly spheres under the guidance of a benevolent emissary from the world of the dead who reveals secrets 'behind the curtain'. The influence of Dante's *Commedia* is apparent and also that of earlier antecedents, in such apocryphal works as *Enoch* and the *Vision of Ezra*, and of the mystical *hekhaloth* literature of the late talmudic period.

With the rise of the 'practical' Kabbalah in the 16th century, the kabbalistic story was invented. The most popular of these was 'The Tale of Joseph de la Reyna', whose earliest version dates from the 15th century. Faust-like in theme, it tells of a Kabbalist who by kabbalistic magic captures Satan; but exploiting Joseph's hubris, Satan turns the tables on him and enslaves him. Ultimately Joseph is metamorphozed into a vicious black dog.

The Hasidim (the pious), while not rejecting the Halacha, objected to the sombre legalism advocated by the communal and religious leadership of the times and turned to a more emotional and joyous expression of their Judaism. Great stress was placed upon the role of the *Tzaddik*, the charismatic leader endowed with supernatural powers, who served as an intermediary between the pious and their God. *Tzaddikism* naturally led to the development of hagiographical tales which told of the wonders which the *Tzaddik* performed. He could penetrate the heavens and influence both the positive and negative forces which determined men's fate by invoking his kabbalistic knowledge or by virtue of his extraordinary piety.

In the world of the Hasidim, the story had a central function at the *Tzaddik's* court and in the prayer-room. This was particularly true of the remarkable stories of Rabbi Nahman of Bratslav. In keeping with the doctrine that even the most earthly phenomenon had a spiritual core (the spark), which had become encrusted with a material shell, and that it was the task of the *Tzaddik* to liberate the spark, Rabbi Nahman felt himself free to draw upon any folk or literary source available to him as material for his imaginative, quasi-allegorical stories.

Although Hasidim spoke Yiddish, the Hasidic tale was written in Hebrew. Since the Hasidic author was primarily concerned with his story and not with style, his Hebrew is highly Yiddishized. For all his violations of classical Hebrew grammar and syntax, he succeeded more than any of his predecessors in conveying the flavour of the folk idiom.

One of the earliest printed Hebrew books was Isaac ibn Sahula's collection of animal fables, with naïve little woodcut illustrations. It was printed probably at Brescia in 1491.

Literature in the secular world

During the 18th century, Hebrew literature underwent a radical transformation, the result of the growing secularization of European Jewry. Works such as these we have been discussing were widely rejected by the intelligentsia. In Galicia, two talented satirists appeared: Josef Perl (1773–1839) and Isaac Erter (1791–1851). Perl fashioned very witty parodies of Hasidic works as a weapon to wield against the Hasidim whom he considered to be the forces of 'medieval Jewish obscurantism'. Erter chose a biblical style for his *The Observer of the House of Israel*. He borrowed from medieval and Hasidic tales the device of a night journey in which the narrator encounters the butts of his wit.

More significant developments took place in Tsarist Russia. Abraham Mapu (1808–67), the first Hebrew novelist, set his two historical novels, *Love of Zion* and *The Guilt of Samaria*, in biblical Palestine. His heroes are gallant and chivalrous Jewish gentry, and villains are devious, social-climbing nouveaux riches or religious obscurantists or hypocrites. His social novel, *The Hypocrite*, constituted the first attempt at depicting contemporary Jewish social life in fiction.

In the following generation, Peretz Smolenskin (1840–85) and Reuben Asher Braudes (1851–1903) were able to edge closer towards more realistic writing. Smolenskin's *A Wanderer in the Paths of Life* is structured more competently than *The Hypocrite*, because the narrative is centred around its protagonist (Joseph), who roams the Jewish Pale of Settlement in quest of the meaning of life. Joseph encounters the underworld of Jewish beggars, studies at a Lithuanian *yeshiva*, joins the court of a Hasidic rabbi and travels as far as London, Paris and Berlin. Smolenskin attempted to draw a panorama of Jewish life as it was lived inside Russia as well as in Western Europe.

In *Donkey's Burial*, he introduced a new hero, the militant *maskil* (literally: enlightened), who is unable to survive within or without the traditionalist world into which he was born. This new hero also appeared in Braudes's unfinished novel, *Religion and Life*, as a young militant *maskil*, struggling to liberate himself from the narrow medievalism of the Jewish hamlet. Braudes approached realism in his novel, *The Two Extremes*. The hero, having liberated himself from tradition, now discovers that the new secularism for which he had yearned lacks the certainty and peace of mind of a traditional society.

The last quarter of the 19th century marks a crisis in European liberalism, and particularly in Eastern Europe. The reformism advocated by the European bourgeoisie, with its promises of emancipation, was abandoned after the assassination of Alexander II. Hebrew authors and readers of the new generation could no longer accept the romanticism of their predecessors. The harsher milieu of the new order demanded a more realistic approach.

Mendele Mokher Sefarim (1835–1917) stands at the cross-roads of the Haskalah and this new period. His penchant for realism led him, in 1867, to abandon the inflexible and euphuistic Hebrew of his peers for the richer and more malleable Yiddish vernacular. But even the Yiddish, he found, had to be recast into a literary language. Mendele is responsible more than anyone else for the development of literary Yiddish. Like the *Maskilim*, he satirized Jewish life in the Pale but in his later works he soothes the sting by interspersing nostalgic passages in praise of the simple piety and the strong sense of family which were the earmarks of the traditional Jewish community. In response to the urging of his younger colleagues, in the 1880s Mendele returned to Hebrew writing, forging a new realistic idiom comprised of rabbinic and biblical Hebrew. Mendele's 'new style' greatly influenced subsequent prose writing.

Less realistic and doctrinaire, Polish writers tended to stress feeling and beauty rather than form and classical syntax. The leading figure, I. L. Peretz (1851–1915), who, like Mendele, wrote in Yiddish and Hebrew, declared: 'In the world of general literature the sun of realism has set.' He uses an impressionist, sentimental style in an attempt to recapture the mystical rapture of his characters.

A foremost proponent of the neo-romantic style was Micah Josef Berdichevski (1865–1921). He questioned the value systems of traditional Judaism, which stressed communal discipline and religious conformism at the expense of individual freedom. Only the freeing of the individual to follow his creative instincts, he believed, can lead to national rebirth. Berdichevski's heroes are individualists who strive to escape the narrow world of their childhood but are frequently psychologically incapable of consummating the break. Their impotence is often accentuated not only by feelings of guilt towards their former system of values but also by their deep group loyalties and their familial love.

The revival of Hebrew

With the rise of Jewish folkism and Zionism the question of literary 'authenticity' became a problem. Modern Hebrew and Yiddish authors had generally adopted European literary models and standards for their works. Should they not return to more 'authentic' Jewish models? Biblical cadences, the blending of biblical and aggadic Hebrew, the use of Jewish and medieval folk-motifs and of the Hasidic story were all seriously attempted. But none of these experiments succeeded in developing indigenous Hebrew literary forms.

In the generation that succeeded Mendele's, the protagonist in Hebrew literature was the *talush* (the uprooted, underground man), who reached his full development as an anti-hero in the works of Joseph Hayyim Brenner (1881–1921). Brenner's was a sombre world of disillusionment in which the old certainties of the tradition are mercilessly if painfully discarded, and the new ideologies, socialism and Zionism, are masochistically unveiled as superficial and inadequate. Yet Brenner was no nihilist. He retained his moral commitment to truth, the brutal truth of man's tragic condition. No Hebrew writer had ever plumbed the tragedy of the early settlers in Palestine, their physical and spiritual agonies, their disillusionment both with the world of the *halutz* (pioneer) and with the world of the old Orthodox community of Jerusalem.

The challenge of Palestine and Israel

The writers of the Second Aliyah (period of settlement, 1905–14) were culturally rooted in Eastern Europe and many of their works were set in the world of their childhood. Their Zionist commitment, however, impelled them to acclimatize to the new scene with a frenzied and almost artificial urgency. At times the romantic mode predominated: the landscape became redolent with biblical memories. But at other times, the economic hardships, the malaria, the hostility of the Arabs, the despondency, disillusionment and loneliness of the young *halutzim* found tragic or bitter expression.

The writers of the 1920s and 1930s shared the common experience of their Eastern European origins, the traditionalist upbringing in the *shtetel* (small town), the revolt against Orthodox religion, the terror and disillusionment of wars, revolutions and pogroms and the ardour of Zionist and Socialist commitments. The background of J. S. Agnon, by far the leading Hebrew novelist of the period, was somewhat different. A Galician rather than a Russian, he had come to Israel during the Second Aliyah, but shortly before World War I had migrated to Germany, where he spent over a decade absorbing German and German Jewish culture. His achievement marked the high spot of the Polish-Galician strain in modern Hebrew literature with its post-naturalist neo-romantic bent towards symbolist and meta-realistic writing. Agnon's fiction is epic in scope and is set in an extensive geographical framework: the Galicia of his ancestors and of his own times, Germany during and immediately following World War I and Ottoman and British Palestine. His main theme is the disintegration of the cultural unity of modern Jews.

In *The Bridal Canopy*, he attempts to develop an indigenous 'Jewish' narrative form built about cyclical motifs drawn from pietistic literature (marriage, gluttony, hospitality, wandering, etc.). But usually his techniques are European, varying from the classical novel (*A Simple Story*) to the involved symbolist stories of his later period (*Until Now* and *Inside the City's Walls*). In *A Guest Comes Visiting*, he depicted the disintegration of the Eastern European Jewish world following World War I. *Not So Long Ago* reflected the clash between tradition and modernity among the earlier Zionist settlers of Ottoman Palestine. The fascinating world of Jerusalem's intellectuals during the 1930s served as background for *Shirah*, an unfinished novel.

More in line with the Russian realist tradition is Hayyim Hazaz, who merged the realism of the Odessan school with a penchant for the grotesque. After he moved to Israel, he shifted to *halutzic* themes and to the depiction of the life of Israel's Yemenite Jews both before and after their migration from the Yemen. A key theme in many of his works is Zionism, which he often associated with Jewish Messianism. Jewish redemption, argue many of his characters, was not achieved in the past because Jews lacked the courage to risk all, to abandon the safety of the ordinary for the challenge of the ideal.

Hebrew literature of the early 20th century was essentially a literature of immigrants. Writers like I. D. Berkowitz and Shimon Halkin had moved from Eastern Europe to America and then to Palestine, depicting each of these cultures in turn and the position of the Jewish migrant within them. The very fact that modern Hebrew authors until the mid-century were not monolingual, but lived in two or more cultures simultaneously, gave Hebrew literature its peculiarly rich texture.

By the 1940s, almost coinciding with the establishment of the State of Israel, a new generation of native Hebrew readers and writers had begun to make its presence felt. They were far less interested in the European past of their parents. 'The new young reader', says Yaacov Rabinowitz, 'now asks: what have we to do with those over there? Give us this land, this moment. Yesterday, the past, what's all that to him? He is not ashamed to admit it; on the contrary, he's proud of it. History begins with him, his generation, where he lives, now!' S. Yizhar's (born, 1916) *Efrayim Returns to Alfalfa* (1938) is the first important work of the new school. Its Hebrew style has a natural rhythm and ring, which distinguishes it from that of the older generation. And the native writer is obsessed with the landscape, which he describes with a freshness and flexibility of language that rarely appeared before.

The arrival of the new school coincided with the final phase of the struggle for national independence. Moshe Shamir's (born, 1921) realistic novel, *Hu Halakh ba-Sadōt* (*He Walked in the Fields*, 1946), was not only a best-seller, in its stage version it became a great hit of the war period. Parent and soldier identified with Uri, the taciturn, life-loving, cocky platoon sergeant whose commitment to the national struggle was not 'ideological' but motivated by social imperatives. S. Yizhar's profounder war novel, *Days of Ziqlag* (1958), written after a 'distance' of almost a decade, explored with greater depth the world of a band of soldiers, their ideals and fears: the strange compound of love of country and alienation that disturbs the native Israeli, only one generation removed from the immigrant, and occasionally puts into question the entire Zionist enterprise.

The 1950s were turbulent years. The native-born had the pick of governmental, university, industrial and army posts but longed for the old certainties of their Zionist ideology. Aharon Megged expressed the disillusionment of the ex- *Palmachnik* in *Hedva va-ani* (*Hedvah and I*), bemoaning the loss of idealism and the careerism which mark the new era.

Among new immigrants were survivors of the holocaust who were young enough to acquire the new Hebrew idiom and join the natives as fellow writers. Itammar Yaoz-Kest (Hungary, 1934), writing almost two decades after his immigration, recollects the sense of inferiority which they felt and their passionate desire to integrate into the world of the native *Sabra* and forget their tragic past. But he avers that the past could not be buried, and rose like a ghost to haunt 'the children of the shade' separating them from the 'others'. Most poignant are the short stories and novellas of Aaron Applefield. Applefield rarely approaches his holocaust frontally. He writes of people and events who live before or immediately after the experience of the death camps. In one of his later novellas, *Badenheim 1939*, the victims, guests at a summer resort that they visit perennially, are hardly aware of the fact that the resort had become converted into a staging camp for their dispatch to the death camps until the trap is sprung. Not that the others had ignored the holocaust. Hanoch Bartov met it and the complex problem of avenging its dead in his novel, *The Jewish Brigade*. Yehudah Amichai (born, 1924), who although born in Germany reached safety before the holocaust, confronts it in his novel, *Not Now, Not here,* by having his hero return to his native city in Germany.

During the mid-1950s a new wave of Hebrew prose writers took the stage, led by Amos Oz (born, 1939) and A. B. Yehoshua (born, 1936). Amos Oz's first book, *The Lands of the Jackal*, is a collection of Kibbutz stories. The Kibbutz becomes a symbol for Israel, a green, cultivated oasis encompassed by a wilderness in which patient jackals roam, awaiting their carrion. This reality of an ever-present threat of annihilation becomes a metaphor for the condition of man surrounded by irrational forces that anticipate his doom.

A. B. Yehoshua drew upon Jewish symbols for an ostensibly secular story, *Galiah's Wedding*: the burning bush, the heavenly chariot, the holy beasts. A story about frustrated love, it is also an allegory of the pilgrim's quest for salvation. After he fails to regain his beloved (the grail?), the hero remounts the empty bus and orders its mysterious driver to drive on into the dark. The quest must continue.

Amalia Kahana-Carmon's stories are psychologically rather than meta-realistically oriented. 'I have nothing to offer but myself' says one of her characters. A major theme is the interrelation of people in the encounter of love. She suggests that sustained human relationships are impossible because nobody can really understand the 'other' or maintain the surrender of independence that is the ultimate price of love.

Yitzhak Orpaz, whose earliest works are heavy with symbolism, and at times tend to quasi-mysticism (*Daniel's Journey*), has moved to a more realistic mode (*Another Man's Home*).

The most recent trend has been back to a new realism. This is apparent in the latest works of Yehoshua (*The Lover*) and Oz (*The Hill of Evil Counsel*) and in the stories and novels of two younger writers, Yitzhak ben Ner and Y. Korn, which are set in the more established communities of rural Israel and are permeated with a harsh, almost Hardy-like naturalism.

It is difficult to predict what directions Hebrew narrative prose will pursue in the near future. Israel's population is increasingly becoming Middle Eastern in its ethnic make-up, but there are no recognizable signs that its writers will be influenced by Arabic literature. The American-European tradition is not only firmly entrenched in Hebrew literature but in the Arab literary world itself. One could expect an increase of writers from Jews of Middle Eastern descent and even the introduction of characters and events drawn from that community, but the techniques will probably remain Western. Above all, much will depend on whether the Arab-Jewish conflict will be resolved. If this occurs, what would be the consequence of the relaxation of the terror and the opening towards the East?

Jewish Literature: Poetry

T. CARMI

THE DISTINCTIVE HISTORICAL FEATURES of Hebrew poetry are its chronological span and geographical distribution. It has been written virtually without interruption from biblical times to the present day. Over the centuries its main centres were in Palestine, Spain, Babylonia, Italy, Germany and Eastern Europe. But it had also had important branches in North Africa, the Balkans, the Yemen and Holland.

This longevity and mobility involved several fresh and, sometimes, false starts. It involved centuries of continuity, followed by bouts of amnesia, and then rediscovery of neglected treasures. It also meant that Hebrew poetry could be at very different stages of its development, during the same period, in different geographical areas.

Yet despite dispersion in time and place, Hebrew poetry maintained its own internal tradition, which both absorbed and transformed the external influences. Once a centre was established, its development was determined by a complex network of relationships and tensions: between its original matrix and the impact of the host literature; between the resultant fusion and the attraction of other Hebrew centres; between the prestige of a revered tradition and the need for innovation; and between its inherited prosody and the local pronunciation of Hebrew.

The flowering of the piyyut

Post-biblical poetry developed in Palestine, under late Roman and Byzantine rule, in the centuries preceding the Muslim conquest (636). This is the period that witnessed the remarkable flowering of the *piyyut*, that is, liturgical poetry, which made Palestine the centre of Hebrew letters until the late 8th century.

The *paytanim*, liturgical poets, were generally cantors. On every Sabbath and on every festival, they surprised their congregations with new compositions which elaborated on the subjects of the biblical lection or the specific theme of the holy day.

Little is known of the origin of the *piyyut*. The first four or five centuries of post-biblical poetry are sparsely represented by the poems in the Talmud (completed *c.* 500 CE), the ecstatic hymns of the Palestinian *Hekhaloth* mystics (*c.* 3rd and 4th centuries), and several alphabetic prayers of great antiquity. In full or partial form, most of the major genres are encountered in the pre-classical period (5th–6th centuries). They were, as yet, unrhymed. The alphabetic acrostic set the limit of the line of verse. Word-metre was often the organizing rhythmic principle. The vocabulary was mainly biblical, though the *paytan* enlarged the semantic field of many words, and did not abstain from coinages. Generally speaking, the pre-classical *piyyut* and the poetry that preceded it are surprisingly modern in tone. Their diction and their rhythms are clear and forceful.

The classical period (mid-6th–late 8th century) established the intricate patterns of the major genres and intensified the use of existing devices. It created an extremely dense texture of epithets, neologisms and midrashic allusions and gradually developed a specialized, inbred vocabulary that often makes the *piyyut* seem abstruse and cryptic. The acrostics became highly intricate, sometimes spelling out not only the name of the author but also his father's name, his place of residence, his occupation, and even concluding formulae such as *ḥazak*, 'be strong!'

The outstanding innovation of the classical period was the introduction of rhyme as a standard feature of liturgical poetry. Rhyme now set the boundary of the line of verse and of the strophe. The gain in resonance was, however, offset by a loss of rhythmical tautness.

The development of the *piyyut* and the changes it underwent in the late Eastern period (*c.* 750–1050) can only be understood in the context of its relationship to public prayer. During the pre-classical and classical periods, the obligatory benedictions that the congregation recited had assumed a fixed form. However, the overall pattern of the liturgy had not yet been standardized, and so the *paytanim* enjoyed a great deal of latitude. In fact, their monumental sequences, which were recited by the cantor, or prayer-leader, could replace entire prose passages of the liturgy.

The *piyyut* forfeited its status as 'versified prayer' when the entire text of the liturgy became sanctified and the first prayer-books were edited in 9th-century Babylonia. Henceforth, it could no longer serve as an alternative to passages of the codified rite; it had to content itself with being an ornamental insertion, an embellishment to a rigidly formulated text.

Almost all Hebrew poetry up to the 10th century is liturgical. This, however, does not mean that it is all 'religious' in the limited sense of the word, requiring the reader's consent to a system of belief or of dogma. Since the *piyyut* is generally linked to the biblical portion of the week and to the appropriate passages from the prophetic books, the range of subjects is almost unlimited. As long as the *paytan* observes the formal links, at the prescribed points, to the liturgical framework, he can, and does, digress at will. He can move, within the confines of the same sequence, from the lyrical to the dramatic, from narrative to supplication, from meditative poetry to mystical hymns.

Though the late Eastern period presided over the disintegration of classical genres and, in general, favoured a less rhythmical line and less demanding forms of rhyming, it also witnessed a classical revival in the

A cantor, from the same Bird-head Haggadah *illustrated on p. 197 The early* paytanim *(liturgical poets) were generally cantors.*

works of its finest poets, Saadya Gaon and Samuel Hashelishi. Samuel (fl. late 10th century) was second to none in his mastery of the taut and melodious Hebrew line. Saadya Gaon (882–942), the most original poet and thinker of his time, was the major link between the Eastern and Spanish schools.

The 'golden age' in Spain

Up to the 10th century, the lineage of Hebrew poetry is fairly clear. All the *paytanim* of the classical period flourished in Palestine. From the middle of the 9th century, Babylonia, with its network of talmudic academies and its highly organized Jewish community, superseded Palestine as the dominant centre of Jewish scholarship. Meanwhile, branches had sprung up in Egypt, North Africa and Syria which, like Palestine, acknowledged the authority of Babylonia and its liturgical customs.

At the end of the 9th century, Hebrew poetry makes its first appearance on European soil, in southern Italy. Germany, under the direct influence of Italy, produces its first major poet, Simeon the Great, in the 10th century.

The complexion of Hebrew poetry is dramatically transformed in the 10th century with the emergence of the Andalusian school (Andalusia, at the time, encompassed most of the Iberian peninsula) and the appearance of secular poetry. When Dunash ben Labrat of Cordoba (he was born in Fez and studied under Saadya in Baghdad) first adapted the quantitative metres of Arabic to Hebrew and wrote the first, almost apologetic, secular poems and the first *piyyutim* in the new style – he performed one of the most drastic operations in the history of Hebrew poetry. Within decades, Hebrew submitted to, and then quickly mastered, the techniques of the Andalusian school.

Hebrew poetry spans some five hundred years in Spain, which are divided into two major periods: the

Muslim period (*c.* 950–1150) and the Christian period (*c.* 1150–1492). By the beginning of the 11th century, the first of the giants of the 'golden age' (*c.* 1020–1150) had arisen: Samuel ha-Nagid – Samuel the Prince, who for twenty years commanded the Muslim armies of Granada, and whose epic and lyrical accounts of military campaigns trace a sudden arc to the 'Song of Deborah'. He was followed by three outstanding figures: Solomon ibn Gabirol, the passionate, introspective poet and major philosopher; Moses ibn Ezra, the virtuoso technician and theoretician; and Yehuda ha-Levi, 'the sweet singer of Zion', perhaps the finest poet of this school.

Secular Hebrew poetry was born at the courts of Jewish grandees who served as courtiers to Muslim rulers. This aristocratic birth set its mark not only on the subjects of the poetry, but also on its style and character. Its main genres were panegyrics, laments on the death of the patron or his relatives, songs of self-praise, invectives aimed at the patron's rivals or, when the need arose, against the hard-fisted patron himself; aphoristic verse; stylized wine songs and love songs which, to the accompaniment of instrumental music, regaled the company gathered for a drinking session in the palace garden in springtime, or the palace courtyard in winter. There were also genres of a more personal nature, such as complaints and meditative poems.

There were other shaping forces as well, namely, the powerful attraction of Arabic verse, and the highly motivated desire to revive biblical Hebrew. This revival of biblical vocabulary and images was stimulated by strong national sentiments and reflected a current of rivalry with the host culture. For the Arabs, the stylistic excellence of the Qur'ān was proof of its veracity and divine inspiration. The Jews countered this by championing the Hebrew of the older Book of Books. Again and again poets expressly state that their intention is to glorify the ancient tongue, to demonstrate that it is equal, if not superior, to the reigning language.

Secular Hebrew poetry's aristocratic upbringing did not confine it within the palace walls; it quickly gained a wide and appreciative public in Spain and in distant lands. Its triumph was complete when it infiltrated the *piyyut* and thus reached the masses in the synagogue. For the first time in Jewish history the *paytan* was not only a 'deputy' or 'delegate' of the congregation (*sheli'ah tsibur*), but a professional poet who was bound by the same conventions and judged by the same aesthetic criteria as the secular poet. The first two generations of *paytanim* after Dunash ben Labrat (died, *c.* 990) hesitated to accept his innovations, but from the time of Ibn Gabirol (born, 1021/22) onwards, the greatest *paytanim* were also the greatest secular poets.

A striking example of the marriage of the sacred and the profane is afforded by a famous poem by Yehuda ha-Levi:

Ever since you were my home-of-love,
my love has camped where you have camped.
For your sake, I have delighted in the reproaches of my admonishers;
let them be, let them torment the one whom you tormented.
It was from you that they learned their wrath, and I love them
for they hound the wounded one whom you struck down.
From the day you despised me, I have despised myself,
for I will not honour what you have despised . . .

260

The poem is written in the classical monorhymed form (the hemistichs are here printed as separate lines). Its vocabulary and imagery are typical of the secular genre. It is only with its last line—

until Your anger has passed and again You will redeem
Your own possession, which You once redeemed—

that the poem reveals itself as a *piyyut*. And it is even more surprising to learn that, except for the last line, this *piyyut* is an adaptation of an 8th-century Arabic love poem.

The speed with which the Andalusian school imposed itself upon the centres of Hebrew poetry throughout the world is one of the most striking phenomena in the annals of Hebrew poetry. By the beginning of the 11th century, poets in Babylonia, Egypt, North Africa and Palestine were already writing in the Spanish style. From the middle of the 12th century, Provence became an adjunct of the Andalusian poetic empire. At the same time, poets in Italy abandoned the Palestinian *paytanic* style, and began to write secular and sacred poetry in the Hispano-Arabic manner. Greece, Turkey and the Yemen followed suit. The conventions of the Spanish school became so pervasive that one is often hard put to identify the geographical provenance of a poem in the Andalusian style.

The only centre that did not pay total homage to the Andalusian school was the German-French, or Ashkenazi centre. Though it produced great poetry in its classical period (10th century) and during its typically Ashkenazi phase (12th and 13th centuries), it was probably the most provincial and insular centre of Hebrew poetry. Historical circumstances – the ravages of successive Crusades and the brutal pogroms during the year of the Black Death (1348–9) – partly account for this. The poetic efforts of the Ashkenazi school concentrated on passionate pentitential verse (*selihot*) and dirges (*kinot*), many of which recorded the harrowing experiences of the Rhineland communities.

The Reconquista

The 'golden age' in Spain was brought to an abrupt end in 1140 with the invasion of the Almohads, a fanatical Berber sect from North Africa. After the destruction of the Jewish centres in Andalusia, the communities moved north, to Christian Spain. New centres of Hebrew poetry now arose in Toledo, Saragossa and Barcelona, as well as in northern areas, such as Navarre, which had never been under Muslim rule.

The patronage of Hebrew poetry did not disappear in Christian Spain. There were Jewish princes, courtiers and administrators in the service of Christian kings, who, like their Andalusian predecessors, spread a protective wing over poets and scholars. However, the extent of patronage and the centrality of the court were considerably diminished. The poetry tended to become more personal, more realistic, reflecting larger areas of individual life and public experience. The language became more catholic, incorporating elements from rabbinic Hebrew and from the terminology introduced by the translators of Jewish Arabic classics. The tensions between the Jewish aristocracy and the masses found expression in social satire, intended for large, popular audiences.

Two pages from the well known Dayyenu poem, from a manuscript of 1397 (an earlier manuscript of the same poem is illustrated on p. 149). In the sequence beginning on the right-hand page and continuing at the top of the left, every line both begins and ends with the same words.

The major innovation of the Christian period was the introduction of narratives in rhymed prose, interspersed with metrical poems. Of these works, the best known genre was the *maqama*, which reached its full stature in the work of Judah al-Harizi (*c.* 1170 – after 1235).

All the poems in the *maqamat* and in the related genres of rhymed narrative strictly adhered to the classical *qasida* form (quantitative metre and uniform rhyme). Though traditional, they had a far-reaching effect on the subject-matter, tone and dramatis personae of secular poetry. The narrative and dramatic framework gave the poets licence to put poetic monologues into the mouths of lovelorn women, impotent greybeards, hospitable yokels, lecherous adulterers and even pathetic roosters fleeing from the butcher's knife. The *maqama* framework also enabled the author to stage poetic duels; to appear in the double guise of counsel for the defence and the prosecution, alternately praising and condemning women or wine; and to record autobiographical experiences.

The Expulsion of the Jews from Spain in 1492, and from Portugal in 1497, signalled the beginning of a new era in Hebrew poetry. The exiles and refugees flooded the shores of the Mediterranean and initiated a re-surgence of poetic creativity in North Africa, Turkey and Palestine. In Safed, the school of mystics gathered around Isaac Luria in the 16th century provided Hebrew poetry with the inspiration of the Kabbalah, and this new source of energy quickly radiated out to the Yemen, Holland and Italy.

Hebrew poetry in Italy
While Hebrew Poetry was being expelled from Spain it was refining the ottava rima in Italy, in some of the most delicate lyrics ever written in Hebrew.

Italy, it will be recalled, was the first European host to Hebrew poetry. It was also, in many ways, the most hospitable. The history of Hebrew poetry in Italy extends from the 9th to the 19th century. It is of particular interest because, in the course of this

millennium, it mirrored all the existing schools and tried out all the Hebrew metrical systems until it finally achieved its distinctive style. Immanuel of Rome (*c.* 1261–*c.* 1332), one of the wittiest and bawdiest of poets, introduced the sonnet into Hebrew around 1300. The thirty-eight sonnets that he interspersed in his famous *maqama* collection (*Mahberot Imanu'el*) reflect both the *dolce stil nuovo* and the burlesque style then current in Italian letters. They also strike an original compromise between Andalusian and Italian prosody.

The characteristic Hebrew-Italian style, which evolved between the 15th and 17th centuries, testified to an unusually close rapport between the two languages. At its extreme, this took the form of 'macaronic' poems, alternating Hebrew and Italian lines; poems that paired Hebrew and Italian rhyme-words; echo-poems, in which the echo of the Hebrew word yields an Italian word (e.g. *yekara* 'dear one' . . . *cara*); and even poems that could be read as both Hebrew and Italian.

Hebrew enjoyed a high status among the humanists, some of whom studied under Jewish scholars and poets. Hebrew presses were founded in Italy as early as the 15th century, in the period of the incunabula. Unlike his predecessor in Spain, the Hebrew poet in Italy was not competing with the dominant culture; he saw himself as a collaborator in a joint venture. Despite the harassing restrictions of the Roman Church, this was the period that witnessed the appearance of bilingual editions of original devotional poetry as well as translations of *piyyutim*.

Given its enormous diversity, chronological range and geographical dispersion, what are the factors that give Hebrew poetry its cohesion and justify the use of that much abused word 'tradition'? First and foremost, the cement of biblical Hebrew. Though Hebrew poetry cultivated different stylistic prejudices at different periods – sometimes preferring the rabbinic idiom, or the specialized allusive usages of the classical *piyyut* – biblical Hebrew remained, and continues to be, the base of the language. This is one of the reasons that Hebrew, despite its multilayered formation, did not develop the schism that characterizes Classical and modern Greek, or literary and vernacular Arabic.

The long, sprawling tradition is held together not only by the infrastructure of biblical Hebrew, but also by the larger cultural frame of reference, the sources studied so intensively, committed to memory, commented upon and reinterpreted in each generation, until they become an almost subconscious layer of the national memory. It is further reinforced by the repetition of central themes and motifs, which are capable of transmitting the traumas of history, whether the martyrdom of entire communities during the Crusades, the *autos-da-fé* of the Inquisition, or the extermination of more than half of the Jewish population in the Yemen in the 17th century. One could, for example, compile an extensive anthology of poems on the theme of the binding of Isaac (*akedot*), from talmudic to modern times, that would mirror these and other events in the idiom of the respective periods. It is as though one were walking through a house of mirrors, constantly catching glimpses of familiar scenes from different angles of vision.

The modern voice of Hebrew

The Haskalah (1781–1881) was a movement that advocated the secularization of Jewish life and the emancipation of the Jewish people. It began in Prussia as a rationalist, cosmopolitan movement and, by the middle of the 19th century, shifted to Eastern Europe. The wave of pogroms that struck Russian Jewry in the 1880s tarnished the ideal of emancipation, undermined its feasibility and initiated the earliest organized Zionist movement, known as *Hibat Tsiyon* ('The Love of Zion').

Though one must admire the courage and tenacity of epic poets such as Judah Lev Gordon (1830–93), and the gentle lyricism of poets such as Micah Joseph Lebensohn (1828–52), the poetry of the period is largely devoid of aesthetic interest, and it is only with Hayim Nahman Bialik (1873–1934) that Hebrew recovers from its stroke of amnesia, begins to rediscover important chapters of its long history and finds its modern voice. In 1890, Odessa was the centre of Hebrew letters. By 1920 it was superseded by Palestine. This critical transition affected the prosody of Hebrew poetry, its musical key and, of course, its themes and locales.

Under the influence of Yiddish, Russian and German, the syllabic system was discarded in favour of the tonic-syllabic or accentual system (the alternation of stressed and unstressed syllables, as in English, German or Russian verse). This change was effected mainly by Bialik, the acknowledged leader of the Odessa circle.

History thoughtfully paired Bialik with Saul Tchernikhovsky (1875–1943), the other major figure of the period. Bialik's life story – his *shtetl* (small town) background, religious education and subsequent encounter with secular culture – was typical of the East European writer. His poetry, his unerring linguistic instincts, seemed to recapitulate successive stages of Jewish history. He was, at times reluctantly, the voice of the people at critical moments in their history. Tchernikhovsky, by contrast, was by far the most European Hebrew poet of his generation. His upbringing was atypical: he received a secular Hebrew education and a thorough grounding in Russian literature. His translations, from fifteen languages, of national epics and of Renaissance and Romantic works, reminded Hebrew poetry of the larger cultural frame of reference within which it had flourished in the Spanish and Italian periods. While Bialik devoted endless energy and erudition to the in-gathering (*kinus*) and editing of forgotten Hebrew sources, Tchernikhovsky was engaged in a parallel venture: the 'in-gathering' of European classics, from Antiquity to his time, from which Hebrew poetry had been severed in the ghetto-centuries.

Compared to Bialik, Tchernikhovsky was an outsider; he seemed to be more at home in the *Odyssey* and *Kalevala* than in the Talmud and Zohar. And though he consistently enlarged the vocabulary of Hebrew – some of his favourite areas were flora, fauna and the female anatomy – his idiom was far less flexible and resonant than Bialik's.

Although Hebrew was not revived as a spoken language in Palestine until the end of the 19th century, it was not, as is commonly thought, 'dead'. It was, of course, the language of prayer and study, but prayer that was generally understood and not recited by rote. And it is important to remember that the prayer-book is actually an anthology of the various layers of Hebrew. It was also the language of family observances and communal fesitivities, of legal and commercial documents, of historical chronicles, municipal records, tombstone inscriptions and irreverent parodies of sacred texts, as well as the *lingua franca* of the Jews from various countries.

Aharon Megged, the Israeli novelist, has admirably summed this up: 'The revival of the Hebrew language is not like Lazarus arising miraculously from the dead. It is more like the Sleeping Beauty awakened by the Prince. . . . Contrary to Eliza Doolittle of *Pygmalion*, she is quite all right at fancy parties, but she misbehaves in the market place. . . .'

The 'market place' was Palestine. There, Hebrew poetry faced one of its harshest trials: the need to adjust to a new geography, to a Mediterranean texture of light and seasons and sounds. The fact that this landscape was also 'familiar', that these hills and rivers had been sung before by poets who inhabited them in real life or in the life of the imagination, was both an advantage and an impediment. The literary memory had to make way for fresh, immediate vision; the individual memory had to contend with a new biography.

Broadly speaking, it was the poets of the Palestinian period (1920–47), such as Karni, Greenberg, Lamdan, Shlonsky, S. Shalom and Alterman, who put the Sleeping Beauty to work in the fields. These were the poets who first introduced the rhythms of the spoken language into Hebrew poetry and brought it, somewhat belatedly, into the 20th century. And as so often in the history of Hebrew poetry, the new surge of creativity was accompanied and catalyzed by an influx of foreign influences; in this case, Russian Futurism and Symbolism, and German Expressionism.

Hebrew poetry's encounter with its homeland often produced poems of an ecstatic, almost Messianic tone, such as Abraham Shlonsky's 'Toil', which was written around 1927, and forms part of a sequence named after Mount Gilboa in the Valley of Jezreel:

Dress me, good mother, in a glorious robe of many colours,
and at dawn lead me to toil.
My land is wrapped in light as in a prayer-shawl.
The houses stand forth like phylacteries. . . .

The trials of the pioneer, the spiritual and physical possession of the land (the landscape became one of the main topics of Hebrew verse and prose), the zeal of the return – these were prominent themes of the Palestinian period. But the fervour was also counterpoised by a starker account of the realities of everyday life. Lea Goldberg (1911–70) shows us the darker side of the picture in her poem 'Tel Aviv 1935' – the year she immigrated to Palestine:

And the kit-bags of the travellers walked down the streets
and the language of an alien land
was plunged into the hamsin-*days*
like the blade of a cold knife. . . .
Like pictures turning black inside a camera
they all turned inside out: pure winter nights,
rainy summer nights of overseas,
and shadowy mornings of great cities. . . .

By now there are several generations of Israeli poets who have not 'known the pain of hovering between two home-lands' – a phrase taken from a poem by Lea Goldberg. Their perception of the desert was not impeded by the memory of soft European mists. The language is their birthright; it was not, consciously or unwittingly, competing with foreign models; it was not compensating or over-compensating for something lost or surrendered; it was not struggling to liberate itself from the gravitational pull of a many-layered tradition. The motto of the Israeli period, in the years following the War of Independence of 1948, could have been a line from a poem by Ayin Hillel: 'I hate rhetoric (*melitsot*) as the forest hates picnickers'; or a line from Yehudah Amichai: 'I, who use only a small part of the words of the dictionary. . . .'

The entire modern period could be studied in terms of the relationship of spoken Hebrew to written poetry. The rate of change, until some twenty years ago, was both exhilarating and unnerving. Shlonsky, the brilliant innovator, whose coinages fill an entire dictionary, had outrageously compared Bialik in the 1930s to a huge bus, blocking a one-way street. But Shlonsky himself turned into a double-decker in his lifetime. And the picture was further complicated in the 1950s, when the younger poets turned to Anglo-American models. This created a fairly distinct cleavage between the poetry – and, one might add, the criticism – of the modernizers and of their at first loyal, and then rebellious, progeny.

Whether the poet wills it or not, there is often an element of counterpoint in Hebrew poetry. However colloquial the rhythms and even the diction, it is heard by the alert reader against the background of biblical poetry and of an uninterrupted poetic tradition. And some of the finest effects of modern Hebrew poetry still result from the tension between everyday speech and the undertones of a shared heritage.

Here, for example, is the opening stanza of a poem by Yehudah Amichai, entitled 'A Sort of Apocalypse':

The man under his fig tree telephones to the man under his vine:
'Tonight they will surely come.
Armour the leaves,
Lock up the tree,
Call home the dead and be prepared.'

The introduction of the anachronistic telephone into the body of a famous biblical idiom for peace and peace of mind – 'They shall sit every man under his vine and under his fig tree and none shall be afraid' – is enough to jolt any Hebrew reader. But something is also happening on the physical, visual level. The peace-loving vine and fig tree shed their symbolic roles and are transformed into routine accessories of field camouflage.

Amichai's lines are representative of the individualistic, anti-dogmatic, anti-ideological tone of many of the younger poets. In some cases, this becomes a desperate attempt to step out of history. The individualization of Israeli society over the past twenty-five years has often led writers to rebel against the sentiment of collectivity, of being an exposed nerve within a very nervous system. And, needless to say, one often finds both impulses, pulling in opposite directions, within one and the same writer.

A poem such as Amir Gilboa's 'Isaac', entirely modern in tone and technique, may serve as a final illustration of the way in which Hebrew, at a given moment, can draw on a wide range of linguistic and historical associations:

At dawn the sun strolled in the forest
together with me and father,
and my right hand was in his left.

Like lightning a knife flashed among the trees.
And I am so afraid of my eyes' terror, faced by blood on the leaves.

Father, father, quickly save Isaac
so that no one will be missing at the midday meal.

It is I who am being slaughtered, my son,
and already my blood is on the leaves.
And father's voice was smothered and his face was pale.

And I wanted to scream, writhing not to believe,
and tearing open my eyes.
And I woke up.

And my right hand was drained of blood.

The father, as the reader discovers, is both the legendary Patriarch, the Father of the tribe, and the poet's own father, who was slaughtered in the European forest. In its language, images and events, the poem shuttles back and forth between the past and the present. The biblical tableau and the real scene dissolve into each other. Personal biography, national memory – all become one in the childlike voice of the nightmare. The biblical motif ceases to be a 'subject', as it would have been a generation before Gilboa. The identification is so total and, at the same time, so ambiguous, that it can hardly be paraphrased.

The simple, day-to-day history of Israel and of the Jewish people conspires to remind the Hebrew poet that he is a point in time, and that time has a way of exploding unexpectedly.

Chapter Thirteen

European Jewry in the 19th and 20th centuries

LIONEL KOCHAN

IN THE WHOLE HISTORY OF the Jewish people, no period was more fateful than that bounded by the French Revolution and the end of the Second World War. The century and a half that gave to European Jewry unexampled opportunity for self-expression ended in the murder of more than one-third of its members. The Jewish rapprochement with Gentile Europe showed itself to be a bloody trap. This must colour any view of those decades.

By the time of the Congress of Vienna the Jews of Europe numbered about 2,250,000. Those living under Russian rule were most numerous, totalling nearly 1,500,000. Under Habsburg rule lived about 400,000 (half in Galicia, 80,000 in Hungary and 70,000 in Bohemia and Moravia). The German states comprised 350,000 Jews. To the west and south the numbers were far fewer – Italy 30,000, France 40,000, Holland 50,000 (half in Amsterdam), England 25,000. Nowhere did these totals reach more than 2 per cent of the general population.

Those Jews embraced every variety of occupation and circumstance but, almost without exception, their places of residence and sources of livelihood were limited. This is to say nothing of a multitude of other restrictive measures – burdensome, trivial, humiliating. In Alsace, a Jew who wished to spend a day in Strasbourg had to pay a special tax; in Rome, he was obliged to attend a number of conversionist sermons each year; in Saxony, only with the king's permission could a tailor take a Jewish apprentice; in Frankfurt, the annual number of marriages was limited to twelve, etc.

Community and state

But a common factor that characterized the status of the overwhelming majority was membership in a Jewish community. This was the body that constituted 'the state within a state', as its 19th-century detractors termed it, for which, however, the political institutions of the *ancien régime* readily made provision, recognizing the community as a corporate estate. The Jewish community in Rome and Vilna, in Amsterdam and Trieste, in Prague and Avignon, in Hamburg and Lvov, and countless smaller rural centres in areas as far apart as Bordeaux and the Ukraine, enabled the Jew to lead a life in accordance with the legal requirements of his religion (subject always to the restrictions of the surrounding polity). This self-governing community provided a political and religious centre for the Jew, beyond which he had no recognized

existence. The community was political, insofar as it was the body that mediated the Jew's relationship, especially financial, with the surrounding Christian world; and it was religious, insofar as it provided a framework for his legal, educational, dietary and hygienic requirements.

For a combination of reasons, internal and external, the community at the end of the 18th century and beginning of the 19th found itself in a state of decline and even disintegration. On the one hand, increasing economic differentiation, especially in Germany and Bohemia, fostered disunity and heterogeneity among its members. Further to the east, in pre-partition Poland, the communities were heavily indebted to the nobility and clergy. Again, rabbinic authority, with all that this connoted for the administration of justice and the arbitration of differences among community members, suffered in the aftermath of the Sabbatean movement (founded by the pseudo-Messiah, Sabbatai Zevi) in the 17th century and the onslaught of the Hasidim a century later. The dissolution of the Council of the Four Lands in Poland, in 1765, removed another bastion of traditional authority. As the reality and tradition of self-government declined, so did Jewish society enter a protracted state of crisis from which, in fact, it never recovered.

The effects of the crisis were compounded in Western and central Europe by the new interest taken by the state (and certain individuals) in the treatment of its Jewish subjects towards the end of the 18th century. Ill-will by no means motivated this interest. On the contrary, in many of its manifestations it corresponded to the humanitarian ideals of the Enlightenment. A mood of this kind animated the Royal Society of Arts and Sciences in Metz, in 1785, when it announced a competition for an essay on the subject: Are there means to make the Jews more useful and more happy in France? Of the nine contestants who submitted entries in 1787, seven advocated Jewish emancipation and two opposed it. The three laureates among the former – abbé Henri Grégoire from Lorraine, Claude-Antoine Thiéry, advocate at the Parlement of Nancy, and Zalkind Hourwitz, a Polish Jew and librarian in the Oriental Section of the Bibliothèque Royale – all saw Jewish life in terms of degradation and superstition from which it could only be rescued by removing those barriers – residential, cultural, linguistic, sartorial and occupational – that prevented the Jews from sharing in, and contributing to, European progress and enlightenment. The incapacity of the 18th century to appreciate the values of other epochs and its self-assertion as the ne plus ultra of enlightenment was nowhere more blatant and misguided than in its confrontation with Jewish society. Here was a culture founded on respect for scholarship and study, on pacific values and on a patient quest for the ideal government that stood in no need of reform – least of all from warring despots.

Moreover, the very idea of emancipation contained within itself a disrespectful ambiguity: it was propounded, not in order that the Jews might be enabled to live freely as Jews, but rather that they might thereby be induced to become converts to Christianity. The abbé Grégoire cherished the hope that the 'regeneration' of the Jews might culminate in their conversion. In Prussia, the liberal reformer, Wilhelm von Humboldt, argued the case for emancipation on precisely those grounds: 'If you will try to weaken the bonds among the various Jewish churches and do not encourage a single orthodoxy among the Jews but rather foster schisms through a natural and justifiable tolerance, the Jewish hierarchy will fall apart of itself. Individuals will become aware that theirs is only a ceremonial order but not really a religion, and they will turn towards the Christian faith, driven by the innate human desire for a higher belief. . . . Their conversion then . . . will become desirable, enjoyable and beneficial.' If not conversion to Christianity, then at least loss of identity was demanded, in favour of complete subjection to the nation state.

This requirement already contained the guidelines of a programme that was common alike to enlightened despot, to French revolutionary and to Napoleon. The Jews of Europe found themselves confronted by a threat to their separate existence – a threat that was also coupled with genuine amelioration of their status. Early examples were the various Letters-Patent issued by the Habsburg emperor, Joseph II, between 1781 and 1789, in which the Jews of Silesia, Bohemia, Moravia, Hungary, Lower Austria and Galicia were, with differences of detail, freed from much of the discriminatory and oppressive legislation which earlier Habsburg rulers had imposed. 'My chief aim', said Joseph, 'is education, enlightenment and better training for this nation. The opening up of

The Jews of the Habsburg Empire were not only conscripted into the army, but had to endure satire on their bad soldiership. In this Viennese broadsheet of 1788, they are shown making various absurd mistakes in drill. 'Ah weh!' says the one in the foreground.

new sources of income, the repeal of hateful constraints, the abolition of the insulting badges on clothes – all this, as well as rational education and the extinction of their language, will serve to weaken their own prejudices, and either will lead them to Christianity or improve their moral character and make them useful citizens.' To this end, Joseph's Letters-Patent, allowing for regional differences, freed Jews from the obligation to wear a yellow badge and to pay a multitude of special taxes, dues, fees, and tolls; allowed them to enter crafts and trades and apprentice themselves to Christian masters; to employ Christian servants; to engage in agriculture; to enter the imperial universities; they were allowed to leave their homes on Sundays and Christian holidays before midday; and Jews were encouraged to enter the haulage trade and to establish factories. But Joseph also confined the use of Hebrew to religious purposes and introduced some degree of supervision over the curriculum in Jewish educational institutions. At the very end of his reign, Emperor Joseph took the revolutionary step of imposing on his Jewish subjects liability to military service (though he did make appropriate modification to the customary oath, omitting reference to Jesus).

Jews or citizens?

In France, the first two years of the revolution gave equality of rights to the Sephardi Jews of Bordeaux and the Ashkenazi Jews of Alsace. But in doing so it exacted a price whereby the Jew lost his independence and membership of a corporate communal body. Indeed, this was the precondition of emancipation. This was made clear in December 1789, when the National Assembly discussed Jewish enfranchizement and Count Stanislaus de Clermont-Tonnerre declared: 'Everything must be refused to the Jews as a nation; everything must be granted to them as individuals. They must be citizens. It is claimed that they do not wish to be citizens. Let them say so and let them be banished; there cannot be a nation within a nation. . . .'

Some fifteen years later, Napoleon underlined the new status of the Jews in France and, indeed, also of others elsewhere in the empire. In 1806 he summoned an Assembly of Jewish Notables of 111 delegates (including fifteen rabbis, the remainder, wealthy individuals in property, banking, commerce and industry) from France, the Rhine provinces of the empire and northern Italy. In response to twelve questions presented by Napoleon, this body assured the emperor that no impediment, religious or otherwise, stood between the Jew and his complete and utter allegiance to his French fatherland: 'All our principles make it a duty for us to love Frenchmen as our brothers.' Rabbinical authority, solidarity with fellow-Jews outside the empire, the laws governing money-lending – nothing prevented a Jew from identifying himself completely with the interests of the French nation. Only in respect of intermarriage with Christians – such as Napoleon wished to encourage – did the Assembly refrain from giving the answer sought, insofar as it declared that no rabbi could sanction such a marriage, although the Jewish spouse would not for that reason cease to be considered a Jew by his brethren.

The following year, in 1807, a Sanhedrin of 71 members (45 rabbis, 26 laymen) met at Napoleon's

The ideals of the French Revolution included religious liberty, with the result that many European Jews suddenly found themselves granted full civil rights. This medal was struck in 1796 to celebrate the granting of such rights to the Jewish citizens of the short-lived Batavian Republic of the Netherlands.

instruction to give religious and universal sanction to the declaration already made by the Assembly, for the Sanhedrin was explicitly directed at the total corpus of Israel. Henceforth, the Jews of France were organized in consistories: there were 7 in France, 6 in the German provinces, 5 in Italy and 4 in Holland. They were to ensure that no unauthorized religious services were conducted, to encourage Israelites 'to exercise useful occupations' and to inform the authorities of the number of Israelite conscripts. The duty of the rabbis in each consistory was to teach religion, to inculcate obedience to the laws, 'particularly those relating to the defence of the country', and to make Israelites regard military service 'as a sacred duty'. It would seem that Napoleon degraded the rabbi, formerly a judge and arbitrator, to the status of recruiting agent for the Grande Armée. But it is true that through the consistorial system he established an enduring structure for the development of religious and communal life in France.

The Tsarist Empire, too, sought to integrate the Jews into the body of the state, to make them useful subjects, to regenerate them and rehabilitate them, in the jargon of the time. The attempt was all the more ludicrous in that the Jews of the Tsarist Empire constituted a nationality whose institutions – linguistic, religious, educational, judicial, charitable – perhaps more than in any other area of Jewish settlement, formed a literate civilization, in contrast with the ignorant and serf-ridden Russian environment. In practical terms, moreover, the establishment of the Pale of Settlement, which, from the 1790s onward, confined the vast bulk of Russian Jewry to the western provinces of the empire, inevitably halted any inroads that assimilation might otherwise have made. Similarly, the growing amount of legislation concerning taxes, residence, occupation, etc. that applied to Jews alone also intensified the differences between them and the rest of the population.

None of this internal contradiction, however, deterred any of the tsars from seeking to assimilate the Jews. The comparatively benign Jewish Statute of 1804, promulgated by Alexander I, reduced the powers of the communities and also sought to encourage Jews to undertake agricultural colonization, particularly in 'New Russia', the southern Ukraine, as a means of reducing their dependence on the liquor trade as a source of livelihood. Later in his reign, Alexander inaugurated the policy of

expelling Jews from rural areas (e.g. from villages in the provinces of Vitebsk and Moghilev) in the supposed interests of the exploited peasants.

Even this hardship was exceeded by Nicholas I, Alexander's successor. He it was who conscripted boys from the age of twelve into special 'cantonist' schools, where they would be prepared for military service of twenty-five years, and converted to Christianity. This would train a new generation to become leaders of their people. In 1835, the liberal Russian émigré, Alexander Herzen, met a battalion of such boys (near Perm, in the Urals):

> Poor unfortunate children! The boys of twelve or thirteen managed somehow to stand up, but the little ones of eight and nine. . . . No artist's brush could paint the horror.

Later in his reign, Nicholas dissolved the Jewish autonomous organizations in a further attempt to uproot Judaism, and to the same end sought to introduce a system of secular schooling, though he did not reveal its ultimate aims of Christianization. He invited a Jewish educationist, Max Lilienthal, the principal of a Jewish school, newly established on Western lines at Riga, to co-operate. Lilienthal accepted and did, indeed, meet with support, not only from the tsarist government, of course, but also from certain wealthy assimilationists, e.g. a certain Nisan Rosenthal of Vilna. Members of the younger generation in Vilna also welcomed Lilienthal, but the overwhelming majority was hostile. 'The course pursued against all denominations but the Greek', said the elders of the community, 'proves clearly that the government intends to have but one church in the whole empire . . . we put no confidence in the new [educational] measures proposed by the ministerial council and we look with gloomy foreboding into the future.'

The tyranny of Nicholas I came to grief in the Crimean War. The liberalizing and modernizing policies of the 1860s – emancipation of the serfs, introduction of elected organs of local self-government, judicial reforms, etc. – had their parallel in the Jewish realm. Not only was the conscription of minors brought to an end, but it also became possible for the better educated and wealthier Jews to live outside the Pale; Jews could enter state services (e.g. as physicians) and live in cities within the Pale formerly closed to Jews (e.g. Kiev). Jewish society responded eagerly to measures such as these. The 1860s was a period that saw a considerable degree of rapprochement between the Jew and his Russian environment. In this heady atmosphere, Judah Lev Gordon wrote his celebrated poem, *Awake, my people*: 'Be a man when you go out and a Jew in your tent, a brother to your fellow citizens and a servant to your king.' Russia, 'this land of Eden', will be open to you and 'her sons will now call you brethren.'

In the economic sphere, a Jewish middle and upper class crystallized out of the incipient industrialization of the empire. Important examples were the participation by Jews in the Ukrainian sugar industry, the enlargement of the Russian railway network, water transport, the oil industry in the Caucasus and in private banking.

At the cultural level, an important development was the increased entry of young Jews into Russian universities. This facility was appreciated to the full.

Take, for example, the case of the eighteen-year-old Vladimir Harkavy, the future Moscow jurist, who in 1864 matriculated, with a friend, at the University of Moscow:

> When we came out of the old university building, we crossed to the other side of the street and, respectfully doffing our hats, bowed before the sanctuary that had opened its doors to us, and we embraced each other. Proudly we walked home, eager to shout to everyone we met: Have you heard? We are students. All at once it was as though the alienation from the Christians around us had gone. We felt like members of a new society in which there were neither Jews nor Greeks.

In this new atmosphere of optimism, engendered by a measure of liberal policy and economic advancement, the Pale of Settlement, especially the urban centres, was the scene of a veritable ferment of ideas and publications (all the more so now that tsarist censorship was relaxed). Reformers and traditionalists, Hebraizers and Russifiers, Yiddishists and Westernizers struggled for a hearing. A dominant trend was that favoured by the Haskalah, the Jewish enlightenment, which preached assimilation into the dominant Russian culture. This trend enjoyed the support of the newly founded Society for the Promotion of Culture among Jews, a body established under the patronage of a circle of wealthy St Petersburg Jews. It functioned under the supervision of the Ministry of Education. It had three aims: to encourage acquisition of the Russian language by Jews, to subsidize poor Jewish pupils in the state schools and to publish works of useful knowledge.

Side by side with these developments, an antisemitic reaction took shape. It was fed by the traditional Christian sources but drew also on more recent phenomena, such as the pan-Slav nationalism inflamed by the Polish rebellion of 1863, the left-wing and populist identification of the Jew with capitalist and exploiter, the right-wing view of the Jew as subversive and trouble-maker. Dostoevsky combined all three hallucinations: 'The Jew and his bank now dominate everything, Europe and Enlightenment, the whole civilization, especially socialism, for with its help the Jew will eradicate Christianity – and destroy the Christian civilization. Then nothing is left but anarchy. The Jew will command everything.'

At the end of the 1870s a discriminatory note already entered certain legislation, e.g. in respect of military and jury service and local government positions. Criticism could also be heard of the number of Jewish students at secondary schools and universities. But not even a pogrom at Odessa in 1871 could have prepared the Jews for the events that took place a decade later, a few weeks after the assassination of Alexander II. Beginning at Elizavetgrad in the Ukraine, pogroms spread to other towns and villages in the southern and eastern Ukraine. Looting, arson, rape and beating were the hallmarks of mob violence. But what finally destroyed the hope of a Russo-Jewish rapprochement, in all save the wealthiest and most assimilated Jewish circles, was the deafening silence with which the majority of liberals, radicals and populists looked on at the pogroms, if indeed there were not some who benignly saw in them welcome signs of peasant revolt.

The West: from Napoleon to 1848

Events in Western Europe took an altogether different path. True, in no country did emancipation proceed without friction. In France, Napoleon's Infamous Decree of 1808 annulled the work of the revolution insofar as it forbade a Jew to engage in trade unless he had first obtained a prefectorial licence; it virtually cancelled all debts owed to Jewish money-lenders; it prohibited Jews from settling in certain départements of Alsace, or elsewhere in France if they did not purchase land and engage solely in agriculture. The decree was valid for ten years, i.e. until 1818, by which time, of course, the Restoration had robbed it of all its power.

In England, there existed few of the occupational and none of the residential restrictions that dominated and obstructed Jewish life elsewhere. The 25,000 English Jews at the beginning of the 19th century enjoyed a measure of social acceptance, religious freedom and economic status that was without parallel in Europe. The Board of Deputies took the lead in agitating for Jewish rights under its president, Sir Moses Montefiore, but mindful of the fact that the most vociferous fighters for emancipation also supported religious reform (e.g. Sir David Salomons) Montefiore moved with caution, 'most firmly resolved not to give up the smallest part of our religious forms and principles to obtain civil rights.'

In Prussia, the Edict of Emancipation of 1812 recognized the citizenship of all Jews living in the state and conferred on them the same civic rights, duties and freedoms that Christians enjoyed. But matters relating to Jewish educational bodies, religious organizations and the admission of Jews to governmental and administrative posts were left to later legislation. What the Prussian state conceded in the wake of defeat and in the context of its rejuvenation did not survive unharmed, and in practice the implementation of the edict was whittled down.

However, measures of this kind could not undo a deepening rapprochement already existing between Jews and Germans in the intellectual and social spheres. An early example was the friendship of Lessing and Moses Mendelssohn. At this time, also, Solomon Maimon, a prodigy and autodidact from Lithuania, was expounding the new philosophy of Kant to German readers. In a later generation, the salons of Rahel Varnhagen and Henriette Herz in Berlin and Fanny Arnstein in Vienna brought together writers, intellectuals, scientists, statesmen, poets and reformers.

Thus the new régime in Western Europe was unquestionably popular among the bulk of Jews affected. Could it be otherwise? Emancipation offered the opportunity to enter the political struggle in person and thereby shape the Jewish future and the future in general; it brought the academic world closer; it offered the opportunity to partake of the advantages offered by the burgeoning capitalist economy. In all these respects the majority of Jews must necessarily find themselves aligned with the forces of change, political and economic. Hence, also, the attraction of the capitalist system of production, for this brought the 'uninterrupted disturbance of all social conditions. . . . All fixed, fast frozen relations, with their train of ancient and venerable prejudices and opinions, are swept away, all new-formed ones become antiquated before they can ossify' (*Com-*

The Emperor Franz Josef's visit to the Goldberger textile factory at Buda in 1859 was proudly recorded by the local Illustriertes Israelisches Jahrbuch.

munist *Manifesto*). Such a revolutionary movement must necessarily have contributed to the political and economic liberation of the Jew.

This latter showed itself in the contrast between the occupational distribution of Jews in undeveloped Posen as compared with the more advanced western provinces of Prussia. In 1834, for example, of every 1,000 Jews engaged in the professions as doctors and teachers there were 30 in Posen and 43 in the rest of Prussia; the figures for bankers, large merchants and manufacturers were, respectively, 6 and 45; for retailers, commercial agents, inn-keepers, the figures were 348 and 493; for artisans, 237 and 100; for unspecified occupations, 213 and 65. What the figures show overall is that there were almost three times as many professional men, rentiers and big business men in the western provinces of Prussia as in Posen; that in Posen there were more than twice as many artisans and a far higher proportion of nondescript workers. This trend away from handicrafts and towards the professions, industry and commerce became more and more marked during the 19th century.

The nature of Jewish participation in politics in Western and central Europe showed itself equally aligned with the new forces causing agitation in Europe, especially in the revolutionary years of 1848–9. The revolutions in central and Western Europe embraced an area inhabited by perhaps around half a million Jews. In France, the revolution in the first cabinet formed after the February uprising brought to power two Jews,

Adolphe Crémieux, Minister of Justice, and Michel Goudchaux, Minister of Finance. In Vienna, Adolph Fischhof, a young doctor, found himself head of the committee on security, the highest governing body of the revolution. The Prussian Assembly included the physicians Jacoby and Kosch. The Frankfurt Parliament included Gabriel Riesser as second vice-president, and other prominent personalities such as Veit, Hartmann and Kuranda, the journalists and publishers. Further to the left, as publicists, pamphleteers and agitators, stood Marx, Hess, Bamberger and Lasker. None of those men fought as Jews, exclusively or primarily, for full Jewish emancipation. Rather, if they considered the matter at all, it was wholly subsumed under the extension of human rights. In no case, however, did the short-lived revolutionary constitutions immediately advance the cause of Jewish emancipation. When this came, it did so through the extension of Prussian rule under Bismarck and associated economic developments, e.g. the Zollverein. In Austria–Hungary, only the liberal constitution of 1867, after many false starts, brought complete equality.

What the revolutions did demonstrate was the sheer difficulty of being a Jew in certain crucial areas. In Posen, for example, where Poles confronted Germans; in Hungary, the battleground of Magyars and Croats; in Bohemia where Czechs stood against Austrians – where did the Jew stand? In general they took the higher culture – German and Magyar – which inevitably provoked the xenophobia of Poles, Croats, Czechs. While the less developed nations were held in check, however, the full consequences of the Jewish dilemma were not apparent.

The ambiguity of emancipation

In the meantime the impulse towards assimilation proceeded apace. It had both positive and negative features. Among the former must certainly be counted that movement of scholarship known as *die Wissenschaft des Judentums* – the science of Judaism – which resulted from the application to Jewish history, philosophy, biblical exegesis, jurisprudence, etc. of those principles of research developed in the Christian world, primarily at the German universities. True, the founder of *die Wissenschaft des Judentums*, Leopold Zunz, had apologetic motives; true, also, that initially he looked on his endeavours as the mere attempt to preserve the memory of a dying culture and belief – for all that, the methods of Zunz and his co-workers stimulated a vast movement of scholarship that revolutionized Jewish learning.

The negative feature of emancipation was manifest in religious reform, which sought to assimilate the form and liturgy of traditional Jewish synagogal worship to the model of the Christian environment. Here the pattern was set by the New Israelite Temple in Hamburg, in 1818, which devised services complete with organ and vocal accompaniment and used a prayer-book in which German texts took the place of Hebrew prayers and from which supplications for the return to Zion, the restoration of the sacrificial cult and a personal Messiah were eliminated.

Despite all attempts at the denationalization of Judaism, despite all identification with the environment, despite the failure of the Halacha (legal tradition) to meet the demands of an unprecedented situation, the Jews continued to exist as a distinct entity, in some sense, irrespective of their political allegiance as Frenchmen, Russians, Englishmen, etc. Indeed, it might be said that in the second half of the 19th century they became more evident than ever before, through the triple processes of urbanization, demographic growth and occupational diversification. The unusual and problematic nature of Jewish existence, which combined citizenship in one country with a world-wide allegiance to, and some degree of solidarity with, fellow-Jews, subject to a different political entity, became more and more pronounced. In 1840–1, English and French Jews, led by Sir Moses Montefiore and Adolphe Crémieux, came together to rescue the threatened Jews of Damascus following a blood libel, in which a number of local Damascus Jews were accused of murdering a Capuchin friar and his Muslim servant in order to use their blood for purposes of the Passover. French Jews founded the Alliance Israélite Universelle in 1860 to safeguard the interests of Jews elsewhere; British Jews in 1870 created a parallel body in the form of the Anglo-Jewish Association. In 1877–8 at the Congress of Berlin, Jewish notables from England, France and Germany came together to try to improve the lot of the Jews of Russia and newly independent Romania. Such phenomena belied the hopes of the emancipationists – the Jews, though weakened and debilitated, had clearly survived emancipation.

But by this very token, of course, they had failed to keep their side of the bargain struck earlier in the century. This realization was undoubtedly one factor behind the resurgence of antisemitism in the decade of the 1880s. Although the term was first used only in 1879 by the German journalist, Wilhelm Marr, the notion rapidly developed such momentum as to constitute on its own a veritable political programme. Antisemitism could be presented as an answer to the malaise endured by a society in which Christianity was increasingly threatened by a materialistic and critical outlook and in which old-established ways of life were yielding to both the spread of large-scale industry and the development of collective labour organizations. But there were also causes specific to individual areas: in France, resentment at defeat by Prussia in 1871; in Austria, the decline of the German element in relation to the Slav; in Germany, the role of Jews in cultural and intellectual life. Drumont's *La France juive*, first published in 1886, with its thesis of the corruption of France by the Jews as part of a plan to dominate the country, was one of the most successful antisemitic works ever published. The Christian-Social party in Germany, organized by the Protestant pastor and court preacher, Adolf Stöcker, sought to combat social-democracy and use antisemitism as a means to reconcile the workers to the throne and the church. Stöcker himself presided over the first International Anti-Jewish Congress, at Dresden in 1882. In Vienna, Lueger was repeatedly elected mayor on an antisemitic programme that exploited the displacement of the Viennese lower middle class and craftsmen; in 1882, a trial for ritual murder took place at Tisza-Eszlar in Hungary. What distinguished the antisemitism of the 1880s from earlier manifestations of anti-Judaism was its biological basis, in that it ascribed to the Jew an inferior and noxious physiological status. This constituted a hereditary and irredeemable taint that rendered all talk of emancipation and assimilation a mortal danger to Christian Europe.

The Jews of Russia bore the main brunt of suffering. The pogrom of 1881 was followed by others in 1883 (Rostov, Yekaterinoslav) and in 1884 (Nizhni Novgorod). Legislative measures accompanied the pogroms: the May Laws of 1882, which forbade the acquisition by Jews of rural property, the expulsion of Jews from Moscow, the imposition of a quota for Jewish students in secondary schools and universities.

The increase in the Jewish population accentuated the misery of the situation. It appears that between 1820 and 1880 the number of Jews in the empire (except the Caucasus) grew from 1,600,000 to 4,000,000. This increase of 150 per cent far exceeded the general increase of 87 per cent. By 1910 the number of Jews had further grown to more than 5,600,000, and this after several decades of mass emigration. There was a direct relationship between population growth and poverty, given the continuing existence of the Pale of Settlement. It meant that an increasing number of artisans and middlemen of various types, who formed the bulk of breadwinners, were forced to ever more fierce competition among themselves for a limited market. Jewish artisans lacked capital, tools, access to credit and stocks of raw materials and were frequently driven into the ranks of those with no secure occupation. In cities such as Odessa, Vilna, Bialystok, Lodz and Warsaw, a Jewish proletariat of some 300,000 did indeed come into existence, but its remoteness from the main centres of Russian industry, outside the Pale, and its consequent marginality, is shown by the fact that only 50,000 were employed in medium- and large-scale factories, mainly related to the textile and tobacco trades. The vast bulk was employed in establishments that were little better than workshops. The mass poverty was such that at the turn of the century about one-third of Russian Jews depended on the relief provided by Jewish organizations.

The first response to a deteriorating economic and political situation was emigration. This was, of course, the classical age of migration from Europe to the West, but its scope in Jewish terms far exceeded that of any other people. About 2,750,000 Jews left Eastern Europe between 1881 and 1914 – slightly under 2,000,000 from Russia, nearly 500,000 from Austria-Hungary, 150,000 from Romania and 200,000 from other countries. Given that the world Jewish population was about 10,000,000 at this time, one in four of world Jewry was on the move. Such a proportion had no parallel elsewhere. Two million Jews settled in the United States. Other major centres of reception were Canada, Argentina, Britain, Palestine and South Africa. The overall result was to produce an entirely new map of world Jewry in which the Western dimension unprecedentedly balanced the Eastern. At the local level, the face of whole communities was transformed.

To those Jews who stayed in Russia, a solution was also sought in socialism and radical political activity. In general the Socialist movement overlooked the national problem and supported the illusion that the problem exemplified a false consciousness that the revolution

The new synagogue in Pest, opened in 1859. Architects searching for a suitably non-Christian style for synagogues often fell back upon Islamic.

would cure. This can be seen as a left-wing pendant to the right-wing illusion of those Liberal and Reform Jews who sought to drain Jewishness of its national content. From Marx, the Social-democratic movement inherited a view that identified Judaism with the characteristics of bourgeois materialism, a problem only to be resolved by a social revolution. Thus: 'the *social* emancipation of Jewry is the *emancipation* of society from Judaism,' Marx wrote. At best, Jews were a caste, already in the process of disappearing under the influence of industrialization. To propose anything in the nature of special Jewish rights, therefore, or even to acknowledge the existence of a distinct Jewish question, was a retrograde and reactionary step, a move that would preserve the very ghetto. This was the attitude of most of the Jewish leaders of European socialism – Lassalle, Luxemburg, the older Martov, Trotsky, Viktor Adler, Otto Bauer, etc.

Only in Russia was the attempt made to take seriously the problem posed by the national dimension. This was the task that the General League of Jewish Workingmen in Lithuania, Poland and Russia – more generally known as the Bund – set itself. The Bund was founded in 1897 at Vilna, and had as its aim, in the programme enunciated by Arkadi Kremer, the Bund's moving spirit, 'not only the struggle for general Russian political demands; it will also have the special task of defending the specific interest of the Jewish workers, carry on the struggle for their civic rights and above all combat the discriminatory anti-Jewish laws. That is because the Jewish workers suffer not only as workers but also as Jews, and we dare not and cannot remain indifferent at such a time.' Within the next few years, however, the Bund, partly under the influence of the historian Dubnow, had to move in a more 'nationalistic' line as its analysis of the Jewish situation was bedevilled by the absence of a Jewish territorial concentration. By way of compensation it began to emphasize the cultural grounds of Jewish nationalism and to demand for Russian Jewry not only civil and political emancipation but also national-cultural

autonomy. This did not inhibit its growth or its role in giving a worthwhile identity to the Jewish worker, who was increasingly alienated from the official or self-appointed leaders of Russian Jewry. The Bund, in other words, was not only a political party but also a way of life that gave a cultural and social framework to individuals caught up within a rapidly changing and hostile environment. The worker had lost his place within the traditional Jewish community, but the Bund preserved for him some of his ancient bonds with the past.

Radical though the Bund's Marxist analysis of the situation in Russia might be, this did not compare in ruthlessness with that propounded by the first spokesman of Russian Territorialism, Leon Pinsker. Pinsker's volte-face in 1882, when he published his *Auto-Emancipation!* at the suggestion of Arthur Cohen, Member of Parliament and president of the Board of Deputies of British Jews in London, epitomizes the role of a generation. Until 1881, Pinsker, a graduate in medicine of the University of Moscow, had been an adherent of the Haskalah and active in the Society for the Promotion of Culture among Jews, but the pogrom of that year forced him to renounce his earlier hopes. His notion of antisemitism conformed so closely to that of an existing proto-Zionist movement that he willingly became associated with it and, indeed, its principal exponent.

The birth of Zionism

This, then, was the third response of Russian Jewry to the events of 1881: there was emigration, there was socialism and there was Zionism. In its initial stages, the Lovers of Zion movement was predominantly successful among professional men and the Jewish middle class. Pinsker himself was a medical man and it is typical that two others present at the meeting in 1883 were Emanuel Mandelshtamm, the ophthalmologist of Kiev University, and Hirsch (Herman) Schapira, a mathematician who later became professor of mathematics at Heidelberg. At a meeting in Kattowitz in 1884, the thirty delegates were mainly middle-aged and middle class; rabbis, free professional men, merchants and manufacturers, and men of letters. Later, the movement broadened its appeal. A socialist Zionist movement developed. This was finally established in 1906 under the name of Poalei Zion – Workers of Zion – under the lead of Nahman Syrkin and Ber Borokhov. With it came the beginning of mass immigration into Palestine. Between 1881 and 1914 the number of Jewish settlers amounted to some 50,000.

In the meantime, a Zionist movement with a decidedly different emphasis came into existence in Western Europe. This had antecedents in the work of Moses Hess, but owed incomparably more to the thought and activity of Theodor Herzl.

Herzl was born in Budapest in 1860, and moved with his family to Vienna where he graduated in law, practised as a lawyer but won far greater fame as a journalist and playwright. His evolution in regard to the Jewish question was more radical but not wholly dissimilar to that of Hess and even Pinsker, in that Herzl at first saw the solution in terms of a mass Jewish conversion to Christianity; however, his experience of antisemitism convinced him that another solution must be found: a Jewish state, a secure haven for those Jews threatened by, or actually subject to, antisemitism. Herzl, unlike those liberals entranced by emancipation, understood that emancipation not only failed to bring with it an increased degree of tolerance, but in fact brought intolerance by virtue of its very success. That a Jewish state might be elsewhere than the Holy Land never became a serious possibility. What did emerge from Herzl's endeavours, and the Basel Conference that he fathered in 1897, was the attempt to win the support of the Great Powers for the principal claim in the Basel Programme: the object of Zionism was 'to establish for the Jewish people a publicly and legally assured home in Palestine.'

In the meantime, the First World War was fast transforming the circumstances of Jewish life, especially in the multi-national empires of Russia and Austria-Hungary. With the collapse of the former in March 1917, emancipation and civil and political equality were at once proclaimed. Russian Jewry seized its chance to implement a system of national autonomy within the liberated empire by summoning a Congress: 'Citizens, Jews! The Jewish people in Russia now faces an event which has no parallel in Jewish history for two thousand years. Not only has the Jew as an individual, as a citizen, acquired equality of rights ... but the Jewish nation looks forward to the possibility of securing national rights.' Elections to the Congress were held in January 1918. The Zionists received some 60 per cent of the vote, the socialist parties in combination 25 per cent, and the Orthodox 12 per cent. Given the fundamental divergences among their standpoints it is difficult to visualize any degree of consensus on the form of Jewish autonomy that might be implemented. But by 1918, of course, the Bolsheviks had formed their government and the projected Jewish Congress never met.

In any case, the future was determined less by political action than by actual violence. In circumstances of civil war, revolution and counter-revolution, the Jews attracted the enmity of all parties involved. This was above all true in eastern Poland and the Ukraine, in 1919–21, where warring gangs perpetrated massacres on a scale that directly anticipated those instigated by the Germans twenty years later. The collapse of the multinational Tsarist Empire, in itself, facilitated the emergence of an antisemitism that derived from a powerful combination of Christianity and hitherto frustrated nationalism. In these years, in more than 500 communities, over 156,000 Jews fell victim to the attack of Ukrainians, White Russians, Poles and the Red Army. The number of separate outrages exceeded 1,200. Thus far, the revolution had brought nothing but suffering and economic catastrophe to the millions of Russian Jews.

Revolution and war

When the revolution did establish itself in power, it brought a decidedly ambiguous message. On the one hand, it made a sincere attempt to repress overt antisemitism and in this it was, apparently, largely successful (though antisemitism was certainly used as a political weapon by Stalin in his struggle against Trotsky in the later 1920s). On the other hand, the Jews of Russia suffered in their dual capacity as a religious entity that was reactionary by definition, and as a national-political entity that lacked the concentrated territorial nature of other ethnic minorities. Moreover, any cultural or political manifestations that smacked of separatism, e.g. Zionism or Bundism or the study of Hebrew, automatically conflicted with the Bolshevik political monopoly and must be suppressed.

The principal agents of Bolshevik policy were the Jewish sections of the Communist Party. Hardly were they formed in 1918 than they formally dissolved the *kehilla* (community) structure of religious Jews. Henceforth, the main functions of the sections were to destroy the old Jewish order, to bring Bolshevism to the 'Jewish street' and to rebuild Jewish national life on the basis of a secular Yiddish culture. In the early 1930s one such 'educator' illustrated precisely the intellectual content of such a national life:

> First, the Sabbath day of rest was abolished. Second all books with a nationalist colouring were removed. Those steps enabled the school to raise the level of instruction and to include anti-religious and international subject-matter in its curriculum. . . . The very concept of 'Jewish history' is alien to the school.

However, cultural impoverishment accompanied occupational advance and diversification. This applied all the more in the conditions of industrialization and labour shortage. The pattern of central and Western Europe reproduced itself in Soviet Russia. In respect of urbanization, for example, the Jewish population of Moscow grew from 8,100 in 1895 to 131,000 in 1926, and to perhaps 350,000 by 1939; that of Leningrad (St Petersburg) from 17,000 in 1895 to 84,500 in 1926, and to some 250,000 in 1939; and that of Kiev from 32,000 in 1895 to 140,000 in 1926. In the main, this process was unaffected by the parallel effort of the establishment of Jewish farming communities in the southern Ukraine and the Crimea, and the establishment in Biro-Bidzhan of a Jewish autonomous region. It is clear that young Russian Jews benefitted from the educational opportunities earlier than their non-Jewish contemporaries, particularly in the less developed constituent republics of the Soviet Union; for example, in White Russia and the Ukraine in 1926–7 Jewish medical students formed 46.6 per cent and 44.8 per cent, respectively, of all medical students. Other heavily favoured faculties were economics, industry and technology. Later, by 1938, the proportion of Jewish students at universities and colleges declined to 13 per cent, though their absolute number continued to grow. Already, on the eve of war, these figures were reflected in the fact that of 1,400,000 gainfully employed Jews in Russia nearly 18 per cent (25,000) earned their livelihood in the liberal professions. Such phenomena are remarkable testimony to the unity of certain aspects of the Jewish experience in Europe; there was not all that much difference between the degree of urbanization and occupational concentration in the totalitarian Soviet Union and that elsewhere in Europe. Paris, London, Vienna, Warsaw and Berlin were as important as Moscow and Leningrad.

Not only did the First World War create the conditions in which Bolshevism could establish itself in Russia, but by encouraging national self-determination it also fostered a number of new political units (e.g. Poland, Hungary, the Baltic States), with the inevitable harmful consequences for minorities without units, such as the Jews. It was this awareness that emboldened the Jews of Lithuania, for example, even before the war had ended, to struggle for either a greater Lithuania that would include the Jewish centres of Grodno and Bialystok, or a Lithuanian federation with Russia, or a Lithuanian 'state of nationals' rather than a 'national Lithuania'.

At Versailles, the attempt was made to safeguard the religious, civil, cultural and political rights of minorities by means of the 'minorities treaties'. In the ephemeral Ukrainian republic and in Lithuania, another solution was sought by way of statutory constitutional provision for a degree of Jewish autonomy. But neither minority rights nor constitutional provision had any great success. With the singular exceptions of Czechoslovakia and Bulgaria, the status and security of the Jews of Eastern, south-eastern and central Europe steadily worsened during the interwar years. The virtual end to all hope of emigration to the Western world aggravated an already desperate situation.

Even in Poland, where these circumstances were at their worst – or, perhaps, especially in Poland – there were attempts to preserve a continuity of Jewish existence. Here, where the three million Jews constituted almost ten per cent of the population, all shades of outlook developed educational and political institutions – Zionist, Yiddish and traditional Orthodox. The *yeshivas* of Mir, Lublin and Kamenetz enjoyed world-wide renown. The cultural level and diversity of Polish Jewry is further shown in Poland's position as a publishing centre. In 1928, for example, 622 Yiddish works were printed. In 1930, 180 Jewish periodical publications were issued, 135 in Yiddish, 28 in Polish, 16 in Hebrew. But none of this could disguise the continuously increasing impoverishment of Polish Jews through the state's policy of eliminating them from the considerable number of sectors of the economy that it controlled, in which it enjoyed the enthusiastic support of the Church. In some communities, as many as half of the Jews were wholly or partly dependent on communal funds.

Towards the holocaust

Not Poland but Germany most fully expressed the polarity of achievement and persecution. German Jewry was already in an advanced state of demographic decline. A noteworthy analysis of intermarriage and sterility by A. Theilhaber (1911) showed that of every 100 Jewish girls born fifty years earlier, the 55 who married Jews produced only 118 children; 18 married non-Jews; 22 remained spinsters or childless; 2 were baptized; and 3 had illegitimate children. By the early 1930s, deaths in the German Jewish community outnumbered births, and almost half the community was over forty-five.

This decline did not, however, prevent German-speaking Jewry from assuming a position of incomparable achievement in the world of thought. It suffices to mention the names of Freud and Einstein. In other fields there was an abundance of outstanding talent, in some cases perhaps genius. Lazarus and Steinthal created the science of social psychology; Hermann Cohen renewed Kantian philosophy in the 19th and 20th centuries; Bloch and Horkheimer accomplished a similar task for Marxism; Simmel and Oppenheimer gave new impetus to the study of society; Kafka, Kraus and Schnitzler brought modernism to the novel, drama and the short story; Schoenberg revolutionized modern music. So far as the science of Judaism is concerned, the tradition of scholarship established in the 19th century was fully maintained in the 20th at institutions such as the Jüdisch-Theologisches Seminar in Breslau and the Rabbiner-Seminar für das orthodoxe Judentum, and the Hochschule für die Wissenschaft des Judentums in Berlin. At Frankfurt, the Freie Jüdische Lehrhaus, an entirely new scholarly centre, came into being, which will always be associated with the person of Franz Rosenzweig. In his *Stern der Erlösung* (*Star of Redemption*, 1921) he produced a striking rationale of Jewish existence in the Diaspora, but subject to Jewish law, such as no Jewish thinker had produced since the problem had first arisen. Jewish achievements outside Judaism proper were of comparable stature; so much so indeed that the intellectual climate of the interwar world, especially in the Weimar Republic, was largely determined by persons of Jewish origin.

Richard Wagner sounded the Gentile alarm as early as 1850 in his *Judaism in Music*, which reviled the Jewish role in the decay of modern art, as Wagner saw it. This was indeed a familiar theme in German thought, and to some extent elsewhere. But only in Germany did it reach murderous dimensions, no matter how many accomplices the Germans found throughout Europe. European history, as a whole, was indeed 'the seedbed of the Holocaust' (J. L. Talmon). In 1933 the age of emancipation came to an end.

This was by no means clear at the time. Even from Germany itself the emigration statistics reveal that it took some years for the full awareness of irreversible exclusion to be accepted. Of the approximately 500,000 Jews in Germany in 1933, about 150,000 left between then and the middle of 1938. Not until the pogrom in

November of that year did the rate accelerate. By the outbreak of war, that is, in one year alone, another 100,000–150,000 emigrated. What also marked the Jewish response in Germany to the onset of Nazism was an efflorescence of educational endeavour, which took shape as a form of resistance to oppression and persecution.

It was outside Germany, however, that the further implications of Nazism and the general plight of European Jews were grasped; Jabotinsky, for example, called for the evacuation of the Jewish community of Poland in the face of accumulated Polish enmity and cruelty. One and a half million Jews must be evacuated to Palestine within the next ten years, Jabotinsky urged. 'Liquidate the *Galut* or the *Galut* will liquidate you.' But this was a forlorn hope. Even in a country such as Great Britain, which had great traditions of tolerance and welcome, there was little disposition to admit refugees from Europe. The Foreign Office argued that to seek to defend the position of a minority in Germany or elsewhere might in fact do positive harm to the minority. Both the Foreign and the Colonial Offices maintained restrictions on immigration to Palestine, fearful lest Arab sympathies be jeopardized. The British colonies in Asia and Africa were also closed, out of deference to the prejudices of the white settlers. The Dominions were sovereign states and the Dominion Office could not bring pressure on them to mitigate a policy of exclusion. As for the Home Office, it could consider only individual cases – whereas the need was collective. Interested pressure groups, such as physicians and dentists, supported this limitation.

If in Britain this was the case, then elsewhere it could certainly be no better. Indeed, so frustrated was the need for refuge that it at length forced a further radical review of the whole political programme of the emancipation that had dominated European Jewish thinking since the Enlightenment. The first such review was the Zionist; the second took shape in 1939. In the year that celebrated the 150th anniversary of the outbreak of the French Revolution, the question was first posed in a Yiddish periodical, *Oifn Sheydeveg* (*At the Crossroads*), as to the value of emancipation. What had it brought to its adherents? Was it not a delusion? Had the time not come to reject the universalist ideals of emancipation and return to the values of Judaism, the world of the ghetto? The reply by the great historian Simon Dubnow, 'What should one do in Haman's Times?', fully accepted the reality of Hitler's 'system of extermination' and mentioned indeed 'the tremendous battle [to] save European Jewry from extinction.' But it refused to take up the challenge, and spoke rather of the economic and moral blockade that world Jewry could impose on its German persecutors. 'We must fight against the plague of the Hitler expulsions and not drop our hands and sigh that emancipation has deceived us. You will say that the German Expulsion may be duplicated in Eastern Europe, but there they have already tasted of Hitlerism and they had to line up with the anti-aggression bloc of the democratic countries against those world bandits. When the anti-aggression movement succeeds in liberating Europe, its Jewish part will also be liberated.'

This was not so. When Europe was liberated, its Jewish inhabitants, save for a remnant, had all been killed. The Germans and their fellow-criminals in what was truly 'the war against the Jews' imposed the common fate of extermination on all Continental Jewry. 'The whole exile became like a sea of fire.' The secularists and the pious, the town-dwellers and the villagers, the rich and the poor – all were consumed alike in a common holocaust, literally so.

The Germans and their accomplices throughout Europe could draw on that accumulated hatred of the Jews fostered by Christian influences over the centuries. The Jews fought back, to be sure: in the Jewish partisan and resistance groups in France, the Ukraine and elsewhere in occupied Europe, and, above all, in the revolt of the Warsaw ghetto in April and May 1943. Here, the Jews mounted the largest and longest act of armed resistance in occupied Europe (outside Yugoslavia). Jewish resistance must also be esteemed in terms of survival at the uttermost edge of death. Rabbi Oshry reports from Kovno:

> On the 6th of Heshvan 5702 [27 October 1941] two days before the great *hurban* [destruction] of the ghetto of Kovno at a time when about ten thousand people, men, women and children, were led to the slaughter before our eyes and every inhabitant of the ghetto was waiting for his bitter end, an honourable man from the town came to me crying bitterly that he was afraid that he might be forced to see his wife, children and grandchildren being slaughtered before his eyes to increase his suffering. The murderers used to take pleasure in seeing the suffering of their victims and therefore killed children in front of their parents, wives in front of their husbands and after that they tortured and killed the head of the family. As he could not stand such suffering (he was sure he would die of a heart attack) he enquired as to whether he was permitted to commit suicide, to be spared the torture and be buried in a Jewish cemetery in the Kovno ghetto.

The rabbi gave his answer:

> One can be sure that he will be subject to terrible sufferings. Nevertheless, one is certainly not permitted to declare it in public as a clear decision that we may commit suicide in such circumstances, as through this action support is given to our enemies, who many times wondered why the Jews did not commit suicide as the Jews of Berlin did. Such an action is a *hillul Ha'Shem* [profanation of the Name] because it shows that the Jews do not trust in God to save them. It should be noted with pride that in the ghetto of Kovno there were no cases of suicide save in three instances. All the other inhabitants of the ghetto believed with perfect faith that God would not forsake his people.... (*The Echo of the Nazi Holocaust in Rabbinic Literature*)

In fact, God did forsake his people, and by the end of the war nearly six million of that people had been put to death. This is not the final answer to the problem of Jewish existence, originally posed in the conditions created by the French Revolution. It is, rather, a dreadful reminder of the precarious nature of that existence which the answer of Rabbi Oshry of Kovno could resolve no better than the optimistic philosophy of Mendelssohn.

Chapter Fourteen

American Jewry

OSCAR HANDLIN

IN THE LAST QUARTER of the 20th century, the United States is home to the largest and most influential community of Jews in the world. The six million men and women who thus identify themselves have reached America from a variety of origins through a continuing process which began in 1654 and still continues in 1979. But it is not only numbers that give these Jews their pivotal position, nor even the wealth and the political leverage that affect their co-religionists in Europe and the Near East as well. Above all, the character of life in their country challenges many traditional assumptions built into the experience of this ancient people. In America, the attitudes, customs and laws of the Old World were almost at once anachronistic. Jews live on terms of equality and intimacy with a vast number of people of other creeds and antecedents; and the freedom of that relationship is a challenge – both a potential opportunity and a potential danger. Both possibilities are evident as the 20th century draws to a close.

Jewish settlement in the United States was long incidental to and co-extensive with the great migration of Europeans to North America. The history of the Jews in the New World reflects the influence of population movements in Europe as well as the nature of the society encountered upon arrival.

In the 17th and 18th centuries, and the first two decades of the 19th, immigration was small in numbers and generally a result of commercial operations. In the sixty years down to 1880, an era of national expansion and integration, and again in the fifty years thereafter, an era of industrialization and urbanization, immigration drew enormous reserves of human beings displaced by technological change from across the face of Europe. The close of immigration in 1924 at first seemed to transform the problems Jews faced; but the expected stability did not materialize. Depression, totalitarianism and war renewed immigration and its attendant problems; the appearance of the State of Israel created, as well as resolved, difficulties; and radical changes in the cultural and social environment threatened tradition and the prospects of survival.

The Colonial period, 1654–1820

Intercontinental trade scattered the seeds of permanent Jewish settlement in the English colonies of the 17th and 18th centuries. The inhabited area reached but a short distance from the coast and held a total population of less than three million on the eve of Independence.

To this wilderness came some Jews from Brazil, the West Indies and Europe, but not many and those almost by accident. They numbered fewer than three thousand in all by 1776. Mostly they were merchants who handled the flow of goods from the farms and plantations to overseas markets. Aaron Lopez and Jacob Rodrique Rivera of Newport traded with the West Indies, the Franks family of Philadelphia had connections in London and Moses Lindo of Charleston developed the indigo exports of the South. The largest groups were in those seaports as well as in New York and Savannah and occasionally in such inland towns as Lancaster, Pennsylvania.

The Touro Synagogue of Newport reflected the wealth of its merchant members. No American congregation, however, was capable of supporting a rabbi. Most Jews were ignorant of the law and ritual and, whatever their national origin, looked for advice and guidance to London, the Imperial capital. They, therefore, tended to take over the Sephardi ritual prevalent in that city.

Laymen controlled the synagogue. Towards the end of the 18th century, though, the only permanent officer, the *hasan*, by imitation of the Christian churches, gradually took on the office of minister and assumed the title of Reverend. The synagogue was a religious organization, but it also maintained cemeteries and administered informal charitable activities. In addition, its officials sometimes supervised religious schools, ritual slaughter and the preparation of matzahs. But no community was yet strong enough to extend its functions beyond those primarily religious.

In the American Revolution, Jews, by and large, took the patriot side, although there was at least one prominent Tory among them. Their reaction was similar to that of the other merchants and other immigrants who also lacked sentimental attachments to England. Old Aaron Lopez risked his property in a flight from Newport rather than co-operate with the British; young Haym Salomon helped finance the war; and men like Benjamin Nones, Mordecai Sheftall and Francis Salvador served valiantly in the ranks.

The first decades of American independence witnessed a slow growth in the number of Jews, which had climbed to about five thousand in 1820. After the revolution, as before, they were mostly traders and enjoyed moderate prosperity.

That period also saw the attainment, almost everywhere, of full political rights. Civil rights had come as far back as 1657, when Asser Levy protested successfully against inferior status in New Amsterdam. But test acts involving an oath as a Christian were persistent impediments to office-holding until the divorce of Church and State under the new state and federal constitutions. Survivals of the old discrimination remained on the statute books in some places until the Civil War – New Hampshire abolished the last in 1877 – but had no practical consequence after 1800, as a growing list of Jewish office holders testified.

Jews were not simply tolerated but equal, a status consolidated under the republic. The Virginia Bill of Rights of 1776 had proclaimed that all men were 'equally entitled to the free exercise of religion according to the dictates of conscience,' a principle thereafter adopted everywhere. The First Amendment to the federal constitution, which forbade Congress from enacting any law 'respecting an establishment of religion, or prohibiting the free exercise of religion', carried the Jews to a plane of almost complete equality with their fellow citizens.

In August 1790, George Washington and the Jewish congregations of the country greeted one another. All Americans, the president pointed out, 'possess alike liberty of conscience and immunities of citizenship. It is now no more that toleration is spoken of, as if it was by the indulgence of one class of people that another enjoyed the exercise of their inherent natural rights. For happily the government of the United States, which gives to bigotry no sanction, to persecution no assistance, requires only that they who live under its protection should demean themselves as good citizens, in giving it on all occasions their effectual support.'

This favourable relationship reflected a romantic conception of the Jews, inherited from the Puritans and buttressed by familiarity with the Bible. Such works as Hannah Adams's *History of the Jews* popularized the image of the wandering Jew, living witness to the truth of the Christian Gospels. The spread of millennial hopes for a quick end to the evils of the world revived emphasis on the conversion of the Jews, by Christian tradition one of the marks of the second coming. The expectation of imminent conversion created a very favourable atmosphere for adjustment; and the social position of the Jews, few in number, prominent in the upper social strata and symbolized by wealthy and philanthropic individuals like Judah Touro, made that adjustment easy.

The mounting tide of immigration, 1820–1880

A mounting tide of immigration from Germany and central Europe, which brought Jews, among others, in unprecedented numbers to the New World, reshaped these gentle conceptions after 1815. These were years of rapid expansion in the United States, of massive displacements in Europe. Americans now pushed across the continent, brought millions of new acres under cultivation, began to exploit vast mineral resources and entered upon the first stages of industrialization. The opportunities for labour thus created attracted an army of peasants and artisans for whom there was no room across the Atlantic. The movement grew steadily to a peak in the 1850s and persisted into the 1870s.

Within it were a significant number of Jews. The Enlightenment and the French Revolution had kindled among the residents of the ghettos exciting hopes of universal improvement. Then, reactionary governments after 1815 threatened to stifle those hopes. In many German states and in the Bohemian, Hungarian and Polish provinces of the Austrian Empire, Jews still lacked civil rights. Excluded from many occupations, and in some places even dependent upon the grace of the authorities for permission to marry, they sought equality in the land of promise across the ocean. They eagerly followed in the train of the Christian neighbours among whom they had lived. As a result, Jewish population in the United States increased to about fifteen thousand in 1840 and to about a quarter of a million in 1880. Contemporaries spoke of these newcomers as German, but that designation applied to any Yiddish-speaking Jew, since language then was the chief token of nationality. The label 'German' certainly covered immigrants from Austria, Bohemia, Hungary, Prussian

The Purim Ball in New York in 1865. Purim commemorates Esther's deliverance of the Jews from Haman.

Poland and Galicia. Besides the number who came from these places, there was a discernible influx of Jews from England and France.

These were not the wealthy merchants of the Colonial period. Among the new arrivals were a few writers, physicians and journalists. But most of them had been petty traders at home. In the New World, an expanding country needed their services and offered them their chance. In many rural districts, goods were hard to get. In the South and in the West, along the receding frontier, few cities or even market-towns filled the needs of commerce.

Here the Jewish immigrants found room as either independent handicraftsmen or petty traders and indeed the two occupational categories overlapped substantially. Social mobility was remarkably rapid and often permitted progress from pedlar's pack to substantial mercantile enterprise. Straus, Gimbel and others started with little stocks of haberdashery, bought with borrowed capital, carried in packs or loaded into rickety wagons. Hard work and ingenuity permitted them to open a shop; and good fortune finally advanced them to the ownership of large department stores. Through the length and breadth of the land the Jewish retailer became a familiar figure.

The Jews did not concentrate in a few large cities as their predecessors had. Although settlement on farms was unusual, they spread throughout the country, and entered unobtrusively into small-town life about them. Where their numbers justified it, they formed synagogues and mutal aid societies to guard against the insecurities of illness or death. But, in most matters, their circumstances compelled them to live in intimate association with neighbours of other creeds.

Even in the larger cities, the Jews could not form a single unified community. The newcomers could rarely identify themselves completely with the old settlers. Differences of language and custom kept them apart. Nor did the Rhinelanders feel as one with the Poles. Rival synagogues appeared, as each new group insisted on worship in its own way.

The attitudes of others remained favourable. Jews were accepted as one of innumerable diverse strands that contributed to a new, distinctively American, culture. Holding a position of full equality with other citizens, they entered prominently into political life, producing such notable figures as Senators David Yulee (Florida) and Judah P. Benjamin (Louisiana) and Judge M. M. Noah (New York).

Jews did not stand entirely apart as a solid group separate from other Americans. Like the German, Scandinavian, and Irish Lutherans and Catholics, they appeared merely to maintain their distinctive heritage while sharing the general rights and obligations of citizens. By and large, the Jews took on the coloration of the people among whom they lived. During the Civil War, those in the North took up the anti-slavery and Unionist cause, while those in the South remained on the side of the Confederacy. August Bondi fought with John Brown in Kansas while Judah P. Benjamin was Secretary of War for Jefferson Davis.

As new communities sprouted in scores of inland cities, communal life developed novel forms. The old centres along the seacoast – New York, Philadelphia and Baltimore – continued to grow. But thriving religious establishments appeared also in Cincinnati, Chicago, Saint Louis and San Francisco. England remained the source of authority in religious matters until the development of a rabbinate in America permitted a considerable degree of autonomy and encouraged significant diversions from Orthodoxy. The first rabbis, and the most influential, were immigrants from Germany and Bohemia, where pressures from secular learning were already modifying tradition. But the process of adaptation to American conditions further influenced drastic changes in belief and practice.

As early as 1824, a group of dissidents who set up the Reformed Society of Israelites in Charleston expressed the urge to adjust the patterns of worship to those practised by the Christians about them. The wish to introduce a more decorous service later, and independently, drew Temple Emanu-El in New York and the congregations of Isaac M. Wise in Albany and Cincinnati in the same direction.

An indefatigable publicist, shrewd thinker and forceful writer, Rabbi Wise gave form and rationale to these spontaneous efforts, and his influence gained followers throughout the country. By 1873, with Kaufman Kohler of New York, he was instrumental in establishing a central agency, the Union of American Hebrew Congregations, and, within the next decade, the Hebrew Union College in Cincinnati, and the Central Conference of American Rabbis. Continued agitation of these new ideas finally culminated in the formal adoption, at the Pittsburgh Conference of 1885, of a statement of principles that defined the Jews as a religious denomination rather than as a national entity.

The Reform movement sought to dispense with portions of the ritual that seemed anachronistic, preferred English as the language of prayer and expected a sermon as part of the service, as it was among Protestants. It also judged the Sabbath and the dietary laws less binding than had tradition. In justification, its leaders argued that Judaism, like other religions, was not static but developed in accordance with the conditions of time and place. What had been obligatory for the Patriarchs had not been obligatory in Spain or Poland; and it need not be in the United States.

The precepts of ethical monotheism, rather than forms of ritual or worship, were the permanent elements of Judaism. Embedded in the Law was a conception of a righteous God who loved justice and mercy and who wished men to conduct themselves in a manner pleasing to him. To lead a moral life, therefore, was more important than adherence to customs. The Jews were heirs to the tradition that had discovered and preserved the faith in such a God. It was also their obligation to communicate it to all men. Believing in the fatherhood of God and the brotherhood of man, the Reform rabbis anticipated that universal enlightenment would soon bring an awareness of the same truths to everyone.

Other communal institutions in the same period grew by adapting to the peculiar conditions of the United States. Thriving communities made room for a succession of weekly newspapers. Among the most prominent early publications, all in English, were the *Jewish Messenger* of New York, the *Israelite* of Cincinnati and the *Occident and Jewish Advocate* of Philadelphia. Although these were personal undertakings, unconnected with the synagogue, their editors, Samuel Myer Isaacs, Isaac M. Wise and Isaac Leeser, were clergymen and the interests of their publications were largely religious.

Jewish institutions, like other American institutions, were, however, in process of secularization. Like other immigrants, the Jews turned their first associational efforts towards the creation of charitable and benevolent societies, of which the most notable were the Independent Order Bnai Brith (1843) and the Independent Order Brith Abraham (1859). These organizations differed from the traditional local sickness, loan and aid societies and adopted many features of the American fraternal lodge. The Young Men's Hebrew Association (1874) even more clearly showed the influence of an American model.

Education likewise responded to the pressures of the environment. The old *heder* or *yeshiva* had encompassed all learning, recognizing no distinction between religious and secular subjects. Students there acquired all the knowledge worth having. Such institutions could not survive the competition in the United States of free state education. Various part-time expedients took their place. Most conspicuous was the spread of the Sunday School, marked in 1886 by the formation of the Sabbath School Union.

Such independent organizations, generally autonomous and subject to no control but that of their sponsors, threatened to plunge Jewish communal life into a state of anarchy as well as penury. By the time of the Civil War, support of hospitals and orphanages as well as of other activities strained limited resources. But efforts at national union were fruitless. The Board of Delegates of American Israelites, founded in 1859 on the model of the English organization, proved short-lived. There were too many diversities in Jewish life to find room for expression in a single body. And the process of acculturation, heavily conditioned by local factors, emphasized the width of the differences rather than the depth of the common elements.

The East European movement, 1880–1930

In 1880, American Jews were a stable, prosperous, if disunited segment of society. But in the decades that followed, unsettling forces, emanating from the Austrian and Russian Empires, rapidly raised the level of Jewish immigration to, and of Jewish population in, the United States. At the same time, industrialization transformed the country that awaited the newcomers.

The dislocations that had earlier set men in motion in the West now had shifted to Eastern Europe; and the Jews who came off the ships in New York or Boston after 1880 began their journeys in the Polish parts of Austria and Germany, in the Ukrainian provinces of Russia and in Romania.

In these regions, difficult times and religious persecution had weakened the old communities; and the Jews were no longer content to accept suffering as their lot divinely decreed. Enlightenment ideas convinced many that they could improve their condition; and America was the golden land that would enable them to do so. There they could live in dignity like other men, enjoying the fruits of their own free labour and opening the doors of education to their children.

As the steamship and the railroad made communications easier after 1880, the number of young people anxious to move rose steadily. In the single year, 1906, fully 150,000 came to the United States. In the entire half-century, some 2,250,000 Jewish immigrants left the Old World for the New. A smaller group of about 50,000 Sephardi Jews, from Greece and the Balkans, from Asia Minor, Turkey and North Africa, followed the same westward course. These arrivals raised the total Jewish population to about 3,500,000 in the 1920s.

The land the newcomers reached no longer offered the earlier opportunities for independent trade. Westward expansion had ended; and shoes or clothing or food were less likely to be products of the shops of individual craftsmen than of great factories in which men did nothing but operate machines. And altogether new branches – steel and automobiles, petroleum and electric power – transformed the economy of the United States.

These factors profoundly affected the Jewish population. The country now demanded industrial labour, and the new immigrants fell into the ranks of the working class. They did not, therefore, spread through the country as their predecessors had, but concentrated in the great cities where the need was.

The largest settlement developed in New York, the most important port of entry. But substantial clusters also appeared in Philadelphia and Boston on the seacoast and in Chicago in the interior. Many men and women found employment in the cigar-making and garment industries, working either at home or in the dismal factories that became known as sweat-shops. By 1900, almost all the country's clothing was produced by the toil of Jews. Others worked in the building trades as painters or carpenters; and a few, who were scarcely better off, struggled for success in tiny grocery or dry goods shops.

These people created problems new to American Jews. A proletariat developed, with signs of permanence, penned up in ghettos made visible by a depressed standard of living. Low wages and frequent periods of unemployment left these people insecure and helpless in illness. Lacking guidance, their children sometimes went astray and contributed to the delinquency and crime of the great cities.

In the 1920s, perhaps three-quarters of all American Jews engaged in proletarian occupations. The remainder, and especially those several generations in the land, were more fortunate. Among them were a few wealthy bankers and merchants, such as the Warburgs, the Kuhns, the Loebs and the Guggenheims, and a somewhat larger contingent of retailers. But relatively few Jews made their way in the large corporations which dominated heavy industry. At the end of the period, *Fortune*, a magazine widely read by businessmen in the United States, concluded that Jews were hardly represented in this sector of the economy.

Jews acquired power only in a few marginal industries, such as small-scale clothing manufacture, requiring little capital, and exploiting a depressed labour force, composed largely of immigrants. Lack of competition from native entrepreneurs proved an advantage there. The same was true of the movie industry, which developed rapidly after 1910. Jews like William Fox, Louis B. Mayer and the Warner Brothers early entrenched themselves in that field because at first it seemed beneath the interest of well-established businessmen.

No single set of institutions met the religious and social needs of all American Jews. The new immigrants struggled to find in the fervour and flavour of the old religion some compensations for and respite from the harsh existence of the tenement slums. In the large cities their synagogues grew rapidly in numbers and in adherents, as did a host of peripheral institutions. In 1896, the *yeshiva*, Rabbi Isaac Elchanan, began to train an Orthodox rabbinate, and two years later the Union of Orthodox Jewish Congregations drew together a group of like-minded organizations.

Orthodox synagogues were, however, jealous of their autonomy. Factional disputes exerted a constant splintering effect. The attempt in New York to establish a central communal organization in 1888 failed despite the prestige of the leadership of Rabbi Jacob Joseph of Vilna. In 1909, the same fate befell the New York *kehilla* led by J. L. Magnes. Ultimately, internal divisions produced five separate organizations of rabbis in the United States and many congregations remained entirely unaffiliated.

American Jews, descended from earlier migrations who remained Orthodox and did not wish to travel the road of the Reform movement, were, however, uncomfortable when set side by side with the newcomers, strangers in everything but adherence to ritual. The emergence of a distinctive American form, Conservative Judaism, provided a release from this awkward situation. The Jewish Theological Seminary, originally founded in 1886 by such pillars of the old Orthodoxy as Sabato Morais and Alexander Kohut, steadily moved in the new direction. Under the leadership of Solomon Schechter, it produced a corps of rabbis which exerted substantial influence in the next half-century.

Conservatives, too, altered the form of the services, introduced an English sermon, and relaxed some of the rigid regulations bearing on personal life. But they insisted upon maintenance of the traditional Sabbath and upon preservation of the dietary laws and other rituals. The Conservative movement also viewed Judaism as a historical religion subject to change from epoch to epoch. But it was not willing to rely upon the unaided power of reason as a guide to what was alterable. Conservatives argued, rather, that only such changes were acceptable as were in accord with a broad consensus among all faithful Jews at any given time.

In truth, centrifugal forces were powerful at every level of Judaism. One extreme of reform led to the Ethical Culture movement; and working class or socialist movements might preserve cultural, but not always religious, allegiances. More generally, erosion of the sense of communal responsibility in the great anonymous cities and lack of any recognized authority permitted a slackness that frequently edged over into abandonment of religion, or outright conversion.

Secular institutional life flourished, although in the same undisciplined and unorganized manner. The Jews long settled in the country differed from the new arrivals in culture and status, but nevertheless did not shirk the obligation to aid and counsel. The problem of teaching an impatient youth heavily influenced by state schools, together with the diversity of religious influences, nurtured a wide variety of Jewish part-time educational establishments, including settlement houses, to further Americanization. New benevolent societies and new charities, in their very number and variety mirroring the complexity and differences of Jewish life in the United States, ministered to the needs of the newcomers. At the practical level of fund-raising, the resultant confusion called forth its own remedy, the Federation, which issued a united appeal and apportioned the collection to constituent agencies. Pioneer efforts in Cincinnati and Boston in 1895 and 1896 proved successful enough to earn imitation in more than sixty other cities.

Internal divisions racked even the bodies formed to protect Jews against discrimination and slander. The Jewish Alliance (1891) quickly fell apart, the American Jewish Committee (1908) and the American Jewish Congress (1917, re-established 1922) represented only segments of organized Jewry, while Bnai Brith carried on its own work through its Anti-Defamation League.

Quite apart from the formal organized Jewish life of the times, the immigrants also created their own communities to cope with their troubles. In the East Side of Manhattan, in Williamsburgh and Brownsville in Brooklyn, in the West Side of Chicago and in the West End of Boston, little spontaneous societies drew men and women together to help one another. A host of tiny synagogues permitted each to worship in the familiar style. Fraternal organizations, called *landsmannschaften*, supplied the folk from various regions of Eastern Europe with mutal assistance in illness or death and with camaraderie in life. Charitable societies aided orphans, widows and the aged. Afternoon schools added religious instruction to the education children received in the state schools. The International Ladies Garment Workers Union, the Amalgamated Clothing Workers of America and other unions not only struggled to improve labour conditions but also extended various social services to their members. Their own daily newspapers interpreted the world to the immigrants and a lively theatre supplied entertainment. A culture expressed in Yiddish, the Old World language of all East European Jews, held all these activities together and somehow lightened the heavy burdens newcomers bore.

New issues offset the underlying causes for fragmentation after the turn of the century. The growth of the Jewish labour movement at first threatened to divide wealthy from poor Jews, German from Russian, uptown from downtown. But common values and communal pressures after 1910 proved stronger than class lines and evoked a protocol that made co-operation of workers and bosses possible.

The great external danger of anti-Semitism drew them together. Through the 19th century, scattered instances of discrimination in resorts and schools or of slurs in popular literature had no deep significance. But as the century drew to a close, Americans, bewildered by change, sought to place the blame for all the nation's troubles on outside conspiratorial forces. Farms, factories and money supply were in perennial disorder; and many troubled citizens believed the fault somehow sprang from the strange cities, monstrous in size and frightening in their combination of wealth and poverty. There, perhaps, was the seat of an alien conspiracy directed by the Pope, or the Jews, or the anarchists or the bankers. Furthermore, it was tempting to ascribe the poverty, slums, criminality and other social disorders created by industrialization to the immigrants and to speculate that, if only the Italians, the Slavs and the East European Jews could be shut out, perhaps the country would revert to its earlier purity.

A new theory of race strengthened hostility towards the foreigner. Some Americans came to deny that all men descended from common ancestors and found scientific support for the idea that ineradicable racial differences set off entirely separate groups, which could not safely mingle with one another. In the past, it was argued, civilizations had declined because of the mixture of these races; this danger now confronted the United States.

This theory was especially attractive to people worried about the place of the Negro in American life, or concerned about the Chinese on the Pacific coast, or eager to undertake the imperialistic conquest of foreign territories. In time, the same logic extended to the Italians, the Slavs and the Jews. If each was a separate race, they ought not to mingle with the original Anglo-Saxon stock of the United States.

For the moment, the hostility was not open except when a Georgia mob lynched Leo Frank, wrongly accused of murder. The tradition of equality was too deep-rooted for immediate reversal. However, a pattern of discrimination began to restrict access to desirable jobs and to professional education. Some private colleges, many engineering schools and almost all medical faculties began to apply a *numerus clausus* to Jews; and the fortunate few who secured the necessary training faced hardship in establishing themselves, often confining their practice to a Jewish clientele.

The First World War made matters worse. The high hopes of the crusade to save the world for democracy gave way to a feeling of disappointment and betrayal when peace led to no noticeable improvement in the state of the world. The disorder of Communism and Fascism spread across Europe and Americans began to wonder why they had failed when their cause had been righteous. Some of them found in both the war and the peace further evidence of an insidious conspiracy against their security. Now the racial dread of the new immigrants grew more intense. It led some Americans into the Ku Klux Klan, a secret movement against Catholics, Jews and Negroes. It led many more to support the laws that put an end to further immigration.

During the war, furthermore, much of the hostility against foreigners focused upon the Jews, as a result of the transmission to the United States of an old line of European anti-Semitism. Early in the 20th century, anti-Semitic propagandists spread the false theory of a great international conspiracy by the Elders of Zion to conquer the world. After the war, these ideas spread across the Atlantic and supplied some with the explanation they sought for the single cause responsible for all the disaster in the world since 1914. It was easier to blame all evil on strangers than to look for its true source.

The background of heightened tension contributed to the sense of the relevance of Zionism. The Federation of American Zionists, established in 1897 after the Basel Congress, grew slowly in the next two decades; and the formation of Hadassah (1912) and the Jewish National Fund (1910) stirred little attention. The concept of a return to Palestine attracted few supporters. The Reform movement explicitly rejected it; labour and the socialists were international in orientation; and the mass of immigrants had made their choice of a promised land in coming to America. The First World War did project American Jews into a position of international leadership and responsibility, and, guided by Louis D. Brandeis and Louis Marshall, they helped evolve the policy that resulted in the Palestine Mandate. In the 1920s, however, there was no consensus in the United States about the future character of the future homeland.

The quest for stability, 1930–1950

American Jews in 1930 longed for the stability that would permit them to deal with the leading issues before them – labour conditions, anti-Semitism and Zionism. They were ill-prepared for further difficulties created by the end of immigration, by a great economic depression and by a second world war.

The close of the immigrant movement dammed up the source of new strength. The First World War had interrupted the flow but for a few years; after peace had reopened the shipping lanes, the United States once more had welcomed thousands of new arrivals. Then American policy changed and, in 1924, the gates finally closed. In any case, the Soviet Union and other European countries now discouraged their people from leaving; and the cost of travel rose steadily.

In the bitter decade of the 1930s, there seemed little possibility of any meaningful revival of immigration. Unemployment mounted to the point at which almost one out of four possible wage-earners lacked a source of livelihood. It was futile to think of reopening the gates to new people who might only complicate the problem. By the time employment picked up significantly in 1939, war in Europe made peaceful traffic across the ocean impossible. American Judaism could no longer rely upon European sources for growth or even to hold on.

Yet, in the same decade the plight of the victims of Fascism strained the conscience of all Americans. The United States had traditionally been a place of refuge for victims of political persecution. It could not now refuse admission to the first of Hitler's victims. From 1933 onward, a trickle of refugees entered and resettled.

The refugees of the 1930s differed markedly from the immigrants of the past. Few were labourers; only the well-to-do had the resources to escape. Among them were many highly educated professional and business people who had held important posts in Germany before their flight. Compelled to take jobs that wasted their talents and training, they adjusted with difficulty and established themselves against great odds.

The end of the Second World War revealed the existence of a much larger problem. The liberating armies discovered thousands of victims of Nazism confined in concentration camps. In addition, immense bodies of homeless men drifted about Europe. Torn away from their homes by the Germans, they often found it impossible to return. Meanwhile, the peace uprooted still others as radical boundary changes displaced masses of people.

Of the fifteen million people whom the Nazis had displaced, some six million had been exterminated and seven million repatriated by the Allies before 1947. In that year, however, a million refugees in Europe still had no homes to which they could return and of that number about one-fifth were Jews. It took strenuous effort to get the United States to take a share of these people. The dominant groups in Congress were afraid to risk any change that might open the country to new immigration and, as a matter of fact, would make the permanent immigration law more restrictive than ever with the enactment of the McCarran-Walter Act of 1952. It proved difficult to secure even emergency legislation until a Displaced Persons Act in 1948 admitted some 400,000 newcomers, of whom 16 per cent were Jews. A supplementary measure in 1953 opened the way for a few more. All in all, about 100,000 Jews came to the United States in the post-war years.

The arrivals were a miscellaneous group drawn from every corner of Europe, among them Germans, Poles, Hungarians, Russians and Romanians of every social level, for war and Fascism were indiscriminate in their choice of victims. Coming in a period of high employment, these people established residence with relatively little difficulty. They were, in any case, few in number, and communal services were now efficiently organized so that the newcomers had dependable advice and assistance from the moment they left the camps of Europe until they finally found homes.

In the 1930s and 1940s anti-Semitism, at home and abroad, shackled the ability of Jews to deal with the refugee problem, raised doubts about the conception of assimilation and gave new attractiveness to Zionism.

The 1930s saw no abatement of anti-Semitism. Indeed, the great depression intensified the sense of hatred. Millions of men were out of work, helpless, desperate and vulnerable to agitation of every sort. Numerous movements aimed at a revolution in American life. Some proposed economic cure-alls of one sort or another; others directed a stream of hostile argument against the Jews. The success of Mussolini and Hitler inspired numerous American fascists with the wish to emulate the Duce and the Führer. Furthermore, the Nazi government immediately set flowing a flood of propaganda aiming to justify its own mistreatment of the Jews by convincing Americans that they ought to do likewise. As the years went by with no relief from the hard times, tension mounted in the United States.

The war had revealed the Nazis as enemies not only of the Jews but of all Americans. Racism was not simply a speculative theory, susceptible to rational argument. Everywhere there was an instinctive revulsion against the blind hatred that had doomed six million Jews to extermination chambers.

But no one could be sure in the immediate post-war years that there would not be a revival of the passions that had once enlisted millions in the Christian Front, the Silver Shirts and the Klan. Hence the reluctance to urge admission of more substantial numbers of refugees. Hence, also, the growing dependence on the one territory, Palestine, likely to offer a home to stateless Jews. Yet, the British government had begun to narrow the meaning of the Balfour Declaration by imposing artificial restrictions upon Jews who wished to go to Palestine. In 1939, to appease the Arabs, it completely halted immigration. Even when the need was greatest, in 1947, it would admit no Jews as long as it was in control.

American Jews then divided into three groups. Confirmed Zionists regarded a Jewish political state as their ultimate goal. In opposition, the anti-Zionist American Council for Judaism maintained a position of complete hostility to any view of the Jews as a separate nationality. But most American Jews refused to take either extreme position. Swayed not by any nationalistic ideology but by the immediate problems of relief, they believed that only migration to Israel could save the victims of the war. British intransigence forced this larger middle group to support the idea of a Jewish state as the only alternative to abandonment of the refugees.

The creation of the State of Israel in 1948 clarified the situation by demonstrating that the interest of Americans was primarily humanitarian. Israel drew its population almost entirely from Europe, Africa and the Near East. Few American Zionists chose to migrate, although they now had the opportunity to do so. Their loyalties were in America and their future relationship to Israel was to be that of philanthropic support.

On the other hand, the anti-Zionists could no longer argue against the reality of a state which actually existed and which became more firmly established year by year. In practice, although they continued to criticize extreme nationalistic tendencies, they also felt an obligation to aid the Jews overseas.

For the middle group, the problem was simpler. They were Americans to whom Israel was a foreign state. But ties of sentiment, religion and philanthropy bound them to the people of Israel, whom they would assist towards democratic development, just as other Americans at the same time were bringing their skills and financial resources to help other underdeveloped countries.

The stability for which so many had longed in 1930 still eluded them in 1950. The depression, war and genocide that had occupied the intervening decades were fresh in the minds of every survivor and none could be sure that these trials were over. Jews still failed to conform to the general configuration of the American population. Of the five million in the United States in 1950, some seventy per cent lived in the eleven largest cities with over two million in New York alone. Furthermore, the distribution of occupations was markedly distorted away from the average American pattern. The percentage of Jews was far higher than that of other Americans in trade, in entertainment and the professions; far lower in the personal services, construction, transportation, finance, public services, utilities and in manufacturing. The situation thus was far from stable, the future uncertain.

The one offsetting factor was the access to political power created by the New Deal and the Fair Deal. The presidencies of Franklin Delano Roosevelt and Harry S. Truman offered a glimmer of hope in those desperate years and won the loyalty of a majority of Jewish citizens. Furthermore, individuals like Felix Frankfurter and Samuel Rosenman were closer to the White House than any of their co-religionists had been before; and a significant number of other Jews entered the administrative bureaucracy. The possibility of turning to government for aid in the struggle for equality and opportunity was one of the few cheerful elements of this trying period.

The consequences of affluence, 1950–1977

The massive social changes that transformed the United States after 1950 affected the Jews as they did every other social group. The depression did not return; instead, the economy boomed in unanticipated directions. In response, the population shifted, from east to west and from central cities to suburbs. New cultural forms first strengthened, then weakened traditional family life. And after an initial revival of religion, young people launched upon a restless search for alternative forms of faith.

The global struggle thrust upon them in 1941 had united Americans, and had totally discredited all who preached the doctrines that had led Germany to destruction. The anti-Semitism of the 1930s, so feared in the 1940s, did not return in the 1950s or 1960s. A new generation of social scientists and biologists had demonstrated the falsity of the old ideas, and a public constantly being educated had become freshly aware of its own heritage and diversity. A few agitators wandered unheeded through the country; a handful of scurrilous journals and books circulated among the still zealous; and an occasional man of new wealth paid to express his own atavistic hatreds. But the anti-Semitism of the past disappeared.

Hardened patterns of discrimination and exclusion fell away more slowly. But growing security enabled Jews to abandon the purely defensive stance of earlier years and move actively to fight for equality. They had learned there was a unity of interests and ideals among all minorities and no longer sought exceptions on their own behalf so much as the affirmation of general rights, the elimination of all prejudices.

The times were propitious both for political action to end discrimination by law and for eliminating prejudice by understanding and education. The expansion of the economy made room for newcomers in numerous desirable posts. Renewed mobility freed many individuals from the binding force of old prejudices. And the necessities of the struggle against totalitarianism gave the ideals of personal equality critical import. The changed attitudes of the period made it possible to enact laws against discrimination, to begin to enforce them and, in significant areas, to level the barriers of exclusion even without legislation.

Older measures against discrimination on account of colour or creed in resorts, places of entertainment and refreshment and transportation, once disregarded, were increasingly effective after 1950. Critical shortages and ethnic sensitivities complicated the housing problem. Some states forbade the housing projects they subsidized to differentiate among applicants on the basis of race or creed, but efforts to incorporate analogous provisions into federal law failed until the 1960s.

Jews welcomed these steps, although they did not ease their own difficulties, which centred in the restrictive covenants in the sale or rental of private quarters. In 1948, the Supreme Court held in *Shelley* v. *Kraemer* that such agreements were not legally enforceable. More important was the general relaxation of hostility. Restrictive covenants continued to be written into deeds of sale on an informal basis. But, increasingly, Americans all over the country found these barriers pointless, and in neighbourhood after neighbourhood the old prejudices dissolved.

Shifts in law and sentiment also undermined the patterns of exclusion in employment. Early federal and state laws ruled out religious discrimination in appointments to the civil service and to jobs connected with the government. After 1940, moreover, defence orders tied an ever larger percentage of American industry to Washington, thus making it subject to regulation. A march on Washington, initiated by Negroes but supported by the Jews and other minorities, on 25 June 1941, elicited Executive Order 8802, which forbade discrimination because of race or creed in government service, defence industries and unions. A Fair Employment Practices Committee appointed to supervise the Order served throughout the war. Efforts to make it permanent failed, however, and the battle then shifted to the states. The laws some of them enacted had enormous importance. Overt discrimination became difficult, especially by employment agencies and large corporations the records of which were readily subject to scrutiny. The F.E.P.C. measures also created a standard of what was legal and just, and called into question the old unthinking practices based on prejudice. In increasing numbers, Jews found employment in professional and clerical occupations that not long before had been barred to them.

The relaxation of the pattern of discrimination also influenced education. The war and the G.I. Bill of Rights brought Jews, in training programmes, to colleges and schools throughout the country where they had scarcely been known before; and that alone earned them wider acceptance. Three states (New York, Massachusetts and New Jersey) adopted fair educational practices laws, and although the enforcement power was weak, the importance of the standards thus set was great. The overall limitation on the number of medical students still justified some restrictive practices. But even in this very tense area, there was progress, particularly in the northeastern states.

For the first time in many years, also, the racist features of the permanent immigration law came under attack. Throughout the war, Jewish organizations had hesitated to reopen the issue. After 1950, they led the fight to bring the law into accord with American principles; and after fifteen years succeeded in eliminating the national origins quota system. They asserted an analogous right to be heard with reference to Israel.

Developments after 1950 also resolved the remaining ambiguities in the relationship between Church and State in America. The apparent apathy of the interwar years induced some ecclesiastical bodies to seek state aid in bringing people back to the churches. The widespread growth of church membership after 1940 made others belligerently intransigent about any measure that threatened the status quo. By then, the more important bodies had effectively mobilized their political strength, often maintaining powerful lobbies in the national and state capitals. The ecclesiastical authorities did not always have their way when they sought action. But they were almost always able to block action they did not approve; and that tended further to preserve the existing situation.

The issue of establishment had long been settled; even the occasional lapses by which officials and public documents had once referred to the United States as a

'Christian nation' no longer occurred. The Christian Amendment Movement continued its futile agitation to secure the mention of Christ in the constitution and Senator Flanders of Vermont introduced such a resolution in 1951. But neither the resolution nor the agitation represented more than local eccentricities.

Although judicial decisions in the 1920s had held that the Fourteenth Amendment transferred to the states the restriction by which the First Amendment bound the Federal government, residues of ancient legislation remained in effect. Old blasphemy and sacrilege laws thus lingered on the statute books until 1952, when the Supreme Court, in the 'Miracle Case', denied their constitutionality. Sunday laws were an unreasonable and unprincipled hodge-podge of compromises. The courts adhered with some rigour to a distinction between 'labour', which observant Jews could perform, and 'selling', which they could not, not for its logic but for fear of being set adrift without any guiding precedents at all.

The most serious difficulties, however, came in the relationship of religion to the state schools. The practice of reading the King James Bible long remained worrisome. Some states barred comments on the part of the teachers; others excused children of objecting parents; and still others compromised by using a variety of expedients. But the constitutional issue was not seriously addressed until the 1950s when, after several attempts at judicial compromise, the courts held against the whole practice.

Protestant clergymen since the beginning of the century had proposed plans for released time from state schools for the purposes of religious education. The Jewish reaction had at first been equivocal. Some Reform groups had opposed all sectarian practices in the state schools. Other Jews, however, were tempted to think that the aid of state schools might solve their own difficulty in supplying adequate religious training to the young. By the same token, and for the same reasons, the Catholics, who had at first opposed the plan, ultimately became its most enthusiastic supporters. After 1947, however, all major Jewish organizations united in opposition. The Supreme Court, however, was not willing to allow the state schools to become the instruments of sectarian instruction, and, in barring various versions of released time, firmly set forth the principles of total separation of Church and State.

The subsidence of prejudice and the attainment of equality seemed to normalize the position of the Jews. Despite some additions from abroad, the percentage of the native-born grew while that of the foreign-born declined; the old immigrant culture disintegrated, and institutions based on the Yiddish language decayed and became the subjects of nostalgic reminiscence.

The old Jewish labouring class also disappeared. The sons of factory workers did not move into their fathers' occupations, nor even the sons of the shop owners. The percentage of the proletariat among Jews declined steadily as the first generation of East European immigrants died off.

Instead, Jews moved into the professional and managerial occupations. The increase in the number of Jewish doctors and lawyers was not as surprising as the expansion of places in organized and institutionalized professional life. Jews appeared with increasing frequency in government bureaucracies, on college faculties, in the ranks of state and private school teachers and as engineers and accountants for industrial firms. The number of Jewish managers, executives, officials and independent proprietors also increased; they were less likely than formerly to be in distinctively Jewish trades, but established themselves in construction, rapid transit, real estate, transportation and communications. It was a sign of changing times in the 1970s when a Jew became chief executive officer of the Dupont Corporation.

As the Jews lost the traces of their immigrant and proletarian origins, they acquired middle class habits and adopted a suburban style of life. Their cultural distinctiveness faded and they became like other Americans. Spread across the nation, no longer concentrated in a few great cities, they seemed at last to have surmounted the difficulties of the past.

The passage of time, however, did little to simplify the complexities of the Jewish situation in America. The underlying divisions, submerged during the war and suppressed immediately thereafter by the requirements of defence against anti-Semitism at home and against the enemies of Israel abroad, re-emerged in the 1960s and 1970s in the face of unexpected new problems.

Viewed from without, Jewish religious and social institutions seemed impervious to change after 1950. Though the Lubovicher and other Hasidic groups added an exotic fringe, the three main branches – Orthodox, Conservative and Reform – went their usual way. A Jewish university (Brandeis) and occasional all-day schools did not alter the expectation that education would be preponderantly secular and universalistic, supplemented as best it could by religious or cultural instruction when there was time for it. The philanthropic, defence and Zionist organizations also remained intact. Yet not so visible were important shifts in function and in meaning.

The effects of immigration now made themselves felt. It was not simply that liberalized laws permitted the entry of any Jews who escaped from Eastern Europe or that perhaps 200,000 *yordim* arrived from Israel. More important, the refugees of the two decades after 1933 and their children played an increasingly important part in communal affairs; and their experiences, therefore their ideas, were not identical to those of either the East Europeans or the native Americans.

New types also moved into leadership positions. Early in the century, lawyers and men of wealth had usually been spokesmen of the various sectors of the community – Jacob Schiff, Louis Marshall, Joseph Proskauer, Louis D. Brandeis and Meyer London, for instance. Those dominant in the trades unions – Sidney Hillman, David Dubinsky or Samuel Gompers – had risen from the ranks. But during the war, organizational professionals, frequently trained in social work or public relations, began to move into positions of authority; and laypeople, occupied with other matters, acquiesced in a role that made them primarily fund raisers.

After 1950, the power of the rabbis in communal affairs also increased. The slightly old-fashioned figure of the past, foreign in appearance and accent, less comfortable in English than in Yiddish, gave way to a modern college graduate as familiar with sociology, psychology and counselling as with Halacha (legal tradition) and capable of dealing on equal terms with clergymen of other denominations and with public officials. Furthermore, by advancing the rabbi as their spokesman, Jews defined themselves as a religious group and acquired a place in public consciousness disproportionate to their numbers, for Americans by then accepted the conventional tripartite division, Catholic-Protestant-Jew.

The new professional-clerical leadership was a source of both strength and weakness. It put control into the hands of dedicated, full-time, workers with a stake in the preservation of their own organizations and also of the community as a whole. Cut off from the day to day life of the lay members, however, the leaders were sometimes unaware of shifts in interest and ideas.

The return to religion of the 1950s gave way to the alienation of the 1960s and to the revived ethnicity of the 1970s without guidance from communal leaders, lay or clerical. The generation that matured in the affluent suburbs, sheltered from want by parents who had suffered through the depression, knew nothing of anti-Semitism and slipped into the comfortable middle class liberalism of their environment. They accepted the obligation of political and financial support for Israel as a good cause, in the same category as civil rights and pacifism. Believing that anti-Semitism was a failing of the political right, they long refused to recognize the realities of the Soviet situation; for their primary articles of faith were tolerance, universalism, disarmament, aid to the oppressed, decolonization, the United Nations and, above all, the certainty that each was compatible with all the others. Habituated to instinctive sympathy for the underdog, they took the affluence of their own society as prima facie evidence of its evil nature and responded readily to criticism of the military and of industry. That is, they accepted the masochistic ideas generally prevalent among Americans of their class and status.

To a very large extent, that accounted for the ability of Jews to articulate the cultural discontent of this generation on more than one level. The novels of Saul Bellow, Bernard Malamud and Philip Roth, the poetry of Delmore Schwartz and Karl Shapiro, the plays of Arthur Miller spoke to readers, with varying degrees of excellence, of the individual as dangling man, perennial outsider, everlasting victim. The popular lyrics of Bob Dylan, the cinematic lamentations of Stanley Kramer, Mike Nichols and Paul Newman sounded the same theme, as did the self-pitying mockery of Woody Allen. The promised land became the land of deceit – Catch 22, all of it – a judgment that came easily to those who did not have to think of purpose or of alternative.

The consequences unfolded slowly. Intermarriage should not have been a surprise among young people reared under these conditions; yet the discovery that some estimates in the 1970s ran as high as forty per cent evoked panicked predictions that the Jews were doomed to ever diminishing numbers and perhaps to disappearance in America.

Late in the 1960s, Jews discovered also the fragility of the alliance of the minorities in which they held a heavy political investment. Responsible Black leaders had checked occasional tendencies towards anti-Semitism among their followers; but no such inhibitions governed the extremist Muslims, Panthers and others who looked East for guidance. More important, as the country moved beyond the first stages of the civil rights struggle, a difference in tactics widened into a difference in objectives. Unity among the disadvantaged minorities had endured as long as their aim was removal of the discriminatory practices that affected them all. When Blacks and then others began to seek the positive intervention of the government on their behalf, especially affirmative action measurable in numerical goals, the result seemed, and in some cases actually was, a restoration of the quotas of the past and a reversion to abhorred discriminatory devices. On the DeFunis and Bakke cases, Jewish and Black communities split apart.

In the aftermath of the 1967 war, also, Jews totally involved with the Israeli cause found themselves abandoned by allies who refused to distinguish between Vietnam and Suez and insisted on regarding both as imperialist conflicts. The following year, a New Left convention took an anti-Zionist position; and, thereafter, support for the Palestinians grew steadily among people who refused to discriminate between one liberation movement and another.

In 1977, puzzlement was the dominant tone among American Jews. They had voted overwhelmingly, the preceding year, for a president who paid slight attention to their interests and seemed ready to sacrifice Israel for the sake of an illusory détente with the Soviet Union and the dubious friendship of the Arabs. The ideal of equality, for which they had long fought, no longer commanded universal assent.

The profound irony of the situation reflected the circumstance that its sources lay not where Jews had long feared it would – in poverty, prejudice and discrimination from the political right – but at the other pole – in affluence, permissiveness and wishful thinking from the political left.

American Jews sometimes yielded to a wistful longing for return to the good old days of the world of their fathers, when problems had been less ambiguous and good stood clearly marked off from evil. In an effort at reassurance, they often rehearsed their contributions to America – Joseph Goldberger, who discovered the cause of pellagra (or Italian leprosy), S. A. Waksman, who discovered streptomycin and coined the word antibiotic, and Jonas Salk, the pioneer of polio vaccine. They recalled the Nobel Prize winners, who have included, among dozens of others, Albert Einstein and I. I. Rabi; the Supreme Court justices, Louis D. Brandeis, Benjamin Cardozo and Felix Frankfurter; and an endless roster of musicians, writers, actors and athletes who had enriched the country's life.

They were less likely to think of the long way they themselves had come, from the first scattered venturers to the wilderness, through the long agonizing process of immigration, to the point at which they had advanced to positions of wealth and power; and what remained – which was most difficult of all – was only to consider how best to use their freedom.

VI
THE MODERN WORLD: CONSTRAINT AND OPTIONS

Judaism and Modernity

Zionism and Israel

The prelude to Zionism is to be sought not only in the hopes and prophecies of the Jewish people themselves, but also in the cultural climate of Western Europe in the mid-19th century. Partly because Palestine was the home of Christianity as well as of Judaism, there was intense interest in the early history of the Jews, and pioneer work was being done in biblical exegesis. Imaginative writers, too, became fascinated by the Jews as survivals from a distant past, guardians of an ancient yet living heritage. The hero of Disraeli's *Tancred* (1847) journeys to the Holy Land in search of religious experience. And George Eliot's *Daniel Deronda* of 1876 is the story of a young man who, on discovering his Jewish parentage, feels compelled to go to Palestine and work for the regeneration of his people. As early as 1842, the Earl of Shaftesbury had suggested the possibility of resettlement, an idea eagerly taken up by a Canadian, Henry Wentworth Monk. Holman Hunt's painting *The Finding of the Saviour in the Temple* (detail *opposite*) is thus only one example – though perhaps the most vivid – of a whole movement. It is virtually an attempt to reconstruct ancient Israel. Hunt had studied the subject deeply, reading the Talmud as well as the

Old and New Testaments. Twice he visited Jerusalem for lengthy periods and his work contains many hints picked up from the contemporary Jewish community there; the costumes, indeed, are very largely Arab. And Jews at the time of Jesus wore the *tallith* as a garment not as a shawl. The scene is an outer chamber of the Temple. In this section, the left-hand half of the picture, we see the circle of rabbis who have been disputing with the young Jesus. On the left sits the Chief Rabbi, very old, and blind. He holds the Torah, rolled on two rollers and wrapped in a red cloth. A richly dressed boy sits beside it with a whisk to guard it from defilement by flies. Behind the old man another boy stealthily kisses the silken mantle of the Torah. The man next to the Chief Rabbi holds a phylactery in his hand, while a third has a scroll of the Prophets which he is about to unroll. The fourth actually wears a phylactery on his head as a sign of piety (custom requires this only at times of prayer) and holds a reed pen in his hand. The next holds a bowl of wine, poured from a jug by the man standing behind him. The rear figures towards the left are musicians, two with harps and one with sistrum. (1)

A more insidious, because more subtle, form of anti-Semitism replaced the blood libel. In this detail from an 18th-century folk-painting showing the Estates of Society and their roles, the Jew has the line: 'I deceive you.' (2)

A wave of anti-Semitism swept France in the wake of the Dreyfus Affair. Captain Dreyfus, a Jew, was accused of selling military secrets to the Germans – so all Jews were guilty of 'selling the flag'. Dreyfus was in fact totally innocent, but for many French readers it was enough that he was a Jew. (3)

'Where are we now, papa Solomon?' asks the German on the other side of the frontier: another anti-Dreyfus cartoon of 1898. Ten years were to elapse before Dreyfus was exonerated by an appeal court and restored to his rank. (4)

A monstrous Jew, his pockets full of gold, writes the laws of France, 1901. (5)

The Nazis (*right*) attributed all the ills of the proletariat to the Jew: a poster of 1924. (6)

'He is to blame for the war.' Nazi propaganda twenty years later (1943), still purveying the same message. (7)

Desecrated Torah scrolls in a synagogue in Kishinev tell of the vicious massacre that has just taken place. Kishinev, formerly part of Russia, now in Romania, was the scene of violent anti-Jewish riots in April 1903. Homes, shops and synagogues were smashed and forty-seven Jews murdered. The brutality of the killings aroused horror all over the world, but official Russian reaction was luke-warm: only a few men were prosecuted, and received lenient sentences. Restriction laws, prohibition of residence in most of Russia, special taxes and other repressive measures continued to multiply. (8)

Hitler's 'final solution' can be seen as the logical continuation of centuries of prejudice and hysterical fear. The major part of European Jewry perished in the holocaust. Its effects, on both the consciousness of Western man and the Jews' own attitude to their identity, have still to be fully realized. *Below:* Belsen 1945. (9)

Tradition and aspiration

Dispersed throughout the world and subjected to renewed pressures to assimilate with their host countries, the Jews of the later 19th century preserved to a remarkable degree a community of religious and, to a large extent, social observance. Tashlik is a rite that takes place on New Year's Day. Verses from Micah and penitential prayers are recited by a stream, river or seashore: 'He will turn again and have compassion upon us; he will tread our iniquities under foot; and thou wilt cast all their sins into the depths of the sea.' This painting (*left*) by Aleksandr Gierymski shows Orthodox Jews reciting the appropriate verses by a Polish river in 1884. (10)

'The Sabbath Candles' by Isidor Kaufmann (*below left*). Kaufmann left many scenes of ordinary life among the Jewish communities of Poland and Hungary. In this one, it is the Friday evening marking the commencement of the Sabbath. The housewife, in her plain room (both bedroom and living room), has just lit the two candles and makes the sign of blessing over them. Under the linen cloth are the two Sabbath loaves. She has her prayer-book ready as she waits for the return of her husband from the synagogue before beginning the meal. (11)

'On the way to Zion' (*above*) by Isaac Levitan. Levitan died in 1900, but this painting showing Jewish Pilgrims approaching Jerusalem can easily be read as an allegory of the Zionist hope. (13)

'Carpatho-Ukranian Jews in the Synagogue' (*left*) by Robert Guttmann. Guttmann was a naïve painter, drawing on childhood memories for much of his art. Between the wars he settled in Prague, at one time knowing Kafka. He died in a concentration camp in 1942. (12)

Eastern Europe: the impasse

Prospects for any Jew living before 1914 in Poland, Hungary or Russia were bleak. All avenues to improvement seemed closed. Restrictions multiplied. Violence increased. And where the urge to emigrate was deep and widespread, Zionism found fertile soil. These photographs show a community with roots in the past but no hope for the future.

The Feast of the Tabernacles requires the building of a *sukkah*, a small hut of palm branches. An alternative, shown in this household in Hungary, is to raise part of the roof and cover the opening with leaves and fruit. (14)

Among the Hasidim a Zadik was a holy man credited with the power to work miracles. *Above right:* Samuel Hirszenberg's painting *The Funeral of the Zadik* (Lodz, Poland, 1905) conveys a sense of impending doom, as though a world is ending and the people are terrified of what is to come. Hands reach out to touch the coffin as it is carried to the grave under a lowering sky. (17)

In Galicia fervent religious commitment overcame economic depression. *Left:* outside the synagogue of Przemysl, 1905. *Below:* encounter between two Jews in a Galician country lane, about 1895. (15, 16)

A Jewish porter, photographed in 1914 at Vladimir Volynsk. (18)

The rabbis exercised a powerful influence, and so-called 'wonder-rabbis' almost attained the status of sainthood. *Above*: young Jews entering the house of one such man, Rabbi Spira of Mukasz, then part of Czechoslovakia, now U.S.S.R. *Below*: members of a Jewish self-defence group at Odessa, an indication of new attitudes. (19, 20).

The Jews of England passed unscathed through the crises of the 19th century. Between 1750 and 1858 they gradually acquired every civic freedom, culminating in the right to sit in the House of Commons without taking the Christian oath. Since then Jews have held practically every high office and are well represented in all the professions. This painting of the New Synagogue, Great Helen Street, London, in 1850, bears witness to their easy relationship with the state. It is the Feast of the Tabernacles, the man on the left carries the Torah, that on the right the *lulab* and *ethrog*. And on each side of the sanctuary is a prayer for the Royal Family, in English and Hebrew. (21)

German Jews patriotically identified themselves with their country in the Franco-Prussian War. This printed handkerchief shows an open-air service on the Day of Atonement, 1870, outside Metz. According to the verses, Christian soldiers kept watch during the ceremony. A 'War Haggadah' service book (*right*) makes the same point for the 1914-18 War. (22, 23)

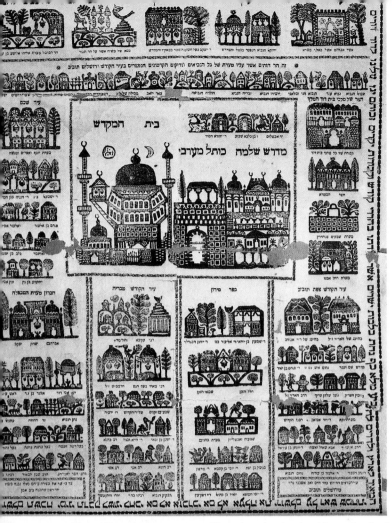

The first steps towards a recolonization of Eretz Israel were taken in the early 19th century. Sir Moses Montefiore, the great Anglo-Jewish philanthropist, founded several institutions, including a printing-press, a textile factory and agricultural communes. He used part of his immense wealth to buy land from the Turks for Jewish settlements. This seal relates to the Kerem Moshe area, a new quarter of Jerusalem – almost a garden suburb – outside the walls. (25)

Eretz Israel, the concept of Israel as the destined homeland of the Jewish people, was an ideal that never faded. Jerusalem was a place of pilgrimage for Jews as much as, if not more than, for Christians and Muslims. This late 19th-century woodcut features Jerusalem in the centre, surrounded by the tombs of kings, prophets, saints and rabbis. The little scene second from the left at the top is the 'throne of the Messiah on Mt Tabor', with throne and *shofar*. (24)

The number of Jews coming to Palestine from Europe (mainly from Eastern Europe) continued to increase up to 1914, when it reached about 100,000. Their achievement in founding a viable community went hand in hand with the political efforts of Zionist leaders to attain statehood. Up to 1917 they lived under Turkish rule. The conquest of Palestine by British forces in that year marked a turning point in Jewish fortunes. *Right:* physical training at a girls' school in Jaffa or Tel-Aviv, 1915. *Below:* three seals from around 1900, of a soap factory, a *yeshiva* (talmudic college) and an agricultural association. (26-29)

The grape harvest in an early commune. The tower in the background is used to keep watch against thieves. (30)

'Produce of Jewish villages in Palestine', reads the sign over this shop (*above right*) at the Berlin World Fair of 1896. The décor is still distinctly Turkish, but Jewish enterprise is already making its mark. (31)

The arts and education were organized on an ambitious scale from the beginning. *Right:* the Rishon-le-Zion Orchestra, founded in 1896. *Below:* the Bezalel School of Arts and Crafts, founded in 1906 (note the portrait of Herzl on the wall at the back). *Below right:* a class in Hebrew at the Bezalel School. (32, 33, 34)

The success of modern Israel has surprised both her friends and enemies. Using advanced methods, land that had been desert for centuries has been brought into cultivation. *Above:* the fields of a Kibbutz at Yotveta, in the Negev. The tremendous problem of lack of water has been tackled and great progress has been made towards solving it. (35)

Industry: Israel's is a fast growing economy. Between 1958 and 1970 industrial output increased by nearly four hundred per cent. Israel Aircraft Industries, one of the country's largest enterprises, produces aircraft and aeroengines (*below*) both for the home market and for export. Three-quarters of Israel's exports go to Europe or America. (36)

Fruit farming has developed into one of Israel's major export industries, specializing in semi-tropical products like dates (*above*) and oranges (*below*). Mass cultivation has entailed the use of a whole range of new equipment for picking, topping, hedging, pruning and shaking. While fruit production is mostly privately owned, communal settlements, comprising about three-quarters of the country's cultivable land, dominate other branches of agriculture. The collectivist Kibbutz movement, with its emphasis on social levelling, played an important part in the early years. (37, 38)

Founding fathers: Moses Hess (1812-75) was a precursor of Zionism, whose book *Rome and Jerusalem* is a perceptive analysis of the Jewish predicament in Europe. Leon Pinsker (1821-91) studied at Odessa and Moscow and at first supported assimilation. The pogroms of 1881 convinced him that the foundation of a Jewish state was the only solution, and under his leadership active steps for settlement in Palestine began.

Theodor Herzl (1860-1904) pulled the movement together, founded the World Zionist Organization and by the time of his early death had given it the momentum to success. Asher Ginsberg (1856-1927) was drawn to Pinsker's circle at Odessa. Writing under the name of Ahad Ha-'Am ('one of the people'), he crystallized an approach to Zionism that emphasized the moral and cultural over the political. (39)

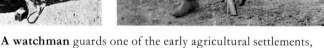

Herzl attends the Sixth Zionist Congress in 1903, only a year before his death; he is seen here with delegates from England. (40)

A watchman guards one of the early agricultural settlements, about 1910. (41)

The Western Wall was – and is – the focus of Jewish devotion in Jerusalem: a photograph taken by Gertrude Bell in 1899. (42)

Tel-Aviv was founded in 1909 (*below*) on the seashore just north of Jaffa. (43)

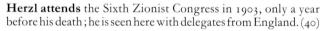

The birth of Israel

'His Majesty's Government view with favour the establishment in Palestine of a national home for the Jewish people, and will use their best endeavours to facilitate the achievement of this object.' The Balfour Declaration of November 1917 seemed to many Zionists the fulfilment of all their hopes. But it was deliberately vague, and it was a statement of intent only. Nevertheless, when a Zionist Commission arrived in Jerusalem the following year (*above right*) it was given an enthusiastic reception (*right*). (44, 45)

The way to nationhood was rough. Between 1922 and 1947 the country was ruled by Britain under a Mandate from the League of Nations. Jewish and Arab expectations were irreconcilable; violence mounted, exacerbated by the war. In 1947 the whole question was referred to the United Nations, which recommended partition. On 15 May 1948, the State of Israel came into being. *Below right*: David Ben-Gurion reading the proclamation beneath a portrait of Herzl. (46)

Modern Israel is a unique phenomenon with unique problems. The great question of physical survival is matched by other, internal questions, less urgent but more complex. How are secular and religious values to be balanced? What will the Jewish past mean to the Jewish future? What is to be the relationship between Israelis and the Jews of the Diaspora?

The top picture shows Tel-Aviv today, the first modern all-Jewish city in the world, with a population approaching a million. More evocative in the context of this book, perhaps, is the shepherd girl (*left*), guarding her sheep with a radio in her hand and gun behind her. It is the sort of disturbing image that has appealed to contemporary Israeli poets – a patriarchal scene brought joltingly up to date, like the opening stanza of Yehudah Amichai's 'A Sort of Apocalypse':

*The man under his fig-tree telephones to the
    man under his vine.
'Tonight they will surely come.
Armour the leaves,
Lock up the trees,
Call home the dead and be prepared.'*

(47, 48)

Chapter Fifteen

Judaism and Modernity

ARTHUR HERTZBERG

THERE IS NO COMMONLY ACCEPTED VIEW as to when the modern era in Jewish history began. In the 19th century 'modernity' was generally held to coincide with political emancipation. The hinge on which history turned was therefore the French Revolution, for it was in the midst of those great events, in 1791, that the Jews of France were granted equality before the law for the first time anywhere in Europe. In recent decades several other definitions have been proposed. Ben Zion Dinur, the 'founding father' of Israeli historiography, and his disciples defined modernity as beginning early in the 18th century with the first stirrings in the Diaspora towards the return to Palestine. Others paid primary attention to the breakdown of normative Judaism, and the increasing disobedience to talmudic Laws in the last two centuries. In the opinion of Gershom Scholem, the pioneer authority on Jewish mysticism and Messianism, the critical breach occurred through Sabbatai Zevi, who appeared in the middle of the 17th century to announce that the Torah was now nullified because he had come to declare the final redemption. Scholem posited Sabbatai Zevi as the direct ancestor of Reform Judaism and even of Zionism. There are other views, which highlight the explosive impact of Western culture on the Jews of the ghetto; in this perspective, what is new in the modern era is that for the first time (at very least since the 'golden age' in Spain, the brief early medieval era of Jewish intellectual symbiosis with high Arabic culture) the advanced intelligentsia of European Jewry was confronted with a problem that had occurred on a world-wide scale only once before, in the Hellenistic era: namely, whether they believed in the divine origin of their own religion and whether they could believe, on any ground, in the superiority of their culture and tradition to that of the majority.

Europe in turmoil

Despite their differences, these views can, without doing them violence, be divided into two contrasting positions: those that emphasize inner factors of self-generated revolt against earlier stages of Jewish history and those that put the accent on outer factors, the world of the Gentiles beckoning to Jews. Without attempting to decide between these two opinions (they are, indeed, more in the nature of ideological assertions about what Jews should be striving towards than assessments of the past) it seems safest, and perhaps even truest, to take a synthetic view. By the middle of the 17th century, both Christian Europe and its pervasive minority, the Jews,

were in serious turmoil. The inner unity of Christendom had been challenged by the Renaissance, with its re-evocation of classic paganism; by the Reformation, which, at least in theory, made every man the judge of religious truth; and by the new science, which was undermining the authority of all inherited knowledge. Within Jewry, enforced conversion in Spain before the Expulsion in 1492 created the Marranos, who in their thousands lived for generations as secret Jews. As time went on, their knowledge of authentic Judaism faded and what remained was a religious identity that was marginal both to Christianity and to their own faith. Uriel da Costa, a representative figure from these circles, escaped, like many others, to Amsterdam and reverted to Judaism, but he could make peace with neither faith; his stormy career ended in suicide in 1647.

In the next year, 1648, perhaps one third of the Jews of Eastern Europe were murdered by the Cossacks under Bogdan Chmielnicki, the leader of the revolt in the Ukraine against the Poles, in pogroms the likes of which had not occurred since the Crusades. Large-scale persecutions had always evoked Messianic stirrings, dreams of a miraculous redemption near at hand. What was different after 1492, and especially after 1648, was an increasing practicality even among the visionaries. In the 1520s, the mysterious David Reubeni appeared as the supposed emissary of an Eastern kingdom of the lost ten Tribes of Israel to negotiate with the Pope for an alliance against the Turks; one of the conditions was to be the restoration of Palestine to the Jews. A generation later, Joseph Nassi, the most prominent of ex-Marranos, treated with the Sultan, to whose court he belonged, to the same end; in 1561 he received the rule of Tiberias and seven nearby villages, but the effort soon petered out. Sabbatai Zevi, although far more mystical, was aware that the return could not take place without an understanding with the Turks. It was the Eastern European followers of that false Messiah who produced the first group of settlers who came to Palestine in 1700 to labour on this earth as part of an ongoing process of restoration.

Most of these themes came together for the first time in the mind and life of Baruch Spinoza. He was born in Amsterdam in 1632 of immediate Marrano extraction (his father had fled from Spain as an adult) and as a youth he attended the famous school of talmudic studies in that city. In early adulthood Spinoza broke radically with the faith in revelation and moved to a philosophical position that asserted that both the physical and the historical world were determined by laws, universally true, that were open to reason. Specific revelations or cultures were, at best, secondary and partial reflections of universal moral laws; more likely they were the enshrining of fantasies and untruths. In a famous scene, the young Spinoza was excommunicated by the Jewish leaders of Amsterdam. He spent the rest of his life supporting himself by grinding lenses for optical use and writing the works for which he will always be remembered, the *Ethics* and the *Tractatus Theologico-Politicus*.

This second work was primarily a criticism of the Bible in the name of reason and universal moral norms. Spinoza made use of medieval Jewish analyses of the biblical text as building blocks for his radical – and new – assertion that the Bible had been written not by Moses but by a variety of men who contradicted themselves and each other. Spinoza thus denied the fundamentals of Judaism, the faith in revelation and in the chosenness of the Jews. He was the first Jew to live outside the Jewish community, both socially and intellectually, without converting to another religion, even pro forma. The destiny of the Jews did concern him. It was a self-conscious implication of his work that the unique disabilities of Jews, and for that matter of all other subgroups in society, would disappear when men achieved the rule of reason. He even envisioned the possibility for the Jewish group as a whole of the re-establishment of their commonwealth in Palestine. They might some day come to live under their own political laws again, which would justify the continuing apartness they might choose to practise.

Most of the problems of Jewish modernity thus existed by the second half of the 17th century. The Jewish roots of Spinoza's criticism of the biblical tradition were in the medieval philosophical rationalists and not in the mystics or in the Messianists. However, Sabbatai Zevi and Chmielnicki, both of whom he never mentioned, were his contemporaries.

In politics and economics it was the age of mercantilism. Jews in Spinoza's own Amsterdam had large economic rights because they were of use to the Dutch state, which thought of itself economically in totally secular terms. In France, in the early years of the 18th century, the Jews of Alsace dared to petition the crown, for the first time not for some increase in their limited rights, but for total economic equality – for the right to trade and work at all economic pursuits on 'the same footing as his Majesty's other subjects'. The demands that the Jews put formally in 1789 to the Estates General, which Louis XVI convoked and which initiated the revolution, were no more extensive. From all perspectives, therefore, it seems just to begin the modern era with the middle of the 17th century and to trace the development of each of its major themes, and their interrelationships, from that period.

This discussion about dating the beginning of the period is no mere exercise in historical theorizing. By pushing back the boundary of the modern age by a century, it becomes clear that in the intellectual realm Jewish modernity, in all its schools of thought, has preceded rather than followed political freedom. From Spinoza through Moses Mendelssohn a century later to the late 19th-century founders of the Jewish Socialist Bund and of Zionism in Russia (the 'Lovers of Zion', of

whom more will be said below), all of these 'modern' Jews lived in regimes in which the law discriminated against them. Every movement and form of Jewish modernity without exception was first defined by unfree Jews. The question of whether to believe in the older tradition or in some other newer faith was indeed intertwined in the last several centuries with the quest by the Jews for political freedom and social acceptance, but intellectual modernization was a precondition of political equality. It was Jews who had already intellectually entered, or half-entered, the non-Jewish world who led the fight throughout the modern age for the completion of their acceptance and, generally, for that of all Jewry. Those who remained, or chose to remain, in the older life, were usually indifferent to or even opposed to political emancipation, which they viewed as a preamble to the breakdown within Jewry of the older values. They were right. Wherever a relatively small group of 'enlightened' Jews succeeded in gaining political emancipation, mass Westernization followed in no more than a generation.

Emancipation – the great dilemma

In the 18th century, a small but highly significant group of Jewish capitalists in Western Europe (court agents, army purveyors, ship owners, bankers and merchants on the stock exchange) adapted themselves not only to the business ways of early capitalism but also to the social ways of their Gentile peers. In this age of Enlightenment the fashionable faiths were either deism or half-veiled atheism. By the middle of the century an increasing number of Jews shared in the prevailing intellectual culture. Such a one was Isaac de Pinto, a French Jew who tried in 1762 to get Voltaire to accept him as a man who belonged to the European world. Voltaire was not totally accepting, although he had no reason to doubt that de Pinto had freed himself of 'Jewish superstitions'. Indeed he had – he was a deist – but de Pinto, like innumerable such figures in the next two centuries, nonetheless remained within Jewry and even served as the lay head of a synagogue.

Moses Mendelssohn in contemporary Berlin was even more conservative. The central issue before him was how to define Judaism in such a manner that it would remain the religion to which Jews adhered and would be held in intellectual respect. For that purpose he persuaded himself that in its basic faith Judaism was, like all other high religions, identical with universal deism, and that the Bible, if rightly understood, was God's lesson in moral virtue for all mankind. What pertains specifically to Jews is an unchanging, divinely ordained commitment to the ritual laws. Mendelssohn, who died in 1786, was involved in the opening stages of the battle for economic and political equality. He was willing to offer on the altar of individual equality before the law the separate Jewish community, with its structure, half willed and half imposed, of a legally established self-government. He and his disciples wanted to change the education and habits of the mass of Jews, to Westernize their mode of life in order to prepare them for political equality and social acceptance by the majority. In the next generation, many of the children of these innovators went radically beyond their parents and left the Jewish community, but this was not the intention of the fathers.

In Tsarist Russia, in which the bulk of world Jewry lived throughout the 19th century, the problems of emancipation, and how to achieve it, did not appear until half a century later, by the third decade of the 19th century. Here, until the pogroms of 1881 put an end to such hopes, the ambition of 'enlightened' Jews (*Maskilim*), following Mendelssohn's maxim, 'Be a Jew at home and a man in society,' was merely to live in, and be treated as part of, the countries of which they were citizens. For that matter, under the radically different circumstances in the 20th century, this continues to be the dominant Jewish self-definition in the Western democracies and especially in the United States. The French and American revolutions have made of religion the private and personal choice of the individual, who regards it as a matter, at least in theory, of no public consequence.

What was fundamental was the change in feeling among the majority of Jews. For many centuries Jews had been willing to live outside society waiting for their supernatural redemption. This was 'normal' in ages when the Gentile world was dominated by other-worldliness, at least in theory. By the middle of the 18th century an emerging Christian middle class was merely paying lip-service, or less, to talk of damnation and predetermination. The accent was now on justifying life even in heaven by successes in this world. The effect of this pervasive atmosphere on Jews, and particularly on those who were being allowed to enter the mercantilist arena, was to make them impatient of other-worldliness and anxious to define Jews and Judaism in terms that would make it possible for them to enter society.

Changes began in France even before the revolution. The Sephardim of Bordeaux, whose leaders were avowed rationalists two generations before the revolution, excluded study of the Talmud from their school for the young as early as the 1760s. In Germany, a lay leader in the town of Seesen in the Rhineland, Israel Jacobson, made changes, in 1810, in the ritual of his synagogue to include the use of an organ, and he added a church-like steeple to the building, with a bell to call the congregation to prayer. In 1818, a group of younger people in Hamburg organized a temple of Jewish worship on a self-consciously reformed basis, holding that all the rituals were subject to modification according to 'the spirit of the times'. By the 1840s, a few younger rabbis in Germany were eager to institutionalize a radical break with the inherited Orthodoxy. In three successive synods in the mid-1840s, Judaism was defined as essentially a theological and moral outlook of universal import, and all the rituals, including, in the view of some, even the Sabbath and circumcision, were declared as past and transcended stages of faith. The door was thus opened to the definition of Jews as Germans or Frenchmen or Englishmen of the Mosaic faith.

Concurrently, in the United States, a parallel development was taking place which owed more to life and less to ideology than the events in central Europe. In 1824 in Charleston, South Carolina, some of the grandchildren of the first colonial settlers, led by a young writer and journalist named Isaac Harby, revolted against their elders in the Sephardi synagogue. This group split off from the parent community and for a few years maintained a synagogue of its own, in the image of a

The title-page to the Book of Psalms, translated into German by Moses Mendelssohn and published in Berlin three years before his death. At the time, Judaeo–German, with its Hebrew script, was still the Jewish medium of expression, and Mendelssohn's mastery of German was a significant step in Jewish emancipation from the ghetto outlook.

proper congregation of the Protestant kind. The announced position was the desire to be rid of older superstitions in order to appear reasonable and similar to their Christian neighbours.

The flood-tide of religious reform in the United States came after the middle of the 19th century, with the arrival of the second wave of immigrants, largely from central Europe. They represented, overwhelmingly, the least educated and least Westernized classes. Their move to reform was motivated much more by adjustment to American conditions than by ideology. It was difficult to adhere to Jewish observances when travelling the roads as an itinerant trader in the frontier areas, as almost every one of these immigrants began by doing. When they began to settle down in a couple of decades, as merchants and even, a few, as bankers, the transition to Protestant-type, bourgeois style even in religion was easy and almost self-evident.

By the time the third major wave of immigrants began to arrive in the United States, after the pogroms in Russia in 1881–2, almost all the American synagogues were Reformed. The dominant figure then, Isaac Mayer Wise, came from Bohemia, but he preached a profound passion for America, a desire that Jews be totally integrated into the new country and that the synagogue on those shores should reflect a new rite (*Minhag America*), different from that of all previous countries of Jewish habitation. He organized the Union of American Hebrew Congregations in 1873 and the Hebrew Union College, the Reformed rabbinic seminary, in 1875.

One of the effects of the Reform movement was an elaboration of synagogue liturgy (adopting some features of Christian worship, such as organs and bells) and a corresponding elaboration of synagogue architecture. This lavishly decorated building is the new Cologne synagogue, by E. F. Zwirner, opened in 1861.

The return to Orthodoxy

From the 1780s to the 1880s, a century of Jewish experience was thus dominated by the drive of Jews into the larger world. But there were those who accepted the basic proposition of the new outlook, that Jews could no longer live in an intellectual or cultural ghetto, and yet reasserted the position of Moses Mendelssohn himself, that Jews could live as modern men and yet obey the tradition. Punctilious ritual Orthodoxy could be a protected and unchanging segment of the life of the individual. This view was restated in the 1830s by the first rabbi in Germany to receive a university doctorate and yet remain Orthodox in his religious practice and conviction, Sampson Raphael Hirsch. In the course of a half-century of activity, which was co-extensive with the heyday of Reform in Germany, he succeeded in creating an alternative community and its institutions based on the neo-Orthodox definition of Judaism. Though German in language and culture, Hirsch and his followers were too Orthodox in religion even to remain in the organized, tax-supported Jewish community, which, in 1856, had accepted the law making the Reform synagogue part of the officially designated Jewish community, entitled to the same rights as the Orthodox synagogue. Hirsch's group completely separated itself from the rest of German Jewry, by law, in 1876.

More fundamentally, however, the underlying outlook of the Enlightenment was being questioned in the 19th century by the new forces of romanticism and nationalism. The histories and traditions of individual communities; their roots in their own pasts and their

hopes for themselves in the future; the sense of the individual as related in the first instance to his own kind, to his ancestors and to those who shared his outlook and destiny – such affirmations challenged and soon replaced the notion of the individual as relating directly to a world-wide human society. In these accents, in the name of history, and of the God who dwelt not in moral and theological abstractions but in the concrete experience of a historic community, a number of Jewish scholars and thinkers challenged Reform in the middle of the 19th century. In Italy, S. D. Luzatto contrasted Jewish and Western culture as eternal opposites; in Galicia in Eastern Europe, Nachman Krochmal wrote his *Guide to the Perplexed of the Times*, which identified God as the Absolute Spirit expressing itself in the recurrent cycles of Jewish history; in Germany, the historian Heinrich Graetz began on his life work, the first great modern synthetic history of the Jews from Maccabean times to the present, in the many volumes of which he tried to demonstrate the uniqueness of Jewish suffering and Jewish creativity, faith and fortitude. Zechariah Fraenkel, a participant in the second synod that defined Reform, made a demonstration out of leaving the synod over the issue of the Hebrew language. He was willing to countenance quite a number of the changes in ritual proposed by the reformers but he could not accept the suggestion that the language of prayer should cease to be Hebrew and become German. To Fraenkel's historical sensibility, a change in language would represent a radical break with the Jewish past. He and his followers soon defined the 'historical school' in modern Judaism, called Conservative Judaism after its transplantation to the United States by Solomon Schechter, half a century later. The rabbinical seminary in Breslau in eastern Germany was founded in 1854 and it continued in Fraenkel's spirit until its end in the Hitler years. It stood for a Judaism of tradition, of moderate change, of intellectual and social Westernization and of the identification of a modern Jewish religious outlook with the commitment to the Jewish people, past and present.

A very substantial part of the Jews in the 19th century either remained untouched by these stirrings in the direction of modernity or resisted them. Even in the stormy days of the French Revolution there were Jewish leaders who did not desire the total entry of Jews into society at the cost of surrendering their own autonomous community. When, in 1807, Napoleon called together a rather melodramatically styled Sanhedrin, in the hope that the rabbis and lay leaders there assembled would redefine Judaism to direct it towards rapid assimilation, there was a firm majority of Conservatives who would not change Jewish Law and practice in any way not sanctioned by the Talmud. The most serious opposition to modernity arose, however, in central and Eastern Europe. Moses Schreiber, who occupied the rabbinic office in the city of Bratislava in the middle years of the 19th century, was a considerable figure of the widest influence in Orthodox circles. He pronounced anathema on the whole of modernity, its ways and its thoughts, in the name of the unchanged and unchangeable life of the inherited Judaism. In Eastern Europe the disciples of the great 18th-century scholar, Elijah of Vilna, organized new centres of talmudic study, the *yeshivas*, in order to counteract the inroads of the new age. The Hasidim remained unshakably committed in all particulars to the ways of the founders of the movement in the middle of the 18th century.

Throughout the 19th century and into the 20th, these groups, which had once fought one another, increasingly learned to co-operate against the common enemy, modernity, especially in its Jewish form. By the early years of the 20th century, bridges were even built to the Western neo-Orthodox, who had been regarded earlier with considerable suspicion. In Eastern Europe the main thrust of the battle was to protect Jews from any taint of Western education, even as various governments attempted to enforce and compel some basic secular learning. The advent of Zionism at the end of the century, and the adherence even of some Orthodox forces to the new movement, precipitated the organization, in 1912, of a new body, the Agudath Israel, which encompassed most of the older forces. This organization stood for unchanging Judaism. It resisted the Zionist attempt to create a Jewish nation state, for it feared secularization.

All of the permutations of modern Jewish religious thought described so far continue to exist to this very day both as theory and in organizational forms, though with some changes because of the traumatic and glorious events of the 20th century. After the Hitler years and the creation of the State of Israel, both Reform Judaism on the religious left and most of the ultra-Orthodox on the right have abandoned their anti-Zionism. Reform now agrees even in theory that the Jews are a people, an ethnic religious community, and not merely a 'church' of believers in Jewish dogma. The bulk of ultra-Orthodoxy operates in practice as part of a world-wide Jewish people. The Agudath Israel is a political party in Israel and it is represented in the Knesset, even though it continues to maintain in theory its unchanged theological outlook. The majority of the Orthodox forces throughout the Jewish world, and the overwhelming majority of the non-Orthodox, go much further: they regard the creation of the State of Israel as an event of epochal religious significance. In most synagogues today the prayer for Israel as ordained by its Chief Rabbinate is repeated every Sabbath. It terms the creation of the state 'the first root of our redemption'.

Ethics for the individual

The major crises and controversies in Jewish religious thought during the last two centuries have thus revolved around two themes: the relationship to tradition, to the laws and practices handed down from the past, and the involvement in the community of Jews. The individual, in his mortality, his fear and his need for personal hope and meaning, has been scanted. In the 19th century, modern theologians had very much less to say in this realm than did the older ones. The Hasidim continued to believe and to teach that God was to be worshipped, no matter what the personal circumstances, in joy and in encounter. Among the talmudic rationalists there arose in the middle of the 19th century a pietistic group which taught *musar*, ethics, a life of fear and trembling, of the most exquisite and critical awareness of the moral import of even the slightest action and of the need for constant self-correction. It was not till the early years of the 20th century, in the works of Martin Buber and Franz

Rosenzweig, that the individual appeared as the centre of two modern Jewish theologies. Buber's Hasidim were depicted as much more individualistic than the real ones were, or had ever been. In Buber's version, man stood alone before God, unbounded by any traditional norms and aided only by the examples of what happened to others before him in their wrestlings with divinity. Rosenzweig moved from nearly abandoning Judaism towards affirming the whole of the tradition ('from the periphery to the centre'). Even at the end of Rosenzweig's journey the Jewish individual remained his own judge of what he had heard and of what he could therefore affirm with integrity. These individualistic religious views of Buber and Rosenzweig have not – by their very nature they could not have – been embodied in institutions, but they remain influential and important even in those circles of the modernists for whom religion is primarily nationalist.

The universalist dimension was equally under-represented in modern Jewish religious thought. To be sure, Reform Judaism in its earliest definitions did conceive of the Jews as a religious denomination that had as its purpose the propagation of ethical monotheism. From this definition was derived the notion that Jews ought to behave, both as individuals and as a community, in such fashion as to be exemplary. Among many Jews this was simply translated into somewhat nervous self-congratulation at having become respectable bourgeois. Among many others, however, such theology was the source of profound passion for social service. In central and Western Europe to a considerable degree, and even more so in the United States, the network of modern Jewish social services to the poor, the ill, broken families and the like, which was constructed in the last hundred years, was largely a creation of 'modern', very often Reform, Jews. In the United States this passion for social service in the name of human decency even spilled over into the creation in the 1870s of a non-denominational, largely Jewish group, Ethical Culture, within which an element of the upper middle class, almost totally Jewish in origin, practised its social concerns while entirely abandoning all specifically Jewish observances.

The major thrust of Jewish universalist concerns was, however, to be found outside the community, among the revolutionaries. In France as early as the 1820s, a number of young Jews from leading families adhered to the new religion of science and technocracy that was proclaimed by St-Simon. In this new dispensation there would be neither Jews nor Gentiles, but only modern men who were together building a new order. The motivations of such figures as the brothers Jacob and Isaac Péreire were far different from those of their contemporaries who simply converted to Christianity because they wanted to assimilate into the existing majority. The Péreires believed, in their youth (they later returned to Jewish affairs), that the prophetic impulse in Judaism itself commanded Jews in the new age to make common cause with all men who would abandon particularisms in the name of an activist universal social ideal. Such a belief is the root of the propensity of Jews for the last century and a half to be in the forefront, in outsize numbers and with markedly prophetic fervour, in almost every movement of political and intellectual revolt.

Movements for social reform in the 19th century included many Jews, and the most fervent for universalist solutions were often those who had rejected Judaism most completely. The foremost example is Karl Marx. In his view, the Jewish problem was due solely to capitalism; abolish the second and the first would disappear. In the new economic order, Jews and non-Jews would work together until the distinction became meaningless.

It is a distinguished line. The most important early figure was Karl Marx. He defined his position on the Jewish question as a young man, in an essay written in 1843. The main thrust of his argument (couched in some unforgivably anti-Semitic rhetoric, with which he distanced himself from his Jewish origins) was that the Jewish question exists because of capitalism. The Jew is the most striking version of the immemorial capitalist. The tensions which the Jew evokes could not disappear through emancipation by the bourgeois society but only in a new order in which capitalism would no longer exist. Therefore, nothing that Jews could do to change their lives or their religion, and, more important, nothing that the bourgeois society could do to change its laws would make any difference whatsoever. The Jewish question would disappear together with the social dysfunctions of capitalism, which had given rise to Jewish existence in the first place. Jews and non-Jews had only one fruitful path, to work for a new economic order.

With essentially minor variations, these views as announced by Marx were the faith for the next century of Jewish revolutionary socialists of many varieties. Some, such as the young Moses Hess, who was a colleague of Marx, and Ferdinand Lassalle, another contemporary, who was the founder of the German Socialist party, were very much aware of their Jewish motivations. On the other hand, such figures as Rosa Luxemburg, murdered in Germany in 1919 after the failure of the left wing revolt in Bavaria, and Leon Trotsky, second only to Lenin among the makers of the Russian Revolution, denied – as Marx had before them – that any Jewish self-awareness coloured their lives and labours.

In the cultural realm too, despite a substantial number of Jewish conservatives, the main thrust of Jewish

intellectuals in the modern age has been towards liberal, untraditional culture. Heinrich Heine, the first important Jewish literary figure in the 19th century, was the leader of Young Germany, the movement of revolt in the 1830s against the authority of older forms and traditions. Very nearly a century later, in Germany after the First World War, Jews were prominent in all the modern 'isms', from architecture through art and literature to opera. Everywhere to this day Jews are present in such movements in significantly large numbers.

This phenomenon is perhaps best understood by examining the Jewish element in Sigmund Freud and his disciples. For him, on psychoanalytic grounds (as for Spinoza more than two centuries earlier on rational grounds and for Karl Marx, on economic grounds), historic communities were secondary and were based on myths and delusions. Human experience could be understood by studying drives and feelings, which are ultimately the same for each individual, regardless of the history of the group into which he was born. Self-understanding would cure man of illusions and neuroses, including that of religion. Freud himself never quite broke his ties with his own Jewishness, though he knew that this part of himself remained an unanalyzed mystery. In this respect too, he was typical of many of his Jewish followers (they were the large majority): self-consciously and avowedly, Freud and his disciples proposed psychoanalysis as a new outlook that could cure men of their hatreds – including, of course, the seemingly unending hostility between Jews and those who persecuted them – and of their self-hatreds.

From what has been said so far it is clear that the major schools of Jewish thought in the modern era were responses to the Enlightenment, and to its universalism. Mendelssohn and Sampson Raphael Hirsch entered European culture while walling off an enclave in their lives for Orthodox Judaism. The early reformers defined Judaism as the most enlightened example of ethical universalism. A variety of Jewish rebels, from the brothers Péreire to recent days, when young Jews were so prominent in the anti-establishment movements in Western universities in the late 1960s, insisted that they, precisely because they were Jews, had a mission to help create a new order for all men.

The nationalist response

There was, however, a powerful particularist, anti-Enlightenment counter-theme in modern Jewish thoughts. It was evoked by nationalism, which began to flourish in Europe in the early years of the 19th century.

The first stirrings towards Jewish political nationalism began around 1830, soon after the successful revolt of the Greeks against the Turks. A Sephardi rabbi and Kabbalist from Sarajevo, Yehudah Alkalai argued, against the weight of Orthodox opinion, that it was permissible for Jews to act politically in this world for their restoration to Palestine and not wait passively for divine miracles. All the nations, especially the oppressed smaller ones, were now arising to fight for their independence; why should not the Jews? Such ideas were to occur, independent of Alkalai, to a number of other rabbinic contemporaries. By 1860, Moses Hess, a completely modern man, a founder of Communism, turned back to his Jewish roots and published a short book entitled *Rome and Jerusalem*. He proposed the restoration of the Jews to Palestine not only as a political necessity but primarily in order to enable a modern generation to live again in its own religio-national culture.

Contrary to accepted clichés among those who have written about Zionism, Hess was not ignored when he published his then startling views. But Hess was no organizer of a movement; the Jewish intelligentsia to which he appealed still believed in the future triumph of either the bourgeois or the socialist revolution in Europe. Indeed, this faith, more implicit in action than expressed in theory, has never been abandoned by the bulk of the Jews of the world, not even in the tragic years of the Hitler era or in the aftermath of the heroic events which attended the creation of the State of Israel. The bulk of world Jewry remained and remains by choice in the Diaspora, confident that their individual lives are secure in the Western world.

As persecution increased in Eastern Europe, culminating in the pogroms of 1881–2 in Russia, and as anti-Semitic parties appeared in France, Austria and Germany, some Jews did conclude that there was no hope in Europe and that the only way that they could enter the political world as equals was through creating their own nation. The way in which this was accomplished, first through the writings of theorists such as Pinsker and then through the practical organization of Herzl and his supporters, is related at length in the next chapter.

Zionism and 'Diaspora nationalism'

Theodor Herzl was, as he had dreamt, the founding father of the Zionist state. Yet, in two fundamental respects, the state and the world-wide Jewish people of which it has been the centre since its creation are quite different from what Herzl imagined. Even more sharply than Pinsker before him, his dominant concern was the 'normalization' of the Jewish people: he wanted to find a way for Jews to be effectively modern, secular people. A Jewish nation state would make it possible for Jewry to behave 'like everyone else', including the choice for some, or many, individuals to assimilate effectively. Those who chose to live outside the borders of the Jewish state would, like Germans who emigrated to the United States or Russians who went to France, easily lose themselves in the community of their choice, because a normal Jewish national community would exist for those who preferred to be Jews. Herzl of course imagined that the majority of the Jews of the world, meaning primarily those of Eastern Europe, would, if given a chance, emigrate to a Jewish state – already in existence, or in the process of formation. Herzl thought also that the cultural and religious content of a renewed Jewish state needed to owe no more, and perhaps even less, to the Jewish heritage than any European liberal state in the modern era owed, or should owe, to its medieval past.

Events in the turbulent half century after Herzl first appeared have not confirmed his prognosis. The large masses of persecuted Jews in Eastern Europe fled westward in their millions before World War I, mostly to the United States, in search of the personal equality denied to them in Russia. Only handfuls, fewer than thirty thousand, went to Palestine in those years. The overwhelming majority of Herzl's contemporaries, the Jewish intelligentsia in Western Europe to whom he had addressed himself initially, refused to follow his lead. They continued to put their political hopes in the liberal state, or to join the revolutionary movements. Herzl attracted people such as the young Martin Buber and Chaim Weizmann, whose motivations were rooted in the soil of Jewish spiritual and religious concern. They had rallied to Herzl because they were troubled about anti-Semitism, but it was not their primary obsession. They wanted to refresh the Jewish spiritual heritage, and the recreation of a national community in the land of their ancestors seemed to such people – they were the bulk of Herzl's followers – to be indispensable for such purpose.

This kind of Zionism had already been defined in Russia a few years before Herzl appeared on the Jewish scene. In the aftermath of 1882, and as a direct result of Pinsker's pamphlet, *Auto-Emancipation!* . . . an organization called Hovevei Zion (Lovers of Zion) was established. It engaged in limited colonization activity in Palestine but its primary endeavours were in the intellectual and spiritual field. After 1889, Asher Ginzberg, who wrote under the pseudonym Ahad Ha-ʿAm ('one of the people'), became the dominant spiritual force in this movement. Jews, he said, had to shore up their national identity by creating a 'spiritual centre' in Palestine. This centre would devise new, authentically Jewish cultural content and modes of behaviour that the rest of world Jewry, continuing to exist in the Diaspora, could adopt and adapt. The world of Ahad Ha-ʿAm was the Hebrew language and the literary and intellectual past in all varieties; his task and burden was to try to translate this heritage into a modern cultural nationalism. Ahad Ha-ʿAm and Herzl met once. As was inevitable, they completely misunderstood each other. Modern Zionism has, however, been the creation of both men. From its very beginning the movement laboured to create a Jewish self-governing entity. It was also from its very beginning the quasi-religion of Jews who wanted to be modern men and yet retain the Jewish loyalties and even build on them in new ways.

Zionism in any of its versions was, however, not the only option or even the dominant one at the turn of the century among those who wanted to affirm themselves as Jews through ethnic or national loyalties. There were a number of other possibilities. In the very year in which Herzl founded the Zionist Organization, 1897, a group of Jewish workers met in Vilna to organize the Jewish Socialist Bund. In theory this body existed for the purpose of furthering universalist socialist aims; the reason for its separate existence was language, Yiddish, for only in that language, the spoken language of the masses, could the Jewish workers be approached. The Bund soon became much more Jewish nationalist. It affirmed the need to preserve a completely secular Jewish national identity in the language of the masses, even in a new socialist dispensation. While the Bund fought against Zionism in the name of the duty of Jews to remain in their native lands and work towards a better society for all, it also insisted on Jewish cultural continuity. There was thus some truth in Lenin's mocking observation that it was a body of Zionists who 'were afraid of seasickness'. Despite its opponents in both the socialist and Zionist camps, the Bund was a great force in Eastern Europe. It was more powerful than Zionism in Russia before the revolution and it remained a major factor in interwar Poland, emerging as the dominant party in the communal elections right before World War II.

In the first two decades of its existence, the Bund had evolved towards a socialist version of Jewish Diaspora nationalism. The principal proponent of this idea was Simon Dubnow, a Russian Jewish historian whose politics were more liberal than socialist. Dubnow's understanding of Jewish history was based on the proposition that the Jewish people had undergone an evolution. It had once in early biblical days been a normal people dwelling on its own land, but only briefly. The Diaspora was not primarily a creation of disaster, of the destruction of Jewish independence first by the Babylonians and then by the Romans, but rather it was a result of the inner dynamics of Jewish history. The Jews had chosen to create other centres, such as the settlements in Babylonia and Egypt, even when Palestine was in their hands. They had chosen long ago to become the first world-wide people united by historic and cultural ties and operating everywhere through self-governing institutions. This was the direction, Dubnow asserted, in which all people were moving, away from land and state towards dispersed peoples co-existing in multiethnic political structures. In each age of Jewish history one community, or at most two, had taken the lead and been the centre for the Jews of the world. Dubnow's programme for his own time consisted of urging the creation of Jewish semi-autonomous communities everywhere, of working to strengthen culture in both Hebrew and Yiddish and of insisting that, though the new Zionist community in Palestine was important, the most critical issues were in the Diaspora where continuity could be guaranteed only by Diaspora nationalism.

Dubnow's thought has had a much greater intellectual and even political effect than has been generally perceived. The Yiddishists, who redefined East European Jewish identity as that of a national group with its own spoken language and culture (in the language that it had acquired to replace Hebrew), were very much under Dubnow's influence. The debt was acknowledged at the founding conference of the Yiddishists in 1908, in Czernowitz. After World War I, one of the two central Jewish demands on which even assimilationists from Western Europe and the United States were willing to agree at the peace conference in Versailles was the request, which was heeded, that minority rights for Jews be written into the treaties with the newly independent states that were being carved out of the Russian Empire.

Dubnow's most lasting and least obvious influence remains in the United States. To be sure, the institutions of an autonomous minority cannot exist in American law. It is also true that Zionist rhetoric has been used in the United States throughout the 20th century to describe what has really amounted to Diaspora nationalism. The dominant Jewish self-definition in the United States has been that of a community operating within 'cultural pluralism'. America as a whole was defined in the early 1900s by two Jewish thinkers, Horace Kallen and Mordecai Kaplan, as a country made up of various immigrant groups which should, while belonging to the general society, maintain their own ethnic traditions. Jews would thus survive in America as one community among the many. What united Jews was not religion but history, culture and fellow-feeling for all Jews everywhere. Kallen and Kaplan both emphasized the importance to contemporary Jewish life of the Zionist effort in Palestine, but their primary emphasis was on continued Jewish existence in America.

The theory of cultural pluralism has had two basic uses: it has provided a rationale against assimilation by countering the 'melting pot' image of America; it has enabled a post-religious community to identify its Jewish emotions and Jewish activities, however they express themselves, as valid forms of continuity with the Jewish past. Horace Kallen understood this best when he distinguished between 'Judaism' and 'Hebraism'. He defined Judaism as the dos and the do nots of traditional Jewish religion; he proposed Hebraism as the term that summed up all those things that Jews choose in their day to do together because it seems to them to be worth doing. Despite his disbelief in Orthodox religion, Ahad Ha-ʿAm belonged to Judaism, for the past as history remained the source of value judgments. Dubnow was much more secular and more permissive. The cultural, communal definition implicit in much – perhaps most – of contemporary Jewish experience is somewhere between these two options.

There is one fundamental respect in which contemporary Jewish experience has followed neither Dubnow nor even Ahad Ha-ʿAm: the realm of the relationship between the Diaspora and the State of Israel. As Dubnow insisted, much of Jewish life today continues to be lived, even creatively, in the major Diaspora communities. As Ahad Ha-ʿAm insisted, Israel is now the centre of the Jewish world, the shared concern of all Diaspora communities. What was unforseen was the nature of that concern. Both Ahad Ha-ʿAm and Dubnow were oriented to culture, but the contemporary situation is pragmatic. The task that all Jews share today is that of working for the upbuilding and support of Israel; the major instrumentalities of world Jewry exist primarily for this task. The Jewish world as a whole is now being sustained by a kind of 'social gospel', in which practical and tangible labours for Israel are based on a common denominator: Jewish loyalty.

The Jewish people entered the modern age facing its own religious doubts and striving for political acceptance. It is still facing these twin problems today in a new key. Those who choose to remain Jews affirm not faith in a revelation but loyalty to a community; the prime task of that community is to labour for the dignity of the Jewish people among the peoples, which a Jewish state symbolizes. None the less, certain perennial questions remain and will not go away. No contemporary Jewish community, either in Israel or in the Diaspora, is free of them. What indeed is the spiritual and ethical content of Jewish ethnicity? For that matter, does the Jewish people require such content? Is being Jewish really just a matter of ethnic or nationalist feeling, which it is not so difficult to discard, or are Jews ultimately created for some profound purpose – and by whom?

The questions were posed some three centuries ago. As we have seen, they have been answered and reanswered, in theory and in life, many times. Like all serious and fundamental questions, they remain open to be rethought and reargued in each new generation.

Chapter Sixteen

Zionism and Israel

DAVID VITAL

THE ESSENTIAL CONTENT OF ZIONISM – and the greatest source of its power to move men's minds – has been the doctrine that the course of Jewish history must be reversed and the familiar patterns of Jewish life in the Dispersion transformed. The Exile must be ended, the Diaspora wholly or largely wound up. By one great stroke – by setting apart a defined territory into which the Jews would gather and in which, as the majority people, they would rule themselves – the scales of the Exile would be made to drop away. Its social, psychological and intellectual distortions would be eliminated, its physical miseries and its humiliations ended and a whole new range of mental and social activity opened up as much for the Jews as a people as for the Jews as individuals. In purpose Zionism was, therefore, revolutionary and in flavour had something of the romantic. In its time, in its formative period towards the end of the 19th century, it was a thoroughly *modern* movement, inconceivable except as a child of the general liberal trend in Europe throughout that century and of liberalism's double impact on the Jews: the fact or promise of civil emancipation and the inroads of secularization on the ancient forms of Jewish communal life and the practices and thinking of individual Jews. But Zionism has to be understood too as a *reaction* to the emancipation, at any rate to its incompleteness, to its unforeseen and undesirable consequences and to the disappointments it engendered. And here, a broad distinction must be made between those parts of the Diaspora where a formal grant of civil liberties and substantial, if not necessarily complete, equality with non-Jews had been made and those where inequality and insecurity remained the rule.

In Western and central Europe it was apparent in the last quarter of the century that the civil and legal emancipation of the Jews had not solved the 'Jewish Problem' – not for the convinced and systematic anti-Semites, nor for the Jews themselves. It had only taken on new, subtler, and in some ways more painful, forms. Certainly, emancipation had allowed the Jews to bring their qualities of industry, thrift and tenacity into play and greatly to improve their material condition. They did not starve. They were now rarely, if ever, subject to persecution at the hands of the mob, let alone of the authorities. They had, as individuals, taken on roles of some importance in economic and intellectual life. And while pockets of tradition remained, so far as externals of dress and habitation, command of the indigenous languages, access to, and avidity for, general education, and, per contra, loss of Hebrew, diminishing command of Jewish learning, and fading interest in, and respect for, the norms of the tradition were all concerned, it was evident that the face of Western Jewry had been transformed. None the less, the Jews, as Max Nordau told the First Zionist Congress (1897) in a classic analysis of their condition, had misunderstood the purpose of the emancipation – which was to bring the formal arrangements of society into line with general liberal principles – and had failed to see that fundamental attitudes to the Jews in the lands of their exile had undergone no change. Then, said Nordau, after

> a slumber of thirty to sixty years, anti-Semitism broke out once more from the innermost depth of the nations and his real situation was revealed to the mortified Jew.... He has lost the home of the ghetto, but the land of his birth is denied to him as his home....
>
> The emancipated Jew is insecure in his relations with his fellow beings, timid with strangers, even suspicious of the secret feelings of his friends. His best powers are exhausted in the suppression, or at least the difficult concealment, of his own real character. For he fears that this character might be recognized as Jewish, and he never has the satisfaction of showing himself as he is in all his thoughts and sentiments. He becomes an inner cripple.

But these were problems for the *individual* which, under the new dispensation (if he accepted it), he had to face alone; while the importance he ascribed to them depended, at this stage, upon his mental make-up, his sensitivity and the company he kept or wished to keep. It followed that a disposition to question openly, let alone reject the post-emancipatory condition – whether on the moral grounds that it was an ignoble one or on the pragmatic grounds that it was founded upon an illusion – was far from common. Zionism in its Western form, the fruit of just such a disposition to question, was, therefore, necessarily the approach of a small and unrepresentative minority; and the established leaders of Western Jewry, judging it to be subversive of their achievements and of their new status, either opposed it with force from every available platform and pulpit or else dismissed it as an affair of cranks and eccentrics. And so, perhaps, it would have remained – at any rate until the full resurgence of systematic anti-Semitism in central and Western Europe in the 1930s and 1940s – had not the

E. M. Lilien's memorial to the victims of the Kishinev massacre in 1903. A martyr, bound to the stake and wrapped in a prayer-shawl, is received by an angel bearing the Torah scroll.

private sorrows and doubts of the Western Zionists been complemented by the growth, to huge dimensions, of the public and entirely concrete miseries to which the Jews of Eastern Europe became subject in the last quarter of the 19th century.

The dilemma of Eastern Jewry

There, in the heartland of Jewry, where three-quarters or so of the total of ten or eleven million lived, no civil emancipation had taken place and none was in prospect. In Romania the Jews were not even admitted to be citizens and fully lawful residents of the state. In Russia and its possessions, which alone contained half of all Jewry, the long-standing system of restrictions, inequalities and constraints under which the Jews lived was in continual process of intensification in scope and severity. Upon the accession of Alexander III in 1881, officially sponsored mob-violence, large-scale expulsions from the countryside into the towns, limits on access to schools and universities and other refinements had been added to the blanket prohibition of residence in most of Russia, the restrictions on occupation, the special taxes and a per capita rate of conscription into the army that was higher than for any other ethnic group and had been in force for a century. By 1888, an official Russian commission of inquiry into the affairs of the Jews found that the law books contained 650 separate restrictive regulations directed specifically at the Jewish subjects of

the Tsar. By the end of the decade, the great migration of Eastern Jewry westwards, which was to change the demographic face of Jewry in less than half a century, was already well under way and the hopes had evaporated of those who had relied on Russia adopting, however slowly, the liberal tendency that was still the rule in Western and even central Europe.

The hostility and violence with which the government of Alexander III had turned upon the Jews had thus produced two clear-cut results. And these – the stimulus to migration and the inculcation into the Jews of a mood of deep and ineradicable hostility to the autocracy – had one thing in common: they evoked responses that ran contrary to the normally stoic manner in which Jews had in the past tended to meet change for the worse in the lands of their dispersion. Characteristically, it was among those who were best equipped to survive economically and socially in Russia itself, and, therefore, under least pressure to leave, that the refusal to take the new developments in their stride was most marked. On the whole, these were Jews who had gone some way towards secularization and even Russification and whose hopes had been highest for a Russia in which they could maintain themselves approximately as Jews then maintained themselves in France or Germany. Their fundamental response, especially to the pogroms of 1881–4, but also to the entire scene as it was now revealed to them, was hurt and fury:

> When we are ill-used, robbed, plundered and dishonoured [wrote Y. L. Pinsker] we dare not defend ourselves, and, worse still, we take it almost as a matter of course. When our face is slapped, we soothe our burning cheek with cold water; and when a bloody wound has been inflicted, we apply a bandage. When we are turned out of the house which we ourselves built, we beg humbly for mercy, and when we fail to reach the heart of our oppressor we move on in search of another exile. . . . We have sunk so low that we have become almost jubilant when, as in the West, a small fraction of our people is put on an equal footing with non-Jews. But he who is *put* on a footing stands but weakly. . . . Though you prove yourselves patriots a thousand times . . . some fine morning you find yourselves crossing the border and you are reminded by the mob that you are, after all, nothing but vagrants and parasites, without the protection of the law.

The classic response to persecution was to accept it as a fact of nature, a manifestation of the inscrutable Divine Will. Pinsker, the Zionist, sought to subject anti-Semitic behaviour to analysis. The fear and hatred that sprang from it were pathological, he contended, and ingrained habits of mind were impervious to argument. For the Gentiles, Jews were eternal and universal aliens, uniquely so in that they had no country of their own from which they had come and none to which they would or could return. Such 'a people without a territory is like a man without a shadow: a thing unnatural, spectral.' To this Judaeophobia the emancipation, a set of legal, not social measures, was largely irrelevant. Besides, what had been granted as a gift could be as easily withdrawn.

But Pinsker's main concern was with the Jews themselves. He attacked them for their timidity and he challenged them to see matters as they really were.

We must reconcile ourselves once and for all to the idea that the other nations, by reason of their inherent natural antagonism, will forever reject us. We must not shut our eyes to this natural force which works like every other elemental force; we must take it into account.

The Jews must, therefore, cease to look to others to emancipate them; they must strive for *auto*-emancipation, they must free themselves by their own efforts. They must form a national organization and take a national resolution. And their goal must be a territory, a homeland, a *single* refuge, a land into which they might enter as of right, which would be 'politically assured', and in which they might finally reconstitute their lives, individually and collectively. This was no more than other peoples had asked for and in many cases obtained – peoples whose claim to territorial and political independence was no greater than the Jews'. The need was urgent. The Western Jews, who alone were free to act, should take the lead without delay.

The Zionist goal

Much of the strength of Zionism, down to the successful establishment of a Jewish territorial state in 1948, lay in the great simplicity of its central purpose. For in this purpose programmatic goal and fundamental *Weltanschauung* were neatly and logically combined. All Zionists were united in their conviction that the drive to assimilate had failed – and deserved to fail; that the condition of all but insignificant portions of Jewry was either morally or materially intolerable, or both; that the Jews must look to themselves, not to others, for salvation; that they must aim at a territorial solution, thus reconstituting themselves as a political nation; and that the only territory on which Jewish life and society could be so remade was the ancestral Land of Israel itself.

But in practice, this unity was qualified and diminished by profound differences on other, albeit related matters and on what might or might not actually be feasible in the light of the resources available to the movement and the opposition to Zionism within Jewry and outside it.

These differences reflected the great variety of conditions and opinions in Jewry itself: the circumstances of the various communities, the extent to which Jews were free to assume public, political roles, the degree of secularization and attitudes to the Orthodox tradition, the pull of other ideologies – socialism notably – which, on the face of it, had nothing to do with the particular problems of the Jews, and, of course, peculiarities of temperament. 'Political Zionism', namely the tendency to work first and foremost for a state with the approval and co-operation of the governments directly or indirectly concerned with Eretz Israel and on a basis of give and take, was first promoted, not unnaturally, by the free Jews of the West. 'Practical Zionism', which amounted to concentration on the piecemeal settlement of Eretz Israel in defiance, if necessary, of the Ottoman authorities, was, perhaps as naturally, the policy favoured by the less self-confident, less sanguine, much less free, more timid but also more patient Zionists of the East, whose somewhat grim determination to pursue a cautious long-term course evinced something of classic Jewish attitudes to public

questions. Distinct religious and socialist tendencies appeared in the movement almost from the first and were soon recognized and institutionalized. In part, they were the inevitable consequences of a belief – which not all adhered to and was itself the subject of debate – that the territorial state was a necessary but not sufficient goal, and that questions relating to the nature of the state, to its ultimate form and internal arrangements, were not merely valid but deserving of immediate discussion. In part, the religious and socialist parties grew out of the circumstance that interim policy frequently touched upon issues to which the Orthodox or the socialists, as the case might be, could not but be sensitive: education, or the precise terms in which the Zionist case was cast for public propagation, or the allies the movement might legitimately seek, or the practices and organization of the various groups of settlers in Eretz Israel. Even the question of Eretz Israel itself was a matter for debate, at any rate until the expulsion of the Turks in 1917–18 and the promise of British support for Zionism (as embodied in the Balfour Declaration) appeared to open the way to political autonomy and large-scale settlement there once and for all.

Eretz Israel: redemption and return

In its initial and simplest form, the question of the attitude of the Zionist movement to Eretz Israel boiled down to a question of matching goals to capabilities. If a recognized foothold in the country was unobtainable, as it appeared to be, after repeated attempts to induce the Ottoman government to mitigate its hostility to the movement, and if the material condition of the Jews in Eastern Europe cried out for cure and the Jews were streaming to other countries anyway, as was certainly the case, was it not incumbent upon the movement to seek a temporary solution, elsewhere? And was it not wiser on general grounds to establish at least the principle of Jewish political autonomy, outside Eretz Israel if need be, if one of the Powers was prepared to co-operate with the Zionists to that end for reasons of its own? For such was the case when, soon after the final dashing of hopes of a change of heart in Istanbul, the British government informed Theodor Herzl that it was ready to consider the establishment of a Jewish settlement with local autonomy in East Africa.

The East Africa proposal, brought by Herzl to the Sixth Congress in 1903, was the subject of the fiercest ideological debate ever held. In the event, it was settled quite rapidly in favour of an absolute demand for the Land of Israel and a rejection of all alternatives, temporary or otherwise. The results were momentous. In the short term the decision represented a victory for the Eastern wing (and variety) of Zionism and presaged a change of leadership and a shift of the movement's centre of gravity to the East, where it could be said to have belonged: for it cannot be stressed too often that it was East European Jewry, particularly the Jews inhabiting the Russian Empire and its successor states, who gave the Zionist movement its strongest raison d'être, its mass following, its greatest source of energy, most of its leaders, many of its governing ideas and much of its special character. In the longer term, unwittingly, it set the Zionists, and ultimately the Jewish people as a whole, on a path of conflict with the Arabs and, to a lesser

The Zionist dream: a design by the Galician artist E. M. Lilien, commemorating the Fifth Congress of Zionists, Basel. An angel, the Star of David on his robe, points from the land of oppression to the new life of work and freedom where the sun is rising.

degree, with Muslims generally. Last and perhaps most fundamental, was the significance of the decision for the essential quality and ethos of Zionism itself as the national movement of the Jewish people.

Zionism, it must be noted, has no authoritative or fundamental text which successive generations may interpret and reinterpret for guidance. The canon, such as it is, consists of less than half a dozen highly individual, quite brief, and for the most part unambitious analyses of the Jewish condition and outlines of programmes for action. Of these, Moses Hess's *Rome and Jerusalem* (1862) and Ahad Ha-ʿAm's running commentary on events, in the form of a series of essays extending from the late 1880s to the early 1920s, are the finest and most original in intellectual quality. Pinsker's pamphlet, *Auto-Emancipation!* (1882), is the most moving and, perhaps, the best reflection of the contemporary mood. Herzl's pamphlet, *Der Judenstaat* (1896), usually called *The Jewish State*, was the most clearly political in intention and, as a plan for action, the one with most practical effect. Generally, the theoretical and programmatic writings of Zionism have been sporadic and disconnected – as is illustrated by the fact that Herzl had read neither Hess nor Pinsker until well after the publication of his own manifesto and his assumption of leadership over the movement. Formal statements of purpose, the most famous of which was the Basel Programme resolved upon at the First Congress of Zionists in 1897, were conceived as political documents addressed to the outside world rather than to the movement's own members, and therefore were studiously written with an eye to what was politic. The Basel Programme makes no mention of the movement's ultimate goal (on which, in any case, there had been no agreement), but speaks cautiously of Zionism aiming 'at the creation of a home for the Jewish people in Palestine to be secured by public law.'

The absence of great comprehensive and systematic works of social analysis, upon which successive generations might draw, and a certain vagueness and fluidity of doctrine, even on matters that were clearly and absolutely central to the entire undertaking, are best explained as the consequence of the Zionists' profound sense of their weakness and isolation, and, with it, the conviction that all concerned were at one in their fondest hopes; that there was, therefore, little need or profit in giving hostages to fortune. Pragmatic considerations, considerations of means, rather than of ends, dominated the thinking of the movement's most influential members over the years and largely governed their behaviour. The ends seemed always to be so remote as to make attention to them appear a little absurd. Besides, the means to which the movement devoted most attention between the death of Herzl and the end of the Second World War – the steady, piecemeal building up of the new *yishuv* (settlement) – seemed to many, and particularly to those on the left, to be of immense value in themselves. For here the transformation of the Jews, their 'normalization', was in process before the eyes of all. In contrast, the proclamation of ultimate purposes and excessive ventilation of the issues involved were judged political acts, liable to have adverse political consequences both for the internal composition and structure of the movement and for the balance of forces between it and its external enemies. It is fair to add that there were always those who thought otherwise, those who thought it entirely politic to say clearly and publicly where you were heading and with whom you wished to travel. As late as the 1930s, when the question whether or not finally to define the *Endziel* (the final goal) still agitated the movement, one of the smaller parties resolved to call itself the Jewish State Party. It was judged, correctly, to have intended an act of defiance and provocation. But radicals of that type were always in the minority and the usual disposition of the majority, at least until the 1940s, was to trim – both on the *Endziel* and, more generally, on the fundamental constituent ideas of the Zionist ideology or rationale. Until, that is, circumstances forced a decision or a stand one way or the other.

This is what happened in 1903, for the really fundamental issue that came to a head, albeit implicitly, in the course of the great debate on the East Africa proposal concerned the possible and desirable relationship between the Jews and the non-Jews. This, of course, was the heart of the contemporary problem of Jewry. It may be said to touch on the inner content of Judaism itself.

The Zionist view on the feasibility and propriety of the integration and assimilation of Jews into non-Jewish society as *individuals* has already been outlined. There remained the question of what might be called the integration (or reintegration) of the Jewish people as such, *collectively*, into the society of nations, its terms and its limits, if any.

At one level, the pro-East Africa faction, the Territorialists, as they came to be called after the decision to reject the project had been taken (and after its chief promoter, Herzl himself, had died, soon after succumbing to the will of the majority), argued pragmatically. Eretz Israel was unobtainable for large-scale settlement and for a self-governing Jewish community. There, only a return to the small-scale methods and humble purposes of pre-Herzlian, 'practical Zionism' could be expected – 'Zion without Zionism', as Israel Zangwill, their leader, put it. So better a 'provisional Palestine', he said, than none at all: 'Any territory which was Jewish, under a Jewish flag, would save the Jew's body and the Jew's soul.'

But there was another level to the argument. Here is Zangwill opening his campaign to reassert the original, Herzlian, Territorialist approach:

We are approaching the season when the pious Russian Jew, sitting at the Passover table, rejoices at his redemption from slavery. . . . A few months ago you might have seen our prisoners of the Pale celebrate their feast of Chanukah, their Thanksgiving or Independence Day. The irony of it! These downtrodden, cringing victims of the Ghetto celebrating the victories of Judas Maccabaeus! The poor, peaceful slum dwellers, who have never known a fatherland, singing paeans of triumph at having won back their Holy Land and Temple from the ancient Syro-Greeks over two thousand years ago! Is it not about time Rip Van Winkle woke up and took stock of things and himself? We have not had a stocktaking for nearly two thousand years. It is eighteen hundred and thirty-five years since we lost our fatherland, and the period of mourning should be about over. We have either got to reconcile ourselves to our loss or set about recovering it. But to choose clearly between one alternative or the other is a faculty the Jew has lost.

It is plain that what Zangwill was after was not the end of the Jewish people, once and for all, but the end of the Jews as a Peculiar People. If elements of the past could be preserved without excessive trouble and, above all, without impeding progress towards what might be termed Redemption through Normalcy, well and good. But whatever threatened to impede such progress must be jettisoned; and this sloughing off of ancient burdens could be done with a good conscience, to say nothing of some, not unjustifiable, relief.

Eretz Israel, however, was central to Jewish history and belief; the Exile is the exile from it; in the Tradition, Redemption and Return imply each other; and it could be argued that it is the bond with the Land as much as anything else that has prevented the Jewish religion from falling easily into line with other faiths as one of several

possible options open to adoption by any decent member of a modern liberal society (outside Israel). Regardless of whatever validity the Territorialist view may have had in its pragmatic aspect, the abandonment of Eretz Israel, even temporarily, was correctly understood as a step implying a revolution in Jewish life far deeper than desired by any but a fraction of the Zionists. The content of Zionism was revolutionary, but its revolution was intended to be of limited and defined degree. The links with the past were not to be cut, but refashioned.

Ahad Ha-ʿAm spoke for the opposing party:

Seven years ago [i.e. just before Herzl appeared on the scene] we had an *ideal*. We already knew that the . . . settlement of Eretz Israel would not solve the problem of the migrants in search of bread, and we knew (and it did not occur to us to complain) that we would not attain to a *new* life (in the political sense) in Eretz Israel for who knows how many generations. But our ideal was the spiritual regeneration of the nation. Seeing the growth of disunion and spiritual ruin all about us we hoped to fight it by the establishment of a national centre in Eretz Israel, slowly, by simple, but well ordered settlement, a *yishuv* founded on the national spirit, such as would give our people back its union and its historic but now weakening bond with the great past . . . .

They had hoped, Ahad Ha-ʿAm recalled, that to this the Turks would agree and that, therefore, this was a purpose requiring no ' "diplomats" from Vienna'. But then came Herzl and

put the matter of the Jews entirely in material terms and turned Eretz Israel into a *political* ideal for present purposes. What he said to you was: Do you want to rid yourselves of all your miseries? Then leave the countries of your exile and found your own, autonomous state, in Eretz Israel. . . . And then in the course of time you underwent a change of heart without noticing the fact. The Zionist ideal took on a purely political significance for you. The moral and spiritual ideal slowly faded and Zion came to signify *only* a solution to the problem of the Jews [as individuals] . . . the *state* became the essential. But if that was the case, [Herzl was right and the state] should indeed be set up without delay; for the exile has become very hard and the power to endure it is at an end. . . . [Yet the truth was that] *we* had never sought a solution for our bodily miseries in Eretz Israel and consequently we had no reason to go elsewhere. What *we* seek in Eretz Israel is not to be found elsewhere.

Zangwill's Territorialism made no great headway; neither did Ahad Ha-ʿAm's notion of a small, ideal, model society, a 'spiritual centre' for Jewry to inspire and edify and pull a disintegrating Diaspora together. Or rather, the Zionists, in their great majority, held both to the Territorialist principle that the state must cope with what Ahad Ha-ʿAm tended to dismiss as the 'bodily miseries' of the Jews and to the Ahad Ha-ʿAmist principle that what they should be about was the moral and social regeneration of the Jewish people, and that *this* could only be done by drawing, however selectively, on the vast storehouse of the nation's history and culture. They refused, by and large, to follow Zangwill's advice

In 1922, a Russian commemorative anthology was published by Jewish emigrés in honour of Theodor Herzl, who had died some twenty years before. His pamphlet (foreground) is Der Judenstaat, *of 1896. Behind him, Zionist pioneers mount to a symbolic new Jerusalem.*

and 'choose clearly between one alternative or the other'. And since, in practice, no political progress could be made for many years, all that was left for the movement to attend to, if it was not to disintegrate into inaction and apathy, was to help build up a small and in many ways superior community in Eretz Israel, in which many of the elements that Ahad Ha-ʿAm sought for his 'centre' were to be found or were in the making.

The Great War and after

But, in the course of time, external circumstances first encouraged and then compelled the Zionists to revert to full-scale political action. The great upheaval precipitated by the outbreak of the World War in 1914 brought the prospect (and, in its wake, the reality) of new rulers over Eretz Israel. To the leaders, it enhanced the value of support from even so weak and scattered a force as the Jews could (or were thought able to) muster. It completed the process whereby emigration from Eastern Europe to Western Europe and overseas to North America and elsewhere was being brought to an end. And it pitched the persecution of the Jews, notably in newly independent Poland and in briefly independent Ukraine, at a practically unprecedented level of death, injury, humiliation and destitution. Together, British imperial interests, a successful reappearance of the Zionists on the international diplomatic stage, led by Weizmann, greater recognition by Jews and non-Jews alike of the desperate *needs* of the Jews, and of the uses of Zionism as a method of dealing with them, combined to give the Zionist movement a new lease on life, as well as renewed hopes and, for the first time, formal international status. Under the new world order the British government's wartime declaration 'in favour of the establishment in Palestine of a national home for the Jewish people' was incorporated bodily into the League of Nations' Mandate; Britain was enjoined to put it into

effect; the 'historic connection of the Jewish people with Palestine and . . . the grounds for reconstituting their national home in that country' were explicitly recognized, as was the Zionist Organization as the 'appropriate Jewish agency . . . for the purpose of advising and co-operating with the Administration of Palestine' to that end.

But the Great War over and its control of Palestine secured, the value of the Jews in Britain's political eyes waned, while that of the Arabs grew. And since, after some initial hesitation, Arab leaders set their peoples on a path of fundamentalist hostility to the Zionists, and, by natural extension, to the Jews in general – a position from which their successors have not really wavered to this day – the Zionist movement soon found itself locked in a triangular conflict with Imperial Britain and Arab neighbours alike, all three sides of which were characterized by a steadily growing intensity of emotion and violence of action. For a while, none the less, the crucial side of the triangle, so far as the Zionists were concerned, was the Jewish-British relationship. Initially, because hope that the erosion of British support might be halted; then, because although Britain had in effect renounced the Mandate and committed itself to the Arab cause by the outbreak of World War II it had not quit Palestine. The ultimate fate of the country still appeared to be in its hands; and it was Britain that could decide whether Eretz Israel might serve as a refuge for those still able to escape the slaughter-house of wartime Europe. When, in the event, regard for Arab opinion led Britain to deny all but a handful of Jews access to the one country that extended a welcome – thus condemning untold thousands to their death – what remained of the original structure of trust and mutual interest between Jews and British crumbled into dust. In the final and protracted crisis between the end of the war and the proclamation of the State of Israel in May 1948, the Jews were to all intents and purposes alone. They had reverted under Ben-Gurion to a clear political, Herzlian thrust, fuelled by greater bodily misery than either Herzl or Zangwill had ever imagined, but relying chiefly on such military and economic resources as the still small, still rather select, still somewhat Ahad Ha-ʿAmian *yishuv* could muster.

The State of Israel

The regaining of political rights over Eretz Israel eighteen centuries after the last vestiges of Jewish autonomy had been obliterated by the Romans must surely be reckoned a stunning achievement. In particular, the success of the Zionists in winning through to their goal must be measured against their own small numbers and absurdly limited resources and the vast forces marshalled against them: Britain, still the preponderant power in the Middle East, her Arab allies and satellites, and, for much of the crucial period, although never with absolute consistency, the United States as well. The opposition to the Jewish cause had many sources, some atavistic and ugly, some heartless, and some – given the terms in which statesmen tend to conceive their function – ostensibly rational and respectable and, in their way, well meaning. But the nub of the matter, at all levels and for all concerned, was the idea of there being a Jewish state at all. To some it seemed an enterprise that was inherently incredible, if not perverse. Some thought it fraught with incalculable and unspeakable dangers. Some judged it (and some still judge it) contrary to the fundamental teachings of (Christian and Muslim) religion. Whatever the argument, its enemies accounted it (and many still account it) a project to be fought very hard and with every available political and military weapon. In 1948, with so much hostile force arrayed against them, with the American Secretary of State's harsh warnings not to proceed with the proclamation of the state ringing in their ears, not all the members of the inner Zionist leadership itself were inclined to support wholeheartedly so momentous and irreversible a decision. Nevertheless, in the end, it was precisely with this sense of historic responsibility and the belief that 14 May 1948 presented an opportunity that might never be repeated, that, led by a few bold spirits, they were impelled to leap into the unknown.

The state the Zionists built bears the marks of its birth. It is an isolated state and in perpetual conflict with its neighbours. It is devoid of natural or formal allies and is forced to make the best of such co-operation as it can muster in the international arena, some of which has been fleeting, some of which has been durable and none of which has been fully reliable, least of all in times of adversity. It has, therefore, been thrown back, as perhaps no modern state has ever been, on its own resources and it relies to a high degree on the loyalty and support of Jewish communities elsewhere. Thus, it has been said that in the Jewish state are perpetuated some of the ancient, peculiar and anomalous characteristics of the Jewish people. But such truth as there may be in this view must be qualifed by the immensely important reservation that the fundamental rationale of Zionism, namely that the Jews assume responsibility for their own lives and fortunes and organize and equip themselves to discharge that responsibility to the full, has been realized – at all events, for those Jews who have chosen to live in the Jewish state. Still, the upshot has been that although Israel serves, as it was always intended to serve, as a refuge to which all Jews may turn as of right and in which they may live as free men and women, it is a country that cannot yet offer the absolutely safe and protected haven its founding fathers originally had in mind.

For those in need of refuge, it is none the less able to offer a great deal. The great wave of immigration, which began in May 1948 when the fighting in the first Jewish–Arab war, the War of Independence, was at its height (over 300,000 by the end of 1949), was spectacular evidence of such a need and of the ability of Israel to meet it. It was followed by subsequent waves, notably Jews from the Islamic lands and from behind the Iron Curtain and in recent years a not insignificant number of Jews from the Soviet Union. The door is always open: on principle and by law, and, it must be added, of necessity. Israel's small population (three million Jews, half a million others, mostly Arabs) sets narrow limits to its economic and military viability and, when compared with the immense populations of its closest neighbours (seventy million in Egypt, Syria, Iraq, Jordan, Lebanon and Saudi Arabia combined), encourages its enemies and disheartens its friends. A question that hangs perpetually over any consideration of the Zionist enterprise today, three decades after achievement of its specific goal is, therefore, why the bulk of Jewry has not seen fit to join the Jewish state. It can be restated as: what has Zionism – and indeed Israel – come to mean for the Jews of the Diaspora? Either way, it leads to what is surely the central issue in contemporary Jewish life, both in Israel and outside it: the problem of the relationship between the Jews of the Diaspora and the Jews of the Jewish state.

Today's Diaspora

It must be remembered that in one cardinal respect the Zionist movement was overtaken by events. East European Jewry was first reduced, for all practical purposes, by the enclosure of some three million inside Communist Russia. It was then subjected to the terrible war of extermination conducted against it by the Germans during the Second World War. Thus the Jewish state came too late for all but a fraction of the very people for whom it had been intended and who were most suited to it by culture, by inner social cohesion, by relative absence of assimilatory tendencies, by basic political and national belief and by need. The contemporary Diaspora consists, for the most part, of a different class of people, differently placed, whose approach to the Jewish national movement necessarily starts from different premises. The Jews of North America and Western Europe (to whom the present remarks are limited: those of the Soviet Union and Latin American require separate treatment) are, before all else, those who have had the full benefit of the emancipation and who, therefore, generally believe that it is for them as individuals to determine the nature and degree of their commitment to Jewish communal and, a fortiori, national concerns. Accordingly, the inner matter of Zionism tends to present itself in their eyes as a free, ideological question and, perhaps inevitably, to be of real and practical interest only to a minority. There is a constant trickle of immigrants into Israel from the Western countries; but, by and large, the demographic balance between the two great sectors of modern Jewry is stable, at least for the time being.

What of the quite fair numbers of committed, self-styled Zionists who retain their residence in the Diaspora and are politically loyal to their countries of residence? Given the classic and basic Zionist rejection of the Diaspora-Exile in favour of a politically autonomous Jewish society, it is no longer clear what Diaspora Zionism can consist of, now that the state exists and its gates are open, and how it may be distinguished, if at all, from the undifferentiated sympathy and support for Israel that is characteristic of the overwhelming majority of Jews in the West regardless of their personal commitments. It could be said that, whereas Zionism was a minority party in Jewry up to the eve of the Second World War and even up to 1948, today most of those who identify themselves with Jewry are, in some – if reduced – sense of the term, Zionists. Moreover, the effect of the extended conflict in which Israel has been involved, given its preponderantly ethno-religious nature and the reliance Israel places on the free Jewish communities to aid it politically as well as materially, has been to involve the Jews of the Diaspora ever more – and to be judged by others to be involved – in Israel's affairs. In one way or another, the war between Israel and the Arab states has increasingly taken on the lineaments of a conflict in which Israel fights not only for itself, but for and with the Jewish people as a whole. And it is this that gives the problems of the relationship between Israel and the Diaspora its particular urgency and its edge. For the more closely the Diaspora is involved in Israel's affairs the stronger the need must become for consultation and, where possible, co-ordination of approach and policy. Whereas Israel has a government, however, the Diaspora has not. It has long been, and it remains, politically invertebrate. Who is to speak for it? Who is entitled to decide for it? The communal institutions, no matter how worthy, no matter how large, do not and cannot enjoy more than a certain vague moral authority, which is at its most persuasive when it is expressed on purely communal issues. And what of the minority that is opposed, if not to Israel, at any rate to some of Israel's policies, or those who go further and wish to disengage from an Israel not only enmeshed in conflict with the Arabs and the Soviet Union, but also, if at a lower level of enmity, with governments of some of the Western states in which the Jews form large and prosperous communities? Would it not be legitimate in these circumstances to demand of the Israeli government that it should make and formulate its policy not only in the light of the interests of the Jewish state, but in the light of the interests and needs of the Jewish communities outside it? May there not be a case for the leaders of Diaspora Jewry – if they can be identified – to participate actively in the Israeli decision-making process?

To none of these questions is any easy and clear answer in prospect. The institutional and legal obstacles to the establishment of a formal and binding system of political co-ordination are immense on both sides of the divide, and the balance of opinion is unfavourable. But the problems raised by the Jews of Israel and the Jews of the Diaspora being thrown ever more closely together will not go away. They are the fruit of the recreation of a Jewish state and may be seen as so much evidence that the Zionist revolution, like all great revolutions, continues to be at work long after the *event* signalling it is past.

What of Israel itself? If, in the final analysis, the hopes and fortunes of the Jewish people now depend upon this small, imperilled society, because it is upon it that the pressures of all the political, social and religious forces hostile to Jewry are focused, its own social evolution cannot but have the most far-reaching effects upon Jewry everywhere and perhaps, ultimately, on Judaism (as a belief-system) itself.

Whereas the most dramatic impact of Israel on the Diaspora has been a function of the establishment of the state as such, Israel's own society reflects the differences of opinion, if not uncertainty, within the Zionist movement from its earliest days, on the shape their future society should take. The great decision to ensure that the Jewish Risorgimento looked backwards with love, not only forwards with hope, ensured that no fully coherent set of answers could be given and that differences of opinion would grow sharper once that state had been brought into being. For, in the first place, there is a sense in which a Jewish *state* must run counter not only to the forms of private and communal life that have evolved since the emancipation, but, still more profoundly, to the norms and practices of Judaism as

they have evolved since the destruction of the Second Commonwealth. Exile has been the Jews' signal characteristic. Their religious practices and doctrines, their forms of communal organization, the sources of their leaders' authority, their fundamental attitudes to one another and, a fortiori, to non-Jews, their typical hopes and fears, their personal fortunes, their occupations – all these and more have been stamped by exile and its corollaries, minority status and the absence of political autonomy. How well can what was evolved in exile or explicitly designed to preserve the Jews as a non-territorial, non-political nation be made to work in antithetical conditions? Can it be made to work at all? Questions of religious observance and its compatibility with, for example, the technical requirements of modern industry, agriculture and administration are perpetual subjects of dispute, because for those who are themselves observant it is unthinkable that due respect for the injunctions of the Jewish religion not be paid in and by a Jewish state. Divisions of opinion on education, the laws of personal status, and the role and position of non-Jews in a Jewish state and a predominantly Jewish society – matters on which religious teaching touches directly – are hardly susceptible to resolution at all. Zionism, the discontented child of late 19th-century liberalism, and Zionism, the national movement of an ancient people in rebellion, are here in conflict with each other. And issue having been joined, no reasonable and informed observer can imagine that the outcome could be anywhere but in the exceedingly distant future. Nor can its nature be anticipated. What can be said is that, given the common tendency to avoid a clash serious enough to divide the country permanently, it is likely that a slow, fluctuating movement towards synthesis will obtain, with Israel emerging as a somewhat more traditionally minded society than it appeared to be in its early years, but in which Orthodoxy will have been forced by circumstances to make an adjustment to the dictates of sovereignty by its own exceedingly slow and laborious methods. In that event, the impact on Diaspora Jewry cannot but be profound. For in the Diaspora, unlike Israel, Jewish society is still largely defined in terms of religion, or religious affiliation, however thinly stretched and nominal they may have become over large areas of the Western world. The probability is, therefore, that at one level religious observance, where it plays any role at all, will tend slowly to become more rigorous. Of this there are already some signs. At a deeper level, the re-emergence of Judaism as the dominant religion and culture of an independent state and its adjustment and reinterpretation to that fundamental circumstance, will impel a parallel adjustment abroad. Some will reject the possibility out of hand, as some, on theological grounds, have already rejected the man-made state. But the modes of Judaism do not encourage schism, if only because there is no line distinguishing Jewry as a civil society from Jewry as a religious community. And the land of Israel looms too large in the religious scheme of things for events within it, particularly in this realm, to be shrugged off. Finally, if things did move this way they would be moving in a direction that, on the whole, suited the religious communities of the Diaspora for whom the problem of religious practice in a modern society is, in some ways, as acute.

Design by E. M. Lilien, around the turn of the century, for the cover of the 'Golden Book', in which the names of people who had donated generously to the Jewish National Fund (Keren Kayemeth) were inscribed.

Where the rise of an authentic and autonomous Jewish society may have its deepest impact – apart from the factor of political involvement to which reference has been made – is on the thinking of those Jews who are the true, latter-day children of the emancipation, those whose fundamental ethical and political ideas are derived, in the first instance, from secular and non-Jewish sources. These, typically, are educated, middle class, and liberal-minded men and women of good will and good intentions. One great problem that Israel presents for them – although it must be an open question whether these are the terms in which they themselves conceive it – is the ancient one of the compatibility of moral dictates and political imperatives. Where, in the past, they have appeared to be in conflict, the liberal, secular Jew tended typically to hold to the line that the resolution must be such as to satisfy private morality. Such was and is the unique position of the Jew, even in the most free and pluralistic of societies, that he could always choose, in some measure, to stand apart when decisions on public issues were reached of which he did not approve and so retain his moral integrity without excessive trouble.

In the past he was free to support Zionism if he so wished, because it could be accounted a *cause* – a justified cause in his view. But a state is not a cause and the governing and preservation of a state (and of the society which inhabits it) requires forms of action which are often at variance with the dictates of private morality – markedly so in the realm of external relations, where truth and goodness, charity and non-violence may add up to nothing but a sure recipe for downfall. In brief, the dilemmas of raison d'état, insoluble at the level of philosophical discourse and undoubted source of anguish to decent men at all times, are unfamiliar to the Jews in a Jewish context. The Israelis are compelled by circumstances to handle their affairs as best they may; the non-Israelis have tended to observe them from afar, sometimes with awe at their daring, sometimes in distress, sometimes, prudishly, with disapproval. But whatever may be their immediate response to acts of public policy by the government of Israel, the cumulative effect on their thinking must, in the end, be substantial.

The Jewish state, in this sense, is a burden to some Jews. To others, of course, the freedom to take great and hard decisions is exhilarating, so much additional proof of the truth of the original Zionist diagnosis of the ills and humiliations of Jewry and of the means by which they might be sloughed off. For however things may turn out, the year 1948 surely marks one of the great watersheds in the history of the Jews. The Zionists' belief that it was in their power to transform the patterns of Jewish life has been borne out, although, of course, it is far too early to assess the likely structure and ethos of Jewry at the culmination of the process. Meanwhile, the effort to infuse a modern state with as much of the heritage of its people as possible and to bring an ancient culture to terms with modern circumstances might well be watched by others for what it may have to teach them.

Chronology

Most of the events of Jewish history before the year 1000 BCE can be dated only approximately. The migration of Jacob and the age of the Patriarchs, if historical, belong to the first half of the second millennium. Exodus, undocumented outside the Bible, is usually placed in the reign of Ramesses II, 1292–1225 BCE. The rule of the judges must lie between the 12th and 11th centuries. At the end of this period we reach the first fairly secure dates: the reign of Saul, c. 1030–1011 BCE.

BCE

1000 1000–960 David
         960–922 Solomon

         922 Division into the two kingdoms of Judah and Israel
900

         859–24 Shalmaneser III king of Assyria
800

         744–727 Tiglath-Pileser III king of Assyria
         722 Conquest of kingdom of Israel by Assyria
700

         611 Assyria conquered by Babylon
600 609 Battle of Megiddo
         586 Capture of Jerusalem by Nebuchadnezzar. First Temple
                     destroyed. Exile. Age of Isaiah, Jeremiah, Ezekiel
         538 Babylon conquered by Cyrus the Great. Return from Exile.
                     Pentateuch probably reaches final form
500

400 400 Beginning of compilation of the Mishnah

         323 Death of Alexander the Great

         320 Invasion of Palestine by Ptolemy
300 301 Battle of Ipsus

         Palestine disputed between Seleucids and Ptolemies

200 199 Seleucid hegemony established
         190–188 Antiochus III (Seleucis) defeated by Rome
         165–160 Uprising under Judas Maccabaeus. Alliance with Rome
         142 Hasmonean kingdom established. Simon. Alexander Yannai
         135–104 John Hyrcanus
100

         67 Civil War between Hyrcanus II and Aristobulus
         63 Hasmonean kingdom passes under Roman control
         40–4 Herod king of Judaea
CE 6 Roman procurator of Judaea appointed
         c. 20–50 CE Philo Judaeus, philosopher
         Shammai and Hillel, founders of 'Houses' or schools
         50 Gamaliel the Elder, supposed son or grandson of Hillel
         66–70 Jewish War. Second destruction of the Temple
100

         132 Rebellion of Bar Kokhba
         170–210 Principal activity of Rabbi Judah the Patriarch, redactor of
                     the Mishnah
200

         Final redaction of the Mishnah and the 'Writings' of the Bible

300

400
         Palestinian Talmud complete

CE
500 Babylonian Talmud complete

         527–65 Reign of Emperor Justinian. Penal laws against Jews

600 612 Beginning of Jewish persecution in Visigothic Spain
         636 Jerusalem occupied by the Muslims

700
         711 Arab conquests of Visigothic Spain

800

         882–942 Saadya Gaon, philosopher
900

         969 Egypt and Palestine conquered by Fatimids

1000 c. 1021/2–c. 1057 (possibly c. 1070) Solomon ibn Gabirol, poet
                                                       and philosopher
         1040–1105 Rabbi Rashi of Troyes
         1080–1141(?) Yehuda ha-Levi, mystic and philosopher
         1096 First Crusade. Massacres of Jews in many countries
1100
         1135–1204 Moses Maimonides, philosopher

1200
         1258 Conquest of Baghdad by Mongols
         1263 Barcelona Disputation
         1270 Zohar composed
         1290 Jews expelled from England
1300
         1306–15 Jews excluded from France

         1348 Black Death comes to Europe. Persecution of Jews in many
                                                                   countries
         1391 Severe pogroms in Spain
1400
         1453 Fall of Constantinople to the Ottomans

         1492 Expulsion of Jews from Spain
         1497–1507 Expulsion of Jews from Portugal
1500
         1516 The first ghetto established in Venice
         1525 Bomberg's Bible printed in Venice
         1534–72 Isaac Luria, Kabbalist
1600
         1626–76 Sabbatai Zevi, pretended Messiah
         1632–77 Spinoza, philosopher
         1648 Chmielnicki massacres in Poland
         1656 Readmission of Jews to England
1700
         1729–86 Moses Mendelssohn, philosopher
         1781 C. W. Dohm's *On the Civil Improvement of the Jews*
         1782 Joseph II's Toleration Edict
         1789 French Revolution
1800 1790–1 Emancipation of Jews in France

         1807 Napoleon's Grand Sanhedrin
         1808 Napoleon's Infamous Decree
         1858 First Jewish MP sits in the House of Commons
         1860 Foundation of the Alliance Israélite Universelle
         1860–1904 Theodor Herzl (*The Jewish State*, 1896)
         1881–4 Pogroms in Russia. Pinsker's *Auto-Emancipation!*, 1882
         1894–1908 Dreyfus Affair
         1897 First Congress of Zionists
1900
         1917 Balfour Declaration
         1939–45 Second World War. Nazi holocaust
         1948 Foundation of the State of Israel

Select Bibliography

General

Encyclopaedia Judaica (Jerusalem, 1972)
Baron, S. W. *A Social and Religious History of the Jews* (2nd ed.; Philadelphia, 1957–67)
Ben-Sasson, H. H. (ed.) *A History of the Jewish People* (London, 1976)
Finkelstein, L. (ed.) *The Jews: Their History, Culture and Religion* (Philadelphia, 1960)
Netanyahu, B., etc. (eds.) *The World History of the Jewish People* (First Series: London, Ramat-Gan, 1964–77; Second Series: London, Ramat-Gan, 1966–76)

1 Pre-Exilic Jewry

Alt, A. 'The God of the Fathers' in *Essays on Old Testament history and religion*, trs. R. A. Wilson (Oxford, 1966)
Bright, J. *A history of Israel* (2nd ed.; London, 1972)
Fohrer, G. *History of Israelite religion* (Nashville, 1972; London, 1973)
Hermann, S. *A history of Israel in Old Testament times* (London, 1975)
Noth, M. *The history of Israel* (London, 1960)
Saggs, H. W. F. *The encounter with the Divine in Mesopotamia and Israel* (London, 1978)
Vaux, R. de *Histoire ancienne d' Israël* (2 vols; Paris, 1971–3)
Vriezen, T. C. *The religion of ancient Israel* (Guildford, 1967)
Wiseman, D. J. (ed.) *Peoples of Old Testament Times* (Oxford, 1973)
Yeivin, S. *The Israelite conquest of Canaan* (Istanbul, 1971)

2 The Bible

Albright, W. F. *From the Stone Age to Christianity* (London, 1957)
Buber, M. *Moses* (Oxford and London, 1946)
Dahood, M. *The Psalms* (3 vols; New York, 1965)
Frankfort, H. *Kingship and the Gods* (Chicago and London, 1948)
Heschel, A. J. *The Prophets* (New York, 1962)
Kaufmann, Y. *The Religion of Israel* (London, 1961)
Sanders, E. P. *Paul and Palestine Judaism* (London, 1977)
Sandmel, S. (ed.) *Old Testament Issues* (London, 1969)
Weinfeld, M. *Deuteronomy and the Deuteronomic School* (Oxford, 1972)
Welhausen, J. *Prolegomena to the History of Ancient Israel* (New York, 1957)

3 The Jews and the Great Powers of the Ancient World

Abel, P. F.-M. *Histoire de la Palestine depuis la conquête d' Alexandre jusqu'a l'invasion arabe*, Vols I–II (Paris, 1952)
Bickermann, E. *Der Gott der Makkabäer* (Berlin, 1937)
- *From Ezra to the Last of the Maccabees* (New York, 1962)
Hengel, M. *Judaism and Hellenism* (Philadelphia, 1974)
Juster, J. *Les juifs dans l'empire romain, leur condition juridique, economique et sociale*, Vols I–II (Paris, 1914)
Osterley, W. O. E. and Robinson, T. H. *History of Israel*, Vol. II (London, 1932)
Osterly, W. O. E. *Jews and Judaism During the Greek Period* (London, 1941)
Radin, M. *The Jews among the Greeks and Romans* (Philadelphia, 1915)
Safrai, S. and Stern, M. (eds) *Jewish People in the First Century* Compendia Rerum Iudaicarum ad Novum Testamentum, Section One (Assen/Amsterdam, I, 1974; II, 1976)
Schürer, E. *The History of the Jewish People in the Age of Jesus Christ*, Vol. I (eds G. Vermes and F. Millar; Edinburgh, 1973)
Smallwood, E. M. *The Jews Under Roman Rule* (Leiden, 1977)
Stern, M. *Greek and Latin Authors on Jews and Judaism*, Vol. I: *From Herodotus to Plutarch* (Jerusalem, 1974)
Tcherikover, V. *Hellenistic Civilization and the Jews* (2nd ed.), trs. S. Applebaum (Philadelphia, 1961)

4 The Talmud

Neusner, J. *Early Rabbinic Judaism* (Leiden, 1975)
- *First Century Judaism in Crisis* (Nashville, 1975)
- *A History of the Jews in Babylonia* (Leiden, 1965–70)
- *A History of the Mishnaic Law of Holy Things* (Leiden, 1978–9)
- *A History of the Mishnaic Law of Purities* (Leiden, 1974–7)
- *A History of of the Mishnaic Law of Women* (Leiden, 1979)
- *Invitation to the Talmud* (New York, 1973)
- *The Modern Study of the Mishnah* (Leiden, 1973)
- *The Rabbinic Traditions about the Pharisees before 70* (Leiden, 1971)
- *Talmudic Judaism in Sasanian Babylonia. Essays and Studies* (Leiden, 1976)

5 The Ritual and Music of the Synagogue

Adler, I. *La Pratique musicale savante dans quelques communautés Juives en Europe au XVIIe et XVIIIe siècles* (Paris, 1966)
- 'Les chants synagogaux notés au XIIe siècle' in *Revue de Musicologie*, LI (Abbeville, 1965)
- *Hebrew writings concerning music* (Munich, 1975)
Avenary, H. *Studies in the Hebrew, Syrian and Greek liturgical recitative* (Tel-Aviv, 1963)
- *Hebrew Hymn Tunes; the rise and development of a musical tradition* (Tel-Aviv, 1971)
- 'Jewish music: Post-biblical history' *Encyclopaedia Judaica*, Vol. 12 (Jerusalem, 1972)
Bayer, B. *The Material Relics of Music in Ancient Palestine and its Environs* (Tel-Aviv, 1963)
Binder, A. W. *The Jewish Music Movement in America* (New York, 1963)
Gerson-Kiwi, E. 'Juedische Musik' in *Musik in Geschichte und Gegenwart* (Tel-Aviv, 1960)
- 'Vocal Folk-Polyphonies of the Western Orient in Jewish Tradition' *Yuval; Studies of the Jewish Music Research Centre*, I (Jerusalem, 1968)
Idelsohn, A. Z. *Jewish Music in its Historical Development* (New York, 1929)
Katz, I. *Judeo-Spanish Traditional Ballads from Jerusalem* (New York, 1972)
Shiloah, A. *Music Subjects in the Zohar, Texts and Indices* (Jerusalem, 1977)
Werner, E. and Sonne, I. 'The Philosophy and Theory of Music in Judeo-Arabic Literature' in *Hebrew Union College Annual* (Cincinnati; 16, 1941; 17, 1942–3)
Werner, E. *The Sacred Bridge; Interdependence of Liturgy and Music in Synagogue and Church during the first Millennium* (London, 1959)
- *A Voice Still Heard . . . The Sacred Songs of the Ashkenazic Jews* (University Park, Pennsylvania, 1976)
RECORDS: A. Shiloah 'Morasha' Traditional Music Heritage (Ethnic Folkways FE 4202, 1978); 'Jewish Music' Unesco Collection Musical Sources (Philips 658001)

6 The Jews in Spain

Baer, Y. *A History of the Jews in Christian Spain*, Vols I–II (Philadelphia, 1961–6)
Baer, F. *Die Juden in christlichen Spanien*, Vols I–II (Berlin 1929–36)
Beinart, H. *Trujillo: A Jewish Community on the Eve of the Expulsion* (Jerusalem, 1979)
Fernandes, F. *Suarez Documents acerca de la Expulsión* (Valladolid, 1964)
Gines, J. V. *Historia de la viencia española* (Madrid, 1975)
Highfield, R. (ed.) *Spain in the fifteenth Century* (London, 1972)
Vives, J. V. *Manual de Historia Económica de España* (3rd ed.; Barcelona, 1964)

7 The Jews in Byzantium and Medieval Europe

Abrahams, I. *Jewish Life in the Middle Ages* (2nd ed.; London, 1932)
Agus, I. A. *The Heroic Age of Franco-German Jewry* (New York, 1969)
- *The Jewish Community* (3 vols; Philadelphia, 1942)
Blumencranz, B. *Juifs et Chrétiens dans le monde occidental, 430–1096* (Paris, 1965)
Bondy, G. and Dworsky, F. *Zur Geschichte der Juden in Böhmen, Mahren und Schlesien, 906–1620* (2 vols; Prague, 1906)
Browe, P. *Die Judenmission in Mittelalter und die Päpste* (Rome, 1942)
Finkelstein, L. *Jewish Self-Government in the Middle Ages* (New York, 1924)
Grayzel, S. *The Church and the Jews in the XIIIth Century* (2nd ed.; New York, 1966)
Jacoby, D. 'Les Quartiers Juifs de Constantinople à l'Époque Byzantine' in *Byzantion*, T. 37 (Brussels, 1967)
Kisch, G. *The Jews in Medieval Germany* (Chicago, 1949)
Parkes, J. *The Conflict of the Church and the Synagogue* (London, 1934)
Richardson, H. G. *The English Jewry under Angevin Kings* (London, 1960)
Roth, C. *The History of the Jews in Italy* (Philadelphia, 1946)
- *A History of the Jews in England* (Oxford, 1941)
Synan, E. A. *The Popes and the Jews in the Middle Ages* (New York, 1965)
Trachtenberg, J. *The Devil and the Jews* (2nd ed.; New York, 1966)
Twersky, I. 'Aspects of the Social and Cultural History of Provençal Jewry' in *Cahiers d'Histoire Mondiale*, Vol. XI (Quebec, 1968)

8 The Jews under Islam: 6th–16th centuries

Ashtor, E. *The Jews of Moslem Spain* (Philadelphia, 1973)
Cahen, C. 'Dhimma' in *Encyclopaedia of Islam*, Vol. II (Leiden, 1965)
Cohen, G. D. *The Book of Tradition by Abraham Ibn Daud* (Philadelphia, 1967)
Cohen, M. R. 'The Jews under Islam' in *Biographical Essays in Medieval Jewish Studies* (New York, 1976)

Fischel, W. J. *Jews in the Economic and Political Life of Medieval Islam* (New York, 1969)

Goitein, S. D. *A Mediterranean Society: The Jewish Communities of the Arab World as Portrayed in the Documents of the Cairo Geniza*, Vols. I–III (Berkeley, Los Angeles, London, 1967–78)

- *Jews and Arabs, Their Contacts Through the Ages* (3rd ed.; New York, 1974)

- *Letters of Medieval Jewish Traders, Translated from the Arabic* (Princeton, 1973)

Hirschberg, H. Z. (J. W.) *A History of the Jews in North Africa*, Vol. I, *From Antiquity to the Sixteenth Century* (Leiden, 1974)

Katsh, A. I. *Judaism in Islam; Biblical and Talmudic Backgrounds of the Koran and its Commentaries, Suras II and III* (New York, 1954)

Mann, J. *The Jews in Egypt and in Palestine under the Fatimid Caliphs* (New York, 1970)

- *Texts and Studies in Jewish History and Literature* (New York, 1972)

Rosenthal, E. I. J. *Judaism and Islam* (New York and London, 1961)

The Jews under Islam:
c. **1500–today**

Cohen, H. J. and Yehuda, Z. *Asian and African Jews in the Middle East, 1860–1971* (Jerusalem, 1976)

Emmanuel, I. S. *Histoire des Israélites de Salonique* (Thonon, 1936)

Franco, M. *Essai sur l'Histoire des Israélites de l'Empire Ottoman* (Paris, 1897)

Galanté, A. *Documents officiels turcs concernant les Juifs en Turquie* (Istanbul, 1931)

- *Histoire des Juifs d'Istanbul* (Istanbul, 1941)

Goodblatt, M. S. *Jewish Life in Turkey in the 16th Century* (New York, 1952)

Hirschberg, H. Z. 'The Oriental Jewish Communities' in *Religions in the Middle East*, ed. A. J. Arberry, Vol. I (Cambridge, 1969)

9   Jewish Philosophy

Agus, A. *Modern Philosophies of Judaism* (New York, 1970)

Albo, J. *Sefer ha-Ikkarim (Book of Principles)*, ed. and trs. I. Husik (Philadelphia, 1946)

Bergman, S. H. *Faith and Reason: An Introduction to Modern Jewish Thought*, ed. and trs. A. Jospe (New York, 1963)

Buber, M. *I and Thou*, trs. W. Kaufmann (New York, 1970)

Guttmann, J. *Philosophies of Judaism: The History of Jewish Philosophy from Biblical Times to Franz Rosenzweig*, trs. D. W. Silverman (New York, 1966)

Halevi, J. *The Kuzari*, trs. H. Hirschfeld (New York, 1964)

Husik, I. *A History of Medieval Jewish Philosophy* (New York, 1960)

Ibn Gabirol, S. *The Kingly Crown*, trs. B. Lewis (London, 1961)

Ibn Pakuda, B. ben J. *Duties of the Heart*, trs. M. Hyamson (New York, 1925)

Katz, S. T. (ed.) *Jewish Philosophers* (Jerusalem, 1975)

Maimonides, M. *Guide of the Perplexed*, trs. S. Pines (Chicago, 1963)

Mendelssohn, M. *Jerusalem and Other Writings*, ed. and trs. A. Jospe (New York, 1969)

Rosenzweig, Franz *Star of Redemption*, trs. W. H. Hallo (New York, Chicago, San Francisco, 1970)

Rotenstreich, N. *Jewish Philosophy in Modern Times: From Mendelssohn to Rosenzweig* (New York, 1968)

Saadiah Gaon, *The Book of Beliefs and Opinions*, trs. S. Rosenblatt (New Haven, 1948)

Wolfson, H. A. *Philo: Foundations of Religious Philosophy in Judaism, Christianity, and Islam* (Cambridge, Mass., 1968)

- *Three Jewish Philosophers*, 'Philo: Selections' ed. H. Lewy; 'Saadya Gaon: Selections from Book of Doctrines and Beliefs' ed. A. Altmann; 'Jehuda Halevi: Selections from Kuzari' ed. I. Heinemann (New York, 1976)

10   Jewish Mysticism

Buber, M. *Tales of the Hasidim* (New York, 1946 and 1968)

Jacobs, L. *Dov Baer of Lubavitch: Tract on Ecstasy* (London, 1965)

- *Seeker of Unity* (London, 1966)

- *Hasidic Prayer* (London, 1972)

Scholem, G. *Major Trends in Jewish Mysticism* (3rd rev. ed.; New York, 1964)

- *Jewish Gnosticism, Merkabah Mysticism and the Talmudic Tradition* (2nd ed.; New York, 1965)

- *Ursprung und Anfänge der Kabbala* (Berlin, 1962)

- *On the Kabbalah and its Symbolism* (New York, 1965)

- *Kabbalah* (Jerusalem, 1974)

11   The Jews and the Enlightenment

Altmann, A. *Moses Mendelssohn* (London, 1973)

Duker, A. G. and Ben-Horin, M. (eds) *Emancipation and Counter-Emancipation* (New York, 1974)

Ettinger, S. 'The Modern Period' in *A History of the Jewish People*, ed. H. H. Ben-Sasson (London, 1976)

Jehouda, J. *The Five Stages of Jewish Emancipation* (Brunswick, N.J., 1966)

Katz, J. *Exclusiveness and Tolerance* (Oxford, 1961)

Mahler, R. *Jewish Emancipation: A Selection of Documents* (New York, 1941)

- *A History of Modern Jewry* (London, 1971)

Maimon, S. *An Autobiography* (New York, 1947)

Meyer, M. A. *The Origins of the Modern Jew* (Detroit, 1967)

Raisin, J. S. *The Haskalah Movement in Russia* (Philadelphia, 1913)

12   Jewish Literature: Fiction

Adar, Z. *Biblical Narrative* (Jerusalem, 1970)

Auerbach, E. *Mimesis* (Princeton, 1953)

Dan, Y. 'Fiction, Hebrew' in *Encyclopaedia Judaica* (Jerusalem, 1972)

- 'Aggadah' in *Encyclopaedia Judaica* (Jerusalem, 1972)

Gunkel, H. *Genesis. The Legends of Genesis* (New York, 1964)

Halkin, S. *Modern Hebrew Literature* (New York, 1950)

Halper, B. *Post-Biblical Hebrew Literature* (New York, 1921)

Spicehandler, E. 'Hebrew Literature, Modern' in *Encyclopaedia Judaica* (Jerusalem, 1972)

Zinberg, I. *A History of Jewish Literature* (Cleveland and London, 1972)

Jewish Literature: Poetry

Amichai, Y. *Selected Poems*, trs. A. Guttmann and H. Schimmel (London, 1971)

- *Amen*, trs. the author and T. Hughes (New York, 1977)

Burnshaw, S., Carmi, T. and Spicehandler, E. (eds.) *The Modern Hebrew Poem Itself* (New York, 1965)

Carmi, T. and Pagis, D. *Selected Poems*, trs. S. Mitchell (London, 1976)

Glatzer, N. N. (ed.) *Language of Faith. A Selection from the Most Expressive Jewish Prayers* (New York, 1967)

Goldberg, L. *Selected Poems*, trs. R. Friend (London, 1976)

Goldstein, D. *The Jewish Poets of Spain* (London, 1965)

Heinemann, J. *Prayer in the Talmud* (Berlin and New York, 1977)

Idelsohn, A. Z. *Jewish Liturgy and its Developments* (New York, 1967)

Kovner, A. and Sachs, N. *Selected Poems*, Kovner's poems trs. S. Kaufman and N. Orchan (London, 1971)

Petuchowski, J. J. *Theology and Poetry* (London, 1978)

Ravikovitch, D. *A Dress of Fire*, trs. C. Bloch (London, 1976)

Schirmann, J. 'Hebrew Liturgical Poetry and Christian Hymnody' in *Jewish Quarterly Review*, N.S., XLIV (Philadelphia, 1953–4)

Silk, D. (ed.) *Fourteen Israeli Poets* (London, 1976)

Spiegel, S. *The Last Trial. On the legends and lore of the command to Abraham to offer Isaac as a sacrifice: the Akedah*, trs. J. Goldin (Philadelphia, 1967)

- 'On Medieval Hebrew Poetry' in *The Jewish Expression*, ed. J. Goldin (Philadelphia, 1967)

Stern, S. M. *Hispano-Arabic Strophic Poetry* (Oxford, 1974)

Vogel, D. *The Dark Gate*, trs. the author and others (London, 1976)

13   European Jewry in the 19th and 20th centuries

Ainsztein, R. *Jewish Resistance in Nazi-occupied Eastern Europe* (London, 1975)

Dawidowicz, L. (ed.) *The Golden Tradition* (London, 1967)

Elbogen, I. *A Century of Jewish Life* (Philadelphia, 1966)

Grayzel, S. *A History of the Contemporary Jews* (Philadelphia, 1960)

Greenberg, L. *The Jews in Russia* (New Haven, 1944, 1951)

Katz, J. *Out of the Ghetto* (Cambridge, Mass., 1973)

Mahler, R. *A History of Modern Jewry 1789–1815* (London, 1971)

Mayer, M. A. *The Origins of the Modern Jew* (Detroit, 1967)

Sachar, H. *The Course of Modern Jewish History* (London, 1958)

Zimmels, J. H. *The Echo of the Nazi Holocaust in Rabbinic Literature* (London, 1975)

14   American Jewry

Birmingham, S. *Our Crowd: The Great Jewish Families of New York* (New York, 1967)

Brandes, J. *Immigrants to Freedom: Jewish Communities in Rural New Jersey since 1882* (Philadelphia, 1971)

Dinnerstein, L. *The Leo Frank Case* (New York, 1968)

Feingold, H. L. *Zion in America: The Jewish Experience from Colonial Times to the Present* (New York, 1974)

Glazer, N. *American Judaism* (rev. ed.; Chicago, 1972)

Grinstein, H. B. *The Rise of the Jewish Community of New York, 1674–1860* (New York, 1954)

Handlin, O. *Adventure in Freedom* (New York, 1954)

Knox, I. *Rabbi in America: The Story of Isaac M. Wise* (Boston, 1957)

Marcus, J. R. *The Colonial American Jew, 1492–1776* (Detroit, 1970)

Rischin, M. *The Promised City, New York's Jews 1870–1914* (Cambridge, Mass., 1962)

Rosenstock, M. *Louis Marshall: Defender of Jewish Rights* (Detroit, 1966)

15   Judaism and Modernity

Arendt, Hannah *The Origins of Totalitarianism* (New York, 1951)

Blau, J. L. and Baron, S. W. *The Jews of the United States: A Documentary History* (New York, 1963)

Dubnov, S. *History of the Jews in Russia and Poland*, Vols I–III (Philadelphia, 1920)

Hilberg, R. *The Destruction of European Jews* (Chicago, 1967)

Kochan, L. (ed.) *Jews in the Soviet Union since 1917* (London, 1970)

Marrus, M. R. *The Politics of Assimilation: A Study of the French Jewish Community at the Time of the Dreyfus Affair* (Oxford, 1971)

Mendelsohn, E. *Class Struggle in the Pale: The Formative Years of the Jewish Workers Movement in Tsarist Russia* (Cambridge, 1970)

Meyer, Michael *The Origins of the Modern Jew* (Detroit, 1967)

Schorsch, I. *Jewish Reactions to German Anti-Semitism* (New York, 1972)

Weizmann, C. *Trial and Error* (New York, 1972)

16   Zionism and Israel

Ahad ha-Am (Asher Ginsberg) *Essays, Letters, Memoirs* (Oxford, 1946)

Bein, A. *Theodore Herzl*, trs. M. Samuel (Philadelphia, 1940)

Berlin, I. *The Life and Opinions of Moses Hess* (Cambridge, 1959)

Böhm, A. *Die Zionistische Bewegung* (2nd ed.; Tel-Aviv, 1935–7)

Halpern, B. *The Idea of the Jewish State* (2nd ed.; Cambridge, Mass., 1969)

Hertzberg, A. (ed.) *The Zionist Idea* (New York, 1968)

Herzl, Theodor *The Complete Diaries*, trs. H. Zohn (New York, 1960)

Laqueur, W. *A History of Zionism* (London, 1972)

Palestine Royal Commission Report (Cmd. 5479; London, 1937)

Ruppin, A. *Memoirs, Diaries, Letters*, ed. A. Bein (Jerusalem, 1971)

Stein, L. *The Balfour Declaration* (London, 1961)

Vital, D. *The Origins of Zionism* (Oxford, 1975)

Sources of Illustrations

References are to sections, followed by illustration numbers (e.g. I. 3 = section I, illustration 3); in the case of text illustrations the page number is given.

Museums and Libraries

Aleppo, National Museum I. 3, II. 28 (photos: Arthaud)
Amsterdam, Jewish Historical Museum p. 225
Avila, Archivo Historico Provincial III. 19
Basel, Historisches Museum III. 27
- Universitätsbibliothek p. 112
Belgrade, Jewish Historical Museum III. 78
Berlin, Islamisches Museum III. 12, IV. 28
- (West) Staatsbibliothek Preussischer Kulturbesitz III. 35–38
Birmingham City Art Gallery VI. 1
Cairo, Museum of Islamic Art III. 52, 55 (photos: Sophie Ebeid)
Cambridge, University Library III. 41, 50, 51, 57, 59
Chicago Oriental Institute I. 2
Cincinnati, Ohio, American Jewish Archives V. 46, 53, 54, 59
Cologne, Stadtmuseum p. 304
Copenhagen, Statens Museum for Kunst V. 20
- Royal Library p. 214
Cracow, National Museum IV. 51
Constance, Rosgarten Museum III. 39a, 39b
Damascus, National Museum I. 20, 32, IV. 11, 26 (photos: Princeton University Press)
Frankfurt A.M. Stadthistorisches Museum V. 21, 27, 28
The Hague, Royal Collection of Coins and Medals p. 266
Hamburg, Staats und Universitätsbibliothek IV. 52, p. 221
Hanover, Kestner Museum I. 28
Heidelberg, Universitätsbibliothek III. 22, 23
Hodonin, Moravia, Museum IV. 49 (photo: Jan Lukas)
Istanbul, Archaeological Museum I. 8, 9, 11, 18, II. 18 (Photos: Josephine Powell)
- Museum of Islamic Art III. 70 (photos: Josephine Powell)
- Topkapi Saray Library III. 66, 67, 68 (photos: Josephine Powell)
Jerusalem, Central Zionist Archives VI. 20, 39a, 39c, 39d, 40, 45, 46

- Historical Archives VI. 26, 30, 31, 32, 33, 34, 41
- Israel Museum I. 29, 31, 33, II. 2–4, 8–12, 21, 22, 23, 29–31, 39, 40, 41, 50, III. 11, 47, 62, 71, 73, 83, 89, 90, 92–94, IV. 4, 5, 6, 13, 24, 32, 33, V. 3, 7, 8, VI. 13, 24, 25, 27–30, pp. 55, 90, 91, 116, 118, 122, 259
- National and University Library IV. 1, pp. 57, 63, 114, 255
Kabul, Museum III. 56 (Photo: Josephine Powell)
Leiden, Rijksmuseum von Oudheden I. 4, 5
Leningrad, Russian Museum V. 31
- Saltykov Schedrin Public Library I. 43, III. 42–44, 48, 49 IV. 30, p. 59
Lisbon, National Gallery III. 15
- University Library p. 64
London, British Library I. 1, 24, 34, 38–42, 47, II. 24, 26, 33, 36, 53, III. 4, 7, 18, 45, 46, 58, 60, 61, 64, 72, IV. 14, 17, 18, 19, 20, 21, 22, 23, 35, 38, V. 4, 40, pp. 66, 109, 162, 183, 212
- British Museum, endpapers, I. 10, 12, 14–17, 19, III. 33, 63, IV. 34, 36, 53, 54, 55, V. 9–16, 22, VI. 3, 39b, p. 226
- Imperial War Museum VI. 9, 44
- Jewish Museum I. 25, 36, 37, III. 20, IV. 56, V. 5, 6, 17, VI. 21, 22, p. 188 (photos: J. R. Freeman)
- Museum of Mankind III. 70b
- Victoria and Albert Museum III. 54
Madrid (near), El Escorial III. 16 (photo: Mas)
Moscow, Tretyakov Gallery V. 30, 34
Naples, National Museum II. 14
New York, Hispanic Society of America II. 43
- Jewish Museum I. 35, V. 55, VI. 17
- Jewish Theological Seminary of America pp. 124, 213
- Museum of the City of New York V. 47, 48, 50, 51–52
- New York Public Library V. 41, p. 275
- Whitney Museum of American Art V. 56
Nuremberg, Germanisches Nationalmuseum p. 189
Oxford, Bodleian Library II. 35
Paris, Bibliothèque de l'Alliance Israélite Universelle II. 34, III. 86
- Bibliothèque Nationale I. 26 44–46, II. 54–56, III. 5, 8, 95, IV. 7, 8, 9, V. 2, 18, 24, 29, pp. 65, 125, 163, 166, 187

- Louvre II. 16, 20
- Musée de l'Homme II. 51, III. 92, IV. 50
- Musée National d'Art Moderne V. 32 (photo: Giraudon)
Parma, Biblioteca Palatina IV. 15, p. 123
Prague Jewish Museum II. 47, III. 34, IV. 39–44, 57, V. 19, VI. 12, p. 170 (photos: Karel Neubert)
- State Archives III. 32
San Paolo, Museo V. 36
Tel-Aviv, Museum of the Jewish Diaspora III. 75–77, 79–80
Tbilisi, The Georgian Museum of Fine Art III. 21 (photo: Karel Neubert)
Trier, Landesmuseum VI. 2
Vatican, Biblioteca Apostolica II. 25, p. 56
Vienna, Osterreichische Nationalbibliothek, half-title, III. 24, V. 37, VI. 14–16, 18, p. 265
Villahermosa, Museo III. 17 (photo: Mas)
Waltham, Mass., American Jewish Historical Society V. 43
Warsaw, National Museum VI. 10 (photo: T. Zoltowska)
Washington, D.C., Cooper Hewitt Museum II. 38
- Hirshhorn Museum, Smithsonian Inst. V. 58
- Library of Congress VI. 6, 7
Wilmington, Delaware Art Museum V. 45
Wolfenbüttel, Herzog August Bibliothek III. 40
Yale University Art Gallery, Beq. Dr C. C. Foole V. 44

By courtesy of the following private collections and galleries

B. M. Ansbacher Haggadah Collection, Jerusalem VI. 23
Mr and Mrs Victor Babin, Cleveland, Ohio p. 127
Dott. F. Bolla, Lugano II. 32
George Eastman House, New York V. 48
Mrs B. Goldberg, New York VI. 11
Kennedy Galleries, Inc., New York V. 1
Keir Collection, London III. 53
Levi Strauss & Co., San Francisco V. 60, 61, 62
Palacio de Liria, Madrid I. 30, II. 44, III. 1, 13, 14
The Montefiore Endowment Committee, London V. 25, 26
Rippon Boswell & Co., London II. 45, III. 84

Galerie Rosengart, Luzern V. 33
Formerly S. D. Sassoon Collection I. 22, 23, 27, II. 37, III. 30, 74, IV. 10, pp. 58, 61, 62, 93, 111, 254, 261
Jacob Schulman Collection, New York V. 57

Photographers

Alinari/Mansell Collection II. 7, p. 97
Gertrude Bell Collection, University of Newcastle-upon-Tyne VI. 42
Benedittini di Priscilla, Rome IV. 3
Bildarchiv Marburg p. 172
Yael Braun, Jerusalem II. 13
Bulloz, Paris V. 23
J. L. Charmet, Paris II. 34, III. 95
Georg Gerster/Magnum I. 6, 7, VI. 47
Glenderman, Würzburg IV. 48
Sonia Halliday I. 13, II. 52, III. 69, IV. 25, 29
David Harris, Jerusalem I. 5, 6, III. 11, 47, 81–83
John Hopf, Newport, R.I. V. 43
Thomas Hopfer/Magnum VI. 37, 38, 48
Franz Hubmann, Vienna V. 38
Jerusalem, Department of Antiquities I. 5, 6, 22, 23, IV. 2, 6, pp. 38, 105
Richard Lannoy II. 17, 19, 48
J. P. Lauer p. 42
Jan Lukas, New York III. 29, IV. 49
Felix H. Man, Rome VI. 19
Mas, Barcelona II. 43, III. 2, 4, 7, 9, 15
Fred Mayer/Magnum II. 15, VI. 35, 36
George Mott, Rome III. 31, IV. 46, 47
Karel Neubert, Prague II. 27, 42, 46, 49, III. 25, 26, 28, IV. 16, 31, VI. 12
Josephine Powell, Rome II. 1, III. 65
Roger-Viollet, Paris III. 85, 87, 88
Scala, Florence II. 14
Ronald Sheridan, London IV. 4, 45
Unesco, Paris IV. 12, 27

We wish to acknowledge the help of Mrs Irene Lewitt, Jerusalem, and Madame M. T. Hirschkoff, Paris, in obtaining pictures.

Special photography at the British Museum by J. R. Freeman, Ray Gardner and John Webb.

A NOTE ON THE CAPTIONS
The publisher wishes to thank all the authors for their unfailing help and constructive comments at all stages of the book. Hyam Maccoby, especially, has provided invaluable advice on subjects connected with Judaism and Jewish literature and iconography. It must be made clear, however, that the illustrations sections and their captions are entirely the responsibility of the publisher.

Index

Page numbers in *italic* refer to illustrations.

V W X Y Z